The Constitution in Congress

The Constitution in Congress

Democrats and Whigs

1829–1861

David P. Currie

The University of Chicago Press • Chicago and London

DAVID P. CURRIE is the Edward H. Levi Distinguished Service Professor of Law at the University of Chicago. He is the author of *The Constitution in Congress: The Federalist Period, 1789–1801* (1997), *The Constitution in Congress: The Jeffersonians, 1801–1829* (2001), and the award-winning two-volume history *The Constitution in the Supreme Court* (1985–1990), all published by the University of Chicago Press.

The University of Chicago Press, Chicago 60637
The University of Chicago Press, Ltd., London

Printed in the United States of America
14 13 12 11 10 09 08 07 06 05   1 2 3 4 5

ISBN: 0-226-12900-4

Library of Congress Cataloging-in-Publication Data

Currie, David P.
The Constitution in Congress : Democrats and Whigs, 1829–1861 / David P. Currie.
p. cm.
Includes bibliographical references and index.
ISBN 0-226-12900-4 (cloth : alk. paper)
1. Executive power—United States—History. 2. Legislative power—United States—History. 3. Constitutional law—United States—History. 4. United States—Politics and government—1815–1861. I. Title.

KF4541.C83 2005
342.7302'9—dc22

2004022457

♾ The paper used in this publication meets the minimum requirements of the American National Standard for Information Sciences—Permanence of Paper for Printed Library Materials, ANSI Z39.48-1992.

Unwissende werfen Fragen auf, welche von Wissenden vor tausend Jahren schon beantwortet sind.

GOETHE

Contents

Preface

This is the third volume in a continuing study of extrajudicial interpretation of the Constitution—interpretation by members of the Legislative and Executive Branches, sworn like the judges to uphold the Constitution, in the course of their duties.[1]

This volume and the one that follows cover the period between the inauguration of Andrew Jackson and that of Abraham Lincoln—from the Jacksonian revolution of 1829 to the outbreak of the Civil War. There was a kind of terrible unity to this period: the apparently inexorable slide toward disunion and rebellion. As always, however, the ordinary business of government had also to go on; the upshot was a rich variety of constitutional issues and debates.[2]

I attempted to treat the entire period in a single volume, until I discovered I could no longer carry it. There is too much material. Fortunately, the period divides itself rather neatly in half. The first sixteen years were dominated by partisan efforts to dismantle Henry's Clay's celebrated American System, the second by conflicts over expansion and slavery. I have divided the study accordingly.[3]

The division, however, is not exact; neither subject confined itself strictly to the years I have attached to it. The first volume pursues the threads of economic controversies

[1]For earlier installments see David P. Currie, The Constitution in Congress: The Federalist Period, 1789–1801 (Chicago, 1997) [hereafter cited as The Federalist Period]; David P. Currie, The Constitution in Congress: The Jeffersonians, 1801–1829 (Chicago, 2001) [hereafter cited as The Jeffersonians].

[2]The title of this series, like many shorthand expressions, fails to reveal the full scope of the study. I have already warned that I shall discuss executive as well as legislative sources. On occasion I shall also examine important contributions by *candidates* for federal office, in addition to party platforms and extracurricular letters, speeches, and other utterances by leading figures of the period. From time to time, moreover, I shall call attention to constitutional questions that *might* have been raised during the debates but were not; to comprehend either the issue itself or how the Constitution was understood at the time we must know not only what the participants saw but also what they did not see. And needless to say I shall put in my own two cents on the merits of the issues, as in earlier volumes; kibitzing comes with the territory.

[3]See David P. Currie, The Constitution in Congress: Descent into the Maelstrom, 1829–1861 (Chicago, 2005) [hereafter cited as Descent into the Maelstrom].

all the way to 1861; the second begins with a skirmish over slavery that flared up during Jackson's first term. Thus I have abandoned my earlier plan to subtitle the third volume "1829–1845" and the fourth "1845–1861"; there are too many departures from this pattern to make the designations credible. It remains true, however, that the present volume is *mostly* about the first half of the Jacksonian period, the next *mostly* about the second half. The time of the battle over the Bank, the roads, and the tariff was not, on the whole, the time of the great battles over expansion and slavery.[4]

The central theme of the present volume is therefore the determined and ultimately successful effort of a succession of largely Democratic Presidents and their congressional allies to limit federal intervention in the economy, whether in the form of support for internal improvements, maintenance of a National Bank, establishment of protective tariffs, or disposition of the public lands. As we shall see, the slavery question often lurked behind Southern insistence on strict interpretation of federal powers, but in the controversies considered in this volume it was seldom overtly discussed. In the great crisis over South Carolina's Nullification Ordinance in 1832, for example, the tariff was in part a proxy for slavery and the incident itself a rehearsal for secession; it took all the wiles of Henry Clay and the spine of Andrew Jackson to restore an uneasy truce.[5]

Expansion, slavery, and the American System were the dominant issues of the period from Jackson to Lincoln, but they by no means exhaust the supply. Others that cropped up ran the gamut from federalism and separation of powers to fundamental rights, and it is not easy to organize them. Somewhat arbitrarily, perhaps, I have consigned to the present volume most controversies over the everyday domestic activities of the Federal Government, from congressional authority over bankruptcy and the seat of Government and a scattering of questions of free speech and establishment of religion to a variety of controversies over the executive and judicial powers and such intramural matters as elections and contempt of Congress. Many but not all of these controversies arose during the first half of the period we are studying; none of them was doctrinally related to slavery or secession in any obvious way.[6]

Reserved for the next volume, in addition to issues of slavery itself, are a concatenation of issues largely repecting foreign affairs, expansion, and the use of force. Not all of these issues have direct relevance to the great controversies of slavery and secession, but a number of them do, and most of them conveniently arose during the latter part of the period between Jackson and Lincoln.

In all these controversies, as always, there is much food for thought, much that is of

[4]Indeed a knowledgeable reviewer reminds me that from 1829 until 1847 constitutional divisions were principally either between East and West or between Democrats and Whigs; thereafter they were mostly between North and South. Even the votes on the annexation of Texas and the Mexican War were essentially partisan, not sectional. The catalyst of this sea change was the Wilmot Proviso. See also Michael A. Morrison, Slavery and the American West 4, 6 (North Carolina, 1997).

[5]In 1847 South Carolina Representative Robert Barnwell Rhett went so far as to perceive a threat to slavery in a proposal to establish a Committee on Internal Commerce to relieve the overburdened Commerce Committee. His colleague Isaac Holmes replied "that he had heard that Union sometimes gave strength, but he could not understand how a mere subdivision of the labours of the present committee . . . could have the effect to give more power to the proposed committee than they already possessed . . . ." David Outlaw to Emily B. Outlaw, Dec 9, 1847, David Outlaw Papers, Southern History Collection, University of North Carolina at Chapel Hill.

[6]Other first-amendment issues that *did* pertain to slavery, however, are dealt with in volume 4.

immediate relevance to modern constitutional disputes, and much that goes beyond what can be found in that proverbial tip of the iceberg, the judicial reports. One general observation should be made at the outset: With the possible exception of a few radicals beyond the fringe on the question of slavery, just about everybody was an originalist during the period of this study.[7] Mr. Madison's notes of the debates in the Constitutional Convention were made public shortly after his death in 1836 and immediately became gospel. That had been equally true of the less informative convention journal, which had been available for some time. The question was not whether to follow the Framers' intentions, but what those intentions were.[8]

Let me briefly describe the landscape in which the events of this period occurred. When Jackson became President in 1829 there were twenty-four states. When Lincoln was inaugurated in 1861 there were thirty-four—if one includes those that had attempted to secede. Most of the new states were created out of territory that already belonged to the United States, from Arkansas in 1836 to Kansas in 1861. But these years witnessed an enormous expansion of U.S. territory as well; Manifest Destiny was the motto of the day. Texas was annexed in 1845. A treaty with Great Britain settled our rights to Oregon as far north as 49°, the present Canadian boundary. The Treaty of Guadalupe Hidalgo, which brought Mr. Polk's Mexican War to a close, added a vast domain in the Southwest

[7]Indeed even those who pretended that slavery was unconstitutional often professed to rely on the original understanding. Hypocrisy, as the philosopher says, is the homage that vice pays to virtue. Nor does it detract from my conclusion that nineteenth-century interpreters made incessant appeals to precedent, whether legislative, executive, or judicial; originalism is not inconsistent with a recognition that questions sometimes do get settled, for better or worse. On the interesting and important question whether the same standards apply or should apply to legislative, executive, and judicial expositors of the Constitution see Keith E. Whittington, Constitutional Construction: Divided Powers and Constitutional Meaning (Harvard, 1999), reminding us (at 210) that "[c]onstructions" by members of the political branches "are made by explicit advocates, not by disinterested arbiters."

[8]"[T]he principle that will govern me in the high duty to which my country calls me," said President Van Buren in his Inaugural Address in March 1837, "is a strict adherence to the letter and spirit of the Constitution as it was designed by those who framed it." James D. Richardson, 3 A Compilation of the Messages and Papers of the Presidents 313, 319 (US Congress, 1900) [hereafter cited as Richardson]. See also Joseph Story, 1 Commentaries on the Constitution of the United States, § 400 (Brown, Shattuck, 1833) [hereafter cited as Story], embracing the "first and fundamental rule" that written instruments should be construed "according to the sense of the terms, and the intention of the parties."

The basic source materials for this study, as in earlier volumes, are statutes, executive orders. congressional journals and debates, reports of Senate and House committees, and presidential messages, supplemented by secondary materials and by such more or less original papers as letters, diaries, and recollections of the principal actors, documents published at congressional direction, and official opinions of the Attorneys General. Presidential messages are generally cited, as before, to Richardson, Attorney General opinions where possible to Opinions of the Attorneys General of the United States (Robert Farnham, 1852–) [hereafter cited as Op AG]. Congressional debates were collected during the first few years of the period in Gales and Seaton's Register of Debates in Congress and its accompanying appendix (1826–37) [hereafter cited as Cong Deb and Cong Deb App respectively] and later (with a brief period during which both were compiled) in Francis P. Blair and John C. Rives's Congressional Globe and its appendix [hereafter cited as Cong Globe and Cong Globe App]. The Register of Debates, cited by volume number in volume 2 of this study, is here cited by Congress and session number to conform with more conventional usage typically applied to the Globe. Senate Reports were not separately numbered or published until the Thirtieth Congress; earlier reports are thus cited as S Doc rather than S Rep.

stretching from New Mexico and Colorado to California, which became a state as part of the Compromise of 1850. The Gadsden Purchase in 1853 rounded out territorial acquisitions within what are now the forty-eight contiguous states.[9]

Politically the years between 1829 and 1861 were dominated by Mr. Jackson's emerging Democratic Party, which claimed to speak for the Common Man.[10] More realistically, perhaps, it spoke for free enterprise, for laissez faire, for states' rights—and increasingly, as witnessed by the eventual defection of a number of influential Northerners, for slavery.[11]

Opposition groups coalesced during the 1830's into the Whig Party, so called to highlight its antagonism to what its variegated adherents regarded as President Jackson's deplorable inclination to expand executive authority. The dominant element of the Whig coalition revolved around such nationalistic leaders as Henry Clay and Daniel Webster, who stood for a broad interpretation of federal powers to promote the economy. But there were other elements too, most notably the essentially Southern states-rights Whigs like John Tyler, who shared with his nationalist fellows little more than a pronounced antipathy to Andrew Jackson and his policies.[12]

Of the nine presidential elections from 1828 to 1860, the Whigs won only two. Each time they ran an embarrassingly unqualified General who assiduously refrained from taking a position on the major substantive issues of the day,[13] and each time he died in

[9]10 Stat 1031 (Dec 30, 1853). The area in question was a narrow strip of land along the Mexican border in what is now Arizona and New Mexico. See Harold M. Hyman & William M. Wiecek, Equal Justice Under Law 161 (Harper & Row, 1982):

> Southerners promoted the acquisition of this otherwise valueless area to facilitate construction of a transcontinental railroad terminating in New Orleans, raising the specter of a new avenue for slavery's western expansion.

[10]See, e.g., Robert V. Remini, Andrew Jackson and the Course of American Democracy, 1833–1845 xvi, 340–42 (Harper & Row, 1984). The standard hagiography is Arthur M. Schlesinger, Jr., The Age of Jackson (Little, Brown, 1953) [hereafter cited as Schlesinger, The Age of Jackson]. As the term "emerging" suggests, to speak of Democrats and Whigs is another exercise in shorthand; neither party sprang fully fledged into existence upon Jackson's taking office in 1829.

[11]See, e.g., Bray Hammond, Banks and Politics in America 328–29, 345–46 (Princeton, 1957); Editors' Introduction to Glyndon G. Van Deusen, The Jacksonian Era xi (Harper & Row, 1959) [hereafter cited as Van Deusen, The Jacksonian Era]; James F. Rhodes, 2 History of the United States from the Compromise of 1850 to the End of the Roosevelt Administration 196, 222 (Macmillan, 2d ed 1928). This is not to say, as some historians have argued, that the Democratic Party was *created* in order to protect slavery. See, e.g., Michael F. Holt, The Political Crisis of the 1850s 29 (Norton, 1983) (first published in 1978) (making the suggestion); Robert V. Remini, The Legacy of Andrew Jackson 83–88 (LSU, 1988) (disputing it). Nor is it to deny that many respectable Northern Democrats believed in states' rights without supporting slavery.

[12]See the revealing observation of Tyler's son, biographer, and editor that when his father became President a real Virginian finally held the reins of state again "after the reign of nationalism for sixteen years"—a period that included the Presidencies of both Jackson and Van Buren. Lyon G. Tyler, 2 Letters and Times of the Tylers 14 (Da Capo, 1970) (first published in 1885) [hereafter cited as Tyler Letters]. For all you could conceivably want to know about the Whigs see Michael F. Holt, The Rise and Fall of the American Whig Party (Oxford, 1999).

[13]William Henry Harrison, first of the two, had occupied a variety of civil offices, serving inter alia as Indiana's Governor during its territorial days and as both Representative and Senator after it became a state. Yet his record of accomplishment in those positions was meager. As his biographer wrote, Harrison "was seldom the initiator of programs, and he was not conspicuous for advocacy of any particular political ideas . . . ."

office. The first time the presidential reins were taken up by Tyler, a closet Democrat who owed his place on the ticket to his narrow conception of federal authority and who was said during his decade of nominal Whiggery to have been "sojourning in a land whose people worshipped strange gods."[14] The short of it was that we had Whig Presidents in more than name for no more than four of the thirty-two years encompassed in this study.

The Whigs were not without talent. Henry Clay was superbly qualified by intellect, temperament, and experience. He ran for President three times, and he invariably got thrashed.[15] For Mr. Clay *stood* for something, and that was a grave handicap in a candidate during this period. Few people who rose above mediocrity had any chance of becoming President. It was a time of great animosities, and anyone who had taken a position on anything was certain to have mortally offended some important segment of the electorate.[16] Who were the Whig Presidents? William Henry Harrison and Tyler, Zachary Taylor and Millard Fillmore. Who, after Jackson, were the Democrats? Martin Van Buren, James Knox Polk, Franklin Pierce, and James Buchanan. Household names, all of them.[17] A nation blessed with Webster, Clay, and John C. Calhoun chose Harrison, Taylor, and Pierce.[18] Amid the puny anonymities who inhabited what we have come to call the White House between Jackson and Lincoln, only Polk seems remotely of presidential timber, and that largely because of his warlike obsession with increasing the size of the country.[19]

He did receive a few kudos for instigating a modest pro-settler reform of the public-land laws as Delegate from the Northwest Territory in 1800. See Dorothy Burne Goebel, William Henry Harrison: A Political Biography 379–80 (Indiana Library, 1926); Roy M. Robbins, Our Landed Heritage: The Public Domain, 1776–1970 18 (Nebraska, 2d ed 1976), citing 2 Stat 73 (May 10, 1800). Daniel Webster reportedly said of Harrison in 1835 that he would not lift a finger to elect a man "who is justly the scorn and ridicule of his foes, and the pity and contempt of his friends." He later denied it. See Merrill D. Peterson, The Great Triumvirate: Webster, Clay, and Calhoun 294 (Oxford, 1987) [hereafter cited as Peterson, The Great Triumvirate]. As for Zachary Taylor (who had no experience at all in civil government), "having no political principles, he had made no political enemies." The principal pronouncement of his presidential campaign "announced his determination to accept the will of Congress regarding the tariff, the currency, and internal improvements; and asserted that he loved peace." Van Deusen, The Jacksonian Era at 252, 255. For further encomiums to Taylor see Descent into the Maelstrom, ch 8, n.1.

[14]See Oliver P. Chitwood, John Tyler: Champion of the Old South 156, 172–73, 208 (Appleton, 1839).

[15]The 1844 election was close, but Clay lost again. "[T]hrashed" is a literary allusion. W.S. Gilbert, The Pirates of Penzance, Act I.

[16]See Alan Nevins, Ordeal of the Union: Fruits of Manifest Destiny, 1847–1852 186–87 (Scribner's, 1947); Holt, The Whig Party at 89, 98 (cited in note 12).

[17]Van Buren and Buchanan, of course, were exceptionally well-known politicians of ample experience and some ability. Yet when Van Buren came out against the annexation of Texas in 1844 he managed to lose a nomination that had been understood to be his by default, while Buchanan's decisive virtue in 1856 was that, having been out of the country during the lacerating debate over Kansas and Nebraska, he had the good fortune not to have taken a position on the central issue of the day.

[18]"[C]onsummate mediocrity" is the term one prominent historian employed to characterize Pierce, who he said had "few qualifications" for the Presidency. Avery Craven, The Coming of the Civil War 312 (Chicago, 2d ed 1957). Pierce's own biographer, anxious to rehabilitate his much-maligned subject, acknowledged that the "sole legislative monument" of Pierce's nine years in the House and Senate was "several hundred reports on individual pension cases" and that he exercised no leadership as President. Roy F. Nichols, Franklin Pierce: Young Hickory of the Granite Hills ix, 98, 111, 538 (Pennsylvania, 2d ed 1958).

[19]While short on "creative political capacities," writes Professor Schlesinger, "Polk has been excelled by few Presidents in his ability to concentrate the energies of his administration toward the attainment of given ends." Schlesinger, The Age of Jackson at 441. Professor Rossiter called Polk "the one bright spot in the dull

The Whigs were more often able to control at least one House of Congress, and especially in the later years enough Northern and Western Democrats strayed from the party line to confront their executive colleagues with a number of measures incompatible with the reigning states'-rights creed. The orthodox Democratic headlock on the Presidency, however, assured that most of these initiatives never made it out of the graveyard on Pennsylvania Avenue. Disgruntled Whigs mounted a concerted attack on the veto itself, but they lacked both the votes and the arguments to prevail. Restrictive interpretation of federal powers was the order of the day, and most Presidents between John Quincy Adams and Lincoln considered it their business to enforce it.[20]

The Whig Party disintegrated under the sectional strains engendered by slavery, and for a short time the Democrats had no serious national rival.[21] By 1856, however, Free-Soil Democrats, antislavery Whigs, and others had combined to form a new political party with real principles in its platform and exclusively Northern support. Their candidate, John C. Frémont, did well enough to give the triumphant Democrats cold chills about the future; and when the Democrats too succumbed to sectional schism in 1860 they were vanquished at last by the first real leader to reach the President's House in a quarter century. They were not to regain the Presidency for another twenty-four years.

Great men continued to serve in Congress and the Cabinet during this period, if less frequently in the President's chair. With the disappearance of the "Great Triumvirate" of Webster, Clay, and the increasingly extremist Calhoun in the early 1850's, the baton passed to such notable successors as Stephen A. Douglas, John J. Crittenden, Jefferson Davis, William H. Seward, and Salmon P. Chase. Abraham Lincoln put in a brief but memorable appearance in Washington during the late forties, and his voice was increasingly heard from the prairies a decade later. But the constitutional history of this era was made not so much by this handful of celebrated statesmen as by an army of largely forgotten tillers of the field—from Ether Shepley of Maine and James Simmons of Rhode Island to George Badger of North Carolina and Emerson Etheridge, the uppity Unionist from Tennessee. I have included two appendices to help keep them straight: an alphabetical roster listing the federal positions and political affiliations of each of the numerous actors who tread our stage and a separate list of the principal federal officers during each relevant Administration.

As in the earlier volumes of this series, I disclaim any pretension to improve upon

---

void between Jackson and Lincoln." Clinton Rossiter, The American Presidency 106 (Harcourt, Brace, 2d ed 1960). Polk left us a magnificent diary of his years as President that affords us the best inside view of the Executive Department since the Memoirs of John Quincy Adams. See Milo M. Quaife, ed, The Diary of James K. Polk During His Presidency, 1845 to 1849 (4 vols.) (McClurg, 1910) [hereafter cited as Polk Diary].

[20]The Democratic Platform of 1840 ("the first national party platform," according to those who collected them) emphasized that "[t]he federal government [was] one of limited powers" and that constitutional grants of federal authority "ought to be strictly construed." Kirk H. Porter & Donald B. Johnson, eds, National Party Platforms, 1840–1964 1, 2 (Illinois, 1966) [hereafter cited as Porter & Johnson, Party Platforms]. With minor stylistic changes, this formulation was repeated in every Democratic platform down to the Civil War. Id at 3, 10, 16, 24, 30, 31.

[21]The so-called Know-Nothings, formally known as the American Party, enjoyed astounding and sudden success at the local and state levels as the Whigs disappeared but never came close to electing a President or a majority of either House.

the work of historians and political scientists who have studied this period.[22] Specialization, as I have said before, is as advantageous in scholarship as in the manufacture of pins. My aim is to examine the same material through a lawyer's lens.

Portions of this book originally appeared in the form of articles in the Green Bag 2d, in the University of Chicago Law Review, and in the Festschrift for Knut Wolfgang Nörr, to the publishers of which thanks are extended for permission to reprint. See His Accidency, 5 Green Bag 2d 151 (2002); President Harrison and the Hatch Act, 6 Green Bag 2d 7 (2002); Miss Otis Regrets, 7 Green Bag 2d 375 (2004); David P. Currie and Emily E. Kadens, President Polk on Internal Improvements: The Undelivered Veto, 8 Green Bag 2d 75 (2004); The Smithsonian, 70 U Chi L Rev 65 (2003); The Constitution in Congress: The Public Lands, 1829–1861, 70 U Chi L Rev 783 (2003); Der Schneesturm vom Jahre 1856, in Mario Ascheri et al, eds, "Ins Wasser geworfen und Ozeane durchquert": Festschrift für Knut Wolfgang Nörr 145 (Böhlau, 2003). I should also like to thank the Paul M. Bator Research Fund, the James H. Douglas, Jr. Fund for the Study of Law and Government, the Jerome F. Kutak Faculty Fund, the Carl S. Lloyd Faculty Fund, the Robert B. Roesing Faculty Fund, and the Law and Government Endowment at the University of Chicago Law School for financial support; Steven J. Duffield, John Eastman, Thomas Hiscott, James C. Ho, Greg Jacob, and Stephanie Smith for seminar papers that stimulated my thinking on the issues here discussed; Barbara Flynn Currie, Stephen F. Currie, David T. Flynn, Douglas G. Baird, Philip Hamburger, Jefferson Powell, and especially Mark A. Graber for invaluable advice and encouragement; Paul Clark, Lyle Elder, John Hendershot, Emily Kadens, and Crista Leahy for exemplary research assistance; Lovetta Holmes for a thousand cheerful and efficient contributions of a secretarial nature; the Southern History Collection at the University of North Carolina at Chapel Hill, where I was privileged to undertake a modicum of archival research; the University of Chicago Library for its splendid collection of nineteenth-century materials; and Greg Nimmo, the indefatigable Book Page of the D'Angelo Law Library, for keeping me supplied with the exorbitant number of ponderous and dusty books that this study required.

[22]The most prominent studies of the period as a whole and of its leading protagonists include Van Deusen, The Jacksonian Era; Peterson, The Great Triumvirate; Samuel Flagg Bemis, John Quincy Adams and the Union (Knopf, 1956) [hereafter cited as Bemis, Adams and the Union]; Charles M. Wiltse, John C. Calhoun: Nationalist, 1782–1828 (Bobbs-Merrill, 1944); Nullifier, 1829–1839 (Bobbs-Merrill, 1949); Sectionalist, 1840–1850 (Bobbs-Merrill, 1951) [hereafter cited as Wiltse, Calhoun]; Glyndon G. Van Deusen, The Life of Henry Clay (Little, Brown, 1937) [hereafter cited as Van Deusen, Clay]; Robert W. Johannsen, Stephen A. Douglas (Oxford, 1973) [hereafter cited as Johannsen, Douglas]; Robert V. Remini, The Life of Andrew Jackson (Harper & Row, 1988) [hereafter cited as Remini, Jackson]. Works pertaining principally to the sectional conflict that led to the Civil War are cited in the Preface to volume four of this series.

Abbreviations and Shortened Titles

The Annotated Constitution	Johnny H. Killian, ed, The Constitution of the United States of America: Analysis and Interpretation (S Doc 99-16, 99th Cong, 1st Sess) (Government Printing Office, 1987)
Bemis, Adams and the Union	Samuel Flagg Bemis, John Quincy Adams and the Union (Knopf, 1956)
Benton, Thirty Years' View	Thomas Hart Benton, Thirty Years' View; or, A History of the Working of the American Government for Thirty Years, from 1820 to 1850 (2 vols) (Appleton, 1854–56)
Biographical Directory	Biographical Directory of the United States Congress 1774–1989 (Government Printing Office, bicentennial ed 1989)
Blackstone	William Blackstone, Commentaries on the Laws of England (4 vols) (Chicago, 1979) (first published in 1765–69)
Calhoun Papers	Robert L. Meriwether et al, eds, The Papers of John C. Calhoun (26 vols to date) (South Carolina, 1959–)
Clay Papers	James F. Hopkins et al, eds, The Papers of Henry Clay (11 vols) (Kentucky, 1959–92)
Cong Deb	Register of Debates in Congress (Gales & Seaton, eds, 1825–37)
Cong Globe	Francis P. Blair & John C. Rives, eds, Congressional Globe (Washington, 1833–73)
Contested Elections, 1789–1834	M. St. Clair Clarke & David A. Hall, eds, Cases of Contested Elections in Congress, 1789–1834 (Gales & Seaton, 1834)

Contested Elections, 1835–1865	D.W. Bartlett, ed, Cases of Contested Elections in Congress, 1835–1865 (HR Misc Doc 57, 38th Cong, 2d Sess) (Government Printing Office, 1865)
Corwin, Office and Powers	Edward S. Corwin, The President: Office and Powers (NYU, 1940)
Davis Papers	Lynda L. Crist, ed, The Papers of Jefferson Davis (10 vols to date) (LSU, 1971–)
Descent into the Maelstrom	David P. Currie, The Constitution in Congress: Descent into the Maelstrom, 1845–1861 (Chicago, forthcoming 2004)
Elliot's Debates	Jonathan Elliot, The Debates in the Several State Conventions on the Adoption of the Federal Constitution (4 vols) (2d ed 1836)
Farrand	Max Farrand, ed, The Records of the Federal Convention of 1787 (4 vols) (Yale, rev ed 1966)
The Federalist	Jacob E. Cooke, ed, The Federalist (Wesleyan, 1961)
The Federalist Period	David P. Currie, The Constitution in Congress: The Federalist Period, 1789–1801 (Chicago, 1997)
The First Hundred Years	David P. Currie, The Constitution in the Supreme Court: The First Hundred Years, 1789–1888 (Chicago, 1985)
Gallatin Writings	Henry Adams, ed, Writings of Albert Gallatin (3 vols) (Antiquarian Press, 1960) (first published in 1879)
Haynes	George H. Haynes, The Senate of the United States: Its History and Practice 123 (2 vols) (Russell & Russell, 1960) (first published in 1938)
Jackson Correspondence	John S. Bassett, ed, The Correspondence of Andrew Jackson (7 vols) (Carnegie, 1926–35)
Jackson Papers	Sam B. Smith et al, eds, The Papers of Andrew Jackson (6 vols to date) (Tennessee, 1980–)
The Jeffersonians	David P. Currie, The Constitution in Congress: The Jeffersonians, 1801–1829 (Chicago, 2001)
Johannsen, Douglas	Robert W. Johannsen, Stephen A. Douglas (Oxford, 1973)
J Cont Cong	Journals of the Continental Congress, 1774–1789 (34 vols) (Government Printing Office, 1904–37)
JQA Memoirs	Charles Francis Adams, ed, Memoirs of John Quincy Adams (12 vols) (Lippincott, 1874–77)
Kent's Commentaries	James Kent, Commentaries on American Law (Da Capo, 1971) (first published in 1826)
Lincoln Works	Roy P. Basler, ed, The Collected Works of Abraham Lincoln (11 vols) (Rutgers, 1953–90)
Madison Writings	Gaillard Hunt, ed, The Writings of James Madison (9 vols) (Putnam, 1900–10)

McLaughlin	Andrew C. McLaughlin, A Constitutional History of the United States (Appleton, 1935)
Op AG	Opinions of the Attorneys General of the United States (Robert Farnham, 1852–)
Peterson, The Great Triumvirate	Merrill D. Peterson, The Great Triumvirate: Webster, Clay, and Calhoun (Oxford, 1987)
Polk Correspondence	Wayne Cutler, ed, Correspondence of James K. Polk (9 vols to date) (Vanderbilt, 1969–)
Polk Diary	Milo M. Quaife, ed, The Diary of James K. Polk During His Presidency, 1845 to 1849 (4 vols) (McClurg, 1910)
Porter & Johnson, Party Platforms	Kirk H. Porter & Donald B. Johnson, eds, National Party Platforms, 1840–1964 (Illinois, 1966)
Rawle	William Rawle, A View of the Constitution of the United States of America (Philip H. Nicklin, 2d ed 1829)
Remini, Jackson	Robert V. Remini, The Life of Andrew Jackson (Harper & Row, 1988)
Richardson	James D. Richardson, A Compilation of the Messages and Papers of the Presidents (10 vols) (US Congress, 1900)
Schlesinger, The Age of Jackson	Arthur M. Schlesinger, Jr., The Age of Jackson (Little, Brown, 1953)
The Second Century	David P. Currie, The Constitution in the Supreme Court: The Second Century, 1888–1986 (Chicago, 1990)
Story	Joseph Story, Commentaries on the Constitution of the United States (3 vols) (Brown, Shattuck, 1833)
Tucker's Blackstone	St. George Tucker, ed, Blackstone's Commentaries: with Notes of Reference, to the Constitution and Laws, of the Federal Government of the United States; and of the Commonwealth of Virginia (5 vols) (Lawbook Exchange, 1996) (first published in 1803)
Tyler Letters	Lyon G. Tyler, ed, The Letters and Times of the Tylers (3 vols) (Da Capo, 1970) (first published in 1884–96)
Van Buren, Autobiography	John C. Fitzpatrick, ed, Autobiography of Martin Van Buren, 1918 Annual Report of the American Historical Ass'n, vol II (Government Printing Office, 1920)
Van Deusen, Clay	Glyndon G. Van Deusen, The Life of Henry Clay (Little, Brown, 1937)
Van Deusen, The Jacksonian Era	Glyndon G. Van Deusen, The Jacksonian Era (Harper & Row, 1959)
Webster Correspondence	Charles M. Wiltse et al, eds, The Papers of Daniel

	Webster: Correspondence (7 vols) (Univ Press of New England, 1974–86)
Webster Diplomatic Papers	Kenneth E. Shewmaker, ed, The Papers of Daniel Webster: Diplomatic Papers (2 vols) (Univ Press of New England, 1983–87)
Webster Speeches	Charles M. Wiltse, ed, The Papers of Daniel Webster: Speeches and Formal Writings (2 vols) (Univ Press of New England, 1986–88)
White, The Jacksonians	Leonard D. White, The Jacksonians: A Study in Administrative History (Macmillan, 1954)
Wiltse, Calhoun	Charles M. Wiltse, John C. Calhoun: Nationalist, 1782–1828 (Bobbs-Merrill, 1944); Nullifier, 1829–1839 (Bobbs-Merrill, 1949); Sectionalist, 1840–1850 (Bobbs-Merrill, 1951)

Part One

Death of a System

Introduction to Part One

Like Alexander Hamilton before him, Henry Clay of Kentucky championed an aggressive role for the Federal Government in promoting the domestic economy. At the urging of Hamilton, first Secretary of the Treasury under the new Constitution, Congress had assumed state Revolutionary War debts, imposed a tariff with protective features, and established a National Bank. It had declined, however, even to debate his proposal of money subsidies for local manufactures, and the Bank's charter had since expired.[1] Clay, longtime Speaker of the House, had set his sights largely on more protective tariffs, a new Bank, and federal support for "internal improvements"—a system of roads and canals supplemented by expenditures for the enhancement of natural waterways.[2]

Clay's economic program crystallized during the days of nationalistic sentiment following the War of 1812, and he called it the American System. In its inception it had the enthusiastic support of the great South Carolina statesman John C. Calhoun, then also serving in the House. As I noted in an earlier installment of this study, Clay's program suffered serious and partly unanticipated reverses at the hands of Presidents Madison and Monroe. In John Quincy Adams, on the other hand, it found a friend, and by March 3, 1829 Clay's renowned System was in full flower. The Bank of the United States was in its second incarnation; tariffs had just been raised to unprecedentedly high levels; internal improvements sprouted like weeds on the Capitol lawn.[3]

On March 4, 1829 Andrew Jackson of Tennessee became the seventh President of

[1]See The Federalist Period, ch 2.

[2]For a succinct description of Clay's program see Charles M. Wiltse, The New Nation 55–58 (Hill & Wang, 1961). It should be noted that Clay, like many another sometime Republican of nationalistic bent, tended to trace his political descent to Jefferson rather than Hamilton; "Federalists" were in bad odor. See Mark A. Graber, Federalist or Friends of Adams, 12 Studies in American Political Development 229, 236 (1998).

[3]See The Jeffersonians, ch 9.

the United States.[4] Before Jackson left office in 1837, Clay's entire System was in shambles.

The contemporary observer might have been forgiven if he found the accession of Jackson a less than auspicious occasion. Unlike all but the most eminent of his predecessors, Jackson had no education worth mentioning. He had sat ever so briefly in Congress,[5] where he made no significant contribution.[6] Like Washington, he had spent much of his life in the Army, where he had shown himself high-handed, insubordinate, and disrespectful of constitutional limits on his authority.[7] His principal claim to fame was that (after scandalously neglecting the city's defenses)[8] he had crushed the British at the battle of New Orleans. Many of the best men of his generation thought him utterly unqualified for the Presidency.[9]

[4]For a comprehensive study of Jackson see the three-volume biography by Robert V. Remini, abridged and updated in his Life of Andrew Jackson (Harper & Row, 1988).

[5]Jackson represented Tennessee in the House and then in the Senate between December 1796 and April 1798 and served again in the Senate from 1823 until 1825. Like other unattributed biographical information in this study, these facts are taken from the Biographical Directory of the United States Congress 1774–1989 (Government Printing Office, bicentennial ed 1989) [hereafter cited as Biographical Directory].

[6]"General Jackson has been so little in public life," wrote Martin Van Buren on the eve of the 1828 election, "that it would be not a little difficult to contrast his opinions on great questions with those of Mr. Adams." Van Buren to Thomas Ritchie, Jan 13, 1827, quoted in John Niven, Martin Van Buren: The Romantic Age in American Politics 178 (Oxford, 1983).

[7]See, e.g., The Jeffersonians, ch 7 (discussing Jackson's role in the first Seminole War).

[8]Henry Adams's assessment, predictably, was as tart as it was readable:

> The record of American generalship offered many examples of misfortune, but none so complete as this. Neither Hull nor Harrison, neither Winder nor Samuel Smith, had allowed a large British army, heralded long in advance, to arrive within seven miles unseen and unsuspected, and without so much as an earth-work, a man, or a gun between them and their object. The disaster was unprecedented, and could be repaired only by desperate measures.

Henry Adams, History of the United States of America during the Administrations of James Madison 1147 (Library of America, 1986) (first published in 1889–91).

[9]See, e.g., Jefferson's views as recorded (and apparently disseminated) by Webster in 1824: "He is one of the most unfit men, I know of for such a place. He has had very little respect for Laws or Constitutions,—& is in fact merely an able military chief. . . . [H]e is a dangerous man." Charles M. Wiltse et al, eds, The Papers of Daniel Webster: 1 Correspondence 370, 375–76 (Univ Press of New England, 1974) [hereafter cited as Webster Correspondence]; see Peterson, The Great Triumvirate at 129. Albert Gallatin, concluding that Jackson was "not fitted for the office of first magistrate of a free people," charged him with "very erroneous opinions on the subject of military and Executive power," with most affecting particulars. Gallatin to Walter Lowrie, May 22, 1824, in Henry Adams, ed, 2 Writings of Albert Gallatin 288, 289–91 (Antiquarian Press, 1960) (first published in 1879) [hereafter cited as Gallatin Writings]. William Plumer recalled Henry Clay's having complained that "a man totally unknown to the civil history of the country—who knew nothing of the constitution or laws of the land—and who, in short, had no other recommendation than that which grew out of his fortunate campaign at New Orleans, should be thought of for president of the United States . . . ." Quoted in Niles' Register, Jul 5, 1828; Peterson, The Great Triumvirate at 127. Calhoun, who had reason to be bitter after Jackson had snookered his supporters out of the Cabinet, spoke of his "incompetency, intellectually and morally," and said the incident had confirmed him "in what I have long believed, that Gen Jackson is unworthy of his station . . . ." Calhoun to Samuel D. Ingham, May 4, 1831, Robert L. Meriwether et al, eds, 11 The Papers of John C. Calhoun 377, 378 (South Carolina, 1978) [hereafter cited as Calhoun Papers]; Calhoun to Ingham, May 25, 1831, id at 390. See also Van Deusen, The Jacksonian Era at 30, describing Jackson as a man of "violent and sometimes ignorant prejudices." Arthur Schlesinger, Jr., one of Jackson's staunchest defenders,

Before his election Jackson had criticized the breadth of his predecessor's program for the exercise of congressional authority. He had focused, however, on such exotica as "lighthouses in the skies, . . . national universities, and . . . explorations round the globe";[10] he had not publicly attacked any essential element of the American System. Indeed, while in the Senate he had voted for the 1824 tariff, supported internal improvements, and said nothing against the Bank.[11]

Jackson's first inaugural address was short and noncommittal.[12] He was for peace, for economy in government, for a "just and liberal policy" toward Indians, for reform of "abuses" of government patronage; he did not expressly add motherhood or apple pie. He promised to respect "the limitations . . . of the Executive power" and "the rights of the separate States." He pledged to devote much attention to "[t]he management of the public revenue," noted the possible desirability of framing taxes in such a way as to encourage the production of goods "essential to our national independence,"[13] and added that "[i]nternal improvement and the diffusion of knowledge, so far as they can be promoted by the constitutional acts of the Federal Government, are of high importance."[14]

In his first Annual Message to the new Twenty-first Congress in December 1829 Jackson was somewhat more specific.[15] The Constitution should be amended to provide for direct election of the President.[16] Members of Congress should be disqualified from appointment to federal office. Circuit Courts should be established in newly admitted states. To avoid "such a multiplication of [judges] as to encumber the supreme appellate tribunal," it might be desirable to divide the Circuit Judges into two classes and to provide "that the Supreme Court should be held by these classes alternately, the Chief Justice always presiding."[17]

Jackson went on to spell out what he meant by a "just and liberal" Indian policy. Article IV provided that "no new State shall be formed or erected within the jurisdiction of any other State" without its consent; "[i]f the General Government is not permitted to tolerate the erection of a confederate State within the territory" of another, "much less could it allow a foreign and independent government to establish itself there."[18] Thus so long as Indians remained within the states they must be subject to state laws.[19] They

---

conceded that his analytical powers were inferior to his judgment and that he took office with neither experience nor program. Schlesinger, The Age of Jackson at 36–45.

[10]Jackson to John Branch, Mar 3, 1828, quoted in Remini, Jackson at 160.

[11]See Bemis, Adams and the Union at 14, 126–27.

[12]2 Richardson at 436–38 (Mar 4, 1829).

[13]In 1824 Jackson had written that "the first design" of tariff legislation should be to protect domestic industry. Jackson to James W. Lanier, May 15, 1824, in Harold D. Moser & Sharon McPherson, eds, 5 The Papers of Andrew Jackson 409 (Tennessee, 1996) [hereafter cited as Jackson Papers].

[14]The President's address, his predecessor generously confided to his diary, was "short, written with some eloquence, and remarkable chiefly for a significant threat of reform." Charles F. Adams, ed, 8 Memoirs of John Quincy Adams 105 (Lippincott, 1876) [hereafter cited as JQA Memoirs].

[15]2 Richardson at 442–62 (Dec 8, 1829).

[16]For previous efforts to reform the presidential election process see The Jeffersonians at 335–43.

[17]2 Richardson at 461. But see US Const, Art III, § 1: "The judicial power shall be vested in one Supreme Court . . . ."

[18]2 Richardson at 457. Among other difficulties with this argument, the provision in question deals with the admission of new states to the Union, which no one contemplated in the case of Indians.

[19]Id at 459. The Supreme Court later held to the contrary. Worcester v Georgia, 31 US 515 (1832); see David P. Currie, The Constitution in the Supreme Court: The First Hundred Years, 1789–1888 181–83

should be offered the alternative of "voluntary" emigration to "an ample district west of the Mississippi, and without the limits of any State or Territory," where they might be "secured in the enjoyment of governments of their own choice, subject to no other control from the United States than such as may be necessary to preserve peace on the frontier and between the several tribes."[20]

Of more immediate interest for present purposes were Jackson's observations on the extent of federal authority. As in his inaugural address, he warned against "all encroachments upon the legitimate sphere of State sovereignty." Not only did he reiterate that the Constitution limited federal power; like Madison before him, Jackson insisted that "the great mass of legislation relating to our internal affairs was intended to be left where the Federal Convention found it—in the State governments."[21]

The time was fast approaching, Jackson observed, when burgeoning federal revenues would extinguish the public debt and leave the Government with "a considerable surplus." What should be done? There was room for reduction of existing tariffs, especially on articles like tea and coffee that "can not come into competition with our own productions." In light of the propensity of other nations to enact "selfish legislation," however, duties should generally be set at such a level as to place U.S. goods "in fair competition with those of other countries," and even higher in the case of "articles which are of primary necessity in time of war." Thus it was unlikely that revenue could be

---

(Chicago, 1985) [hereafter cited as The First Hundred Years]. Connecticut Representative Jabez Huntington, in the 1830 debate on the removal bill, anticipated the Court's arguments based on the right of occupation as confirmed by statutes and treaties. Cong Deb, 21st Cong, 1st Sess, Omitted Speeches at 5-18 (following p 1148).

[20] 2 Richardson at 458. President Monroe had made similar proposals to Congress as early as 1824, and an 1820 treaty negotiated by Jackson himself had already begun to carry out this policy. See, e.g., id at 234–37 (Mar 30, 1824); Treaty with the Choctaws, 7 Stat 210 (Oct 18, 1820). Six months after Jackson's address Congress responded by authorizing him to convey Western land to Indian tribes in exchange for their existing claims within the several states, to assist them in moving to their new territory, to support them during their first year there, and to protect them against "all interruption or disturbance." 4 Stat 411, 411–12, §§ 1, 2, 5, 6 (May 28, 1830). In the House, John Quincy Adams objected that Congress's authority extended only to commerce with the Indians, not to their internal affairs. Cong Deb, 21st Cong, 1st Sess 365; see also id at 1114 (Rep. Lamar). Indiana Representative John Test added that Congress could not authorize the President to make agreements with Indian tribes without Senate consent, id at 1108; Georgia Senator John Forsyth argued the Constitution gave no authority to make Indian treaties, id at 336, although as Maine's Peleg Sprague responded Presidents had done so, with Senate approval, from the beginning. Id at 348–50. The treaties were made, an 1834 statute set aside all unorganized territories for exclusive Indian use, and removal was accomplished, at great human cost. See, e.g., Treaty with the Choctaws, 7 Stat 333 (Sep 27, 1831); Treaty with the Chickasaws, 7 Stat 450 (May 24, 1834); Treaty with the Cherokees, 7 Stat 478 (Dec 29, 1835); 4 Stat 729 (Jun 30, 1834); Francis P. Prucha, 1 The Great Father: The United States Government and the American Indians 183–242 (Nebraska, 1984); Van Deusen, The Jacksonian Era at 49–50. For an assessment less unsympathetic than most see Robert V. Remini, The Legacy of Andrew Jackson 56–57 (LSU, 1988), quoting a letter from Jackson to John C. Calhoun, Sep 2, 1820, that defended removal of the Indians as "the only means we have in preserving them as nations, and of protecting them."

[21] 2 Richardson at 452. Cf The Federalist No 45 (Madison): "The powers delegated by the proposed Constitution to the federal government are few and defined. Those which are to remain in the State are numerous and indefinite." Even the great nationalist Joseph Story conceded this principle: "The jurisdiction of the general government is confined to a few enumerated objects, which concern the common welfare of all the states." 1 Story, § 509.

sufficiently reduced to eliminate the anticipated surplus; the question of its disposition would have to be faced.[22]

Federal appropriations for internal improvements, the President continued, had always been attended by "difficulties"; many thought them unconstitutional or inexpedient, and they were certainly divisive. "To avoid these evils," he said, it would be preferable to distribute the anticipated surplus among the states "according to their ratio of representation" in the House, so that improvements might be constructed "in a mode which will be satisfactory to all." If necessary, he added, the Constitution should be amended to make this distribution possible. For "in cases of real doubt" one should always appeal to the people for explicit authorization rather than "undermine the whole system by a resort to overstrained constructions."[23]

Finally, the charter of the Bank of the United States would expire in 1836, and Jackson thought it was none too soon to consider whether it ought to be renewed. For "[b]oth the constitutionality and the expediency of the law creating this bank are well questioned by a large portion of our fellow-citizens, and it must be admitted by all that it has failed in the great end of establishing a uniform and sound currency."[24]

> Under these circumstances, if such an institution is deemed essential to the fiscal operations of the Government, I submit to the wisdom of the Legislature whether a national one, founded upon the credit of the Government and its revenues, might not be devised which would avoid all constitutional difficulties and at the same time secure all the advantages to the Government and country that were expected to result from the present bank.[25]

[22] 2 Richardson at 450–51.

[23] Id at 451–52. Jackson repeated this recommendation in his second Annual Message the following year. 2 id at 500, 514 (Dec 6, 1830).

[24] Former Treasury Secretary Albert Gallatin, who ought to have known, said the Bank had succeeded admirably. Considerations on the Currency and Banking Systems of the United States (1831), 3 Gallatin Writings at 231, 236. See also South Carolina Representative George McDuffie's well-documented rebuttal of Jackson's assertion (HR Rep 358, 21st Cong, 1st Sess 14–15 (1830), noting i.a. that the Bank's own bills were "invariably and promptly redeemed in specie" and that the Bank had provided "a currency of absolutely uniform value in all places, for all the purposes of paying the public contributions, and disbursing the public revenue"); Bray Hammond, Banks and Politics in America 374 (Princeton, 1957), characterizing Jackson's suggestion as "preposterous."

[25] 2 Richardson at 462. Not long after delivering this message, Jackson explained that what he had in mind was a National Bank of deposit, as others had recommended. See Jackson to Moses Dawson, Jul 17, 1830, John S. Bassett, ed, 4 The Correspondence of Andrew Jackson 161–62 (Carnegie, 1929) [hereafter cited as Jackson Correspondence]; Samuel Ingham to Jackson, Nov 26, 1829, id at 92; James Hamilton to Jackson, Jan 4, 1830, id at 111. Later in 1830, in his second Annual Message, he suggested that the Bank might be "a branch of the Treasury Department, based on the public and private deposits, without power to make loans or purchase property" but with authority to sell bills of exchange. 2 Richardson at 500, 529 (Dec 6. 1830). In 1833, noting that both Congress and the public had been cool to his suggestion, he abandoned it, concluding that any adequate federal institution would be too powerful and that state banks could fill Government needs. Jackson to William Duane, Jun 26, 1833, 5 Jackson Correspondence at 111, 114; Jul 17, 1833, id at 131, 133. In 1841–42 he protested that nothing in his own messages supported President Tyler's proposal to establish an institution with authority to issue notes as currency: He had spoken only of a depository for Government funds. Jackson to William B. Lewis, Dec 28, 1841, 6 Jackson Correspondence at 130; Jan 15, 1842, id at 134.

We shall return to this tantalizing suggestion in due course. For now let it be noted that in his first Annual Message President Jackson specifically addressed each of the three principal elements of the American System. While rather firmly endorsing the principle of a protective tariff, he plainly suggested constitutional as well as policy objections both to internal improvements and to the Bank. Soon enough he would reveal the strength of those objections.

1

Intercourse

Federal support for transportation began in 1789, when Congress, apparently without pausing to talk much about the source of its authority, took over the lighthouses.[1] Then, in 1802, it promised to dedicate a portion of the proceeds from public land sales to build a highway to and through the new state of Ohio—the beginning of the famous Cumberland Road. Once again there was little effort to explain.[2]

As advocates unsuccessfully urged federal support for additional transport projects—canals to connect Chesapeake and Delaware Bays, to bypass rapids on the Ohio River, to traverse New York State—they developed plausible constitutional arguments to support them. Roads and canals were necessary and proper to the regulation of commerce, to delivery of the mails, to the national defense. Alternatively, as John C. Calhoun told the Senate in proposing that the bonus the second National Bank paid for its charter be set aside to fund a comprehensive system of roads and canals, Congress could tax and therefore spend for anything that served the "general welfare of the United States," as many such "internal improvements" plainly did.[3]

As I have related elsewhere, President Madison took a narrower view of congressional authority, vetoing Calhoun's ambitious Bonus Bill on constitutional grounds on his last day in office, to everyone's great surprise.[4] When Congress voted to charge tolls to finance repair of the Cumberland Road in 1822, President Monroe vetoed that too. Unable to reconcile earlier congressional expenditures with the traditional narrow Republican understanding of federal authority, however, Monroe conceded that Calhoun had been right about the spending power: Congress could spend for anything that benefited

[1] 1 Stat 53–54, §§ 1–2 (Aug 7, 1789); see The Federalist Period at 69–70.

[2] 2 Stat 173, 175, § 7 (Apr 30, 1802); see The Jeffersonians at 90–92.

[3] See id at 119–22, 258–65.

[4] 1 Richardson at 584 (Mar 3, 1817); see The Jeffersonians at 265–66.

the country as a whole.[5]

Monroe's reading of the commerce, postal, and war powers, I have suggested, was unduly grudging. His interpretation of the spending power, in contrast, was too broad, and traditional Jeffersonians refused to accept it. The second President Adams, on the other hand, shared none of his predecessors' constitutional reservations. Internal improvements were a centerpiece of his recommendations for legislation, and a Congress too undisciplined to consider a comprehensive program sent him a flurry of bills to promote particular projects, which he resignedly approved.[6] As we have seen, President Jackson had begun by raising both constitutional and policy questions about federal aid for such improvements, and a few months later he slammed on the brakes.

I. THE MAYSVILLE ROAD

On May 27, 1830 Jackson vetoed a bill to authorize the Government to purchase stock in the Maysville, Washington, Paris, and Lexington Turnpike Road Company, which had been organized to construct a road between Lexington and the Ohio River, all within the state of Kentucky.[7] The bill, he said, was unconstitutional.

As an original matter, Jackson argued, there was much to be said for the position that federal money could be spent only to carry out Congress's enumerated powers.[8] But this interpretation, he said, had been abandoned during Jefferson's Administration by the purchase of Louisiana and by appropriations for the Cumberland Road; Madison had acknowledged the breadth of the spending power in vetoing the Bonus Bill; Monroe had recognized an authority "restricted only by the duty to appropriate [revenue] to purposes . . . of general, not local, national, not State, benefit." It was too late, Jackson concluded, to go back:

> for although it is the duty of all to look to [the Constitution] instead of the statute book, to repudiate at all times encroachments upon its spirit, . . . it is not less true that the public good and the nature of our political institutions require that individual differences should yield to a well-settled acquiescence of the people and confederated authorities in particular constructions of the Constitution on doubtful points. Not to concede this much to the spirit of our institutions would impair their stability and defeat the objects of the Constitution itself.[9]

[5]2 Richardson at 142 (May 4, 1822); see The Jeffersonians at 278–82.

[6]Id at 282–83.

[7]2 Richardson at 483–93.

[8]In a draft message written in his own hand four months before the actual veto Jackson had expressed exactly this position. See 4 Jackson Correspondence at 137, 138–39 (May 19–26?, 1830). So had Madison in 1791, with apt references to the use of the same terminology in the Articles of Confederation. See The Federalist Period at 79, 169. Jackson seemed to return to this position in his Farewell Address in 1837: "Congress has no right under the Constitution to take money from the people unless it is required to execute some one of the specific powers intrusted to the Government . . . ." 3 Richardson at 292, 299 (Mar 4, 1837).

[9]2 Richardson at 487. Without relying on precedent, Jackson had endorsed Monroe's position in 1824:

Madison had said much the same thing with respect to the Bank of the United States in 1815.[10]

But the established broad interpretation of the spending power, Jackson continued, was not enough to save the bill that was before him. For the understanding was only that Congress could finance improvements that benefited the nation as a whole, and the Maysville Road was one "of purely local character":

> It has no connection with any established system of improvements; is exclusively within the limits of a State, starting at a point on the Ohio River and running out 60 miles to an interior town, and even as far as the State is interested conferring partial instead of general advantages.[11]

Lest this argument create false impressions, Jackson added that he did not mean to imply that he would approve appropriations for improvements that *were* of "national" character. Though it might not be unconstitutional to support such improvements, it would be inexpedient to do so "at this time." Until the debt was paid off, there would be no surplus to expend on them. Thereafter it would seem good policy to spend federal dollars on national improvements, but only on two conditions. First, it should be done pursuant to a "general system of improvement" (one is reminded of Albert Gallatin's comprehensive 1808 plan), not by ad hoc legislation "which tolerates a scramble for appropriations." Second, the Constitution should first be amended, as Jefferson and Madison and Monroe had all recommended, to make clear the existence and limits of federal authority.[12]

For even if Congress already had power to spend for the purpose of constructing roads and canals of national importance, the scope of that power was unclear. Moreover,

---

> As regards internal improvements, Congress can constitutionally apply their funds to such objects as may be determined National. They may erect fortresses and make roads and canals, where they are of a character National, not local.

Jackson to James W. Lanier, May 15, 1824, 5 Jackson Papers at 409; 3 Jackson Correspondence at 253.

When Van Buren sent Madison a copy of the Maysville veto message, Madison responded that the President had misunderstood his Bonus Bill argument: "It was an object of the Veto to deny to Congress as well the appropriating power, as the executing and jurisdictional branches of it. And it is believed this was the general understanding at the time . . . ." Madison to Van Buren, Jun 3, 1830, Gaillard Hunt, ed, 9 The Writings of James Madison 375–76 (Putnam, 1908) [hereafter cited as Madison Writings]. Van Buren was caustic about Monroe's concession: In his expansive view of federal spending the formerly rock-ribbed Jeffersonian had "embraced all that Alexander Hamilton had ever contended for." John C. Fitzpatrick, ed, Autobiography of Martin Van Buren, 1918 Annual Report of the American Historical Ass'n, vol II 304 (Government Printing Office, 1920) [hereafter cited as Van Buren, Autobiography].

[10]See 1 Richardson at 555 (Jan 30, 1815); The Jeffersonians at 255. As one commentator has recently emphasized, however, Jackson had prefaced his Maysville statement with a pointed warning of "the necessity of guarding the Constitution with sleepless vigilance against the authority of precedents which have not the sanction of its most plainly defined powers"—an admonition that would bear dramatic fruit in his veto of the bill to recharter the National Bank a scant two years later. 2 Richardson at 487; Gerard N. Magliocca, Veto! The Jacksonian Revolution in Constitutional Law, 78 Neb L Rev 205, 229 (1999); see section I of chapter 3.

[11]2 Richardson at 487.

[12]Id at 488–92. Jackson repeated this suggestion in his fourth and sixth Annual Messages, id at 591, 602 (Dec 4, 1832); 3 Richardson at 97, 121 (Dec 1, 1834). For Gallatin's plan see The Jeffersonians at 118.

as the history of the Cumberland Road showed, it was plainly inadequate to the purpose: "The right to exercise as much jurisdiction as is necessary to preserve the works and to raise funds by the collection of tolls to keep them in repair cannot be dispensed with," and Congress had no such authority. In the teeth of experience he expressed confidence that an appropriate amendment could be adopted: "The difficulty and supposed impracticability of obtaining an amendment to the Constitution in this respect is, I firmly believe, in a great degree unfounded."[13]

What are we to make of this message? Plainly the new President meant to make a sharp break with the past.[14] His predecessor had approved a raft of internal improvements. Jackson made clear he would have vetoed on constitutional grounds any of them he did not deem of national importance and seemed to suggest that on policy grounds he would disapprove even a second Cumberland Road.[15]

Congressional advocates of the Maysville Road had insisted that it was indeed of national significance, although (as opponents such as future Presidents Tyler and Polk emphasized) it lay entirely within a single state.[16] In the first place, they argued, it was designed as part of a projected interstate highway extending from Zanesville, Ohio to Florence, Alabama; if the highway as a whole was national, each part of it must be national too.[17] Moreover, the road itself connected the interior of Kentucky to the Ohio River and thus served as a major artery for the transportation of goods to and from other states. It was also "the great national mail route from the East to Kentucky," and in the

[13]2 Richardson at 490–92. For earlier vain efforts to amend the Constitution to authorize internal improvements see The Jeffersonians at 115–17, 267–69. Jackson took pains to add that he saw "no necessary connection" between internal improvements and protective tariffs, which others had linked as twin evils. Each, he said, should be considered on its own merits; the protection of domestic industry, within reason, was both constitutional and expedient, and sustained by long-standing precedent as well. 2 Richardson at 493. In his Farewell Address seven years later, after the Compromise of 1833 (see chapter 4), Jackson rediscovered the connection he had denied in the Maysville message: "The abuse of the power of taxation was to be maintained by usurping the power of expending the money in internal improvements," and "[t]hus one unconstitutional measure was intended to be upheld by another." 3 Richardson at 292, 300 (Mar 4, 1837).

[14]By his own later account he succeeded admirably. "Nearly four years have elapsed," Jackson wrote in 1834, "and several sessions of Congress have intervened, and no attempt within my recollection has been made to induce Congress" to authorize the construction of roads or canals. Sixth Annual Message, 3 Richardson at 97, 120 (Dec 1, 1834). See also his Farewell Address, 3 Richardson at 292, 300:

> The good sense and practical judgment of the people when the subject was brought before them sustained the course of the Executive, and this plan of unconstitutional expenditures for the purpose of corrupt influence is, I trust, finally overthrown.

[15]For those interested in the motives of political actors as contrasted with the principles they profess to follow, the Maysville Road veto has been attributed both to "a personal grudge against Henry Clay" and to a desire (in the interest of Martin Van Buren) "to preserve . . . the trade monopoly of the Erie Canal." Carlton Jackson, the Improvement Vetoes of Andrew Jackson, 25 Tenn Hist Q 261, 262 (1966); Charles M. Wiltse, The New Nation 114 (Hill & Wang, 1961).

[16]See Cong Deb, 21st Cong, 1st Sess 433–35 (Sen. Tyler); id at 831–33 (Rep. Polk). See also id at 820, 827 (Rep. Foster).

[17]Id at 828 (Rep. Coleman); see also HR Rep 77, 21st Cong, 2d Sess 15 (1831) (Rep. Hemphill). Cf Gibbons v Ogden, 22 US 1, 194 (1824), confirming that the power to regulate commerce among the states embraced those portions of an interstate journey that lay within one or another state.

event of war it would "again become an important military road."[18] Congress had funded intrastate improvements before when they benefited the entire nation: "Every inch of the Delaware Canal . . . is in the State of New Jersey; and every inch of the Louisville canal is in one county . . . ."[19] Such reasoning, opponents responded, would make every road a national road; there would be no limit to federal authority.[20]

II. RIVERS AND HARBORS

Four days after his Maysville veto Jackson torpedoed a second turnpike bill on identical grounds,[21] and he soon pocket-vetoed an omnibus bill for the construction of navigation aids and the improvement of harbors because "it also contains appropriations for surveys of a local character, which I can not approve."[22] At the same time, however, while admonishing Congress that it had been "improviden[t]" and perhaps "extravagant" in spending for navigation improvements in the past, Jackson made clear he thought federal expenditures for many navigation projects not only constitutional but also expedient:

> The practice of defraying out of the Treasury of the United States the expenses incurred by the establishment and support of light-houses, beacons,

[18]Cong Deb, 21st Cong, 1st Sess 828–29 (Rep. Coleman) (adding, id at 829–31, that the road would also serve national ends by promoting Western settlement, enhancing the value of public lands, and strengthening the bonds of union). See also id at 820 (Kentucky Rep. Robert Letcher):

> The road . . . is intended to intersect the great national [Cumberland] road in the State of Ohio. It connects itself also with the Ohio river. These two connexions most certainly and justly entitle it to the appellation of a national work.

[19]Id at 828 (Rep. Coleman). Every lighthouse, as Professor Peterson later wrote, was local; "it was mainly by the assemblage and interconnection of local works that the national interest was advanced." Peterson, The Great Triumvirate at 157, 195.

[20]See Cong Deb, 21st Cong, 1st Sess 831–32 (Rep. Polk); id at 822 (Rep. Foster); id at 433 (Sen. Tyler): "[I]t is the easiest thing imaginable to make a road a national road. Every road in the country . . . is connected with every other . . ."). Tyler went on to deplore the acceptance of *any* federal authority over internal improvements:

> This harmless and beneficent power was yielded; and what has followed, let the whole South testify. She can bear witness throughout her borders; measure after measure has followed; until powers as supreme as universal are claimed for this Government, as if the parchment upon your table had never been executed. The internal policy of the States prescribed, the industry of the country regulated, and all the mere charities of life exercised as fully by this Government as by an imperial monarch. The States sinking every day with accelerated velocity into the condition of mere provinces, and a great national government to grow out of the ruins of the confederacy.

Cong Deb, 21st Cong, 1st Sess 434. Utterances such as this help to explain how it was that a decade or so later Tyler, as a President elected under the Whig label usually associated with the nationalistic Henry Clay, could assume the role of defender of state rights against a Whig-dominated Congress. See section III of this chapter, and chapter 3.

[21]See 2 Richardson at 493–94 (May 31, 1830).

[22]Second Annual Message, id at 500, 509 (Dec 6, 1830). His simultaneous pocket veto of additional aid for the canal around the Ohio River rapids, which Congress had assisted in the past, was based upon the distinct ground that it was bad policy for the Government to buy shares in private corporations. Id at 509.

> buoys, and public piers within the bays, inlets, harbors, and ports of the United States, to render the navigation thereof safe and easy, is coeval with the adoption of the Constitution, and has been continued without interruption or dispute.

As foreign commerce penetrated the interior, the President continued, Congress had provided not only for similar navigational aids on inland waters but also, "upon the same principle," for "the removal of sand-bars, sawyers, and other partial or temporary impediments in the navigable rivers and harbors which were embraced within the revenue districts from time to time established by law . . . ." And that, President Jackson concluded, was as it should be:

> It is indisputable that whatever gives facility and security to navigation cheapens imports, and all who consume them are alike interested in whatever produces this effect. . . . The consumer in the most inland State derives the same advantage from every necessary and prudent expenditure for the facility and security of our foreign commerce and navigation that he does who resides in a maritime State. . . . From a bill making *direct* appropriations for such objects I would not have withheld my assent.[23]

Indeed, barely a month before vetoing appropriations for the Maysville Road on the ground that its benefits were "local," Jackson had unprotestingly signed a bill appropriating over $300,000 for no fewer than twenty-two rivers and harbors projects, including one "[f]or the preservation of Plymouth Beach, Massachusetts," which on its face appeared to have no connection with navigation or commerce at all.[24]

Jackson continued to approve river and harbor improvements throughout his Presidency,[25] although, as Kentucky Representative Robert Letcher had implied in debating the Maysville bill,[26] most of them too were located in a single state. Jackson's argument that they were nevertheless of national importance was basically the same as that made by

[23]Id at 508–9.

[24]4 Stat 394, 395 (Apr 23, 1830). President Polk later suggested that the purpose of this grant too was to protect an existing harbor, though it is not clear that it served either foreign or interstate commerce. 4 Richardson at 619. Two years later, however, Jackson pocket-vetoed a second rivers and harbors bill as inconsistent with the principle he had laid down in the Maysville Road case:

> [T]here is a class of appropriations in the bill for the improvement of streams that are not navigable, that are not channels of commerce, and that do not pertain to the harbors or ports of entry designated by law, or have any ascertained connection with the usual establishments for the security of commerce, external or internal.

2 Richardson at 638, 639 (Dec 6, 1832). In this message Jackson also suggested an interesting understanding of the veto process itself, which is briefly considered in section I of chapter 6.

[25]E.g., 4 Stat 488 (Mar 3, 1831); 4 Stat 550 (Jun 28, 1832); 4 Stat 702 (Jun 28, 1834); 4 Stat 719 (Jun 30, 1834); 4 Stat 753 (Mar 3, 1835); 5 Stat 67 (Jul 2, 1836); 5 Stat 128 (Jul 4, 1836); 5 Stat 181 (Mar 3, 1837); 5 Stat 187 (Mar 3, 1837).

[26]See Cong Deb, 21st Cong, 1st Sess 835.

supporters of the Maysville Road.[27]

As President Jackson observed in his Maysville veto message, the distinction between "national" and "local" improvements was pretty elusive,[28] and people might reasonably differ as to the national interest in a particular project.[29] It was more difficult, however, to understand why Jackson declared himself so much more willing to approve expenditures for national river and harbor improvements than for national roads and canals, since he acknowledged that long-standing precedent supported them both.[30] Comparison of the highway and harbor messages suggests he thought the two classes of improvements were based upon different congressional powers: While navigation aids and the removal of obstructions to natural watercourses were necessary and proper to the regulation of foreign commerce, roads and canals were not; they could be aided, if at all, only by appropriations pursuant to the power to tax (and thus to spend) to promote the general welfare.

As I have argued elsewhere, this distinction is unconvincing.[31] In the first place, canals and roads may also promote foreign commerce. One need only think of land traffic between the United States and Mexico, or of the St. Lawrence Seaway, which permits ships from Europe and Asia to reach Chicago. More important, Congress may regulate interstate as well as foreign commerce, and roads are as necessary as harbors for the purpose. If Jackson was right that (as had been said at the time) congressional authorization of lighthouses and other navigational facilities in 1789 was based on the commerce power, it was good precedent for any improvements that promoted interstate or foreign intercourse, including roads and canals.[32]

[27]Notwithstanding his highly visible Maysville veto, a leading historian of the period has said that Jackson "sanctioned expenditures for transport developments during his first term at a rate nearly double that of the expenditures under Adams," and that some of the improvements he sanctioned were "fully as local as the Maysville Road." Van Deusen, The Jacksonian Era at 51–52.

[28]See 2 Richardson at 487: "That even this [distinction] is an unsafe use, arbitrary in its nature, and liable, consequently, to great abuses, is too obvious to require the confirmation of experience." The later observer is reminded of efforts to determine which local activities had such an impact upon interstate or foreign commerce as to bring them within Congress's regulatory powers. See David P. Currie, The Constitution in the Supreme Court: The Second Century, 1888–1986 222–26, 236–38 (Chicago, 1990) [hereafter cited as The Second Century]; United States v Lopez, 514 US 549 (1995).

[29]With regard to navigation improvements Jackson had offered a standard of his own in a letter to Van Buren in October 1830, objecting to federal surveys of local tributaries of navigable rivers, "which cannot be considered national; nothing can be so considered, but those great leading and navigable streams from the ocean, and passing through two or more states." 4 Jackson Correspondence at 185.

[30]Jackson reiterated his preference for river and harbor improvements in his sixth Annual Message in 1834. 3 Richardson at 97, 121–22 (Dec 1, 1834). He did so in the course of explaining the pocket veto of a bill to improve navigation of the Wabash River on the ground that it contradicted "a limitation for the government of my own conduct by which expenditures of this character are confined to places below the ports of entry or delivery established by law." Id at 122. In so saying he appeared to favor foreign over interstate commerce, though Congress had power over one as well as the other, and though both would appear to be of equally national importance. We shall hear more of this distinction; but Jackson, at least, did not state it as a matter of constitutional law.

[31]The Jeffersonians at 122, 276. See also S Doc 268, 28th Cong, 1st Sess 5 (1844) (Michigan Sen. Augustus Porter) (urging an appropriation to construct a canal around the rapids at Sault Ste. Marie): "[I]t surely will not be insisted, that a power to remove impediments to an extended natural navigation may not be exerted to overcome them by a canal . . . ."

[32]So were many of the twenty-seven federal hospitals for merchant seamen constructed before the Civil War on the basis of legislation dating from 1798, whose most plausible constitutional justification was the

President Jackson did sign several bills to pay for repair of the Cumberland Road and other existing improvements;[33] once a road had been built, it could hardly be permitted to go to ruin. He also approved bills to extend the road into Indiana and Illinois.[34] He did so, however, with the intention of handing the completed highway over to the states through which it ran; for with his blessing Congress had begun the process of ceding responsibility for the road to the states, which under Monroe's and Jackson's view of the Constitution had sole authority to levy tolls for its continued support.[35] Thus, although Congress with Jackson's approval continued to finance lighthouses and other aids to the navigation of rivers and harbors, the Federal Government was well on the way to divesting itself of its first and most conspicuous investment in roads and canals. "[T]he Era of National Projects," as one commentator has written, "may be thought of as ending in [Jackson's] administration.[36]

III. EBB TIDE

Succeeding Democratic Presidents—and John Tyler, who had turned Whig because he thought Jackson too *generous* in his interpretation of federal power[37]—took increasingly narrow views of congressional authority over internal improvements.[38]

In loudly vetoing an omnibus rivers and harbors bill in 1844, for example, Tyler echoed Jackson's distinction between national and local improvements,[39] but he went further. Unable to swallow Jackson's distinction between roads and canals on the one hand

---

commerce clause. See, e.g., 1 Stat 605 (Jul 16, 1798); George R. Taylor, The Transportation Revolution, 1815–1860 368–69 (Holt, 1964).

[33] 4 Stat 551, 553–54, § 1 (Jul 3, 1832); 4 Stat 680 (Jun 24, 1834); 5 Stat 71 (Jul 2, 1836); 5 Stat 195, § 3 (Mar 3, 1837).

[34] 4 Stat 427, § 2 (May 31, 1830); 4 Stat 469 (Mar 2, 1831); 4 Stat 551, 557, § 1 (Jul 3, 1832); 4 Stat 680 (Jun 24, 1834); 5 Stat 195, § 1 (Mar 3, 1837). See also Jackson's fourth Annual Message, 2 Richardson at 591, 602 (Dec 4, 1832), urging Congress to refrain from subsidizing improvements "in doubtful cases, except in relation to improvements already begun." Several of these Acts also provided for extension and repair of roads in the territories and one "military" road, which arguably stood on different constitutional foundations. 4 Stat 427, § 1; 4 Stat 551, 555–57, § 1; 5 Stat 195, § 3.

[35] 4 Stat 483 (Mar 2, 1831); 4 Stat 551, 553–54, § 1 (Jul 3, 1832); 4 Stat 655 (Mar 2, 1833); 4 Stat 680, 681, § 4 (Jun 24, 1834); 5 Stat 71, 72, § 2 (Jul 2, 1836): "[T]he moneys hereby appropriated . . . [shall] be expended in completing the greatest possible continuous portion of said road in the said States, so that such finished parts thereof may be surrendered to the said States, respectively." See Jeremiah S. Young, A Political and Constitutional Study of the Cumberland Road, ch VII (Chicago, 1902); Carter Goodrich, Government Promotion of American Canals and Railroads, 1800–1890 42 (Columbia, 1960).

[36] Id.

[37] Tyler, who had favored Jackson over John Quincy Adams in 1828 as the lesser of two evils, broke with him over the question of coercion of South Carolina during the Nullification crisis. The breach became "irreparable" after Jackson removed Government deposits from the Bank of the United States, though both agreed the Bank was unconstitutional. See Oliver P. Chitwood, John Tyler: Champion of the Old South 83–84, 112–15, 124–28 (Appleton, 1939).

[38] There was little activity in this area during the Presidency of Martin Van Buren, who in his Inaugural Address had pledged "a strict adherence to the letter and spirit of the Constitution as it was designed by those who framed it," 3 Richardson 313, 319 (Mar 4, 1837). Although Van Buren did sign yet another appropriation to extend the Cumberland Road (5 Stat 228 (May 25, 1838)) and a land grant to the Wisconsin Territory for a canal to connect Lake Michigan with the Rock River (5 Stat 245 (Jun 18, 1838)), Congress was safely in Democratic hands and sent him precious few improvement bills.

[39] 4 Richardson at 330, 331–32 (Jun 11, 1844).

and the improvement of natural waterways on the other, he concluded that Congress properly had no authority over either. Rightly interpreted, he argued, the commerce clause gave Congress authority only to "adopt rules and regulations prescribing the terms and conditions on which" commerce should be conducted. And thus, he declared, as an original matter Congress should have been found to have no more power to improve existing rivers or harbors than to build roads or canals.[40]

Like Jackson, however, Tyler was prepared to bow to long-standing precedent. Because some of the appropriations in the bill were of purely local import, he said, he had no choice but to reject them. Others, however (such as that for "the Delaware breakwater"), he could have approved if they had been presented separately, for—deplorable though it might be—the country had long accepted the validity of navigation improvements that benefited the nation as a whole.[41] Indeed the same day he vetoed one rivers and harbors bill President Tyler signed another, providing for continuation of works on the Great Lakes (and Lake Champlain) that had already been undertaken as well as new projects to improve navigation of the Mississippi and its tributaries[42]—for, as he said in his veto message, the very purpose of the Louisiana Purchase was to secure the free navigation of that river.[43]

[40]Id at 331. In contrast, not even the most parsimonious President had the slightest hesitation during this period in approving actual regulation of what the Supreme Court would later refer to as the "instrumentalities" of interstate or foreign commerce. See section I of chapter 5. For doubts as to the validity of Tyler's distinction between regulation and promotion see S Rep 340, 33d Cong, 1st Sess 1 (1854) (Maryland Sen. Thomas Pratt), urging an appropriation to clear obstacles from the Baltimore Harbor:

> It would be a singular anomaly to assume that a government possessing the power to regulate commerce, and in fact regulating it in such manner as to derive from it almost its entire revenue, should be deprived of the power of appropriating a part of that revenue to the removal of such natural or artificial obstructions as might destroy or impair it.

[41]4 Richardson at 331–32.

[42]5 Stat 661 (Jun 11, 1844).

[43]4 Richardson at 332. John C. Calhoun, in an apparent bid for Western support for a last vain effort to capture the Presidency, would also argue that the Mississippi and its major tributaries were a special case, but for a different reason. Because neither individuals nor states were in a position to ensure the navigability of those waters, he said, it was up to Congress to do so:

> It is the genius of our Government to leave to individuals what can be done by individuals, and to individual States what can be done by them, and to restrict the power of the General Government to that which can only be effected through its agency and the powers specifically granted.

Speech to the Memphis Convention, Nov 13, 1845, 22 Calhoun Papers at 276, 281. For Calhoun's later unsatisfactory effort to demonstrate why on this standard the Mississippi was different see S Doc 410, 29th Cong, 1st Sess 15–17 (1846), reprinted in 23 Calhoun Papers at 193, 213–15; for discussion of subsidiarity as a constitutional doctrine see David P. Currie, Subsidiarity, 1 Green Bag 2d 359 (1998). See also Avery Craven, The Coming of the Civil War 10 (Chicago, 2d ed 1957): "A harbor might extend far up an inland river when Calhoun wanted to be President!"

Daniel Webster roundly rejected Calhoun's distinction:

> Of the power of the Government to make appropriations for erecting harbors and clearing rivers, I never entertained a particle of doubt. This power, in my judgment, is not partial, limited, obscure, applicable to some uses and not to others, to some States and not to others, to some rivers and not to others, as seems to have been the opinion of gentlemen connected with the Memphis

Thus in deference to perceived errors of the past President Tyler brought himself to accept "national" river and harbor improvements that Jackson had urged as a matter of conviction.[44] In the course of his argument Tyler was also at pains to condemn the practice of combining appropriations for national and local improvements in a single bill, which he said "necessarily . . . embarrass[ed] Executive action"; for in such a case, he complained, he had no choice but to veto the entire bill.[45] Thus Tyler implicitly reaffirmed Washington's unimpeachable determination that the President possessed no item veto: Under Article I, § 7 each bill was a unit that must be approved in toto or not at all.[46]

Tyler was replaced in 1845 by James Knox Polk of Tennessee, a former Speaker of the House and a Democrat to the core.[47] President Polk vetoed appropriations for river and harbor improvements in 1846[48] and again in 1847.[49] The first time he sounded very much like Tyler. Congress could not provide for purely local improvements, and in principle there was no difference between improving existing ways and constructing new ones. Like his predecessors, however, Polk was prepared to accept venerable precedents:

> Congress have exercised the power coeval with the Constitution of establishing light-houses, beacons, buoys, and piers on our ocean and lake

---

> Convention. . . . In my opinion, the authority of the Government in this respect, rests directly on the grant of the Commercial power to Congress; and this has been so understood from the beginning . . . .

Webster to Samuel L. Smith et al, Jun 26, 1847, 6 Webster Correspondence at 239–40.

[44]On his last day in office Tyler also signed legislation providing subsidies for oceangoing steamships in the form of contracts for the carriage of mail. 5 Stat 748–50, §§ 1, 7 (Mar 3, 1845). This statute too, on which there was no reported debate, plainly served to promote commerce, and any part of the consideration beyond the value of the service could fairly be justified by the postal power only if that authority too was broadly construed. The requirement that ships built with federal assistance be convertible into warships (id at 750, § 7), however, suggested that the statute might also be necessary and proper to providing a Navy. Some $14,500,000 were expended under this statute before the subsidy was repealed in 1858. See 11 Stat 364, § 4 (Jun 14, 1858) (limiting compensation under future contracts to the applicable rate of postage); Taylor, The Transportation Revolution at 129–31 (cited in note 32).

[45]4 Richardson at 331. President Polk would say much the same thing in a veto message he drafted in 1848 and never needed to use. See Polk Papers (microfilm), Reel 61, series 5 (Library of Congress, 1964). Other elements of this undelivered message are discussed in sections IV and VI of this chapter.

[46]See The Federalist Period at 32. In 1849 the Senate committee announced that henceforth it would present each new request for improving rivers or harbors separately, so that each could be evaluated on its own merits. S Rep 284, 30th Cong, 2d Sess 1–3.

[47]As a budding politician in Tennessee, Polk had made cautious noises in support of federal improvements for his own state. "This," wrote his biographer, "was the most serious departure from Old Republican orthodoxy of Polk's entire career," and he quickly recanted. Charles G. Sellers, Jr., James K. Polk, Jacksonian, 1795–1843 85, 97, 120–21, 152–55 (Princeton, 1957).

[48]4 Richardson at 460 (Aug 3, 1846). In this message Polk fully endorsed the restrictive position taken in every Democratic Party platform from 1840 down to the Civil War: Congress had no authority "to construct works of internal improvement within the States, or to appropriate money from the Treasury for that purpose." Id at 461; see Porter & Johnson, Party Platforms at 2, 3, 10, 16, 24, 30, 31. No such authority was expressly given, said Polk, and it could not be found necessary and proper to the execution of Congress's explicit powers. Here Polk revisited (and rejected) *McCulloch v Maryland:* Necessary and proper measures included only those "without which such principal power can not be carried into effect," and internal improvements were not indispensable to the execution of any federal power. 4 Richardson at 461. Contrast *McCulloch,* 17 US 316, 421 (1819).

[49]4 Richardson at 610 (Dec 15, 1847).

> shores for the purpose of rendering navigation safe and easy and of affording protection and shelter for our Navy and other shipping. . . . After the long acquiescence of the Government through all the preceding Administrations, I am not disposed to question or disturb the authority to make appropriations for such purposes.[50]

In 1847, however, Polk revealed that his position was even more restrictive than it had initially appeared. Once any authority to improve rivers and harbors was conceded, he now argued, there was no tenable way to contain it; and the commerce power did not justify such improvements at all. As Tyler had acknowledged, "to 'regulate commerce' does not mean to make a road, or dig a canal, or clear out a river, or deepen a harbor"; it meant to "prescrib[e] general rules by which commerce should be conducted." Nor was there, as Tyler had believed, long-standing precedent for the existence of such power, for the first appropriation for harbor improvements had been made in 1823 and the first for river improvements in 1826.[51]

Polk's earlier bow to precedent, in other words, was to be taken most literally. "[L]ight-houses, beacons, buoys, and piers" had been accepted since 1789 and could still be approved; "to clear out or deepen" a waterway was a recent perversion that must be abandoned.[52] Federal authority over the improvement of transportation facilities had never been more narrowly conceived.[53]

[50]Id at 462. Even in this message, however, Polk found Jackson's test for distinguishing national from local improvements too lenient. It was not enough that the improvement be undertaken "below the ports of entry or delivery established by law," as Jackson had argued (see note 30), for many ports of entry existed only on paper:

> If the restriction is a sound one, it can apply only to the bays, inlets, and rivers connected with or leading to such ports as actually have foreign commerce—ports at which foreign importations arrive in bulk, paying the duties charged by law, and from which exports are made to foreign countries.

Id at 463.

[51]Id at 614, 625–26, 619–20.

[52]Even Calhoun, an ardent states'-righter in his later years, had rejected this distinction: Where Congress could build lighthouses, it could remove snags. See his Senate Report, S Doc 410, 29th Cong, 1st Sess 15 (1846), reprinted in 23 Calhoun Papers at 193, 212–13. See also Cong Globe App, 30th Cong, 1st Sess 57–58 (Tennessee Rep. F.P. Stanton): "When the purpose is to facilitate navigation, it cannot be important what means are adopted, provided they be calculated to produce the desired effect." The House countered Polk's message with two resolutions affirming congressional authority, first "to construct such harbors and improve such rivers as are 'necessary and proper' for the protection of our navy and our commerce, [or] for the defenses of our country" and then "to appropriate money to open and improve harbors, and remove obstructions from navigable rivers, in all cases where such improvements are necessary to the protection and facility of commerce with foreign nations or the commerce among the States." Cong Globe, 30th Cong, 1st Sess 62; Cong Globe App, 30th Cong, 1st Sess 750.

[53]Polk was equally firm in opposing the notion that Congress might support the construction of roads or canals overseas. After the conclusion of a treaty giving U.S. citizens a right of transit across the Isthmus of Panama, Secretary of State James Buchanan recommended that federal engineers be sent to survey a possible route. Polk put his foot down:

Polk had a ready answer for those who might fear that rivers and harbors would not be improved if Congress did not improve them. Article I, § 10 empowered Congress to consent to the imposition of state tonnage duties on vessels plying navigable waters; that was how river and harbor improvements had been paid for until Congress began to usurp state authority.[54]

IV. THE UNDELIVERED VETO

Anticipating that Congress might present him with yet another rivers-and-harbors bill during the last year of his term, President Polk in 1848 prepared what he described as an "elaborate" third veto message designed to "add to the strength" of his earlier pronouncements. Having no occasion to use it, he vowed to "preserve it with my other valuable papers," for he regarded it "as one of the ablest papers I have ever prepared."[55]

Preserve it he did. A lengthy set of fragments in Polk's own hand, it nestles snugly among other Polk papers in the Library of Congress.[56] It does indeed add to his previous observations on internal improvements, and it reflects impressive research efforts hardly to be expected of a busy President even in the nineteenth century. Polk was a hands-on executive who insisted on running his own show.[57]

> I told him that he was aware that I denied the power to make internal improvements, & that I could not see upon what principle we possessed the power to make external improvements in a foreign country.

Buchanan tried again a few days later and ran into the same stone wall:

> He then enquired of me if the Minister of New Granada should request the services of one of our officers of Topographical Engineers to make the survey for his Government & at their expense, [whether] I would agree to detail such an officer. I replied that the time and services of such an officer belonged to his own Government, which paid his salary, and that I must in such case decline giving my sanction to such an application. I added that if we had no employment for our officers they had better be disbanded.

4 Polk Diary at 139–40, 154. Even a bill to pay for private construction of a road on which to "transport[] the mails & public property across the Istmus" [sic] was met with the assurance of a veto: "I consider that the Government possesses no constitutional power to apply the public money either within or without the U.S. for any such purpose." Id at 314. The Panama Railroad was completed in 1855, without federal subsidy. See Goodrich, American Canals and Railroads at 175 (cited in note 35).

[54] 4 Richardson at 615–18. This suggestion is pursued in section VI of this chapter.

[55] 4 Polk Diary at 157–58, 364.

[56] Polk Papers (microfilm), Reel 61, series 5 (Library of Congress, 1964). The essential portions are printed in David P. Currie and Emily Kadens, President Polk on Internal Improvements: The Undelivered Veto, xx Green Bag 2d xx (2004).

[57] A number of diary entries confirm this conclusion. E.g., 1 Polk Diary at 73, noting that he had asked Cabinet members for their annual reports by November 15 "as I wished to examine them fully and minutely before they were communicated to congress"; id at 124, rejecting the suggestion that the Secretary of the Treasury had written portions of his annual address: "[T]he tariff part and every other part of it is my own. . . . I wrote the whole message"; 4 id at 261, musing that the public could not imagine the burdens of the Presidency:

> No President who performs his duty faithfully and conscientiously can have any leisure. . . . I prefer to supervise the whole operations of the Government myself rather than entrust the public business to subordinates, and this makes my duties very great.

Apart from the usual platitudes,[58] Polk's undelivered message consists largely of a detailed and masterly exposition of congressional precedents designed to demonstrate that his conclusion that Congress had no authority to improve rivers and harbors was in accord with the original understanding. His first exhibit was an excerpt from House debates on the initial bill to establish the national capital in 1789.

Convinced of the importance of ensuring that the seat of Government be accessible by water from the Atlantic Ocean, Polk wrote, the House of Representatives had initially voted to locate the capital on the Susquehanna River—on condition that "the States of Pennsylvania and Maryland shall pass acts (not including any expense to the said States) providing for the removing of the obstructions" downstream.[59] James Madison had urged adoption of this proviso to prevent Pennsylvania from "defeat[ing the] object" of the bill;[60] James Jackson of Georgia had rhetorically inquired "what would become of Congress" if (by Pennsylvania's revoking its designation of the river as a public highway) the capital was "cut off from a water communication with the Atlantic."[61] "[N]o member of Congress," Polk concluded, intimated at the time that Congress itself could provide for removal of the offending obstructions; "every member either expressly or [word illegible] conceded that the power rested entirely and exclusively with the States . . . ."[62]

Without more, the House's insistence that the states provide for clearing the Susquehanna might prove only that it did not believe the Federal Government should bear the cost.[63] The fact that the proviso specified that the condition might be met without "any expense to the said States," however, casts considerable doubt upon this hypothesis; and thus Polk seems right that it never occurred to anyone during the seat-of-Government debate that Congress had authority, without state consent, to remove obstructions from otherwise navigable streams.

The troublesome precedent of lighthouses, beacons, buoys, and piers, however, could not be so lightly dismissed. Congress had acquired, erected, and operated such navigational aids since 1789; it was far from obvious why, if the Federal Government could warn travelers of obstructions, it could not remove them as well. In 1847 Polk had said only that he would not extend this precedent to the removal of obstructions, which Congress had not undertaken for another twenty-five years. Now he asserted that the two

---

This theme is developed at length in Charles A. McCoy, Polk and the Presidency, passim (Texas, 1960).

[58]The message begins with the policy argument that the country could not afford a general program of internal improvements, which would increase the already burdensome national debt rather than paying it off. Noting the risk that members of Congress might be tempted to promote undeserving projects in their own districts to facilitate reelection, Polk proceeded to state a general principle of constitutional interpretation: "If there be one construction of the Constitution which is entirely safe, and another on the same subject which is full of danger, it is fair to conclude, that the safe construction is that, which was intended by its framers." Polk Message (cited in note 56). A variant of John Marshall's familiar argument that the Framers were reasonable people and would not have prescribed rules whose consequences were absurd, this passage stamped Polk, like so many of his contemporaries, as what would be called an originalist today. For Marshall see, e.g., Marbury v Madison, 5 US 137, 178 (1803); Cohens v Virginia, 19 US 264, 377 (1821); The First Hundred Years at 71, 97.

[59]1 Annals of Congress at 929, 932.

[60]Id at 930.

[61]Id at 931.

[62]Polk Message at "Permanent Seat of Government" (cited in note 56).

[63]Cf Congress's 1790 decision not to pay for removing obstructions in the Savannah River, noted in The Federalist Period at 70 n.116.

cases were distinguishable in principle too. Contrary to popular rumor, he argued, federal authority over lighthouses and other navigational installations was based not on the inapposite power to "regulate" commerce but rather on that clause of Article I, § 8 giving Congress the right of "exclusive legislation" over the seat of Government and other places ceded by the states "for the erection of forts, magazines, arsenals, dockyards, and other needful buildings."[64] And that clause, he did not have to point out, lent no support to the dredging of harbors or the removal of snags.

The argument itself was not new. Virginia Representative Philip Barbour had made it in 1817, and others had echoed it with conviction. As a textual matter, I have said before, there was little to recommend this position. The clause was plainly designed to permit the United States to ensure the security of their own operations by excluding state jurisdiction over them; nothing its language or origin suggests that it was intended to limit the competence of Congress, without going to such lengths, to construct or acquire facilities necessary and proper to the exercise of other federal powers.[65]

What was new about Polk's 1848 draft veto was his effort to demonstrate that in voting to acquire and construct lighthouses and other navigational facilities Congress had *actually relied* on the exclusive-jurisdiction clause rather than on the commerce power. Every statute on the subject from 1789 until 1819, he insisted, had been expressly conditioned on a prior cession of jurisdiction by the state; an 1820 law, which was "still in force," flatly provided in the most general terms that "no light-house, beacon nor landmark, shall be built or erected on any site, previous to the cession of jurisdiction over the same being made to the United States."[66] The obvious inference, Polk concluded, was that "Congress did not . . . feel at liberty to exercise these powers over any territory but its own . . . ."[67]

Much as I admire Polk's assiduousness and legal skill, I remain unconvinced. That Congress demanded cession of lighthouse sites may indicate nothing more than the desire to obtain exclusive jurisdiction over them.[68] In none of the relevant debates, so far as Polk's researches reveal, was Congress's right to dispense with this condition clearly denied.

Moreover, I think it most improbable that the cession clause was intended to permit the United States to acquire territory for purposes otherwise foreign to federal authority, as Polk appeared to assume.[69] "[F]orts, magazines, arsenals, [and] dockyards" are necessary and proper to exercise of the military and naval powers granted to Congress; "other

[64]Polk Message at "Lighthouses, Beacons, Buoys, and Piers" (cited in note 56); see US Const, Art I, § 8, cl 17.

[65]See The Jeffersonians at 275–76. See also 3 Story, § 1141: "[S]urely it will not be pretended, that congress could not erect a fort, or magazine, in a place within a state, unless the state should cede the territory." But that was indeed what Polk asserted: "The United States can no more put a spade into the soil of the States . . . without purchase of title and a grant of jurisdiction than they can dig or legislate over the soil of Great Britain or France." Polk Message at "Lighthouses, Beacons, Buoys, and Piers" (cited in note 56).

[66]3 Stat 598, 600, § 7 (May 15, 1820).

[67]Polk Message at "Lighthouses, Beacons, Buoys, and Piers" (cited in note 56).

[68]Moreover, neither the marine hospitals first provided for in 1798 nor the subsidies for transatlantic steamships authorized in 1845 could be explained on the basis of the clause in question; for the hospitals were to be built on any land ceded, sold, or donated to the United States, while the subsidy involved no land at all. See notes 32, 44; 1 Stat 605, 606, § 4 (Jul 16, 1798).

[69]F.P. Stanton of Tennessee had effectively made this argument in response to Polk's 1847 veto. Cong Globe App, 30th Cong, 1st Sess 58.

needful buildings" are those incident to the exercise of some legitimate federal function. Perspicuous guardians of state rights had made this point repeatedly with respect to the District of Columbia, and before an incident to be discussed in a later chapter they had invariably prevailed.[70] Until then one would have thought it inconceivable that Polk himself would have countenanced the acquisition by cession of territory on which to establish, for example, a national bank.[71]

V. CONGRESS INSISTS (A LITTLE)

Presidents Taylor and Fillmore, who behaved like true Whigs, took a broader view: Congress had ample power to improve rivers and harbors and ought to do so;[72] it should also take steps to improve intercourse with the Pacific coast by opening a "line of communication."[73] With one important exception soon to be noted, however, little was accomplished in the field of internal improvements during this fleeting period of Whig ascendancy. It was not until 1855, during the Democratic Administration of Franklin Pierce, that Congress authorized construction of a private telegraph line across public property from the Mississippi or Missouri River to San Francisco[74]—which could easily be justified on the innocuous ground that Congress, like any other proprietor, could grant easements over its own land.[75]

President Pierce, like his Democratic forebears, took a dim view of federal power

[70]See The Jeffersonians at 255, 298–302 and the discussion of the Smithsonian Institution in chapter 5 of this volume.

[71]In his fourth Annual Message Polk summed up his philosophy by condemning as unconstitutional every element of Clay's American System: the National Bank, the protective tariff, internal improvements, and the distribution of land revenues to the states. 4 Richardson at 629, 658 (Dec 5, 1848).

[72]See 5 Richardson at 4, 6 (Mar 5, 1849) (Taylor); id at 77, 90–91 (Dec 2, 1850) (Fillmore). "This authority," wrote Fillmore,

> I suppose to be derived chiefly from the power of regulating commerce with foreign nations and among the States and the power of laying and collecting imposts. Where commerce is to be carried on and imposts collected there must be ports and harbors as well as wharves and customhouses.

Id at 90. It will be noted that Fillmore drew no distinction between interstate and foreign commerce in this respect, or between inland and coastal waters.

[73]5 Richardson at 9, 20 (Dec 4, 1849) (Taylor); id at 77, 86 (Dec 2, 1850) (Fillmore); id at 163, 178 (Dec 6, 1852) (same).

[74]10 Stat 610, § 1 (Feb 17, 1855). Five years later Congress passed a second statute authorizing competitive bidding to construct a telegraph to San Francisco to carry Government messages, on condition the line also be open to public use. 12 Stat 41 (Jun 16, 1860); see Robert L. Thompson, Wiring A Continent: The History of the Telegraph Industry in the United States, 1832–1866 348–69 (Princeton, 1947). Carrying official dispatches was obviously necessary and proper to the conduct of Government business (see Cong Globe, 36th Cong, 1st Sess 1695 (Rep. Conkling)); carrying messages for the general public was not. See also 11 Stat 187 (Mar 3, 1857), authorizing the Secretary of State to contract for construction of a submarine cable *from Newfoundland to Ireland* on similar terms.

[75]Scarcely more difficult for a strict constructionist to justify was a provision of the same law making it a federal crime to damage the line "within the territories of the United States," 10 Stat at 611, § 2, since (despite Southern arguments respecting the prohibition of slavery) it was widely conceded that Congress had considerable authority to protect private property (including slaves) in the territories. See Descent into the Maelstrom, chs 7, 10.

with respect to internal improvements.[76] His first Annual Message, in 1853, while conceding that Congress could build roads in the territories and that some improvements within the states might be necessary and proper to the exercise of congressional war powers,[77] suggested that in most other cases Congress consider getting out of the business of coastal as well as internal improvements.[78] Another warning came in 1854, when in signing a garden-variety bill for the removal of obstructions from the Cape Fear River he took the unusual step of informing the Senate that he did so only because "the obstructions which the proposed appropriation is intended to remove are the result of acts of the General Government."[79] The United States, in other words, could rectify their own earlier mistakes, but that was not to say they had general authority to improve the navigability of streams.

Later that year, in explaining his reasons for vetoing yet another bill for the improvement of rivers and harbors, Pierce embraced Polk's distinction between warning mariners of obstructions and eliminating them. Lighthouses, beacons, and buoys (as Polk had said) were a special case because of their long pedigree; when not necessary for naval purposes, they might perhaps be justified "as incident to the revenue power." The removal of obstructions, as Polk had said, was another matter:

> It is a remarkable fact that for a period of more than thirty years after the adoption of the Constitution all appropriations of this class were confined, with scarcely an apparent exception, to the construction of light-houses, beacons, buoys, and public piers and the stakage of channels; to render navigation "safe and easy," it is true, but only by indicating to the navigator obstacles in his way, not by removing those obstacles nor in any other respect changing, artificially, the preexisting natural condition of the earth and sea.[80]

In other words, it was all right for Congress to illuminate obstructions but not to remove

[76]As a member of the House during the 1830's Pierce had been more Catholic on this subject than the Pope, voting against a rivers-and-harbors bill that President Jackson signed. See Roy F. Nichols, Franklin Pierce: Young Hickory of the Granite Hills 73 (Pennsylvania, 2d ed 1958): "[T]he federal government was one of limited powers and among them Pierce never found any to help the West."

[77]5 Richardson at 207, 216, 220. It was on the basis of territorial and military authority that Pierce repeated Taylor's and Fillmore's request for consideration of a railway to the Pacific coast. Id at 220–22.

[78]Id at 218–20.

[79]Id at 243 (Jul 22, 1854); see 10 Stat 307 (Jul 22, 1854). That had been the reason given by numerous members of Congress for supporting this and other similar appropriations. See, e.g., Cong Globe, 33d Cong, 1st Sess 1654, 1657 (North Carolina Rep. William Ashe); Cong Globe, 32d Cong, 1st Sess 1420 (Georgia Sen. John Berrien, on a bill (10 Stat 640 (Mar 3, 1855)) "to remove the obstructions in the Savannah River . . . placed there during the revolutionary war, for the common defence"); Cong Globe, 31st Cong, 1st Sess 198, 211 (Mississippi Sen. Jefferson Davis, on a bill to repair a crumbling dam): "I hold that the Federal Government, having put an obstruction in the natural navigation of the river, is bound to remove that obstruction . . . ."

[80]5 Richardson at 257, 263–65 (Dec 30, 1854). Pierce did not quite say it was unconstitutional to remove obstructions, though he speculated that constitutional doubts might have underlain the distinction. Id at 264. He had vetoed the bill on August 4, just before Congress adjourned, noting that time did not then permit a full statement of his reasons. Id at 256.

them, except perhaps in cases of national security.[81]

As if to illustrate what he had in mind, Pierce vetoed five bills for the improvement of rivers within a three-month period in 1856. One was designed "to render the port of Baltimore accessible to the war steamers of the United States," two to deepen channels over the flats of the St. Clair and St. Mary's Rivers connecting Lakes Erie, Huron, and Superior, and two to improve navigation of the Mississippi—in one case by removing impediments to commerce to and from the Gulf of Mexico.[82] All were liable, he said, to the objections voiced in his 1854 message; two he expressly denounced as beyond Congress's authority.[83] But Congress would have none of it; it thumpingly overrode all five of President Pierce's 1856 vetoes.[84]

That was more remarkable than it may appear to the later observer. We have become accustomed to the override of presidential vetoes, and it was plainly contemplated by the Framers. The President's veto is suspensive only; Congress may pass a law despite the President's objection.[85] But *it had never done so until 1845.* Indeed only a few years earlier prominent critics had predicted that no veto would ever be overridden: The untraversable two-thirds barrier, they complained, had transformed the intended suspensive veto into an absolute one.[86]

James Buchanan, who had never had much use for federal improvements,[87] shared Pierce's constitutional views. As late as 1860 he vetoed additional bills to dredge both the St. Clair flats and the Mississippi's mouth.[88] This time Congress, though its advocates of federal authority had been augmented by the election of numerous Republicans, did nothing about it. And thus on the eve of the Civil War Congress found itself unable even to remove obstructions to naturally navigable waters, which Andrew Jackson himself had conceded it not only could but ought to do.

VI. TONNAGE DUTIES

In his 1847 veto message, as I have noted, President Polk had suggested that his narrow interpretation of federal authority with regard to navigational improvements would not prevent them from being undertaken: Congress might permit the states to finance them by laying tonnage duties otherwise interdicted by Article I, § 10.[89] He returned to this theme

[81]Pierce closed by admonishing Congress (as Tyler and Polk had also urged) "to make appropriation for every work in a separate bill," so that each could be examined "on its own independent merits" (5 Richardson at 270–71)—and thus Pierce, like more than one of his predecessors, clearly indicated that he understood he had no item veto. For the similar views of Presidents Tyler and Polk see notes 45–46 and accompanying text.

[82]5 Richardson at 386–88 (May 19, May 22, Aug 11, and Aug 14, 1856).

[83]Those respecting the St. Clair and St. Mary's Rivers, id at 387. Even the appropriation to open the mouth of the Mississippi he dismissed as nothing but "part of a general system of internal improvements" and therefore not deserving of his approval. Id at 386.

[84]11 Stat 24 (Jul 8, 1856); 11 Stat 25 (Jul 8, 1856); 11 Stat 44 (Aug 16, 1856); 11 Stat 51 (Aug 16, 1856).

[85]US Const, Art I, § 7.

[86]See section I of chapter 6.

[87]He had been among the first, for example, to urge that the Federal Government divest itself of the Cumberland Road. See The Jeffersonians at 283.

[88]5 Richardson at 599 (Feb 1, 1860); id at 607 (Feb 6, 1860).

[89]See note 54 and accompanying text. Abraham Lincoln, then representing his Illinois district in the House, took the floor to differ with Polk. Tonnage duties might be adequate to keep existing facilities in repair, he said, but how were they to finance new ones? It would be inequitable to charge users of one harbor for the cost of

in his undelivered 1848 message, citing additional examples of congressional consent to such measures in order to establish "the contemporaneous construction of the Constitution on this point"[90] and attempting to counter arguments against the legitimacy of his suggestion that he said others had raised.[91]

There were two objections that Polk chose to refute, and they were closely related. First, the Northwest Ordinance had provided in 1787 that "navigable waters leading into the Mississippi and St. Lawrence [Rivers], and the carrying places between [them]" should be "common highways, and forever free" to all U.S. citizens, "without any tax, impost or duty therefor."[92] Second, Congress had imposed the same requirement on a number of Western states as a condition of their admission to the Union.[93] State taxes on vessels plying the waters in question, it was argued, contravened both the Ordinance and the later statehood provisions.

I think it can fairly be said that Polk blew these objections out of the waters they professed to protect. The Ordinance, if valid, was "nothing more than an act of legislation" by Congress under the Articles of Confederation and thus subject to later modification or repeal. The Constitution had modified it by authorizing Congress to consent to state tonnage taxes and to impose its own, and the Constitution was supreme. The Ordinance itself, pursuant to a stipulation in the Act by which Virginia had ceded the Northwest Territory to the United States, required that new states carved out of that territory be admitted on "an equal footing with the original states," all of which had power to levy tonnage duties with congressional approval. The Ordinance further provided that the guarantee of free navigation, like other elements of what it termed a "compact" between the original states and the people of the territory, might be altered "by common consent"; if Congress and the relevant state agreed to the imposition of duties, the consent requirement was satisfied.[94]

Polk wielded similar arguments against the objection based on conditions in the statutes admitting Western states to the Union. Since the equal-footing doctrine was of constitutional rank, he said, Congress could not condition admission on the surrender of powers possessed by other states.[95] In any event, the statehood Acts too were subject to modification by common consent of the parties.[96] Finally, the "settled construction" of all

---

building another. And thus Polk's proposal involved "the same absurdity of the Irish bull about the new boots—'I shall niver git 'em on,' says Patrick, 'till I wear 'em a day or two, and stretch 'em a little.'" Cong Globe App, 30th Cong, 1st Sess 710. Lincoln forgot one thing: the possibility of borrowing money to be repaid out of future tonnage revenues.

[90]The earliest examples, dating from 1790, are cited in The Federalist Period at 56 n.6.

[91]Not, to my knowledge, in Congress; my notes, at any rate, do not reveal them. The debates on internal improvements during the period under examination are not only enormously repetitive; they are voluminous, if not to the point of actual impracticability, well beyond that of diminishing returns. In contrast to those relevant to earlier installments of this study, I cannot claim to have read them all, though I have glanced at all the pages. Thus the absence of an argument from this volume, alas, is no absolute warranty that the argument was never made.

[92]32 J Cont Cong 334, 341, Art IV (Jul 13, 1787), 1 Stat 51, 52 n.(a).

[93]E.g., 2 Stat 701, 703, § 1 (Apr 8, 1812) (Louisiana).

[94]Polk Message at "Tonnage Duties" (cited in note 56).

[95]See the debates on the admission of Missouri, discussed in The Jeffersonians at 243–45.

[96]Congress in 1828 had finessed the question of its power to repeal a similar condition on grants made to Alabama at the time of statehood by consenting to the imposition of tolls to pay for improvements, presumably under Article I, § 10. 4 Stat 308 (May 24, 1828); see The Jeffersonians at 232.

relevant free-navigation provisions was that they applied, in the words of a federal Circuit Court, only "to the navigable rivers and the carrying places, as they then were": "It would seem to be no violation of the compact if the Legislature should exact a toll, not for the navigation of the rivers in their natural state, but for the increased facilities established by the funds of the State."[97]

Additional objections to Polk's proposal surfaced as consent to state tonnage duties was debated in Congress over the next several years. To permit a single state to impose such duties, it was suggested, might give its ports a "preference" over those of other states, contrary to Article I, § 9;[98] to allow them to be levied on vessels engaged in interstate commerce would require ships "bound to, or from, one State" to "pay duties in another," which the same clause forbade.[99] Defenders of congressional consent pointed to the unqualified language of the following section authorizing Congress to permit state tonnage taxes,[100] argued that preferences were benefits while taxes were burdens,[101] and insisted that the purpose of the latter clause was to prevent Congress from requiring that a ship bound from one state to another be diverted to a third.[102]

Polk's defenders, I think, had the better of these arguments too, and as he said precedent nearly as old as the Constitution supported him. He was right that Congress could consent to state tonnage taxes to finance internal improvements.[103] That did not

[97]Polk Message at "Tonnage Duties" (cited in note 56), citing Spooner v McConnell, 22 F Cas 939, 944–45 (No 13, 245) (CCD Ohio 1838). The Supreme Court would later conclude that a charge for use of state-constructed improvements such as wharves was not a tonnage duty within Article I, § 10 but a mere service fee the states were free to impose without congressional consent. Packet Co v Keokuk, 95 US 80 (1877). See also Cannon v New Orleans, 87 US 577, 581 (1874), defining a tonnage duty as "a contribution claimed for the privilege of arriving or departing from a port."

[98]See Cong Globe, 31st Cong, 1st Sess 960 (New York Rep. Harvey Putnam). A moment later, anticipating rebuttal, Putnam qualified his assertion: He was arguing only that such consent was contrary to the "spirit" of the Constitution. Id at 961. Delaware Senator James Bayard went to the opposite extreme: Congress could *only* approve individual requests for permission to impose tonnage duties, not grant it in gross as Senator Douglas had proposed; for Congress had an obligation to examine the merits of a particular state request. Cong Globe App, 32d Cong, 1st Sess 1127 (Sen. Douglas); id at 1146 (Sen. Bayard). See also Cong Globe, 36th Cong, 2d Sess 537, 541 (Sen. Trumbull), arguing that to give blanket consent in advance was to repeal the constitutional prohibition. Compare the question whether Congress may consent in advance to the future admission of states, Descent into the Maelstrom, ch 5.

[99]Cong Globe App, 30th Cong, 1st Sess 59–60 (Rep. F.P. Stanton); Cong Globe, 35th Cong, 1st Sess 2350 (Sen. Jefferson Davis).

[100]Cong Globe, 31st Cong, 1st Sess 961 (Maryland Rep. Robert McLane).

[101]Id. See also Cong Globe, 35th Cong, 1st Sess 2383 (Vermont Sen. Jacob Collamer), noting that experience had shown tonnage taxes drove ships to other ports, thus explaining why few states any longer asked permission to impose them. This, I think, was the weakest argument in the series; for although the tax itself might be a burden, the *privilege* of collecting revenue that was off limits to others was a tangible benefit whose desirability repeated requests for congressional consent had amply confirmed.

[102]Id at 2350 (Georgia Sen. Robert Toombs): "If a vessel was bound from Buffalo for Michigan City, . . . this clause would prohibit the paying of duties at Chicago." See also Cong Globe, 36th Cong, 1st Sess 3095–96 (Sen. Toombs again, citing Story (see 2 Story, § 1011) and the debates in the Constitutional Convention). The full text of the provision tends to confirm this common-sense interpretation: "[N]or shall vessels bound to, or from, one State, be obliged to enter, clear, or pay duties in another." The same objection had been rejected on the same ground in 1789, when *Congress* imposed tonnage duties on ships engaged in interstate as well as foreign commerce. See The Federalist Period at 58 n.26.

[103]An additional argument supports the conclusion that the provision respecting duties in other states did not apply. As the existence of separate ex post facto and bill of attainder clauses in the following section makes clear, Article I, § 9 limits federal, not state action. Its evident goal is to protect states against federally imposed

mean, however, that Congress was without power to finance them itself; as Tennessee Representative F.P. Stanton pointed out in 1848, Article I, § 10 limited state, not federal authority.[104]

VII. THE IRON HORSE

During the same period of largely Democratic hegemony, as rivers and harbors bills were dropping like flies under the blows of states'-rights Presidents, the rise of the railroad prompted a number of Democrats in Congress, especially those of the Western persuasion, to reexamine their party's traditional hostility to federally subsidized improvements.

As early as 1830 the nationalistic Daniel Webster, in light of the understandable reticence of South Carolina's Democratic Senators, had presented a petition inviting Congress to aid in the construction of a railroad that would ultimately connect that state to Cincinnati on the Ohio River.[105] He got nowhere in the adverse climate of the Jackson years, and for two decades railroad construction proceeded essentially without federal bounty.[106] Requests for assistance multiplied, however, and by mid-century Western Democrats had settled on a new formula that would permit Congress to subsidize their pet projects without tearing down the barriers that states'-rights partisans had erected to federal spending for other internal improvements. The breakthrough came in 1850, during a rare hiatus in Democratic control of the Executive Branch, with the authorization of land grants to aid in construction of the Illinois Central Railroad.[107]

The resourceful and indefatigable sponsor of the Illinois Central was the young Stephen A. Douglas, who had represented Illinois in one House or the other since 1843,[108] and of whom we shall have much to say in the next volume. Mr. Douglas, a lifelong Democrat, had an abiding interest in the development of the West in general and his state in particular, and for what it is worth the railroad in question was to pass through his own property.[109]

---

disabilities; if a state elects to place itself at a disadvantage by taxing access to its own ports, and if Congress concludes that the resultant burden on interstate and foreign commerce is not excessive, I see no reason why the Framers would have wanted to interfere.

[104]Cong Globe App, 30th Cong, 1st Sess 59.

[105]Cong Deb, 21st Cong, 1st Sess 21–22. See William Aiken to Webster, Jan 9, 1830, 3 Webster Correspondence at 4–5; South Carolina Sen. Robert Hayne to Webster, Jan 15, 1830, id at 9; Peterson, The Great Triumvirate at 172.

[106]Railroads were given, however, "either full or partial rebates on the duties on iron imported for rails"; and three railroads "received free right of way through federal lands and the use of stone and timber from them." See Goodrich, American Canals and Railroads at 169–70 (cited in note 35). In addition, railroads benefited from Government surveys made at federal expense until the relevant statute was repealed in 1838. 4 Stat 22, 22–23 (Apr 30, 1824); 5 Stat 256, 257, § 6 (Jul 5, 1838); see Taylor, The Transportation Revolution at 94–95 (cited in note 32).

[107]9 Stat 466 (Sep 20, 1850). A similar bill, also sponsored by Senator Douglas, had passed the Senate in 1848 but narrowly failed in the House. See Cong Globe, 30th Cong, 1st Sess 214, 723, 1071.

[108]Born in Vermont in 1813, Douglas was elected to the Illinois legislature in 1836 and then sat for two years on the Illinois Supreme Court before going to Congress; he moved from the House to the Senate in 1847. His most comprehensive biography is Robert W. Johannsen, Stephen A. Douglas (Oxford, 1973). As Johannsen tells us, Douglas spelled his name with two s's until 1846. Id at 876 n.7.

[109]See id at 335, reporting that Douglas sold a portion of his land to the railroad for $21,300—"about ten times what he had paid for the entire acreage" not long before.

In addition to allowing the state of Illinois a right of way over public lands for a railroad from Chicago and Galena to "a point at or near the junction of the Ohio and Mississippi Rivers," the Act granted the state, "for the purpose of aiding in making the railroad, . . . every alternate section of land designated by even numbers, for six sections in width on each side of said road . . . ." Similar provisions were made for Alabama and Mississippi, in order to subsidize extension of the road from the Ohio to Mobile, on the Gulf coast.[110]

When Senator Douglas introduced his bill in April 1850, Georgia Senator William C. Dawson objected. The United States held the public lands in trust, said Dawson, "either for the people at large or for the States"; it had no right to donate any part of the trust property "to any portion of the *cestui que trusts* to the exclusion of the other."[111]

William H. Seward of New York disputed his premise: Congress had express authority to dispose of public lands,[112] "without any limitations prescribed upon our discretion." The Constitution imposed no specific trust; there was no need to distribute lands or their proceeds equally among all citizens. Congress should exercise its power, "like every other power of the Government, . . . with judgment, wisdom, and a due regard to the best interests of the country." It was in the country's best interest to dispose of land for the construction of railroads that would promote settlement and cultivation of the public domain.[113]

Douglas, in contrast, conceded Dawson's premise that public lands were held in trust for the entire nation, but he disputed Dawson's conclusion. Like any trustee, he argued, Congress might lawfully dispose of public lands in any manner that increased the value of the trust fund, and by granting land to promote railroads the Government enhanced the value of the remaining soil.[114] "[B]y running this road through [the Pine Barrens] of Mississippi and Alabama," explained the venerable Henry Clay, "you will . . . bring into market an immense amount of lands, increasing their value to the benefit of the

[110] 9 Stat at 466–67, §§ 1, 2, 7. There was precedent for this plan: While the sympathetic John Quincy Adams was President, Congress had granted lands to Illinois, Indiana, and Ohio to subsidize the construction of canals. 4 Stat 234 (Mar 2, 1827) (Illinois); 4 Stat 236 (Mar 2, 1827) (Indiana); 4 Stat 305 (May 24, 1828) (Ohio); see Goodrich, American Canals and Railroads at 142, 169 (cited in note 35). A later grant to Wisconsin for the same purpose under Democratic auspices (5 Stat 245, § 1 (Jun 18, 1838)) was distinguishable, as Wisconsin at the time was still a territory, over which no state had authority. Thus, despite periodic efforts at revival in Congress (see, e.g., HR Rep 510, 23d Cong, 1st Sess 1–2 (1834); S Doc 203, 25th Cong, 2d Sess 1 (1838)), the device employed in the Illinois Central case had basically lain dormant for a full twenty years; and thus, as Goodrich wrote (supra at 169–70), the Illinois Central grant introduced a new era of federal aid for internal improvements in the states.

[111] Cong Globe, 31st Cong, 1st Sess 849.

[112] US Const, Art IV, § 3.

[113] Cong Globe, 31st Cong, 1st Sess 851. See also id at 850 (Sen. Clay); 3 Story, § 1321, arguing that constitutional objections to spending tax revenues for unenumerated purposes "ha[ve] not been supposed to apply to an appropriation of the proceeds of the public lands."

[114] Cong Globe, 31st Cong, 1st Sess 849. To ensure that the Government be none the poorer for having parted with some of its acreage, the Act required that alternate sections not granted to the states "shall not be sold for less than double the minimum price of the public lands." 9 Stat at 466, § 3; see Cong Globe, 31st Cong, 1st Sess 845 (Sen. Douglas). "This arrangement," Illinois Representative John McClernand had said two years earlier in debating a similar bill, "will secure to the Government as much for one-half of the land as it otherwise could obtain for the whole." Cong Globe App, 30th Cong, 1st Sess 1137.

treasury of the United States."[115]

Dawson had begun the debate by observing that he could perceive no distinction between granting land to subsidize a railroad and appropriating money for the same purpose.[116] As South Carolina Senator Andrew Butler noted, the Democratic Party was on record as denying (in its Baltimore Platform of 1844) that Congress had power to establish a general system of internal improvements;[117] if Congress could evade this limitation by simply granting land instead of money, said Dawson, "all controversy about internal improvements will have ceased . . . ."[118]

Alabama Democrat William R. King, whose state was to benefit from Douglas's bill pursuant to an amendment he himself had offered,[119] thought there was a difference:

> As regards our constitutional power on this subject, we have always drawn a distinction between appropriations out of the Treasury direct, and the right of the Government to dispose of the public domain for the internal improvements of the States, so that the part not so disposed of will be increased in value, or as a great land owner would dispose of part of his own lands for the benefit of the remainder.

The same distinction, King added, had been explicitly embraced two years before by that latter-day high priest of states' rights, the late John C. Calhoun.[120]

Other good Democrats bought the distinction as well. Lewis Cass of Michigan, the party's 1848 presidential candidate, stated it concisely that year in the Senate.[121] President Pierce would soon swallow it hook, line, and sinker.[122] Nor was support for railroad land grants among congressional Democrats confined to those from the North. As we have seen, King of Alabama supported the Illinois Central bill; so did both Jefferson Davis and Henry Foote of Mississippi, through whose state the road would also run.[123] The principal division on this question—as it had been on many others before the slavery question monopolized the limelight—was between East and West, not between North and South.[124]

[115]Cong Globe, 31st Cong, 1st Sess 850. The argument was not new; a House committee had suggested as early as 1806 that Congress support improvement of Ohio River navigation in part because it would enhance the value of the public lands. See The Jeffersonians at 119 n.235.

[116]Cong Globe, 31st Cong, 1st Sess 845.

[117]Id at 845–46; Democratic Party Platform of 1844, in Porter & Johnson, Party Platforms at 3. Substantially identical provisions appeared in all Democratic platforms from 1840 to the Civil War. See note 48.

[118]Cong Globe, 31st Cong, 1st Sess 849. See also Cong Globe App, 30th Cong, 1st Sess 535 (1848) (Connecticut Senator John Niles, opposing an earlier Illinois Central proposal): "To say that we can get round the Constitution by granting the public lands, instead of taking the money directly out of the treasury, is certainly trifling with the judgment of this body."

[119]Cong Globe, 31st Cong, 1st Sess 845.

[120]Id at 846. Indeed it had. In debating the 1848 counterpart of the Illinois Central bill ultimately adopted, Calhoun noted that on this ground, as Vice-President, he had cast the deciding vote in favor of a land grant to finance construction of the Illinois and Michigan Canal. Cong Globe App, 30th Cong, 1st Sess 537. See also S Doc 410, 29th Cong, 1st Sess 21–22 (1846).

[121]Cong Globe App, 30th Cong, 1st Sess 537.

[122]See 5 Richardson at 207, 216–17 (Dec 5, 1853); id at 247, 253–54 (May 3, 1854).

[123]See Cong Globe, 31st Cong, 1st Sess 870 (Sen. Davis); id at 847 (Sen. Foote).

[124]See id at 849 (Sen. Dawson): "It is remarkable, that if a citizen and politician goes from any part of the Union to the western States, he forgets all that he may have learned in early life of the powers of the Gov-

Mississippi and Alabama spokesmen were thus prepared to help themselves to federal land, but they drew the line at helping Kentucky and Tennessee. To reach the Gulf Coast the road had to cross those states as well, but both were devoid of unappropriated federal land.[125] Tennessee Senator John Bell, a respected Whig who would run for President on the Constitutional Union ticket in 1860, accordingly proposed to grant both Tennessee and Kentucky proceeds from the sale of land in Alabama, Mississippi, and Illinois.[126] King protested at once: To give land to states other than that in which it was situated was a different matter entirely.[127] Davis agreed: Congress could grant land "to build a road through its unsettled domain, with a view of bringing it into the market, or rendering it saleable." To do so in order to build roads elsewhere, he argued, was a "new feature" that could not be condoned, for he was unable to perceive "any difference between thus granting land or taking money from the Treasury to build these works"—and that, of course, orthodox Democratic interpretation forbade.[128]

The rift thus opened was detrimental to the cause of internal improvements, since it meant that Congress could subsidize them only in Florida and the West, where there were abundant federal lands.[129] As Bell suggested, the distinction was also without constitutional foundation.[130] For the argument in favor of grants to Illinois was that they would enhance the value of property still owned by the United States; grants to Kentucky and Tennessee were equally important to improving the value of Illinois land. Indeed Davis was right that there was no way of distinguishing grants of money for this purpose from grants of land: *Any* federal subsidy that promoted the Illinois railway was necessary and proper to improving the marketability of Illinois public land.

VIII. THE GOLDEN GATE

It was not long before Congress granted public lands for additional railroads in Iowa, Florida, Alabama, Louisiana, Wisconsin, and Michigan—all states embracing goodly quantities of federal land.[131] President Pierce signed them all.[132] He also reiterated his

ernment in relation to internal improvements, and comes back here a thorough internal-improvement man . . . ."

[125]Kentucky had never belonged to the Federal Government, and Tennessee was "almost entirely covered by [private] claims." See Benjamin H. Hibbard, A History of the Public Land Policies 10, 12 (Peter Smith, 1839).

[126]Cong Globe, 31st Cong, 1st Sess 868.

[127]Id at 869.

[128]Id at 870. For the defeat of Bell's amendment see id at 900.

[129]Even if the Constitution did not (as Tennessee Senator Hopkins Turney argued) require that all states benefit proportionally from the disposition of public lands, there was certainly something to his policy argument that the benefits should not accrue exclusively to those states in which the land was situated. Cong Globe, 31st Cong, 1st Sess 871–72. See also Cong Globe App, 30th Cong, 1st Sess 535 (Sen. Niles).

[130]See Cong Globe, 31st Cong, 1st Sess 869: "If it be constitutional to give land to Mississippi, why is it not constitutional to give it to Tennessee or Kentucky? . . . The only constitutional question that I know of, rests alone upon the question of appropriation, whether of lands or money, for works of this description . . . ." As a good Whig, Bell had no doubt of Congress's power to appropriate money as well as land for this purpose. Id at 867.

[131]11 Stat 9 (May 15, 1856); 11 Stat 15 (May 17, 1856); 11 Stat 17 (Jun 3, 1856); 11 Stat 18 (Jun 3, 1856); 11 Stat 20 (Jun 3, 1856); 11 Stat 21 (Jun 3, 1856).

predecessors' request for aid in the construction of a railroad to the Pacific coast, "by all constitutional means."[133] In that connection he hinted strongly that such a project might be necessary and proper for purposes of national defense.[134]

The Pacific railroad was always viewed as a special case. Some defended it, unsurprisingly, on the controversial theory that had prevailed in the case of the Illinois Central: Land grants for building the road would enhance the value of remaining public lands.[135] Some argued it was enough that the rails would pass largely through territory with respect to which the United States had broad power (under Article IV, § 3) to make all "needful rules and regulations."[136] Some invoked the postal power, on the entirely plausible ground that the railroad (like the Illinois Central, it should be added)[137] would carry the mail.[138] But a special appeal was made to those who found the road not sustainable on any of these theories: A railway was indispensable to protect the West Coast from possible invasion.

As noted, Presidents Taylor, Fillmore, and Pierce had all taken that position. Maryland Whig Thomas Pratt spelled it out for the Senate in 1853: "Without a railroad con-

---

[132]He did so although earlier doubts whether (constitutional questions to one side) the country was going "too fast and too far" in this direction had led him to reopen for public sale more than 30,000,000 acres that had been reserved in anticipation of future grants. Second Annual Message, 5 Richardson at 273, 290–91 (Dec 4, 1854).

[133]Id at 207, 221 (Dec 5, 1853).

[134]Id at 220. See generally Robert R. Russel, Improvement of Communication with the Pacific Coast as an Issue in American Politics, 1783–1864 (Torch, 1948).

[135]E.g., Cong Globe, 33d Cong, 1st Sess 876 (California Sen. William Gwin).

[136]E.g., id (Sen. Gwin); Cong Globe, 32d Cong, 2d Sess 280 (1853) (Texas Sen. Thomas Jefferson Rusk) (suggesting that portions of the road within the state of California be left to the state to build); Cong Globe App, 34th Cong, 1st Sess 477 (California Sen. John Weller). But see HR Rep 439, 31st Cong, 1st Sess 2 (1850) (Tennessee Rep. F.P. Stanton), dismissing the territorial power as inadequate, since the road would have to pass through states as well, and pointing out that before the project was completed much of the territory in question would have been admitted to statehood.

As we shall see, the extent of congressional authority to legislate for the territories had become a matter of fierce dispute (see Descent into the Maelstrom, ch 7). Indeed in 1852 North Carolina Representative Abraham Venable went so far as to question the power of Congress to build roads in the Minnesota Territory, astoundingly asserting that he could see no difference in this regard between a territory and a state. Cong Globe, 32d Cong, 1st Sess 1453–54. David Seymour of New York made hash of him, as William Bissell of Illinois and Minnesota Delegate Henry Rice did of other anarchist members two years later in debate on a similar territorial bill. Cong Globe, 32d Cong, 1st Sess 1454; Cong Globe, 33d Cong, 1st Sess 564–67. See also the parallel response of Senator Jefferson Davis, Cong Globe, 35th Cong, 2d Sess 445, 480 (1859) (also maintaining the distinction), and his 1854 letter to Bissell, Lynda L. Crist, ed, 5 The Papers of Jefferson Davis 57–59 (LSU, 1985) [hereafter cited as Davis Papers], finding military justification for the Minnesota road. The bill to authorize construction of that road was passed in June 1854 and repealed less than two months later after allegations of corruption were made. See 10 Stat 302 (Jun 29, 1854); 10 Stat 575, § 2 (Aug 4, 1854); Rice v Railroad Co., 66 US 358 (1861) (upholding the repeal); Roy M. Robbins, Our Landed Heritage: The Public Domain, 1776–1970 164 (Nebraska, 2d ed 1976).

[137]See 9 Stat at 467, § 6, and the discussion in Cong Globe, 31st Cong, 1st Sess 844.

[138]Cong Globe, 33d Cong, 1st Sess 876–77 (Sen. Gwin). Senator Seward offered a variant of this theme that he thought would appeal even to those who denied that the power to establish post roads included power to build them: Surely the Government could contract for carriage of the mail, and the prospect of compensation would induce private entrepreneurs to construct the road. Cong Globe, 32d Cong, 2d Sess 766. Cf the earlier subsidies granted to oceangoing steamships that carried the mail, discussed in note 44. Wisconsin Democrat Isaac Walker denied even this authority: What Congress could not do directly it could not do indirectly. Cong Globe, 32d Cong, 2d Sess 767.

necting the valley of the Mississippi with the Pacific, it would be impossible for the United States, in the event of a war with a foreign maritime Power, to defend California from a common enemy."[139] Democratic President James Buchanan picked up this theme in his inaugural address in 1857:

> Under the Constitution Congress has power "to declare war," "to raise and support armies," "to provide and maintain a navy," and to call forth the militia "to repel invasions." Thus endowed, in an ample manner, with the war-making power, the corresponding duty is required that "the United States shall protect each of them [the States] against invasion." Now, how is it possible to afford this protection to California and our Pacific possessions except by means of a military road . . . , over which men and munitions of war may be speedily transported from the Atlantic States to meet and repel the invader? . . . It is impossible to conceive that whilst the Constitution has expressly required Congress to defend all the States it should yet deny to them, by any fair construction, the only possible means by which one of these States can be defended.[140]

Buchanan made this argument in the very next paragraph after solemnly rehearsing the traditional Democratic credo that "strict construction of the powers of the Government is the only true, as well as the only safe, theory of the Constitution."[141]

Many roads, it had long been argued, had potential military uses;[142] the Pacific railroad, Pratt and Buchanan insisted, was a case of military necessity.[143] Not everyone was persuaded. Virginia's influential Senator James M. Mason, for instance, protested even in this context that Congress had no power to appropriate either money or land for internal improvements.[144] After a series of amendments had so enfeebled one bill for the construc-

[139]Id at 679.

[140]5 Richardson at 430, 434–35 (Mar 4, 1857). It should be noted that, like Pratt before him (Cong Globe, 32d Cong, 2d Sess 679), Buchanan went beyond saying that Congress *could* build a military road to California; in his view Article IV, § 3 made it Congress's *duty* to do so.

[141]5 Richardson at 434.

[142]See, e.g., the argument unsuccessfully urged in support of the Maysville Road, text accompanying note 18.

[143]Before his election, in an effort to win California support, Buchanan had written that Congress had the same power to finance a Pacific railroad as to fortify the San Francisco harbor. Buchanan to Col. B.F. Washington, Sep 17, 1856, John Bassett Moore, ed, 10 The Works of James Buchanan 93 (Lippincott, 1910).

[144]Cong Globe, 32d Cong, 2d Sess 676. See also Cong Globe App, 33d Cong, 1st Sess 406–7 (1854) (Virginia Rep. Thomas Bayly) (suggesting that the defense argument was a mere "pretext" and that land, like money, could be appropriated only to execute powers elsewhere enumerated). Jefferson Davis, in an animated exchange with Louisiana Senator Judah Benjamin, argued strongly that the war powers justified construction of the Pacific road but oddly only in the territories. Cong Globe, 35th Cong, 2d Sess 444–46, 480 (1859). In the states, he had said earlier, Congress could support a military road, like those designed to enhance the value of the public domain, by grants of land. Speech at New York, Jul 20, 1853, in Dunbar Rowland, ed, 2 Jefferson Davis: Constitutionalist. His Letters, Papers and Speeches 246–51 (Miss Dept of Archives & History, 1923). See also Davis's firm endorsement of the Pacific road on military grounds in his Speech at Philadelphia, 5 Davis Papers at 29–31; his 1855 annual report as Secretary of War, Cong Globe App, 34th Cong, 1st Sess 17, 19–21 (Dec 3, 1855); his letter to the Chairman of the Committee on Military Affairs, House Exec Doc 1, pt 2, 34th Cong, 1st Sess 16–17 ("the most imposing argument for the railroad as a military necessity ever presented," Russel at 199); and his letter to William R. Cannon, Dec 7, 1855, 5 Davis Papers at 141–42,

tion of the Pacific road that one of its chief proponents said he would have to oppose it,[145] North Carolina's Whig Senator George Badger declared in frustration that Democratic principles made any transcontinental railroad impossible.[146]

The proponents had the better arguments, and their numbers were legion.[147] Later bills succumbed less to lingering constitutional doubts than to interminable sectional quibbling over what route the road should follow.[148] Then the project was overtaken by the Civil War;[149] not until 1862, when Southern objections no longer carried much weight, would Congress finally authorize the California railroad.[150]

IX. THE TELEGRAPH

In connection with the campaign for adequate communications with the Pacific coast we have seen that Congress in 1855 authorized a private company to construct a telegraph line across public lands.[151] Some years earlier, however, in a time of equally strict construction of federal powers respecting internal improvements generally, Congress after continued executive prodding had taken a far more aggressive step: It had established a telegraph line between Washington and Baltimore and opened it for a brief period for public use.[152]

It was in 1837, during the Van Buren Administration, that Treasury Secretary Levi Woodbury, a good Democrat from New Hampshire, first recommended expanding the postal service to include telegraphy.[153] House committees responded favorably in 1842

---

suggesting that a Southern route to the Pacific might be the best means of promoting the admission of additional slave states. No friend of federal improvements generally, Davis had supported both land grants for continuation of the Illinois Central line through Mississippi and President Pierce's vetoes of river and harbor improvements. See text accompanying note 123; Speech at Jackson, Nov 4, 1857, 6 Davis Papers at 157, 158.

[145]Cong Globe, 32d Cong, 2d Sess 774 (Sen. Rusk).

[146]Id at 775.

[147]Even the 1860 platform of the states'-rights Breckinridge Democrats pledged "to use every means in their power" to secure legislation, "to the extent of the constitutional authority of Congress," to ensure construction of a Pacific railroad "at the earliest practicable moment," branding it "[o]ne of the greatest necessities of the age, in a political, commercial, postal and military point of view." Porter & Johnson, Party Platforms at 31.

[148]See Goodrich, American Canals and Railroads at 179–82 (cited in note 35); Alan Nevins, The Emergence of Lincoln: Douglas, Buchanan, and Party Chaos, 1857–1859 335–36 (Scribner's, 1950); Russel, Communication with the Pacific Coast, passim (cited in note 134). A War Department survey authorized by Congress, while preferring the most southerly route, found two others practicable as well. See 10 Stat 214, 219, § 10 (Mar 3, 1853); House Ex Doc XVIII, No 129, 33d Cong, 1st Sess (1855); Russel, Communication with the Pacific Coast at 168–83.

[149]Even Senator Crittenden of Kentucky, a firm supporter of federal improvements, voted to postpone the 1861 version of the bill. How can Congress debate ordinary legislative questions, he inquired, while Rome burns? Cong Globe, 36th Cong, 2d Sess 387.

[150]12 Stat 489 (Jul 1, 1862).

[151]See note 74 and accompanying text.

[152]See Thompson, Wiring a Continent 11–34 (cited in note 74); Leonard D. White, The Jacksonians: A Study in Administrative History, 1829–1861 456–58 (Macmillan, 1954) [hereafter cited as White, The Jacksonians].

[153]HR Doc 15, 25th Cong, 2d Sess 1 (Dec 6, 1837). Woodbury had been stimulated to this course by a letter from the inventor himself, who thought the Government ought to control his discovery. Samuel F.B. Morse to Woodbury, Sep 27, 1837, HR Doc 15, 25th Cong, 2d Sess 28. Ten years earlier, Postmaster General John McLean had waxed enthusiastic over the prospect that the Post Office might transmit messages by the more

and 1845.[154] Congress appropriated $30,000 to build an "experimental" line to Baltimore in 1843, transferred it to the Post Office in 1845, and made it available for commercial use.[155]

President Tyler, notwithstanding his narrow perception of federal improvement authority, signed both bills. Why? He did not say. The fact that it was the Post Office to which operation of the embryonic system was ultimately entrusted may suggest the answer: The telegraph is a modern variant of the mail. The Post Office was created to carry messages throughout the country; the telegraph was a means of carrying them.[156] The words of the Constitution are general enough to allow for technological progress; if photographs are "writings" within the copyright clause and an air force is an army or navy, telegraph offices are post offices and telegraph lines are post roads, which Congress may establish under Article I.[157] European practice confirms that telegraphy is an outgrowth of the mails, and that telephones are too; before the modern wave of privatization, the Post Office there typically operated all three.[158]

An enthusiastic House committee said all this and more in recommending that the line be extended to New York in 1845. The postal power made the Government "a public or common carrier" of information. The means of conveying that information that were available when the Constitution was written were painfully slow; the steamboat and the railroad were faster. "[T]hough not anticipated or foreseen, these new and improved modes were as clearly within the purview of the constitution, as were the old ones with which our ancestors were familiar." So it had come to pass that the post office had long dispatched information by steam, and it should equally do so now by wire; for the telegraph was a great advance over even the steam engine, and it would be a dereliction of duty not to keep up with improving technology.[159]

Under traditional Democratic doctrine the fact that telegraph lines might be considered post roads did not mean Congress could build them; it was party dogma that to

---

primitive method of visual signals known as optical telegraphy. See Richard R. John, Spreading the News: The American Postal System from Franklin to Morse 86–87 (Harvard, 1995).

[154]HR Rep 17, 27th Cong, 3d Sess 3 (Dec 30, 1842); HR Rep 187, 28th Cong, 2d Sess 5–6 (Mar 3, 1845). See also the favorable reports of Democratic Postmaster General Cave Johnson, S Doc 1, 29th Cong, 1st Sess 861 (Dec 1, 1845); S Doc 1, 29th Cong, 2d Sess 689 (Dec 7, 1846).

[155]5 Stat 618 (Mar 3, 1843); 5 Stat 752, 757 (Mar 3, 1845).

[156]See William Rawle, A View of the Constitution of the United States of America 103 (Philip H. Nicklin, 2d ed 1829) [hereafter cited as Rawle], associating the postal power with "a regular system of free and speedy communication"; see also Postmaster General Johnson's 1845 report, House Ex Doc 2, 29th Cong, 1st Sess 861, characterizing telegraphy as "the business of transmitting intelligence," which the Constitution confided to the United States.

[157]US Const, Art I, § 8, cl 7. See Burrow-Giles Lithographic Co v Sarony, 111 US 53 (1884), construing the next clause of the same section to include photography; The First Hundred Years at 435. Cf US Const, Art I, § 8, cl 12–13, giving Congress authority "[t]o raise and support armies" and "[t]o provide and maintain a Navy."

[158]In Germany, for example, "postal and telecommunications services" are one of the few subjects of exclusive federal legislative power, and "posts and telecommunications" were administered directly by the central authority until 1994; they have since been largely privatized. Basic Law for the Federal Republic of Germany, Art 73, cl 7; Art 83, ¶ 1 (earlier version); Art 87f, ¶ 2 (since 1994).

[159]HR Rep 187, 28th Cong, 2d Sess 1–7 (Mar 3, 1845) (adding, id at 6, that even apart from the postal power there was no doubt the United States could establish telegraph service "for its own use in the transmission of official orders and communications"). Alas, this report was filed on the last day of the expiring Congress, and it was never acted upon; the new Congress, as we shall see, turned in another direction.

"establish" post roads was only to designate those routes on which the mail was to be conveyed.[160] The transmission of information by telegraph, however, was a different matter: Even Mr. Jefferson's loyal disciples should have had no trouble in concluding that the Post Office could be authorized to transport messages by wire as well as wagon.

The experiment with public administration of telegraph services lasted little over a year; without fanfare, Congress in 1846 directed that the Baltimore line be leased or placed in private hands, and it was eventually sold.[161] There was no suggestion that the reason was constitutional compulsion. It was a deeply held policy preference for private enterprise, not a constitutional limitation on federal power, that in this case precluded our following the European model.

[160] See The Jeffersonians at 263.
[161] 9 Stat 19 (Jun 19, 1846).

2

The Public Lands

When Virginia ceded the Northwest Territory to the United States in 1784, it ceded title as well as sovereignty.[1] For much of the land beyond the Ohio River was inhabited only by Indians; once their rights were extinguished by treaty, the United States became owner of most of the soil.[2] The same pattern prevailed when the United States acquired additional territory from North Carolina, from Georgia, from France, and from Spain. Thus over the years the United States became the proprietor of vast areas of land that came to be known as the public domain.[3]

From the beginning it was contemplated that the territory thus acquired would eventually be admitted to statehood. The celebrated Northwest Ordinance, adopted by the Confederation Congress in 1787, expressly provided for division of the territory it covered into states, as Virginia in response to congressional suggestion had stipulated;[4] the treaties by which Louisiana and Florida were acquired prescribed prompt "incorporation" of the inhabitants into the United States.[5] Before 1829 eight new states had been estab-

[1]See the deed of cession, 11 Va Stat 571, 574 (Mar 1, 1784), and the authorizing statute, id at 326, 327 (Dec 20, 1783).

[2]See Johnson v M'Intosh, 21 US 543, 593–94 (1823).

[3]General studies of public-land policy during this period include George M. Stephenson, The Political History of the Public Lands from 1840 to 1862 (Badger, 1917); Benjamin H. Hibbard, A History of the Public Land Policies (Peter Smith, 1939); Roy M. Robbins, Our Landed Heritage: The Public Domain, 1776–1970 (Nebraska, 2d ed 1976).

[4]See Northwest Ordinance, 32 J Cont Cong 334, 342 (Jul 13, 1787), 1 Stat 50, 53 n.(a); Virginia's deed of cession, 11 Va Stat at 572–73; and the earlier congressional resolution inviting the states to cede their Western claims, 17 J Cont Cong 806–7 (Sep 6, 1780). All of this was in accord with Maryland's request in making the cession of Western claims a condition of ratifying the Articles of Confederation. 14 J Cont Cong 619, 621–22 (May 21, 1779).

[5]Treaty between the United States and the French Republic, Art III, 8 Stat 200, 202 (Apr 30, 1803); Treaty of Amity, Settlement, and Limits, between the United States and his Catholic Majesty, Art 6, 8 Stat 252, 256–58 (Feb 22, 1819) (ratified as modified Feb 19, 1821).

lished in what had once been territories: Tennessee, Ohio, Louisiana, Indiana, Mississippi, Illinois, Alabama, and Missouri.[6]

Statehood put an end to federal sovereignty over the territories, but not to federal ownership of the land. Statutes admitting new states not only reserved federal title to the public domain within their borders; they contained explicit provisions designed to insulate federal lands from state taxation.[7]

From the beginning it was also contemplated that the Federal Government would make conveyances of public lands. Virginia's 1784 deed of cession for the Northwest Territory, for example, declared that the grant was made on the following condition, among others:

> [t]hat all the lands within the territory so ceded to the United States, and not reserved for, or appropriated to [other purposes] . . . , shall be considered as a common fund for the use and benefit of such of the United States as have become, or shall become members of the confederation . . . , according to their usual respective proportions in the general charge and expenditure, and shall be faithfully and bona fide disposed of for that purpose, and for no other use or purpose whatsoever.[8]

The Confederation Congress accordingly provided in 1785 that land in the ceded territory be surveyed and sold at auction for not less than one dollar per acre,[9] and Article IV, § 3 of the new Constitution provided that "Congress shall have power to dispose of and make all needful rules and regulations respecting the territory or other property belonging to the United States."

As I have related in earlier installments of this study, Congress made early and frequent use of its authority to dispose of the public lands. The First Congress made grants to Revolutionary veterans and to French settlers at Vincennes, as the Virginia cession had envisioned.[10] The Fourth Congress reaffirmed the policy of the 1785 Ordinance, authoriz-

[6]See The Federalist Period at 217–22; The Jeffersonians at 87–94, 219–49. Kentucky, originally a part of Virginia, had been admitted, with that state's consent, without passing through territorial status; Maine's case was similar. See also the peculiar case of Vermont, which likewise was never a territory. Kentucky and Vermont are considered in The Federalist Period at 97–101.

[7]E.g., the Louisiana Enabling Act, 2 Stat 641, 642, § 3 (Feb 20, 1811); see The Jeffersonians at 223. For brief consideration of the persistent question whether this arrangement was consistent with the equal-footing principle that many nineteenth-century Congressmen and the Supreme Court in 1911 (Coyle v Smith, 221 US 559) found implicit in Article IV see The Jeffersonians at 294–95. See also President Van Buren's first Annual Message to Congress, 3 Richardson at 373, 384 (Dec 5, 1837):

> The position at one time assumed, that the admission of new States into the Union was incompatible with a right of soil in the United States and operated as a surrender thereof, notwithstanding the terms of the compacts by which their admission was designed to be regulated, has been wisely abandoned.

[8]11 Va Stat at 574 (1784). For the corresponding language of the authorizing statute see id at 328.

[9]See 28 J Cont Cong 375, 377–78 (May 20, 1785).

[10]See The Federalist Period at 107 n.412; 11 Va Stat at 573.

ing the Government to sell off individual parcels for not less than two dollars per acre.[11] It also directed the transfer of a named tract to "the society of United Brethren for propagating the gospel among the heathen."[12]

When Ohio became a state in 1803, Congress granted it certain salt springs within its borders for public use, one section in each township "for the use of schools," and a percentage of the proceeds of federal land sales to build roads to and through the state.[13] Subsequent statutes respecting the admission of other new states contained similar provisions.[14] Later Congresses built upon this precedent to grant lands to subsidize additional roads and canals.[15] In 1815 Congress authorized a grant of land for the relief of earthquake victims at New Madrid, in the Missouri Territory.[16] In 1819 and in 1826 Congress made land grants to support "asylums" for the deaf and dumb—not in the territories but in the states of Connecticut and Kentucky.[17] Not all these transfers were effected without constitutional controversy. Yet by the time Andrew Jackson became President in 1829 there was an impressive body of legislative precedent for a wide variety of dispositions of public land.

As we saw in the preceding chapter, in 1850 Congress over strenuous constitutional objection made the first of a series of land grants to finance the construction of railroads.[18] Controversies over the constitutionality of other dispositions of public lands pervaded the entire period from 1829 to 1861.

[11]1 Stat 464, 466–67, § 4 (May 18, 1796); see The Federalist Period at 207. For Alexander Hamilton's 1790 report, urging that lands continue to be sold to produce revenue, see 1 Am St Papers (Public Lands) 4, 8 (Jul 20, 1790).

[12]See The Federalist Period at 207 n.5. For a later grant in a similar vein see 12 Stat 22 (Jun 1, 1860), authorizing sale of a specified tract in Wisconsin to an Episcopal Missionary Society; for President Madison's veto of an intervening bill to grant public land to a religious institution see the Jeffersonians at 323–24.

[13]See 2 Stat 173, 175, § 7 (Apr 30, 1802); The Jeffersonians at 90–92.

[14]See id at 219–49. The Indiana Act added a grant for purposes of establishing a seminary of higher learning. Id at 226 & n.51.

[15]See id at 282 & n.205.

[16]3 Stat 211 (Feb 17, 1815); see The Jeffersonians at 291. Congress's extraordinary powers over the territories, where federalism concerns were absent, may likewise help to explain the later grant of land in the Florida Territory to promote "the propagation and cultivation of valuable tropical plants." 5 Stat 302, §§ 1–4 (Jul 7, 1838). It should be noted, however, that although the experiments in question were to be conducted in the Territory, one stated reason for subsidizing them was to determine the suitability of such plants for "gradual acclimation throughout all our southern and southwestern States." Id, Preamble; see HR Rep 454, 22d Cong, 1st Sess 1–3 (1832). Compare the ongoing dispute over Congress's power to establish institutions for national purposes in the District of Columbia, The Jeffersonians at 291–92, 313–15, and see section III of chapter 5 of the presesnt volume.

[17]6 Stat 229 (Mar 3, 1819); 6 Stat 339 (Apr 5, 1826); see The Jeffersonians at 292–94. Proposals to benefit a similar institution in New York were defeated in 1830 and again in 1832 after the usual debate over congressional authority. See Cong Deb, 21st Cong, 1st Sess 302–4 (Reps. Livingston, Barton, and Marks); Cong Deb, 22d Cong, 2d Sess 912–16 (Rep. Root and Sen. Mason). In addition, sizeable tracts were withheld from sale and reserved for military or naval purposes or for the use of Native Americans. E.g., 3 Stat 347 (Mar 1, 1817) (timberlands for the Navy); Treaty with the Creek Nation, 7 Stat 120, 121 (Aug 9, 1814). This practice continued during the period of this study. E.g., 4 Stat 729, § 1 (Jun 30, 1834), reserving the entire area west of Arkansas and Missouri for Native Americans displaced from the East; 10 Stat 226, 238, § 1 (Mar 3, 1853).

[18]See section VII of chapter 1.

I. THE 1833 DISTRIBUTION BILL

In conformity with Virginia's specification that land in the ceded territories constitute "a common fund" for the benefit of all states, Congress in 1790 required that the proceeds of Western land sales be employed to pay off the national debt[19]—thus making land revenues in essence a substitute for federal taxes. By 1829, as noted in the introduction to this part, President Jackson was able to envision that the debt would soon be extinguished,[20] and it was not long before major debate erupted over what to do with the remaining public lands.

In his 1829 message Jackson had already suggested that anticipated tax surpluses be distributed among the states "according to their ratio of representation"—after amending the Constitution, if necessary.[21] Three years later, in his fourth Annual Message, he suggested a similar but subtly different disposition of the public domain.

Lands had been ceded to the United States, Jackson asserted, "for the purposes of general harmony and as a fund to meet the expenses of the [Revolutionary] war." Those purposes "having been accomplished," he argued, it no longer made sense to regard the public lands as a source of revenue; they should rather "be sold to settlers . . . at a price barely sufficient to reimburse" the Government for its costs, and ultimately any remaining parcel should be "surrendered to the State[] . . . in which it lies."[22]

The following year, however, essentially on constitutional grounds, President Jackson vetoed a bill that would for a time have distributed the proceeds of public land sales to the states.[23]

His first objection was that the distribution scheme was unequal. The bill would have given an initial 12.5 percent of the revenue from public land sales to those states in which the lands were situated. That, the President argued, was improper. For the lands were held for the common benefit of the whole country; states in which public lands lay had no special claim.[24]

[19] 1 Stat 138, 144, § 22 (Aug 4, 1790).

[20] 2 Richardson at 442, 451; see text accompanying notes 21–22 of the Introduction to Part One.

[21] 2 Richardson at 452; see also his second Annual Message, id at 500, 514 (Dec 6, 1830), and the Introduction to Part One. A House committee promptly proposed a similar disposition of public-land revenues, arguing it was nothing more than an "equitable distribution of the proceeds of a common fund, already belonging to the people." HR Rep 312, 21st Cong, 1st Sess 1, 5 (1830).

[22] 2 Richardson at 591, 600–601 (Dec 4, 1832). In the meantime a resolution by Connecticut Senator Samuel Foot to limit the sale of public lands had provoked not only an important debate over public-land policy but the famous exchange between Daniel Webster and South Carolina's Robert Y. Hayne over the very nature of the Union. For the resolution in its original and amended forms see Cong Deb, 21st Cong, 1st Sess 3, 35; for the Hayne-Webster debate see section II of chapter 4.

[23] 3 Richardson at 56, 64–66 (Dec 4, 1833).

[24] Id at 64. Only the year before Henry Clay had made the same objection to Jackson's own proposal to cede unsold lands to the situs states. S Doc 128, 22d Cong, 1st Sess 2–3 (1832). So had Daniel Webster, protesting what he perceived as the creeping heresy "that these lands, by right, belong to the States respectively in which they happen to lie":

> The lands are well known to have been obtained by the United States, either by grants from individual States, or by treaties with foreign powers. In both cases, and in all cases, the grants and cessions were to the United States, for the interest of the whole Union; and the grants from individual States contain express limitations and conditions, binding up the whole property to the common use of all the States forever.

Jackson's reservations, however, went deeper. The bill directed that initial grants to the public-land states be applied "to objects of internal improvement and education" and the balance of revenues "to such purposes as the legislatures of the said respective States shall deem proper." Thus the bill in both respects offended the principles Jackson had laid down in vetoing the bill for support of the Maysville Road:

> The leading principle then asserted was that Congress possesses no constitutional power to appropriate any part of the moneys of the United States for objects of a local character within the States. . . . If the money of the United States can not be applied to local purposes through its own agents, as little can it be permitted to be thus expended through the agency of the State governments.[25]

Questions of consistency aside,[26] there was much to be said for Jackson's objections. The notion of equality in the distribution of public-land benefits, to be sure, seems not to have risen to constitutional proportions. As Treasury Secretary Albert Gallatin had argued in his notable 1808 report on internal improvements, pro rata distribution of federal tax revenues among the states made no sense, and nothing in the Constitution seemed to require it. Tax revenues were to be spent where the general welfare demanded, not by mathematical adherence to state lines.[27] The history adumbrated above suggested that land revenues were meant to be an alternative to taxes, and they had long been so employed. In light of the absence of *any* explicit limitation on Congress's authority to "dispose of" the public domain, it is hard to find Congress *more* constrained in disbursing land revenues than in spending money raised by taxation.

But Jackson was on firmer ground in insisting that Congress was no *less* constrained when disbursing the proceeds of public lands. As we have seen, South Carolina Senator Andrew Butler would repeat the point in 1850 in the debate over the Illinois Central Railroad: The Framers could hardly have intended to permit Congress to evade

---

Speech at Worcester, Oct 12, 1832, Charles M. Wiltse, ed, The Papers of Daniel Webster: 1 Speeches and Formal Writings 531, 545 (Univ Press of New England, 1986) [hereafter cited as Webster Speeches]. After the President's veto, however, it was Clay's turn to defend discrepancies in distribution: Congress had always made special grants for the benefit of new states. S Doc 323, 23d Cong, 1st Sess 7 (1834).

[25]3 Richardson at 65–66. Jackson also complained that the bill distributed the proceeds according to "Federal representative population" rather than "the general charge and expenditure provided by the compacts" of cession, id at 64, but this subtle distinction hardly seems of constitutional dimension in light of the general language of Article IV. In support of his interpretation Jackson invoked the concluding clause of that Article, which provides that "nothing in this Constitution shall be so construed as to prejudice any claims of the United States, or of any particular state" (id). His detractors seem right that this provision was meant only to reserve boundary questions, not to limit disposal of what were concededly federal lands. See Cong Deb, 22d Cong, 2d Sess 134 (Mississippi Sen. George Poindexter, citing The Federalist No 43 (Madison)).

[26]Nothing in his present veto message, Jackson argued, impaired his earlier suggestion that (as he now for the first time explained) the *worthless* ("refuse") lands remaining unsold ultimately be surrendered to the states in which they lay. 3 Richardson at 69. He said nothing about his more radical 1829 suggestion that Congress consider distributing the *general Treasury surplus* among the states. Not surprisingly, Clay did: it was "hardly to be anticipated" that the President would shrink from giving land revenues to the states after proposing to hand them the whole federal Treasury. S Doc 323, 23d Cong, 1st Sess 11 (1834).

[27]See The Jeffersonians at 282–83, 293–94.

restrictions on federal spending by the simple expedient of substituting land for money.[28] His predecessor Robert Y. Hayne had taken the same stance in opposing the distribution bill in 1832: If land proceeds were not subject to the limitations that applied to the disposition of tax revenues, there was no limit to congressional spending.[29] Tennessee's veteran Senator Felix Grundy echoed Hayne's argument a few months later:

> My proposition is . . . that the lands belong neither to the new nor the old States, nor to both of them combined, but to the Federal Government; and that their proceeds cannot be applied to other objects than those to which the United States can constitutionally appropriate money.[30]

As Jackson would say in his veto message, Congress could spend tax moneys neither for education nor for local improvements. Therefore, Grundy concluded, it could not accomplish the same end indirectly by distributing land proceeds to the states.[31] In the words of Illinois Senator Elias Kane, federal funds could be expended only for national purposes; and Congress could not delegate to the states its authority to determine what the general welfare required.[32]

Subsequent generations have been attuned to the argument that by attaching certain conditions to grants Congress invades rights reserved to the states.[33] Jackson and his congressional supporters took the sharply contrasting position that grants *without* strings exceeded congressional authority.[34]

Citing as precedent earlier land grants to support asylums for the deaf and dumb,[35]

[28]See text accompanying notes 117–18 of chapter 1.

[29]Cong Deb, 22d Cong, 1st Sess 1163.

[30]Cong Deb, 22d Cong, 2d Sess 112. See also id at 1905–14 (Alabama Rep. Clement Clay) (emphasizing that the public lands constituted a fund for the United States, not for the separate states); id at 217–18 (Missouri Sen. Thomas Hart Benton, adding that tax revenues too were "property" of the United States of which Congress had power to "dispose" under Article IV).

[31]Id at 114–15. Representative Polk had made the same argument in 1831 in rejecting Jackson's own proposal to distribute general tax revenues to the states for local improvements: "[W]hat the Federal Government does not possess the power to do directly, it cannot do indirectly"; the General Government was not meant to be "tax-gatherer of the States." HR Rep 51, 21st Cong, 2d Sess 7–9.

[32]Cong Deb, 22d Cong, 2d Sess 66. Calhoun too argued that Congress could not "denationalize" federal funds by distributing them pell-mell to the states. Id at 234. This argument is independent of the question whether President Monroe was right that Congress was authorized to spend for any subject of national import, or whether it could do so only when necessary and proper to the execution of other express or implied powers. See The Jeffersonians at 280–81.

[33]See, e.g., United States v Butler, 297 US 1, 72–73 (1936); South Dakota v Dole, 483 US 203, 206–9 (1987).

[34]Cf *Butler,* 297 US at 83 (Stone, J, dissenting) ("Expenditures would fail of their purpose and thus lose their constitutional sanction if the terms of payment were not such that by their influence . . . the permitted end would be attained."). This was not the first time such arguments had been made against unconditional grants to the states. See The Jeffersonians at 294–95.

[35]See note 17 and accompanying text. Opponents of the 1833 distribution bill ignored these precedents; later advocates of limitations on the power to dispose of public property tended to dismiss them as aberrations. See text accompanying notes 93–94. Representative Clement Clay distinguished the more common grants made in connection with the admission of states on a ground later to become familiar: As others would say in defense of grants to construct railroads, these transfers were consistent with the trust imposed on Congress because they tended to enhance the value of other public lands. See Cong Deb, 22d Cong, 2d Sess 1912 and text accompanying notes 113–24 of chapter 1.

nationalist leader Henry Clay (like Seward in the later railroad dispute) insisted that Congress had unlimited authority to dispose of the public lands.[36] Clay persuaded Congress but not the President, and Jackson had the last word. Clay and others stormed and fumed over Jackson's pocket veto,[37] but they lacked the competence to override it and the votes to try again;[38] there would be no general distribution of land proceeds to the states while a Democrat was President.[39]

II. THE 1841 DISTRIBUTION LAW

In 1840, however, when the Whigs rejected their leader in favor of the sphinx-like William Henry Harrison,[40] the Democrats finally lost the Presidency. With the cat on vacation, the mice got down to work. In 1841 Congress passed another distribution law, and this time the President signed it.[41] Harrison having died in the interim, the President was John Tyler.[42]

President Tyler, though as we have seen grudging in his interpretation of Congress's power to appropriate tax revenues for internal improvements,[43] took a broad view of its authority to dispose of public lands. Finding that in the straitened financial circumstances that had prompted his predecessor to call the legislature into special session a number of states suffered from a crushing burden of debt, Tyler invited Congress to relieve them:

> [A] distribution of the proceeds of the sales of the public lands, provided such distribution does not force upon Congress the necessity of imposing upon commerce heavier burthens than those contemplated by the act of 1833, would act as an efficient remedial measure by being brought directly in aid of the States. As one sincerely devoted to the task of preserving a just balance in our system of Government by the maintenance of the States in a condition the most free and respectable and in the full possession of all their power, I can no otherwise than feel desirous for their

[36]Cong Deb, 22d Cong, 1st Sess 1114–15, 1163. See also, e.g., Cong Deb, 22d Cong, 2d Sess at 129–36 (Sen. Poindexter); id at 161 (Sen. Ewing); S Doc 323, 23d Cong, 1st Sess 10 (1834) (Sen. Clay) (adding, id at 6, that land grants had been made in the past "for almost every conceivable purpose"). In 1832, in dismissing the possibility of reducing the surplus by distributing *tax* revenues to the states, Clay himself had said he knew of "no principle in the constitution which authorizes the Federal Government to become [tax] collector for the States." Cong Deb, 22d Cong, 1st Sess 69.

[37]See the discussion of the pocket-veto question in section I of chapter 6.

[38]The bill had passed the Senate by only three votes the first time. While Henry Clay maintained that several absentees might have been persuaded to vote to pass it over the veto, he acknowledged that intervening changes in membership had dimmed the prospects of ultimate success. His new distribution bill, though favorably reported, was never taken up. Cong Deb, 23d Cong, 1st Sess 1599–1606.

[39]But cf the 1836 "deposit" provision, discussed in section III of chapter 3, whose transparent purpose and effect were to transfer general funds of the Government to the states. Democratic platforms from 1844 to 1860 insisted that land revenues be "sacredly applied to the national objects specified in the Constitution" and that it was unconstitutional to distribute them among the states. Porter & Johnson, Party Platforms at 4, 11, 17, 24, 30, 31.

[40]See note 13 of the Preface and accompanying text.

[41]5 Stat 453 (Sep 4, 1841).

[42]Or was he? See section IV of chapter 6.

[43]See note 20 and text accompanying notes 38–46 of chapter 1.

> emancipation from the situation to which the pressure on their finances now subjects them. And while I must repudiate, as a measure founded in error and wanting constitutional sanction, the slightest approach to an assumption by this Government of the debts of the States, yet I can see in the distribution adverted to much to recommend it. The compacts between the proprietor States and this Government expressly guarantee to the States all the benefits which may arise from the sales. The mode by which this is to be effected addresses itself to the discretion of Congress as the trustee for the States, and its exercise after the most beneficial manner is restrained by nothing in the grants or in the Constitution so long as Congress shall consult that equality in the distribution which the compacts require.[44]

No, Mr. Tyler was not gifted in his use of the written word. Paraphrasing is risky at best, but let me try. (1) The states were unable to pay their debts, and Congress ought to help them to the extent it could. (2) Congress had no power to assume state obligations directly. (3) To distribute the proceeds of land sales to the states would enable them to pay their debts and thus serve the same purpose as a forbidden assumption. (4) The Federal Government held the public domain for the benefit of the states, and to that end Congress could dispose of it however it liked, provided that the states were treated equally. (5) It was imperative, however, that tariffs not be increased beyond the levels agreed upon in the Compromise of 1833. (6) Congress ought therefore to think seriously about distributing land revenue to the states, but only so long as it was not needed to meet federal expenses. Tyler's conception of Congress's power to dispose of the public lands was as capacious as that of Henry Clay.

Legislative debate was brief and offered little that was new.[45] Congress took Tyler's advice, and he signed the resulting bill.

Following the pattern of the bill Jackson had vetoed in 1833, the 1841 statute granted an initial percentage of land proceeds to Western states in which the land was

[44]4 Richardson at 40, 47 (Jun 1, 1841). Earlier, we are told, some Whigs had urged that Congress assume debts that the financially strapped states had incurred, largely to finance ambitious internal-improvement schemes that Jacksonian philosophy forbade Congress to subsidize directly. Democratic platforms from 1840 through 1860 uniformly denied that Congress could achieve the same goal by assuming state obligations (see Porter & Johnson, Party Platforms at 2, 3, 10, 16, 24, 30, 31), and by the time of Tyler's message the Whigs had largely abandoned assumption in favor of the indirect means of distributing federal largesse. See Robbins, Our Landed Heritage at 78–79 (cited in note 3). In the disillusionment that followed their initial enthusiasm, a number of states would soon adopt constitutional provisions severely restricting state and even local support for internal improvements. See Carter Goodrich, Government Promotion of American Canals and Railroads, 1800–1890 59, 71–72, 80, 138–39, 145–49 (Columbia, 1960).

[45]Nathan Clifford in the House and Silas Wright and Levi Woodbury in the Senate repeated that the source of funds was irrelevant; Congress could spend land proceeds only for those purposes for which it could spend tax money. Cong Globe, 27th Cong, 1st Sess 128, 325–26; Cong Globe App, 27th Cong, 1st Sess 247. Senator Benton added that land revenues distributed to the states would have to be replaced by taxation; he seemed to be suggesting that Congress was indirectly financing local projects with tax money. Id at 228. Most interesting was Calhoun's observation that many of the public lands had been purchased with tax revenues to begin with: "By what art, what political alchymy [sic], could the mere passage of the money through the lands free it from the constitutional shackles to which it was previously subject?" Id at 333. Supporters of the distribution had the votes and largely held their tongues; Robert Winthrop of Massachusetts, in the House, echoed Tyler's argument that Congress could dispose of land for whatever purpose it wished. Id at xi.

sold.[46] This time, however, there was no restriction on how these funds should be used.[47] After deducting administrative expenses, the remaining revenue was to be divided among the states, the territories, and the District of Columbia "according to their respective federal representative population" and "applied by the Legislatures of the said states to such purposes as the said Legislatures may direct."[48] These provisions were wholly inconsistent with President Jackson's 1833 veto message, but the Democrats had lost both Congress and the Presidency.[49]

The Distribution Act was to be permanent,[50] but its operation was to be suspended if foreign war broke out[51] or if customs duties were increased beyond the levels provided for in the 1833 compromise.[52] For the expenses of war might create a need for land revenues, and Tyler had supported distribution only on condition that it be accomplished without imposing additional duties.[53] Tariffs had to be raised in 1842 to cover Government expenses, and distribution was accordingly suspended.[54] The Mexican War, which would have suspended distribution in any case, "buried it under a national debt sufficiently

[46]5 Stat 453, § 1. This time the states' share was 10 percent, and the new states of Arkansas and Michigan were included.

[47]The Senate committee explained that to tell the states how to spend the money would look like "an assumption of a guardianship over the states, to which the General Government has no claim." S Doc 46, 27th Cong, 1st Sess 2. A later section, however, granted the same states additional lands "for purposes of internal improvement," which the statute defined as "[r]oads, railways, bridges, canals and improvement of water-courses, and draining of swamps." Id at 455, §§ 8, 9.

[48]Id at 453, § 2. Section 4, id at 554, required that such grants be first applied to the payment of debts owing to the United States (with the conspicuous exception of sums deposited in state banks under Jacksonian legislation discussed in chapter 3), but that did not remove the constitutional objection; as opponents argued, Congress had no general authority to pay state obligations. See the discussion of the 1790 assumption of state revolutionary debts in The Federalist Period at 76–78; Thomas Hart Benton, 2 Thirty Years' View; or, A History of the Working of the American Government for Thirty Years, from 1820 to 1850 241 (Appleton, 1854) [hereafter cited as Benton, Thirty Years' View].

[49]See Donald B. Cole, Martin Van Buren and the American Political System 372–73 (Princeton, 1984). South Carolina, at Calhoun's urging, initially refused to accept its share of the money, and the 1844 Democratic Platform denounced distribution as "alike inexpedient in policy and repugnant to the Constitution." See Wiltse, 3 Calhoun at 59; Porter & Johnson, Party Platforms at 4.

[50]See 5 Stat at 454, § 5: "This act shall continue and be in force until otherwise provided by law . . . ."

[51]Id.

[52]Id at 454, § 6.

[53]See his Special Session Message, quoted in the text accompanying notes 43–44. Indeed Tyler vetoed no fewer than three bills for violation of this condition. Two would have increased tariffs while overriding the suspension of distribution; the third would have repealed the proviso itself so as to permit both distribution and higher tariffs in the future. See 4 Richardson at 180, 183, 255. See Tyler's concise explanation of the first of these vetoes in the message accompanying the second:

> I did not think that I could stand excused, much less justified, before the people of the United States, nor could I reconcile it to myself to recommend the imposition of additional taxes upon them without at the same time urging the employment of all the legitimate means of the Government toward satisfying its wants.

Id at 185. To give away land revenues for state purposes at a time when the Federal Government needed them to meet current expenses, he added, was "highly impolitic, if not unconstitutional." Id at 187. For the story of these vetoes see Stephenson, Political History of the Public Lands at 73–87 (cited in note 3); see also the brief discussion in chapter 4.

[54]See 5 Stat 548, 567, § 30 (Aug 30, 1842).

heavy to keep it down for many years."[55] In 1848, after the war was over, President Polk spoke of distribution in the past tense and branded it an unconstitutional element of the discredited American System;[56] although the statute was not repealed, distribution was apparently never resumed.[57]

III. THE MAD

President Polk had no difficulty, however, in approving the usual land grants to the new states of Florida, Iowa, and Wisconsin for such apparently local purposes as state government, transportation, and schools.[58] Two days before leaving office, in March 1849, he signed a bill granting Louisiana most "swamp and overflowed lands . . . unfit for cultivation" within its borders, in order "to aid the State . . . in constructing the necessary levees and drains to reclaim" them.[59] Whig President Millard Fillmore did the same for other states in 1850[60]—the same year in which he approved the grant to support construction of the Illinois Central Railroad.[61] On the same day on which he signed the second swamp bill Fillmore also endorsed the grant of forty to one hundred sixty acres to veterans of the War of 1812, the Mexican War, and various Indian wars, and to their immediate survivors.[62] Democratic Presidents Pierce and Buchanan, however, would apply the veto with vigor over the ensuing decade to enforce their narrow views of Congress's constitutional authority to dispose of the public domain.

The first of these vetoes came in 1854, when Congress in a moment of weakness was persuaded to grant land to the states to support asylums for the indigent insane. Various bills to this effect had passed one or the other House, and in one case both Houses, in 1851, 1852, and 1853.[63] Proponents predictably pointed out that Congress had already granted land for an enormous variety of purposes; opponents predictably argued that the

[55]Stephenson, Political History of the Public Lands at 90 (cited in note 3).

[56]4 Richardson at 629, 656, 658.

[57]The 1842 suspension "proved to be permanent, for the tariff never again went back to the twenty per cent level" prescribed by the 1833 statute. Matthias N. Orfield, Federal Land Grants to the States with Special Reference to Minnesota 101 (1915). The total amount distributed under the 1841 law was somewhat more than $600,000. See S Doc No 64, 50th Cong, 1st Sess (1888); Thomas Donaldson, The Public Domain: Its History 256, 753, 1260 (Government Printing Office, 1884).

[58]See 5 Stat 788, § 1 (Mar 3, 1845) (Florida); 5 Stat 789, § 6 (Mar 3, 1845) (Iowa); 9 Stat 56, 58, § 7 (Aug 6, 1846) and 9 Stat 233, § 2 (May 29, 1848) (Wisconsin). No such grants were made to Texas, which (having never been a territory) retained its public lands on admission to the Union. 5 Stat 797, 798 (Mar 1, 1845); 9 Stat 108 (Dec 29, 1845). Similar grants were later made to California (10 Stat 244, 246, 248, §§ 6, 12–13 (Mar 3, 1853)), Minnesota (11 Stat 166, 167, § 4 (Feb 26, 1857)), Oregon (11 Stat 383–84, § 4 (Feb 14, 1859)), and Kansas (12 Stat 126, 127–28, § 3 (Jan 29, 1861)).

[59]9 Stat 352, § 1 (Mar 2, 1849).

[60]9 Stat 519, §§ 1, 4 (Sep 28, 1850). The celebrated editor Horace Greeley, who was serving a single term in the House, supported swampland grants in 1849 but later came to regret them as "a farce and a sham" whose "consequence was a reckless and fraudulent transfer . . . of millions on millions of choice public lands, whole sections of which had not muck enough on their surface to accommodate a single fair-sized frog." Horace Greeley, Recollections of a Busy Life 231 (J.B. Ford, 1868).

[61]See section VII of chapter 1.

[62]9 Stat 520, § 1 (Sep 28, 1850).

[63]See Cong Globe, 31st Cong, 2d Sess 522 (Feb 12, 1851) (Senate); Cong Globe, 32d Cong, 1st Sess 2229 (Aug 16, 1852) (House); id at 2466 (Aug 30, 1852) (Senate); Cong Globe, 32d Cong, 2d Sess 1091 (Mar 3, 1853) (House). The 1852 House and Senate bills were not identical; neither was sent to the President.

precedents were either erroneous or not in point.[64] These arguments were repeated at greater length in the Senate debate on the bill that passed both Houses in 1854.[65]

President Pierce's veto message neatly encapsulated the arguments against the bill.[66] If Congress could provide for the indigent insane, it could provide for "all those among the people of the United States who by any form of calamity become fit objects of public philanthropy"—whether victims of idiocy, destitution, or disease.

> I readily and, I trust, feelingly acknowledge the duty incumbent on us all as men and citizens, and as among the highest and holiest of our duties, to provide for those who, in the mysterious order of Providence, are subject to want and to disease of body or mind; but I can not find any authority in the Constitution for making the Federal Government the great almoner of public charity throughout the United States.[67]

The general welfare clause, Pierce safely concluded, was a limitation on the tax power, not a grant of authority to do whatever was good for the United States. A bill to spend money from the Treasury to support the indigent insane "would have attracted forcibly the attention of Congress"—i.e., no one would have thought it constitutional.[68] That was enough, he thought, to dispatch the bill that Congress had passed; for from "a constitutional point of view" it was "wholly immaterial whether the appropriation be in money or

[64]See Cong Globe, 31st Cong, 2d Sess 508–10 (Sens. Jefferson Davis (con), James Pearce, and Solon Borland (both pro)); Cong Globe, 32d Cong, 1st Sess 2467 (Mississippi Sen. Stephen Adams, pointedly inquiring whether care of the insane was a federal or a state responsibility); Cong Globe, 32d Cong, 2d Sess 1091–93 (Sens. John Bell (pro) and Adams (con)).

[65]For arguments in support of the bill see Cong Globe, 33d Cong, 1st Sess 455–56 (Sen. Foot); id at 507–8 (Sen. Walker); id at 509 (Sen. Badger); id at 560 (Sen. Brown). For arguments in opposition see id at 507 (Sen. Mason); id at 508 (Sen. Hunter); id at 556 (Sen. Adams); id at 557–61 (Sen. Bayard).

[66]5 Richardson at 247 (May 3, 1854).

[67]Id at 249.

[68]Cf President Polk's draft veto of a bill to appropriate funds for relief of the great Irish famine:

> I deeply regret that I cannot perceive in the Constitution of the United States the authority of Congress to appropriate the public money for the purpose of relieving the suffering of our own fellow citizens much less the subjects of foreign Governments. . . . [I]t cannot be maintained that the Government of the United States possess the power to make mere donations for charitable purposes.

Final draft message to the Senate, Mar 3, 1847, in James K. Polk Papers (microfilm), Reel 60, series 5 (Library of Congress, 1964); see also 2 Polk Diary at 396–98. Compare Polk's denial of congressional authority to support roads or canals overseas, discussed in note 53 of chapter 1; contrast Congress's 1812 appropriation to aid victims of an earthquake in Venezuela (The Jeffersonians at 290–92), which like the Irish proposal (Cong Globe, 29th Cong, 2d Sess 534 (Sen. Calhoun)), was sensibly defended as an exercise of federal authority over foreign affairs.

At the request of Virginia Senator James Mason, who thought the original Irish proposal exceeded Congress's power, it was amended to authorize the Secretary of the Navy to make two ships available, with or without Navy crews, to transport private gifts to the victims—as if that made it any easier to sustain, which Senators Dayton and Crittenden appropriately denied. Id at 534–35. Both Houses passed the amended resolution, and Polk signed it without a murmur, although he had elsewhere said with much justice that Congress could no more lend federal officers to Panama to survey a railroad across the isthmus than build the railroad itself. See 9 Stat 207 (Mar 3, 1847) and note 53 of chapter 1.

in land." As the Virginia Act of cession had expressly provided, the public lands were to constitute "a common fund" for all of the United States and to be disposed of for that sole purpose—not, said Pierce, to achieve "objects which have not been intrusted to the Federal Government, and therefore belong exclusively to the States."[69]

Finally, wrote Pierce, the only precedents in point were grants made in 1819 and 1826 to subsidize asylums for the deaf and dumb, and those grants should never have been made. For those institutions were of no more national significance than "any establishment of religious or moral instruction," or for that matter "every ear of corn or boll of cotton," or anything else that "promotes the material or intellectual well-being of the race."[70] Pierce did not mention the general distribution law Tyler had approved in 1841; he obviously shared Polk's view that it had been unconstitutional too.[71]

Other land grants, Pierce concluded, could easily be distinguished. The public land, he asserted,

> is distinguished from actual money chiefly in this respect, that its profitable management sometimes requires that portions of it be appropriated to local objects in the States wherein it may happen to lie, as would be done by any prudent proprietor to enhance the sale value of his private domain. All such grants of land are in fact a disposal of it for value received, but they afford no precedent or constitutional reason for giving away the public lands.

Thus the various grants to new states were not only consideration for preserving federal rights (including tax immunity) in the remaining public lands but also "a way to augment the value of the residue and in this mode to encourage the early occupation of it by the industrious and intelligent pioneer."[72] Thus the grant of swamp lands for draining served both to eliminate a "nuisance to the inhabitants of the surrounding country . . . which the United States could not justify as a just and honest proprietor" and in so doing to "enhanc[e] the value of the remaining lands belonging to the General Government."[73] And thus, Pierce had suggested in an earlier message to Congress, grants for the construction of railways "enhanc[ed] the value and promot[ed] the rapid sale of the public domain"[74]—

[69] 5 Richardson at 250–54.

[70] Id at 255. The refusal of the Framers to include a provision expressly authorizing Congress to establish a university in the District of Columbia, the President added, demonstrated that the Convention considered such matters as local and therefore (except in the District, where Congress possessed the power of "exclusive legislation") they were reserved to the states. Id at 255–56.

[71] For Polk's view see note 56 and accompanying text.

[72] Grants to military veterans, Senator Adams twice explained, were not gratuities either; they were additional compensation for services rendered, and thus, he seemed rightly to imply, necessary and proper to the raising of armies and the conduct of war. Cong Globe, 33d Cong, 1st Sess 556, 570–71.

[73] 5 Richardson at 253–56. See also S Rep 19, 31st Cong, 1st Sess 3 (1850) (Sen. Borland).

[74] First Annual Message, 5 Richardson at 207, 216–17 (Dec 5, 1853). See also Pierce's message of December 30, 1854, id at 257, 260, acknowledging, in the course of explaining an earlier veto of a rivers and harbors appropriation, that the property clause "authorize[d] Congress, in the management of the public property, to make improvements essential to the successful execution of the trust." Douglas distinguished railroads on this ground in the Senate debate on overriding the veto of the bill to provide for the indigent insane. Cong Globe, 33d Cong, 1st Sess 1066–67.

as Senator Douglas in 1850, we may add, had argued with such signal success.[75]

Pierce's veto message was a definitive repudiation of President Monroe's 1822 argument that Congress could spend for anything that benefited the whole nation[76] and an equally definitive endorsement of the position that federal lands were merely an alternative source of revenue for otherwise legitimate federal goals. Lewis Cass of Michigan, Democratic candidate for President in 1848 and later Buchanan's Secretary of State, expressed that position clearly and concisely in defending the President's veto. North Carolina Senator George Badger had professed to find it odd that Pierce thought it unconstitutional to distribute public land to the states:

> It is strange, when we have heard, time and again here, that these lands are held by the General Government as the trustee for the States; when we have been told so often, in very glowing terms, that they have been procured by shedding the common blood, or they have been purchased by applying the common treasure; that we are then also told that it is utterly unconstitutional in the trustee to use a portion of the lands which he holds for the benefit of those for whom he holds them.[77]

Indeed, added Wisconsin Senator Isaac Walker, if the public lands were "the patrimony of all the States," as opponents of the bill argued, grants for insane asylums everywhere were far less objectionable than the various grants to individual states that Congress had routinely approved; for the present bill was, he believed, "the first bill . . . which has ever been before Congress proposing to make an equitable and equal distribution of this patrimony among the whole of the States."[78]

Cass made mincemeat of the argument that either land or tax revenues should be distributed equally among the states. "If, as the Senator says, [Delaware received] four times as much . . . [as] North Carolina, it is because the interest or common benefit of the Confederated Government required it." Forts, for example, could be built only where an enemy might otherwise invade the country:

> Because the city of New York draws largely upon the public resources for its defenses, it would be a strange pretension that Frankfort, in Kentucky, must be equally fortified, or that there must be a naval dock-yard in Iowa, because there is one in Virginia. Such a demand, if acceded to, would hazard the benefit of all, by the pretense of seeking the benefit of each.[79]

Badger's argument that Congress was trustee for the states and could therefore distribute the land to them was more troublesome, for the famous Virginia cession designated the ceded lands as a fund for "such of the United States, as have become, or shall

[75]See section VII of chapter 1. Another debate ensued on a motion to override Pierce's veto of the asylum bill, but the motion failed to attract even a simple majority. See Cong Globe, 33d Cong, 1st Sess 1620–21.

[76]See the introductory paragraphs of chapter 1.

[77]Cong Globe, 33d Cong, 1st Sess 509.

[78]Id at 508. President Jackson had stressed the requirement of equality in vetoing the general distribution bill in 1833. See text accompanying notes 23–24.

[79]Cong Globe App, 33d Cong, 1st Sess 982.

become, members of the confederation"—and thus arguably for each of the states rather than for the nation.[80] But Cass had an answer for that too, and it was a good one. When the cession was made, he explained, the United States had no taxing power; the Federal Government was dependent upon contributions from the several states. To end this dependency was one of the reasons for the adoption of the new Constitution; it was also one of the purposes of the cession.

> Now, what is the meaning of the terms employed in it, that the land should become a fund for the use and common benefit of the members of the Confederation, according to their usual proportions in the general charge and expenditure, and should be faithfully applied to that purpose, and to no other? That this fund should go towards defraying the expenses of the Confederation, and should be fairly appropriated to that purpose. . . .

Thus the cession was "designed . . . for the benefit of the Confederation as such," not to make the United States a conduit for distributing wealth to the individual states.[81]

On this interpretation the bill to finance asylums for the insane was an easy case; grants for this purpose were not necessary and proper to the exercise of any federal powers, not even to management of the public domain. The harder case of a homestead law was soon to reach the desk of Pierce's successor. In the meantime, however, President Buchanan would have yet another opportunity to express his views on the purposes for which Congress might legitimately dispose of the public lands.

IV. THE LEARNED

On December 14, 1857 Representative Justin S. Morrill, Republican of Vermont, introduced a bill to distribute public lands to each of the states for the purpose of establishing colleges whose "leading object shall be . . . to teach such branches of learning as are re-

[80] 11 Va Stat 571, 574. President Tyler had made the same argument in proposing a general distribution in 1841. See text accompanying note 44. See also S Doc 323, 23d Cong, 1st Sess 9 (Sen. Clay) (1834): "The grant is not for the benefit of the confederation, but for that of the several States . . . ."

[81] Cong Globe App, 33d Cong, 1st Sess 982. Felix Grundy of Tennessee had spelled this out in a committee report several years before. Now that the quotas for state contributions under the Articles of Confederation had been abolished, he argued, there was

> but one mode by which the compacts of cession can be carried into effect; that is, by the payment of the proceeds of the public land sales into the common Treasury, thereby lessening the amounts which have to be raised from the people of the several States, in exact proportion as they contribute to the general charge and expenditure.

The purpose was "to make [the lands] the property of the United States, collectively, and not separately, and to secure the application of the proceeds to the common benefit, in the same manner as other public money should be applied." In other words, the public domain should be regarded "as a source of revenue, for the ordinary purposes of the General Government"; there was thus "no difference between the power which Congress possesses over the revenue which arises from customs and the money received from the sales of the public lands." S Doc 153, 26th Cong, 1st Sess 11–14 (1840).

lated to agriculture and the mechanic arts."[82] Congress's power to dispose of public lands, Morrill argued, was plenary; Congress had made grants for a variety of purposes, including education. If Congress could make educational grants to individual states, it could make them to all states at once; and it was time for Congress to do something to promote agriculture as well.[83]

Opponents made the usual objections both in the House and in the Senate.[84] Ohio Senator George Pugh pointed out with much justice that there was no way to distinguish the present bill from the one President Pierce had just vetoed, for agriculture was no more a federal subject than was the care of the indigent insane.[85]

Pugh made an additional argument that to my knowledge had not been heard before in the context of federal grants. The bill attached a variety of conditions to the grants it authorized: The states were to establish colleges to teach agriculture and the mechanical arts; the corpus of the land proceeds was to be preserved as an endowment for those institutions; the interest was to be expended for their support, but not for the construction of buildings; and so on.[86]

> Now, sir, if we have the right to require the things which are specified in this section, if they are incident to, or a part of any of the powers possessed by Congress, let us do it directly by legislation; but the section proceeds upon the hypothesis, . . . that these . . . are things which Congress has no right to require, except as conditions to a gift; and in order to acquire that authority, in order to usurp that power from the State Legislatures, we propose to bribe them, by the donation of public lands—bribe them to surrender powers which they did not surrender at the time the Constitution was established.[87]

Virginia Senator James Mason echoed Pugh's concern: The states were to be "bribed by Federal power to conform their domestic policy to Federal will."[88]

This was a different argument from that which Pierce had made against the asylum bill and Pugh and others had repeated above. Pugh made the distinction plain in later moving to eliminate the conditions from the bill:

> If you choose to grant public lands to the States in aid of agriculture and

[82]Cong Globe, 35th Cong, 1st Sess 32. The bill itself is printed, with minor modifications, in id at 1697; the quoted language is taken from § 4. States in which there were no federal lands were to be given their proportional share in the form of "land scrip" to be redeemed by private purchasers with land from any other state. Id, § 2.

[83]Cong Globe, 35th Cong, 1st Sess 1692, 1695–96.

[84]See id at 1741–42 (adverse report of the House Committee on Public Lands, presented by Alabama Democrat Williamson Cobb); Cong Globe, 35th Cong, 2d Sess 720–21 (Missouri Sen. James Green); id at 721–22 and 856–57 (Sen. Jefferson Davis, appropriately distinguishing the military and naval academies as necessary and proper to the maintenance of armies and navies); id at 852–54 (Alabama Sen. Clement Clay).

[85]Id at 714–15.

[86]See Cong Globe, 35th Cong, 1st Sess 1697.

[87]Cong Globe, 35th Cong, 2d Sess 716.

[88]Id at 719. See also id at 785–86 (Delaware Sen. James Bayard); id at 852 (Alabama Sen. Clement Clay) (comparing this feature of the bill to the Devil's temptation of Christ).

> for the establishment of colleges, as the first and second sections of the bill provide, do so; but leave it to the wisdom of the States how to apply it, and not undertake to fetter them by conditions imposed in this bill. In fact, objectionable as the whole grant is to my mind, this attempt of Congress to assume control over the legislation of the States, in virtue of the condition, is altogether the worst feature of the bill . . . .[89]

Even if Congress had power to grant lands for educational purposes, Pugh was saying, it had no right to condition the grant on state action that Congress could not require. This was the argument that would later be made in such conditional-grant cases as *United States v Butler*[90] and *South Dakota v Dole*.[91] It had been made in Congress in connection with conditions attached to federal employment and to naturalization.[92] It had prevailed there in the context of Missouri's admission to the Union.[93] It was the now familiar argument of unconstitutional conditions.

It was not to prevail in Congress in 1858 or 1859. Each House approved the land-grant college bill,[94] and President Buchanan killed it on the basis of the argument his predecessor had employed in rejecting grants for insane asylums: Neither agriculture nor education was an appropriate object of federal bounty.[95] Buchanan's veto message is a major pronouncement on Congress's power to dispose of the public lands and deserves to be more widely read.

It was clear, Buchanan wrote, that Congress could not appropriate tax revenues to establish colleges; Congress could tax only for federal, not state purposes. The public lands, he continued, were subject to the same restriction:

> It would require clear and strong evidence to induce the belief that the framers of the Constitution, after having limited the powers of Congress to certain precise and specific objects, intended by employing the words "dispose of" to give that body unlimited power over the vast public domain. It would be a strange anomaly, indeed, to have created two funds—the one by taxation, confined to the execution of the enumerated powers delegated to Congress, and the other from the public lands, applicable to all subjects, foreign and domestic, which Congress might designate; that this fund should be "disposed of," not to pay the debts of the United States, nor "to raise and support armies," nor "to provide and maintain a navy," nor to accomplish any one of the other great objects enumerated in the Constitution, but be diverted from them to pay the debts of the States, to educate their people, and to carry into effect any other measure of their domestic policy. . . . The natural intendment would be that as the Constitution confined Congress to well-defined specific

[89]Id at 785.

[90]297 US 1, 74 (1936).

[91]483 US 203, 212 (1987) (Brennan, J, dissenting).

[92]See The Federalist Period at 62, 193–95.

[93]See The Jeffersonians at 232–43.

[94]Cong Globe, 35th Cong, 1st Sess 1742 (House); Cong Globe, 35th Cong, 2d Sess 857 (Senate).

[95]5 Richardson at 543 (Feb 24, 1859).

> powers, the funds placed at their command, whether in land or money, should be appropriated to the performance of the duties corresponding with these powers. . . .
>
> The question is still clearer in regard to the public lands in the States and Territories within the Louisiana and Florida purchases. These lands were paid for out of the public Treasury from money raised by taxation. Now if Congress had no power to appropriate the money with which these lands were purchased, is it not clear that the power over the lands is equally limited? The mere conversion of this money into land could not confer upon Congress new power over the disposition of land which they had not possessed over money. . . . The inference is irresistible that this land partakes of the very same character with the money paid for it, and can be devoted to no objects different from those to which the money could have been devoted.

Earlier land grants for educational purposes were distinguished as Pierce had distinguished them five years before: Made "chiefly, if not exclusively, . . . to the new States as they successively entered the Union," these grants had rendered nearby retained lands more valuable by enhancing their attractiveness to potential settlers.

> No person will contend, [Buchanan concluded,] that donations of land to all the States of the Union for the erection of colleges within the limits of each can be embraced by this principle. It can not be pretended that an agricultural college in New York or Virginia would aid the settlement or facilitate the sale of public lands in Minnesota or California.[96]

And so Representative Morrill's noble plan to educate farmers and mechanics, like the earlier effort to care for the indigent insane, foundered on sound Democratic conceptions of the boundaries of federal power. The land-grant colleges that were to bear his name were not to be authorized until 1862, when the Presidency was in other and more sympathetic hands.[97]

V. THE FOOTLOOSE

Our survey of public-land controversies during the pre–Civil War period comes to a close with President Buchanan's veto of a homestead bill passed by both Houses in 1860.[98]

Homestead proposals had been percolating in Congress at least since 1835.[99] The

[96]Id at 547–50. Congress had granted land to Wisconsin "for the use and support of a university" in 1838 (5 Stat 244 (Jun 12, 1838)), but the precedent was not in point. In the first place, Wisconsin encompassed additional public lands whose value might be enhanced by the existence of an institution of higher learning. Furthermore, the grant was made while Wisconsin was a territory, over which only Congress had legislative authority.

[97]12 Stat 503 (Jul 2, 1862) (Morrill Act); see also 26 Stat 417 (Aug 30, 1890).

[98]5 Richardson at 608 (Jun 22, 1860).

[99]Franklin Plummer, a Jacksonian from Mississippi, presented a petition seeking a homestead law to the House in that year and spoke in its favor, though he apparently offered no bill for its implementation. Cong Deb, 23d Cong, 2d Sess 1566–70. Robert Smith of Illinois asked that the House Committee on Public Lands

1841 distribution law had given actual settlers a "pre-emptive" right to buy public lands at the minimum statutory price of $1.25 an acre.[100] The homestead proposals went further, commonly offering the land scot-free (or on payment of administrative costs) to any citizen who would settle on the land and cultivate it for five years. The purpose was to encourage settlement of underpopulated areas.[101]

Opponents attacked the homestead bills on grounds familiar to those who have followed the discussion of land grants for agricultural colleges and care of the insane. To President Buchanan those precedents were squarely in point. In his veto of the Morrill bill he had made clear that to "dispose of" the public lands meant to sell them, not to give them away; and the nominal consideration of twenty-five cents per acre for a homestead (to be paid at the end of five years) was "so small that [the transaction] can scarcely be called a sale." Beyond that Buchanan had nothing new to say on the constitutional question; he contented himself with quoting the meaty parts of his veto message of the year before.[102]

But the homestead bill was not, as Buchanan imagined, a carbon copy of the ill-fated bills to finance insane asylums and agricultural schools. It differed in one critical respect, as repeatedly emphasized by its most irrepressible advocate, Democratic Representative (and then Senator) Andrew Johnson of Tennessee.[103]

Mr. Johnson, the reader knows, would later bear the dubious distinction of being the first President ever impeached. A staunch Unionist who would remain at his congressional post after his state had attempted to secede, he would subsequently incur the wrath of congressional radicals by opposing on powerful constitutional grounds their efforts to abolish civilian government in ten Southern states. When we first encounter him in the 1840's, Johnson was a green populist legislator with a penchant for demagoguery.[104] His

---

consider proposing such a bill in 1844. Cong Globe, 28th Cong, 1st Sess 103. President Polk suggested something of the sort for Oregon settlers in his first Annual Message in 1845. 4 Richardson at 385, 397 (Dec 2, 1845).

[100] 5 Stat 453, 455–56, § 10 (Sep 4, 1841). This was not the first time Congress had taken pity on the plight of trespassers who had invested sweat equity in developing the Government's land. Earlier preemption statutes, however, had only forgiven past trespasses, not invited additional ones in the future. See Robbins, Our Landed Heritage at 50 (cited in note 3). For a brief consideration of the history and policy of preemption laws see President Van Buren's first Annual Message, 3 Richardson at 373, 388–89 (Dec 5, 1837); for the strange politics of the 1841 provision see Robbins at 72–91.

[101] In the later years of this struggle the vote on these proposals was almost perfectly divided on sectional lines. Southerners had discovered, it is said, that "free land meant free soil." Robbins, Our Landed Heritage at 109, 179 (cited in note 3). A Canadian newspaper neatly summed up the reason: "The most effective way to shut out slavery is to people the new lands . . . with men whose position places them in natural antagonism to the plantation system." See id at 209, quoting an editorial from the Montreal Herald as reprinted in the New York Tribune, May 26, 1862.

[102] 5 Richardson at 609–11.

[103] See Cong Globe App, 32d Cong, 1st Sess 518 (Rep. McMullen) (giving principal credit for the progress of homestead legislation to Johnson, "for having had the head to conceive, and the energy and perseverance to consummate, so important and philanthropic a measure").

[104] Johnson's first major speech in the House, in 1844, was a tasteless defense of slavery replete with biblical citations and racial slurs. In 1846 he proposed that no federal officer be permitted to serve longer than eight years and that appointments be apportioned among the states according to population. Later the same year, attempting to tar the Whig Party with the discreditable Hartford Convention, he impugned the loyalty of those who questioned the legitimacy of the Mexican War. In 1851 and again in 1852 he proposed a constitutional amendment to limit federal judges to twelve-year terms. See Cong Globe, 28th Cong, 1st Sess 212; 29th

homestead project was a worthy one, however, and he defended it with admirable tenacity and skill.

The best congressional debate on the constitutionality of homestead legislation took place in the House of Representatives during the Thirty-second Congress, in 1852. The bill, as usual, was Johnson's.[105] Pennsylvania Democrat John Dawson supported it with the broad argument that Congress could dispose of the public lands for any reason it liked[106]—an argument that Presidents Pierce and Buchanan would rightly reject in connection with asylums and colleges in the next few years. Thomas Averett of Virginia protested on grounds later to be invoked by Pierce and Buchanan: The purpose of the constitutional provision was to provide a source of revenue to discharge Government obligations; Congress had no power to give away the public lands.[107] For those who agreed with Averett that Congress must receive something in return for its land Joseph Chandler of Pennsylvania had an answer: There could be no better compensation for federal grants than settlement, and under the bill "no man shall come into possession of a single acre of the soil until he enters upon its occupation or improvement."[108]

Standing alone, this argument was unpersuasive. It was not enough to sustain the constitutionality of homestead grants that the Government got what it wanted in return. It would have got lunatic asylums and agricultural schools if grants for those purposes had been approved. What was crucial was whether what the Government got was something it had the constitutional right to seek. It was essential to show that settlement and cultivation of the public domain were necessary and proper to the exercise of some federal power.

That indeed several Representatives proceeded to show. Johnson began the demonstration, taking California as an example. California had been acquired under the treaty power. Why? "[F]or settlement and cultivation." Having acquired land in California, Congress was empowered to dispose of it—to promote the purposes for which it was acquired.

> Is not the passage of a law to induce settlement and cultivation carrying out one of the highest objects contemplated by the Constitution in regard to the acquisition of territory? . . . [I]f the great object of the acquisition of territory is settlement and cultivation, to give power and potency to the country, is it not strange that, under that other provision of the Constitution "to dispose" of the territory, you cannot dispose of it to accomplish and carry out the very object for which you acquired it?[109]

That the treaty power authorized the acquisition of territory had been accepted ever since

---

Cong, 1st Sess 193; 29th Cong, 2d Sess 38; 31st Cong, 2d Sess 627; 32d Cong, 1st Sess 443. Even with respect to homesteads Johnson would make the aberrant argument that the Constitution *required* Congress to distribute land to settlers free of cost, on the ground that the land belonged neither to the United States nor to the states but to the people. Cong Globe, 31st Cong, 1st Sess 1449 (1850).

[105]HR 7, 32d Cong, 1st Sess; see Cong Globe, 32d Cong, 1st Sess 58.

[106]Id at 670. The published text of his speech, Cong Globe App, 32d Cong, 1st Sess 258, 259–60, is not quite so categorical.

[107]Cong Globe, 32d Cong, 1st Sess 1018. See also Cong Globe App, 32d Cong, 1st Sess 582–85 (Texas Rep. Volney Howard).

[108]Cong Globe, 32d Cong, 1st Sess 1021.

[109]Cong Globe App, 32d Cong, 1st Sess 528.

the Senate approved the Louisiana treaty in 1803;[110] Johnson was right that it was not unreasonable to interpret Article IV to permit disposition of property for the purpose for which it had been acquired.

Other speakers applied the same argument to lands that had been ceded to the Federal Government by the states. "The very object for which the cessions were originally sought," quoth David Disney of Ohio, "was for the purpose of causing this territory to be settled, and formed into republican States."[111] Mississippi's John D. Freeman expanded on this theme:

> The object of the States in ceding the lands was, first, to pay the debt incurred by the war of the Revolution and, second, to settle the public lands and construct them into separate republican States. Now, the debt of the war of Independence has been paid, and the Treasury reimbursed for the purchase of the lands; and I maintain that the Constitution, in connection with the articles of cession, authorizes Congress *to dispose of,* and make all needful rules and regulations in regard to this land, for the purpose of building up the new States of the Confederacy. . . .
>
> Thus the Government has the power to settle these lands. And in order to encourage their settlement, we have the right to grant one hundred and sixty acres to each actual settler. And why? I do not sustain the bill upon the ground that we have the right to convert the Federal Government into a great alms-house for the support of the poor and indigent. . . . I sustain the principle of the bill on the ground that we have the right to pay for public services rendered. . . .[112]

A splendid argument, n'est-ce-pas? Opponents of various donations of public lands had argued, with considerable success, that the scope of Congress's power to dispose of property was defined by the purposes for which the land was acquired.[113] As they had argued, those purposes included the raising of revenue to defray expenses incident to the execution of its other powers. But what the defenders of homesteads added to the debate was a recognition that this was not the only purpose for which territory had been acquired;

[110] See The Jeffersonians at 87–122.

[111] Cong Globe, 32d Cong, 1st Sess 1283. See also Disney's elaboration of this argument, id at 1313.

[112] Id at 1283–84. I have divided the quotation into paragraphs for purposes of clarity. See also id at 1312 (Missouri Rep. Willard Hall):

> For what purpose has any Government upon the face of God's earth ever acquired territory? Was it not solely and exclusively for the purpose of peopling it? . . . And, sir, we have recognized that this is the only purpose for which we have acquired this [territory], because, from time to time, we have passed laws with reference exclusively to its settlement. We have passed preemption laws to induce people to go and live upon the land. We have established a credit system at one time, and then we have established the cash system at another time, all the time selling the land at a comparatively low price, . . . with a view of encouraging people to go and live upon it. If we acquire these lands for the purpose of peopling them, I ask the gentleman from Virginia [Mr. Averett] . . . why Congress cannot, in the exercise of a sound discretion, pass a bill, the object of which is to settle the public lands?

[113] See, e.g., id at 1315 (Rep. Howard).

another was to promote settlement and the erection of new states.[114]

The Northwest Ordinance itself made this clear. The territory was to be divided into states, and there could be no states without inhabitants. Disposing of land to encourage settlement promoted the original purpose of admitting additional members to the Union. But the 1780 resolutions of the Continental Congress, paraphrased but not quoted by Representative Freeman, are even more directly in point.

On September 6, 1780 that Congress passed a resolution urging the several states to surrender their Western claims, as New York had already done, "for the general benefit," and to promote "the stability of the general confederacy."[115] A month later Congress enacted the clincher:

> *Resolved*, that the unappropriated lands that may be ceded or relinquished to the United States, . . . pursuant to the recommendation of Congress of the 6 day of September last, shall be disposed of for the common benefit of the United States, and be settled and formed into distinct republican states, which shall become members of the federal union . . . ;
>
> That the said lands shall be granted and settled at such times and under such regulations as shall hereafter be agreed on by the United States in Congress assembled . . . .[116]

It was in vain that Georgia's Alexander Stephens protested that neither the Virginia, the North Carolina, nor the Georgia cession expressly mentioned settlement.[117] As the states had unanimously agreed in Congress, settlement was one of the express purposes to which the land was to be applied; and this history informs the meaning of the corresponding later provision authorizing the new Congress to dispose of the public lands.

Like land-grant colleges (and the Pacific railroad), homesteads were finally authorized under Republican auspices in 1862.[118] In terms of congressional power, however, the two measures were by no means analogous, as Buchanan believed they were; the constitutional basis of homesteads was far more secure.

[114]"The great object of government, in respect to [public] lands," Daniel Webster had argued in 1825, "was not so much the money derived from their sale, as it was the getting of them settled." Cong Deb, 18th Cong, 2d Sess 252, quoted in Robert V. Remini, Daniel Webster: The Man and His Time 636 (Norton, 1997).

[115]17 J Cont Cong 806–7 (Sep 6, 1780). The resolution also noted the necessity of strengthening the public credit—an oblique reference, perhaps, to the utility of land as a source of public funds. Representative Disney would later explain what Congress had in mind with its reference to "stability" by suggesting that retention of state claims would have endangered our security: "[T]he possession of such large tracts made one State [Virginia] too powerful for the safety of the rest." Cong Globe, 32d Cong, 1st Sess 1313; see also id at 1283.

[116]18 J Cont Cong 914, 915 (Oct 10, 1780).

[117]Cong Globe, 32d Cong, 1st Sess 1313–14. See also id at 1314 (Rep. Woodward) (arguing that although settlement may have been the reason for the cessions, their condition was the payment of debts).

[118]12 Stat 392 (May 20, 1862). Cf 12 Stat 489 (Jul 1, 1862) (Union Pacific); 12 Stat 503 (Jul 2, 1862) (colleges). See text accompanying notes 150 of chapter 1 and 97 of this chapter.

3

The Bank War

President Madison, as I reported in an earlier volume, signed the bill establishing the Second Bank of the United States in 1816, yielding his constitutional scruples in deference to the general understanding.[1] The Supreme Court sustained it three years later in *McCulloch v Maryland*.[2] But the charter of the Second Bank, like that of the first, was to last only twenty years. It thus would expire in 1836; and as we have seen one of the first things Andrew Jackson did upon assuming the Presidency was to raise the question whether that charter should be renewed.[3]

The suggestion was premature, said Missouri Senator Thomas Hart Benton not long afterward;[4] the charter had several more years to run. But Nicholas Biddle, the Bank's capable and combative President, chose to fight sooner rather than later. As a result, like Aesop's dog, he lost the bone he had as well as the one to which he aspired. Congress passed a bill to renew the charter, but Jackson vetoed it. He proceeded to have the Government's money removed from the Bank before its charter ran out, prompting a major brouhaha in Congress over executive "despotism" and presidential control of the Executive Branch. The Senate censured the President, Jackson replied in kind, and a more Democratic Senate voted to "expunge" the censure after a vigorous debate over the constitutionality of falsifying the public record that Article I, § 5 required each House to

[1]See The Jeffersonians at 257. For the constitutional debates surrounding creation of the First Bank see The Federalist Period at 78–80.

[2]17 US 316 (1819); see The First Hundred Years at 160–65.

[3]See text accompanying notes 23–25 of the Introduction to Part One.

[4]Cong Deb, 22d Cong, 1st Sess 966. Treasury Secretary Louis McLane, a friend of the Bank, had urged that the Bank not apply for renewal until after the 1832 election lest the President veto it. Henry Clay had initially taken the same position but then had changed his mind. See Nicholas Biddle's memorandum of a conversation with McLane, Oct 19, 1831, in Reginald C. McGrane, ed, The Correspondence of Nicholas Biddle dealing with National Affairs, 1807–1844 128, 130–31 (Houghton, Mifflin, 1919); McLane to Biddle, Jan 5, 1832, id at 165, 166–67; Clay to Biddle, Sep 11, 1830, id at 110–14; Clay to Biddle, Dec 15, 1831, id at 142.

maintain.

The country stumbled along without a national bank, the Government first parking its funds in state banks and then retaining custody of its own money in a "sub-treasury" system that basically meant the Treasury acted as its own depository. Then the Whigs captured both ends of Pennsylvania Avenue and promptly voted (twice) to establish a new national bank—only to see their efforts frustrated by "His Accidency" John Tyler, who, as we have seen,[5] was anything but a true Whig in his conception of federal power. National banks were not to be reestablished until the Democratic era was over, in 1863.[6]

I. PRESIDENT JACKSON'S VETO

In January 1832 Pennsylvania Senator George M. Dallas submitted the Bank's memorial requesting an extension of its charter;[7] two months later he reported a committee bill to extend the Bank by a full fifteen years.[8] The usual arguments were made as to the constitutionality and expediency of the Bank—briefly, for the question was not new.[9] Daniel Webster emphasized the Bank's utility in the collection and distribution of revenue and its role in promoting a stable and uniform currency.[10] South Carolina Representative George McDuffie, the House sponsor, placed unusual weight on a contention that, for reasons both textual and historical, had been relatively slighted in the past. The arguments from the powers to tax, borrow, and spend were powerful, he said, but the strongest case for the Bank was that Congress had authority to coin money—which in his view included bank notes as well as coins.[11]

More novel than the dispute over the Bank itself was Alabama Senator Gabriel Moore's proposal to permit the states to tax it to the same extent as competing institutions established under state law.[12] The Supreme Court had held the Bank immune from state taxation in *McCulloch,*[13] and Webster objected that Congress could not authorize what the Constitution forbade.[14] Stephen Miller of South Carolina responded that it was up to Congress to specify the conditions of the charter, but he failed to explain why the

[5]See note 20 and text accompanying notes 37–46 of chapter 1.

[6]12 Stat 665 (Feb 25, 1863).

[7]Cong Deb, 22d Cong, 1st Sess 53. A former solicitor of the Bank and a Democrat, Dallas would later serve as Vice-President under Polk. He spent less than two years in the Senate.

[8]Id at 530. McDuffie's parallel House bill, id at 1780, would have extended the charter for twenty years. It was the Senate bill that Congress would pass and send to the President.

[9]For the earlier arguments see The Federalist Period at 78–80; The Jeffersonians at 254–58.

[10]Cong Deb, 22d Cong, 1st Sess 954–64.

[11]Cong Deb App, 21st Cong, 1st Sess 109. Clay and Calhoun had made this argument in 1816, see The Jeffersonians at 256–57. See also McDuffie's 1830 committee report, HR Rep 358, 21st Cong, 1st Sess 6 (1830): "'Coin' was regarded, at the period of the framing of the Constitution, as synonymous with 'currency,' as it was then generally believed that bank notes could only be maintained in circulation by being the true representative of the precious metals." But see the minority report of Representatives Alexander and Gaither on the 1832 bill, HR Rep 283, 22d Cong, 1st Sess 55: "Coin is a term known all over the world, as applied to metallic substances as money, in contradistinction to paper." For further objections see Cong Deb, 23d Cong, 1st Sess 1073–76 (Sen. Benton).

[12]Cong Deb, 22d Cong, 1st Sess 980.

[13]17 US at 425–37.

[14]Cong Deb, 22d Cong, 1st Sess 982–83.

condition Moore proposed was constitutional.[15] To the extent that the immunity recognized in *McCulloch* was based upon the Bank's initial charter,[16] there was no difficulty; what Congress giveth, Congress (in this context) may surely take away. Moreover, even if the immunity was derived from the Constitution itself, it was for the benefit of the Government, and thus should be waivable—as the Court had already concluded, and would later reaffirm, in the analogous arena of state immunity from suit in federal court.[17]

Moore's motion to waive the Bank's immunity was defeated,[18] and the bill went to the President. Citing both constitutional and policy objections, he sent it back.[19]

On the merits of the constitutional question Jackson's veto message can perhaps best be described as uninspiring and bizarre.[20] Eschewing familiar attacks on the Bank as an institution[21] or on the power to establish corporations,[22] the President sniped uncon-

[15]Id at 994.

[16]See The First Hundred Years at 165–67.

[17]Bank of the United States v Planters' Bank, 22 US 904, 907–8 (1824); Clark v Barnard, 108 US 436, 447–48 (1883). That, in somewhat different words, was John Marshall's suggestion in a letter expressing surprise at Webster's objection:

> This may be considered not as granting power of taxation to a state, for a state possesses that power; but as withdrawing a bar which the constitution opposes to the exercise of this power over a franchise created by Congress for national purposes . . . .

Marshall to Webster, Jun 16, 1832, 3 Webster Correspondence at 177, 178.

[18]Cong Deb, 22d Cong, 1st Sess 1005. Later Congresses, following Moore's lead, permitted certain state taxes to reach national banks, e.g., 42 Stat 1499 (Mar 4, 1923); in 1969 national banks were equated with state banks for purposes of state taxation. 83 Stat 434 (Dec 24, 1969), 12 USC § 548 (2003). See generally First National Bank v State Tax Comm, 392 US 339 (1968).

[19]2 Richardson at 576–91 (Jul 10, 1832).

[20]Much of the message consists of populistic ranting against monopolies, giveaways, and foreign influence, as well as animadversions on "the rich and powerful," id at 576–81, 590. One prominent commentator described it as "legalistic, demagogic, and full of sham." Bray Hammond, Banks and Politics in America 405 (Princeton, 1957). I do not mean to deny that there may have been legitimate reasons for concern over abuses in the actual administration of the Bank.

The message was written, we are told, by Amos Kendall (a minor Treasury official prominent in Jackson's Kitchen Cabinet and soon to be Postmaster General), "with an assist from [Attorney General Roger] Taney." Peterson, The Great Triumvirate at 210. For a more expansive view of Taney's role see Carl B. Swisher, Roger B. Taney 194 (Archon, 1961), quoting Taney's own later unpublished account of the entire Bank War.

[21]Several months after the veto Taney would write the President that the Constitution did not authorize Congress to establish a bank "if the fiscal operations of the government can be carried on with safety and convenience" without it, and that they could be. Taney to Jackson, Mar ?, 1833, 5 Jackson Correspondence at 33, 40. For Taney's earlier list of provisions in the bill he thought unnecessary see Swisher, Taney at 191–92 (cited in note 20), quoting an unpublished letter from Taney to Jackson, Jun 27, 1832.

[22]2 Richardson at 583. Nicholas Biddle, however, in a memorandum of a conversation with the President around the end of 1829, reported him as saying "I do not think that Congress has a right to create a corporation out of the ten mile square," i.e., the District of Columbia. McGrane, Biddle Correspondence at 93 (cited in note 4). Van Buren, in an 1836 letter, agreed. See A Letter from the Hon. Martin Van Buren, Vice-President of the United States, Relative to the Bank of the United States 13 (Miller, 1836). Representative McDuffie, in his 1830 report urging recharter, gave a crushing response to such objections. "The power of creating corporations," he argued, was "one of the lowest attributes . . . of sovereign power"; incorporation "d[id] not authorize the corporation to do any thing, which the individuals composing it might not do without the charter." If Congress could pass laws inflicting the death penalty on the ground that it was necessary and proper to the execution of federal authority, McDuffie concluded, it was "difficult to conceive why it may not pass a

vincingly at details of the bill. Congress could not give the Bank a monopoly, for it could surrender neither its authority to create another nor its power to legislate "in all cases" for the District of Columbia.[23] The express power to grant "exclusive" copyrights and patents to "authors and inventors"[24] implied that Congress could not give exclusive rights "as a means of accomplishing any other end."[25] It was neither "necessary" nor "proper" to the legitimate purposes of the Bank to permit foreigners to purchase its stock or to exempt their interests from state taxation: The first would "impoverish our people . . . [and] endanger our independence," while the second was "vitally subversive of the rights of the States."[26] Nor could Congress give the Bank authority to purchase land within the states, for the Government itself could acquire land only for the limited purposes enumerated in the penultimate clause of Article I, § 8, and then only by cessions from the states.[27] The requirement that the Bank pay the United States a "bonus" in exchange for its privileges showed that it had been given more powers than were "necessary," for the "use and emolument" of the shareholders, and not "for the advantage of the Government."[28] Finally, the bill implicitly deprived the states of authority to tax the Bank, "in subversion of one of the strongest barriers which secured [the states] against Federal encroachment"; while the Government itself was concededly immune to state taxes, its private agents were not, and "it can not be *necessary* to the character of the bank as a fiscal agent of the Government that its private business should be exempted" from state taxation.[29] Maybe

---

law, under the same authority, for the more humble purpose of creating a corporation." HR Rep 358, 21st Cong, 1st Sess 5.

[23] 2 Richardson at 583–84. The Supreme Court had already rejected this argument in holding that a state could give contractual tax exemptions. New Jersey v Wilson, 11 US 164 (1812); see The First Hundred Years at 136–37. Jackson's argument was weaker still in the Bank context, for no contract clause (as in *Wilson*) required the United States to live up to its promises; the bill would not have divested Congress of its power to create additional banks after all. Congress had given the Post Office a monopoly in 1792. 1 Stat 232, 236, § 14 (Feb 20, 1792).

[24] US Const, Art I, § 8, cl 8.

[25] 2 Richardson at 584. Even Justice Peter Daniel, arguably the most states'-rights-minded jurist ever to inhabit the Supreme Court, acknowledged that the express provisions respecting counterfeiting and offenses on the high seas or against the law of nations did not preclude Congress from making additional conduct criminal when necessary and proper to the exercise of other federal powers. United States v Marigold, 50 US 560 (1850); The First Hundred Years at 323 n.269.

[26] 2 Richardson at 585. Whether a measure was "necessary and proper" was a question of degree; in this passage Jackson seemed to transmute it into a pure question of policy. Along the same line see Jackson's further complaint, id at 585, that the bill allowed the Bank more capital than it needed to carry out its federal functions.

[27] The clause in question has generally been understood not to limit the acquisition of land necessary and proper to the exercise of other granted powers but only to provide a means of obtaining exclusive jurisdiction over it, as in the District of Columbia. US Const, Art I, § 8, cl 17; see The Jeffersonians at 275–77 and section IV of chapter 1.

[28] 2 Richardson at 586. Without some financial inducement, private investors could hardly be expected to buy shares in the Bank. Furthermore, Jackson had begun by complaining that the Bank should be required to pay for its monopoly, id at 577; it was a bit thick for him then to object that it was.

[29] Id at 586–89. State taxes would increase the cost of the Bank's operations; immunity was as necessary in the case of a private bank as in that of a public one. Later Congresses have granted federal instrumentalities exemptions from state taxation, and the Supreme Court has upheld them—quite apart from the Supreme Court's apparent conclusion in *McCulloch,* 17 US at 425–26, that they were implicit in the Constitution itself. E.g., Bank v Supervisors, 74 US 26, 30–31 (1869). Contrast Webster's equally untenable argument (recounted in the text at note 14) that it would be unconstitutional to *repeal* the Bank's exemption.

the Government could constitutionally establish *some* bank, Jackson concluded, but not this one.[30]

For reasons sketched in the footnotes, I think there was little to any of the foregoing objections. There was equally little to Jackson's further suggestion that Congress could not even delegate to the Bank the decision where to establish branches.[31] Other agencies carrying out statutory directions had been permitted without objection to determine where to locate their offices; this seems the sort of ministerial detail that Congress might legitimately leave to those entrusted with executing the law.

Hidden among the detritus of Jackson's message, however, was the germ of a related contention that was more worthy of notice: If Congress had power to regulate paper money, it could not transfer that authority to a corporation.[32] A year after the veto, during the ensuing controversy over removing Government money from the expiring Bank, Jackson would fulminate once more against entrusting fiscal responsibility to a private company: How would it be, he asked, if Congress created corporations to run the Army and Navy, or to conduct foreign affairs, and thus deprived the President of his constitutional authority?[33]

This was not a frivolous concern. Before the much regretted decision in *Morrison v Olson,* which upheld the appointment of a special prosecutor insulated from presidential supervision,[34] it had been generally understood that, as Madison had argued in 1789, executive power could not be placed beyond presidential control.[35] If that was so, surely it would not avoid the problem to place such authority in private hands.[36] This is not to deny that the Government may contract out such ministerial functions as the construction of public buildings and the storage of federal funds, but to the extent the Bank was authorized to make federal policy—by controlling the currency, for example—Jackson's worries were by no means misplaced.

On the whole, however, Jackson's objections to the Bank were not especially convincing. More noteworthy than these idiosyncratic essays on the merits, in any event, was his famous argument that he was not bound by the Supreme Court's conclusion in *McCulloch* that the Bank was constitutional. First of all, he wrote, the Court had "not decided that all the features of this corporation are compatible with the Constitution." The opinion had expressly declared that it was not for the judges "to inquire into the degree of . . . necessity" for any particular provision. To paraphrase this argument in modern terms, the Court had said that was a political question.

[30]2 Richardson at 589. Democratic platforms from 1840 through 1860 would take the argument a giant step further: "[C]ongress has no power to charter a national bank." Porter & Johnson, Party Platforms at 2, 4, 11, 17, 24, 30, 31.

[31]2 Richardson at 585–86.

[32]Id at 586.

[33]Draft statement to the Cabinet, Sep 18, 1833, 5 Jackson Correspondence at 192, 196. See also Robert V. Remini, Andrew Jackson and the Bank War: A Study in the Growth of Presidential Power 44 (Norton, 1967), arguing that what really troubled Jackson about the Bank was his fear of the concentration of power in private hands and beyond either executive, legislative, or popular control.

[34]487 US 654 (1988).

[35]See The Federalist Period at 38; The Second Century at 591 n.223 (discussing *Morrison*). See US Const, Art II, §§ 1, 3: "The executive power shall be vested in a President of the United States of America. . . . He shall take care that the laws be faithfully executed . . . ."

[36]Cf Carter v Carter Coal Co, 298 US 238, 311 (1936), confirming the common-sense conclusion that Congress can no more delegate its legislative powers to private parties than to a governmental agency.

> Under the decision of the Supreme Court, therefore, it is the exclusive province of Congress and the President to decide whether the particular features of this act are *necessary* and *proper* to enable the bank to perform conveniently and efficiently the public duties assigned to it as fiscal agent, and therefore constitutional . . . .[37]

That was clever. It was also true. And what was left to Congress was also, as Jackson said, left to the President; for in deciding whether to sign a bill the President, unlike a reviewing court, was a participant in the legislative process.

That was enough to justify Jackson (or Congress, for that matter)[38] in taking a fresh look at the constitutionality of the Bank, unembarrassed by the constraints that had limited Supreme Court review. But Jackson had a more sweeping and better-known argument as well, and it was equally convincing:

> If the opinion of the Supreme Court covered the whole ground of this act, it ought not to control the coordinate authorities of this Government. The Congress, the Executive, and the Court must each for itself be guided by its own opinion of the Constitution. Each public officer who takes an oath to support the Constitution swears that he will support it as he understands it, and not as it is understood by others. It is as much the duty of the House of Representatives, of the Senate, and of the President to decide upon the constitutionality of any bill or resolution which may be presented to them for passage or approval as it is of the supreme judges when it may be brought before them for judicial decision. The opinion of the judges has no more authority over Congress than the opinion of Congress has over the judges, and on that point the President is independent of both. The authority of the Supreme Court must not therefore, be permitted to control the Congress or the Executive when acting in their legislative capacities, but to have only such influence as the force of their reasoning may deserve.[39]

[37]2 Richardson at 583.

[38]In this connection it should be noted that Congress itself continued to debate the constitutionality of the Bank after the Court had upheld it in *McCulloch*.

[39]2 Richardson at 582. Justice Story, writing shortly afterward, echoed Jackson's conviction that every federal officer was bound by his oath to determine for himself the constitutionality of his proposed actions, but he spoke only of cases "not hitherto settled by any proper authority," and (in response not to the President's message but to the nullification doctrine) he insisted that the Supreme Court's interpretation of the Constitution was binding and conclusive. 1 Story, §§ 374–75, 385, 387.

Jackson's Bank veto message is also notable for its rejection of the deference to *legislative* precedent reflected both in Madison's 1815 Bank pronouncement and in *McCulloch* itself. Insisting appropriately enough that "mere precedent" should be decisive only "where the acquiescence of the people and the States can be considered as well settled" (2 Richardson at 581–82),

> the President totally ignored Madison's prior veto declaring that practice had settled the bank constitutionality question. The most relevant precedent of all—Madison's acquiescence on the question of constitutionality—does not appear anywhere in Jackson's veto message, and this "see

Back in the Senate, Daniel Webster and Henry Clay disputed the President's conclusion: The Supreme Court's decision was binding.[40] Jackson's message, Webster thundered, "denies to the judiciary the interpretation of law."[41]

It is not my custom to take the part of Andrew Jackson against the likes of Daniel Webster and Henry Clay. On the merits of the Bank most of his arguments were not worth a continental—whatever one might think about the more fundamental questions that had been raised by such early and worthy opponents as Thomas Jefferson and James Madison. On the issue of the President's responsibility to obey the Constitution, however, Jackson had the better of the argument. His was not Franklin Roosevelt's obviously improper proposal (which Roosevelt fortunately did not have to communicate) that the Government disobey a court order directed to it as a party, which would have denied the power of the courts to decide cases at all.[42] It was not Abraham Lincoln's more debatable but still troubling assertion that Congress was free to reenact a law the Supreme Court had just declared invalid, which while based on the truism that a judgment binds only the parties[43] might if indiscriminately followed sorely undermine the efficacy of judicial review.[44] Far from subverting the judicial check on unconstitutional legislation, Jackson's bold pronouncement added three more. Jefferson, in private correspondence, had taken the same position in explaining his decision to pardon Sedition Act offenders on constitutional grounds;[45] Jackson performed a major service in restating it publicly,

---

> no evil, hear no evil" methodology belies the President's assertion that he considered himself bound by well-settled understandings.

Gerard N. Magliocca, Veto! The Jacksonian Revolution in Constitutional Law, 78 Neb L Rev 205, 232–33 (1999). For Madison's message see 1 Richardson at 555 (Jan 30, 1815); The Jeffersonians at 255; for *McCulloch* see 17 US at 401.

[40]Cong Deb, 22d Cong, 1st Sess 1231–32 (Sen. Webster); id at 1273 (Sen. Clay) (significantly branding the President's action "nullification" of Congress's decision). Clay argued that one might as well say an inferior court could ignore Supreme Court precedent or a customs agent a Treasury order (id at 1273), but those cases were not in point: The hierarchical principle amply explains them, since the subordinate's action can simply be reversed.

[41]Cong Deb, 22d Cong, 1st Sess 1240. Clay also chose to challenge Jackson's understanding of the veto power in other respects, arguing that the power had been intended as a check on "precipitate legislation"; to employ it on grounds of mere expediency was irreconcilable with "the genius of representative government." Id at 1265. This was an early salvo in a Whig campaign against the veto power that would continue until Congress finally mustered the votes to start overriding the President's negative over a decade later. Suffice it for now to say that Clay's argument was pure moonshine, and immaterial at that; for Jackson had based his veto primarily on grounds of unconstitutionality, not policy. See the further discussion of the veto power in section I of chapter 6.

[42]See Elliott Roosevelt, ed, 1 F.D.R.—His Personal Letters, 1928–1945 459–60 (1950).

[43]Tennessee Senator Hugh Lawson White made this point in defending Jackson's position during the debate on overriding the veto. Cong Deb, 22d Cong, 1st Sess 1243. Attorney General Taney had said much the same thing in suggesting that a state might continue to enforce a statute limiting the rights of free black seamen within its ports even though he expected the Supreme Court to strike it down: "If the judgment pronounced by the court be conclusive it does not follow that the reasoning or principles which it announces in coming to its conclusions are equally binding and obligatory." Taney to Secretary of State Edward Livingston, May 28, 1832, quoted in Swisher, Roger B. Taney at 157 (cited in note 20).

[44]See Herbert Wechsler, The Courts and the Constitution, 65 Colum L Rev 1001, 1008 (1965). For Lincoln's argument see Descent into the Maelstrom, ch 9.

[45]See The Jeffersonians at 5–6.

plainly, and persuasively.[46]

It was one of Mr. Jackson's finest hours. The finest of them all came a few months later, when he took a position that seemed in considerable tension with the one I have just applauded. We shall explore that occasion in due course,[47] but we have miles to go in the meantime.

II. REMOVAL OF THE DEPOSITS

Jackson was not yet through. The Bank had been killed, but it was not yet dead; and it still had the Government's money. In his next Annual Message Jackson asked Congress to investigate whether Government deposits were safe in the Bank's hands.[48] The House proceeded to make the requested investigation (presumably incident to determining whether new legislation was needed) and concluded, over sharp dissent, that the deposits were indeed safe.[49]

On December 3, 1833 Secretary of the Treasury Roger B. Taney nonetheless reported to Congress that he had ordered the Government's deposits to be withdrawn from the Bank as needed and not to be replaced.[50] Opposition Senators went berserk.

A. The Statute

It is not at all obvious what they had to go berserk about. The statute creating the Bank, which Taney appropriately quoted at the outset of his report, provided that (wherever the Bank had offices) the Government's money be deposited there, "unless the Secretary of the Treasury shall at any time otherwise order and direct."[51] The Secretary had otherwise ordered and directed; on the face of it he had acted squarely within his statutory powers.[52]

Both Clay and Webster had crossed swords with President Jackson over the Bank veto. In the case of removal of the deposits they were joined by the equally formidable John C. Calhoun. The Secretary's power was not unlimited, they argued. His authority should be interpreted in light of its purpose, which was to ensure safe and faithful custody

[46]Both Webster and Clay argued that the President was arrogating to himself power to determine which laws to enforce. Cong Deb, 22d Cong, 1st Sess 1232 (Sen. Webster); id at 1273 (Sen. Clay). He did no such thing. Far from violating his duty to take care that the laws be faithfully executed (Art II, § 3), or as a House committee would argue many years later transforming a suspensive veto into an absolute one by refusing to execute an unconstitutional provision already enacted (HR Rep 138, 99th Cong, 1st Sess 13 (1985)), Jackson was exercising his independent authority to prevent a bill from becoming law. Indeed, as Attorneys General and their subordinates have often maintained, it is at least arguable that Jackson's reasoning equally proves that the Constitution requires the President not to *enforce* unconstitutional laws. See the discussion in chapter 6, section II.

[47]See the discussion of Jackson's rejection of state nullification of allegedly unconstitutional laws in chapter 4.

[48]2 Richardson at 591, 600 (Dec 4, 1832).

[49]For Representative Gulian Verplanck's committee report in support of this conclusion and Representative Polk's interminable dissent see HR Rep 121, 22d Cong, 2d Sess (1833); for the House vote, which was a resounding 109–46, see Cong Deb, 22d Cong, 2d Sess 1936. An 1834 report from Senator Tyler would reaffirm that the Government's money was "abundantly safe" in the Bank's hands. S Doc 17, 23d Cong, 2d Sess 14 (1834).

[50]See Cong Deb App, 23d Cong, 1st Sess 59–68.

[51]3 Stat 266, 274, § 16 (Apr 10, 1816).

[52]See Cong Deb, 23d Cong, 1st Sess 235–36 (Sen. Shepley).

of the funds. Taney had conceded that the Bank was faithful and the money safe, as the House had already concluded; he had therefore acted beyond his statutory authority in removing the funds.[53]

Taney had anticipated this objection. "[T]he plain terms" of the statute, he argued, revealed

> that the power reserved to the Secretary over the deposites [sic] shall not be restricted to any particular contingencies, but be absolute and unconditional. . . . [I]t must be the duty of the Secretary of the Treasury to withdraw the deposites . . . whenever the change would, in any degree, promote the public interest. . . . The safety of the deposites, the ability of the bank to meet its engagements, its fidelity in the performance of its obligations, are only a part of the considerations by which his judgment must be guided.[54]

To confirm his textual argument Taney quoted a letter from William H. Crawford, who had been Secretary of the Treasury under Monroe, asserting a willingness to withdraw money from the National Bank if necessary to support the credit of its state competitors.[55] It was absurd to think, added Maine's freshman Senator Ether Shepley, that Congress had meant to keep the money in the Bank if doing so seriously inconvenienced the Government.[56] "[N]othing seems to be more natural," said William C. Rives of Virginia, "than that the power of withdrawing" the deposits "should be reserved to the Government, as a means of control over the conduct of the bank, as well as to provide for the safety of the public moneys." The Bank's behavior, Rives continued, fully justified this broad authority; for the Bank had made such use of Government funds for its own profit that it had proved "unable to meet the demand of the United States for their own money."[57] Rather than limiting the Secretary's discretion, Taney concluded, the statute merely required him to report to Congress the reasons for his decision.[58]

[53]See id at 51 (Sen. Clay); id at 206–7 (Sen. Calhoun); Cong Deb App, 23d Cong, 1st Sess 148–50 (Sen. Webster). See also Webster's committee report, S Doc 72, 23d Cong, 1st Sess 7 (1834), adding that removal would also have been proper had the Bank defaulted on its obligation to transfer funds.

[54]Cong Deb App, 23d Cong, 1st Sess 60.

[55]Id.

[56]If those who urged a narrow interpretation of the Secretary's authority were correct, said Shepley,

> What would be the consequence? Why, sir, the bank might be ever so unaccommodating, it might in every possible way inconvenience the Government, and you could not help yourself; your hands would be tied up; for the money would be safe, sir—it would be safe. The deposites may be used by the bank for its own purposes; it may openly exhibit that power, and yet you cannot remove them; they are safe . . . . They may corrupt your press; they may bribe your electors; they may come into your legislative department, and interfere with the enactment of your laws; and yet, because the deposites are safe, you have not a word to say . . . .

Cong Deb, 23d Cong, 1st Sess 246–47.

[57]Id at 267–69.

[58]Cong Deb App, 23d Cong, 1st Sess 60. Even Justice Story, much to Webster's chagrin, agreed with this conclusion. Story to Webster, Dec 25, 1833, in William W. Story, 2 Life and Letters of Joseph Story 155–56 (Little, Brown, 1851). The reasons for withdrawal, which Jackson had revealed to his Cabinet in September of the same year, included the Bank's alleged misconduct and the need to ensure an orderly transition to the time

I am inclined to think Taney and his supporters had the better of this argument. Although Calhoun was certainly right that general statutory terms may sometimes be cut down to conform to their purpose,[59] neither he nor anyone else succeeded in demonstrating that Congress had been concerned only with the Bank's fidelity and the safety of the deposits. But the statutory controversy was trivial; Senators do not commonly become so exercised over the mere fact that a Cabinet officer has arguably misinterpreted an ambiguous statutory provision. The real source of Senatorial ire was not that the decision to remove the deposits was wrong; it was that the President had made the decision.

B. The President's Powers

Jackson had raised the question of removing the deposits in his fourth Annual Message in December 1832.[60] Even earlier, it seems, he had made up his mind that the deposits should be withdrawn. When Louis McLane, his second Treasury Secretary, reportedly balked at the removal, he was transferred to the State Department—"with the expectation," one student of the controversy asserted, "of securing a more pliable secretary of the treasury."[61] His replacement was William Duane, a longtime opponent of the Bank, who in turn concluded that there was no reason to remove the deposits, that to do so would amount to "a breach of the public faith," and that it would "tend to shake public confidence, and promote doubt and mischief in the operations of society."[62] For this bout of honesty the President unceremoniously removed him, giving the accommodating Mr. Taney a recess appointment to his place.[63]

Henry Clay solemnly moved that the Senate censure President Jackson for causing the deposits to be removed. The statute, said Clay, vested authority to remove them in the Secretary, not the President; in discharging Duane for refusing to do so Jackson had usurped the Secretary's authority.[64] Moreover, Clay roared, this action did not stand alone. It was just one element in a "revolution" designed to consolidate power in a single man. The President had paralyzed Congress by excessive use of the veto and by withholding bills instead of returning them so that Congress might override his objections. He had circumvented constitutional checks on the appointing power by giving recess ap-

---

when the Bank would no longer exist. See id at 60–68, 284–89. See also HR Rep 312, 23d Cong, 1st Sess 9 (1834) (Rep. Polk): "If want of safety was the only reason which could justify a removal of the deposites, why was the Secretary required to report his reasons at all?"

[59]Consider, as one of many examples, Blackstone's famous case of the law forbidding "bloodletting" in the streets of Bologna. See William Blackstone, 1 Commentaries on the Laws of England *61 (Chicago, 1979) (first published in 1765–69) [hereafter cited as Blackstone].

[60]See note 48 and accompanying text.

[61]See Ralph Catterall, The Second Bank of the United States 292 (1902). Taney's biographer denies that this was the President's motivation: Jackson had not made up his own mind that the deposits should be removed, and McLane wanted his new job. Swisher, Roger B. Taney at 214, 221 (cited in note 20).

[62]See two of the four letters from Duane to Jackson dated September 21, 1833, in Cong Deb App, 23d Cong, 1st Sess 306, 309.

[63]See Jackson to Duane, Sep 23, 1833, id at 309; Jackson to Martin Van Buren, Sep 23, 1833, 5 Jackson Correspondence at 207. Congress was not in session; when the Senate met again it rejected Taney's appointment. Sen Exec Journal, 23d Cong, 1st Sess 427 (Jun 24, 1834). He became Chief Justice in 1836. Sen Exec Journal, 24th Cong, 1st Sess 520 (Mar 15, 1836).

[64]Cong Deb, 23d Cong, 1st Sess 58, 64–65.

pointments to nominees for federal office after the Senate had rejected them.[65] He had ignored both judicial decisions and treaties. "The premonitory symptoms of despotism are upon us," Clay shouted; we were well on our way to an elective monarchy.[66]

Henry Clay was a great statesman, but even great statesmen have bad days. Whatever may be said for Clay's other accusations, it was not true that Jackson had "usurped" the authority of his own Secretary of the Treasury. It was true that the statute had said the Secretary should make the decision and that the President had effectively done so. But as Taney had said in explaining his action to Congress, the Secretary presided over an executive department, and in disposing of the deposits he was exercising an executive function. Thus, Taney concluded, "the manner in which it is exercised must be subject to the supervision of the officer to whom the constitution has confided the whole executive power, and has required to take care that the laws be faithfully executed."[67]

Benton of Missouri, Shepley of Maine, Rives of Virginia expanded on Taney's point. Yes, the statute made it the Secretary's duty to look after the deposits, "but the Constitution makes it the duty of the President to see that the Secretary performs his duty."[68] The President could not take care that the laws be faithfully executed if he could not control the action of those who actually execute them; "there can be no constitutional law making the Secretary of the Treasury independent of the executive power."[69] As James Madison had told the House in 1789, the President's obligation to see that the laws were faithfully executed implied "a power of superintendence and control" over officers who carried out the law.[70]

For indeed these arguments were not new. Madison, Fisher Ames, and others had made them with great effect in the First Congress, during the famous debate on the President's right to remove the Secretary of Foreign Affairs. As I have argued elsewhere, it is too much to conclude (as Shepley and others did)[71] that Congress (or even the House) adopted Madison's position in 1789. The statutory language finally adopted found favor with those who thought Congress could decide whether the President should be able to fire the Secretary as well as those who thought the Constitution gave him that authority.[72] But Madison's and Ames's arguments in 1789 were as unanswerable as Benton's and Shepley's in 1834. Not only would the creation of an independent Treasury make it impossible for the President to take care that the laws be faithfully executed, as Article II

[65]As Attorney General, Taney had attempted to justify this practice: A new vacancy had occurred at the end of the intervening session, and the President had a duty to ensure that the laws were enforced. 2 Op AG 525, 526 (1832).

[66]Cong Deb, 23d Cong, 1st Sess 59, 94. Cf Luigi Illica & Giuseppe Giacosa, La Bohème, Act I (1896): "Già dell'Apocalisse appariscono i segni." Senator Benton tried to suggest that the nation had approved Jackson's action by reelecting him, Cong Deb, 23d Cong, 1st Sess 136, but as Clay said the people had only thought him preferable to his opponent, not endorsed his every action; and in any event the election of a President could not amend the Constitution. Id at 65–66. See also Remini, Jackson and the Bank War at 45 (cited in note 33), asserting that Jackson was reelected *in spite of* his campaign against the Bank.

[67]Cong Deb App, 23d Cong, 1st Sess 60. See US Const, Art II, §§ 1, 3.

[68]Cong Deb, 23d Cong, 1st Sess 100 (Sen. Benton).

[69]Id at 241 (Sen. Shepley).

[70]Id at 283–84 (Sen. Rives). The whole point of vesting the executive power in a single President, Rives added, was to ensure a unitary executive. Id at 279–82 (quoting both Madison and Jefferson); see also id at 418 (Sen. Grundy); id at 892 (Sen. Tallmadge).

[71]See, e.g., id at 238 (Sen. Shepley); id at 418 (Sen. Grundy).

[72]See The Federalist Period at 40–41.

requires him to do; it would vest a portion of the executive power in someone other than the President, in whom the same Article declares it shall be vested.[73] Finally, even if the 1789 legislative decision was consistent with a congressional power to free the Secretary from presidential control, Congress had not exercised that power. On the contrary, as Senator Shepley pointed out, the statutes explicitly recognized the President's power to remove, and thus to control, the Secretaries of Foreign Affairs, War, and the Treasury.[74] All of this, of course, had been good Federalist dogma in 1789—until their ideological successors, those who believed in broad federal power to establish banks, impose protective tariffs, and finance internal improvements, lost the Presidency in 1829.

Clay and company were on the ropes. Calhoun deserted them on the constitutional question: Firing Duane was an abuse of authority, but it was not unconstitutional, for the President had power to supervise and remove him.[75] Webster uncomfortably endeavored to divide the baby: The President could fire the Secretary but not tell him what to do.[76] Why Webster thought this argument promoted his cause is a mystery, for Jackson had done what Webster conceded was in his power: He had fired Duane. Moreover, Webster's distinction made no sense. If the President possesses authority to remove the Secretary, it is for the reason suggested by Shepley and Madison: Without it he cannot effectively tell the Secretary what to do.[77]

Clay tried to suggest that the Secretary was not an executive officer but an agent of Congress,[78] but Shepley buried him once again. The Constitution, said the unsung Senator from Maine,[79] recognized only "three branches of power[:] . . . legislative, judicial, and executive." No one suggested that the Secretary's authority over the deposits was judicial. Nor was it legislative, for legislative power was "the power to ordain the laws," while the

[73]Virginia Representative Henry A. Wise, who thought the President's reasons for removing the deposits inadequate, made both of these arguments. Cong Deb, 23d Cong, 1st Sess 2671–74, 2679–81. See also id at 417–18 (Sen. Grundy). Clay and Webster responded that the vesting clause granted no executive powers but merely designated who the Executive was, id at 1173, 1676, but that was precisely the point: It was the President who was to exercise those executive powers elsewhere granted.

[74]Cong Deb, 23d Cong, 1st Sess 238. The Treasury provision appears at 1 Stat 65, 67, § 7 (Sep 2, 1789).

[75]Cong Deb, 23d Cong, 1st Sess 216.

[76]Id at 1664. See also id at 161–62 (Sen. Southard); id at 307 (Sen. Ewing). In an earlier letter Webster had denied the President's removal power as well, but Chancellor Kent advised him that "after a declaratory act of Congress and an acquiescence of half a century" it was too late to complain. Webster to Joseph Hopkinson, Jan 15, 1830, 3 Webster Correspondence at 8; James Kent to Webster, Jan 21, 1830, id at 11, 12. See also James Kent, 1 Commentaries on American Law 289–90 (Da Capo, 1971) (first published in 1826) [hereafter cited as Kent's Commentaries].

[77]See 1 Annals of Congress at 394 (Rep. Madison): "[I]f the head[] of [an] executive department[] . . . does not conform to the judgement of the president in doing the executive duties of his office, he can be displaced." (quoted by Rives in Cong Deb, 23d Cong, 1st Sess 288). See also Clinton Rossiter, The American Presidency 20 (Harcourt, Brace, 2d ed 1960): "It is the power of removal . . . that makes it possible for the President to bend his 'team' to his will." Kendall v United States ex rel Stokes, cited by Professor Corwin to refute Jackson's claim of authority to direct his subordinates, is not to the contrary; the Court's whole point was that the statute in question left no discretion to either the President or his subordinate. 37 US 524, 610 (1838); Edward S. Corwin, The President: Office and Powers 82–83 (NYU, 1940) [hereafter cited as Corwin, Office and Powers].

[78]Cong Deb, 23d Cong, 1st Sess 65.

[79]Educated at Dartmouth, Shepley had served twelve years as U.S. District Attorney for Maine before his election to the Senate as a Jacksonian in 1833; he resigned in 1836 to take a position on Maine's highest court, where he remained (as Chief Justice the last seven years) until 1855.

Secretary's task was to carry them out.[80] No, Shepley concluded, the Secretary's duties were of an executive nature, and thus he could not be an agent of Congress; for Congress could employ agents only in aid of its own functions. Nor did the mere fact that the Secretary was required by law to report to Congress make him a tool of Congress; as Rives added a few pages later, the Constitution required the President to report to Congress too, and there was no doubt that he was an executive officer.[81]

The President's assailants grew wilder and wilder.[82] The President could not withdraw money from the Treasury, said Calhoun, without an appropriation by Congress.[83] Of course not, Shepley replied, but he had not done so; he had merely instructed the Treasurer where to keep it.[84] The appropriation clause was a limitation on spending money, not on moving it from one place to another.[85] The President was behaving, complained the legendary Webster, as if the entire executive power had been vested in him.[86] Well, it had been—by the explicit terms of Article II.[87] Jackson had inverted the constitutional scheme, said Clay; for he was supposed to ask Department heads for their opin-

[80]See also Cong Deb, 23d Cong, 1st Sess 419–20 (Sen. Grundy); id at 275 (Sen. Rives):

> But while the general powers to raise and appropriate money for the public service were vested in Congress, it certainly never could have been intended that Congress itself was to collect, to receive, to keep, to disburse, the public money. These are subordinate ministerial functions, which must, of necessity, be performed by Executive agents under the general provision of the law.

[81]See id at 239–40 (Sen. Shepley); id at 287 (Sen. Rives). Clay acknowledged that the Secretary's duties, while not "executive," were purely "administrative," and that Congress could not give him legislative authority, id at 80–81. Clay's distinction was feeble. As Forsyth observed, to administer the law was to execute it; "what are administrative duties but executive duties?" id at 348.

[82]Calhoun even attacked the President for having attempted to communicate with the public by publishing his own memorandum to the Cabinet, id at 211. Shepley's response was withering: "I did not know that our constitution had closed all communication between the President and the people who elect him." Id at 235.

[83]Id at 215. See also id at 312 (Sen. Ewing). The implicit reference was to US Const, Art I, § 9: "No money shall be drawn from the Treasury, but in consequence of appropriations made by law . . . ." Related was the more abstract argument that in assuming control of the Treasury the President was improperly seeking to combine authority over the sword and the purse. Id at 60 (Sen. Clay); id at 219 (Sen. Calhoun). Actually, as Rives said, it was Congress that had both powers, for only Congress could tax and spend, and only Congress could raise armies and declare war. Keeping money during the interval between collecting and spending it was a largely ministerial function for the executive under law. Id at 275, 278.

[84]Id at 237.

[85]Id at 243–44. The Bank was not the Treasury within the meaning of the appropriation provision, the President's defenders sensibly added; the Treasury was wherever the Government kept its money. Id at 248 (Sen. Shepley); id at 276 (Sen. Rives); id at 423 (Sen. Grundy). Calhoun also argued that to deposit Government money in state banks, as Taney planned to do, was to distribute surplus revenues to the states, id at 222. To deposit them without expectation of withdrawing them, as at Calhoun's urging Congress would later require the Government to do (see section III of this chapter), would indeed pose a constitutional problem. (See the discussion of the related issue of the proceeds of public land sales in chapter 2.) Simple storage of federal money, however, was a mere service that so far as the Constitution was concerned might as well be performed by state banks as by anyone else.

[86]Cong Deb, 23d Cong, 1st Sess 1683. See also id at 835 (Sen. Clay); id at 1341 (Sen. Sprague).

[87]See US Const, Article II, § 1: "The executive power shall be vested in a President of the United States . . . ." South Carolina Representative Henry Laurens Pinckney, whose father had been at the Constitutional Convention, branded presidential control of the executive "despotism" (Cong Deb, 23d Cong, 1st Sess 3106). If it was, it was a despotism expressly erected by the Constitution.

ions, not offer them his own.[88] He was authorized to solicit those opinions, explained Rhode Island Representative Tristam Burges, in order that he might conform to them, not overrule them[89]—a topsy-turvy world in which the subordinate controlled his superior. Maine Senator Peleg Sprague, exhibiting a rare talent for understatement, calmly summed up the attackers' case: "It was just such a meeting [of the Executive and the people against the Legislative and Judicial Branches] that crushed the Senate and the liberties of Rome, and placed the blood-stained Caesar upon the throne."[90]

I think there was much to be said for Secretary Duane's conclusion that it was a mistake to remove the deposits. But the merits of that position were obscured by the torrent of untenable and implausible arguments against presidential authority. Clay and his fellow conspirators had performed the singularly difficult task of making a strong case look weak, and they had made themselves look ridiculous in the process.[91]

C. Censure and Protest

Jackson's critics may have lacked arguments, but they had plenty of votes. The Senate adopted both of Mr. Clay's resolutions: The President's reasons for removing the deposits were inadequate, and he had usurped the Secretary's authority.[92] The President promptly fired back a protest: In censuring him for acting beyond his powers the Senate had condemned him without notice or hearing; it had acted as both prosecutor and judge. It had exercised a judicial function not entrusted to it by the Constitution; it had arrogated to itself the House's exclusive power of accusation; it had found him guilty of impeachable offenses without conforming to constitutional procedures; it had prejudged matters that might later come before it if the House chose to impeach him. It was irrelevant that the Senate had not attempted to remove or disqualify him, as it might have done after impeachment; the stigma of censure was punishment too. Appending an elaborate defense of his conduct on the merits, Jackson closed with the assertion that Senate censure of the President was incompatible with the independence of the executive.[93]

Several of the President's arguments had been made earlier during the Senate debate. Senator Benton had put the case with characteristic pungency:

> The constitution gives to the House of Representatives the sole power to

[88] Id at 30, 62, 66.

[89] Id at 3193–94. Appointed Chief Justice of the Rhode Island Supreme Court but rejected a year later by the voters, Burges was an expert on pensions. He was the great-great-uncle of Theodore Green, a Rhode Island Senator of the following century, who is said to have replied to an inquiry as to how it felt to be eighty years old by saying "Pretty good, considering the alternative."

[90] Cong Deb, 23d Cong, 1st Sess 387. A product of Harvard and of the law school at Litchfield, Sprague later sat as a federal District Judge for nearly twenty-five years. For the aimless ravings of Senator Tyler on the subject see id at 663–79. It was over the removal of the deposits that Tyler irreparably broke with Jackson, whom he had supported in 1832. See note 37 of chapter 1.

[91] The sober and knowledgeable John Quincy Adams, now serving in the House, acknowledged the President's control over the Treasury but found his reasons for the withdrawal wanting. Cong Deb, 23d Cong, 1st Sess 3011–12.

[92] Id at 1187. The vote on the first resolution was 28–18, on the second 26–20. Id. The Jacksonian revolution had not yet conquered the Senate, only a third of whose members were elected at one time. US Const, Art I, § 3.

[93] 3 Richardson at 69–93 (Apr 15, 1834).

> originate impeachments; yet we originate this impeachment ourselves. The constitution gives the accused the right to be present; but he is not here. It requires the Senate to be sworn as judges; but we are not so sworn. It requires the Chief Justice of the United States to preside when the President is tried; but the Chief Justice is not presiding. It gives the House of Representatives a right to be present, and to manage the prosecution; but neither the House nor its managers are here. It requires the forms of criminal justice to be strictly observed; yet all these forms are neglected and violated. It is a proceeding in which the First Magistrate of the republic is to be tried without being heard, and in which his accusers are to act as his judges![94]

We accuse the President of no crime, said Theodore Frelinghuysen of New Jersey in response. We merely say he was wrong on a debatable question of constitutional interpretation.[95] Impeachment requires intentional wrongdoing, Clay added; we do not allege that here.[96] Yes you do, said Jackson in his protest: "The charge is not of a mistake in the exercise of supposed powers, but of the assumption of powers not conferred by the Constitution and laws, . . . and nothing is suggested to excuse or palliate the turpitude of the act."[97] But if the President usurps the Senate's authority, Clay asked, must we stand idly by?[98]

Poindexter of Mississippi moved that the President's protest not be received. The Constitution authorized the President to address the Senate only to recommend legislation and to report on the state of the Union; the protest did neither and thus lay beyond his powers.[99] That was silly; Presidents communicated with the Senate on a plethora of topics relating to their respective powers. The protest was an interference with the Senate's prerogatives, other Senators argued, and a threat to its independence. The Senate was not accountable to the President, they said, and thus he had no right to question what Senators did in exercising their right to speech and debate.[100]

Others attacked the merits of the President's protest and in so doing reviewed the earlier debate on the Senate's right to criticize him. Webster solemnly proclaimed the protest "ominous": It was shocking for the President to argue that the people's representatives had no right to express their opinion of his official acts.[101] More Senators chimed in:

[94]Cong Deb, 23d Cong, 1st Sess 98. See also Benton's later argument, id at 1347–53, adding that the censure resolution fell within none of the Senate's affirmative powers.

[95]Id at 449.

[96]Id at 75.

[97]3 Richardson at 74. See also Cong Deb, 23d Cong, 1st Sess 98 (Sen. Benton), noting that if the terms of the resolution left any doubt that the President was being accused of crime it was dissipated by "the whole tenor of the argument, and especially that part of it which compared the President's conduct to that of Caesar, in seizing the public treasure, to aid him in putting an end to the liberties of his country . . . ."

[98]Id 75. Suppose the President commissioned an officer the Senate had rejected, Webster later inquired, or turned the Senators out of the Capitol, or declared war. Id at 1401, 1671.

[99]Id at 1339–40. See also id at 1341 (Sen. Sprague); id at 1383 (Sen. Leigh); id at 1389 (Sen. Clayton); id at 1523 (Sen. Bibb); id at 1641 (Sen. Calhoun).

[100]See id at 1345 (Sen. Frelinghuysen); id at 1395 (Sen. Poindexter); id at 1523 (Sen. Bibb); id at 1566–67 (Sen. Clay); id at 1641 (Sen. Calhoun).

[101]Id at 1397. See also Carl Schurz, 2 Life of Henry Clay 40 (Houghton, Mifflin, 1887):

The Senate had authority to comment on public questions; it had a right to rebuke executive encroachment upon its own prerogatives; it had a duty to evaluate the adequacy of the Secretary's reasons for removing the deposits; it was entitled to adopt resolutions as a prelude to possible legislation.[102]

By the same token, replied Georgia Senator John Forsyth, the President had a corresponding right to defend himself against the Senate's attack.[103] Webster employed the same argument in reverse to defend the Senate's action: If he can criticize us, we can criticize him.[104] Thomas Ewing of Ohio took the middle road: The President may protest if he likes, as the Senate did; but the Senate should not enter his protest in its records, any more than he would enter its protest in his own.[105]

The Senate voted 27–16 to adopt Poindexter's resolutions, which as revised declared the President's protest a breach of the Senate's privileges inconsistent with its authority and with the Constitution; the President had no right to object to the Senate's proceedings.[106]

D. Expungement

The ink was hardly dry on Clay's resolutions attacking the President than Senator Benton vowed to see that they were expunged from the Senate record.[107] When Congress met again he moved to have them expunged: The censure resolutions were illegal, unjust, indefinite, vague, and unconstitutional.[108]

Poindexter objected on the spot. Article I, § 5 required each House to keep a journal of its proceedings, so that the public would know what Congress had done. Unconstitutional laws were repealed, not expunged. If the Senate had erred in adopting the resolution, it should adopt a new and contrary one, not falsify the record the Constitution required.[109] Even some Senators who had voted against censure supported this analysis: The journal must reflect what actually happened, whether we approve it or not.[110]

> [T]he pretension . . . that the Senate, because it might have to sit as a judicial body in cases of impeachment, had, as a legislative body, no constitutional right to express an unfavorable opinion about an act of the Executive . . . was altogether incompatible with the fundamental principles of representative government.

[102]See Cong Deb, 23d Cong, 1st Sess 1346 (Sen. Frelinghuysen); id at 1356–57 (Sen. Southard); id at 1390 (Sen. Clayton); id at 1405, 1409 (Sen. Ewing); id at 1520–21 (Sen. Bibb); id at 1569 (Sen. Clay); id at 1647–48 (Sen. Calhoun); id at 1659 (Sen. Preston); id at 1668 (Sen. Webster).

[103]Id at 1399, 1652–53. See also id at 1463–64 (Sen. Kane). Senator Wright suggested that the President had the same right as anyone else to petition the Senate for redress of grievances, id at 1618. The President's protest, Calhoun countered, was not an individual petition; it was an official communication that required some connection to presidential powers. Id at 1644.

[104]Id at 1671–72.

[105]Id at 1405.

[106]Id at 1712.

[107]Id at 1347.

[108]Cong Deb, 23d Cong, 2d Sess 510.

[109]Id at 510–11. See also id at 665 (Sen. Southard); id at 723 (Sen. White); Cong Deb, 24th Cong, 1st Sess 935–37 (Sen. Porter); id at 1060–61 (Sen. Leigh); id at 1886 (Sen. White); Cong Deb, 24th Cong, 2d Sess 417 (Sen. Calhoun); id at 458–62 (Sen. Bayard); id at 499–501 (Sen. Webster); id at 435 (Sen. Clay).

[110]See Cong Deb, 23d Cong, 2d Sess 724 (Sen. White); Cong Deb, 24th Cong, 2d Sess 471–72 (Sen. Hendricks).

To "keep" a journal, Benton weakly replied, was not to preserve it; it was enough to write it down.[111] Wisely, he tried again: The Senate had already published and distributed copies of the journal; it was not necessary to keep the original.[112] Better, but still no cigar: Copies were only prima facie evidence, subject to contradiction by the original.[113] William Rives of Virginia supported Benton: To correct errors in the journal was not inconsistent with keeping it.[114] As Rives himself said at one point, however, there was a difference between correcting the record and expunging the truth;[115] to falsify the record was not to correct it.[116] The Constitution did not specify *how* the journal should be kept, Rives continued; the first two Congresses had included the full text of bills, while later practice revealed only their titles.[117] But it is one thing, I should think, to abbreviate references to actual Senate proceedings; it is another to leave them out altogether. Legislatures in both Massachusetts and England, Benton asserted, had expunged records of what had actually occurred;[118] but Massachusetts, said Samuel Southard of New Jersey, did not require a journal, and England had no written Constitution at all.[119] Finally, Benton stressed that he did not insist on actually obliterating the original reference to the offending resolution; he asked only that black lines be drawn around it and the word "expunged" written across it in heavy black letters.[120] No dice, said Webster. It was just as improper to add to the original record as to subtract from it; black lines falsified the journal too, since they were not part of the original record.[121]

Benton's motion to expunge the censure resolution failed in 1835 and again in 1836.[122] It passed by a vote of 24–19 in early 1837[123]—after Democratic victories in the intervening elections. The Secretary of the Senate, pursuant to Benton's resolution, then ceremoniously drew the prescribed lines and wrote the prescribed words;[124] the censure of President Jackson was officially "expunged." There was a rumpus in the gallery; one

[111]Cong Deb, 23d Cong, 2d Sess 632; Cong Deb, 24th Cong, 1st Sess 880–81. For Porter's obvious riposte see id at 937. See also Schurz, 2 Life of Clay at 101 (cited in note 101): "[I]f the record was to be 'kept,' it could not be expunged."

[112]Cong Deb, 24th Cong, 1st Sess 885–86.

[113]Id at 940 (Sen. Porter). See also id at 1062 (Sen. Leigh); Cong Deb, 24th Cong, 2d Sess 394 (Sen. Dana).

[114]Cong Deb, 24th Cong, 1st Sess 982, 992.

[115]Id at 990–91. Rives's example showed that he had something else in mind when he spoke of "expunging the truth"; for he related with approval that the House had excised from its journal an erroneous report of the death of Senator Pinckney, though the report had actually been made.

[116]Subject to the same refutation was the House Clerk's testimony that his predecessors had regularly destroyed the rough notes they had used in preparing the official journal, see Cong Deb, 24th Cong, 1st Sess 1593–94 (Sen. Hill); no falsification was there involved.

[117]Id at 983.

[118]Cong Deb, 23d Cong, 2d Sess 633.

[119]Id at 672. This response was incomplete, since English practice remained relevant to show what was understood by keeping a journal.

[120]Cong Deb, 24th Cong, 1st Sess 879. See also id at 994 (Sen. Rives); Cong Deb, 24th Cong, 2d Sess 453 (Sen. Buchanan). Buchanan, who as Clay noted had argued as a state legislator that the record could not be expunged even with unanimous consent (see Cong Deb, 24th Cong, 1st Sess 1908 n.*; Cong Deb, 24th Cong, 2d Sess 437), said he still thought it would be wrong actually to obliterate a journal entry. Id at 451–53.

[121]Cong Deb, 24th Cong, 2d Sess 500–501. See also id at 472 (Indiana Sen. William Hendricks).

[122]Cong Deb, 23d Cong, 2d Sess 727; Cong Deb, 24th Cong, 1st Sess 1907.

[123]Cong Deb, 24th Cong, 2d Sess 504.

[124]Id at 504–5.

protester was brought to the bar of the Senate and then released.[125]

E. Ruminations

Shall we take stock? Jackson may well have exercised bad judgment in removing the deposits from the Bank of the United States; Duane thought so, and Duane was an enemy of the Bank. The Secretary had the right to remove them, however, and the President did not usurp authority in making the decision; Article II vests in him the executive power and makes him responsible for execution of the laws.

The shouting match over the rights of the President and the Senate to comment on one another's actions, I think, ended pretty much in a draw. Neither has express authority to criticize the other, but it may reasonably be thought implicit in either's office to defend its prerogatives. Federal officers of all types habitually sound off on topics unrelated to their substantive authority, and nobody tends to complain; we are wont to dismiss the release of hot air as not rising to the level of an exercise of power.[126]

Finally, Poindexter was plainly right that expunging the record of what actually happened in Congress would be incompatible with the constitutional requirement that Congress keep a journal of its proceedings and with its unmistakable purpose.[127] Drawing black lines around the entry and writing "expunged" across it were not so flagrant, since they did not prevent the reader from ascertaining what actually occurred.[128] Yet the spirit was wrong, for as Webster said the record no longer reflected *only* what happened on the date in question.[129] Hugh Lawson White of Jackson's own Tennessee, one of several re-

[125]Id at 505–6. "Never before and never since," wrote Professor Corwin, "has the Senate so abased itself before a President." Corwin, Office and Powers at 267.

[126]See Andrew C. McLaughlin, A Constitutional History of the United States 421 (Appleton, 1935) [hereafter cited as McLaughlin]: "No one would dare say unhesitatingly that the Senate has no authority to pass such resolutions of opinion as it chooses." Contrast the decision of the German Constitutional Court that by authorizing advisory referenda on matters of foreign affairs and national defense a state legislature had impermissibly intruded on turf reserved exclusively to the Federation. 8 BVerfGE 104, 116–18 (1958); see David P. Currie, The Constitution of the Federal Republic of Germany 79 (Chicago, 1994). See also National Foreign Trade Council v Natsios, 181 F3d 38 (1st Cir 1999), striking down a Massachusetts law that restricted the right of state agencies to purchase goods or services from companies doing business with Burma and pointedly noting (id at 61 n.18): "We do not consider here whether Massachusetts would be authorized to pass a resolution condemning Burma's human rights record but taking no other action with regard to Burma." The Supreme Court affirmed the First Circuit decision without commenting on the constitutionality of hot air. 530 US 363 (2000).

[127]See also James Wilson's argument in the Convention in favor of the journal requirement, which was borrowed from the Articles of Confederation: "The people have a right to know what their Agents are doing or have done, and it should not be in the option of the Legislature to conceal their proceedings." Max Farrand, ed, 2 Records of the Federal Convention of 1787 260 (Yale, rev ed 1966) [hereafter cited as Farrand].

[128]See William M. Meigs, The Life of Thomas Hart Benton 244 (Lippincott, 1904):

> It is hard to see how there can be any constitutional objection to what was actually done in the case, for the Senate journal of March 28, 1834, exists to-day and has been "kept." To draw lines around it and to write certain words across its face, as was done, has not at all destroyed it, and that day's original journal can be read now as well as before . . . .

[129]The terminology was wrong too, for the entry was not in fact expunged and (as even Buchanan conceded) could not constitutionally have been.

gional Whig candidates in the peculiar election of 1836, got it about right when he moved to rescind the censure resolution as erroneous rather than to expunge it, but his sensible proposal ultimately attracted only two votes.[130]

One nagging doubt remains. Maybe the Senate and the President both have implicit power to comment on public affairs even when they have no power to take coercive action, and maybe each is within its rights in protesting when it believes its rights have been infringed. But was there not something to Jackson's complaint that by censuring him for usurping authority the Senate had condemned him without a hearing and assumed the House's authority to impeach?

Like most constitutional questions, this one had come up before. In 1793 Representative William Giles had asked the House to censure Alexander Hamilton for his conduct as Secretary of the Treasury.[131] In 1814 Christopher Gore of Massachusetts had asked the Senate to declare that President Madison had exceeded his powers in giving recess appointments to envoys to negotiate peace with Great Britain.[132] In each case there were vigorous arguments that the proposed censure was unconstitutional. Neither House, it was argued, had authority to make abstract pronouncements unconnected with the exercise of its legislative duties; censure amounted to condemnation and punishment without trial.

Later Supreme Court decisions confirm the existence of a problem. Branding an individual as guilty of unlawful conduct without hearing can indeed offend the due process clause;[133] exposure for its own sake may be unrelated to any enumerated power of Congress.[134] But there is another case much closer to home. Only three months after condemning President Jackson for removing the deposits, the Senate *unanimously* resolved that Postmaster General William Barry had unconstitutionally borrowed money without authority from Congress.[135] If it was all right to censure the Postmaster General, numerous speakers argued, it was all right to censure the President too.[136]

The starting point for analyzing this question may lie in a constitutional provision that seems not to have been invoked in the 1834 debate or in earlier related controversies but that played a prominent role in the spat over possible censure of President Clinton more than a century and a half later: the clause of Article I, § 9 forbidding passage of any "bill of attainder."[137]

[130]Cong Deb, 24th Cong, 1st Sess 1884, 1897. Benton himself reported that at an earlier point White's language had actually been substituted for his own; the report of the debates seems ambiguous on this score. See 1 Benton, Thirty Years' View at 550; Cong Deb, 23d Cong, 2d Sess 723–27; Sen Journal, 23d Cong, 2d Sess 225.

[131]See The Federalist Period at 164–68.

[132]See The Jeffersonians at 188.

[133]Jenkins v McKeithen, 395 US 411 (1969); see also the various opinions in Joint Anti-Fascist League v McGrath, 341 US 123 (1951) (involving the "Attorney General's List" of allegedly subversive organizations).

[134]Watkins v United States, 354 US 178, 187 (1957).

[135]For passage and text of this resolution see Cong Deb, 23d Cong, 1st Sess 2120 (Jun 27, 1834). The vote was 41–0. Barry's defense was that he had borrowed on the credit of the Post Office alone, not of the United States. After the censure Jackson appointed him minister to Spain, "ostensibly to improve his health"; but "Barry died at sea, a broken man." Richard R. John, Spreading the News: The American Postal System from Franklin to Morse 241–47 (Harvard, 1995).

[136]See, e.g., Cong Deb, 23d Cong, 2d Sess 670 (Sen. Southard); Cong Deb, 24th Cong, 1st Sess 951–52 (Sen. Porter); id 1087–89 (Sen. Leigh).

[137]See, e.g., 144 Cong Rec H12035 (daily ed) (Rep. Pease); id at H11789 (Rep. Buyer); 145 Cong Rec S1490 (daily ed) (Sen. Biden).

A bill of attainder, the Supreme Court has since said, is "a legislative act which inflicts punishment without a judicial trial."[138] Thus if Congress were to enact a law fining Jane Smith (or Andrew Jackson) for mail robbery it would offend the bill of attainder clause. Apart from disciplining its own members, in other words, Congress may punish an individual for wrongdoing only in accordance with the substantive and procedural provisions governing impeachment, or in the exercise of the implicit contempt powers of either House.[139]

Did the Senate in 1834 punish either the Postmaster General or the President? Neither resolution imposed any coercive sanction such as imprisonment or removal from office.[140] Official condemnation, however, may also amount to punishment. Hester Prynne was punished by being forced to publicize her own adultery. "Shaming penalties" are much in vogue as this chapter is written.[141] Censure not only inflicts direct harm to reputation but may also bring adverse practical consequences in its train as others decide to forgo normal personal or professional relations with the asserted offender. The Supreme Court acknowledged the punitive nature of public condemnation when it held that a Louisiana commission could not brand an individual as a criminal without trial.[142] Justice Hugo Black, in a separate opinion attacking the constitutionality of the notorious "Attorney General's list" of "subversive" organizations, which imposed no penalty beyond exposure, flatly defined "the classic bill of attainder" as "a condemnation by the legislature"—with no requirement of additional sanctions.[143]

If this interpretation is correct, it would appear unconstitutional for Congress (or for either House)[144] to convict the President or his Postmaster General of crime, even if it imposed no penalty beyond the stigma of the conviction itself.[145] But did the Senate in effect convict either Jackson or his Postmaster General of crime? The President was said to have "assumed upon himself authority and power not conferred by the constitution and laws, but in derogation of both,"[146] his subordinate to have borrowed money "without authority given by any law of Congress" and thus illegally, "as Congress alone possesses the power to borrow money on the credit of the United States."[147]

[138]Cummings v Missouri, 71 US 277, 323 (1867).

[139]See US Const, Art I, §§ 2, 3; Art II, § 4; Anderson v Dunn, 19 US 204 (1821); The Federalist Period at 232–38 (discussing the case of Randall and Whitney).

[140]Contrast *Cummings,* 71 US at 320 (disqualification from various positions); Ex parte Lovett, 328 US 303 (1946) (termination of salary).

[141]E.g., Dan M. Kahan, What Do Alternative Sanctions Mean? 63 U Chi L Rev 591 (1996). See Richard A. Posner, An Affair of State: The Investigation, Impeachment, and Trial of President Clinton 193 (Harvard, 1999): "No one doubts that these [shaming penalties] are *penalties;* if Congress imposed them on individual malefactors . . . , they would be bills of attainder."

[142]Jenkins v McKeithen, cited in note 133.

[143]Joint Anti-Fascist Refugee Comm v McGrath, 341 US at 144 (cited in note 133).

[144]There is no reason to think that in forbidding passage of a bill of attainder, which under Article I, § 7 would in any event require the concurrence of both Houses, the Framers meant to allow a single House to accomplish the forbidden result. Cf the related question whether the first amendment, which on its face limits only "Congress" in the enactment of "law," applies to the action of a single House. The Federalist Period at 12 (discussing legislative chaplains).

[145]See James Ho, Misunderstood Precedent: Andrew Jackson and the Real Case against Censure, 24 Harv J L & Pub Pol 283, 290 (2000).

[146]Cong Deb, 23d Cong, 1st Sess 1187.

[147]Id at 2120.

In neither case did the Senate expressly employ terms like "convict," "condemn," or even "censure." There was no explicit finding of criminal responsibility. And thus at least one careful observer has concluded that in neither case was there legislative condemnation, that the resolutions were therefore neither bills of attainder nor end runs around the requirements for impeachment, and indeed that neither President Jackson nor his Postmaster General could properly be said to have been "censured" at all.[148]

Can it really be so easy? The author just cited reaches the same conclusion with respect to Alexander Hamilton, whom Representative Giles had unsuccessfully sought to hound from the Treasury by a resolution declaring him in violation of his official duties—but again omitting the magic words of condemnation or censure. Yet, as President Jackson said in his protest, the resolution's finding that he had "assumed" unconstitutional powers drips with condemnation; usurpation is pejorative. Nor did the language of the Hamilton and Barry resolutions leave much room for doubt that those endorsing them intended to express moral indignation at their actions. It is not, I think, as if the Senate had merely said it respectfully disagreed with one or another's interpretation of the Constitution and laws.[149]

Thus although it would seem wrong to deny either the House, the Senate, or the President the right to comment on the correctness of another's interpretation of the law, a case can be made that in their attempts to stigmatize Hamilton, Jackson, and Barry for flagrant abuses of authority Representative Giles in 1793 and the Senate in 1834 may have crossed the line that, however obscurely, separates legitimate commentary from a forbidden bill of attainder.

The most troubling argument against this line of reasoning is that it is based upon a modern understanding of the bill of attainder clause that is without support in its history and thus unfaithful to its original sense. When the Supreme Court in 1867 defined a bill of attainder broadly to include any form of legislative punishment without trial, Professor Pomeroy attacked it: "Bill of attainder" was a technical term that should be interpreted in accord with its established meaning; legislative punishment was a bill of attainder only if the penalty was death; any lesser legislative punishment was a bill of pains and penalties.[150] Professor Raoul Berger vehemently echoed Pomeroy's criticism a century later.[151]

Stated in this form, the argument strikes me as singularly unconvincing. I have nothing against looking either to the words of the Constitution or to their history to inform interpretation. Nor do I deny that the distinction trumpeted by Pomeroy and Berger existed in England or in this country. To conclude that the Framers banned only conventional attainder and not pains and penalties, however, seems to me literalism at its most wooden and unthinking, for it makes no sense. Why would a rational Framer have wanted to ban bills imposing capital punishment but not those imposing imprisonment or fines? The Framers had no particular qualms about the death penalty; the due process clause

[148]Ho, Misunderstood Precedent at 296 (cited in note 145). In contrast, Ho notes, the proposed resolution in President Clinton's case would expressly have "censure[d]" its target. Id at 286.

[149]Compare the much-mooted question whether Marc Antony's feigned praise of Brutus can fairly be read as an invitation to insurrection. W. Shakespeare, Julius Caesar, Act III, scene 2.

[150]John N. Pomeroy, An Introduction to the Constitutional Law of the United States, § 511 (7th ed 1883).

[151]See Raoul Berger, Bills of Attainder, A Study of Amendment by the Court, 63 Corn L Rev 355 (1978).

contemplates that the state may deprive persons of life.[152] Professor Berger himself declared, as Wilson Cary Nicholas had said in the Virginia ratifying convention, that the vice in a bill of attainder was condemnation without trial.[153] Thus it seems to me the Supreme Court was right to conclude that "bills of attainder" within the meaning of Article I included what would have been called bills of pains and penalties before.

The more serious obstacle is to establish that mere condemnation or censure, without coercive sanctions of any kind, fit even within the more capacious bounds of traditional bills of pains and penalties. My hunch is that it did not, and that may be why neither Hamilton, nor Madison, nor Jackson, nor any of their defenders invoked the bill of attainder clause against what they argued was congressional censure. If this supposition is correct, then the argument that censure amounts to a bill of attainder may be a modern perversion that ought not to influence our thinking about the Senate's ostensible "censure" of President Jackson.

You want answers? I don't have one. My tentative conclusion is that either House of Congress may state its position that the President has violated the Constitution without running afoul of constitutional limitations, and that the President may return the favor—at least when in so doing they protesting an invasion of their own prerogatives.

III. STATE BANKS AND STATE TREASURIES

The Government receipts that Treasury Secretary Taney decided not to deposit in the Bank of the United States were placed in selected state banks instead—initially one in Philadelphia, one in Baltimore, two in Boston, and three in New York.[154] The House Ways and Means Committee, in a report made by its Chairman, James K. Polk, approved this course of action but called for congressional legislation to ensure the safety of the deposits.[155] The House obliged,[156] but Webster applied the kibosh in the Senate: To regulate deposits in state banks would ratify the President's unconstitutional act in withholding them from the Bank of the United States.[157]

It was 1836, and Jackson's Presidency was approaching its end, before the law regu-

[152]US Const, Amend 5.

[153]See Berger, Bills of Attainder, 63 Corn L Rev at 380 (cited in note 151); Jonathan Elliot, 3 The Debates in the Several State Conventions on the Adoption of the Federal Constitution 236 (2d ed 1836) [hereafter cited as Elliot's Debates]; The First Hundred Years at 293–94 n.40.

[154]See Hammond, Banks and Politics at 419 (cited in note 20) and the documents appended to Taney's report to Congress of December, 1833, Cong Deb App, 23d Cong, 1st Sess 59, 74–77. See also President Jackson's contemporaneous fifth Annual Message to Congress, 3 Richardson at 19, 30 (Dec 3, 1833).

[155]See HR Rep 312, 23d Cong, 1st Sess 29–31 (1834), Cong Deb App, 23d Cong, 1st Sess 161, 175–76. The House adopted the committee's proposed resolution, Cong Deb, 23d Cong, 1st Sess 3474, 3475, and the committee proposed a corresponding bill, Cong Deb App, 23d Cong, 1st Sess 156.

[156]Cong Deb, 23d Cong, 1st Sess 4760.

[157]S Doc 487, 23d Cong, 1st Sess 1–5 (1834); Cong Deb App, 23d Cong, 1st Sess 282. Polk tried again the following year, equally without success. See Cong Deb, 23d Cong, 2d Sess 1266 (Rep. Polk); id at 630 (sending the bill to third reading in the Senate). The bill is printed in id at 621. In the House, New York Democrat Churchill Cambreleng argued that if Congress could not create a bank it could not employ state banks for the same purpose, but he got nowhere. See id at 1325–28, 1333. That was just as well: The principal objections to the National Bank ran to its ancillary powers and its federal charter; if the Government could collect tax money, it was obviously necessary and proper to put it somewhere. There was no suggestion that state banks would be *required* to accept the Government's money.

lating deposits was finally adopted.[158] The statute confirmed the principle that federal revenues should be deposited in local banks in the states, in the District of Columbia, and in the territories.[159] It laid down a number of conditions that banks were required to meet in order to qualify to receive deposits, most of which were plainly necessary and proper to ensure the safety and availability of federal funds.[160] More noteworthy were two further conditions imposed by § 5 of the statute:

> [N]o bank shall be selected or continued as a place of deposite [sic] of the public money which shall not redeem its notes and bills on demand in specie; nor shall any bank be selected or continued as aforesaid, which shall after the fourth of July, in the year one thousand eight hundred and thirty-six, issue or pay out any note or bill of a less denomination than five dollars . . . .[161]

These restrictions may or may not have represented sound public policy, but it was not obvious what they had to do with protecting deposits of federal money. This provision bore a close family resemblance to typical conditional grants of a later period: The Government extends a benefit it is free to deny on condition that the recipient agree to terms the Government could not impose directly. Unless Congress somehow had authority to dictate to state banks that they were to pay their creditors in coin and that they might not issue small bills and notes,[162] the provision posed a question of unconstitutional conditions.[163] No one seems to have objected on this ground; the adoption of the provision stands as a precedent of sorts, though not a strong one, on the breadth of Congress's authority to impose conditions on the award of privileges.

But this difficulty was as nothing compared to the storm raised by a further provision initially proposed by Senator Calhoun:[164] Any surplus beyond $5,000,000 remaining in the Treasury on the first day of 1837 was to be "deposited" with the several states.[165] For the surplus that President Jackson had foreseen at the beginning of his Presidency[166]

[158]5 Stat 52 (Jun 23, 1836). Webster had realistically thrown in the towel: State banks were a poor substitute for the lamented national Bank, but there was nowhere else to deposit the Government's money; regulation of the current state of affairs was indispensable. Cong Deb, 24th Cong, 1st Sess 1650–51.

[159]5 Stat at 52, § 1.

[160]For example, the banks had to agree to pay government creditors, to transfer funds from place to place, to provide the Government with all services previously required of the Bank of the United States, to make financial reports, and to permit inspection of their records. Id at 53, § 4. The Secretary was permitted to select a bank as a depository only if he found it "safe" and willing to satisfy the prescribed conditions; he was authorized to require "collateral or additional securities" to those ends; no bank could receive deposits totaling more than three-fourths of its paid capital stock; on deposits exceeding one-fourth of the bank's capital it was to pay the Government interest at 2 percent. Id at 52–55, §§ 1, 2, 6, 11.

[161]Id at 53.

[162]The Supreme Court would ultimately conclude that Congress did have the latter authority, Veazie Bank v Fenno, 75 US 533, 548–49 (1869), but the answer was far from clear in 1836.

[163]Cf United States v Butler, 297 US 1, 70–72 (1936); South Dakota v Dole, 483 US 203 (1987). See also the discussion of the antislavery condition unsuccessfully sought to be imposed on the admission of Missouri, The Jeffersonians at 235–45.

[164]Cong Deb, 24th Cong, 1st Sess 1577.

[165]5 Stat at 55, § 13.

[166]See Introduction to Part One, note 22 and accompanying text.

was indeed in sight. The debts had been paid; revenues from customs duties and land sales were soaring; Webster estimated that by the end of 1836 there would be $40,000,000 in the Treasury.[167] Congress had the enviable task of deciding what to do with the extra money.[168]

Jackson had opined in 1829 that it would be impracticable to eliminate future surpluses by reducing the tariff, since to do so would harm domestic industries needing protection from foreign competition. The famous Compromise of 1833, which resolved the nullification crisis (of which more hereafter),[169] had provided for progressive tariff reduction, but it had not obviated the surplus. Senator Benton thought the money should be spent on coastal fortifications and other defense measures.[170] Others pooh-poohed the suggestion: There was no responsible way to curtail the expected surplus either by reducing revenue or by increasing spending.

Jackson, who had reached the same conclusion in 1829, had suggested distributing the surplus to the states—after amending the Constitution, if necessary, to ensure the necessary authority. Calhoun picked up this suggestion in 1835, after he had broken with the President—giving as an additional argument for his proposal the desirability of depriving the President of a powerful tool of patronage and influence. He got nowhere at the time; the Senate never took up his proposed amendment to empower Congress to distribute federal money to the states.[171]

In the meantime, as related in an earlier chapter, Congress had passed a kindred measure to give the states the revenue from sales of public land. Jackson had vetoed it on grounds that left no doubt he would veto a distribution of tax revenues as well: Federal funds could be spent only for national, not for local purposes.[172] When Calhoun offered his amendment to the 1836 bill to regulate deposits of federal money, he changed his tune in an effort to circumvent the President's objection: The money was to be *deposited* with the states, not given to them outright; they were to be required to repay it on demand. Thus the proposal was not a distribution to the states but a mere arrangement for custody of the Government's money.[173]

Calhoun's critics were unimpressed. Once the states got their hands on the money they would never give it back, and their spokesmen in Congress would never demand it. The "deposit" was a gift in disguise; federal taxes were to be levied to support the

[167]Cong Deb, 24th Cong, 1st Sess 1651–52.

[168]See generally Edward G. Bourne, The History of the Surplus Revenue of 1837 (Burt Franklin, 1968) (first published in 1885).

[169]See section V of chapter 4.

[170]Cong Deb, 23d Cong, 2d Sess 383–88.

[171]See Calhoun's committee report, S Doc 108 23d Cong, 2d Sess 1–4, 18–22 (1835), reprinted in Cong Deb App, 23d Cong, 2d Sess 219–31; Wiltse, 2 Calhoun at 255–60; Cong Deb, 23d Cong, 2d Sess 361.

[172]See section I of chapter 2. See also Jackson's eighth Annual Message, 3 Richardson at 236, 239–45 (Dec 5, 1836), denying that the surplus could be given to the states because Congress could tax only to promote the general welfare; Bourne, History of the Surplus Revenue at 20 (cited in note 168).

[173]Cong Deb, 24th Cong, 1st Sess 1577, 1630, 1745. See also id at 1836–43 (Sen. Tallmadge). Tallmadge had a second argument, which he borrowed from Jackson's message explaining his veto of the 1833 bill to distribute land proceeds: It was true that Congress could not impose taxes in order to accumulate a surplus to distribute to the states, but there was no reason why Congress could not distribute a surplus that already existed. Id at 1835; see 3 Richardson at 66. The distinction seems tenuous. The argument had been that Congress could not *spend* for local objects, and in any event the money in question had been raised by taxation—or by the sale of public lands, which Jackson said were subject to the same limitations.

states.[174] The money was safe in the state banks, said Benton; there was no point in transferring it to the states themselves.[175]

James Buchanan of Pennsylvania had a more subtle objection. All agreed that the states would be free to use the deposited funds to pay their debts or to finance local improvements.[176] Even if the principal was ultimately repaid, the transaction therefore amounted to a loan without interest. It followed that, if Congress could not donate the money outright to the states, it could not make the proposed deposits either; for "[i]f you have not the power to give the principal, whence can you derive your power to give the interest?"[177]

Calhoun might conceivably have responded that free use of the money was fair compensation for storing it, but there is reason to believe his pious assurances that no giveaway was intended were disingenuous. In explaining his proposal he linked it directly with his earlier attempt to distribute the money to the states; he acknowledged that the Government, if it operated with a modicum of efficiency, might well never want its money back; he flatly declared it unjust for the Government to keep money it did not need.[178] There was no satisfactory answer to Benton's question: If all that was wanted was a safe place to store the Government's money, why not leave it in the state banks?[179]

House amendments offered additional assurances that the United States could get their money back.[180] Buchanan declared himself satisfied;[181] Benton did not.[182] The bill passed the Senate by an overwhelming vote of 40–6.[183] If Calhoun's "deposit" language was a ruse, it worked; President Jackson signed the bill, although he was on record—correctly—that Congress had no power to transfer federal money to the states (or anyone else) for local purposes.[184]

[174]See Cong Deb, 24th Cong, 1st Sess 1611–12, 1614 (Sen. Wright); id at 1644–45, 1744 (Sen. Walker). These objections were repeated in the House. See id at 4360–61 (New York Rep. Abijah Mann); id at 4372–73 (Maine Rep. Gorham Parks).

[175]Id at 1744.

[176]Calhoun had specifically endorsed this use of the money. See id at 1632.

[177]Id at 1638–39.

[178]Id at 1630, 1633, 1745. See also his triumphant speech of Aug 12, 1836 in Pendleton, South Carolina, 13 Calhoun Papers at 266, 269–71, equating deposit with distribution once again and exulting that the new law would make money available to the states to build railroads. This time (in contrast to the 1841 distribution, see note 73 of chapter 2) South Carolina accepted its share with alacrity—investing it, as Calhoun suggested, in railroads. 6 SC Acts 555 (No 2704) (1836); see Bourne, History of the Surplus Revenue at 107, 123 (cited in note 168).

[179]Buchanan, who had come around to the view that the deposit was constitutional after all, weakly suggested that placing the money in state hands would make it available to benefit the people rather than shareholders of the banks. Cong Deb, 24th Cong, 1st Sess 1803.

[180]See 5 Stat at 55, § 13. Calhoun advised his colleagues that the House amendments did not alter the principle of the bill: "No Secretary of the Treasury will ever call for this money." Cong Deb, 24th Cong, 1st Sess 1859.

[181]Id at 1800–1801.

[182]Id at 1809–12.

[183]Id at 1845–46.

[184]Indeed Taney (whose appointment as Chief Justice had already been confirmed, see Sen Journal, 24th Cong, 1st Sess 584) had drafted a veto message for Jackson on this ground, only to disown it once the bill was amended and signed. Even then Taney could not refrain from expressing disapproval on what he lamely described as policy grounds: If Congress could tax beyond its needs and leave the money on deposit with the states forever, there would be no limit to federal powers. See 5 Jackson Correspondence at 404–7 (draft message); Taney to Jackson, Jun 27, 1836, id at 409–10. Taney's draft, incidentally, repeated the standard un-

The surplus was to be paid to the states in four installments during the year 1837. Unfortunately, the nation's financial health was rapidly declining—in part, some said, because of Jackson's removal of the deposits from the National Bank. In October Congress postponed payment of the fourth installment,[185] and it was never made.[186] At the same time, however, Congress forbade the Treasury to recall the money already deposited with the states,[187] and apparently it has never been reclaimed. As a leading commentator wrote in 1957,

> [t]he amounts distributed aggregated about $28,000,000, and on the books of the Treasury, in accordance with an act of Congress so late as 1910, they are still technically due the federal government from the states with which they were "deposited."[188]

Benton opposed the deposit scheme; Clay supported it. Both considered the "deposit" terminology a sham. In Clay's words: "If in form it was a deposit with the states, in fact and in truth it was a distribution. So it was then regarded. So it will ever remain."[189]

IV. AND TYLER TOO

Not all good Jacksonians were content to leave the Government's money (after liquidation of the surplus) in state banks. Some of them wanted the Government to sever its connections with banks entirely.[190] For banks, in their view, were the embodiment of evil.

Among them was Andrew Jackson, now in retirement, who was outraged when many state banks, pinched by the defensive action of the Bank of the United States in calling in loans after losing the federal deposits, suspended specie payments to their creditors. "Now is the time," Jackson wrote, "to separate the government from all banks," state or federal; the Government should "receive and disburse the revenue in nothing but gold and silver coin."[191]

Martin Van Buren, Jackson's faithful lieutenant and successor, took office on March

---

derstanding that the President had no authority "to approve one portion of a Bill and to disapprove another." Id at 405. See notes 45–46 and 81 of chapter 1 and accompanying text.

[185]5 Stat 201 (Oct 2, 1837).

[186]See Hammond, Banks and Politics at 488 (cited in note 20); Ex parte Virginia, 111 US 43, 45–48 (1884).

[187]5 Stat at 201.

[188]Hammond, Banks and Politics at 488 (cited in note 20).

[189]Quoted in id at 455. For Benton's similar words see Cong Deb, 24th Cong, 1st Sess 1810.

[190]A plank to this effect was written into the first Democratic platform in 1840 and repeated every four years until the Civil War. See Porter & Johnson, Party Platforms at 2, 4, 11, 17, 24, 30, 31.

[191]Quoted in Hammond, Banks and Politics at 491 (cited in note 20). Jackson had taken a step in the direction of his professed hard-money policy (his only step, in Hammond's view) with the issuance of the famous Specie Circular in 1836, essentially requiring the Government and its depositories to accept only gold and silver in payment for public lands, as the document said the governing statutes already required. Congress repealed the Circular in 1838; it was reinstated and generalized when Congress established the so-called Independent Treasury in 1840. See 8 Am St Papers, Public Lands 910; Cong Deb App, 24th Cong, 2d Sess 107–8; 5 Stat 310 (May 31, 1838); 5 Stat 385, 390, § 19 (Jul 4, 1840); Hammond, Banks and Politics at 455; Van Deusen, The Jacksonian Era at 104–6.

4, 1837.[192] Finding the country in financial extremis, he called a special session of the new Twenty-fifth Congress. The 1836 Act regulating deposits, he informed Congress, required him to withdraw federal funds from banks that refused to redeem their obligations in specie, and suddenly none of them could do so. What should he do with the money?[193]

Van Buren had a suggestion for Congress, and it built upon that which his predecessor had made in private correspondence. The Treasury should keep its own money, not deposit it in banks; and it should accept nothing but specie, as the Constitution intended.[194] A bill to this effect passed the Senate in 1837 but died in the House.[195] It became law in 1840.[196]

The Whigs won both Congress and the Presidency later that year. One of the few things President William Henry Harrison had time to do before meeting his Maker was to follow Van Buren's example by calling another special session of Congress to consider financial matters,[197] for the economy remained rotten. John Tyler, on whom in his own words "the powers and duties" of the Presidency had devolved,[198] took up the cause. Not only should Congress make some "temporary provision" to cover an anticipated budget deficit of over $11,000,000;[199] it should also provide for "a suitable fiscal agent" to collect, hold, and disburse public money, for "[u]pon such an agent depends in an eminent degree the establishment of a currency of uniform value, which is of so great importance to all the essential interests of society . . . ."[200] The Bank of the United States, the state banks, and a self-sufficient Treasury, Tyler said, had all been tried and found wanting; he proclaimed his willingness to approve whatever solution Congress might come up with, "reserving to myself the ultimate power of rejecting any measure which may, in my view of it, conflict with the Constitution or otherwise jeopardize the prosperity of the country . . . ."[201]

Congress took Tyler at his word, sending him bills repealing the 1840 statute that required the Treasury to keep its own money and incorporating a "Fiscal Bank of the United States." Tyler signed the former[202] and vetoed the latter;[203] there was now no pro-

[192]Born in 1782, Van Buren had been Senator from New York, Secretary of State, and (on a recess appointment that was not confirmed) Minister to Great Britain before serving as Vice-President during Jackson's second term. According to the acidulous editor Horace Greeley, he owed his elevation to the Chief Magistracy to President Jackson, "with whom 'love me, love my dog' was an iron rule." Greeley, Recollections of a Busy Life 113 (J.B. Ford, 1868).

[193]3 Richardson at 324 (Sep 4, 1837).

[194]Id at 332–42. See Hammond, Banks and Politics at 496–99 (cited in note 20).

[195]See Cong Deb, 25th Cong, 1st Sess 511, 1685.

[196]5 Stat 385. Existing deposits were to be withdrawn from the state banks. Id at 389, § 15. Van Buren's struggle to establish these principles, we are told, "consumed most of his time in the White House"—which may help to explain why, to borrow the words of the same author, in the present study too Van Buren's remains a "relatively neglected administration." James C. Curtis, The Fox at Bay: Martin Van Buren and the Presidency ix, vii (Kentucky, 1970).

[197]4 Richardson at 21 (Mar 17, 1841).

[198]Id at 40 (Jun 1, 1841). See the discussion of Tyler's actual status in section IV of chapter 6.

[199]4 Richardson at 42–43. He was pretty vague as to how this should be done, saying only that it would be advisable not to disturb the tariff reductions provided for by the Compromise of 1833. Id at 43.

[200]Id.

[201]Id at 45–46.

[202]5 Stat 439, § 1 (Aug 3, 1841). Section 3 of this statute, id at 440, also repealed the 1836 law authorizing and regulating deposits in state banks, with the exception of the controversial provisions for "deposit" of the 1837 surplus with the states themselves.

vision to direct the Treasurer what to do with federal funds.[204]

His own opinion, wrote Tyler, had always been against the creation of "a national bank to operate *per se* over the Union."[205] By clumsiness or design he managed to leave some doubt whether this opinion had been based on a want of constitutional power,[206] but he left no doubt that Congress had exceeded its authority in passing the bill before him:

> Without going further into the argument, I will say that in looking to the powers of this Government to collect, safely keep, and disburse the public revenue, and incidentally to regulate the commerce and exchanges, I have not been able to satisfy myself that the establishment by the Government of a bank of discount in the ordinary acceptation of that term was a necessary means or one demanded by propriety to execute those powers.[207]

In short, Congress might set up an entity to look after public money, but not to engage in the purely private business of making loans.[208]

Congress tried again, sending the President a bill to establish a "Fiscal Corporation

---

[203]4 Richardson at 63 (Aug 16, 1841).

[204]The 1789 statute establishing the Treasury Department said only that the Treasurer should "receive and keep the monies of the United States" and "disburse" them "upon warrants" properly drawn; this provision was assumed to be still in force. 1 Stat 65, 66, § 4 (Sep 2, 1789); see HR Rep 244, 27th Cong, 2d Sess 2–5 (1842).

[205]4 Richardson at 63.

[206]The question of Congress's power, wrote Tyler, had been disputed from the beginning; he himself had always been "against the exercise of any such power," and he had taken an oath to support the Constitution. Id at 64.

[207]Id. Senator Clay's committee report, in contrast, cursorily reciting the usual justifications for the Bank, had said (in the teeth of President Jackson's recent veto, which he ignored) that the constitutional question should be considered "settled." S Doc 32, 27th Cong, 1st Sess 1–5 (1841).

[208]See also Secretary of State Webster's discussion of this issue in a letter to Hiram Ketchum, Jul 17, 1841, 5 Webster Correspondence at 134, 135–36. The scheme was not saved from unconstitutionality, Tyler added, by the requirement of state consent to the establishment of an office of discount and deposit within its borders. For the consent requirement was a sham: Unless the state unconditionally assented or dissented at the very next session of its legislature, consent would be conclusively presumed. 4 Richardson at 65–68. He might better have said simply that if Congress lacked authority to establish discount banks no state could give it the power. See the discussion of the analogous issue of state consent to federal internal improvement projects, The Jeffersonians at 118, 264–66. Tyler's own initial plan, however, would have permitted the "local" institution he proposed for the District of Columbia to establish branches elsewhere with state consent. When Virginia Governor John Rutherfoord protested that state permission could not expand federal power, the President ingeniously responded that one government could allow a corporation created by another to operate within its borders:

> The local legislature here tenders to the local legislature of the States a scheme of banking for their acceptance or rejection. Both have full power to create a bank or banks, either in the form of substantive creations, or in a secondary form. Reverse the proceeding. Suppose Virginia to create a bank of $30,000,000 with leave to the directors to establish a bank here if Congress shall consent, will you furnish me any constitutional objection to the procedure?

See Rutherfoord to Tyler, Jun 21, 1841, 2 Tyler Letters at 48; Tyler to Rutherfoord, Jun 23, 1841, id at 50. See also Cong Globe App, 27th Cong, 1st Sess 351–52 (Virginia Sen. William Rives), adding that with consent a bank chartered in one state might do business in another, as the Supreme Court had recently recognized in Bank of Augusta v Earle, 38 US 519 (1839): "[C]ould it be pretended, in such a case, that the permission thus given by Virginia had, in any manner, enlarged the legislative power of New York . . . ?"

of the United States"—omitting the inflammatory term "Bank" and the explicit authority to engage in discount operations, which Tyler had singled out for disapproval. Tyler struck again: This bill was unconstitutional too. For it purported to give the new corporation unrestricted authority to deal in "bills of exchange drawn in one state and payable in another," even when the transaction was essentially local; it thus "may justify substantially a system of discounts of the most objectionable character."[209]

Whigs in Congress understandably hit the ceiling. For this, they cried, we won both the Legislative and Executive Branches—to have our own legislative program vetoed by our own President? Clay and others mounted a major attack on the veto power itself (of which more hereafter),[210] and nearly the whole Cabinet resigned.[211] Tyler promised a proposal of his own to flesh out his original suggestion of "a fiscal agent which, without violating the Constitution, would separate the public money from the Executive control and perform the operations of the Treasury . . . ."[212] He outlined his plan in general terms in his first Annual Message in December 1841, reiterating that his principal concern was "to relieve the Chief Executive Magistrate, by any and all constitutional means, from a controlling power over the public Treasury"[213]—an echo of the great debate over Jackson's removal of the deposits from the National Bank and of questionable constitutionality for reasons given in connection with that dispute.[214]

[209]4 Richardson at 68, 70 (Sep 9, 1841). This corporation was to be established in the District of Columbia, where Congress had general legislative authority; Tyler rightly denied that Congress could "invest a local institution with general or national powers." Id. See The Federalist Period at 222–23; The Jeffersonians at 298, 300, 302.

[210]See section I of chapter 6.

[211]Webster remained Secretary of State, ostensibly (in part) to complete negotiations with Great Britain over the boundary between New Brunswick and Maine. The resulting Webster-Ashburton Treaty, it is generally agreed, justified his perseverance. See, e.g., Webster to Hiram Ketchum, Sep 11, 1841, 5 Webster Correspondence at 149, 150; Van Deusen, The Jacksonian Era at 173–76. The treaty itself is considered in Descent into the Maelstrom, ch 3.

[212]4 Richardson at 71.

[213]Id at 74, 86–87 (Dec 7, 1841). He repeated this suggestion the following year. Second Annual Message, id at 194, 204–7 (Dec 6, 1842). Albert Gallatin, widely respected Secretary of the Treasury under both Jefferson and Madison and a staunch supporter of the National Bank, thought Tyler's plan unconstitutional for reasons the President himself had given in his two veto messages:

> I have believed, contrary to the opinion of many respected friends, that the power of the government of the United States to select its own agent for transacting its own business did, in the present general use of banks for all fiscal purposes by the States and by individuals, imply the power to incorporate a bank of its own. But I cannot perceive from which power vested in the general government that of government to deal in exchange for the benefit of individuals is derived.

Gallatin to Caleb Cushing, Jan 7, 1842, 2 Gallatin Writings at 572, 575.

[214]See section II of this chapter. In this same message Tyler, who had taken such a restricted view of Congress's power to establish anything that quacked like a bank, tempted Congress to take a broad view of its authority to control the evils of paper money: "Whether this Government, with due regard to the rights of the States, has any power to constrain the banks either to resume specie payments or to force them into liquidation, is an inquiry which will not fail to claim your consideration." 4 Richardson at 83. Van Buren had made a similar suggestion in 1837. See section II of chapter 5.

Congress had had enough of Tyler, however,[215] and nothing more was done until the Democrats were safely back in power.[216] Then, in 1846, they resurrected Van Buren's Subtreasury system, by which the Government kept its money idle in its own vaults.[217] There it remained, for better or worse, until the Civil War—a costly monument to the narrow views taken by most Presidents from Jackson to Buchanan of what was necessary and proper to the collection, custody, and disbursement of federal funds.[218]

[215]Though a divided House committee basically endorsed the President's plan in 1842, a second report presented by New York Representative Millard Fillmore savaged it on a variety of policy grounds the following year, and it was never heard from again. See HR Rep 244, 27th Cong, 2d Sess (1842); HR Rep 35, 27th Cong, 3d Sess (1843).

[216]And thus, one recent observer concludes, President Harrison's untimely death paradoxically prevented the overruling of *McCulloch v Maryland,* for Harrison would have signed the new Bank bill, and a Supreme Court packed with orthodox Jacksonians would have struck it down. Magliocca, Veto!, 78 Neb L Rev at 254–55 (cited in note 39).

[217]9 Stat 59 (Aug 6, 1846). The Constitution, President Polk had told the lawmakers in his first Annual Message, required the Government to keep its own money. 4 Richardson at 385, 406–8 (Dec 2, 1845). See Abraham Lincoln's speech in Springfield, Illinois, Dec 26, 1839, Roy P. Basler, ed, 1 The Collected Works of Abraham Lincoln 159, 160 (Rutgers, 1953) [hereafter cited as Lincoln Works], complaining that under the Subtreasury plan the money would be "kept in iron boxes until the government wants it for disbursement, thus robbing the people of the use of it, while the government does not itself need it . . . ."

[218]For a brief and caustic treatment of these latter events see Hammond, Banks and Politics at 542–45 (cited in note 20).

4

Customs

You remember protective tariffs. The First Congress passed one, and President Washington signed it. At the urging of the great South Carolina nationalist (as he then was) John C. Calhoun, Congress passed another in 1816, and President Madison signed it. In the 1820's, as the rates grew steeper, a number of Southern Senators and Representatives, believing the tariff inflicted a disproportionate burden on their part of the country, discovered constitutional limits to Congress's authority to impose it. Incidental protection for domestic industry might be all right, but taxes could be levied only to produce revenue—and then only if necessary to cover expenditures. The South Carolina and Virginia legislatures passed resolutions declaring the 1824 and 1828 tariffs unconstitutional.[1]

Very well. One could argue about the constitutionality of purely protective tariffs. And state legislatures, like Presidents, were free to protest when they thought Congress had exceeded its powers. That was what Virginia and Kentucky had done in 1798, with the help of Madison and Jefferson, after Congress had passed the Alien and Sedition Acts.[2] As early as 1827, however, at least one South Carolina hothead had urged that his state go beyond mere protest:

> Situated as we are, and forever must be, to wit, in a minority, and with no hope of changing the national councils in our favour, I cannot see how we

[1]This portion of the story is quickly told in The Jeffersonians at 283–89. For more complete expositions of early tariff history see F.W. Taussig, The Tariff History of the United States (Putnam, 8th ed 1931); Edward Stanwood, 1 American Tariff Controversies of the Nineteenth Century (Houghton, Mifflin, 1903). The South Carolina resolutions are printed in 1 SC Stats at 228 (Dec 16, 1825) and 244 (Dec 19, 1828); the earlier ones are reprinted, along with Virginia's, in Herman V. Ames, State Documents on Federal Relations 139–44 (Da Capo, 1970) (first published in 1900–1906).

[2]See The Federalist Period at 269–71. Compare President Jackson's 1834 protest against the Senate resolution censuring him for removing Government deposits from the Bank of the United States, discussed in chapter 3 of this volume.

> are to get rid of the growing usurpations of Congress, but by RESISTANCE.

South Carolina should make clear "that she will not *submit* to the tariff."[3]

That, as the proverbial schoolgirl knows, is what South Carolina did. Presidential vetoes killed other elements of the American System; South Carolina killed the protective tariff.[4]

I. THE SOUTH CAROLINA EXPOSITION

It was the 1828 "Tariff of Abominations"—the tariff some say no one wanted[5]—that transformed nullification from a gleam in the eye of occasional firebrands into a serious campaign. That tariff, which among other things raised nominal duties on imported woollens to as much as fifty per cent, became law on May 19, 1828.[6] A few months later Representative James Hamilton, Jr., who would soon be South Carolina's Governor, publicly urged that the state nullify the statute. Madison and Jefferson, he argued, had pointed the way in their Virginia and Kentucky Resolutions:

> Mr. Madison says—"in the case of a deliberate, palpable and dangerous exercise of powers not granted by the compact, the States who are parties thereto, have the right, and are in duty bound to interpose for the purpose of arresting the progress of the evil, and for maintaining, within their respective limits, the authorities, rights and liberties appertaining to them." . . . But how are we to interpose for the purpose of "arresting the progress of the evil?" Let Mr. Jefferson answer this question: . . . "That the several States who formed the Constitution being sovereign and independent, have the unquestionable right to judge its infractions; and that a nullification of all unauthorized acts, done under colour of that instrument, is the rightful remedy."[7]

Enter John C. Calhoun, Vice-President of the United States. Born in 1782, Calhoun graduated from Yale College and from Tapping Reeve's pioneer law school in Litchfield, Connecticut. After serving briefly in the South Carolina legislature, he entered the federal

[3]Robert J. Turnbull, The Crisis, reprinted in William W. Freehling, ed, The Nullification Era: A Documentary Record 26, 46 (Harper & Row, 1967).

[4]The best account of the nullification controversy is William W. Freehling, Prelude to Civil War: The Nullification Controversy in South Carolina, 1816–1836 (Harper & Row, 1966). See also Merrill D. Peterson, Olive Branch and Sword: The Compromise of 1833 (LSU, 1982); Richard E. Ellis, The Union at Risk: Jacksonian Democracy, States' Rights, and the Nullification Crisis (Oxford, 1987).

[5]See The Jeffersonians at 287 and authorities cited; Stanwood, 1 American Tariff Controversies at 243–90 (cited in note 1). But see Robert V. Remini, Martin Van Buren and the Tariff of Abominations, 63 Am Hist Rev 903, 906–9 (1958), arguing that Van Buren indeed wanted the bill to pass.

[6]4 Stat 270. The provisions respecting woollens (id at 271–72, § 2) included controversial minimum rates that augmented the actual percentage still further. Any goods whose value was less than fifty cents per square yard, for example, "shall be deemed to have cost fifty cents the square yard." Id at 271, § 2 Second.

[7]James Hamilton, Jr., Speech at Walterborough (Oct 21, 1828), reprinted in Freehling, The Nullification Era at 48, 57–58 (cited in note 3).

House of Representatives in 1811. There he distinguished himself as a leading advocate of war with England and later of the entire American System: protective tariffs, internal improvements, and the Bank of the United States. He resigned from Congress in 1817 to become President Monroe's superlative Secretary of War; he had been Vice-President (under John Quincy Adams) since 1825.[8]

Like so many of his compatriots, Calhoun had grown disenchanted with increasingly protective tariffs. Having cast the tie-breaking vote against another increase in duties in 1827,[9] he revealed his understanding of the relevant constitutional provisions in a letter written soon after the 1828 law was enacted:

> According to my construction of the Constitution, the only power invested in Congress, as it regards the subject under consideration, is incidental to that of raising revenue, and regulating commerce. In exercising either of these powers, Congress may undoubtedly take into consideration the effect of any particular measure proposed on the industry of the country, and may give a preference [to] that, which is calculated to transfer manufacturing skill to our country. But I hold, that all such regulations must be the incident of acts really intended to raise revenue, or regulate commerce, and must be consistent with them. When it transcends this, and when Congress converts the incident into the principal [sic], and instead of revenue, or commerce, aims at the distruction [sic] of both in exercising a power intended to increase and cherish them, I hold it not only unconstitutional but most dangerously so.[10]

Continuing pressure to raise tariffs had also induced Calhoun, even before the Tariff of Abominations was enacted, to begin pondering the question of what to do about it. "[I]n the main," he had written in 1827,

> [t]he freedom of debate, the freedom of the press, [and] the division of power into the three branches . . . afford . . . efficient security to the *constituents against rulers,* but in an extensive country with deversified [sic] and opposing interest[s], another and not less important remedy is required, *the protection of one portion of the people against another*. . . .
>
> After much reflection, it seems to me, that the despotism founded on combined geographical interest, admits of but one effectual remedy, a veto on the part of the local interest, or under our system, on the part of the States.

"[H]ow far such a negative would be consistent with the general power"—that is, with the authority given the central Government by the existing Constitution—was, he added, "an important consideration, which I waive for the present."[11]

[8]All of this information and a great deal more can be found in the first volume of Charles M. Wiltse's comprehensive three-part biography, John C. Calhoun, Nationalist, 1782–1828 (Bobbs-Merrill, 1944).

[9]Cong Deb, 19th Cong, 2d Sess 496.

[10]Calhoun to Samuel Smith, Jul 28, 1828, 10 Calhoun Papers at 403–4.

[11]Calhoun to Littleton W. Tazewell, Aug 25, 1827, id at 300, 300–301.

In November 1828 Calhoun accepted an invitation to draft a statement for the South Carolina House of Representatives in response to the tariff. By this time he had made up his mind. "The remedy you refer to," he wrote to the legislator who had extended the invitation, "is the only safe and efficient one, and is abundantly adequate. . . . *It alone can save the Union.*"[12] The remedy he had in mind was nullification, as the resulting statement shows.

Calhoun's "Rough Draft of What is Called the South Carolina Exposition" began with the assertion that the 1828 law "imposing duties on imports, not for revenue but for the protection of one branch of industry at the expense of others," was "unconstitutional, unequal and oppressive," for the tax power had been given "for the sole purpose of revenue—a power in its nature essentially different from that of imposing protective, or prohibitory duties." Precedent would deserve "little weight" even if in point, for "[o]urs is not a government of precedents"; "[t]he only safe rule is the Constitution itself, or if that be doubtful, the history of the times." But precedent was not in point; earlier tariffs had been legitimate revenue measures affording only "incidental" protection to domestic industry.[13]

After a lengthy disquisition on the unequal and oppressive nature of the 1828 tariff, Calhoun turned at last to the question of remedy. Section 25 of the Judiciary Act, which empowered the Supreme Court to set aside unconstitutional state legislation, efficiently protected the Federal Government against state encroachment on its powers. To give the Court final say as to the extent of *federal* authority, however, "would raise one of the departments of the General Government, above the sovereign parties, who created the Constitution," and "enable it in practice to alter at pleasure the relative powers of the States and General Government."[14] The states themselves must therefore decide:

> If it be conceded, as it must by every one who is the least conversant with our institutions, that the sovereign power is divided between the States and General Government, and that the former holds its reserved rights, in the same high sovereign capacity, which the latter does its delegated rights; it will be impossible to deny to the States the right of deciding on the infraction of their rights, and the proper remedy to be applied for the correction. The right of judging, in such cases, is an essential attribute of sovereignty of which the States cannot be divested, without losing their sovereignty itself; and being reduced to a subordinate corporate condition. In fact, to divide power, and to give to one of the parties the exclusive right of judging of the portion allotted to each, is in reality not to divide at all; and to reserve such exclusive right to the General Government (it

[12] Calhoun to William C. Preston, Nov 6, 1828, id at 431. "Excise," Calhoun added, "will not do." Id. The reference apparently was to the contemporaneous suggestion that Southern states retaliate for the tariff by imposing duties on goods imported from other states—a course of action the Supreme Court would later hold forbidden by the commerce clause, though oddly not by the more obviously apposite express ban on state import duties in Article I, § 10. See Woodruff v Parham, 75 US 123 (1869); Welton v Missouri, 91 US 275 (1876).

[13] 10 Calhoun Papers at 444–46.

[14] Id at 500, 501–3. This section of Calhoun's original draft being in somewhat parlous condition, I have taken the language last quoted from the revised draft approved by a committee of the state House of Representatives.

> matters not by what department it be exercised,) is in fact to constitute it one great consolidated government, with unlimited powers, and to reduce the States to mere corporations. . . . But the existence of the right of judging of their powers, clearly established by the sovereignty of the States, as clearly implies a veto, or controul on the action of the General Government on contested points of authority; and this very controul is the remedy, which the Constitution has provided to prevent the encroachment of the General Government on the reserved right of the States . . . .[15]

Familiar? This is another application of the checks and balances theory of *Marbury v Madison:* Constitutional limitations are worthless if those meant to be limited have the last word in their interpretation. Foxes are not appointed to guard the henhouse. "[F]or surely," Calhoun wrote two years later, "there is not the least practical difference between a government of unlimitted [sic] powers, and one of limitted powers on paper, but with unlimitted right of construction."[16]

There was a good deal to this argument in the abstract, but it cut in both directions. If the states had the last word, they might deny Congress powers the Constitution had actually given. Calhoun had an answer for that too: If one state abused its power to nullify unconstitutional laws, the others could correct it by amending the Constitution to confirm the disputed authority.[17] It was true, he later conceded, that this interpretation permitted one-fourth of the states to deprive Congress of its rightful powers (as opposed, one might add, to the three-fourths expressly required by Article V); but that was not so bad as the risk that Congress might usurp powers the Constitution did not give.[18]

As Calhoun had earlier suggested,[19] his draft concluded that South Carolina had cause to nullify the tariff but that, "out of respect for the other members of the confederacy and the necessity of great moderation and forbearance," it would be best for the time simply to present the legislature's views, "in the hope that a returning sense of justice on the part of the majority" might lead to repeal of the obnoxious provisions "and thereby prevent the necessity of interposing the sovereign power of this State."[20]

A committee of the South Carolina House approved Calhoun's exposition with minor changes.[21] The House ordered four thousand copies printed and distributed.[22] Both chambers followed Calhoun's advice, protesting the adoption of an unconstitutional tariff

[15]Id at 507. Once again I have quoted the committee's cleaner version in preference to the original, which is substantially the same.

[16]Calhoun to Samuel D. Ingham, Oct 30, 1830, 11 Calhoun Papers at 250, 255. He repeated this point a few weeks later in a draft address intended to be issued by the Legislature to the people of South Carolina, id at 264, 271.

[17]10 Calhoun Papers at 520.

[18]Calhoun to James Hamilton, Jr., Aug 28, 1832, 11 Calhoun Papers at 613, 637–38. Webster justly ridiculed Calhoun's suggestion: "In short, the result of the whole is, that, though it requires three fourths of the States to insert any thing in the Constitution, yet any one State can strike any thing out of it." Speech at New York, Mar 24, 1831, 1 Webster Speeches at 448, 461.

[19]See Calhoun to William C. Preston, Nov 6, 1828, 10 Calhoun Papers at 431, 432.

[20]Id at 529–31 (committee version).

[21]See id at 445–553 (odd pages); 1 SC Stats 247–73 (Dec 19, 1828).

[22]See 10 Calhoun Papers at 443.

but saying nothing further about nullification.[23]

II. THE HAYNE-WEBSTER DEBATE

Among the considerations that led Calhoun to refrain from suggesting immediate nullification in 1828 was the hope that the incoming Administration, headed by "an eminent citizen, distinguished for his services to his country and his justice and patriotism," might "under his influence" effect "a complete restoration of the pure principles of our government."[24] If Calhoun believed what he wrote, he was in for a shock; for as already noted protective tariffs were the one element of the American System in which Andrew Jackson believed.

The "first design" of a tariff, Jackson had written in 1824, was protection:

> The domestic industry and labor of the Country, coextensive with our National independence, and national defense in a State of war, should be encouraged & protected. This should be the first design of a Tarriff [sic], & the second a reasonable increase of imports with a view to paying the debt of the Nation . . . .[25]

As we have seen, Jackson reaffirmed this commitment both in his Inaugural Address and in his first Annual Message.[26] He returned to the subject in his second Annual Message in December 1830. Some tariffs were too high and should be reduced, but there was a need for protection, and only Congress could provide it; there was nothing to the argument that protective tariffs were unconstitutional.[27] In declaring that "the chief object of duties should be revenue"[28] Jackson appeared to have softened his views somewhat,[29] but it nevertheless appeared that no major revolution in tariff policy was to be expected from his quarter.

Thus the election of Calhoun's "eminent citizen" had not rendered the nullification question moot, and indeed that question had been dramatically debated in the Senate earlier in 1830 in the unlikely context of a proposal by Connecticut Senator Samuel Foot to limit the sale of public lands.[30]

Opposing the resolution in what historians describe as an effort to forge an alliance between the South and the West,[31] South Carolina's Robert Y. Hayne deprecated the re-

[23] 1 SC Stats at 244 (Dec 19, 1828). This is the protest cited in note 1. For a committee version see 10 Calhoun Papers at 535–39. Calhoun's purpose in all this, his biographer insisted, was to save the Union. Wiltse, 1 Calhoun at 396.

[24] South Carolina Exposition, 10 Calhoun Papers at 531 (committee version); see also Calhoun to William C. Preston, Nov 6, 1828, id at 431, 432.

[25] Jackson to James W. Lanier, May 15, 1824, 3 Jackson Correspondence at 253.

[26] See the Introduction to Part One.

[27] 2 Richardson at 500, 523–25 (Dec 6, 1830).

[28] Id at 524.

[29] This subtle change of emphasis did not escape the notice of advocates of protection in the House. See HR Rep 36, 21st Cong, 2d Sess 3, 12 (1831) (Rep. Mallary).

[30] The Foot Resolution appears at Cong Deb, 21st Cong, 1st Sess 3.

[31] See, e.g., Van Deusen, The Jacksonian Era at 40–42. Jackson having said nothing about tariff reform, Professor Wiltse explained, "Southern leaders . . . responded with a quick offer to the West: unrestricted and

tention of lands (or any other policy conducive to "a great permanent national treasury") as tending toward "consolidation" of the Federal Government—a favorite pejorative for the centralization of power—at the expense of "the sovereignty and independence of the States."[32] Daniel Webster, the majestic orator from Massachusetts, elected to perceive in Hayne's argument against "consolidation" a lack of devotion to the Union:

> I cannot but feel regret at the expression of such opinions as the gentleman has avowed; because I think their obvious tendency is to weaken the bond of our connexion. I know that there are some persons in the part of the country from which the honorable member comes, who habitually speak of the Union in terms of indifference, or even of disparagement. The honorable member himself is not, I trust, and can never be, one of these. They significantly declare, that it is time to calculate the value of the Union; and their aim seems to be to enumerate, and to magnify all the evils, real and imaginary, which the Government under the Union produces.
>
> The tendency of all these ideas and sentiments is obviously to bring the Union into discussion, as a mere question of temporary expediency; nothing more than a mere matter of profit and loss. . . . Sir, I deprecate and deplore this tone of thinking and acting. . . . . [I] believe, that the Union of the States is essential to the prosperity and safety of the States . . . .[33]

Hayne elected to interpret Webster's remarks as an attack on the principle of nullification: "The Senator from Massachusetts, in denouncing what he is pleased to call the Carolina doctrine, has attempted to throw ridicule upon the idea that a State has any constitutional remedy, by the exercise of its sovereign authority, against 'a gross, palpable, and deliberate violation of the constitution.'" Yet the doctrine proclaimed by a committee of South Carolina's legislature in its "exposition" of December 1828, said Hayne, was nothing more than "the good old Republican doctrine of '98" as propounded by Madison and Jefferson in their Virginia and Kentucky Resolutions and in Madison's subsequent report to the Virginia legislature, from all of which Hayne proceeded to quote profusely. He went on to paraphrase the checks-and-balances argument made in the Exposition itself: "If the Federal Government, in all or any of its departments, [is] to prescribe the limits of its own authority, and the States are bound to submit to the decision, . . . this is

---

virtually free public lands in return for tariff reduction." Charles M. Wiltse, The New Nation 110 (Hill & Wang, 1961).

[32]Cong Deb, 21st Cong, 1st Sess 33–34. Western objections, on the other hand, were exemplified by Thomas Hart Benton's later charge that the effect of Foot's resolution would have been "to check emigration to the new States in the West—to check the growth and settlement of these States and territories—and to deliver up large portions of them to the dominion of wild beasts." Benton, 1 Thirty Years' View at 130.

[33]Cong Deb, 21st Cong, 1st Sess 38. As Hayne observed (id at 50), Webster's allusion to "calculat[ing] the value of the Union" was a reference to an incendiary pamphlet distributed in 1827 by a South Carolina professor named Thomas Cooper, who had first achieved notoriety when prosecuted by the Federalists under the Sedition Act. For his earlier adventures see 25 F Cas 631 (No 14,865) (CC D Pa, 1800); his 1827 diatribe is reprinted in substantial part in Freehling, The Nullification Era at 20–25 (cited in note 3).

practically 'a government without limitation of powers.'"[34]

We have now set the stage for one of the most famous and justly admired speeches ever made in Congress, Webster's Second Reply to Hayne.

South Carolina, said Webster, was threatening to break up the Union over tariffs and internal improvements that her own representatives had advocated in 1816 and 1824.[35] Of course, he continued, unconstitutional laws were not binding; "[t]he great question is, whose prerogative it is to decide on the constitutionality or unconstitutionality of the laws?"[36] In maintaining that individual states had the ultimate right to decide, Hayne had relied heavily on the Virginia Resolutions.[37] But, said Webster, Hayne may have misread them:

> In the case of the exercise, by Congress, of a dangerous power, not granted to them, the resolutions assert the right, on the part of the State, to interfere, and arrest the progress of the evil. This is susceptible of more than one interpretation. It may mean no more than that the States may interfere by complaint and remonstrance [which, parenthetically, was all that Virginia and Kentucky had done in 1798 and South Carolina had done in 1828];[38] or by proposing to the people an alteration of the Federal constitution. This would all be quite unobjectionable; or, it may be, that no more is meant than to assert the general right of revolution, as against all governments, in cases of intolerable oppression.[39] This no one doubts; and this, in my opinion, is all that he who framed the resolutions could have meant by it; for I shall not readily believe that he was ever of opinion that a State, under the constitution, and in conformity with it, could, upon the ground of its unconstitutionality, however clear and palpable she might think the case, annul a law of Congress, so far as it should operate on

[34]Cong Deb, 21st Cong, 1st Sess 56–58. Predictably, Hayne also brought up the Hartford Convention, in which delegates from several New England states had come uncomfortably close to embracing nullification and secession in opposition to certain measures taken or threatened during the War of 1812. Id at 50–52; see The Jeffersonians at 180–86. Webster dismissed the Convention as "tame" in comparison to the tariff controversy and more convincingly added that to whatever extent the Convention had expressed views resembling those recently emanating from South Carolina "I shall be as ready as any one to bestow on them reprehension and censure." Cong Deb, 21st Cong, 1st Sess 62–63.

[35]Id at 68.

[36]Id at 73.

[37]Indeed, after Webster restated the nullification doctrine, Hayne interrupted to reread the relevant passage of the Resolutions, which he said stated his own position. Id at 73.

[38]Of course, said Clayton and Livingston later in the debate, a state might protest that an Act of Congress was unconstitutional; that did not mean it could veto its enforcement. Id at 228 (Sen. Clayton); id at 267–68 (Sen. Livingston). See also St. George Tucker, ed, 1 Blackstone's Commentaries: with Notes of Reference, to the Constitution and Laws, of the Federal Government of the United States; and of the Commonwealth of Virginia, App 153 (Lawbook Exchange, 1996) (first published in 1803) [hereafter cited as Tucker's Blackstone], suggesting that if the Central Government usurped authority a state might "sound the alarm," send new spokesmen to Congress, or propose amendments to the Constitution; Tucker said nothing about nullifying federal law.

[39]Webster had suggested this interpretation a few minutes earlier in language paraphrasing the Declaration of Independence, and Hayne had hastened to say that was not what he had in mind. Cong Deb, 21st Cong, 1st Sess 73.

herself, by her own legislative power.[40]

This was a good lawyer's argument, for the phrasing of the Resolutions was slippery enough to permit Webster's interpretation. Indeed by this time "he who framed the resolutions" was himself busily disclaiming both nullification and the assertion that he had embraced it in 1798.[41] Both Madison and Webster would have had an easier task, however, if the Resolutions had been formulated with greater restraint; they certainly invited, though they did not compel, Hayne's more belligerent reading.[42]

Having attempted to deal with the precedents, Webster turned to the merits of the constitutional question. Nullification, he thundered, was an absurd doctrine that the Framers could never have intended.

> In Carolina, the tariff is a palpable, deliberate usurpation; Carolina, therefore, may nullify it, and refuse to pay the duties. In Pennsylvania, it is both clearly constitutional, and highly expedient; and there, the duties are to be paid. And yet we live under a Government of uniform laws, and under a constitution, too, which contains an express provision, as it happens, that all duties shall be equal in all the States! Does not this approach absurdity? . . .
>
> And, sir, if we look to the general nature of the case, could any thing have been more preposterous than to make a government for the whole Union, and yet leave its powers subject, not to one interpretation, but to thirteen, or twenty-four, interpretations? . . . Would any thing, with such a principle in it, or rather with such a destitution of all principle, be fit to be called a government? No, sir. . . . It would not be adequate to any practical good, nor fit for any country to live under."[43]

Hayne argued, Webster continued, that permitting the Federal Government to de-

[40]Id at 77. Webster might have added that, whatever the Virginia and Kentucky Resolutions may have meant, they had scarcely represented the general understanding of the country; for a number of other states had taken the trouble to disagree formally with the Resolutions, while not one was recorded in their support. Ames, State Documents on Federal Relations at 16–26 (cited in note 1). See, e.g., the emphatic response of the Vermont legislature (Oct 30, 1799), id at 25, 26: "It belongs not to State Legislatures to decide on the constitutionality of laws made by the general government; this power being exclusively vested in the judiciary courts of the Union."

[41]In an 1829 letter Madison had arguably left the door open in principle to interposition of the South Carolina sort by insisting, inter alia, that the resolutions had been intended for "extreme cases only," not for mere "inequality in the operation of a tariff." James Madison to Joseph C. Cabell, Aug 16, 1829, 9 Madison Writings at 341, 342–44. By 1830, however, he equivocated no more. Nullification was inconsistent with the Constitution; even "in the extremity supposed" a state would have only the "extra & ultra constitutional right" to self-preservation. Madison to Edward Everett, Aug 28, 1830, id at 383, 398, 31 N Am Rev 537, 542 (Oct 1830). See also Madison's memorandum of June ?, 1835, 9 Madison Writings at 573 (insisting, id at 589–90 n.1, that Jefferson too had asserted only a natural right of revolution); Benton, 1 Thirty Years' View at 347–60, quoting from the Virginia legislative debates of 1799.

[42]See The Federalist Period at 269–71. Webster himself, during the War of 1812, had declared that if Congress adopted the "unconstitutional" conscription bill it would be the duty of the state governments to take the "constitutional" step of "interpos[ing] between their citizens and arbitrary power." 1 Webster Speeches at 30; see The Jeffersonians at 175.

[43]Cong Deb, 21st Cong, 1st Sess 74, 78.

termine the limits of its own authority would subvert state sovereignty. "This the gentleman sees, or thinks he sees, although he cannot perceive how the right of judging, in this matter, if left to the exercise of State Legislatures, has any tendency to subvert the Government of the Union." Yet to recognize a right of nullification would mean the Constitution would exist only at the pleasure of each state.

> Sir, the very chief end, the main design, for which the whole constitution was framed and adopted was, to establish a Government that should not be obliged to act through State agency, or depend on State opinion and State discretion. The people had had quite enough of that kind of government, under the Confederacy.

And if individual states could nullify federal laws, "[a]re we not thrown back again, precisely upon the old Confederation?"[44]

Yes, said Webster, he himself had opposed the 1824 tariff, but he had not sought to nullify it.[45] Nor had Massachusetts nullified Jefferson's 1807 Embargo, which it believed unconstitutional; it had challenged the offending statute in court and acquiesced in the adverse decision.[46] For the Constitution itself, said Webster, answered the crucial question who was to decide whether a law was constitutional: the Supreme Court. Article VI made the Constitution and federal law supreme; Article III extended federal judicial power to all cases arising under the constitution or laws of the United States.

> These two provisions, sir, cover the whole ground. They are, in truth, the key-stone of the arch. With these, it is a constitution; without them, it is a confederacy. In pursuance of these clear and express provisions, Congress established, at its very first session, in the Judicial Act, a mode for carrying them into full effect, and for bringing all questions of constitutional power to the final decision of the Supreme Court.

Hayne was welcome to believe that the power ought not to have been given to the Supreme Court, but it had been; the Constitution was clear.[47]

[44]Id at 79, 77, 74.

[45]Id at 69.

[46]Id at 75–76. See The Jeffersonians at 145–55. Several of the New England resolutions opposing the Embargo and the harsh provisions adopted to enforce it had echoed the ambiguous bluster of their Virginia and Kentucky predecessors, but all had stopped short of threatening actual interference with federal execution of the laws. Ames, State Documents on Federal Relations at 26–44 (cited in note 1).

[47]Cong Deb, 21st Cong, 1st Sess 77–79. Not only that, Webster later added, but the Framers were right to give ultimate authority to the Supreme Court:

> [C]an any reasonable man doubt the expediency of this provision, or suggest a better? Is it not absolutely essential to the peace of the country that this power should exist somewhere? Where can it exist, better than where it now does exist? The national judiciary is the common tribunal of the whole country. It is organized by the common authority, and its places filled by the common agent. . . . The great question is, whether we shall provide for the peaceful decision of cases of collision. Shall they be decided by law, or by force?

Let there be no mistake, said Webster: "[B]etween submission to the decision of the constituted tribunals, and revolution, or disunion, there is no middle ground . . . ." The customs officer would attempt to collect the tariff; the state would try to stop him. "Direct collision, therefore, between force and force, is the unavoidable result"; and forcible resistance to the enforcement of law was treason.[48]

> Talk about it as we will, these doctrines go to the length of revolution. They are incompatible with any peaceable administration of the Government. They lead directly to disunion and civil commotion; and therefore it is, that, at their commencement, when they are first found to be maintained by respectable men, and in a tangible form, I enter my public protest against them all.[49]

Webster closed with a tribute to the Union. I know, I'm an incurable romantic; I can't read it with dry eyes.

> I profess, sir, in my career, hitherto, to have kept steadily in view the prosperity and honor of the whole country, and the preservation of our Federal Union. It is to that Union that we owe our safety at home, and our consideration and dignity abroad. It is to that Union that we are chiefly indebted for whatever makes us most proud of our country. . . . When my eyes shall be turned to behold, for the last time, the sun in heaven, may I not see him shining on the broken and dishonored fragments of a once glorious Union; on States dissevered, discordant, belligerent; on a land rent with civil feuds, or drenched, it may be, in fraternal blood! Let their last feeble lingering glance, rather, behold the gorgeous ensign of the republic, now known and honored throughout the earth, still full high advanced, its arms and trophies streaming in their original lustre, not a stripe erased or polluted, nor a single star obscured, bearing for its motto no such miserable motto as, What is all this worth? Nor those other words of delusion and folly, Liberty first, and Union afterwards;[50] but every where, spread all over in characters of living light, blazing on all its ample folds, . . . that other sentiment, dear to every true American heart—Liberty *and* Union, now and forever, one and inseparable![51]

Speech at New York, Mar 24, 1831, 1 Webster Speeches at 448, 460–61. See also The Federalist No 39 (Madison), acknowledging that "the tribunal which is ultimately to decide" questions respecting the boundary between federal and state authority "is to be established under the general government" and adding that this resolution was better than "an appeal to the sword."

[48]Cong Deb, 21st Cong, 1st Sess 76, 78–79, invoking the case of John Fries, who in the 1790's had indeed been found guilty of treason for armed resistance to the collection of federal taxes. See The Federalist Period at 227 n.173.

[49]Cong Deb, 21st Cong, 1st Sess 79.

[50]Calhoun, whom protocol constrained to sit mutely in the presiding officer's chair as Webster methodically destroyed his henchman's efforts, would repeat the very slogan Webster here disparaged in his famous toast at the Jefferson Day dinner in April 1830. See note 93 and accompanying text.

[51]Cong Deb, 21st Cong, 1st Sess 80.

Magnificent, isn't it? There is more. Poor Hayne felt called upon to scrape himself off the floor and respond. Webster having revealed his checks and balances argument to be a double-edged sword, he fell back upon the alternative argument of sovereignty.[52] As Madison had asserted in 1799, Hayne said, the Constitution was a "compact" between sovereign states; and, as Madison had also argued, "the parties to the compact must, themselves, be the rightful judges whether the bargain has been pursued or violated."[53]

Webster leveled him once again. The Constitution was no compact. The Articles of Confederation had been a compact; they were abandoned because a mere compact was insufficient to the country's needs. Nor did it matter. A compact too might vest final decision-making authority in the Supreme Court, as the Constitution had done.[54] Finally, said Webster, Hayne was right that if the Constitution had been a mere agreement among sovereign states they might have modified or interpreted it as they pleased, but only by agreement; one party to a contract could not unilaterally establish its meaning.[55]

III. THE NULLIFICATION ORDINANCE

The Supreme Court was the Achilles' heel of the nullification movement. Calhoun had worried about it from the beginning.

In 1827, as already noted, he had wondered aloud whether his nullification thesis was consistent with the powers given to the General Government—by which he appeared to mean the federal courts. For only one statute, he insisted, stood in the way of nullification:

> If the appellate power from the State courts to the U[nited] States court provided for by the 25th sec[tio]n [of the Judiciary Act] did not exist, the practical consequence would be, that each government would have a negative on the other, and thus possess the most effectual remedy, that can be conceived against encroachment.[56]

Calhoun was content to live with the supremacy of federal law; he demanded only final authority to say what federal law was. His candid assertion was ample confirmation of Justice Story's argument in *Martin v Hunter's Lessee* that Supreme Court review of state-court judgments was indispensable to the vindication of federal rights.[57]

Calhoun had suggested that it was not too late to review the constitutionality of § 25 itself, and it was not long before his creatures in Congress reported a bill to repeal the provision as unconstitutional.[58] The bill got nowhere, of course,[59] and Calhoun turned to

[52]See Freehling, Prelude to Civil War at 163–65 (cited in note 4), giving a parallel explanation for a similar shift in Calhoun's own argumentation two years earlier.

[53]Cong Deb, 21st Cong, 1st Sess 86, quoting Madison's 1799 Report, at 20.

[54]Accord 1 Story, §§ 371, 375. Compare the modern practice of specifying in which forum suits on a contract shall be brought, or providing for arbitration. See The Bremen v Zapata Off-Shore Oil Co, 407 US 1 (1972); United States Arbitration Act, 9 USC §§ 1–14 (2000).

[55]Cong Deb, 21st Cong, 1st Sess 92–93; see also 1 Story, § 364.

[56]Calhoun to Littleton W. Tazewell, Aug 25, 1827, 10 Calhoun Papers at 300, 301.

[57]14 US 304, 347 (1816).

[58]For Calhoun's suggestion see his letter to Tazewell, 10 Calhoun Papers at 301; for the bill see HR Rep 43, 21st Cong, 2d Sess (Jan 24, 1831); for Calhoun's complicity in the project see his letter to James H. Ham-

the daunting task of demonstrating that § 25 did not give the Supreme Court authority to determine the limits of federal power after all.

Hayne had endeavored to make this argument during his debate with Webster, but with notable lack of success. Questions of "conflicting sovereignty," he had declared, were "political," not judicial.[60] But of course the Supreme Court had undertaken from the outset to define the boundaries between federal and state authority,[61] partly on the basis of the same checks and balances argument that Hayne had urged in favor of nullification.[62] Hayne seemed to admit later in the same speech that federal courts could invalidate Acts of Congress;[63] it is not at all clear what he had in mind.

In later writings Calhoun reiterated Hayne's suggestion that questions of congressional power were "political" rather than judicial; he too seemed willing to cast doubt upon an established check on Congress in hopes of securing a new and more effective one. The judicial power over "cases in law and equity," he wrote in 1831, extended "only to questions, to which there may be parties amenable to the process of the court, and excluding those of a political character."[64] The reference to "parties amenable to . . . process" seemed to evoke sovereign immunity, which would indeed preclude an action against the Government itself; for as Calhoun would later point out the clause extending federal judicial power to "suits to which the United States is a party" did not permit the

mond, Jan 15, 1831, 11 Calhoun Papers at 298, 299. See also his letter to Tazewell of Nov 9, 1827, 10 Calhoun Papers at 312, 313, noting that in an intervening letter Tazewell had failed to consider "whether the appellate power of the Supreme Court can be reconciled to the acknowledged theory of our system, that the States are as sovereign and independent, as to their reserved rights, as the Union is, as to the delegated."

[59]The bill was rejected by a vote of 138–51. See Cong Deb, 21st Cong, 2d Sess 542; Ed Note, 11 Calhoun Papers at 300. Representative Davis's committee report in favor of repeal contained nothing new. Buchanan's minority report, invoking Hamilton's assurance that "an appeal would certainly lie" from state courts to the Supreme Court (The Federalist No 82), added that without it the central flaw of the Articles of Confederation would remain: The states could effectively nullify federal law. HR Rep 43, 21st Cong, 2d Sess 16 (1831). For the merits of the constitutional issue regarding § 25 see The First Hundred Years at 91–98.

[60]Cong Deb, 21st Cong, 1st Sess 87–88.

[61]See, e.g., United States v Fisher, 6 US 358 (1805); McCulloch v Maryland, 17 US 316 (1819); Gibbons v Ogden, 22 US 1 (1824)—not to mention a flock of cases respecting the contract clause and other limitations on state power collected in The First Hundred Years at 127–93. A later Supreme Court would pointedly proclaim that the political-question doctrine was a principle not of federalism but of separation of powers. Baker v Carr, 369 US 186, 210 (1962). Occasional later scholars would indeed renew the heretical suggestion that the courts ought not to determine whether federal statutes invaded states' rights, but on a theory the opposite of Hayne's: that the states were adequately protected by the political check of their representation in Congress. E.g., Jesse H. Choper, Judicial Review and the National Political Process: A Functional Reconsideration of the Role of the Supreme Court (Chicago, 1980); Larry Kramer, Putting the Politics Back into the Political Safeguards of Federalism, 100 Colum L Rev 215 (2000). (For partial acceptance of this thesis by a bare majority in the rarefied context of state immunity from federal regulation see Garcia v San Antonio Metropolitan Transit Auth, 469 US 528, 556 (1985).) The last thing Hayne wanted was that Congress be left to define the limits of its own authority. See Cong Deb, 21st Cong, 1st Sess 88–89.

[62]See, e.g., Martin v Hunter's Lessee, 14 US 304, 347 (1816); The First Hundred Years at 91–93. When Justice Story, the author of *Martin*, announced in his treatise that "political" questions such as Congress's "mode of executing" its tax powers were not subject to reexamination in court, he could scarcely have meant that tax laws were exempt from judicial review altogether, for the Supreme Court had passed upon the validity of the federal carriage tax as early as 1796. See 1 Story, § 374; Hylton v United States, 3 US 171.

[63]Cong Deb, 21st Cong, 1st Sess 89.

[64]Calhoun to Charles J. McDonald, Jun 29, 1831, 11 Calhoun Papers at 406, 407. He repeated this argument almost word for word in another draft report for the South Carolina legislature, written around Nov 20, 1831, id at 485, 492.

Government to be sued without its consent.[65] This fell short of proving Calhoun's point, however, for the constitutionality of the tariff, like that of the Bank and of federal steamboat licensing, might be raised in litigation against a private party.[66]

On the political-question issue Calhoun invoked the authority of John Marshall, who as a member of the House had argued that it was for the executive and not the courts to decide whether to extradite an accused offender,[67] and who as Chief Justice had just dismissed a suit by the Cherokee Nation challenging Georgia's authority over its lands.[68] Neither case cited by Calhoun, however, had anything to do with the limits of congressional power, and when the question of "sovereignty" avoided in *Cherokee* reappeared in an action between "parties amenable to . . . process" the Court resolved it on the merits[69]—just as it had always resolved questions of the extent of federal authority.[70]

Of the significance of Supreme Court review as an argument against nullification we shall have more to say directly. For the moment let us resume the chronological thread of our story.

"From a sense of propriety connected with my relation to the General Government," as Calhoun explained privately in September 1830, he had kept a low profile in the nullification contest.[71] In December of that year he quietly drafted a second statement for the state legislature, this time designed as an "Address to the People of South Carolina."[72] On the subject of nullification it contained nothing new;[73] on the subject of the tariff it was most revealing. Forty years after adoption of the Constitution, Calhoun argued, "[s]carcely a restraint in fact is left on the will of the General Government, and doctrines are openly and boldly avowed, which, if not successfully resisted, will give it unlimited powers, and reduce the States to mere corporations."[74]

[65]Id. See, e.g., United States v McLemore, 45 US 286 (1846). Both Jay and Cushing had suggested this possibility in Chisholm v Georgia, 2 US 419, 469, 478 (1793); see The First Hundred Years at 18.

[66]McCulloch v Maryland, 17 US 316 (1819); Gibbons v Ogden, 22 US 1 (1824). An effort to test the tariff law in a suit to collect on a bond posted by an importer failed, however, when at the Government's request (as directed by the President himself) the judge excluded evidence of the purpose for which the bond was given. See James A. Hamilton to President Jackson, Jul 28, 1831, 4 Jackson Correspondence at 322; 41 Niles' Weekly Register 119–24 (Oct 8, 1831); Wiltse, 2 Calhoun at 113. A suit against the collector either to enjoin collection of the tariff or to recover property taken or held to satisfy it would also have been permissible under Osborn v Bank of the United States, 22 US 738, 847–48 (1824); see United States v Lee, 106 US 196 (1883).

[67]11 Calhoun Papers at 407. For Marshall's argument (in the case of Jonathan Robbins) see 10 Annals of Congress 596, 613–14 (1800).

[68]11 Calhoun Papers at 492. The case is Cherokee Nation v Georgia, 30 US 1 (1831).

[69]Worcester v Georgia, 31 US 515 (1832).

[70]Still later, Calhoun earnestly contended that giving the Supreme Court the last word as to the boundaries between federal and state power would be inconsistent with the Convention's rejection of a plan to give *Congress* authority to veto state legislation. Calhoun to James Hamilton, Jr., Aug 28, 1832, 11 Calhoun Papers at 613, 620–22. The Convention record, however, rebuts this contention: The Framers decided to give this authority to the courts rather than to Congress, and to limit it to cases of unconstitutionality. See, e.g. 2 Farrand at 27 (Messrs. Sherman and Gouverneur Morris).

[71]Calhoun to Virgil Maxcy, Sep 11, 1830, 11 Calhoun Papers at 226, 227. Calhoun remained Vice-President, having been reelected when Jackson won the Presidency in 1829.

[72]Id at 264–79.

[73]See id at 270: "To us, it seems an inevitable consequence, that a State, as a party to the compact, . . . has the right to Judge of its infractions and to interpose her authority for the maintenance of her reserved rights . . . ."

[74]Id at 266–67.

> The majority, under the power in the Constitution to lay taxes, claims the right of laying duties not only to raise revenue, but to regulate the industry of the country, that is, to convert the duties in reality, into a system of penalties, and rewards, by which one branch of industry is repressed, that another may be rewarded. . . . [T]he same principle . . . may be applied to any species of taxes, external & internal, (the direct excepted) and to any purpose, that the majority may think to be, for the G[e]n[era]l Welfare; to the Colonization society, as well as to cotton & woollen manufactures. . . .
>
> Such a power in the hands of the General Government is itself sufficient to control the whole industry and institutions of the country. That it would forever be wielded against us, if we should permit it to be exercised, requires but little sagacity to perceive. On all questions connected with the monied action of the Government, we have been, and must forever continue to be a minority. Our peculiar productions, and peculiar domestick institutions, mark us, as its certain victim, unless we can be protected by the interposed sovereignty of the States.[75]

"Our . . . peculiar domestick institutions" was a favorite euphemism for slavery. As Calhoun had recently explained in private correspondence, the tariff was only "the occasion, rather than the real cause of the present unhappy state of things"; nullification was really about slavery.[76]

The legislature did nothing with this report, but in July 1831, in his celebrated Fort Hill Address, Calhoun finally came out of the closet to explain his position to the people.[77] In November of that year he produced a third draft report for the legislature, which did not adopt it.[78] The following year, in response to a request from Governor Hamilton, he composed what he described as "a fuller developement" [sic] of his views.[79]

In the main these three documents repeated and elaborated upon arguments that Calhoun and his disciples had made before. In the Fort Hill address he made a new ar-

[75]Id at 269–70 (paragraphing added for clarity).

[76]Calhoun to Virgil Maxcy, Sep 11, 1830, id at 226, 229. See also Richard B. Latner, The Nullification Crisis and Republican Subversion, 43 J So Hist 19 (1977). A single premise, Professor Wiltse argued, underlay "every state rights argument advanced between 1798 and the ratification of the 13th Amendment in 1865":

> If a majority in Congress could pass laws, for whatever purpose, against the convictions and interests of a substantial portion of the Union, it could also pass laws for the destruction of slavery.

Wiltse, The New Nation at 117 (cited in note 31). But see Robert V. Remini, The Legacy of Andrew Jackson 86–87 (LSU, 1988): "Had the issue involved slavery, . . . other southern states would surely have sided with South Carolina"; Ellis, The Union at Risk at 190 (cited in note 4), noting that commitments to states' rights had arisen "well before slavery became a national issue" and were not confined to advocates of slavery.

[77]Calhoun to Frederick W. Symmes, Jul 26, 1831, 11 Calhoun Papers at 413–39. Symmes was editor of the Pendleton, S.C. *Messenger*. The letter was intended to be published, and it was.

[78]Draft Report on Federal Relations, Nov 20 [?], 1831, id at 485–509.

[79]Calhoun to James Hamilton, Jr., Aug 28, 1832, id at 613–49. The leading student of the nullification crisis has described the Hamilton letter as the most comprehensive statement of Calhoun's matured position. Freehling, Prelude to Civil War at 165 (cited in note 4).

gument on the critical issue of Supreme Court review, to which we shall recur.[80] In the Hamilton letter he set forth the outlines of his theory of the "concurring majority," which would lay the apparent intellectual foundation of a constitutional amendment he would suggest in his valedictory speech in the Senate nearly twenty years later as a condition of the South's continued membership in the Union.[81]

In the meantime, however, something momentous had occurred. In 1828, it will be remembered, Calhoun had urged the legislature to endorse nullification in principle but not to nullify the tariff: The new Administration should be given a chance to eliminate the problem. In July 1832 he threw down the gauntlet. Congress had shown it was willing to do "nothing, that [would] give satisfaction to the South in regard to the Tariff"; South Carolina must act on her own.[82]

In fact Congress had done something that one with less of a chip on his shoulder might well have considered a significant gesture toward the South. It had moved to third reading in the Senate, and soon would pass, a new tariff law, sponsored by former President John Quincy Adams, that essentially reduced customs duties to 1824 levels.[83] But that was not enough for John C. Calhoun, and South Carolina prepared to nullify federal law.

The legislature authorized the election of delegates to a state convention to consider the nullification question.[84] Nullifiers won by a substantial margin, and Calhoun drafted yet another statement,[85] which this time was adopted. It was the basis of an address designed to accompany South Carolina's Ordinance of Nullification, which the Convention promulgated November 24, 1832.[86]

On nullification the Address repeated the familiar argument that it was for the states,

[80]See 11 Calhoun Papers at 422 and the discussion accompanying notes 119–30.

[81]11 Calhoun Papers at 640–48. See also Cong Deb, 22d Cong, 2d Sess 547–48 (1833), where Calhoun briefly laid out his theory for the Senate. For the final version of this thesis see his undated Disquisition on Government, in Richard K. Crallé, ed, 1 The Works of John C. Calhoun 1 (Appleton, 1854), and his complementary Discourse on the Constitution and Government of the United States, id at 109, in which he applied what he now called the "concurrent majority" theory to the United States and said (id at 391) the Constitution should be amended to give the South a veto on federal legislation. For his amendment proposal see Descent into the Maelstrom, ch 8. In the context of Calhoun's letter to Hamilton, however, this theory served only to counter the objection that nullification was inconsistent with the widely accepted principle of majority rule. 11 Calhoun Papers at 640.

[82]Calhoun to Samuel D. Ingham, Jul 8, 1832, 11 Calhoun Papers at 602, 603. See also Calhoun to Waddy Thompson, Jr., Jul 8, 1832, id at 603, 604: "Let every Carolinian do his duty."

[83]4 Stat 583 (Jul 14, 1832); see Van Deusen, The Jacksonian Era at 59–60. But see Wiltse, The New Nation at 116–17 (cited in note 31), arguing that "[f]rom the standpoint of the South" the new law "was no better than the reprobated bill of abominations." The debates leading to the 1832 statute are reported in Cong Deb, 22d Cong, 1st Sess 66 et seq and Cong Deb, 22d Cong, 2d Sess 6 et seq. On the principal questions they add nothing to what we already know, save that South Carolina Representative William Drayton bravely argued that nullification was unconstitutional, Cong Deb, 22d Cong, 1st Sess 3266–67. There was also a little squeaking about the propriety of asking the executive to draft a bill, Cong Deb, 22d Cong, 2d Sess 6–59. The Senate, argued Maine Senator Peleg Sprague, should not be "merely the recorder of the decrees of the Executive." Id at 18. For earlier barking up the same tree see The Federalist Period at 29–31.

[84]1 SC Stats 309 (Oct 26, 1932).

[85]Address to the People of the United States, 11 Calhoun Papers at 669–81 (Nov 1 [?], 1832).

[86]1 SC Stats 329, reprinted in Freehling, The Nullification Era at 150 (cited in note 3). The final form of the Address can be found at 1 SC Stats 346–54. For the Convention's additional address to the people of South Carolina see id at 334–45.

as parties to the compact, to determine the constitutionality of federal law.[87] On the tariff it made the equally familiar argument of pretext: Neither the tax power nor the commerce power could be employed for the ulterior purpose of promoting manufacture.[88]

Here is the essence of the Ordinance itself:

> Whereas the Congress of the United States, by various acts, purporting to be acts laying duties and imposts on foreign imports, but in reality intended for the protection of domestic manufacturers, . . . hath exceeded its just powers under the Constitution, . . .
>
> We, therefore, the People of the State of South Carolina in Convention assembled, do Declare and Ordain . . . That the several acts and parts of acts of the Congress of the United States, purporting to be laws for the imposing of duties and imposts on the importation of foreign commodities . . . are null, void, and no law, nor binding upon this State, its officers, or citizens; and all promises, contracts, and obligations, made or entered into . . . with purpose to secure the duties imposed by the said acts, and all judicial proceedings which shall be hereafter had in affirmance thereof, are, and shall be held, utterly null and void.
>
> And it is further ordained, That it shall not be lawful for any of the constituted authorities, whether of this State or of the United States, to enforce the payment of duties imposed by the said acts within the limits of this State; but it shall be the duty of the Legislature to adopt such measures and pass such acts as may be necessary to give full effect to this Ordinance, and to prevent the enforcement and arrest the operation of the said acts and parts of acts . . . within the limits of this State, from and after the first day of February next. . . .
>
> And it is further Ordained, That in no case of law or equity, decided in the Courts of this State, wherein shall be drawn in question the authority of this Ordinance, or the validity of such act or acts of the Legislature as may be passed for the purpose of giving effect thereto, or the validity of the aforesaid acts of Congress, imposing duties, shall any appeal be taken or allowed to the Supreme Court of the United States, nor shall any copy of the record be permitted or allowed for that purpose; and if any such appeal shall be attempted to be taken, the courts of this State shall proceed to execute and enforce their judgments, without reference to such attempted appeal, and the person or persons attempting to take such appeal may be dealt with as for a contempt of the Court.
>
> And it is further Ordained, That all persons . . . holding any office of honor, profit, or trust, civil or military, under this State (members of the Legislature excepted), shall . . . take an oath, well and truly to obey, execute and enforce this Ordinance, and such act or acts of the Legislature as may be passed in pursuance thereof . . . ; and no juror shall be empannelled [sic] in any of the Courts of this State, in any cause in which shall

[87] 11 Calhoun Papers at 670.

[88] Id at 673.

> be in question this Ordinance, or any act of the Legislature passed in pursuance thereof, unless he shall first . . . have taken an oath that he will well and truly obey, execute, and enforce this Ordinance, and such act or acts of the Legislature as may be passed to carry the same into operation and effect . . . .
>
> And we, the People of South Carolina, . . . Do further Declare that we will not submit to the application of force, . . . to reduce this State to obedience; but that we will consider the passage, by Congress, of any act . . . to coerce the State, shut up her ports, destroy or harass her commerce, or to enforce the acts hereby declared to be null and void, otherwise than through the civil tribunals of the country, as inconsistent with the longer continuance of South Carolina in the Union; and that the people of this State will thenceforth hold themselves absolved from all further obligation to maintain or preserve their political connexion with the people of the other States, and will forthwith proceed to organize a separate Government, and do all other acts and things which sovereign and independent States may of right do.[89]

Cry, the beloved country! The Ordinance indeed went beyond mere protest against the enactment of unconstitutional laws. It purported to deprive federal officers of their right to institute judicial proceedings and federal courts of their jurisdiction to decide them. It authorized the imposition of penalties for exercising a right of appeal given by federal law. It required state executive officers, judges, and jurors to disobey federal statutes. It promised secession if nonjudicial steps were taken to collect the tariff.

Not all of this followed even if South Carolina was correct that the tariff exceeded Congress's powers and that a state had the right to resist unconstitutional legislation. The Ordinance in effect nullified a whole raft of federal laws it did not pretend were invalid; the supremacy clause made clear they had the right of way.[90]

IV. President Jackson's Response

"I had supposed," wrote President Jackson in October 1830, "that every one acquainted with me knew, that I was opposed to the nullifying doctrine, and my toast at the Jefferson dinner was sufficient evidence of the fact."[91]

[89]1 SC Stats at 329–31, reprinted in Ames, State Documents on Federal Relations at 170–73 (cited in note 1).

[90]As applied to state officers the South Carolina Supreme Court, by a 2–1 vote, struck down the oath requirement (after the crisis was over), essentially because it conflicted with a state constitutional provision on the same subject. State ex rel McCready v Hunt, 2 Hill (SC) 1 (1834). As the reporter's note discloses, the state constitution was subsequently amended to require officers to swear "allegiance . . . to the State of South Carolina." Id at 1 n.(a).

[91]Jackson to Robert Oliver (a pseudonym of Joel Poinsett), Oct 26, 1830, 4 Jackson Correspondence at 191. Poinsett, who would serve four years as Secretary of War under Van Buren, was a leader of the Unionist party in South Carolina. For his courageous role in opposing nullification see J. Fred Rippy, Joel R. Poinsett, Versatile American 134–56 (Greenwood, 1968) (first published in 1935). A state had no more right to withdraw from the Union, said Poinsett in a widely reported campaign speech in 1832, "than an individual living in

Martin Van Buren, who was there, told the story of the Jefferson Day dinner in his autobiography.[92] Having become suspicious that Calhoun and his friends were planning to turn a celebration in honor of Thomas Jefferson into a forum to promote nullification, Jackson and his Secretary of State (as Van Buren then was) decided he should counter them with a toast of his own, and he did: "Our Federal Union—it must be preserved." Jackson's message, Van Buren continued, was not lost on his audience. One opposition newspaper observed that

> it was as much as to say, in reply to the authors of some of the preceding sentiments,—"you may complain of the tariff and perhaps with reason, but so long as it is the law it shall as certainly be maintained as my name is Andrew Jackson."

And that, wrote Van Buren, "was precisely what the President's toast was designed to say."[93]

Jackson continued to deny the legitimacy of nullification in letters to his friends.[94] To Senator Hayne, one of the leaders of the nullifying faction, he was equally blunt. Hayne had written rather testily to inquire whether the President's failure to select one of the Senator's protégés as District Attorney meant that those "of the party in S Carolina, who assist and maintain State rights" were to be "excluded from a fair participation in offices."[95] Jackson began quite properly by denying that he was accountable to anyone for his decision; the Constitution left nominations to his discretion. He went on to say that the applicant in question had been represented to him as a nullifier. He would be the first to insist that state rights be maintained, but "not by conceding to one state authority to declare an act of Congress void"; if Congress and the President should overstep their

---

a community of laws has a right to withdraw himself from their jurisdiction . . . because they appear to him tyrannical and oppressive." Id at 141.

[92]Van Buren, Autobiography at 413–17. See also Van Deusen, The Jacksonian Era at 44–45; Remini, Jackson at 195–97.

[93]Calhoun followed with the revealing parry "The Union—next to our liberty the most dear . . . ," which Webster had repudiated in his second reply to Hayne (see text accompanying note 50). Van Buren's riposte would for the moment carry the day: "Mutual forbearance and reciprocal concessions . . . ," which Clay and Calhoun would ultimately arrange.

Jackson is also reported to have told a South Carolina Congressman about this time that he indeed had a message for the people of that state:

> [P]lease give my compliments to my friends in your State, and say to them, that if a single drop of blood shall be shed there in opposition to the laws of the United States, I will hang the first man I can lay my hand on engaged in such treasonable conduct, upon the first tree I can reach.

Quoted in James Parton, 3 Life of Andrew Jackson 284–85 (Mason, 1860); Remini, Jackson at 197.

[94]E.g., Jackson to Joel Poinsett, Nov 7, 1832, 4 Jackson Correspondence at 485, 486 ("The duty of the Executive is a plain one, the laws will be executed and the union preserved by all the constitutional and legal means he is invested with"); Jackson to Poinsett, Dec 2, 1832, id at 493, 494 ("Nullification . . . means insurrection and war; and the other states have a right to put it down"); Jackson to Gen. John Coffee, Dec 14, 1832, id at 499, 499–500 (branding nullification an "absurdity" that would turn the Constitution into "a rope of sand" and saying that although many powers were reserved to the states neither nullification nor secession was among them); Jackson to Van Buren, Dec 23, 1832, id at 504–5.

[95]Hayne to Webster, Feb 4, 1831, 4 Jackson Correspondence at 238–39.

powers, the remedy was the next election.

> That a state has the power to nullify the Legislative enactments of the General Government I never did believe, nor have I ever understood Mr. Jefferson to hold such an opinion. That ours is a Government of laws, and depends on a will of the majority, is the true reading of the Constitution .... These being my opinions, religiously entertained, situated as I am, charged with the Executive of the laws, and the preservation of the union and the Constitution, it could not be expected that I would select any one to prosecute for a violation of them, who holds that a portion of our revenue laws is not binding, and who would declare that the Union should be dissolved rather than that these laws should be permitted to be enforced.[96]

On the broader question whether he would rule out all members of South Carolina's "state right party" Jackson was equally incisive: "I proscribe no man for honest difference of opinion, and I shall be the last to withhold from any portion of my fellow Citizens the privileges of the Constitution for an honest exercise of opinions which they sincerely entertain ...."[97]

It should have come as no surprise, therefore, that, after a conciliatory start, Jackson came out against the Nullification Ordinance with all guns blazing.[98] His fourth Annual Message, delivered only ten days after the Ordinance was adopted, offered an olive branch and downplayed the danger. Since the debt was about to be extinguished and protective tariffs were divisive, he wrote, it was time to begin reducing them. In the meantime, however, opposition to the revenue laws "in one quarter of the United States" had "arisen to a height which threatens to thwart their execution, if not to endanger the integrity of the Union." He hoped that "moderation and good sense would prevail," and if they did not he thought existing laws "fully adequate to the suppression of such attempts as may be immediately made." If that proved wrong, he said, he would ask Congress for

[96]Jackson to Hayne, Feb 8, 1831, id at 241–42.

[97]Id at 242. Compare the various versions of an apparently unused memorandum prepared by Secretary of War Jefferson Davis in 1853, declaring it the policy of the Pierce Administration to appoint or retain no officer who "assail[ed]" or "agitate[d] against" slavery "as it exists in some of the states" or who sought to dissolve the Union. 5 Davis Papers at 22–23.

[98]Nor did the President confine himself to mere verbal protest. Warned that nullification was coming and urged to take steps to protect the revenue, he ordered the Secretary of War to exercise special vigilance to protect forts at Charleston from capture and to "defend them to the last extremity." He dispatched a special agent to investigate possible disloyalty among federal officers in South Carolina and sent 5,000 muskets and two warships to Charleston. If things got worse, he said, he would order federal troops to South Carolina, collect customs duties at one of the forts or on an island, and prosecute leaders of the resistance for treason. See Poinsett to Jackson, Oct 16, 1832, 4 Jackson Correspondence at 481; Jackson to Lewis Cass, Oct 29, 1832, id at 483; to George Breathitt, Nov 7, 1832, id at 484; to Poinsett, Dec 2, 1832, id at 493; to Poinsett, Dec 9, 1832, id at 497, 498; to Van Buren, Dec 15, 1832, id at 500. As Commander in Chief, he wrote soon afterward, he could send regular troops wherever he pleased. Jackson to Poinsett, Jan 24, 1833, 5 Jackson Correspondence at 11 and Feb 7, 1833, id at 16. In all of this Jackson's actions compared very favorably with those of President Buchanan the next time there was a threat to the Charleston forts. See Descent into the Maelstrom, ch 10.

additional authority.[99]

Less than a week later the President revealed the steel within his glove in a no-nonsense proclamation directed chiefly to the people of South Carolina.[100] Even under the Articles of Confederation, Jackson wrote, "no state could legally annul a decision of the Congress or refuse to submit to its execution," for the Articles had required every state to "abide by the determinations of Congress on all questions which by that Confederation should be submitted to them." Alas, he added, the Articles had provided no means of enforcing Congress's decisions. The new Constitution, on the other hand, designed to form "a more perfect Union," expressly made federal law supreme and required state judges to respect it. It could not have been the aim of those who approved that Constitution, said Jackson, to substitute for the old Confederation "a form of government dependent for its existence on the local interest, the party spirit, of a State, or of a prevailing faction of a State."

> I consider, then, the power to annul a law of the United States, assumed by one State, incompatible with the existence of the Union, contradicted expressly by the letter of the Constitution, unauthorized by its spirit, inconsistent with every principle on which it was founded, and destructive of the great object for which it was formed.[101]

The tariff, Jackson went on, was not unconstitutional. It had been enacted pursuant to the express authorization to levy taxes, duties, and imposts, and the motives of those who passed it were immaterial.

> However apparent this purpose may be in the present case, nothing can be more dangerous than to admit the position that an unconstitutional purpose entertained by the members who assent to a law enacted under a constitutional power shall make that law void. For how is that purpose to be ascertained? Who is to make the scrutiny? How often may bad purposes be falsely imputed, in how many cases are they concealed by false professions, in how many is no declaration of motive made? Admit this doctrine, and you give to the States an uncontrolled right to decide, and every law may be annulled under this pretext.

If a state could nullify federal law on such a flimsy ground, said Jackson, it was in vain that the Framers had invested Congress with the tax power and with authority to pass laws necessary to carry it into execution, in vain that they had made federal law supreme and

[99] 2 Richardson at 591, 596–99 (Dec 4, 1832). Jackson had spelled out this approach in a letter to Van Buren on November 18, saying that he planned to say little of nullification but to treat it as "a mere buble [sic]." 4 Jackson Correspondence at 493. That Jackson knew of the Ordinance when he sent his Annual Message to Congress is shown by his letter of the same date to Edward Livingston, id at 494–95, in which he mentioned the Ordinance and asked whether in his forthcoming proclamation on the subject, which he was already preparing, he should threaten those who actually resisted enforcement with prosecution for treason.

[100] 2 Richardson at 640–56 (Dec 10, 1832). This proclamation, it is said, was drafted by Secretary of State Edward Livingston. Van Deusen, The Jacksonian Era at 74.

[101] 2 Richardson at 642–43. See Articles of Confederation, Art 13, 1 Stat 4, 8 (1778).

required state officers to take a oath to support it.[102]

But the Ordinance did not stop at nullifying the tariff. It equally nullified both the supremacy clause and the Judiciary Act's provision for Supreme Court review of state-court decisions, which had "never been alleged to be unconstitutional."[103] Moreover, it threatened secession; and a state had no constitutional right to secede.

The theory of the Ordinance, the President said, was that the Constitution was a compact that each state could dissolve if it concluded that others had departed from its provisions. But the Constitution "forms a *government,* not a league"; secession "destroys the unity of a nation."

> Secession, like any other revolutionary act, may be morally justified by the extremity of oppression; but to call it a constitutional right is confounding the meaning of terms . . . .

Even if the states were sovereign, he added, and if the Constitution had been formed by compact, "there would be no right in any one State to exonerate itself from its obligations."[104]

Jackson ended with a warning. The Constitution, he observed, made it the President's duty to "take care that the laws be faithfully executed," and he intended to do so. "Disunion by armed force," he concluded, "is *treason.*"[105]

But South Carolina did not recede from its position,[106] and five weeks later Jackson reported to Congress that the emergency to which he had referred in his Annual Message had indeed arisen. The South Carolina legislature had adopted implementing statutes that

[102] 2 Richardson at 644. Any objection to the purposes to which the revenue raised by the tariff would be applied, Jackson added, should be directed against subsequent appropriations, not against the tax itself. Id at 646. Cf Massachusetts v Mellon, 262 US 447, 485–87 (1923).

[103] 2 Richardson at 647.

[104] Id at 648–50. See also id at 649:

> Because the Union was formed by a compact, it is said the parties to that compact may, when they feel themselves aggrieved, depart from it; but it is precisely because it is a compact that they can not. A compact is an agreement or binding obligation.

[105] Id at 652, 654. The concept of treason figured prominently in Jackson's writings at this time. In one draft of his proclamation he proposed to say that resistance to the laws would constitute treason; in three letters he said the same of the mere raising of an army. Jackson to Edward Livingston, Dec 4, 1832, 4 Jackson Correspondence at 494–95; to Joel Poinsett, Dec 9, 1932, id at 497–98; to Van Buren, Dec 15 and 25, 1832, id at 500, 505, 506. The first assertion, while questionable as an original matter, was in accord with some lower-court decisions; the second had been rejected by the Supreme Court. See The Federalist Period at 190 n.129, 227 n.173; Ex parte Bollman, 8 US 75, 127 (1807); see The Jeffersonians at 137, discussing the Burr conspiracy. Van Buren gently dissuaded the President from stating his conclusions aloud, noting that constructive treason was "justly unpopular in the United States." Van Buren to Jackson, Dec 27, 1832, 4 Jackson Correspondence at 506, 507. Thereupon Jackson took steps to conform his rhetoric to constitutional standards, urging his friend Poinsett to advise him as soon as South Carolina troops assembled "in hostile array in opposition to the execution of the laws." Jackson to Poinsett, Jan 16, 1833, 5 Jackson Correspondence at 5–6.

[106] Indeed the state legislature formally protested that in issuing the proclamation the President had exceeded his powers, and Senator Stephen Miller presented the protest to Congress. See 1 SC Stats at 356–57; Cong Deb, 22d Cong, 2d Sess 80–81. Robert Hayne, now Governor of South Carolina, issued a counter-proclamation of his own, 1 SC Stats 358–70 (Dec 21, 1832).

laid bare its determination to obstruct collection of the revenue;[107] the Governor had begun to raise an army; it was time for Congress to make additional provision to ensure execution of the law.[108]

If the United States could not defend themselves against nullification, said Jackson, "the supremacy of the laws is at an end."[109] If Congress exceeded its powers, "the proper remedy is a recourse to the judiciary."

> The law of a State can not authorize the commission of a crime against the United States or any act which, according to the supreme law of the Union, would be otherwise unlawful; and . . . if there be any case in which a State, as such, is affected by a law beyond the scope of judicial power, the remedy consists in appeals to the people, either to effect a change in the representation or to procure relief by an amendment to the Constitution.[110]

It was not unworthy of notice, Jackson added, that while purporting to nullify federal law South Carolina claimed still to be part of the Union,

> to participate in the national councils and to share in the public benefits without contributing to the public burdens, thus asserting the dangerous anomaly of continuing in an association without acknowledging any other obligation to its laws than what depends upon her own will.[111]

Jackson closed with a few specific recommendations for legislation to ensure enforcement of the laws. The President should be authorized if necessary to eliminate ports of entry (such as Beaufort and Georgetown) in order "to establish the custom-house at some secure place." Federal officers should be authorized to remove to federal court actions brought on account of acts performed in the course of their duties. Existing statutes should be amended to permit the President to employ the militia to execute the laws while Congress was in session and without "the ceremony" of a prior proclamation.[112] Finally, Jackson took the occasion to remind Congress that he had already asked it to lower the offending tariff.[113]

It was time for Congress to get cracking.

[107]See 1 SC Stats 371 and 375 (Dec 20, 1832).

[108]2 Richardson at 610–12 (Jan 16, 1833). For details of South Carolina's actions see id at 614–17. Jackson at one point had contemplated asking Congress to define and punish the keeping of state troops in peacetime. See his memorandum of Nov ?, 1832, 4 Jackson Correspondence at 493. The relevant provision of Article I, § 10 says nothing of legislative implementation; cf the controversy over the Fugitive Slave Act of 1850, discussed in Descent into the Maelstrom, ch 8.

[109]2 Richardson at 617.

[110]Id at 623.

[111]Id at 625.

[112]Id at 629–31.

[113]Id at 611, 624.

V. THE COMPROMISE OF 1833

President Jackson had brandished both stick and carrot: The law must be enforced, but the tariff should be reduced. Congress began to work on both halves of his proposal at once. New York Representative Gulian Verplanck offered a bill to reduce customs duties;[114] Pennsylvania Senator William Wilkins reported one (popularly known as the Force Bill) to reinforce execution of the law.[115]

Most of the shouting was over the latter, and most of it was about nullification. No sooner was the bill reported than Calhoun, who had resigned the Vice-Presidency to lead South Carolina's defense in the Senate, offered a set of resolutions restating South Carolina's position: The Constitution was a compact, and each state had the right to determine whether Congress had exceeded its powers.[116] Felix Grundy of Tennessee, who had supported nullification three years before,[117] offered a competing set of resolutions: The states having surrendered to Congress the power to tax imports "without any reservation," the tariffs of 1828 and 1832 were constitutional; South Carolina had no right to nullify them or to obstruct their enforcement.[118] John M. Clayton of Delaware, thinking Grundy had conceded nullification in principle, had an alternative of his own: The Supreme Court, not the individual states, must determine the limits of congressional power.[119]

Like others before him, George Bibb of Kentucky responded that the Supreme Court could decide only "cases in law and equity," not "political" cases.[120] This argument was no better than it had been before; as Clayton said, in a suit to collect the tariff unconstitutionality would be a defense.[121] More troubling was a suggestion that drew strength from the fact that President Jackson had employed a related argument against *state* invalidation of the tariff: Even if it had jurisdiction, Bibb argued, the Court could not effectively determine the constitutionality of the law, because "the judicial tribunals cannot go out of the act to look for the motives of members of the Congress"; the Court itself had so decided in *Fletcher v Peck* in 1810.[122]

[114]See HR Rep 14, 22d Cong, 2d Sess (1832); Cong Deb, 22d Cong, 2d Sess 958 (Jan 8, 1833). A Jacksonian Democrat who served in the House from 1825 until 1833, Verplanck was a man of considerable literary attainments and much ability. Despite his firm opposition to protective tariffs as a matter of policy, he wrote a widely disseminated letter defending federal authority to impose them under the commerce power. "Regulations of commerce" had *meant* high tariffs in colonial days, he argued, and Congress's reasons for exercising its express powers were immaterial. Dropped by his party for apostasy during the Bank war, he retired after a few adventures in New York politics to prepare a complete edition of Shakespeare's plays and look after impoverished immigrants in New York City. See Robert W. July, The Essential New Yorker: Gulian Crommelin Verplanck 148–55, 177, 238–43, 256–60 (Duke, 1951).

[115]Cong Deb, 22d Cong, 2d Sess 244–46 (Jan 28, 1833). As Professor Freehling has argued, "Force Bill" was something of a misnomer, as Jackson mostly sought means of collecting the tariff *without* force. Freehling, Prelude to Civil War at 285 (cited in note 4).

[116]Cong Deb, 22d Cong, 2d Sess 191–92.

[117]See Cong Deb, 21st Cong, 1st Sess 210, 213–14 (Mar 1, 1830).

[118]Cong Deb, 22d Cong, 2d Sess 192–93.

[119]Id at 231–32.

[120]Id at 283–90.

[121]Id at 389.

[122]Id at 290–91; see *Fletcher*, 10 US 87, 130–31 (1810). Calhoun had raised this point in his Fort Hill Address in 1831. Calhoun to Frederick W. Symmes, Jul 26, 1831, 11 Calhoun Papers at 413, 423. Other aspects of this letter are noted in the text accompanying notes 77–80. Justice Story, of all people, appeared to endorse Calhoun's position:

John Marshall, who had written *Fletcher,* had also written in *McCulloch v Maryland* that the Court would strike down any law enacted as "a pretext . . . for the accomplishment of objects not entrusted to the government."[123] Congress had never made a secret of its desire to protect domestic industry; the preamble to the very first tariff law had proclaimed protection as one of its purposes.[124] A court that thought such a purpose illegitimate would surely be in a position to say so, just as the Supreme Court was later able (quite rightly) to invalidate a penalty on the use of child labor wrapped in the "verbal cellophane" of a tax.[125]

That said, it must be conceded that the Court's ability to ferret out improper purposes is limited,[126] as both Marshall and Jackson argued, and moreover that its willingness to undertake the quest has been notably inconstant in later years.[127] Whether or not the tariff was among them, there was (as Hayne had said in his debate with Webster) a set of constitutional questions the Supreme Court could never effectively decide. Hayne rightly mentioned issues respecting the scope of congressional power to spend,[128] most of which still escape review for want of a plaintiff with standing.[129] Indeed, whether or not the courts *could* determine the validity of the tariff, they had not done so. The real question presented by nullification was therefore not the easy one whether a federal judgment upholding the tariff would be conclusive between the parties; the unmistakable grant of jurisdiction made clear that it would.[130] It was rather whether the states were obliged to

---

> Yet cases can readily be imagined, in which a tax may be laid, or a treaty made, upon motives and grounds wholly beside the intention of the constitution. The remedy, however, in such cases is solely by an appeal to the people at the elections; or by the salutary power of amendment, provided by the constitution itself.

1 Story, § 374.

[123]17 US 316, 423 (1819).

[124]1 Stat 24 (Jul 4, 1789).

[125]Bailey v Drexel Furniture Co, 259 US 20 (1922); The Second Century at 173–74. Similarly, the Court has had modest but significant success in rooting out unacknowledged and improper considerations of race or religion in cases in which the challenged action could hardly have been based on anything else. E.g., Guinn v United States, 238 US 347 (1915) (grandfather clause); Stone v Graham, 449 US 39 (1980) (posting of the Ten Commandments).

[126]See, e.g., Lassiter v Northampton County Board of Elections, 360 US 45 (1959), upholding a literacy test for voters against the widely accepted contention it was designed as a means of evading the fifteenth amendment.

[127]See, e.g., United States v Kahriger, 345 US 22 (1953) (refusing to invalidate a tax obviously designed to suppress the business of wagering); United States v O'Brien, 391 US 367 (1968) (disregarding evidence that prohibition of draft-card burning was intended to silence opposition to the Vietnam War).

[128]Cong Deb, 21st Cong, 1st Sess 88 (Jan 27, 1830). Calhoun repeated the general point in 1833, Cong Deb, 22d Cong, 2d Sess 769.

[129]Massachusetts v Mellon, 262 US 447, 485–87 (1923).

[130]Nothing in Jackson's Bank veto message (see section I of chapter 3) or in Lincoln's later assertion of legislative freedom to reexamine the issues determined in the *Dred Scott* case (Descent into the Maelstrom, ch 9) even remotely called this obvious conclusion into question. More embarrassing was the suggestion that Jackson had permitted Georgia in effect to nullify Supreme Court judgments respecting state authority over Indians. See, e.g., Cong Deb, 22d Cong, 2d Sess 454 (South Carolina Sen. Stephen Miller). Jackson never explained why he thought the cases distinguishable, though he worked hard to isolate South Carolina by placating the Georgia authorities. See Robert V. Remini, Andrew Jackson and the Course of American Democracy, 1833–1845 9 (Harper & Row, 1984). Georgia Senator John Forsyth, while lamely suggesting that the cases

respect federal law whose constitutionality the courts had not resolved.

The supremacy clause did not answer the question, for federal law was supreme only if it was constitutional. The issue, as Webster had said in 1830 and as Calhoun repeated in 1833, was who should determine the question of constitutionality.[131]

Webster addressed this issue in a major reply to Calhoun during the Force Bill debate in February 1833. The Supreme Court had the last word in cases that came before it, said Webster, and if no case could be brought Congress was the ultimate judge of its own powers. For otherwise, he argued, either federal law would vary from state to state or the minority would rule.[132]

To buttress this conclusion Webster recurred to the contrast between the Constitution and the Articles of Confederation. The whole point of the Constitution, he said, was to permit the Central Government to impose taxes without state consent and to execute its own laws. The trouble with the Articles, as Oliver Ellsworth had said in the Connecticut ratifying convention, was that they allowed a single state to veto federal law.[133]

That really is the heart of the matter, isn't it? To give the states the last word, even if only when no court has spoken, would contradict the Framers' central principle—made explicit, as Jackson said, by the necessary and proper and take care clauses—that the Government may execute its own laws.[134]

As Webster had earlier conceded, no one was required to obey an unconstitutional law. In most cases the courts were open to afford redress. But the right to challenge unconstitutional laws has seldom been understood to justify resisting arrest, obstructing enforcement, or fomenting rebellion. If the Constitution is to accomplish its central goals, the President must be free to execute federal laws until some competent court tells him not to.[135] Alexander Hamilton had said it in The Federalist:

> [I]f the execution of the laws of the national government should not require the intervention of the state legislatures, if they were to pass into

---

were different because Georgia was right on the merits, bravely conceded that in her case too the President could have used force to enforce an adverse decision. Id at 593–94. The most the incident can prove is that Jackson (like Clay with respect to the Bank, see The Jeffersonians at 253, 256–57) had learned from experience.

[131]See text accompanying note 36; Cong Deb, 22d Cong, 2d Sess 767.

[132]Id at 575–76.

[133]Id at 560, 568. See also id at 502, 505 (Virginia Sen. William Rives); id at 668 (Sen. Grundy); Jackson to Nathaniel Macon, Sep 2, 1833, 5 Jackson Correspondence at 177–78 (adding that the Constitution had formed a "more perfect Union" by enabling the United States to enforce their own laws); The Federalist, Nos 15, 21; 1 Story, § 248. For Ellsworth's argument see 2 Elliott's Debates at 197. Mississippi Senator George Poindexter protested that the problem with the Articles was that the states had vetoed *valid* legislation, Cong Deb, 22d Cong, 2d Sess 634, but Calhoun had already answered him: A government with unlimited authority to interpret has unlimited power. See text accompanying notes 15–16.

[134]US Const, Art I, § 8, cl 18; Art II, § 3; see also the militia clause of Article I, § 8, cl 15, quoted in note 141. For Jackson's argument see 2 Richardson at 625, 643; see also 1 Story, § 322. That the Framers had chosen judicial review rather than nullification as the principal check on federal usurpation provided a strong argument against broad interpretation of the political-question doctrine, for if there was no court to act as censor nothing stood in the way of excess but the self-denying patriotism of the President and Congress.

[135]South Carolina Senator Stephen Miller predictably pointed out that (in vetoing extension of the Bank charter) Jackson himself had insisted that the President could interpret the Constitution for himself (Cong Deb, 22d Cong, 2d Sess 454), but the cases were not parallel; a presidential check is entirely consistent with the Framers' decision that the United States could execute their own laws. See section I of chapter 3.

> immediate operation upon the citizens themselves, the particular governments could not interrupt their progress without an open and violent assertion of an unconstitutional power.[136]

Calhoun tabled his nullification resolutions without asking for a vote.[137] Outside South Carolina, nullification of the tariff had precious little support.[138]

The Force Bill itself, as Senator Wilkins explained, closely tracked the President's recommendations.[139] There were only occasional objections to its provisions, and there was no merit to any of them. Calhoun and Bibb denied that the United States could use coercive power against a state,[140] but nothing in the bill suggested action against South Carolina itself, and there was no doubt that Congress could authorize the use of force to execute the laws.[141] To require payment of duties in cash, some argued, would give a preference to the ports of other states or offend the requirement that duties be uniform.[142]

[136]The Federalist No 16. Elsewhere in the same papers, as defenders of nullification hastened to point out, Hamilton had made noises that previewed the Virginia and Kentucky Resolutions. The state legislatures would be "suspicious and jealous guardians . . . against incroachments [sic] from the Foederal government"; they would be ever prepared "to sound the alarm to the people and not only to be the VOICE but if necessary the ARM of their discontent." If Congress should "betray" its constituents by usurping authority, the remedy would be a resort to "that original right of self-defence, which is paramount to all positive forms of government"; state governments would provide "complete security against invasions of public liberty" by adopting "a regular plan of opposition, in which they can combine all the resources of the community." Id, Nos 26, 28. So far this sounds to me like an invocation of the extraconstitutional right of revolution, especially in light of the explicit assertion, quoted in the text, that resistance to the enforcement of federal law would be unconstitutional.

More problematic is Hamilton's insistence in The Federalist No 33 that only those laws enacted "*pursuant to* the Constitution" would be the supreme law of the land; those that invaded the rights of the states would be "merely acts of usurpation and deserve to be treated as such." It is possible to read this passage as qualifying Hamilton's earlier assurance that states had no right to interfere with the execution of federal law: As Senator Bibb would suggest in 1833, the states were free to nullify *unconstitutional* laws. The trouble with this interpretation is that it effectively nullifies Hamilton's express declaration that under the Constitution the United States would no longer be dependent on the states; if individual states determine the validity of federal law, we are back to the Confederation.

[137]Cong Deb, 22d Cong, 2d Sess 785.

[138]Felix Grundy, who in the past had made nullification noises himself, called attention to this fact during the Senate debate. Id at 667. See also id at 470 (Sen. Clay). Some opponents, to be sure, argued only that South Carolina had no just basis for nullification on the facts (see, e.g., Cong Deb, 22d Cong, 2d Sess 282, 302, 305 (Sen. Bibb); id at 370–71 (Sen. Tyler)), while the Virginia legislature ambiguously announced that it found no support for South Carolina's actions in its Resolutions and report of 1798–99. Ames, State Documents on Federal Relations at 187 (cited in note 1). The legislatures of Georgia, Alabama, North Carolina, and Mississippi, however, all joined Webster and Jackson in condemning nullification itself in terms ranging from "unsound . . . , dangerous . . . , [and] unconstitutional" (Alabama) to "revolutionary" and "subversive" (North Carolina) and a "heresy, fatal to the existence of the Union" (Mississippi). See id at 178–85.

[139]Cong Deb, 22d Cong, 2d Sess 247.

[140]Id at 190 (Sen. Calhoun); id at 280 (Sen. Bibb).

[141]See US Const, Art I, § 8, cl 15: "The Congress shall have power . . . [t]o provide for calling forth the militia to execute the laws of the Union . . . ." As Wilkins observed, Congress had exercised these powers in 1792, 1795, and 1807. Cong Deb, 22d Cong, 2d Sess 262. Similar arguments would be made and disputed at the time of secession nearly thirty years later. See Descent into the Maelstrom, ch 10. The arguments in the text equally refute Senator Bibb's peculiar suggestion (Cong Deb, 22d Cong, 2d Sess 270) that to authorize the President to use force was to permit him to declare war.

[142]Id at 269 (Sen. Bibb); id at 372 (Sen. Tyler); id at 535 (Sen. Calhoun); id at 1867–69 (Rep. Foster); HR Rep 85, 22d Cong, 2d Sess 3, reprinted at Cong Deb App, 22d Cong, 2d Sess 201 (Tennessee Rep. John Bell). See US Const, Art I, § 9, cl 6; Art I, § 8, cl 1.

Since there was no other practicable means of collection in South Carolina, however, *not* to require cash would create far more serious problems of both preference and disuniformity, as Webster had already shown.[143] Calhoun suggested in passing that the bill would delegate to the President Congress's power to regulate commerce and extend the jurisdiction of federal courts to cases outside Article III.[144] But the authority given the President (such as to move custom houses when necessary to ensure collection) seemed the sort of detail that could fairly be deemed execution of congressional policy; and for constitutional purposes suits against revenue officers arising from their duties arose under the laws of the United States, since in each case the officer's defense would be that he had acted in accord with federal law.[145]

The Force Bill passed the Senate 32–1 and the House 149–48.[146] South Carolina's attempt at nullification could hardly have been more decisively rejected.[147]

South Carolina had postponed the effective date of nullification in hopes that Congress would find a way to avoid conflict, and Calhoun had spelled out how that could be done. Lower the tariff, he said, and you'll hear no further complaint.[148] Representative Verplanck had already introduced a bill to do just that, but it was not moving. A few Northerners objected that Congress ought not to give in to South Carolina extortion,[149] but debate was desultory in the extreme. Everyone knew the constitutional arguments; the country was waiting to see what the Senate would do.

Henry Clay, the Great Pacificator, made the critical move on February 12, proposing a reduction of tariffs to the revenue level over a period of nine years in order to avoid both the perceived injustice of the existing law and the hardship of immediate repeal. In nine years, he said, American industry would be able to take care of itself; he did not advocate perpetual protection. "Let us have peace," he adjured his colleagues, "and become once more united as a band of brothers"; let us "heal, before they are yet bleeding, the wounds of our distracted country."[150]

Calhoun responded at once. "He who loves the Union must desire to see this agitating question brought to a termination." He liked the principles of Clay's bill; he had no desire to destroy manufacturers by a sudden removal of protective duties. "Here," the re-

[143]See text accompanying note 43. See also Cong Deb, 22d Cong, 2d Sess 415 (Pennsylvania Sen. George Dallas).

[144]Id at 536. See also id at 372 (Sen. Tyler); id at 458 (Sen. Miller).

[145]Id at 260 (Sen. Wilkins); see Tennessee v Davis, 100 US 257 (1879).

[146]Cong Deb, 22d Cong, 2d Sess 688, 1903; the statute appears at 4 Stat 632 (Mar 2, 1833). The lone dissenter on the final Senate vote was John Tyler. Seven others had opposed sending the bill to third reading, Cong Deb, 22d Cong, 2d Sess 601; Calhoun said some had left the chamber to protest holding the final vote in the absence of several opponents, to avoid giving a false impression of their weakness. Id at 688.

[147]A detailed study by Richard Ellis, however, concludes that opposition to the employment of force against South Carolina (and to the tone of Jackson's nationalistic proclamation) was far broader than the final tally disclosed. Thirteen Southern Senators had voted to postpone debate on the Force Bill; by February 1833 many observers were convinced it had no chance of adoption; it was passed only as a sop to the "defeated" President, and only after it became clear that because the tariff was to be reduced it would never be used. Ellis, The Union at Risk at 162–63, 171–73, 181 (cited in note 4). For discussion of the widespread objections in state legislatures to the use of force see id at 102–16.

[148]Cong Deb, 22d Cong, 2d Sess 239.

[149]See id at 974–75 (Rep. Huntington); id at 1050 (Rep. Dearborn); id at 1795 (Rep. Stewart).

[150]Id at 462–63, 467, 473.

porter recorded, "there was a tumultuous approbation in the galleries";[151] the nightmare was over.

What followed was an anticlimax. Webster protested that Congress ought not to abandon the protective principle,[152] but it was too late. Calhoun complained that to base tariffs on the value of articles at the point of importation would produce disuniformity, but in light of the overriding need for settlement he acquiesced.[153] Senate discussion centered largely on the ancillary question whether a bill reducing taxes was a "bill[] for raising revenue" and thus had to originate in the House;[154] the issue was mooted when the House substituted Clay's bill for Verplanck's and passed it. Senate approval quickly followed.[155]

Clay had done it again; he had sacrificed the centerpiece of his American System, the cornerstone of his whole legislative program, to save his beloved Union.[156] He had been accused, he said late in the debate, of ambition, and he pleaded guilty:

> Yes, I have ambition; but it is the ambition of being the humble instrument . . . to reconcile a divided people, once more to revive concord and harmony in a distracted land; the pleasing ambition of contemplating the glorious spectacle of a free, united, prosperous, and fraternal people.[157]

Clay was a man for all seasons, and once more he had earned the nation's gratitude. But the man of the hour was Andrew Jackson, the hero of New Orleans. In most respects he was not one of my favorite American statesmen. Willfully heedless of limitations on military and executive authority during the Seminole War, ignorant of the most fundamental economic principles, and painfully cramped in his interpretation of federal authority, Jackson wreaked untold harm in dismantling those two admirable elements of the American System, internal improvements and the National Bank. In the controversy over removal of the deposits, however, he stood up manfully for the constitutional powers of

[151] Id at 477–78.

[152] Id at 483–84. The Massachusetts legislature, we are told, had earlier threatened to take unspecified retaliatory measures if tariffs were reduced: "[T]he danger to the Union was not all on one side." Peterson, Olive Branch and Sword at 64 (cited in note 4).

[153] See Cong Deb, 22d Cong, 2d Sess 694, 697, 716.

[154] US Const, Art I, § 7, ¶ 1. To reduce revenue, said Maine Senator John Holmes, was not to raise it. Cong Deb, 22d Cong, 2d Sess 479. Clay said much the same thing, id at 477. Even a bill that lowered rates, replied Mahlon Dickerson of New Jersey, might increase revenue by stimulating demand; whether it raised or lowered revenue, Clay's bill was one for "collecting and bringing money into the treasury." Id at 478. It was under this bill if enacted, Dickerson later added, that revenue would be raised in the future. Id at 720. See also id at 722 (Sen. Webster). As a linguistic matter the latter arguments sounded plausible enough, but the evident purpose of the provision was to ensure that only the people's representatives could initiate an increase in the tax burden. One provision of Clay's bill, however, would actually have increased the rate of duty on certain cotton cloth; it was plainly not for the Senate to originate. Id at 717–19. A Senate committee later resolved that a bill to reinstate the compromise tariff after a subsequent statute had increased it was "a bill[] for raising revenue" and thus could be originated only in the House. S Doc 30, 28th Cong, 1st Sess 1 (1844).

[155] Cong Deb, 22d Cong, 2d Sess 1772, 1810, 809. The House vote was 119–85, the Senate vote 29–16. For the statute itself see 4 Stat 629 (Mar 2, 1833).

[156] More precisely, perhaps, he had sacrificed *part* of his tariff program to save the rest of it, along with the Union; his formula "traded *time,* which was of first importance to manufacturers, for *principle,* which was of first importance to the South." Peterson, Olive Branch and Sword at 52–53, 80 (cited in note 4).

[157] Cong Deb, 22d Cong, 2d Sess 742.

the executive, and in the nullification crisis he stood up just as manfully for the Union. That he was a headstrong general and a states'-rights Southerner lent credibility to his position. In the end South Carolina rescinded the Nullification Ordinance and accepted the new tariff;[158] it was Jackson's finest hour.

VI. CADENZA

When tariffs reached their nadir under the Compromise in 1842, the Government was strapped for money, and Clay's Whigs controlled both Houses of Congress. Twice, at President Tyler's request,[159] they voted to increase duties once again; twice Tyler himself stopped them.[160] This time he was right, though his reasons were not of constitutional caliber. Tyler had approved distribution of the proceeds of public land sales to the states only on condition that tariffs not be raised; he believed the Government ought to exhaust its own resources before asking the public to bear additional burdens.[161] Congress later tried to uncouple the tariff from distribution entirely, but Tyler vetoed that too.[162]

Congress finally succeeded in raising tariffs by agreeing to suspend distribution,[163] but the Whig victory was short-lived. Democrats regained both Congress and the Presidency in 1845, and the Walker Tariff of the following year[164] reduced duties considerably while not eliminating protection entirely.[165] They were reduced once more in 1857 and

[158]See 1 SC Stats 390 (Mar 15, 1833). As a last empty gesture of defiance South Carolina nullified the Force Bill, which its own actions had rendered superfluous. 1 SC Stats 400 (Mar 18, 1833); Ames, State Documents on Federal Relations at 189 (cited in note 1).

[159]A big deficit was his justification. See 4 Richardson at 106, 108 (Mar 25, 1842).

[160]Id at 180 (Jun 29, 1842); id at 183 (Aug 9, 1842).

[161]See section II of chapter 2.

[162]4 Richardson at 255 (Dec 14, 1843).

[163]5 Stat 548 (Aug 30, 1842). See id at 567, § 30, noting that by the terms of the earlier statute enactment of the increase automatically suspended distribution.

[164]Robert Walker, a former Senator from Mississippi, was Polk's Secretary of the Treasury.

[165]9 Stat 42 (Jul 30, 1846). Taking umbrage at the fact that the tariff reduction had passed only because one Senator had subordinated his own views to those of the state legislature that elected him, Daniel Webster in an editorial took aim at what he considered the pernicious (he did not say unconstitutional) doctrine of "*Legislative Instructions*":

> Last year a member of the French Chamber of Deputies was actually *expelled the Chamber* [sic], because he had promised his constituents to vote in a particular way, on a question interesting equally to the whole Kingdom. The general sense of the Chamber was, that one who had already made up his mind, & engaged his vote, in a particular way, was not fit to sit in a Council, assembled for deliberation, & mutual consultation on high matters of State.

National Intelligencer, Mar 13, 1847, 6 Webster Correspondence at 215–16. John Tyler, in contrast, was a firm believer in the right of instruction, as he wrote in drafting a resolution for the Virginia House of Delegates in 1812 to censure Senators who had thumbed their noses at directions to oppose renewal of the first Bank of the United States:

> [F]rom the nature of a representative democracy, the representative can be considered in no other light than as a servant, and necessarily bound at all times to obey the will of his superiors, unless that will tend to the manifest violation of the Constitution . . . . And although the right to instruct is not expressly given by the Constitution of the United States to the State Legislature, yet it is evidently inferrable therefrom, inasmuch as without this right the power of electing would be

not raised again until the eve of the Civil War.[166]

Relatively free trade was thus the new order of the day. On the whole I think that was a good thing, but not for constitutional reasons. Yes, if limits on federal authority are to mean anything, Congress must refrain from imposing pretextual taxes; the *Child Labor Tax Case*[167] was rightly decided. The protective tariff, however, was not a pretext for a prohibition Congress had no power to impose. As Webster implied, Congress could have outlawed the offending imports directly under the commerce clause;[168] it was immaterial that it chose to do so in the form of a tax.[169]

The method by which free trade was achieved also left something to be desired. It is true that Jackson's firmness and the enactment of the Force Bill put an end to the respectability of nullification as constitutional doctrine[170]—until something like it was revived in the unworthy name of racial segregation in the 1950's.[171] Even secessionists in the terrible winter of 1860–61 disowned it: While the Union was a voluntary association from which one might withdraw at will, so long as one was a member one had to play by the rules.[172] But Calhoun maintained that it was nullification that had slain the tariff,[173] and he was right. It may have been the better part of wisdom in 1833 to give in to blackmail, but it had its down side. As any police chief will tell you, paying ransom to kidnappers only encourages them.[174]

> imperfect and incomplete, and the senator, instead of being a servant, would be the uncontrolled sovereign during the period of his constitutional service.

1 Tyler Letters at 274. True to his principles, Tyler later resigned his seat in the Senate when the legislature instructed him to vote to expunge the censure of President Jackson:

> I dare not touch the Journal of the Senate. The Constitution forbids it. . . . [A]s an evidence of the sincerity of my convictions that your resolutions cannot be executed without violating my oath, I surrender into your hands three unexpired years of my term.

Id at 536. For the expungement controversy see section II D of chapter 3.

[166]11 Stat 192 (Mar 3, 1857); 12 Stat 178 (Mar 2, 1861). The 1861 statute modestly restored 1846 levels; a series of wartime measures escalated the tariff to an "extravagant" level of protection that was to persist for another twenty years. See Taussig, Tariff History of the United States at 114–15, 158–70 (cited in note 1). See Keith E. Whittington, Constitutional Construction: Divided Powers and Constitutional Meaning 103–6 (Harvard, 1999), concluding that the 1833 Compromise established a quasi-constitutional understanding about tariffs that basically prevailed until the Civil War.

[167]Bailey v Drexel Furniture Co, 259 US 20 (1922).

[168]Cong Deb, 22d Cong, 2d Sess 582; see United States v Darby, 312 US 100, 115 (1941); The Second Century at 238. See also The Jeffersonians at 145–55, discussing the 1807 Embargo.

[169]Veazie Bank v Fenno, 75 US 533 (1969).

[170]Adoption of the Force Bill, Jackson wrote at the time, "gives the death blow to Nullification or Secession." Jackson to Joel Poinsett, Mar 6, 1833, 5 Jackson Correspondence at 28.

[171]See Bush v Orleans Parish School Board, 364 US 500, 501 (1960).

[172]See, e.g., Cong Globe, 36th Cong, 2d Sess 487 (Mississippi Sen. Jefferson Davis). See also Alexander H. Stephens, 1 A Constitutional View of the Late War Between the States 421, 449–51 (Nat'l Pub Co, 1968); Descent into the Maelstrom, ch 10.

[173]See Calhoun to Samuel D. Ingham, Mar 25, 1833, 12 Calhoun Papers at 148; Speech at Charleston, Nov 22, 1833, id at 180, 181; Speech at Pendleton, Aug 1, 1836, 13 id at 266, 269–70. See also Horace Greeley, Recollections of a Busy Life 108 (J.B. Ford, 1868), complaining that "nullification was abandoned, rather than suppressed, and this only after the main point had been yielded . . . by a gradual reduction of the Tariff. . . ."

[174]See Carl Schurz, 2 Life of Henry Clay 21 (Houghton, Mifflin, 1887):

[A]ttempts to terrorize the rest of the Union into compliance with the behests of the South became a settled policy when the slavery question came to the foreground; and this was owing in a large measure to the encouragement given to the spirit of resistance in 1833.

Part Two

The Kitchen Sink

5

Enumerated and Limited Powers

The first half of the period between 1829 and 1861 was dominated by the death throes of the American System, the second by expansion and the swan song of slavery. Throughout the period, however, Congress and executive officers were confronted, as always, with an extraordinary medley of other constitutional controversies.

We begin with issues of federalism, for apart from the great debates over the American System and slavery the period of this study presented the usual range of questions concerning the limits of congressional authority. We then confront a few stray first-amendment issues before moving on to consideration of matters pertaining more directly to the Executive and Judicial Branches.[1]

I. ADMIRALTY AND COMMERCE

First another word about those perennial sources of contention, the commerce provisions of Article I, § 8, clause 3. Democratic legislators and executives who insisted that the power to regulate interstate and foreign commerce did not include authority to facilitate it by constructing improvements tended (not surprisingly) to be less grudging when it came to actual regulation. As early as 1833, for example, President Jackson called attention to "the many distressing accidents which have of late occurred" aboard steamboats, opined that they were "in a great degree the result of criminal negligence," and urged Congress to consider "precautionary and penal legislation" on the subject, "[s]o far as [it] can be regarded as within [their] constitutional purview."[2] President Van Buren repeated this

[1]For reasons that will become apparent, religion-clause questions respecting efforts to suppress polygamy in the territories are considered in chapter 9 of Descent into the Maelstrom, other freedom of expression considerations in chapters 1 and 2 of that volume and chapter 8 of this one.

[2]Fifth Annual Message, 3 Richardson at 19, 34 (Dec 3, 1833). Webster chimed in at once with a plea for protection against boiler explosions and for federal rules of the road. Only Congress could act, he said, and

exhortation in 1837, curiously suggesting that Congress deal with the problem of steamboats "by means of severe provisions connected with their custom-house papers"[3]—which in the end seems more likely to indicate that he believed a denial of clearance would be an effective sanction than that he thought the prevention of accidents a tax matter and not a subject for commercial regulation.

Congress responded, without significant debate, by enacting a comprehensive code of steamboat safety that embraced everything from licensing and boiler inspection to engineers, lifeboats, fire engines, and signal lights.[4] Subsequent pre–Civil war Congresses appended a congeries of additional statutes designed to protect passengers on vessels of all kinds, including what must have been the first federal law against sexual harassment—making it a crime for a member of the ship's crew to seduce a passenger by means of threat, promise, or authority or to visit a passenger's quarters for nonbusiness purposes.[5] Thus even the most traditional of mid-century Democrats appeared to acknowledge that Congress could regulate what a later Supreme Court would call the "instrumentalities of commerce" for reasons of public safety. Chief Justice Marshall's famous distinction between commercial and police powers[6] was apparently understood only to confirm state authority, not to limit federal. There was nothing really new in all this; Congress had passed its first law to protect passengers in 1819.[7]

A further measure tacked onto the end of the 1842 tariff law introduced an important variation on the theme of regulations of commerce serving police-power goals. The steamboat and passenger laws promoted the safety of commerce itself by protecting persons and property moving from one state or country to another. The 1842 provision, which forbade importation of "indecent and obscene prints, paintings, lithographs, engravings, and transparencies,"[8] did not; it was meant to prevent offenses to public morals after the interstate or foreign journey was over. Perhaps the nearest precedent was the protective tariff, which restricted commerce for the ulterior purpose of promoting industry. Opponents of the tariff had protested that regulations of commerce had to foster commerce,[9] but nobody peeped when Congress ignored that precept in 1842. The obscenity law slipped through without raising an eyebrow and furnished a conspicuous precedent when a divided Supreme Court upheld a federal ban on the interstate shipment of lottery tickets in 1890.[10]

---

there was no doubt such regulations fell within the commerce power. Cong Deb, 23d Cong, 1st Sess 54–57 (Dec 23, 1833).

[3]First Annual Message, 3 Richardson at 373, 394 (Dec 5, 1837).

[4]5 Stat 304 (Jul 7, 1838).

[5]12 Stat 3 (Mar 24, 1860). See also 9 Stat 127 (Feb 22, 1847) (limiting the number of passengers); 9 Stat 220 (May 17, 1848) (requiring ventilation, cleanliness, discipline, and adequate meals); 10 Stat 715 (Mar 3, 1855) (revising and supplementing the earlier provisions).

[6]See Gibbons v Ogden, 22 US 1, 203–10 (1824).

[7]See The Jeffersonians at 301.

[8]5 Stat 548, 566–67, § 28 (Aug 30, 1842). This Act was later amended to embrace photographs, 11 Stat 168–69 (Mar 2, 1857).

[9]See chapter 4. An 1825 provision making it a crime to import counterfeit coins might appear to be a second precedent for the obscenity ban, were it not for the fact that Congress has express power to prohibit counterfeiting. US Const, Art I, § 8, cl 6; 4 Stat 115, 121, § 20 (Mar 3, 1825); United States v Marigold, 50 US 560, 566 (1850).

[10]Champion v Ames (The Lottery Case), 188 US 321; see The Second Century at 28–29. See also 9 Stat 237 (Jun 26, 1848), providing for the inspection of imported medicines to ensure quality, purity, and fitness

Other regulations of commerce proved equally noncontroversial. In 1837 Congress responded to a dispute that allegedly disrupted navigation in New York harbor by authorizing ships in "any port situate upon waters, which are the boundary between two States," to take on pilots certified by either one.[11] Two later measures went beyond regulation of navigation itself to encourage the shipping industry by protecting bona fide purchasers of ships against unrecorded conveyances[12] and by limiting tort liability in most cases to the value of the offending vessel.[13] Kentucky Senator Joseph Underwood objected that the latter bill would regulate contracts rather than commerce, but nobody bothered to refute him or to explain the basis of federal authority.[14]

The final section of the Limitation Act, which exempted from its operation not only canal boats, barges, and lighters but also "any vessel . . . used in rivers or inland navigation," might be thought to reflect a congressional determination that the law was sustained not by the commerce clause but by the provision of Article III, § 2 extending federal judicial power to "cases of admiralty and maritime jurisdiction." For Daniel Webster had explained in 1825 that the admiralty and necessary and proper clauses gave Congress a legislative competence as broad as the jurisdiction itself,[15] which even in 1851 was not understood to include all navigable inland waters.[16] In fact, when the Supreme Court came to uphold the Limitation Act in 1889, it did so on the basis of the admiralty provision; it did not reach the commerce-clause question.[17]

The debates do not reveal the reason for the statutory exemption of inland waters, but it seems poorly designed to reflect constitutional reservations. For even in 1825 the Supreme Court had acknowledged that admiralty jurisdiction extended, as it generally had in England, to all waters within the ebb and flow of the tide.[18] Moreover, Congress had significantly extended that jurisdiction in the celebrated Great Lakes Act of 1845.[19]

That statute gave federal District Courts "the same jurisdiction in matters of contract

---

and banning the introduction of those found improper, unsafe, or dangerous. The House report on this last bill invoked the precedent of the ban on indecent images and argued that government had an obligation to protect health as well as morals; it said nothing about the source of congressional authority. HR Rep 664, 30th Cong, 1st Sess 19 (1848).

[11]5 Stat 153 (Mar 2, 1837). New York had established a "monopoly" that was said to provide inadequate service; after the statute was passed, "New Jersey began to license pilots to compete with the New Yorkers and some of the packet operators and other big shipowners retained a group of their own . . . ." See Robert G. Albion, The Rise of New York Port, 1815–1860 215–16 (Scribner's, 1939). Cf Gibbons v Ogden, 22 US 1 (1824), upholding an earlier federal statute that had broken up another New York monopoly.

[12]The statute was a straightforward recording act of the Massachusetts type, protecting all purchasers without notice of the unrecorded instrument. 9 Stat 440 (Jul 29, 1850).

[13]9 Stat 635 (Mar 3, 1851). The purpose of the law, explained Maine Senator (and later Vice-President) Hannibal Hamlin, was to make U.S. carriers competitive with the British, which already enjoyed such protection. Cong Globe, 31st Cong, 2d Sess 332, 715.

[14]Id at 719. Since the contracts in question concerned the carriage of goods, there seemed little merit in Underwood's distinction.

[15]See The Jeffersonians at 303.

[16]See text accompanying notes 17–22.

[17]Butler v Boston & Savannah SS Co, 130 US 527, 557 (1889); see also In re Garnett, 141 US 1, 12 (1891).

[18]The Thomas Jefferson, 23 US 428.

[19]5 Stat 726 (Feb 26, 1845). More likely, therefore, inland shipping was exempted because it was not subject to foreign competition—although the coasting trade, which was likewise closed to foreign vessels, was not exempted. See 3 Stat 351, § 4 (Mar 1, 1817).

or tort" in certain cases arising "upon the lakes and navigable waters connecting said lakes" as they had in traditional maritime cases. Again there was no significant reported debate; the decisive argument had been made in the House twenty years before.[20] That the law applied only to vessels engaged in interstate or foreign commerce and provided for jury trials not indigenous to admiralty testifies to doubts whether Congress could enlarge the admiralty jurisdiction itself, which the Court had held limited by tradition to tidewaters.[21] When the Supreme Court upheld the statute in 1852, however, Chief Justice Taney would convincingly conclude that the commerce power did not permit Congress to extend federal jurisdiction beyond the limits of Article III; Great Lakes cases could be included only because they were admiralty cases for purposes of Article III.[22]

II. THE BROKEN BENCH

The fourth clause of Article I, § 8 empowers Congress, among other things, to adopt "uniform laws on the subject of bankruptcies." The Federalist Congress had adopted a bankruptcy law in 1800, but the Republican Congress had repealed it in 1803.[23] During their brief period of hegemony in the early 1840's the Whigs went them one better: They passed a new bankruptcy law in 1841 and repealed it themselves less than two years later.[24]

Hard times breed demands for bankruptcy legislation, and times had been hard since the Panic of 1837. The then incoming President, Jackson's loyal sidekick Martin Van Buren, had called a special session to deal with the financial crisis, which he blamed on

[20]See The Jeffersonians at 304.

[21]The Thomas Jefferson, cited in note 18.

[22]The Genesee Chief v Fitzhugh, 53 US 443; see The First Hundred Years at 257–59. Congressional power over commerce extended to that with the Indian tribes as well as with foreign nations and among the several states, and a statute adopted early in Jackson's Presidency (along with measures already noted in the Introduction to Part One) suggests that Congress continued to take a broad view of its authority under this provision. Having recognized a decade earlier that vaccinating the populace at large against smallpox was none of its business (see The Jeffersonians at 295–301), Congress modestly resolved in 1832 to vaccinate the Indians. 4 Stat 514 (May 5, 1832). Section 5 of the statute, id at 515, appropriated money from the Treasury to finance the operation. President Monroe's interpretation of the spending power, which Jackson had accepted as precedent, would have supported appropriations for any program of national proportions. See Monroe's memorandum accompanying his veto of the 1822 Tollgate Bill, The Jeffersonians at 279–81, and the discussion of Jackson's Maysville road veto in chapter 1. Several of Jackson's successors, however, took a more orthodox view of the spending power, as we have seen in chapter 2. That the vaccination program was limited to Indians not only made it uncertain that the statute met even Monroe's more permissive criterion; it also suggested that Congress may have been relying instead on a broad reading of the Indian commerce power or legislating to implement treaties with the various tribes. In any event the passage of this law seems to testify to an emerging tendency of Congress to assume that it had plenary authority over Indian affairs, as Jackson argued and as the Supreme Court would ultimately conclude without invoking any particular constitutional provision. See The Federalist Period at 86–87, 169 n.284; Jackson to James Monroe, Mar 4, 1817, quoted in Robert V. Remini, The Legacy of Andrew Jackson 48–49 (LSU, 1988); United States v Kagama, 118 US 375 (1886); The First Hundred Years at 432–34.

[23]See The Federalist Period at 274; The Jeffersonians at 4. For discussion of unsuccessful efforts to revive the law after the Panic of 1819 see The Jeffersonians at 304–7.

[24]5 Stat 440 (Aug 19, 1841); 5 Stat 614 (Mar 3, 1843). Indeed, since by its own terms the law did not go into effect until February 1842, it was actually in force for little more than a year. See 5 Stat at 449, § 17; Charles Warren, Bankruptcy in United States History 85 (Beard, 1999) (first published in 1935). Chapter II of Professor Warren's fine book contains a thorough account of the background and history of the 1841 statute.

"excessive issues of bank paper and . . . other facilities for the acquisition and enlargement of credit."[25] Good Democrat that he was, Van Buren abjured any direct effort to ameliorate private distress attendant upon the depression. That was not what the Federal Government was for.

> If, therefore, I refrain from suggesting to Congress any specific plan for regulating the exchanges of the country, relieving mercantile embarrassments, or interfering with the ordinary operations of foreign or domestic commerce, it is from a conviction that such measures are not within the constitutional competence of the General Government . . . .[26]

But state bank notes, Van Buren argued, should never have been tolerated; they offended the bills of credit, legal tender, and contract provisions of Article I, § 10. Congress could not outlaw them directly, but it could reduce their abundance by providing for the liquidation of any bank that could not redeem its obligations. And thus it came to pass that President Van Buren, apostle of states' rights, proposed enactment of a bankruptcy law applicable to banks as a means of combating "a depreciated paper currency."[27]

Senator Daniel Webster, high-church Whig and patron of broad federal powers, affected to find in Van Buren's proposal an infringement of state sovereignty. Borrowing a page from opponents of the protective tariff, he denounced the resulting bill as a pretext for regulating state bank notes, which the President had conceded Congress could not do.[28] In a learned reply Missouri Democrat Thomas Hart Benton not only dredged up

[25]See 3 Richardson at 321; id at 324, 325 (Sep 4, 1837).

[26]Id at 345. He coupled this disclaimer with the typically Jacksonian general admonition that "the less government interferes with private pursuits the better for the general prosperity," id at 344, and repeated it in his last Annual Message in 1840, id at 614.

[27]Id at 342.

[28]Cong Deb, 25th Cong, 1st Sess 534 (as quoted by Senator Benton):

> The object of bankrupt laws, sir, has no relation to currency. It is simply to distribute the effects of insolvent debtors among their creditors; and I must say, it strikes me that it would be a great perversion of the power conferred on Congress, to exercise it upon corporations and bankers, with the leading and primary object of remedying a depreciated paper currency.

Benton disputed Webster's premise: Congress *could* suppress state bank notes directly and had a duty to do so in order to prevent violations of Article I, § 10, which Van Buren had invoked in his message. Id at 548. Unlike the full faith and credit clause of Article IV, the clause in question gave Congress no express authority to enforce its provisions. Neither, however, did the extradition and fugitive slave clauses of Article IV, § 2, which Congress had implemented by legislation in 1793. See The Federalist Period at 170–71. Three years later Benton would propose a steep tax on small bank notes for the candid purpose of suppressing them, restating his argument from Article I, § 10 and quoting at length from an 1830 article by Albert Gallatin in the American Quarterly Review in support of such a tax. Cong Globe, 26th Cong, 2d Sess 54–57 (1840); see 3 Gallatin Writings at 324–25. Reminded that only the House could originate a bill to raise revenue (see Cong Globe, 26th Cong, 2d Sess 57 (Sens. Huntington and Webster)), Benton vowed to attach his proposition to the next tax bill that arrived from that chamber (id at 59). In the next Congress he tried again (without curing the origination problem), Cong Globe, 27th Cong, 2d Sess 153 (1842); Cong Globe App, 27th Cong, 2d Sess 81–82, provoking Calhoun and Alabama's William King to complain that although they agreed state bank notes were bad Congress had no right to impose taxes for ulterior purposes. Cong Globe, 27th Cong, 2d Sess 153–55. Benton withdrew his amendment in order not to imperil the treasury-note bill to which it was to be appended (id at 155). Enacted in 1866 (14 Stat 98, 146, § 9 [bis], (Jul 13, 1866)), the tax he had sponsored was upheld in

British legislation that had pushed failed banks into bankruptcy and thus protected the currency[29] but delivered himself of a latitudinarian construction of congressional authority that would have done justice to Webster himself. Congress's power was not restricted, as Webster had argued, to "the usual objects, the usual subjects, and the usual purposes of bankruptcy laws in England." The constitutional grant of power was "without limitation or qualification" and left Congress "at full liberty to pass any kind of bankrupt laws they please[d]," provided they were "uniform in their operation throughout the United States."[30]

Van Buren's proposal died quickly.[31] The next bankruptcy bill to be seriously considered bore a distinctly different cast, and the parties were reversed.

The date was 1840, and the chief defender of the proposal was Webster. As reported by Delaware Whig John M. Clayton, the bill provided exclusively for voluntary bankruptcy, and it applied to all debtors other than corporations. Clayton frankly stated its purpose:

> A majority [of the Judiciary Committee] thought, indeed he might say they all thought, that some immediate relief should be provided for all those persons who have already, by the misfortune of trade, or by other means, failed in business, and become unable to meet their engagements, and to pay their debts, and who are willing to make a full and fair surrender of their property for the benefit of their creditors; and not only for those who are at present laboring under this misfortune, but for all those who may hereafter be in a similar situation . . . .
>
> If passed, [the bill] . . . will emancipate from a species of bondage a vast number of active, intelligent, and enterprising men, who are now struggling against hope, with spirits worn down and energies paralyzed. It is not they only who are interested in this matter; the country has an interest in their activity, and industry, and talents, that they may be again set free to add to its general wealth and prosperity.[32]

Veazie Bank v Fenno, 75 US 533 (1969), partly on the ground that Congress indeed could regulate state banknotes directly by virtue of its various powers over the currency.

[29]Cong Deb, 25th Cong, 1st Sess 544.

[30]Id at 536–38. Thus in Benton's view there was nothing to Webster's doubts whether a bankruptcy law could be made applicable to bankers, or to bankers alone, for the English themselves had borrowed the term "bankrupt" from the civil law:

> *Bancus* and *ruptus* signifies a broken bank; and the word *broken* is not metaphorical but literal, and is descriptive of the ancient method of cashiering an insolvent or fraudulent banker, by turning him out of the exchange or market place, and breaking the table to pieces on which he kept his money and transacted his business. The term *bankrupt,* then, . . . not only applied to bankers, but was confined to them; and it is preposterous in us to limit ourselves to an English definition of a civil law term.

Id at 538.

[31]Shortly after Benton's remarks the Senate voted to discharge the committee from further consideration of the bill, id at 551; it was not revived.

[32]Cong Globe, 26th Cong, 1st Sess 345.

Thus the 1840 bill was revolutionary. The 1800 law (and Van Buren's 1837 proposal) had given creditors the tool of involuntary bankruptcy to facilitate access to their debtors' assets; the 1840 bill would give debtors the option of voluntary bankruptcy as a means of relieving themselves of their obligations.

It was the voluntary nature of the 1840 proposal that attracted the most enemy fire. For it was not only the 1800 statute that limited relief to cases in which creditors requested it; in so providing Congress had followed the pattern of English law as it stood when the Constitution was new.

Senator Benton, who had championed Van Buren's 1837 proposal, vociferously opposed the 1840 bill. He found the very idea of voluntary bankruptcy repugnant:

> The principle of the bill is, that every person owing debts may, at his own will, and by going through a process which he himself commences, be absolved from all liability for his debts. This is the principle; and the details are such as to deprive the creditor of all effective agency in the conduct of a proceeding which is commenced without his consent. The present effect, as gentlemen say, is to release 500,000 debtors from future obligation to pay their debts; of course to deprive an equal number of rights and means on which they relied. Its future effect must be to set an example for the repetition of such laws as often as the debtor class becomes numerous and powerful; and to teach the rising generation a facile way to get rid of their obligations, after squandering the money and property which they had obtained upon the faith of paying for it. Nothing, in my opinion, could be more objectionable than the principle of the bill.[33]

Indeed, although he had initially insisted that any new bankruptcy law should include voluntary provisions,[34] Benton now said they were unconstitutional. The contract clause forbade states to discharge preexisting debts, and Congress was empowered to do so

> [n]ot by passing acts . . . for the abolition of debts at the will of the debtor, but by making the discharge of the debt the joint act of the creditor and debtor; the creditor instituting the proceeding, or being ruled into it by a majority in interest, and thereby assenting to it.[35]

[33]Cong Globe App, 26th Cong, 1st Sess 503. Pennsylvania Senator James Buchanan, who thought Congress could constitutionally enact a voluntary bankruptcy law, opposed it in 1841 on much the same basis: The availability of painless relief from one's obligations would encourage "profligacy." Cong Globe App, 27th Cong, 1st Sess 206. See also Benton's own later condemnation of the 1841 bill as "a cheat, and a falsehood, as well as a base immorality" that would encourage "plunder and spoliation" by allowing debtors to evade their obligations. Cong Globe App, 27th Cong, 2d Sess 90, 91.

[34]Cong Globe, 26th Cong, 1st Sess 237.

[35]Cong Globe App, 26th Cong, 1st Sess 503. It seems difficult to reconcile with this argument Benton's concession that he would accept the bill if it was amended to provide also for involuntary proceedings against corporations and other traders. Id at 505. See also Georgia Senator Wilson Lumpkin's assertion (Cong Globe, 26th Cong, 1st Sess at 484) that he could "find no power in the Constitution which authorizes Congress to impair the obligation of individual contracts." Whether the bankruptcy clause filled that bill was the question that Benton had answered in the negative.

Just why this was so Benton left for the moment in shadow. He could not very well contend that the contract clause was a limitation on Congress; its plain words showed it was not.[36] He said only that Congress was bound to exercise its power "according to the intent of the grant."[37]

All right, Mr. Benton was yet another originalist in constitutional interpretation. But what was the "intent" of the bankruptcy clause? John C. Calhoun, an originalist himself, provided an answer:

> [A]t the time of the formation of the Constitution, there existed, both in this country and in England, from which we derived our laws, two separate systems of laws, growing out of the relation of creditor and debtor; the one known as the system of bankruptcy, and the other of insolvency. . . .
>
> The system of insolvent laws grew out of the debtor side of the relation, and originated in motives of humanity for the unfortunate but honest debtor . . . . [T]he laws of bankruptcy . . . grew out of the creditor side of the relation[;] . . . [t]heir leading object is to strengthen the system of commercial credit . . . .
>
> [I]s it to be supposed, that if [the members of the Constitutional Convention] intended to delegate to Congress power over both systems, these able and cautious men, so familiar with the distinction between them, would not have included both by name? And is it not conclusive, that in not doing so, and in limiting the grant to bankruptcy alone, that it was their intention to grant that only, to the exclusion of insolvency?

As a measure for the relief of debtors, Calhoun concluded, "voluntary bankruptcy" was oxymoronic; the bill sounded in insolvency, not bankruptcy, and it lay beyond Congress's authority.[38]

Senator Clayton's bill cleared the Senate by the narrow margin of 21–19[39] but was never taken up in the House. Little over a year later, when the Whigs controlled both Houses of the new Twenty-seventh Congress, a similar bill (revised to include involuntary

[36]US Const, Art I, § 10: "No state shall . . . pass any . . . law impairing the obligation of contracts." In 1862, while concluding that Congress had not conveyed land to a Minnesota corporation, the Supreme Court added in dictum that if it had it could not have taken it back. Rice v Minnesota & NW Ry, 66 US 358, 373–74. The operative clause of the Constitution was not identified. Though the opinion cited a contract clause case (Fletcher v Peck, 10 US 87 (1810)), the provision that unambiguously justified the Court's conclusion was found in the fifth amendment: "[N]or shall private property be taken for public use without just compensation." Equivocations like that in *Rice* nevertheless encouraged the illusion that the contract clause itself somehow limited federal as well as state authority. See Mark A. Graber, Naked Land Transfers and American Constitutional Development, 53 Vand. L. Rev. 73, 82–85 (2000).

[37]Cong Globe App, 26th Cong, 1st Sess 503.

[38]Id at 690–91. On Calhoun as originalist see also his letter to Robert S. Garnett, Jul 3, 1824, 9 Calhoun Papers at 198, 199, rejecting the suggestion that doubts should always be resolved against the existence of federal authority: "[A]ny doubtful portion of the Constitution, must be construed by itself, in reference to the true meaning and intent of the framers of the instrument."

[39]Cong Globe, 26th Cong, 1st Sess 487. Nearly all Whigs supported the bill; nearly all Democrats opposed it. So much for the ubiquitous legend that Jacksonianism meant sympathy for the common man.

as well as voluntary proceedings) became law.[40] There was little debate of any kind, and none of note with respect to the voluntary provisions. When Congress met again in December 1841, however, those who had opposed the law found their voices once again. The statute's effective date should be postponed, said Benton. The statute should be repealed, said Richard Bayard of Delaware. Why? Because it was unconstitutional: Bankruptcy laws were for creditors, not debtors; voluntary bankruptcy did not exist.[41]

Amplifying the argument that Calhoun had made on the earlier bill, Bayard commendably recited English statutes from 1542 to 1764 to demonstrate his point, assigning the 1759 Act for the relief of debtors to the distinct category of insolvency.[42] Finding confirmation of his conclusion in Congress's decision to adopt only involuntary bankruptcy provisions in 1800 and in Madison's explanation in The Federalist that federal bankruptcy laws would "prevent . . . frauds,"[43] Bayard added the intermediate premise that Calhoun had found it unnecessary to aver. In order to determine the scope of the bankruptcy power, he declared,

> we must have recourse, as we are constantly obliged to have, in expounding other phrases of the same instrument, to the laws of that country which furnished the language as well as the model of our legal institutions. . . . [W]hen it is remembered that a bankrupt system had existed for more than two hundred years in England, . . . it is impossible to believe that, in using the term, [the authors of the Constitution] did not mean to refer to that system for its explanation. He did not mean to say that the use of that term, with reference to the English system, required that we should adopt all its details; but the great questions which were of its essence, namely as to the persons whom it should embrace and the purpose which it contemplated, were clearly intended to be settled.[44]

Appropriately, Bayard closed with an argument based on the subsidiarity principle the Framers had expressly employed in constructing the list of congressional powers: Like the diversity jurisdiction, federal remedies were necessary to ensure out-of-state creditors "the fair administration of justice"; there was no comparable need for federal legislation to relieve debtors from obligations imposed by their own states' laws.[45]

[40]5 Stat 440 (Aug 16, 1841). President Tyler, if that is what he was, had recommended passage of a bankruptcy law. 4 Richardson at 54–55 (Jun 30, 1841). Initially rejected by the House, the bill was revived and passed after a hasty exercise in log-rolling had purchased Western support in exchange for Eastern votes for the distribution of land revenues to the states. See Cong Globe, 27th Cong, 1st Sess 345, 350; Warren, Bankruptcy in United States History at 76–78 (cited in note 24).

[41]Cong Globe App, 27th Cong, 2d Sess 29 (Sen. Benton); id at 149–50 (Sen. Bayard). Richard Bayard was a Whig who served a total of seven years in the Senate between 1836 and 1845. His brother James, Jr. was a Democrat who served in the same position for most of the years 1851–69. Their father, James Bayard, Sr., was the Federalist who made Jefferson's election possible in 1800. James, Sr.'s father was a member of the Continental Congress; James, Jr.'s son and grandson would also represent Delaware in the Senate.

[42]Cong Globe App, 27th Cong, 2d Sess 149–50.

[43]Id at 150, citing The Federalist No 42.

[44]Cong Globe App, 27th Cong, 2d Sess 149.

[45]Id at 151. See David P. Currie, Subsidiarity, 1 Green Bag 2d 359 (1998). Anything in Sturges v Crowninshield, 17 US 122, 194–95 (1819), that might support the constitutionality of voluntary bankruptcy provisions,

Benton, who in 1837 had ridiculed the notion that British precedents controlled the reach of the bankruptcy power, embraced it without reservation in 1841. "The bankruptcy clause," he now argued,

> authorizes nothing but the establishment of the system of bankruptcy known in England at the time of our Constitution; namely, an act for the benefit of creditors, to enable them to secure something out of a debtor's estate which was going to ruin . . . .[46]

Like habeas corpus, ex post facto laws, trial by jury, bills of attainder, and numerous other technical terms the Constitution had borrowed from English law, Benton added a few weeks later, bankruptcy "must be understood according to [its] then established definition[]; or there is an end to all limitations upon the powers of Congress."[47]

In his general approach to the bankruptcy clause Benton had now approximated the position Webster had taken in 1837. But Webster too had reversed his field, and much of what Benton said in 1841 and 1842 was a direct attack on Webster's new position. The Godlike Daniel was in top form as he defended Congress's power to establish a system of voluntary bankruptcy in a major address in May 1840.[48]

It was true, said Webster, that the bill differed from English and American precedents both by extending beyond traders and by permitting the debtor himself to initiate proceedings. But that did not mean the bill exceeded congressional authority. The power was "granted to Congress in the most general and comprehensive terms," subject only to the requirement that the law be "uniform throughout the United States."[49] That was what Benton had said in 1837.[50]

But what was "the subject of bankruptcies," with respect to which Congress was to have legislative power?

> Bankruptcies are the subject, and the word is most certainly to be taken in its common and popular sense—in that sense in which the people may be supposed to have understood it when they ratified the Constitution. . . .
>
> Bankruptcies, in the general use and acceptation of the term, mean no more than failures. . . . When a man cannot pay his debts, we say he has

Bayard added, was worthy of no consideration: It was "a mere occasional observation, touching a point which had not been discussed, and which was not before the court." Cong Globe App, 27th Cong, 2d Sess 151.

[46]Id at 31.

[47]Id at 125, quoting Blackstone's definition of a bankrupt as "a trader who secretes himself, or does certain other acts, tending to defraud his creditors" (2 Blackstone at *285, *471). See also Benton's third speech of this session on the subject, expanding once more on his arguments and adding Blackstone's definition of "insolvent laws" as those providing for the discharge from suits and imprisonment of debtors "not included within the laws of bankruptcy." Cong Globe App, 27th Cong, 2d Sess 740; 2 Blackstone at *484.

[48]Cong Globe App, 26th Cong, 1st Sess 793–97. "The attitude of the Democrats on this issue," Charles Warren wrote, "was only another example of the fact, so often illustrated in our history, that the dogma of State Rights is conveniently reversible, and that it has been a party doctrine only when its application would suit the party." Warren, Bankruptcy in United States History at 66 (cited in note 24).

[49]Cong Globe App, 26th Cong, 1st Sess 793.

[50]See text accompanying note 30.

> become bankrupt, or has failed. . . . A learned judge[51] has said that a law on the subject of bankruptcies, in the sense of the Constitution, is a law making provision for cases of persons failing to pay their debts.

It was argued, said Webster, that in granting authority over bankruptcy the members of the Convention must have referred to the English laws, which permitted nothing but involuntary proceedings against traders. The proper analogy, however, was not to existing British statutes but rather to "the power of Parliament":

> All saw that Parliament possessed and exercised a power of passing bankrupt laws, and of altering and amending them, from time to time, according to its own discretion, and the necessities of the case. This power they intended to confer on Congress. . . . There is no reason to suppose that it was intended to tie up the hands of Congress to the establishment of that particular bankrupt system which existed in 1789, and to deny to it all power of future modification and amendment; it would be just as reasonable to say that the United States laws of copy-right, of patents for inventions, and many others, could only be mere transcripts of such British statutes on the same subjects as existed in 1789. . . .
>
> The bankrupt system of England, as it existed in 1789, was not the same which had previously existed, nor the same which afterwards existed, or that which now exists. . . . [I]t is preposterous to contend that we are to refuse to ourselves not only the light of our own experience, and all regard to our own peculiar situation, but that we are also to exclude from our regard and notice all modern English improvements, and confine ourselves to the English bankrupt laws as they existed in 1789.[52]

Of course it was; but there was a faint odor of straw in Webster's (equally originalist) argument. Bayard would soon explain, as Webster himself had insisted in 1837, that nobody was arguing Congress could only copy those English statutes that were in force in 1789; the argument was only that the laws Congress adopted had to deal with the subject of bankruptcies.[53] And the subject of bankruptcies, in the opponents' view, did not include the historically separate subject of insolvency—any more, we might add, than it included such distinct subjects as domestic relations, wild animals, or estates in land.

Our outlandish examples, however, illustrate the weakness of the opposition argument as well as its generic plausibility. The constitutional language itself excludes child custody and divorce; not even in Webster's "common and popular sense" could "bankruptcies" conceivably embrace them. Not so insolvency; as Webster said, bankruptcy laws afforded a remedy for insolvency. All agreed that English law provided relief for debtors as well as creditors; the question was whether the fact that English statutes had placed the label "bankruptcy" only upon one class of remedies meant that in selecting that term the Framers had meant to exclude the other.

[51]The reference is to Justice Joseph Story. See 3 Story, § 1108 n.3.

[52]Cong Globe App, 26th Cong, 1st Sess 794. See also Cong Globe App, 27th Cong, 2d Sess 100–101 (Georgia Sen. John Berrien).

[53]See text accompanying notes 27–30, 44.

There is no definitive answer to this question. In arguably analogous cases the Supreme Court has given differing replies. "Bills of attainder" have been held to include what in England formed the distinct category of bills of pains and penalties;[54] "ex post facto laws," an example cited by Benton, had been held on British authority to include only criminal provisions.[55] A Supreme Court dictum in *Sturges v Crowninshield* had suggested that the bankruptcy power was all Webster said it was, and Story had elaborated this conclusion in his treatise;[56] but as Bayard said a dictum is not a holding,[57] and a treatise is only a treatise.[58] That Madison in The Federalist mentioned only absconding debtors[59] does not prove he thought only creditors' remedies were allowed; he was not addressing that issue. The records of the drafting and ratifying conventions reveal nothing of significance on the question.[60]

In analyzing the bill of attainder clause we asked whether the purpose of the provision extended to bills of pains and penalties, and both Clay and Webster pursued a similar inquiry in the case of bankruptcy. There was an obvious need for remedies to relieve innocent insolvents, Webster said; and state law could not afford them, for the Supreme Court had held that the contract clause forbade the states to discharge preexisting debts.[61] Clay, arguing that the bill should contain (as it originally had) *only* voluntary provisions, took the argument a step further, turning Bayard's subsidiarity argument on its head. As Webster had said, there was need for a federal system of voluntary bankruptcy, since the states could not supply it. But there was nothing to prevent their providing remedies for creditors, and the states were the best judges of their own needs: "[T]he extent and measure of Federal legislation should be limited by the extent of the deficiency of State authority to provide for the exigency."[62]

Clay fell short of saying that subsidiarity imposed limits on the bankruptcy power, but his statement was one of the strongest yet in respect to the importance of that principle in guiding congressional discretion. And indeed, although it is possible that the Framers employed the term "bankruptcy" either because they shared Benton's repugnance for relieving debtors or because they believed the states could adequately protect them, there is a good deal to the argument that in addressing the problem of failed debtors the Convention was likely to have given Congress ample power to remedy the deficiencies of

[54]Ex parte Garland, 71 US 333, 377 (1867); see the discussion in chapter 3.

[55]Calder v Bull, 3 US 386 (1798); The First Hundred Years at 42–44. Oddly, opponents of the voluntary bankruptcy bills neglected to cite this well-known decision.

[56]17 US at 122, 194–95; 3 Story, § 1106. See also Rawle at 137, concluding that the bankruptcy power was "limited to two objects, the relief of honest insolvency and the equal distribution of the remnants of property among the creditors."

[57]See note 45.

[58]Story's argument, while powerful, adds nothing to Webster's; since Story said it first, it would be more accurate to state it the other way around.

[59]See note 43 and accompanying text.

[60]In discussing the full faith and credit clause of Article IV, § 1 two delegates to the Convention suggested that acts of the legislatures should be included "for the sake of Acts of insolvency &c," and another followed immediately with the proposition that Congress should also be empowered, as it ultimately was, "[t]o establish uniform laws on the subject of bankruptcies." 2 Farrand at 447. It is not clear from Madison's cryptic report whether any of the delegates in question meant to assimilate insolvency laws to bankruptcy laws, to distinguish them, or neither.

[61]Cong Globe App, 26th Cong, 1st Sess 796; see *Sturges,* 17 US at 194.

[62]Cong Globe App, 26th Cong, 1st Sess 816–17.

state authority. That, after all, was the general plan of the Constitution. On that hypothesis it seems fair to conclude that Congress can adopt both voluntary and involuntary bankruptcy laws.[63] For Bayard and Webster were both right: Neither for creditors nor for debtors could the states provide adequate relief.[64]

Charles Warren, the leading student of the 1841 bankruptcy law, describes it as a success but adds that it soon became unpopular and that as a result "the third session of the 27th Congress witnessed the curious sight of the Whig leader who introduced the Act in the first session supporting the bill for its repeal."[65] The Act was retracted on March 3, 1843, "members of both parties uniting to form the heavy majorities" in each House.[66]

There were conflicting lower-court decisions as to the constitutionality of the 1841 statute. The Supreme Court resolved several issues of its interpretation but not of its validity.[67] Despite the fervent objections of Benton and Bayard at the time of repeal, however, Congress's initial decision to enact the law seems effectively to have settled the long-disputed constitutional question. Let Warren have the last word, as he said it first:

> [B]efore the next bankruptcy law was enacted after the Civil War (in 1867), everyone, lawyers and Courts alike, had so thoroughly accepted the

[63]If this was so, it followed a fortiori that Congress could depart from British precedents limiting bankruptcy to "traders" employed principally in the purchase and resale of goods. The first English bankrupt law had not been so limited; and in any case whether to include nontraders seemed merely a matter of substantive detail, not one of those basic characteristics that defined what was meant by bankruptcy laws.

[64]Repeated efforts were made to attach to the various bills Van Buren's earlier proposal for the involuntary bankruptcy of banks incorporated under state law. See Cong Globe, 26th Cong, 2d Sess 144, 153 (New Hampshire Sen. Henry Hubbard); Cong Globe, 27th Cong, 1st Sess 241 (Tennessee Sen. Alfred Nicholson). Proponents of this amendment echoed Van Buren's argument that bankruptcy would help control undesirable paper money and added that states should not be able to immunize their citizens from federal law by giving them corporate charters. See, e.g., Cong Globe, 26th Cong, 2d Sess 156 (Mississippi Sen. Robert Walker); Cong Globe, 27th Cong, 1st Sess 242 (Sen. Nicholson) (citing a recent pamphlet by former Treasury Secretary Albert Gallatin). Calhoun replied that Congress could no more interfere with state banks than the states could interfere with the Bank of the United States, which the Supreme Court had held immune from state taxation. Cong Globe, 26th Cong, 2d Sess 154; McCulloch v Maryland, 17 US 316, 428–36 (1819). Silas Wright, Democrat of New York, responded that the supremacy clause was a one-way street; Calhoun countered (as the Court would later hold) that the state and Federal Governments were each autonomous in their respective spheres. Cong Globe, 26th Cong, 2d Sess 154; Collector v Day, 78 US 113 (1870). Walker's next argument was more convincing: The National Bank was a fiscal agent of the Government, not (like the state banks) an ordinary private business; and the Court had held that even the state lost its sovereign immunity when it became a shareholder in a private company. Cong Globe, 26th Cong, 2d Sess 157; United States v Planters Bank, 22 US 904, 907–8 (1824); The First Hundred Years at 106–8. The Senate was not impressed; whether for reasons of constitutionality or expediency, the statute as enacted did not contain the banking provision.

[65]Warren, Bankruptcy in United States History at 81–85 (cited in note 24).

[66]Id at 85. The Senate voted 32–13, the House 140–71. See Benton, 2 Thirty Years' View at 463:

> The spectacle was witnessed in relation to the repeal of this act which has rarely been seen before—a repeal of a great act of legislation by the same Congress that passed it—by the same members sitting in the same seats—and the repeal approved by the same President who had approved the enactment. It was a homage to the will of the people, and the result of the general condemnation which the act received from the community.

[67]As late as 1861 a House committee remained unconvinced. The bankruptcy power, wrote Ohio Congressman John Bingham, was "nothing more nor less than a power to enforce the payment of debts through the action of Congress . . . ." HR Rep 92, 36th Cong, 2d Sess 9 (Mar 1, 1861).

principle of voluntary bankruptcy as being within the Constitutional power of Congress, that the question was not even raised, when the Act of 1867 was being debated. That which was of doubtful constitutionality in 1841 had become unquestioned law in 1867—and without any specific decision by the Supreme Court.[68]

III. THE SMITHSONIAN

Congress continued during the period of this study to take a broad view of its authority under the eighth clause of Article I, § 8 "to promote the progress of science and the useful arts, by securing for limited times to authors and inventors the exclusive right to their respective writings and discoveries." Copyright protection had been extended to maps and charts in 1790 and to etchings and prints in 1802;[69] it was accorded to "musical composition[s]" in 1831.[70] Similarly, Congress provided for design patents in 1842.[71] It had already provided for the recording both of patents[72] and of copyright assignments,[73] which seems necessary and proper to the "securing" of "exclusive rights." More startling in terms of the expressly stated purpose of the constitutional provision was Congress's decision in 1831 to extend the life of copyrights that had already been issued.[74] The Supreme Court endorsed the constitutionality of this strange practice nearly 170 years later;[75] I have indicated elsewhere my reasons for suggesting that this decision may be easier to swallow than it appears.[76]

As members of the House had pointed out when the First Congress refused to finance an expedition to Baffin's Bay, however, the clause in question gave Congress power only to provide for patents and copyrights, not to promote knowledge generally.[77] Congress's most significant contribution to science and learning in the years under our microscope was based upon quite another grant of authority.

[68]Warren, Bankruptcy in United States History at 87 (cited in note 24). The Supreme Court would confirm the constitutionality of voluntary bankruptcy legislation in upholding the 1867 statute. Hanover National Bank v Moyses, 186 US 181, 185 (1902).

[69]See The Federalist Period at 92; The Jeffersonians at 5. A bill to add paintings and drawings had failed in 1824, but apparently not for constitutional reasons. See The Jeffersonians at 312–13 n.191.

[70]4 Stat 436, § 1 (Feb 3, 1831).

[71]5 Stat 543 (Aug 29, 1842).

[72]5 Stat 191 (Mar 3, 1837). See also 5 Stat 117, 121, § 11 (Jul 4, 1836) (patent assignments).

[73]4 Stat 728 (Jun 30, 1834).

[74]4 Stat 436, 439, § 16 (Feb 3, 1831). For an entertaining exposition of the origins of this provision see Thomas B. Nachbar, Constructing Copyright's Mythology, 6 Green Bag 2d 37 (2002).

[75]Eldred v Ashcroft, 537 US 186 (2003).

[76]See The Jeffersonians at 312 n.191. For the surprising suggestion that the purpose of the copyright clause was not to encourage creativity after all see Nachbar, Copyright's Mythology at 44 (cited in note 74). It was also during this time that Congress, abandoning any thought of exercising its explicit constitutional power to establish a system of weights and measures (US Const, Art I, § 8, cl 5), directed that the standards previously adopted by the Treasury for customs purposes be distributed to the states in hopes that they would make them generally applicable. 5 Stat 133 (Jun 14, 1836); see The Jeffersonians at 308–9. See also HR Rep 285, 27th Cong, 3d Sess 1 (1843), rejecting a request that the United States adopt the metric system: "[T]he advantages of decimals and regularity of nomenclature, proposed by the new system, would not overcome the attachment of the people to long-established names, usages, and habits, which they are slow to relinquish." We are still paying the price for this short-sighted decision.

[77]See The Federalist Period at 93.

Ever since George Washington was President there had been proposals to establish in the District of Columbia, over which Congress had the power of "exclusive legislation," institutions it might not have authority to set up elsewhere—such as a university, a vaccine agency, or a bank. So long as the institution was truly local, bien entendu, there was no constitutional difficulty. Every endeavor to employ authority over the seat of Government as a pretext for evading limits on congressional powers within the states, however, had so far been rightly rejected.[78]

Then, in 1829, an Englishman named James Smithson died, bequeathing to the United States (on certain contingencies that need not concern us here) a substantial sum of money "to found, at Washington, under the name of the Smithsonian Institution, an Establishment for the increase & diffusion of knowledge among men."[79] The requisite preconditions having occurred, President Jackson in late 1835 called Congress's attention to the legacy.[80] Congress promptly passed a statute authorizing the President to appoint an agent to pursue the claim before the British courts and appropriating up to $10,000 to cover the attendant expenses. Once collected, the legacy was to be applied, "as Congress may hereafter direct," to the object specified in Mr. Smithson's will.[81]

Two years later President Van Buren reported that the money had been duly collected and deposited in the Treasury, where it awaited Congress's further orders.[82] Nearly a decade elapsed before Congress responded, and the passage was rocky. But in August 1846 President Polk finally signed the bill establishing the Smithsonian Institution according to the terms of the bequest.[83]

Part of the delay stemmed from differences of opinion over the nature of the projected institution. Rhode Island Senator Asher Robbins, reflecting the views of several prominent sages consulted at the President's request, proposed a university; former President John Quincy Adams plumped for an observatory, which he had once urged

[78]See id at 71–72, 79 n.190, 222–23; The Jeffersonians at 255, 297–98, 300, 302. As late as 1841 President Tyler vetoed a bill to establish a "Fiscal Corporation of the United States" in the District partly on the ground that Congress could not "invest a local institution with general or national powers." See section IV of chapter 3. See also 3 Elliot's Debates at 439–40 (Edmund Pendleton), assuring the Virginia ratifying convention that Congress's power over the seat of Government was purely local and therefore harmless: It granted no authority to make laws that would "operat[e] without the limits of that district" or "affect the interests of the citizens of the Union at large."

[79]The will is printed in George B. Goode, ed, The Smithsonian Institution, 1846–1896: A History of its First Half Century 19–20 (City of Washington, 1897). See also id at 22:

> The motives which actuated Smithson in mentioning the United States as his residuary legatee, rather than any other government or institution, must remain in doubt, for he is not known to have had any correspondent in America, nor are there in his papers any reference [sic] to it or its distinguished men.

[80]"The Executive having no authority to take any steps for accepting the trust and obtaining the funds, the papers are communicated with a view to such measures as Congress may deem necessary." 3 Richardson at 187 (Dec 17, 1835).

[81]5 Stat 64 (Jul 1, 1836). Sections 1 and 3 of the statute repeated the terms of the bequest almost verbatim. The amount of money paid into the Treasury was reported to be $515,169. See 9 Stat 102, § 2 (Aug 10, 1846).

[82]3 Richardson at 506 (Dec 6, 1838).

[83]9 Stat at 102.

Congress to establish with its own money.[84] "In 1846, however, the country was prepared to expect it to be a general agency for the advancement of scientific interests of all kinds—. . . catholic, . . . unselfish, . . . [and] universal . . . ."[85]

And so it was. The statute directed the Board of Regents of the new Institution to construct a building in Washington containing "suitable rooms" for

> objects of natural history, including a geological and mineralogical cabinet; also a chemical laboratory, a library, a gallery of art, and the necessary lecture rooms.

All relevant objects belonging to the United States and located in Washington, as well as Smithson's own collection, were to be transferred to the Institution. The Regents were also authorized to acquire "new specimens" and instructed to compile "a library composed of valuable works pertaining to all departments of human knowledge." Interest from the bequest was appropriated to cover the Institution's expenses, together with an unspecified sum from general revenues to help cover the cost of construction. The principal was to remain untouched.[86]

Thus Mr. Smithson's money was to be used chiefly to establish a museum, a library, and other facilities not for the Government's own use but rather, in the terms of the will itself, "for the increase and diffusion of knowledge." From the outset there had been some who denied that that was any of the Government's business.

When President Jackson first referred Smithson's bequest to Congress, both Calhoun and his South Carolina colleague William C. Preston predictably objected that Congress could not accept it since it had no power to establish a national university.[87] Adams predictably replied in the House that Congress had full authority to put the money to use in the District of Columbia.[88] South Carolina Representative Alexander Sims

[84]See George B. Goode, The Founding of the Institution, in Goode, The Smithsonian Institution at 25, 32–36 (cited in note 79). For Adams and the observatory see The Jeffersonians at 310–12; for his active role in promoting the Smithsonian see Bemis, Adams and the Union, ch XXIII.

[85]George B. Goode, The Founding of the Institution, in Goode, The Smithsonian Institution at 49 (cited in note 79).

[86]9 Stat at 102–5, §§ 2, 5, 6, 8. Advances from the Treasury were to be repaid out of accumulating interest, but that did not make the project easier to sustain; even a loan must be justified as necessary and proper to some enumerated power. Interest not needed for purposes of the Institution itself was to be expended as the Regents thought best "for the promotion of the purpose of the testator." Id at 105–6, § 9. The following section (id at 106) required the holder of any future copyright to deliver copies of the copyrighted work to the Institution and to the Library of Congress, with no mention of compensation. The acquisition of books and other works is necessary and proper to the establishment of libraries, but why it did not offend the taking clause to make contributions to the Government a condition of copyright protection seemed to call for explanation.

[87]Cong Deb, 24th Cong, 1st Sess 1375 (Sen. Preston); id at 1376 (Sen. Calhoun). Calhoun repeated his objection in 1839. See National Intelligencer, Apr 8, 1839, p 2, 14 Calhoun Papers at 576–78. Preston added the quaint argument that the United States could not receive legacies even for national purposes, Cong Deb, 24th Cong, 1st Sess 1374, but that was singularly unpersuasive; acceptance of private funding as an alternative to taxation would seem necessary and proper to the exercise of each of the enumerated powers. On the other hand, the fact that in the end the Institution would soak up no tax revenues made it harder rather than easier to sustain, for it meant one could not defend it on the basis of President Monroe's broad reading of the spending power. See The Jeffersonians at 300.

[88]Cong Deb App, 24th Cong, 1st Sess 79. See also Cong Deb, 24th Cong, 1st Sess 1375 (Virginia Sen. Benjamin Leigh); id at 1376–77 (New Jersey Sen. Samuel Southard). Buchanan of Pennsylvania said it was all

returned to the attack in 1846: Only a local legislature in the District could administer such a legacy, as "the Government was not instituted for any such purpose as the administration of charities"; and "[i]t was never intended that this fund should be applied to the exclusive purpose of the use of the District of Columbia."[89]

Congress passed the bill anyway, and that strict constructionist James K. Polk signed it into law. One can hardly avoid the conclusion that in so doing they played fast and loose with the power to legislate for the seat of Government. For nobody pretended that the Institution was especially intended to serve the few residents of Washington; the debate was about creating a great national resource for the whole country. The same was true when Congress established a national art gallery in 1860.[90] These were at least arguable cases, for District people would benefit from these institutions in common with everyone else. The ruse had been laid bare, however, two months before the National Gallery bill was adopted, when Congress brazenly established the United States Agricultural Society in the District of Columbia—which even at that time was hardly renowned for either its produce or its pigs.[91]

One final aspect of the Smithsonian legislation deserves mention. Section 1 of the statute described the Institution as an "establishment" consisting of an assortment of ranking federal officials, from the President, Vice-President, and Cabinet through the Chief Justice, the Commissioner of Patents, and the Mayor of Washington.[92] Their task was "the supervision of the affairs of [the] institution and the advice and instruction of [the] board of regents,"[93] to whom the conduct of "the business of the . . . institution" was

---

right because the United States would be acting as trustee for Smithson's estate, id at 1377; he failed to explain how that fiction connected the proposal with any of Congress's powers.

[89]Cong Globe, 29th Cong, 1st Sess 738. F.P. Stanton of Tennessee repeated the simplistic answer: "[T]his institution, located within a territory over which Congress has exclusive jurisdiction, surely cannot involve the exercise of a power unauthorized by the Constitution . . . ." Cong Globe App, 29th Cong, 1st Sess 891.

[90]12 Stat 35 (Jun 15, 1860). The same Congress, over vigorous states'-rights objections, also passed a joint resolution directing the Superintendent of the United States Coast Survey to send a vessel to Labrador to observe a solar eclipse—for reasons, it was suggested, of facilitating naval operations as well as commerce. 12 Stat 117 (Jun 15, 1860); see Cong Globe, 36th Cong, 1st Sess 1959–60 (Sens. Pearce and Iverson, pro and con respectively).

[91]12 Stat 12 (Apr 19, 1860). The House committee report reveals that what was involved was the incorporation of a private association. HR Rep 66, 36th Cong, 1st Sess 1 (1860). Private enterprise does not become public simply by obtaining a corporate charter, but on the theory we are discussing the District power can be exercised only for local purposes. The Bank of the United States, you remember, was a largely private corporation. President Taylor, without identifying any source of congressional authority, had earlier urged the establishment of an "agricultural bureau" in the Department of the Interior. First Annual Message, 5 Richardson at 9, 18 (Dec 4, 1849). President Fillmore repeated this request in his own first Annual Message the following year. Id at 77, 85–86 (Dec 2, 1850).

[92]9 Stat at 102.

[93]9 Stat at 105, § 8. The early members of the Establishment set a precedent of taking their responsibilities lightly:

> The Establishment, though exercising constant supervision over the affairs of the Institution, being represented upon the Board of Regents by two of its members, . . . has never deemed it necessary to take any formal action at its meetings, save to adopt . . . a code of by-laws, and to listen from time to time to general statements by the Secretary in regard to the condition and affairs of the Institution.

entrusted.[94] Three members of the Establishment (the Vice-President, the Chief Justice, and the Mayor) were to sit on the Board of Regents, along with three members of each House (to be chosen by their respective chambers) and "six other persons" to be appointed "by joint resolution of the Senate and House of Representatives."[95] The Regents in turn were to elect a "secretary" who among other things was to "take charge of the building" and "discharge the duties of librarian and of keeper of the museum"; in effect he was to be chief executive officer of the entire Institution.[96]

What was this Institution, anyway? If it was a Government agency, the provisions for its governance posed a nightmare of separation of powers problems. "Officers of the United States" were supposed to be appointed by the President and the Senate (or sometimes by the President alone, the heads of departments, or the courts), not by Congress or one of its Houses.[97] No one was supposed to hold "an office of the United States" and a seat in Congress at the same time.[98] No member of the House or Senate was supposed to be appointed to "any civil office under the authority of the United States" created during his term.[99] Yet under the statute Congress named members of the Board of Regents, Congressmen served as Regents, and several were appointed during the term in which the Institution was established. If Regents were federal officers, all of this was flatly unconstitutional.[100]

The statute did not say whether the Institution was a Government agency. Not every organization created by Congress is. The Bank of the United States was not; it was a largely private corporation. The House committee appeared to think the Smithsonian was similar: Its managerial positions were "offices or trusts of a corporation," not "civil offices" of the United States.[101] But the Smithsonian, unlike the Bank, was financed with money that had been given to the United States, and its "Establishment" was made up entirely of federal officers.[102] Both they and the Regents were unpaid for their services to

---

George B. Goode, The Establishment and the Board of Regents, in Goode, The Smithsonian Institution at 59, 60 (cited in note 79).

[94]9 Stat at 103, § 3.

[95]Id.

[96]Id at 103, 105, §§ 3, 7; see Goode, The Smithsonian Institution at 61 (cited in note 79). The provisions respecting the Establishment, the Board of Regents, and the Secretary remain substantially unchanged today. 20 USC §§ 41–43, 46 (2000).

[97]US Const, Art II, 2. See Buckley v Valeo, 424 US 1, 124–41 (1976).

[98]US Const, Art I, § 6.

[99]Id.

[100]Moreover, arguments against the inclusion of the Chief Justice can be made on the basis of Article III, § 2, which limits federal courts to the decision of judicial "cases" and "controversies." From the beginning, however, judges for better or worse have accepted nonjudicial responsibilities to be exercised outside the court itself; there is no explicit bar to their holding two offices at once, so long as they do not serve in Congress. See Mistretta v United States, 488 US 361, 397–408 (1989); The Federalist Period at 209–10, 274 n.310 (discussing the diplomatic adventures of Chief Justices Jay and Ellsworth). If the Regents could be characterized as "heads of departments" there was no difficulty with the Secretary's selection, but the supervisory powers of the Establishment suggested that its members, rather than the Regents, might occupy that position. For objections to the appointment of members of Congress based on the ineligibility and incompatibility clauses see Cong Globe, 29th Cong, 2d Sess 191 (Florida Sen. James Westcott); Cong Globe, 30th Cong, 2d Sess 23 (Tennessee Rep. Andrew Johnson). The appointments clause argument was apparently not made.

[101]HR Rep 63, 29th Cong, 2d Sess (1847).

[102]Stressing "the substantial federal funding" of the Institution and "the important supervisory role played by governmental officials," the District of Columbia Circuit held in 1977 that the Smithsonian, as an

the Institution,[103] but that seems immaterial; compensation is not central to the purposes of any of the relevant provisions.[104] More pertinent, perhaps, is the fact that the Institution's functions were proprietary rather than governmental; as an original matter one might argue that the separation-of-powers provisions with which we are concerned, like certain intergovernmental immunities, apply only to the business of governing, not to government-run business.[105] One might also take refuge once again in the argument that if the Smithsonian was an agency of government it was one of the District of Columbia: Territorial precedents had evinced the conviction that constitutional concerns over separation of powers were more attenuated in local than in national matters, and the official line was that the Smithsonian was a creature of Congress's authority to legislate for the seat of Government.[106]

Overall the whole transaction was pretty shady from a constitutional point of view. But we got a pretty good set of museums out of it, didn't we?[107]

"independent establishment of the United States," was a "federal agency" for purposes of the Federal Tort Claims Act, 28 USC § 2671 (2000). Expeditions Unlimited Aquatic Enterprises, Inc v Smithsonian Institution, 566 F2d 289, 296 & n.6. Subsequently the same court held that the Smithsonian was neither an "establishment in the executive branch of the Government" (because not entrusted with the execution of laws or subject to presidential direction) nor an "authority of the Government of the United States" (because not exercising "governmental authority") within the meaning of the Privacy Act, 5 USC § 552a et seq (2000). Dong v Smithsonian Institution, 125 F3d 877, 879–82 (DC Cir 1997). Cf Cotton v Adams, 798 F Supp 22 (DDC 1992) (holding the Smithsonian a federal agency within the Freedom of Information Act, whose definitions the Privacy Act incorporates). As of November 2002 (on a website since replaced) the Smithsonian described itself as an "independent trust instrumentality of the United States."

[103] 9 Stat at 103, § 3.

[104] See The Jeffersonians at 72, discussing this question in the context of the incompatibility clause of Article I, § 6.

[105] Cf Dong v Smithsonian Institution, 125 F3d at 877–92. See also Bank of the United States v Planters Bank, 22 US 904, 907–8 (1824) (immunity from suit); South Carolina v United States, 199 US 437, 452 (1905) (tax immunity); United Transportation Union v Long Island RR, 455 US 678, 685 (1982) (erstwhile immunity from federal regulation). The dangers of generalization in this field, however, are suggested by the wholly inappropriate application of the same distinction in the so-called "market participant" exception to the negative effect of the commerce clause on state authority. Reeves v Stake, 447 US 429, 436–39 (1980); The Second Century at 583–84. Doubts as to the immunity of proprietary activities from separation-of-powers concerns under present law, moreover, are suggested by Springer v Philippine Islands, 277 US 189, 203 (1928), and Metropolitan Washington Airports Authority v Citizens for the Abatement of Aircraft Noise, Inc, 501 US 252, 267 (1991), both of which struck down on general separation-of-powers principles provisions that envisioned the presence of legislators on managerial boards of public entities engaged in proprietary activities.

A House committee in 1899, building on congressional precedents subsequent to the establishment of the Smithsonian, concluded that members of advisory commissions, regents of public institutions, and similar animals were not "officers of the United States" within the meaning of the incompatibility provision. HR Rep 2205, pt 3, 55th Cong, 3d Sess 2–3 (1899). See also Johnny H. Killian, ed, The Constitution of the United States of America: Analysis and Interpretation (S Doc 99-16, 99th Cong, 1st Sess) at 131 (Government Printing Office, 1987) [hereafter cited as The Annotated Constitution] and the precedents there cited; Buckley v Valeo, 424 US 1, 138–39 (1976), where the Court said that officers appointed by Congress could be authorized to act "in an area sufficiently removed from the administration and enforcement of the public law to permit their being performed by persons not 'Officers of the United States.'"

[106] For the territorial analogy see The Jeffersonians at 109–13.

[107] We also got that observatory that Mr. Adams had been pushing, but in an indirect (not to say underhanded) way. In authorizing the President to hire astronomers for continuation of the Coastal Survey in 1832, Congress had gone so far as to specify that nothing in the statute should "be construed to authorize the construction or maintenance of a permanent astronomical observatory." 4 Stat 570–71, § 2 (Jul 10, 1832). On the same day, however, Congress appropriated $487.80 to reimburse Lieutenant Charles Wilkes for the expenses of

IV. RETROCESSION

The Smithsonian controversy was not the only one of the period under examination respecting congressional authority over the seat of Government. Indeed the District of Columbia itself had been significantly reduced in size when Congress ceded its Virginia portions, including the city of Alexandria, back to the state in 1846.[108] That territory, the statute explained, would not be needed for Government purposes in the foreseeable future, and Virginia had agreed to accept it. A referendum called for by the legislation approved the retrocession, and Alexandria was once more a part of Virginia.[109]

A victory for self-government, for democracy?[110] Perhaps; and for slavery too, as there had recently been fears that Congress might attempt to abolish slavery in the District.[111] On the substantive constitutional question there was little to say, and little was said. One lawmaker argued that Congress had exhausted its authority when it created the District, another that Congress could move the capital but not cede part of it, a third that if Congress could surrender part of the District it could surrender all of it and thus frustrate the purpose of the constitutional provision.[112] That was all hogwash. Even if Congress had to maintain a seat of Government free from state authority (which it did not), and even if a capital once established could not be moved (which it could), Virginia Representative Robert M.T. Hunter was surely right that nothing in the Constitution required that the

---

building "astronomical instruments" for a naval exploring expedition, 4 Stat 569, § 2. Before embarking, Wilkes, who was superintendent of the Navy's Depot of Charts and Instruments in Washington, had constructed a small observatory at his own expense to aid in the rating and repairing of chronometers. His successor was directed by the Secretary of the Navy to make astronomical observations in aid of the expedition. When he reported that existing facilities were inadequate, Congress authorized the expenditure of $25,000 for construction in the District of Columbia of "a suitable house for a depot of charts and instruments of the navy" (5 Stat 576, §§ 1, 3 (Aug 31, 1842))—on the basis of a committee report making clear that an observatory was a principal object of the bill. HR Rep 449, 27th Cong, 2d Sess 3 (1842). The Secretary took this as authorization to construct what came to be known as the Naval Observatory, and thus Adams was able to say in 1846 that he was "delighted that an astronomical observatory . . . had been smuggled into the number of institutions of the country, under the mask of a small depot for charts." Cong Globe, 29th Cong, 1st Sess 738. See Charles O. Paullin, Early Movements for a National Observatory, 1802–1842, in John B. Larner, ed, 25 Records of the Columbia Historical Society 36, 49–56 (1923); G. Brown Goode, The Origin of the National Scientific and Educational Institutions of the United States 55–66 (Putnam, 1890).

[108] 9 Stat 35 (Jul 9, 1846).

[109] See Va Laws 1845–46, ch 64, p 50, and President Polk's proclamation of September 7, 1846, 9 Stat 1000.

[110] See Cong Globe App, 29th Cong, 1st Sess 894 (Rep. Hunter), adding that certain constitutional provisions such as the privileges and immunities, port preferences, and fugitive slave clauses did not apply to the District and noting the continuing temptation to use congressional authority over the District as a pretext for meddling with matters the Constitution had reserved to the states. We have just noted the same tendency, but unfortunately shrinking the District would do nothing to alleviate it; so long as the District exists, so does Congress's power.

[111] See Descent into the Maelstrom, ch 1. When retrocession of the entire District had been proposed a few years earlier, Virginia Representative Henry Wise had argued that it was the duty of every Southerner to support it, as abolitionists wanted to retain the District for their own nefarious purposes. Cong Globe, 25th Cong, 2d Sess 297 (Apr 11, 1838). See also the letter of John L. O'Sullivan to President Polk, Feb 15, 1845, 9 Polk Correspondence at 105–6.

[112] See Cong Globe, 29th Cong, 1st Sess 778 (Rep. Payne); id at 780 (Rep. McClernand); id at 1043 (Sen. Miller).

District remain a full ten miles square.[113]

The provision for a referendum on retrocession, however, suggested a novel constitutional issue that cried out for congressional discussion. The Constitution makes no provision for direct democracy, and it seems unlikely that in any case of *national* legislation Congress could reconvey to the people the legislative authority they had vested in it by Article I, § 1.[114] Nor can one say with any degree of confidence, as one can in the case of delegation to local legislatures in the District or the territories, that the Framers contemplated even local lawmaking by initiative or referendum.[115] Nevertheless one suspects the Supreme Court might be more receptive to direct democracy in the District or the territories, both of which lie outside many of the ordinary provisions respecting the organization of government; if under the necessary and proper clause Congress may delegate its authority to a local legislature, why not to the people as well?[116]

These questions would have made excellent fodder for constitutional debate in Congress; unfortunately no one seems to have raised them at all.[117]

V. PRAYERS

Thanksgiving proclamations had been largely out of favor since President Jefferson took office,[118] and President Jackson continued the negative tradition. As he wrote to an inquiring religious association in 1832, he felt unable to exhort his fellow citizens to pray

[113]Cong Globe App, 29th Cong, 1st Sess 894, 897; HR Rep 325, 29th Cong, 1st Sess 3–4 (1846). The dimensions specified in the Constitution are a ceiling, not a floor: "Congress shall have power . . . [t]o exercise exclusive legislation . . . over such District (not exceeding ten miles square) as may . . . become the seat of Government of the United States . . . ." US Const, Art I, § 8, cl 17. For earlier arguments over the power to abolish the District or move the Government see The Jeffersonians at 66–70. When the question of the validity of retrocession finally reached the Supreme Court some thirty years later, the Court concluded that the passage of time precluded its consideration. Phillips v Payne, 92 US 130 (1875).

[114]Cf. A.L.A. Schechter Poultry Corp. v United States, 295 US 495, 530–37 (1935) (striking down what the Court viewed as a delegation of legislative authority to the President); Carter v Carter Coal Co., 298 US 238, 311 (1936) (striking down a delegation to private interest groups).

[115]Although popular legislation was endemic in the colonies, it had fallen largely into disfavor by the time the Constitution was adopted, except for continuing town meetings in New England and for the arguably distinguishable precedent of popular ratification of state constitutions, first required by Massachusetts in 1778. Popular ratification of *statutory* law was reintroduced in Massachusetts by express constitutional amendment in 1820; when it was later prescribed by state legislatures without express constitutional sanction it tended to be struck down. See, e.g., Parker v Commonwealth, 6 Pa St 507, 527 (1847) (invalidating a local-option provision with respect to the sale of liquor); Charles S. Lobingier, The People's Law; or Popular Participation in Law-Making 68–104, 163–79, 349–66 (Macmillan, 1909). But see Wales v Belcher, 20 Mass (3 Pick) 508, 511 (1826), upholding a statutory referendum provision without reliance on the recently adopted constitutional authorization and invoking the analogy of popular ratification of state constitutions: "Why may not the legislature make the existence of any act depend upon the happening of any future event?"

[116]Cf City of Eastlake v Forest City Enterprises, Inc., 426 US 668, 675 (1976), upholding a requirement that zoning changes be approved by referendum and distinguishing delegations to executive officers: The nondelegation doctrine was "inapplicable where, as here, . . . we deal with a power reserved by the people to themselves."

[117]Whether silence on this issue suggests inattention or an understanding that there was no constitutional problem I cannot say. Compare The Jeffersonians at 295–301 (discussing the case of the Vaccine Agent) and chapter 3 of this volume (discussing the censure of President Jackson).

[118]Of Presidents from Jefferson through the second Adams only Madison proclaimed a day of Thanksgiving, and he later repented. See The Jeffersonians at 325.

> without transcending those limits which are prescribed by the Constitution for the President and without feeling that I might in some degree disturb the security which religion now enjoys in this country in its complete separation from the political concerns of the General Government.[119]

The only Presidents to break this tradition between Jackson's inauguration and Lincoln's were John Tyler and Zachary Taylor.[120]

There was vocal opposition to Thanksgiving proclamations in Congress as well. Cholera having broken out in Canada in 1832, two proposals were made to keep it out of the country: Money should be spent to combat the disease,[121] and the President should be asked to proclaim a day of fasting and prayer.[122] A respectable number of Representatives protested on constitutional grounds, several invoking President Jackson's recent letter. William Archer of Virginia said "[h]e presumed there was no gentleman in that House who could believe that either the General or the State Governments had, as such, any thing to do with the subject of religion at all."[123] His Senate colleague Littleton Tazewell took the same position: "Congress had no more power to recommend [a day of prayer] by joint resolution, than to enact by law, any matter or thing concerning any religious matter or right whatsoever."[124] The most impressive argument, however, came from Representative Gulian Verplanck of New York.[125]

He made no constitutional objection, Verplanck said, because the proposal involved a mere recommendation: "The question of constitutional power seems to me, in strictness, to arise only in matters of proper legislation, of binding law, or of any other action of the Government, which is obligatory upon the citizen."

> But in another point of view it seems to me clear, that whenever

[119]Jackson to Synod of the Reformed Church, Jun 12, 1832, 4 Jackson Correspondence at 447.

[120]For Tyler see 4 Richardson at 32 (Apr 13, 1841). The occasion was the death of President Harrison. Taylor's proclamation called for a day of fasting and prayer for victims of a cholera epidemic in 1849; it is not reported in Richardson. See K. Jack Bauer, Zachary Taylor: Soldier, Planter, Statesman of the Old Southwest 268 (LSU, 1985); Charles E. Rosenberg, The Cholera Years 101–24 (Chicago, 1962).

[121]See Cong Deb, 22d Cong, 1st Sess 3677 (Rep. Howard). Hall and Polk complained that Congress had no authority to spend for this purpose, id at 3697, and the suggestion perished.

[122]Id at 1128 (Sen. Clay).

[123]Id at 3833.

[124]Id at 1131–32. See also id at 3833 (South Carolina Rep. Warren Davis); id at 3834 (North Carolina Rep. Samuel Carson); id at 3859 (Mississippi Rep. Franklin Plummer). Massachusetts Representative Henry Dearborn noted that the first two Presidents had done it, Virginia's Robert Craig that such a proclamation would be "extra official" and not binding. Id at 3834. But the whole point of the proposed resolution, said Plummer wisely, was to put the weight of the Government behind the recommendation. Id at 3859. Recall the controversy over the constitutionality of congressional hot air in connection with Senate criticism of President Jackson during the Bank War, discussed in chapter 3. Archer's motion to table the prayer proposal before third reading failed 63–104. Cong Deb, 22d Cong, 1st Sess 3833.

[125]A classicist and theologian as well as a lawyer, Verplanck was a man of "deeply religious feeling" and an active member of the Episcopal Church. In the New York legislature he had successfully sponsored a bill to do away with the oath of office previously required of a number of petty officials on the ground that it was "an act of public irreverence" that "tended to cheapen the institution." See Robert W. July, The Essential New Yorker: Gulian Crommelin Verplanck 81–82, 211 (Duke, 1951). Further biographical information on Verplanck is given in note 114 of chapter 4.

> Congress or any other political body in this country meddles in affairs of religion, they must run counter, more or less, to the spirit of our free institutions, securing equal religious rights. In this land, where every man's faith is protected, and no man's faith is preferred, even a resolution or a proclamation for a fast from the civil authority may offend the consciences or wound the feelings of some or other of our citizens. . . . Nay, the very language employed by us, or the Executive, and the religious opinions thus expressed or implied, however just and pious we may deem them, as they may truly be, can hardly fail of giving offence to some, perhaps many, of our constituents, of other creeds, whose patriotism is as pure as our own, and whose rights are as sacred. . . .
>
> The observation of my whole life . . . has taught me that you cannot make religion a party and an actor in the halls of human legislation without infinite and incalculable evil—evil to religion, evil to the State. You inflame the rancor of party politics, by adding to it the fervor of religious zeal, or that of sectarian fanaticism, or else you do worse. You pollute and degrade religion by making her the handmaid of human power, or the partisan of personal ambition. You mix her heavenly aspirations with earthly passions. You turn her meekness into gall. . . .
>
> I shall, therefore, not upon constitutional, still less upon party grounds, vote . . . against this resolution in all its forms. . . . There is no need of our action here. Let it be left to the ecclesiastical authority, or to the voluntary arrangement of private citizens, guided by the recommendations of those whose age and virtue give them the right to advise others. Let not such a subject become the theme of party. Let us not make out of it a new precedent for interfering hereafter upon subjects which we cannot touch without polluting them. Let us leave prayer and humiliation to be prompted by the devotion of the heart, and not the bidding of the State.[126]

Mr. Verplanck is not widely remembered today. He seems to me, on this issue at least, to have been a very wise man.[127]

[126]Cong Deb, 22d Cong, 1st Sess 3884–86.

[127]Having previously passed the Senate, the resolution was tabled after third reading in the House on motion of John Quincy Adams. House Journal, 22d Cong, 1st Sess 1182 (Jul 14, 1832)—for what reason the record does not reveal. The session ended two days later. Cong Deb, 22d Cong, 1st Sess 3916.

A pair of related incidents twenty years apart documents the prevalence, during the period of this study, of the idea that Government neutrality is central to the question whether a measure passes muster under the religion clauses of the first amendment. New York Representative William Hogan objected in 1832 to a modest proposal to remit customs duties on a painting and furniture given to the Catholic Bishop of Chicago by the King of France. What public benefit, he asked, would such a tax break produce, and did the Constitution permit such a connection between church and state? Charles Wickliffe of Kentucky replied that the Bishop was engaged in educational good works and that duties had been remitted in similar cases before; it should not be held against the beneficiary that he was a Catholic bishop. Our friend Verplanck added that the general principle was that Congress "ought not to tax the donations of learned or pious men abroad to institutions of religion or literature in this country," which he characterized as "fruits of philanthropy and proofs of goodwill." Hogan withdrew his objection, and the bill was adopted. Cong Deb, 22d Cong, 2d Sess 2201–3; 6 Stat 484 (Mar 31, 1832). Cf Walz v Tax Commission, 397 US 664 (1970); The Second Century at 527–28. Conversely, in 1852, when it was proposed to exempt a box of religious vestments from customs duties in order, as Senators

In contrast to the deafening presidential silence with respect to Thanksgiving the appointment of congressional chaplains continued, but not without periodic objection. The first came from Georgia Representative Mark Cooper in 1839. By what authority, he asked, were chaplains appointed and funds appropriated for their salaries? "[T]his matter of religious denominations," he said, "should not be agitated in this House." With this in mind he moved to reconsider the decision to name a chaplain, "that we may not exercise powers not granted, and may prevent a union of Church and State."[128] In vain. Virginia's Robert Craig replied that a chaplain was like a doorkeeper, an "officer" the Constitution (in Article I, § 2) expressly authorized the House to appoint.[129] Invoking long precedent, Eugenius Nisbet of Georgia urged the House not to banish the influence of Christianity, which, he said, "ought to pervade . . . all the departments of Government."[130]

> The appointment of a Chaplain to this House, [Nisbet continued,] is a declaration, by the nation itself, that the Bible is true. . . . Does not this act proclaim, through the length and breadth of the land, that, according to the belief of the American Congress, God reigns in Heaven and upon earth?[131]

Apparently this was thought to be an argument in favor of the appointment. Without a hint of irony Nisbet observed that he too would view any union of church and state as "abhorrent" but that he had no fears on that score: "The very freedom of religious opinion and action guarantied [sic] to the people must operate as an insurmountable bar to such a union."[132] Cooper's motion received a measly twelve votes.[133]

During the 1840's an Indiana Congressman named John Pettit waged a lonely battle against appropriations for congressional chaplains.[134] If members wanted spiritual solace, he argued, they ought to pay for it themselves.[135] Payment of official compensation tended to establish religion and indeed to prefer one or two sects.[136] It was unconstitutional to

---

Mallory and Pratt argued, to avoid taxing the exercise of religion, Delaware Senator James Bayard objected that the tax was general and the requested exemption particular, and the bill narrowly failed to pass. Cong Globe, 32d Cong, 1st Sess 880–85. The two cases may not be reconcilable on their facts, but the principle that prevailed in both seemed to be that, while religious organizations did not have to be excluded from generally available Government benefits, they ought not to be granted what were perceived as special favors.

[128]Cong Globe, 26th Cong, 1st Sess 83–84. If Congress had power to pay chaplains, Cooper added, "he would be the first man to persuade the people to take it away, and thus sever all connection between Church and State." Id at 85.

[129]Id.

[130]Cong Globe App, 26th Cong, 1st Sess 65. "What, sir," Nesbit rhetorically inquired, "does not liberty owe to Christianity?" Christianity had brought us the Pilgrims and the Huguenots (id)—both refugees, he did not add, from state-sponsored religions.

[131]Id.

[132]Id at 66. "Our denominational divisions," he added (id), "constitute a system of sleepless and enterprising vigilance over the encroachments of the church."

[133]Cong Globe, 26th Cong, 1st Sess 85.

[134]David Outlaw, a North Carolina Congressman of more conventional views, professed to believe Pettit could not be serious: "The fellow makes the same opposition at every session, with no other object I am satisfied but to gain notoriety . . ." David Outlaw to Emily B. Outlaw, Dec 9, 1847, David Outlaw Papers, Southern History Collection, University of North Carolina at Chapel Hill.

[135]Cong Globe, 28th Cong, 2d Sess 2 (1844); Cong Globe, 30th Cong, 1st Sess 16 (1847).

[136]Cong Globe, 28th Cong, 2d Sess 2. Repeated pleas by Pettit and others to drop the requirement that the House and Senate chaplains be of different denominations came to nothing. Virginia Senator James Mason

spend public money to advance religion.[137] It was not for Congress "to prescribe the form of religion" or to make appropriations for religious purposes.[138] The power to spend was no broader than the power to legislate, and Congress could not legislate with respect to religion.[139] Congress could not take a taxpayer's money to support a religion with which he disagreed.[140] Recurring petitions to Congress expanded on Pettit's objections. As a group of Arkansas citizens put it in 1857,

> Inasmuch as [the chaplain] is made an officer of Government, the doctrines preached by him in his official capacity must be considered those of the Government, whose acknowledged agent he is, and by whom he is paid for promulgating his sectarian views, with money drawn from the whole people, nine tenths of whom, perhaps, hold sentiments entirely at variance with those they are thus by law compelled to support.

And thus, the petition concluded, the appointment and remuneration of congressional chaplains offended both the establishment and free exercise clauses of the first amendment.[141]

Unfazed, Congress continued overwhelmingly to vote itself chaplains at taxpayer expense. George Badger of North Carolina had enunciated what appeared to be the definitive justification of the time in urging rejection of yet another petition against the practice in 1853: The term "establishment of religion" referred to the English model, which in his view had three principal features: "endowment at the public expense, peculiar privileges to its members, [and] disadvantages upon those who should reject its doctrines." Any one of these features, Badger acknowledged, would suffice to condemn a measure under the first amendment, but the appointment of chaplains involved none of them; the Framers had not meant to forbid mere expressions of devotion.[142]

Congress likewise authorized the appointment of *military* chaplains during this period, and although there were a few objections to this practice too Georgia Senator John M. Berrien argued powerfully that the military was a special case.

> The Constitution forbade [Congress] from interfering with matters of religion. But had they, therefore, the right to send the soldiers beyond the pale of religion?

---

actually defended the requirement in 1854 on the ground that it showed Congress favored no particular religion. Cong Globe, 33d Cong, 2d Sess 31.

[137]Cong Globe, 29th Cong, 1st Sess 92 (1845).

[138]Cong Globe, 29th Cong, 2d Sess 40 (1846).

[139]Cong Globe, 30th Cong, 1st Sess 15–16 (1847).

[140]Id at 16. Cf Madison's famous Memorial and Remonstrance against Religious Assessments, Jun 20, 1785, William T. Hutchinson et al, 8 The Papers of James Madison 298–304 (Chicago, 1973).

[141]Cong Globe, 35th Cong, 1st Sess 25. See also the 1850 petition from a group of Maine citizens arguing that the appointment of chaplains at federal expense was "neither more nor less than the establishment of a national religion." Cong Globe, 31st Cong, 1st Sess 100. An 1856 petition from Tennessee citizens added a third basis of objection: Appointment of a chaplain offended the provision of Article VI, ¶ 3 proscribing any religious test for federal office. Cong Globe, 34th Cong, 1st Sess 479.

[142]S Rep 376, 32d Cong, 2d Sess 1–4 (Jan 19, 1853).

Congress had an affirmative duty, Berrien said, to provide ministers for soldiers who could not provide them for themselves.[143] One is reminded of much later decisions respecting such matters as food and medical attention for prisoners.[144]

A final incident concerning the religion clauses arose in 1851. In sending a treaty with Switzerland to the Senate for possible approval, President Fillmore called attention to a provision warning that, "on account of the tenor of the federal constitution of Switzerland, Christians alone [were] entitled to the enjoyment of the privileges guaranteed by the present article in the Swiss Cantons." The President denounced this provision in no uncertain terms:

> It is quite certain that neither by law, nor by treaty, nor by any other official proceeding is it competent for the Government of the United States to establish any distinction between its citizens founded on differences in religious beliefs. Any benefit or privilege conferred by law on one must be common to all, and we are not at liberty, on a question of such vital interest and plain constitutional duty, to consider whether the particular case is one in which substantial inconvenience or injustice might ensue. It is enough that an inequality would be sanctioned hostile to the institutions of the United States and inconsistent with the Constitution and the laws.[145]

At the President's suggestion the Senate consented to the treaty on condition that the offending provision be amended, and it was; two years later Fillmore submitted the revised agreement without the discriminatory reference to Christians, and the Senate approved it.[146] Chalk up another modest victory for religious freedom.[147]

[143]Cong Globe, 29th Cong, 2d Sess 222 (1847).

[144]See The Second Century at 472 n.51. Two minor statutes enacted during the period of this study suggested that Congress was still somewhat more tolerant of connections between church and state than President Madison had been. Madison had vetoed a bill to incorporate a church partly on the ground that it authorized the religious corporation to engage in charitable works; Congress in 1858 issued a corporate charter to a "benevolent association" of churches "to relieve the wants of the destitute poor." 11 Stat 266 (May 4, 1858). Madison had vetoed a bill to donate public land to a church; Congress in 1860 authorized an Episcopal missionary society to enter a specified tract of land "at the rate of one dollar and twenty-five cents per acre." 12 Stat 22 (Jun 1, 1860). That the latter statute required the society to pay the statutory minimum price for the land does not distinguish the two cases, for individual parcels sometimes sold for considerably more at auction. See Benjamin H. Hibbard, A History of the Public Land Policies 80, 102 (Peter Smith, 1839). The debates reveal no discussion of these provisions. For Madison's vetoes see The Jeffersonians at 318–24.

[145]5 Richardson at 98, 99. Fillmore also objected to provisions giving Swiss citizens all the privileges and immunities of citizens of other states of the United States, including the right to acquire land. It was not for the President and Senate, said Fillmore, to remove the disabilities of aliens respecting land ownership; "[t]he authority naturally belongs to the State within whose limits the land may lie." Id at 98. The Senate rejected these provisions too, and they were accordingly amended. 11 Stat 587, 590, Art V (Nov 25, 1850). Caleb Cushing, Attorney General under the states'-rights Democrat Franklin Pierce, would take a broader view: The states could not make treaties, and it was not to be supposed that the power "exist[ed] nowhere"; the Jay Treaty had given British subjects the right to own land in the United States, and the Supreme Court had sustained it. 8 Op AG 411, 415–17 (Feb 26, 1857); 8 Stat 116, 122, Art 9 (Nov 19, 1794); Fairfax's Devisee v Hunter's Lessee, 11 US 603, 627 (1813).

[146]See 5 Richardson at 187 (Feb 3, 1853); 11 Stat at 588, Art I. Along the same lines see President Polk's journal entry for January 31, 1846, 1 Polk Diary at 205–6:

VI. SPOILS

There are three things every schoolchild learns (or used to learn) about Andrew Jackson. He was the hero of the Battle of New Orleans; he stood for greater democracy and the rights of the common man; and he introduced the spoils system. If you win the election, you turn your opponents out of Government jobs, and you appoint your political friends. To the victor belong the spoils.[148]

I have already suggested that there are questions about the accuracy of the first two prongs of this conventional wisdom and that there are other things about Jackson that are more important and more admirable as well.[149] Historians remind us that Jackson did not simply replace all officers and employees who were of a different political persuasion either. He did, however, dislodge enough of them to provoke bellows of indignation from opposition speakers in Congress, together with a few choice propositions for reform.[150]

Nor was the patronage system restricted to filling offices with adherents of the right political party. "Before 1829," wrote Leonard D. White, "few federal officeholders had been required to discharge any obligation to the party or faction in power." Thereafter, however,

> they were progressively brought under the dominion of the local party machine and subjected to various party requirements as a condition of

---

> After night Senator Semple called and held a conversation with me in relation to the intended emigration of the Mormons of Illinois to Oregon. I had examined Gov. Ford's letter on the subject, . . . and informed him that as President of the U.S. I possessed no power to prevent or check their emigration; that the right of emigration or expatriation was one which any citizen possessed. I told him I could not interfere with them on the ground of their religious faith, however absurd it might be considered to be; that if I could interfere with the Mormons, I could with the Baptists, or any other religious sect; & that by the constitution any citizen had a right to adopt his own religious faith. In these views Mr. Semple concurred . . . .

[147]The victory was all the more modest because the final version granted rights only insofar as they did not conflict with Swiss law, whether cantonal or federal. 11 Stat at 588, Art I; see Ed Note, Kenneth E. Shewmaker, ed, The Papers of Daniel Webster: 2 Diplomatic Papers 157, 160 (Univ Press of New England, 1983–87) [hereafter cited as Webster Diplomatic Papers], pointing out that this formulation still permitted religious discrimination. Neither Fillmore nor Secretary of State Webster had perceived any difficulty with the original treaty until Jewish leaders pointed out that the first amendment "would appear to exclude the right or power of the Senate to ratify any treaty confering [sic] exclusive rights to any religious denomination," but they quickly came around. See id at 158–60; Joseph Abraham et al to Webster, Feb 25, 1851, id at 167–68; Webster to Joseph Abraham et al, Mar 5, 1851, id at 169.

[148]This familiar phrase has been attributed to New York Democrat William Marcy, who served, inter alia, as Senator, Governor, and Secretary of War and of State. See White, The Jacksonians at 320.

[149]See text accompanying notes 6–7 of the Preface; text accompanying note 8 of the Introduction to Part One; and chapters 3 and 4.

[150]See, e.g., White, The Jacksonians at 300–308; Van Deusen, The Jacksonian Era at 35–36; Remini, Jackson at 185–86; Schlesinger, the Age of Jackson at 45–47. For the traditional view see, e.g., Carl Schurz, 1 Life of Henry Clay 332–37 (1887). Below the policy level, White assures us, necessity protected many career public servants: "The actual conduct of the public business remained after 1829 as before largely in the hands of old-timers who 'knew the ropes.'" White, The Jacksonians at 349. The Postmaster General and the Secretary of the Treasury, however, disclosed to the Senate that no fewer than 491 Deputy Postmasters and 151 subordinate Customs officers (mostly inspectors) had been removed during the first year or so of Jackson's Administration. S Docs 106 and 120, 21st Cong, 1st Sess (1830).

> continuing their employment. Among these were obligations to pay party assessments, to do party work at election time, and to "vote right."[151]

It was such practices as these that drew the particular attention of congressional critics.

An 1835 bill offered by Senator Calhoun would have attacked the spoils system itself by requiring the President to state his reasons for discharging federal officers.[152] As Calhoun explained, no President would admit that he had fired a public servant on crass political grounds.[153] Henry Clay would have gone further, proposing to amend the bill to require Senate consent to remove an officer whose appointment the Senate had approved.[154] All of this prompted a rerun of the 1789 debate over the President's power of removal, which added nothing of significance on the basic question.[155]

Several speakers denied Congress's power even to require the President to state his reasons. Since the President had sole authority to remove executive officers, said Ether Shepley of Maine, he was not accountable to the Senate for his actions.[156] Congress could no more require the President's reasons for firing a subordinate, added James Buchanan of Pennsylvania, than the President could demand the Senate's reasons for rejecting a nomination to federal office.[157] Wrong, said Delaware's John M. Clayton: To pass intelligently on a successor's appointment the Senate needed to know why the previous incumbent had been fired.[158]

Calhoun's bill twice passed the opposition-controlled Senate but died in the Democratic House.[159] In the next three Congresses the Whigs tried a new tack: Political removals should be condemned outright, and federal officers should be forbidden to "intermeddle" in federal elections.

The first of these proposals reminds us of the Supreme Court's much later decision in *Elrod v Burns,*[160] the second of the Hatch Act, which Congress adopted a century afterward.[161] The leading protagonist of both was Whig Representative John Bell of Ten-

[151]White, The Jacksonians at 332.

[152]Cong Deb App, 23d Cong, 2d Sess 219, 229. The bill would also have repealed an 1820 law (3 Stat 582, §§ 1, 2 (May 15, 1820)) limiting the tenure of specified executive officers to four years.

[153]Cong Deb, 23d Cong, 2d Sess 558. See also id at 523 (Sen. Clay). Such a requirement, Carl Schurz added many years later, would also protect the President from political pressure to discharge a subordinate for improper reasons. Schurz, 2 Life of Clay at 67 (cited in note 150).

[154]Cong Deb, 23d Cong, 2d Sess 455.

[155]Felix Grundy of Tennessee did proffer a plausible justification for the Framers' apparent decision to require Senate consent for appointment but not for removal: Local Senators might know a candidate's qualifications best before he was appointed, but the President was in a better position to judge his performance in office. Id at 529.

[156]Id at 454. On similar grounds President Tyler would refuse to provide the House with a list of members of Congress who had sought federal office, and President Cleveland would decline to reveal his reasons for discharging federal officers. See House Journal, 27th Cong, 2d Sess 421; Cong Rec, 49th Cong, 1st Sess 1585 (1886); Edward C. Mason, The Veto Power 40–42 (Russell & Russell, 1967) (first published in 1890).

[157]Cong Deb, 23d Cong, 2d Sess 502.

[158]Id at 504, 538.

[159]Id at 576; Cong Deb, 24th Cong, 1st Sess 367. This proposal was revived by a House committee in 1842 but not adopted. HR Rep 741, 27th Cong, 2d Sess 4 (Virginia Rep. Thomas Gilmer) (adding that the committee had "no doubt" of Congress's power).

[160]427 US 347 (1976).

[161]54 Stat 767 (Jul 19, 1940), 18 USC § 61h (1940). This prohibition has since been watered down considerably. See 5 USC §§ 7323–25 (2002).

nessee, who would run for President on the Constitutional Union ticket in 1860. He made his case in major speeches to the House in 1837 and 1840.

To remove officers or employees (other than the heads of departments or other "constitutional advisers of the President") on political grounds, Bell's 1840 bill recited, was "manifestly a violation of the freedom of elections; an attack upon the public liberty; and a high misdemeanor."[162]

> I am not left free to vote as I please, [Bell told the House in 1837,] . . . when I am made to understand that the office or employment which gives me bread, or supplies my family with the comforts of life, will be taken from me if I do not vote for a particular candidate; and the election is not free in which one hundred thousand such votes are given.[163]

Since free elections were "the foundation stone of liberty," he added, any attack on free exercise of the franchise was an assault on freedom; and Madison himself, in supporting the President's constitutional right to remove federal officers, had insisted that "'the wanton removal of meritorious officers would subject him to impeachment and removal from his own high trust.'"[164]

Bell's rhetoric flirts with *Elrod*'s conclusion that to discharge a public servant for partisan political reasons (with exceptions similar to Bell's own) infringes his expressive freedom. To outlaw intimidation of federal workers at the polls might well have been necessary and proper to the conduct of federal elections,[165] or (like later Civil Service legislation) to the operation of the Government itself;[166] yet Bell explicitly refrained from proposing that political dismissal be made a crime. It would be "injudicious," he initially suggested, to attempt to limit the President's power by statute.[167] (Not unconstitutional: Three years later he would argue that the Constitution gave the President no right of removal.)[168] In 1840 he advanced a different explanation: Congress had no authority to punish the President "for any violation of the duties of his station, in any other form than by impeachment—the mode prescribed by the Constitution."[169]

If Bell meant the constitutional clauses respecting impeachment made it the exclusive remedy for presidential offenses, he should have taken another peek at them. Because the penalties the Senate may inflict in such a proceeding are insufficient to vindicate the public interest, Article I, § 3 expressly provides that an officer impeached and convicted

[162]Cong Globe App, 26th Cong, 1st Sess 830.

[163]Cong Deb, 24th Cong, 2d Sess 1465.

[164]Id at 1466, quoting 1 Annals of Congress at 517.

[165]See Ex parte Siebold, 100 US 371, 382–94 (1880); Ex parte Yarbrough, 110 US 651, 660–62 (1884). Like Civil Service, such a restriction would leave the President free to discharge officers who failed to carry out his instructions, which is the essence of his removal power. See The Second Century at 193–95, discussing Myers v United States, 272 US 52 (1926).

[166]22 Stat 403 (Jan 16, 1883); 5 USC §§ 1101 et seq (2003). Alternatively, Congress might have tried to justify such a prohibition as a means of preventing violations of the Constitution. Unlike the later fourteenth amendment, the first contains no explicit enforcement clause. Neither do the fugitive clauses of Article IV, but Congress had found such authority implicit, and the Supreme Court would soon confirm its conclusion. Prigg v Pennsylvania, 41 US 539 (1842); Kentucky v Dennison, 65 US 66 (1860); see The Federalist Period at 170.

[167]Cong Deb, 24th Cong, 2d Sess 1474.

[168]Cong Globe App, 26th Cong, 1st Sess 830, 832.

[169]Id at 830.

"shall nevertheless be liable and subject to indictment, trial, judgment, and punishment, according to law."[170] Nor was Bell's argument the same as that which would be bruited about much later in connection with President Clinton's alleged perjury and obstruction of justice, namely that he could not be distracted from his duties to defend himself in a criminal trial.[171] If Bell's argument against the spoils system anticipated *Elrod v Burns,* his suggestion of presidential immunity from prosecution anticipated *Nixon v Fitzgerald,* where the Supreme Court would hold that the constitutional independence of the Chief Executive demanded his freedom from damage liability, even after he left office, for even deliberate wrongs committed in the course of his official duties.[172]

Instead, like Madison in 1789, Bell's bill threatened Presidents with impeachment if they discharged subordinates on political grounds. Whether Congress's advance definition of "high crimes and misdemeanors" would bind the House or Senate in a later impeachment proceeding may be doubted; one might expect them to insist on interpreting the Constitution for themselves.[173]

Bell's distinct proposal to prevent public servants from intermeddling in elections, he explained, was intended to protect federal officers and employees from pressure by their superiors to do so and thus to preserve their political freedom.[174] The difficulty was that his bills—and a similar Senate measure debated at length in the intervening Congress—went far beyond merely forbidding the Administration to control the political activities of its cadres. The proposed prohibition insulated workers from coercion by forbidding them to act of their own free will. It denied the very rights it was professedly meant to preserve. To borrow a phrase from Mr. Hammerstein's King of Siam, it protected federal officers out of all they owned. Yes, a categorical ban would spare enforcers the daunting burden of demonstrating actual intimidation. The price of prophylaxis, however, was high. The specific examples of "intermeddling" listed in the bill, such as buying votes and using the franking privilege to affect them, were appropriate enough, and Bell disclaimed any intention to forbid the mere expression of opinions. In the same breath, however, he acknowledged that by "intermeddling" with elections he meant to in-

[170]It is not uncommon for officers subject to impeachment for acts committed in the course of their official duties to be convicted of crimes on the basis of the same conduct. See, e.g., Nixon v United States, 506 US 224 (1993).

[171]Cf Clinton v Jones, 520 US 681, 694–96 (1997), rejecting a parallel argument of temporary immunity from civil damage actions. See also The Jeffersonians at 133–35, discussing President Jefferson's claim of immunity from a subpoena in the case of Aaron Burr.

[172]457 US 731 (1982). Immunity seems an incomplete excuse for the absence of an express prohibition in the bill. Injunctive sanctions pose no comparable risk of chilling the exercise of official duty, and the same Court that held the President absolutely immune from damages in *Nixon* reaffirmed that other executive officers were insulated only if they acted in good faith. See Pulliam v Allen, 466 US 522 (1984); Harlow v Fitzgerald, 457 US 800 (1982).

[173]Cf Marbury v Madison, 5 US 137 (1803); City of Boerne v Flores, 521 US 507, 535–36 (1997); see also The Jeffersonians at 137–39, discussing a congressional effort to define treason. Bell seemed to assume his definition would not be binding if enacted, stressing only the deterrent value of his proposal:

> I shall feel quite well assured that no President or head of a Department will venture upon so gross an abuse of his high trust, if it shall once be solemnly settled by a vote of Congress that it is an impeachable offense.

Cong Globe App, 26th Cong, 1st Sess 830.

[174]Id at 833. See also id at 708 (Tennessee Rep. Meredith P. Gentry).

clude the "distribution of electioneering matter."[175] Political speech, opponents vociferously argued during the 1839 debates, was the lifeblood of democracy; citizens could not be required to surrender first-amendment rights as a condition of federal employment.[176]

Proponents argued that the power not to appoint an individual implied the lesser power to determine the conditions of his employment. They pointed out that the Constitution itself deprived officeholders of the right to serve in Congress. They denied that freedom of expression was absolute: Congress could forbid bribery, jury tampering, and challenges to duels. They reported that Thomas Jefferson himself, the paragon of political freedom, had issued a comparable order when he was President:

> The President of the United States has seen, with dissatisfaction, officers of the General Government taking, on various occasions, active parts in elections of the public functionaries, whether of the General or of the State Governments. Freedom of election being essential to the mutual independence of governments, and of the different branches of the same Government . . . , it is deemed improper for officers depending on the Executive of the Union to attempt to control or influence the free exercise of the elective right. . . . The right of any officer to give his vote at elections, as a qualified citizen, is not meant to be restrained, nor, however given, shall it have any effect to his prejudice; but it is expected that he will not attempt to influence the votes of others, nor take any part in the business of electioneering, that being deemed inconsistent with the spirit of the constitution, and his duties to it.[177]

Bell's focus, as we have seen, was on protecting federal workers from interference with their right to vote. Jefferson's was on the integrity of the election itself, as he had emphasized in an earlier letter to Pennsylvania Governor Thomas McKean: Even voluntary participation by federal officers could "smother[]" the electoral process "by the enormous patronage of the General gov[ern]me[n]t."[178]

None of the Whig proposals to limit the political activities of federal officers had a prayer of success so long as the Democrats controlled the Administration and Congress. No sooner was the first of our handful of Whig Presidents ensconced in the executive

[175]See id at 833. The principle of ejusdem generis, strengthened by a presumption against encroachment on constitutional rights, might nevertheless have avoided a construction that would prohibit mere speech.

[176]S Doc 168, 25th Cong, 3d Sess (1839), reprinted in Cong Globe App, 25th Cong, 3d Sess 157–60 (Sen. Wall); id at 175–79 (Sen. Strange); id at 181–83 (Sen. Norvell); id at 185–86 (Sen. Roane); id at 203–6 (Sen. Buchanan); id at 234 (Sen. Calhoun). Even the Sedition Act, opponents argued, had forbidden only false statements; the present bill proscribed ordinary political discussion. Id at 204 (Sen. Buchanan); id at 182 (Sen. Norvell). On the other side of the ledger, Bell's bills had the advantage of what later generations would call viewpoint neutrality; they might muffle the political debate, but they would not distort it by placing a government finger on one side of the scale.

[177]See Cong Deb, 24th Cong, 3d Sess 1474 (Rep. Bell), quoting from an unidentified circular he attributed to Jefferson. See also Cong Globe App, 25th Cong, 3d Sess 407–8 (Sen. Rives); Cong Globe App, 26th Cong, 1st Sess 708 (Rep. Gentry). Jefferson's directive, tardily unearthed, was published out of order in 10 Richardson at 98–99.

[178]Jefferson to McKean, Feb 2, 1801, Paul Leicester Ford, ed, 7 The Writings of Thomas Jefferson 486–87 (Putnam, 1896), quoted by Representative Bell at Cong Deb, 24th Cong, 2d Sess 1473–74. See also Cong Globe App, 25th Cong, 2d Sess 408 (Sen. Rives).

mansion, however, than he took the matter into his own hands without waiting for Congress to act. In his Inaugural Address on March 4, 1841 President Harrison indicated his intended course of action:

> The influence of the Executive in controlling the freedom of the elective franchise through the medium of the public offices can be effectually checked by renewing the prohibition published by Mr. Jefferson forbidding their interference in elections further than giving their own votes, and their own independence secured by an assurance of perfect immunity in exercising this sacred privilege of freemen under the dictates of their own unbiased judgments. Never with my consent shall an officer of the people, compensated for his services out of their pockets, become the pliant instrument of Executive will.[179]

Two weeks later Daniel Webster, the new Secretary of State, issued the following order to all Department heads at the President's direction:

> The President is of opinion that it is a great abuse to bring the patronage of the General Government into conflict with the freedom of Elections, and that this abuse ought to be corrected wherever it may have been permitted to exist, and to be prevented for the future.
>
> He therefore directs that information be given to all officers and agents in your department of the public service that partisan interference in popular elections, . . . or the payment of any contribution or assessment on salaries, or official compensation for party or election purposes, will be regarded by him as cause of removal.
>
> It is not intended that any officer shall be restrained in the free and proper expression and maintenance of his opinions respecting public men or public measures, or in the exercise to the fullest degree of the constitutional right of suffrage. But persons employed under the Government and paid for their services out of the public Treasury are not expected to take an active or officious part in attempts to influence the minds or votes of others, such conduct being deemed inconsistent with the spirit of the Constitution and the duties of public agents acting under it; and the President is resolved, so far as depends upon him, that while the exercise of the elective franchise by the people shall be free from undue influences of official station and authority, opinion shall also be free among the officers and agents of the Government.[180]

Brave words. Self-denying words, in a commendable cause: political freedom and the integrity of the democratic process. Harrison's sources of inspiration were obvious: Jefferson's earlier circular and John Bell's proposals for legislation. Were the costs greater than the first amendment would allow? John Vining in the First Congress had said

[179] 4 Richardson at 5, 13.

[180] See id at 52 (Mar 20, 1841). President Tyler, in his own Inaugural Address a scant three weeks later, vowed to continue his predecessor's policy. Id at 36, 38 (Apr 9, 1841).

they were;[181] the Supreme Court in sustaining the Hatch Act a century later would say they were not.[182] Webster, like Bell, had improved on Jefferson by making clear that he did not mean to proscribe the mere expression of opinion. Drawing the line between simple expression and "active or officious attempts to influence" voters, however, promised both uncertainty and severe limitations on expressive activities normally within the ambit of constitutional protection. We have come to understand that public employment often gives rise to governmental interests that justify restraints on the activities of public servants that could not be imposed on citizens at large.[183] To forbid overt electioneering by *judges* seems to me entirely appropriate in light of the overriding interest in judicial neutrality.[184] Reasonable minds may and do differ as to where the line should be drawn; my own view is that the case for restriction is much weaker when dealing with executive personnel.

Webster's anti-electioneering directive, however, also raised a perplexing question of the separation of powers. Congress might well have authority to enact such provisions, but could they be adopted by executive order? Article I, § 8 vests federal legislative power in Congress, not the President. As Justice Hugo Black would write in the *Steel Seizure Case* a hundred years later, the President's job is to execute the laws, not to make them.[185]

Faithful to the central Whig creed, President Harrison took a generally dim view of executive authority. Presidential interference with the legislative process, in particular, was to be kept at a minimum. The express veto power, he said, should be employed only to prevent unconstitutional or hasty legislation and to protect the rights of minorities; the explicit constitutional injunction that the President recommend measures to Congress did not permit him to draft bills for congressional consideration.[186] It seemed a little ironic that a President with such a cramped view of his authority to recommend laws should so strikingly assert his power to make them.

A cheap shot, right? For there is a respectable argument that (first-amendment concerns to one side) in limiting the political activities of executive agents Harrison acted within his constitutional authority. Article II vests the executive power in the President and instructs him to see to the faithful execution of the laws. He is thus the boss of the Executive Branch, the manager of the entire Administration. As President Jackson so stoutly maintained during the crisis over removal of the deposits from the National Bank,[187] that means he can tell his subordinates, within the bounds of existing statutes, how to execute the laws. Absent contrary legislation, he can require bureaucrats to be at

[181]See The Federalist Period at 62.

[182]United Public Workers v Mitchell, 330 US 75, 94–104 (1947); US Civil Service Comm'n v National Ass'n of Letter Carriers, 413 US 548, 556 (1973).

[183]For an exemplary explication of the governing considerations, if applied to produce an arguably less exemplary result, see American Communications Ass'n v Douds, 339 US 382, 393–412 (1950); The Second Century at 355–56.

[184]See, e.g., ABA Model Code of Judicial Conduct, Canon 5A. But see the Supreme Court's much later decision striking down limits on campaigning by *candidates* (including those who are already sitting judges) in judicial elections. Republican Party v White, 536 US 765 (2002). It may still be permissible to restrict electioneering by judges for third parties. See id at 796 (Kennedy, J, concurring).

[185]Youngstown Sheet & Tube Co v Sawyer, 343 US 579, 587–89 (1952).

[186]See his Inaugural Address, 4 Richardson at 5, 9–14 (Mar 4, 1841).

[187]See chapter 3.

their desks from nine to five. He can direct them to travel by coach rather than first class. He can forbid them to make decisions in matters in which they have a conflict of interest. He can discharge them for any reason the Constitution and laws do not prohibit; he can therefore declare in advance what he will deem grounds for their removal. Thus, at least arguably, he can protect them from improper interference with the exercise of their political rights and (subject to the same first-amendment constraints that would limit Congress) forbid them to do anything that would impede the public service, compromise the integrity of elections, or reflect adversely upon the Government.[188]

In short, Webster's circular may not have been inconsistent with Congress's legislative monopoly after all.[189] Unfortunately, however, neither the Secretary of State who penned and distributed that directive nor the President who ordered it paused to explain how it could be reconciled with the Constitution—or with their own narrow conception of executive authority.[190]

[188]Similar considerations may help to explain both President Van Buren's unelaborated executive order prescribing a ten-hour day for persons employed on federal public works (3 Richardson at 602 (Mar 31, 1840)) and the broad managerial authority that Presidents have traditionally exercised, in the absence of meaningful legislative direction, over the use and protection of public lands. See, e.g., United States v Midwest Oil Co, 236 US 459 (1915); United States v Grimaud, 220 US 506 (1911). See United States v Mazurie, 419 US 544, 556–57 (1975):

> [L]imits on the authority of Congress to delegate its legislative power . . . are . . . less stringent in cases where the entity exercising the delegated authority itself possesses independent authority over the subject matter . . . .

President Jackson's famed Specie Circular, requiring most purchasers of public lands to pay in gold or silver (see note 191 of chapter 3), was issued on a theory even easier to sustain: The order merely directed its addressees to conform to existing law. Calhoun, who evidently thought it did nothing of the kind, proclaimed that the President had "undertaken to legislate on the subject" and denounced the order as "unconstitutional, without law, without precedent, without any authority whatever." Cong Deb, 24th Cong, 2d Sess 85, 375. Van Buren's ten-hour order is briefly considered in Donald B. Cole, Martin Van Buren and the American Political System 367–68 (Princeton, 1984), without reference to the constitutional question.

[189]But cf the 1854 opinion of Attorney General Caleb Cushing declaring unconstitutional an executive order of President Fillmore promulgating what Cushing accusingly labeled "a code of regulations for the government of the naval service." The distinction between "legislative" action and mere "directions and orders" that the President might legitimately issue as Commander-in-Chief might be fuzzy at the edges, Cushing wrote, but Fillmore's code clearly crossed the line; Congress, not the executive, was authorized "to make rules for the government and regulation of the land and naval forces." 6 Op AG 10; US Const, Art I, § 8, cl 14.

[190]A leading student of administrative history has told us that Harrison's order, while "officially repeated from time to time," was often ignored:

> Official orders and instructions were too feeble to withstand the pressure from the party machines, and officeholders, especially in the large cities, became both the leaders of tens and hundreds and filled the rank and file.

White, The Jacksonians at 338–39.

6

President, Vice-President

Article II, § 1 vests "the executive power . . . in a President of the United States," elected by a cumbersome indirect process soon modified by adoption of the twelfth amendment in 1804.[1] The same article and amendment provide for the simultaneous choice of a Vice-President, similarly selected, whose principal responsibility is to assume the reins of government in case the President becomes unable to retain them.

A number of issues respecting the powers and privileges of President and Vice-President arose in the course of executive and legislative activities during the years we are now examining. The Whigs, perennially locked out of the executive mansion, mounted a prolonged assault upon the President's veto power in the interest of congressional hegemony. Presidents from Jackson to Buchanan felt called upon to protest repeatedly against what they perceived as legislative curtailment of their discretion to nominate individuals to public office and unwarranted legislative prying into confidential executive affairs. The untimely death of President Harrison gave birth to a heated debate over just what became of the Vice-President when the melancholy circumstance for whose eventuality he existed actually occurred. Questions were even raised about the Vice-President's measly constitutional role while the President still functions, namely as presiding officer of the Senate. When is the Vice-President entitled, under Article I, § 3, to break a tie vote in that chamber? Finally, under what circumstances and for what period of time must the Senate elect a President pro tempore under the same provision?

These issues form the subject of the present chapter.

I. THE VETO

I have promised you an examination of the Whigs' quixotic and protracted assault on the veto power. This is a good spot for it, as I have just referred yet again to their narrow

[1]See The Jeffersonians, ch 2.

understanding of executive authority.

Opposition to executive presumption was the only thing the Whigs had in common; it was their raison d'être. Their very name was chosen to highlight it: A similar attitude had characterized the English Whigs.[2] Andrew Jackson was a headstrong President, and he rode roughshod over opponents both in and out of Congress. I have already read you Henry Clay's 1833 point-by-point indictment of his actions on the occasion of the removal of Government deposits from the Bank of the United States: The President was usurping authority right and left, and pretty soon all power would be concentrated in his hands.[3]

Among the evils Clay assailed in this harangue was abuse of the veto power conferred by Article I.[4] The first section of that article vests legislative powers in Congress; the seventh subjects them to one of the Constitution's famous checks and balances. Here is the heart of that provision:

> Every bill which shall have passed the House of Representatives and the Senate, shall, before it becomes a law, be presented to the President of the United States. If he approve he shall sign it, but if not he shall return it, with his objections, to that House in which it shall have originated, who shall enter the objections at large on their journal, and proceed to reconsider it. If after such reconsideration two thirds of that House shall agree to pass the bill, it shall be sent, together with the objections, to the other House, by which it shall likewise be reconsidered, and if approved by two thirds of that House, it shall become a law.

Additional portions of this lengthy section will be quoted when we need them.[5]

A. The President's Pocket

It was true that Jackson had wielded the veto with vigor. By 1833, when Clay lashed out at him, he had already employed it to chop down three pillars of the American System: internal improvements, distribution of land revenues, and the National Bank. As each blow had fallen, opposition reaction had become progressively severe.

When Jackson vetoed the Maysville Road bill in 1830, disappointed Congressmen contented themselves with impugning his motives; they made no general attack on the

[2]Henry Clay had given this explanation in a speech in March 1834. See Carl Schurz, 1 Life of Henry Clay 44–45 (1887). See also Michael F. Holt, The Rise and Fall of the American Whig Party 27–28 (Oxford, 1999); Thomas Brown, Politics and Statesmanship: Essays on the American Whig Party 29 (Columbia, 1985); John P. Kennedy, A Defence of the Whigs, in his Political and Official Papers 317, 323, 348, 354 (Putnam, 1872). Kennedy was a Whig Representative from Maryland; he wrote this tract in connection with the election of 1844.

[3]Cong Deb, 23d Cong, 1st Sess 58–94; see note 76 of chapter 3 and accompanying text.

[4]Cong Deb, 23d Cong, 1st Sess 59.

[5]A useful list of presidential vetoes from 1789 to 1889, together with brief descriptions of each controversy, is found in Edward C. Mason, The Veto Power (Russell & Russell, 1967) (first published in 1890). Most of the early veto messages are reprinted in S Misc Doc 53, 49th Cong, 2d Sess (1886).

veto power or on the President's stated criteria for employing it.[6] Two years later, when Jackson blocked extension of the Bank charter, Clay made a more sweeping argument that would become a central Whig tenet in the developing debate: The veto had been designed for the extraordinary case of "precipitate legislation"; to use it frequently on grounds of mere "expediency" would be irreconcilable with "the genius of republican government."[7]

Jackson's 1833 veto of Clay's pet bill to distribute the proceeds of land sales to the states raised a distinct and novel question, for it was a pocket veto.[8] Having received the bill on the last day of the Twenty-second Congress, the President neither signed it nor returned it to that body. When the next Congress met the following December, he sent it back to the Senate with a comprehensive statement of his reasons for disapproval.[9]

Opposition Senators climbed the wall. The President's veto message, snarled Mississippi Senator George Poindexter, was out of order: A bill could be returned only to the House that had originated it, not to its successor.[10] That, I think, was both trivial and silly; Jackson's message was at worst a harmless courtesy.[11] Moreover, although the relevant constitutional language did not quite cover the case, the President was *supposed* to advise Congress with respect to possible legislation; Jackson's objections might well be helpful to Congress in determining whether to try again.[12]

[6]See Cong Deb, 21st Cong, 1st Sess 1140–48. Clay, out of Congress for the moment to tend his fortune, began to promote a constitutional amendment to weaken the veto. See, e.g., Clay to Webster, Jun 7, 1830, 3 Webster Correspondence 80, 81; Clay to Adam Beatty, Jun 8, 1830, 8 Clay Papers at 220–21; Van Deusen, Clay at 238.

[7]Cong Deb, 22d Cong, 1st Sess 1265. Webster repeated this argument, with emendations, at the National Republican Convention in October: The power had been given "as a guard against hasty or inconsiderate legislation, and against any act, inadvertently passed, which might seem to encroach on the just authority of other branches of the government." Speech at Worcester, Oct 12, 1832, 1 Webster Speeches at 533, 559. Jackson had said the Bank was unconstitutional, but Webster and Clay were unimpressed: He should have deferred to the Supreme Court on the constitutional question. Cong Deb, 22d Cong, 1st Sess 1231–32 (Sen. Webster); id at 1273 (Sen. Clay).

[8]It was not the first. Madison had pocket-vetoed a naturalization bill in 1812; Jackson had done the same with two improvement bills as early as 1830. See House Journal, 12th Cong, 2d Sess 544; 2 Richardson at 500, 508; notes 22–23 of chapter 1 and accompanying text.

[9]3 Richardson at 56 (Dec 4, 1833).

[10]Cong Deb, 23d Cong, 1st Sess 15–16. See also the report of the Senate Committee on Public Lands, S Doc 323, 23d Cong, 1st Sess 1–18 (1834), reprinted at Cong Deb App, 23d Cong, 1st Sess 205, and North Carolina Representative David Outlaw's private objection when President Polk sent a pocket-veto message to Congress in 1847: "His right to do so, is in my opinion very questionable. The subject is not before this Congress . . . ." David Outlaw to Emily B. Outlaw, Dec 15, 1847, David Outlaw Papers, Southern History Collection, University of North Carolina at Chapel Hill.

[11]Madison had reported the reasons for his pocket veto to the next session of the same House in 1812. See House Journal, 12th Cong, 2d Sess 544; Mason, The Veto Power at 54 (cited in note 5). At one point Webster went so far in the other direction as to condemn pocket vetoes on the ground that they permitted the President to frustrate congressional action *without* giving his reasons. Speech at Worcester, Oct 12, 1832, 1 Webster Speeches at 533, 561.

[12]See US Const, Art II, § 3: "He shall from time to time give to the Congress information of the state of the Union, and recommend to their consideration such measures as he shall judge necessary and expedient . . . ." Jackson had informed Congress of his earlier pocket vetoes in his second Annual Message on the state of the Union (2 Richardson at 500, 508), and he could have done the same in the case of the distribution bill. Compare the earlier flap over President Monroe's unsolicited revelation to Congress of his doubts respecting congressional authority over internal improvements, The Jeffersonians at 270–71; and see the discussion of President Jackson's protest against Senate censure in chapter 3.

Clay's objection, while more substantive, was equally lacking in merit: By retaining the bill until the Congress that had passed it expired, he argued, Jackson had unconstitutionally deprived Congress of its right to override the veto.[13] Perhaps we had better quote more of Article I's veto provision:

> If any bill shall not be returned by the President within ten days (Sundays excepted) after it shall have been presented to him, the same shall be a law, in like manner as if he had signed it, unless the Congress by their adjournment prevent its return, in which case it shall not be a law.[14]

This is the provision on which pocket vetoes are based. It seemed to say that the President had ten days in which to decide whether or not to approve a bill, and that if the session came to an end before ten days had passed he had no need to return it at all. If the President failed to return a bill within ten days, and Congress was still in session, the bill would become law; if Congress no longer sat, it would die. As John Forsyth of Georgia argued in the President's defense, it was Congress's own fault that it was unable to reconsider the distribution bill; if it had wanted a chance to override the veto, it should not have waited until the end of the session to pass it.[15]

Clay initially professed doubt whether this interpretation was correct. It was not clear, he said, whether the distribution bill had died or rather become law.[16] The constitutional provision, he explained a few moments later, did not mean what I have just suggested it meant, for it distinguished between cases in which Congress voluntarily concluded one of its sessions and those in which a particular Congress expired.

> Mr. C. denied that the constitution gave to the President ten days to consider bills, except at the long session. At that session, the period of its termination is uncertain, and dependent upon the will of Congress. To guard against a sudden adjournment, by which the President might be deprived of due time to deliberate on an important bill, the constitution provides for ten days at that session. But, at the short session, it is not an adjournment but a dissolution of Congress, on the 3d March, and the day

[13]Cong Deb, 23d Cong, 1st Sess 18, 1604; see also S Doc 323, 23d Cong, 1st Sess 1–3, reprinted at Cong Deb App, 23d Cong, 1st Sess 205. Noting that Congress had sent the bill to the President on the last day of the session in violation of its own rules, Senator Benton praised Jackson for not acting before he had time to examine it; Clay retorted that the President had known about the bill for months and needed no time for further study. Cong Deb, 23d Cong, 1st Sess at 16–18.

[14]US Const, Art I, § 7.

[15]Cong Deb, 23d Cong, 1st Sess 1605. See Benton, 1 Thirty Years' View at 364–65:

> I told [the President] . . . that such a measure ought not to be passed in the last hours of a session, in a thin Senate, and upon an imperfect view of his objections; and that the public good required that it be held up. It was so; and during the long vacation of nine months which intervened before the next session, the opposition presses and orators kept the country filled with denunciations of the enormity of his conduct in "*pocketing*" the bill—as if it had been a case of "flat burglary," instead of being the exercise of a constitutional right . . . .

[16]Cong Deb, 23d Cong, 1st Sess 14–15.

of that dissolution is fixed in the constitution itself, and known to all.[17]

By withholding the bill until the end of the Twenty-second Congress, Clay concluded, the President had thus deprived the Senate and House of their "constitutional right of passing on the bill, after the President had exercised his powers."[18]

Ingenious, no? The language of the provision could indeed support a distinction between the end of a mere session and the end of the Congress that was sitting; since Congress had no choice but to close its doors in the latter case, it could be said that it was not Congress that, by its "adjournment," had "prevent[ed]" the President from returning the bill. If that was so, however, Clay drew the wrong conclusion. If he was right, the President's failure to act had not deprived Congress of the right to override his veto; unless Congress precludes the bill's return, under the plain terms of Article I, § 7 the consequence of executive inaction is that the bill becomes law—as Clay had initially suggested.

More fundamentally, Clay's premise was flawed. The obvious basis of the ten-day grace period, as Clay himself implied, was the President's need for time to think about what he was doing, and deliberation was as essential at the end of a Congress as at the end of an earlier session.[19] There was no reason to think the Framers would have wanted to distinguish voluntary from involuntary adjournment; the purpose of the provision patently covered both.[20]

[17]Id at 18. Congress, you recall, was required to meet at least once a year. US Const, Art I, § 4, cl 2. The "long session" was the first regular session of each Congress, which could sit for the whole year if it liked; the second regular session was "short" because the Congress itself expired with the terms of many of its members two years after it began. Id, Art I, § 2, cl 1; § 3, cl 1, 2.

[18]See also S Doc 323, 23d Cong, 1st Sess 2.

[19]James Madison, with whom Clay had shared his doubts about the effect of presidential inaction as Congress expired, said the bill did not become law but opined that a President who "abused" his grace period to prevent Congress from acting would be justly subject to impeachment. See Clay to Madison, May 28, 1833, 8 Clay Papers at 643; Madison to Clay, Jun ?, 1833, id at 646.

[20]The converse problem had arisen in the context of a bill for the improvement of rivers and harbors in 1832. The bill having been presented too late to permit careful examination before Congress adjourned, President Jackson said he had "maturely considered [it] within the time allowed me by the Constitution," only to conclude that he ought not to give it his approval. 2 Richardson at 638 (Dec 6, 1832). In other words, Jackson interpreted Article I, § 7 to permit him to sign a bill within ten days after Congress went home, even though it was too late to override his veto.

Both Secretary of State John Quincy Adams and Attorney General William Wirt had taken this position in 1824, but they had been overruled. See 6 JQA Memoirs at 379–80; The Jeffersonians at 317 n.214. The text of the Constitution can be read either way: "If any bill should not be returned by the President within ten days . . . , the same shall be a law, unless the Congress by their adjournment prevent its return, in which case it shall not be a law." (If he does not *want* to return the bill, we would not normally say he was prevented from doing so.) The apparent purposes of the provision seem to support Jackson's interpretation: Whatever may be said for making the President's veto absolute when Congress has gone home, there is no evident reason to prevent his signing a bill thereafter. See the Pocket Veto Case, 279 US 655 (1929); The Second Century at 197. The Supreme Court would later agree with this conclusion. Edwards v United States, 286 US 482, 492–94 (1932). See also Lindsay Rogers, The Power of the President to Sign Bills after Congress has Adjourned, 30 Yale LJ 1 (1920).

B. Tippecanoe

While Clay zeroed in on the particular characteristics of pocket vetoes, Maryland Senator Joseph P. Kent returned to the more general theme Clay had sounded in his attack on Jackson's Bank veto in 1832 and would sound again in his speech on removal of the deposits: The veto itself was being abused. As early as 1833 Kent proposed a constitutional amendment that would permit Congress to override the veto by a simple majority of its elected members;[21] in 1835 he took out his pipes to play it again.

The veto power, Kent intoned, had been designed to protect the executive against legislative encroachment and to guard against "inadvertent" legislation, not to permit the President to frustrate the general will for reasons of mere expediency. Good government required only that the President be authorized to require Congress to reexamine the fruit of its labors; there was no justification for taking legislative authority from the representatives of the people.[22]

Kent's proposed amendment went nowhere, and opposition resentment over the veto simmered quietly under the surface while Van Buren was President; with his party firmly in control of Congress, Van Buren had virtually no occasion to obstruct legislation. When the Whigs finally installed a President of their own in 1841, his inaugural observations, as I have suggested, were music to their ears.[23]

"The great danger to our institutions," said President Harrison, "does not appear to me to be in a usurpation, by the Government, of power not granted by the people, but by the accumulation, in one of the departments, of that which was assigned to others." He was less worried about federalism, in other words, than about the separation of powers. Good Republicans, he explained, had feared in the beginning that the Government might "terminate in virtual monarchy." He would not say their fears had yet been realized, but "the tendency . . . , for some years past, ha[d] been in that direction," and he pledged to arrest it to the extent of his ability.[24]

The Constitution was itself to blame in part, said Harrison, for it ought not to have permitted the President to serve for more than four years. No one, he insisted, should remain in office so long that he forgets that he is the people's servant, not their master. Until the Constitution could be amended, he selflessly vowed, he would do his part to avoid the evil: As he had promised before, he would never consent to serve a second term.[25]

But misinterpretation of the Constitution, Harrison continued, had added another dimension to the problem—and with that he launched yet another sally in the continuing Whig assault on the veto. No constitutional provision, he began, could fairly be construed to give the President "a[ny] part of the legislative power." To recommend legislation, as Article II enjoined him to do, was a mere "privilege which he holds in common with

[21]Cong Deb, 23d Cong, 1st Sess 58.

[22]Cong Deb, 23d Cong, 2d Sess 540–49. At another point in his oration Kent appeared to narrow the veto power still further: It was "incontestable" that the sole legitimate basis for its exercise was to protect the executive. Id at 546.

[23]See section VI of chapter 5.

[24]4 Richardson at 5, 7–8 (Mar 4, 1841).

[25]Id at 8–9. With a little help from Providence, this was one promise that President Harrison kept in spades, for within a month he was dead. With all due respect, a thirty-day presidential term seems to me to be carrying a good thing too far.

every other citizen"; in every case it was Congress that made the legislative decision.[26] The power to annul legislation, in turn, was shared with the courts; and, while the judges could set aside legislation only on constitutional grounds, the President's veto power was limited too. For the very idea of authorizing a single individual to negate the action of Congress seemed "an incongruity in our system." The veto was such a departure from the basic principle of majority rule that it could not have been intended to permit the President to interfere in "the ordinary course of legislation."[27] Intimating that his first two predecessors had agreed with him, Harrison then summed up his understanding of the President's authority:

> I consider the veto power, therefore, given by the Constitution to the Executive of the United States solely as a conservative power, to be used only, first, to protect the Constitution from violation; secondly, the people from the effects of hasty legislation, where their will has been probably disregarded or not well understood; and, thirdly, to prevent the effect of combinations violative of the rights of minorities.[28]

C. Mr. Tyler and the Bank

Thus did the self-effacing new President proclaim his party's credo to the world, only to perish after a scant month in harness—leaving the Whig legislative program at the mercy of that Democrat in Whig clothing, John Tyler, who turned out not even to share his party's jaundiced view of the veto power. In his first two years in office this professed enemy of executive excess, who had castigated Jackson for presuming to run his own Administration, vetoed no fewer than five bills precious to the legislative leaders of his own power-starved party, three of them on grounds of mere expediency. It was during this barrage that congressional Whigs formally read him out of the party.[29]

[26]As I have noted above, even here President Harrison went out of his way to dump on his predecessors for going so far as to draft possible legislation for Congress to consider, especially in the field of finance: Not even the Senate was supposed to initiate revenue bills. US Const, Art I, § 7. The analogy is not in point; when the Senate originates a bill it does more than recommend it. Objections to executive drafting of bills went all the way back to the First Congress, though there was nothing to them. See The Federalist Period at 30–31. The practice, by the time explored in the present study, was common. See White, The Jacksonians at 147–48.

[27]See 4 Richardson at 10:

> [I]t is preposterous to suppose that a thought could for a moment have been entertained that the President, placed at the capital, in the center of the country, could better understand the wants and wishes of the people than their own immediate representatives, who spend a part of every year among them, living with them, often laboring with them, and bound to them by the triple tie of interest, duty, and affection.

[28]Id at 11; Cong Globe, 26th Cong, 2d Sess (Special Senate Session) 232–33.

[29]See the so-called Whig Manifesto of September 13, 1841, 61 Niles' National Register 35–36 (Sep 18, 1841). Apart from the cardinal sin of consorting with Democrats ("those who have been busy to prostrate our purposes"), the principal ground for excommunication was Tyler's exercise of "that power in the constitution which has ever been regarded with suspicion, and often with odium, by the people," and which the signers vowed to confine, if they could, to cases of "hasty or unconstitutional legislation." The vote in favor of this screed was said to be unanimous. Id.

The first blow fell on August 16, 1841, when Tyler vetoed the Senate bill to establish a "fiscal bank."[30] Three days later Clay lit into him. The President, said Clay, had led Congress to believe he would sign the bill; Clay himself had worked very hard to find a compromise; if Tyler could not sign it in good faith he could have let it become law without his signature, or he could have resigned. Clay took some comfort in the fact that Tyler had left room for Congress to try again, and if that failed he could only hope that the veto power would be curtailed by amendment or that new elections would produce a majority large enough to override presidential objections.[31]

William C. Rives of Virginia, who hailed from Tyler's branch of the party, responded to Clay's attack. For the President to allow a bill he believed unconstitutional to become law without his signature would be no better than signing it, "an ignominious retreat from duty," "a perversion of the ten-days' provision." Vetoing a bill was nothing to be ashamed of; was not the President "intended to check, when occasion require[d], an improper exercise of the legislative authority?" Resignation, in turn, was out of the question. It was one thing for Tyler to resign his Senate seat, as Clay pointed out he had done, when he could not in good conscience follow the state legislature's instructions: The legislators were his constituents, and according to Virginia practice "he was bound to obey or resign." It was quite another to suggest that the President ought to resign if he differed with Congress, for he was not intended to be "subservient to the Legislative department . . . ; [t]he President never was meant to be the mere tool of legislative will." Finally, Rives concluded, the fiscal-bank case fit into all three of the categories in which the late President Harrison, notwithstanding his allergy to executive pretension, had said a veto was proper, for in Tyler's view the bill "violates the Constitution, it disregards the rights of the States, and it has been passed without allowing time for a sufficient manifestation of the popular will."[32]

Rives had reduced the great Clay's ill-digested arguments to a pile of rubble. A month later Tyler struck again, returning (this time to the House) Congress's effort to create a "fiscal corporation" that would satisfy his earlier objections. He sounded a little defensive: It was the President's *duty,* he said, to veto unconstitutional legislation.[33] Samson Mason, a mainstream Ohio Whig, responded by mounting yet another spirited effort to limit the veto by construction. The Framers, he said, had borrowed the practice from England, where Blackstone had explained that its purpose was to protect the executive from legislative encroachment.[34] Hamilton had said the same of the constitutional provision itself: "The primary inducement to conferring the power in question upon the Executive is to enable him to defend himself."[35] Hamilton had added that the veto was also "calculated to guard the community against the effects of faction, precipitancy, or of

[30]4 Richardson at 63; see the discussion in section IV of chapter 3.

[31]Cong Globe App, 27th Cong, 1st Sess 364–66.

[32]Id at 366–68. For the story of the Virginia legislature's "instructing [Tyler] out of his seat" and of his earlier insistence on the right of instruction see note 165 of chapter 4; Oliver P. Chitwood, John Tyler: Champion of the Old South 83–84, 112–15, 133–39 (Appleton, 1939). See also Clement Eaton, The Freedom-of-Thought Struggle in the Old South 356, 369 (Harper, rev ed 1964), lamenting that by the 1830's instruction had "developed virtually into a form of recall of Senators" and praising those who defied it. For the earliest congressional debates on the alleged right of instruction see The Federalist Period at 15–16.

[33]4 Richardson at 68–69 (Sep 9, 1841).

[34]1 Blackstone at *154.

[35]The Federalist No 73.

any impulse unfriendly to the public good," but Tyler had made no such charge in the case of the fiscal corporation, said Mason, and if he had it could not have been supported: "A Bank of the United States, by whatsoever name it may be called, is no offspring of a momentary or hasty impression. It is an institution whose existence is coeval with the Government itself. . . ."[36]

D. Mr. Clay's Amendment

When Congress met again for its regular session in December 1841, Senator Clay offered yet another constitutional amendment in order, among other things, to water down the veto power. Clay's proposal was in two parts. First, as Senator Kent had earlier proposed, Congress should be permitted to override a veto by a simple majority of all its members; a two-thirds vote should no longer be required. Second, the pocket veto should be abolished. If Congress adjourned before the President had had ten days to consider a bill, he should be required to return it within three days after the next session began, so that Congress could override his objections. His "motive of action," Clay candidly revealed, was "the curtailment of executive power."[37]

Clay defended his proposed amendment in a relatively brief speech that reiterated earlier arraignments of executive excesses generally and of the veto power in particular. The Executive Branch, he moaned,

> was eternally in action; it was ever awake; it never slept; its action was continuous and unceasing, like the tides of some mighty river which continued flowing and flowing on, swelling and deepening and widening in its onward progress, till it swept away every impediment and broke down every frail obstacle which might be set up to impede its course.

"On principle," Clay concluded, "the Executive ought to have no agency in the formation of laws."[38]

As New Hampshire Democrat Levi Woodbury pointed out, Clay's amendment went far beyond the usual Whig position as represented in President Harrison's inaugural address. Harrison would have reserved the veto for such special cases as unconstitutionality, undue haste, and the rights of minorities; Clay's proposal would effectively do away with the power itself.

> Suppose the law to be vetoed is an encroachment on Executive privileges; will it not, when sent back, be repassed by the same bare majority who at first intended to assail him? Suppose the law involves a constitutional

[36]Cong Globe App, 27th Cong, 1st Sess 391–92.

[37]Cong Globe, 27th Cong, 2d Sess 69. Other sections of the proposed amendment would have forbidden the appointment of members of Congress to civil office during their terms and made the Treasury independent of the President by subjecting its principal officers to appointment and removal by Congress. Id. Clay's Kentucky colleague Joseph Underwood introduced a similar but more extensive package of amendments in the House. Id at 350.

[38]Id at 164–66. For Senator Berrien's speech in favor of a modified version of Clay's amendment that would require that the bill be repassed in the following session see id at 417–18.

> question, which was fully debated, and a bare majority voted against the scruples in that respect. Would not the same persons repass the law, if sent back? So of a bad law, passed through corruption, or impulse. I admit that a mistake, through haste, in a law, if sent back, they might correct. But that could be corrected by a new law. Thus every important and vital object of the veto power would be prostrated by a change like that contained in this amendment.[39]

Pennsylvania Senator James Buchanan parried Clay's proposal with a fine speech in defense of the existing constitutional provision. The veto power, he said, was "one of the most effectual safeguards of the union, and one of the surest means of carrying into effect the will of the people." The Convention had adopted it without dissent.[40] "A principle thus settled," he argued, "ought never to be rashly assailed under the excitement of disappointed feelings occasioned by the veto of two favorite measures at the extra session, on which Senators had fixed their hearts."[41]

Far from being (as Clay had asserted) a "monarchical" prerogative, Buchanan continued, the veto was "peculiarly democratic" by nature as well as origin. First conceived to afford the Roman people "a safeguard against the oppression and encroachments of the aristocracy," it provided "a mere appeal by the President," himself popularly chosen, "from the decision of Congress to the people themselves." Presidents had exercised this authority with great restraint: Of some six thousand Acts of Congress in fifty years, only twenty had been annulled, more than half of them relating to various elements of Clay's own American System.

The presidential veto, Buchanan insisted, was an essential element of the constitutional system of checks and balances.

> The true philosophy of Republican Government, as the history of the world has demonstrated, consists in the establishment of such countervailing powers . . . as shall render it morally certain that no law can be passed by [the people's] servants which shall not be in accordance with their will, and calculated to promote their good.

That, said Buchanan, was why every state had established a Senate "to control the House of Representatives." No one doubted the necessity of such a check, and yet it departed far more sharply than the executive veto from the purported standard of majority rule.

> A bill may pass the House of Representatives by a unanimous vote, and yet be defeated here by a majority of Senators representing but one-fourth

[39]Cong Globe App, 27th Cong, 2d Sess 160. See also Rawle at 61:

> If [the President] sent back the bill, . . . and the same numbers that originally passed it, were sufficient to give it the effect of a law, the reference to him would be an empty form.

[40]Senator Woodbury added that no one was reported to have questioned the veto in any of the state ratifying conventions either. Cong Globe App, 27th Cong, 2d Sess 157.

[41]Clay had gone out of his way to insist (truthfully) that his opposition to the veto was of long standing and not simply a knee-jerk response to Tyler's recent vetoes. Cong Globe, 27th Cong, 2d Sess 164.

> of the people of the United States. Why does not the Senator from Kentucky propose to abolish the Senate? His argument would be much stronger against its existence than against that of the veto power of the Chief Magistrate, who, in this particular, is the true representative of the majority of the whole people.

"The best security which the people can have against abuses of trust by their public servants," Buchanan said again, was "to ordain that it shall be the duty of one class of them to watch and restrain another." And thus both bicameralism and the suspensive veto were components of a set of "mutual restraints which the people have imposed on their public servants, to preserve their own rights and those of the States from rash, hasty, and impolitic legislation."

Why were such restraints necessary?

> All that we have to suppose [said Buchanan] is, what our ancestors, in their acknowledged wisdom, did suppose; that Senators and Representatives are but mortal men, endowed with mortal passions and subject to mortal infirmities; that they are susceptible of selfish and unwise impulses, and that they do not always, and under all circumstances, truly reflect the will of their constituents.

To prove his point Buchanan offered a single telling example, which (as he did not remind his hearers) had escaped even the safety net provided by the veto power: "the odious and unconstitutional alien and sedition laws." Finally, he concluded, "of all the Executive powers," that of the veto was "the one least to be dreaded."

> It cannot create; it can originate no measure; it can change no existing law; it can destroy no existing institution. It is a mere power to arrest hasty and inconsiderate changes, until the voice of the people, who are alike the masters of Senators, Representatives and President, shall be heard.[42]

No, Buchanan's arguments were not novel. Hamilton, among others, had said much the same thing in The Federalist.[43] But that only made Buchanan's argument all the stronger: Even before the Government was established, the Framers had appreciated the

[42]Cong Globe App, 27th Cong, 2d Sess 133–41. Senator Woodbury, in a speech already cited, repeated many of Buchanan's arguments without adding much of substance. Id at 157–64. So did Calhoun, id at 164–68, in a pedantic and largely arithmetical effort to demonstrate the many respects in which the Constitution endeavored to counteract "the fatal tendency of the Government to the absolute and despotic control of the numerical majority."

[43]The Federalist No 73. Former Mississippi Senator Henry Foote, writing after the Civil War, concurred—revealing as he did so why the veto was so popular with Democrats of Southern sympathies during the 1840's and '50's: The veto was "the very sheet-anchor of the public safety," the best guarantee of what he delicately called "southern institutions." Foote, War of the Rebellion 284 (Harper, 1866). See also Jefferson Davis to H.R. Davis et al, Oct 6, 1848, Dunbar Rowland, ed, 1 Jefferson Davis, Constitutionalist: His Letters, Papers and Speeches 213, 215 (Miss Dept Archives & Hist 1923), arguing that "[t]he veto of the president gives to a considerable minority a power which may be relied upon to shield it from legislative invasion of a vital right," such as slavery.

benefits of the presidential veto. The difficult question was whether those benefits were outweighed by its costs. Jackson's and Tyler's vetoes had deprived the country of a useful financial institution that even Madison had ultimately been persuaded Congress had power to create; Madison, Monroe, and Jackson had severely and unnecessarily curtailed the Government's ability to provide an adequate system of roads and canals. One is reminded of the eternal debate over the costs and benefits of judicial review; my own opinion is that in both cases the dangers against which the check protects us are greater than the harm it is likely to inflict.[44]

Lost in the shuffle, I am sorry to say, was the one element in Clay's package of amendments that had real merit: the proposal to do away with the pocket veto. Of course Congress could not be permitted, by premature adjournment, to deprive the President of his veto power or to require him to act without time for deliberation. But the existing constitutional provisions, in my view, placed altogether too much importance on the end of a legislative session. There was no good reason why a rejected bill should not be returned to a subsequent session, or even to a subsequent Congress; there was no good reason why the veto should be made absolute simply because a congressional session had expired.[45]

E. Mr. Tyler and the Tariff

Clay's proposed amendment to eviscerate the veto power never came to a vote; his Whigs were not even close to a two-thirds majority in either House, and they were divided. Safe behind gleeful congressional Democrats and the portals of what was beginning to be called the White House,[46] Tyler fired off another three salvos, intercepting two tariff measures and one to uncouple customs increases from distribution of the revenues from sales of public land.[47] Not one of these later vetoes was on constitutional grounds, or designed to prevent encroachment on the executive; all were based on simple disagreement with congressional policy. Each provoked a recrudescence of howls over Tyler's interpretation of the existing veto power.

When Tyler sent the first (interim) tariff bill back to the House, Kentucky Senator John Crittenden flatly declared that he had no power to veto a bill for mere expediency.[48] Virginia Representative Alexander Stuart said Tyler was the first President to do so,[49] but

[44]In arguing for a later version of Clay's proposal Massachusetts Representative John Quincy Adams, by his own account an initial supporter of the veto power, said he had changed his mind on the basis of experience: "He did not know one out of the whole number of vetoes (so called) that had been given since the establishment of this Constitution, that it would not have operated better for the country, if the measures they prevented had become laws." He was not much in favor of constitutional amendments either, he added, but "evils . . . of an intolerable nature" might justify an exception. Cong Globe, 27th Cong, 2d Sess 906. I am not sure I can find many vetoes during the first fifty-three years of which I approve either (except for that of the distribution bill and, ironically, for those cast simply on policy grounds), but I would not be prepared to jettison one of our most important checks and balances.

[45]See The Second Century at 196–98, discussing the Pocket Veto Case, 279 US 655 (1929).

[46]See Cong Globe, 27th Cong, 2d Sess 166 (Sen. Clay).

[47]4 Richardson at 180 (Jun 29, 1842); id at 183 (Aug 9, 1842); id at 255 (Dec 14, 1843) (explaining an earlier pocket veto); see the discussion in section VI of chapter 4.

[48]Cong Globe, 27th Cong, 2d Sess 706.

[49]Cong Globe App, 27th Cong, 2d Sess 824.

that was not true. As several of Stuart's colleagues pointed out, both Washington and Madison had done the same thing; and Washington, Virginia Democrat William Smith mildly observed, must have known what the Framers had intended.[50] As further proof of the original understanding North Carolina Representative Romulus M. Saunders quoted the Federalist Papers, where Hamilton, while suggesting (as orthodox Whigs had selectively indicated) that "the primary inducement" for the veto was to permit the Executive "to defend himself," had added that the power was also meant "to increase the chances . . . against the passing of bad laws, through haste, inadvertence, or design."[51] Finally, said Alabama Congressman William Payne, the text of the Constitution suggested no limits on the permissible grounds for a veto:

> The Constitution . . . expressly declared, if [the President] does not approve a bill, he shall veto it. Not on constitutional grounds—not on the ground of expediency—but simply on the ground of non-approval. It was an obligatory duty, and made so by the same Constitution as required him to sign a bill if he approved it . . . .[52]

No further discussion, I think, is required. A handful of mostly obscure Representatives succeeded in burying the Whigs' entire argument in just a few words, for there was nothing to it. Contemporaneous understanding confirmed what the constitutional language appeared to say: The President was given the power to veto legislation on any ground he saw fit, in order to protect the people against bad laws.[53]

[50]So, we may add, must Madison. See Cong Globe, 27th Cong, 2d Sess 714 (Rep. Smith); Cong Globe App, 27th Cong, 2d Sess 581 (Rep. Hunter); id at 586 (Rep. Saunders). For Washington's policy veto (of a bill to demobilize a body of dragoons) see The Federalist Period at 208 n.12; for Madison's (of the first attempt to charter the second Bank of the United States) see The Jeffersonians at 255.

[51]Cong Globe App, 27th Cong, 2d Sess 586, quoting The Federalist No 73. See also 4 Elliot's Debates at 75 (James Iredell):

> [A]t the same time that it serves to protect the executive from ill designs in the legislature, it may also answer the purpose of preventing many laws passing which would be immediately injurious to the people at large.

[52]Cong Globe, 27th Cong, 2d Sess 714.

[53]These and other debates on the veto power, wrote Professor Corwin, reflected "the early talent of Americans for conjuring up constitutional limitations out of thin air." Corwin, Office and Powers at 283. President Washington, as Tennessee Representative Robert Caruthers informed the House, had by his own account often deferred to congressional judgment in deciding whether to exercise the veto power: "From motives of respect to the Legislature, and, I might add, from my interpretation of the Constitution, I give my signature to many bills with which my judgment is at variance." Washington to Edmund Pendleton, Sep 23, 1793, John C. Fitzpatrick, ed, 33 Writings of George Washington 94, 96 (Government Printing Office, 1940), quoted at Cong Globe App, 27th Cong, 2d Sess 743. As we know, however, on one occasion he nevertheless vetoed a bill because he thought it bad policy.

Without disputing the breadth of presidential discretion intended by the Framers in conferring the veto power, one recent commentator insists that, essentially by abandoning the deference to legislative practice exhibited by Madison in his 1815 Bank message, Jackson managed to transform the previously insignificant veto power into a major vehicle for constitutional change. Gerard N. Magliocca, Veto! The Jacksonian Revolution in Constitutional Law, 78 Neb L Rev 205, 234, 262 (1999); see the discussion of Jackson's Bank veto in section I of chapter 3.

A motion to override Tyler's first tariff veto failed miserably.[54] Congress passed a second tariff bill (this one intended to be permanent), and Tyler returned it too, again invoking not the Constitution but "the soundest considerations of public policy."[55] Over the tired objection that the House could do nothing with a vetoed bill except "proceed to reconsider it" at once,[56] a select committee was appointed, at the request of the venerable John Quincy Adams, to consider the President's message.[57]

Adams's report, filed a scant five days later, eschewed the familiar argument that mere expediency could never justify a veto and reargued the merits of the slain tariff. There was no prospect, Adams conceded, of passing it over the veto; it was up to the House "to determine what further measure they may deem necessary and practicable, by the legislative authority, in the present calamitous condition of the country." The committee, he continued,

> perceive that the whole legislative power of the Union has been, for the last fifteen months, with respect to the action of Congress upon measures of vital importance, in a state of suspended animation, strangled by the *five* times repeated stricture of the Executive cord.[58] . . . The will of one man has frustrated all their labors, and prostrated all their powers. The majority of the committee believe that the case has occurred, in the annals of our Union, contemplated by the founders of the Constitution by the grant of the power to impeach the President of the United States . . . .

Conscious of the fact that "resort to that expedient might, in the present condition of public affairs, prove abortive," the committee contented itself with a renewal of Senator Clay's request that the Constitution be revised to permit vetoes to be overridden by a simple majority of "the whole number" in each House.[59]

What? Impeach the President? Why? For having "annulled, by the mere act of his will, [Congress's] commission from the people to enact laws for the common welfare

[54]The vote was 114–97, far short of the necessary two-thirds. Cong Globe, 27th Cong, 2d Sess 717.

[55]4 Richardson at 183, 184, Cong Globe, 27th Cong, 2d Sess 867, 868 (Aug 9, 1842). Professing to find it "painful" to have to require Congress to reconsider its decision, Tyler took the occasion to defend himself again: "The exercise of some independence of judgment in regard to all acts of legislation, is plainly implied in the responsibility of approving them." 4 Richardson at 183, Cong Globe, 27th Cong, 2d Sess 867.

[56]Cong Globe, 27th Cong, 2d Sess 873 (Georgia Rep. Thomas Foster); see also the subsequent report of a minority of the select committee, id at 896–99 (Virginia Rep. Thomas Gilmer). For earlier arguments to the same effect see The Jeffersonians at 319 n.11. In 1856 Speaker Nathaniel Banks formally ruled that the Constitution required the House to reconsider a vetoed bill right away, and the House did so. Cong Globe, 34th Cong, 1st Sess 1563.

[57]Cong Globe, 27th Cong, 2d Sess 873, 875, 877. See also id at 871, where as a prelude to listing Tyler's numerous sins Adams declared that his latest veto message had placed "the executive and legislative branches of the Government . . . in a state of civil war."

[58]Tyler had so far vetoed two bank bills and two tariff bills; the fifth to which Adams referred was presumably the bill to reapportion seats in Congress, which Tyler had signed with such reservations as to the constitutionality of its central districting provision that Adams had earlier characterized his action as "a veto under a mask," Cong Globe, 27th Cong, 2d Sess 872. See 4 Richardson at 159–60 (Jun 25, 1842). The districting controversy is discussed in chapter 10.

[59]HR Rep 998, 27th Cong, 2d Sess 28, 35–36, Cong Globe, 27th Cong, 2d Sess 894, 896.

. . . ."[60] Translation: for having vetoed several bills the committee thought ought to have become law. Was that a "high crime[] or misdemeanor[]," for which alone Article II provides that the President (or any other civil officer) shall be impeached and removed?[61] Fallible forsooth is mortal flesh! The sturdy and upright ex-President Adams, who as a young Senator nearly forty years before had set his cap firmly against deposing federal judges who had committed no impeachable offense,[62] was now found at the head of a lynch mob prepared to impeach President Tyler for nothing more than disagreement over the desirability or constitutionality of legislation.

Motions to override the second tariff veto and to propose the suggested amendment were defeated,[63] but the House approved Adams's report, with its blistering indictment of the President's conduct.[64] Like Jackson before him in the controversy over removal of the deposits, Tyler fired back a protest against this "condemnation" without trial; like the earlier Senate, the House voted not to receive his protest.[65]

After Tyler's next veto (of the bill to uncouple tariff increases from distribution of land proceeds), John Minor Botts of Virginia introduced a hyperbolic resolution in no fewer than nine counts to impeach "acting President" John Tyler for, among other things, exercising the veto power the Constitution gave him. Eighty-three members of the House, including Adams, voted to send this appalling proposition to committee. Fortunately 127 members voted not to, and the motion was lost. It was true, as Thomas Marshall of Kentucky argued, that the motion was only that the committee consider the proposed resolution, not that Tyler be impeached; it was nonetheless a blessing that the proposal died aborning.[66]

F. Winding Down

Undeterred by censure and vain threats of impeachment, Tyler continued to man the battlements against what he considered improvident legislation. In December 1843, in the

[60]Id at 896.

[61]US Const, Art II, § 4. See Tyler to Robert McCandlish, Jul 10, 1842, 2 Tyler Letters at 172, 173, suggesting that he was apparently to be impeached for the high crimes of "sustaining the Constitution of the country," of preventing a giveaway of federal assets when the Treasury was empty, and of "daring to have an opinion of my own." For discussion of the question whether the reference to "high crimes and misdemeanors" was intended as a limitation on the grounds of impeachment see The Jeffersonians at 29–30.

[62]See id at 27–28, 35, 38.

[63]The vote on the bill was 91–87, on the amendment 98–90. Id at 906, 907–8.

[64]Id at 907. See Senator Crittenden's letter to Henry Clay, Jul 15, 1842, 9 Clay Papers at 734, arguing that "[a] vote of a want of confidence would amount almost, to an impeachment in all its moral consequences"; Clay to Crittenden, Jul 16, 1842, id at 735, 736, agreeing that such a vote by the House (the Senate as a court of impeachment being disqualified) would be better than nothing. Neither Crittenden nor Clay indicated the source of the House's authority.

[65]See 4 Richardson at 190 (Aug 30, 1842); Cong Globe, 27th Cong, 2d Sess 974–75. Senator Benton, ringleader of the successful campaign to expunge the censure of President Jackson, argued that the two cases were distinguishable: While the Senate's action in the earlier case had been unrelated to its responsibilities, "in its action upon [Tyler's] veto messages, the House was clearly acting within its sphere . . . ." Benton, 2 Thirty Years' View at 418. For the controversy over removal of the deposits see chapter 3.

[66]4 Richardson at 255–56 (Dec 14, 1842); Cong Globe, 27th Cong, 3d Sess 134, 146. Henry Clay, who thought Botts's motion "ill timed," nevertheless opined that the time might be approaching for a test of the "dormant power" of impeachment. Clay to John Quincy Adams, Jul 24, 1842, 9 Clay Papers at 741, 742. See also Clay to Willie Mangum, Jul 11, 1842, id at 731, 732.

same message in which he announced the pocket veto just noted, he informed Congress that he had also allowed a bill regulating procedure in congressional election disputes to expire without his signature because it invaded the prerogatives of the individual Houses.[67] A year later he announced the pocket veto of a bill respecting the payment of claims under an Indian treaty.[68] In June 1844, as related in chapter 1, he vetoed an appropriation for river and harbor improvements, announcing his own narrow interpretation of congressional authority.[69] Finally, shortly before leaving office in March 1845, Tyler defiantly refused his assent to a bill to prevent him from constructing revenue cutters until Congress had appropriated money to pay for them, as the Constitution at least arguably required.[70] That was finally too much for Congress, which roused itself for the first time ever to override a presidential veto. The vote in the Senate was 41–1.[71]

President Polk, as a good Democrat, was no more shy than Tyler to exercise the veto power to keep Congress from traipsing upon states' rights.[72] Zachary Taylor, on the other hand, turned out to be a real Whig, though he seems not to have known it until the Whigs decided to run him for President, and he faithfully espoused the party line with respect to the veto power in his first Annual Message in 1849:

> The check provided by the Constitution in the clause conferring the qualified veto will never be exercised by me except in the cases contemplated by the fathers of the Republic. I view it as an extreme measure, to be resorted to only in extraordinary cases, as where it may become necessary to defend the executive against the encroachments of legislative power or to prevent hasty and inconsiderate or unconstitutional legislation.[73]

[67]4 Richardson at 255, 256 (Dec 14, 1843). President Fillmore quietly signed a bill on the same topic a few years later. 9 Stat 568 (Feb 19, 1851). See also the brief discussion in section I of chapter 9.

[68]4 Richardson at 329 (Dec 18, 1843). Again the grounds for Tyler's action were purely prudential.

[69]Id at 330 (Jun 11, 1844). See the discussion in section V of chapter 1.

[70]4 Richardson at 366–67 (Feb 20, 1845). See US Const, Art I, § 9: "No money shall be drawn from the Treasury, but in consequence of appropriations made by law . . . ." Tyler presumably would have waited for appropriations before actually forking over the money, but there was a question whether it was consistent with the spirit of the clause for the President to commit the Government by contract before Congress had provided the funds. See The Federalist Period at 165; The Jeffersonians at 106.

[71]Cong Globe, 28th Cong, 2d Sess 391. In the House, where Virginia Representative Thomas Bayly repeated Tyler's argument that the bill would effectively repudiate "a contract, which the President had a right to make," the vote was 126–31. Id at 396. The statute appears at 5 Stat 795 (Mar 3, 1845).

[72]See, inter alia, the examples of internal-improvement bills noted in chapter 1. Polk also blocked a bill respecting the settlement of citizens' claims against France on purely prudential grounds, although he said only "an extreme case" could justify him in doing so. 4 Richardson at 466, 469 (Aug 8, 1846). Polk's actions provoked another rehearsal of Whig objections to nonconstitutional vetoes. See Cong Globe, 30th Cong, 1st Sess 1011 (Pennsylvania Rep. Andrew Stewart); Cong Globe App, 30th Cong, 1st Sess 808–12 (Indiana Rep. Caleb Smith). In his last Annual Message Polk treated Congress, in turn, to a spirited defense of the veto power. 4 Richardson at 629, 662–69 (Dec 5, 1848).

[73]5 Richardson at 9, 23 (Dec 4, 1849). Taylor had previewed this anti-executive statement in a famous letter to Captain J.S. Allison, Apr 7, 1848, printed in George R. Poage, Henry Clay and the Whig Party 176, 177 (North Carolina, 1936). See Alan Nevins, Ordeal of the Union: Fruits of Manifest Destiny 212 1847–1852 (Scribner's, 1947). Without invoking constitutional constraints, Abraham Lincoln in an undated memorandum had opined that candidate Taylor ought to say pretty much what he did say: "[W]ere I President, I should desire the legislation of the country to rest with Congress, uninfluenced by the executive in it's origin or progress, and undisturbed by the veto unless in very special and clear cases." Roy P. Basler, ed, 1 The Collected Works of Abraham Lincoln 454 (Rutgers, 1953).

True to his word, Taylor never found an occasion to exercise the veto power during the year or so in which he survived his presidential duties. Neither did Fillmore, last of the true Whigs in the executive mansion, who filled out the remainder of Taylor's term and adopted his predecessor's crabbed view of the veto as his own.[74]

The Democrats regained the Presidency in 1853. As I have noted, both Pierce and Buchanan brandished the veto with characteristic Democratic zeal.[75] Following the precedent set in 1845, however, a Congress stuffed with advocates of river and harbor improvements overrode a series of presidential vetoes in 1856.[76] Along the way the Senate after brief debate formally decided that the majority required by Article I, § 7 was two-thirds of those voting on the question, not of all elected or authorized members.[77]

In proposing the twelfth amendment in 1803 the Senate (and maybe the House) had reached the same conclusion with regard to the substantially identical language of Article V respecting amendment of the Constitution.[78] Most of the arguments had thus been made before, and I shall largely refrain from repeating them. Once again the central objection was the incongruity of reading a provision plainly designed to require extraordinary consensus to permit action by less than a majority of the relevant House.[79] On the other side there was one powerful argument that could not have been made in the case of an amendment: Under Article I, § 7 the House that was to reconsider a vetoed bill was the same as that which had originally passed it, and it was universally accepted that a majority of a quorum sufficed for initial passage of a bill.[80]

What was perhaps most noteworthy about this incident was that it appeared to be a rare example of Senate ignorance of its own precedents. In most cases before the Civil War, not least in those concerning elections,[81] the Senators' knowledge of their predecessors' actions was extraordinarily complete. In the 1856 veto controversy, however, not one speaker brought up the obviously relevant precedent of the twelfth amendment. After the debate was over, Louisiana Senator Judah Benjamin, in presenting a resolution to report repassage of the vetoed bills to the Secretary of State, disclosed that in the interim he had discovered that (according to the respective clerks, as we know) the Bill of Rights itself had been approved by two-thirds of those present in each House.[82] Even then Benjamin did not mention the far better precedent of the twelfth amendment, in which the issue was openly discussed and unambiguously decided, and thus the Senate in 1856 found it necessary to reinvent the wheel.

[74]See Fillmore's first Annual Message, 5 Richardson at 77, 79 (Dec 2, 1850), listing the same three justifications that Taylor had given: unconstitutionality, haste, and encroachment on other branches.

[75]For examples respecting internal improvements and the disposition of public lands see chapters 1 and 2.

[76]See the discussion in section V of chapter 1.

[77]The presiding officer so ruled, and the Senate sustained him by the one-sided vote of 34–7. Cong Globe, 34th Cong, 1st Sess 1544, 1550.

[78]See The Jeffersonians at 58–64.

[79]See Cong Globe, 34th Cong, 1st Sess 1546 (South Carolina Sen. Andrew Butler); id at 1547 (Alabama Sen. Clement C. Clay).

[80]Id at 1544 (Tennessee Sen. John Bell); id at 1545–46 (Louisiana Sen. Judah P. Benjamin). The Supreme Court would later confirm the Senate's determination that two-thirds of those voting would suffice in either case. Missouri Pac Ry v Kansas, 248 US 276 (1919) (veto); National Prohibition Cases, 253 US 350, 386 (1920) (amendment).

[81]See the discussion in chapter 9.

[82]Cong Globe, 34th Cong, 1st Sess 1574.

II. THE APPOINTING POWER

As an essential element in the system of checks and balances, the President's veto power injects him conspicuously into the legislative process. The bulk of his authority, of course, is executive. Article II, § 1 vests in him "the executive power" of the United States; § 2 of the same Article declares him "Commander in Chief" of its armed forces; § 3 enjoins him to "take care that the laws be faithfully executed." We have examined the first and third of these provisions in some detail in connection with the Bank War and with President Harrison's in-house antecedent of the Hatch Act;[83] we shall look closely into the demarcation between presidential and congressional war powers in the next volume.[84]

Section 2 also gives the President authority both to make treaties and to appoint federal officers, in each case "by and with the advice and consent of the Senate"— conversely to the veto, establishing a legislative check on presidential power. Treaties too we shall consider in the next volume;[85] we must take a moment here for a couple of observations on the parallel power to appoint "officers of the United States."

First, in 1833 the Senate rejected several of President Jackson's nominees for federal office on the apparent basis of an earlier resolution terming it "inexpedient," absent "some evident necessity," to appoint officers who resided outside the state in which they were to serve. In an arguably analogous case members of the House would later complain that that body could not limit their right to vote for Speaker by laying down qualifications for his election.[86] President Jackson objected to the Senate resolution not because it restricted the freedom of individual Senators but because he viewed it as "an unconstitutional restraint upon the authority of the President in relation to appointments to office . . . ."[87]

Was Jackson mistaken in this assertion? The Constitution specifies qualifications for members of the House and Senate, but not for presidential appointees. Reasonable requirements designed to ensure that a nominee is capable of performing her duties may well be necessary and proper to creation of her office and thus to the legislation the officer is to carry out. The First Congress, for example, had sensibly required that federal District Attorneys be "learned in the law."[88] Moreover, Article II, § 2 appears to give the Senate discretion to reject nominations for any reason it thinks sufficient, or for no reason at all. In the absence of statutory qualifications, perhaps the President is entitled to have the Senate pass on the merits of each nomination at the time it is made, and perhaps no Senate rule can diminish the right of individual members to do so.[89] So long as the

[83]See section II of chapter 3 and section VI of chapter 5.

[84]See especially Descent into the Maelstrom, chs 5 and 6.

[85]See id, chs 3–5.

[86]See section II of chapter 10.

[87]2 Richardson at 636 (Mar 2, 1833).

[88]See The Federalist Period at 43 n.255.

[89]Compare the arguments made with respect to the admission of states in the cases of Texas and Tennessee. Descent into the Maelstrom, ch 5, § IV; The Federalist Period at 218–21; and see the parallel argument of Senator Seward in connection with the election of Senators in note 130 of chapter 9.

President's discretion is not unreasonably restricted, however,[90] there seems little reason to preclude the Senate from giving the President advance warning of the criteria it intends to apply.

A more egregious example along the same lines occurred in 1860, when Congress appropriated funds "for the completion of the Washington Aqueduct, . . . to be expended according to the plans of Captain Meigs and under his superintendence."[91] This time Congress had clearly gone too far; it had left the executive no discretion whatever in determining whom to appoint. In signing the bill President Buchanan made clear that he did so only because he could not believe Congress had meant either to appoint Meigs to a new office or to interfere with the authority of the Commander-in-Chief to determine the duties to which military officers should be assigned—neither of which, he rightly insisted, Congress had power to do.[92]

It was in connection with this latter episode that Attorney General Jeremiah Black, supporting his superior's position, uttered the important dictum that the President was bound to disregard unconstitutional provisions even after signing a law:

> Every law is to be carried out so far forth [sic] as is consistent with the Constitution, and no further. The sound part of it must be executed, and the vicious portion of it suffered to drop.[93]

President Jefferson had asserted the right to pardon convicts on the ground that the law under which they had been prosecuted was unconstitutional, President Jackson the right to veto on constitutional grounds legislation both Congress and the Supreme Court had found kosher.[94] Black's diktat went beyond both Jefferson and Jackson, and it has not received universal approval. For the President has broad discretion both to pardon offenders and to disapprove bills sent to him by Congress, while as Professor Corwin would write in this connection many years later Article II, § 3 requires him to execute the laws.[95] For the President to refuse to carry out an unconstitutional provision already enacted, a House committee would argue later still, would offend Article I, § 7 as well by transforming a suspensive veto into an absolute one.[96]

Nevertheless, as later Attorneys General and their lawyers have frequently maintained, it is at least arguable that the logic of Jackson's Bank veto message equally demonstrates that the Constitution does not require the President to enforce unconstitutional laws.[97] For as we know from *Marbury v Madison* an unconstitutional statute is no law at all,[98] and the Constitution itself is one of the laws the President has sworn to en-

[90]Compare the fears of those opposing additional qualifications for election to Congress in 1807 that states might limit eligibility to the wealthy, to adherents of a specified party, or even to persons residing at a particular address. The Jeffersonians at 79.

[91]12 Stat 104, 106, § 1 (Jun 25, 1860).

[92]5 Richardson 597, 598 (Jun 25, 1860).

[93]9 Op AG 462, 468–69 (1860).

[94]See The Jeffersonians at 5–6 and section I of chapter 3 of this volume.

[95]See Corwin, Office and Powers at 252–54.

[96]HR Rep 138, 99th Cong, 1st Sess 13 (1985).

[97]E.g., 18 Op OLC No 35 (1994), in H. Jefferson Powell, The Constitution and the Attorneys General 577–80 (Carolina Academic Press, 1999) (claiming Supreme Court support for this conclusion).

[98]5 US 137, 176–80 (1803); The Fitst Hundred Years at 69–74.

force. Like Jackson's veto and Jefferson's pardon, Black's assertion of the President's obligation not to execute unconstitutional laws offers us an additional check to ensure that the Constitution is respected; it does nothing to impair the alternative safeguard of judicial review. James Wilson, second only to Madison as sculptor and initial expositor of the Constitution, had prefigured Black's interpretation during the Pennsylvania ratifying convention: Just as the judges would declare unconstitutional statutes void, the President would refuse to enforce them.[99]

III. THE SANCTITY OF THE CABINET

Presidents have express powers, as we have seen, to execute laws, veto legislation, and (with Senate consent) to make appointments and treaties. They also enjoy certain implicit immunities and privileges deemed indispensable to the effective exercise of their functions, and we have encountered them obliquely in an earlier chapter.[100] President Jackson forcefully asserted one of them during the Bank War, and successors of both political persuasions would soon echo his justifiable concerns.

Only a week after Treasury Secretary Roger B. Taney had filed his report announcing the removal of Government funds from the Bank of the United States, Henry Clay provoked a minor tempest by moving that the Senate ask President Jackson for a copy of a paper he had allegedly read to his Cabinet on the subject of the deposits.[101] Georgia Senator John Forsyth objected that the Senate had no legitimate reason to ask for the paper: If it revealed misconduct by the President, only the House would have authority to impeach him.[102] George Poindexter of Mississippi weakly replied that the Senate had a responsibility to inform the public how the Government was conducted;[103] Clay more convincingly added that the paper might show the need for further legislation.[104]

The more acute difficulty lay in the domain of what we have come to call executive privilege. The Senate had no right to pry into communications between the President and his Cabinet, argued Forsyth and Missouri Senator Thomas Hart Benton.[105] If the paper had been kept confidential, Clay conceded, the Senate would have had no right to demand it; but it had been given to the newspapers with the President's apparent approval and thus, he seemed to imply, Jackson had waived his privilege.[106] The Senate voted 23–18 to ask the President to produce the controversial paper,[107] and he angrily refused:

> The executive is a coordinate and independent branch of the Government equally with the Senate, and I have yet to learn under what constitutional authority that branch of the legislature has a right to require of me an account of any communication, either verbally or in writing, made to the heads of Departments acting as a Cabinet council. As well might I be re-

[99]See 2 Elliot's Debates at 446.
[100]See section VI of chapter 5.
[101]Cong Deb, 23d Cong, 1st Sess 25 (Dec 10, 1833).
[102]Id at 31, 33.
[103]Id at 32.
[104]Id at 35.
[105]Id at 31–32.
[106]Id at 30, 36.
[107]Id at 37.

> quired to detail to the Senate the free and private conversations I have held with those officers on any subject relating to their duties and my own.[108]

When President Washington objected to the House's request for information pertaining to the Jay Treaty in 1796, he did so largely on the ground that since only the Senate was required to consent to a treaty the information was not relevant to the House's legitimate functions.[109] Jackson's message invoked a distinct and equally critical constitutional principle, later recognized by the Supreme Court, based on the obvious need for confidentiality to promote frank deliberation within the Executive Branch.[110] Since Jackson himself had already spilled the beans in this case by giving his statement to the press, his invocation of privilege seems hollow on the facts. The principle he asserted, however, was unassailable.

Presidents Tyler and Polk likewise staunchly defended the executive's right to confidentiality, the former invoking English precedent and analogizing to privileges against self-incrimination and disclosure of communications to attorneys or confessors,[111] the latter vigorously applying the principle in the sensitive field of foreign affairs.[112] Responding to Tyler's 1843 message, a House committee mounted a frontal attack on the entire concept of executive privilege: The House was entitled to any information relevant to the exercise of its legitimate powers, whether or not it would be admissible in court. The House of Representatives, the report explained, could be trusted to keep secrets; and it could not do its job (the committee made particular reference to impeachment cases) without obtaining information that was in executive hands.[113] President Polk, while standing up stoutly for confidentiality in other cases, expressly acknowledged that impeachment fell outside the usual rule: "In such a case the safety of the Republic would be the supreme law, and the power of the House in the pursuit of this object would penetrate into the most secret recesses of the Executive Departments."[114]

IV. HIS ACCIDENCY

Quick, who was the tenth President of the United States? John Tyler, of course. Or was

[108] 3 Richardson at 36 (Dec 12, 1833); Cong Deb, 23d Cong, 1st Sess 37.

[109] See The Federalist Period at 214. He had also stressed the need for secrecy in foreign negotiations, and Madison had conceded the legitimacy of this concern. See id & n.70.

[110] See United States v Nixon, 418 US 683 (1974). President Jefferson had made noises of this nature in resisting Chief Justice Marshall's subpoena duces tecum in Aaron Burr's case, in addition to asserting a blanket immunity from judicial process that might distract him from his official responsibilities. See The Jeffersonians at 133–36. Cf US Const, Art I, § 5, making an exception from the requirement that each House of Congress publish its Journal for "such parts as may in their judgment require secrecy"; 4 Elliot's Debates at 73 (James Iredell), explaining the need for confidentiality with respect to military and diplomatic affairs.

[111] 4 Richardson at 220–25 (Jan 31, 1843). See also id at 227, 228 (Feb 18, 1843) (also noted in Descent into the Maelstrom, ch 6, § I) (reserving the right to determine which military orders might safely be communicated to Congress).

[112] 4 Richardson at 565, 566–67 (Jan 12, 1848).

[113] HR Rep 271, 27th Cong, 3d Sess 6–8 (1843). Cf the third count later approved by the Judiciary Committee against President Richard Nixon, charging him with disobedience of a subpoena served in furtherance of the impeachment inquiry itself. 120 Cong Rec 29219, 29220 (1974).

[114] 4 Richardson at 431, 434 (Apr 20, 1846).

he? President Harrison, inaugurated on March 4, died on April 4.[115] Two days later Tyler, who had been elected Vice-President, took an oath to "execute the office of President of the United States."[116]

In an "Inaugural Address" to the people on April 9 Tyler observed that his position was unique: "For the first time in our history the person elected to the Vice-Presidency . . . , by the happening of a contingency provided for in the Constitution, has had devolved upon him the Presidential office."[117]

During his brief tenure as Chief Executive, Harrison had called a special session of Congress to consider "sundry important and weighty matters, principally growing out of the condition of the revenue and finances of the country."[118] When Congress accordingly met on May 31, Virginia Representative Henry A. Wise moved appointment of the usual committee "to wait upon the President of the United States, and inform him that a quorum of the two Houses is assembled, and that Congress is now ready to receive any communication he may be pleased to make."[119]

New York Democrat John McKeon moved to amend the resolution "by striking out the word 'President' and inserting the words 'Vice-President, now exercising the office of President.'"[120] Democrat William Allen of Ohio made a similar motion in the Senate: Tyler should be described as "the Vice-President, on whom, by the death of the late President, the powers and duties of the office of President have devolved."[121] For Mr. Tyler was not the President, McKeon argued. No one could become President except by election. Article I, in providing for the selection of Senate officers, made clear what Tyler's position was, for it specified that the Senate should choose a President pro tem "in the absence of the Vice-President, or when he shall exercise the office of President of the United States."[122]

Nonsense, said Tyler's defenders. Tyler was President. "The office of President," said Wise, "devolved on the Vice President" when Harrison died.[123] No it didn't, said McKeon: It was the President's "powers and duties," not his "office," that were devolved.[124] Indeed, said McKeon, all earlier drafts of the constitutional provision had spec-

[115]See the public announcement by five members of the Cabinet in 4 Richardson at 22.

[116]Id at 31. He did so "for greater caution," reported Judge William Cranch, who administered the oath, "although he deems himself qualified to perform the duties and exercise the powers and office of President . . . without any other oath than he has taken as Vice-President . . . ." Id at 31–32. "In other words," wrote Professor Corwin, "it was clearly Tyler's original belief that he was Vice-President acting as President, and not President." Corwin, Office and Powers at 54. If that was Tyler's initial view, he changed it soon enough. See 2 Tyler Letters at 12–13.

[117]4 Richardson at 36, 37.

[118]See id at 21 (Mar 17, 1841).

[119]Cong Globe, 27th Cong, 1st Sess 3. The text of the resolution appears in id at 4.

[120]Id at 3.

[121]Id at 4.

[122]Cong Globe App, 27th Cong, 1st Sess 13.

[123]Cong Globe, 27th Cong, 1st Sess 4.

[124]Cong Globe App, 27th Cong, 1st Sess 13–14. John Quincy Adams, without stating reasons, agreed with this interpretation. 10 JQA Memoirs at 463–64. See also id at 456–57, disparaging Tyler as "a political sectarian of the slave-driving, Virginian, Jeffersonian school, . . . with talents not above mediocrity" and declaring that his accession "brings to the test that provision of the Constitution which places in the Executive chair a man never thought of for it by anybody." Mr. Adams, it should be added, tended to disparage most people of whom he spoke in his diary.

ified that the Vice-President merely exercise the President's functions; the final version was the work of the Committee of Style, which had no authority to make substantive changes.[125]

Perhaps we had best look to the Constitution itself. When we do we find that it is indeed unclear whether the Vice-President assumes the President's office or only his powers:

> In case of the removal of the President from office, or of his death, resignation, or inability to discharge the powers and duties of the said office, the same shall devolve on the Vice-President . . . .[126]

Mississippi Senator Robert Walker thought rules of grammar resolved the difficulty.

> The language is, "*the same* shall devolve." . . . The immediate antecedent is "the said office," and it is a rule of grammatical construction, as well as of common sense, that the immediate antecedent is connected with the adjective which follows.[127]

Walker drew further strength for his conclusion by contrasting the language of the succeeding constitutional provision. If *neither* the President nor the Vice-President could fulfill the President's duties, another officer designated by statute should "act as President," not become President; there was no such provision when the Vice-President was available.[128]

The constitutional text, I fear, did not answer the question.[129] Consequential arguments were also rolled out to support the competing positions.

"Is Mr. Tyler still the Vice President," asked Walker, "discharging additional duties? If so, why is he not here performing the duties of Vice President? Could he come here and act as Vice President for a single moment? Surely not . . . ."[130] The implication was that the Framers, with their solicitude for the separation of powers, could not have intended to make the de facto head of the Executive Branch President of the Senate. Of course not; but as Senator Allen replied they had not done so. Vice-President Tyler could not preside over the Senate "because the Constitution had assigned him duties which re-

[125]Cong Globe App, 27th Cong, 1st Sess 14. For what it's worth, McKeon was right about those earlier drafts. See 2 Farrand at 186, 495, 575. Ohio Senator Benjamin Tappan added analogies to suggest it would have been unusual to make the Vice-President President when his predecessor was eliminated. A senior judge did not become Chief Justice by presiding in the latter's absence; the subordinate of a fallen officer did not become colonel by assuming command; nor did the Senate President pro tem become Vice-President in Tyler's absence, thus vacating his seat and losing his right to vote. Cong Globe, 27th Cong, 1st Sess 4–5. The Framers might of course have meant to depart from these models, but they were nevertheless suggestive.

[126]US Const, Art II, § 1.

[127]Cong Globe, 27th Cong, 1st Sess 5.

[128]Id; see US Const, Art II, § 1.

[129]Clinton Rossiter confidently tells us that "[c]onstitutional historians are in unanimous agreement that the framers intended the Vice-President to act as President but not to be President," but he cites nothing for this conclusion, and except for such inferences as may be drawn from the language of earlier drafts (see note 125 and accompanying text) the records of the Constitutional Convention are singularly uninformative as to the Framers' intentions. See Clinton Rossiter, The American Presidency 209 (Harcourt, Brace, 2d ed 1960).

[130]Cong Globe, 27th Cong, 1st Sess 5.

quired his presence elsewhere, viz: the duties of the Presidential office. He was now an executive, not a legislative officer."[131] Allen did not say so, but Article I, § 3 made it perfectly clear that the Vice-President was not to wear legislative and executive hats concurrently by providing that another officer preside over the Senate whenever the Vice-President "shall exercise the office of President of the United States."

Allen had a better consequential argument of his own. As McKeon also observed in the House, the same constitutional provision that prescribed the Vice-President's role when the President died applied when he suffered a temporary disability.[132] Surely, "if the late President had been afflicted with a disease producing, for time, a state of mental alienation, he would on his recovery have been reinstated in all the powers of that high office to which the People had elected him."[133] But if the Vice-President had become President by virtue of his predecessor's disability, he would remain in office; for there would be no way short of death, incapacity, or impeachment to get rid of him.[134] This result, we might add, would not only be bizarre in itself; it would contradict the explicit scheme the Framers spelled out for the analogous case in which some other officer substitutes for a disabled President; for in that case the surrogate acts, as we would expect, only "until the disability be removed."[135]

Persuaded? But there is one further twist. In an effort to assuage the fears of their adversaries, both Allen and McKeon declared their willingness to vote Mr. Tyler the President's full salary while he exercised the President's functions.[136] But both seemed clearly to understand that to do so was an act of grace, not of constitutional compulsion. "There was nothing in the Constitution," said McKeon, to guarantee the Vice-President the President's compensation; "he was given only 'the power and duties' of the office, but not the salary."[137] Troubling? It gets worse. For if Mr. Tyler was not President, he was not protected by the provision of Article II, § 1 forbidding Congress to reduce the President's wages during his service—a result quite incompatible with that clause's purpose of ensuring an independent executive.

Thus it is inconceivable either that Tyler became President or that he did not; I see no satisfactory way out of the box.[138] Tyler's friends had the votes in both Houses, and the

[131]Id.

[132]Id at 4 (Sen. Allen); Cong Globe App, 27th Cong, 1st Sess 14 (Rep. McKeon).

[133]Cong Globe, 27th Cong, 1st Sess 4.

[134]Id at 5. Professor Rossiter argues that the possibility that a transfer of power to the Vice-President might be irrevocable made it unthinkable for Vice-Presidents Arthur and Marshall to assume responsibility on the disability of Presidents Garfield and Wilson, respectively. Rossiter, The American Presidency at 216 (cited in note 129).

[135]US Const, Art II, § 1.

[136]Cong Globe, 27th Cong, 1st Sess 4 (Sen. Allen); Cong Globe App, 27th Cong, 1st Sess 14 (Rep. McKeon). See also Cong Globe, 27th Cong, 1st Sess 5 (Sen. Tappan).

[137]Cong Globe App, 27th Cong, 1st Sess 14.

[138]One might conceivably conclude, by construing each clause in light of its purpose, that Tyler was President under one clause but not under another: He would cease to exercise the President's functions if the President recovered, but in the meantime Congress could not reduce his salary. The same word need not mean the same thing throughout the Constitution; corporations are treated as "citizens" for purposes of the diversity jurisdiction but not under the privileges and immunities clause. Marshall v Baltimore & Ohio RR, 57 US 314 (1853); Blake v McClung, 172 US 239 (1898). Consider also the varying interpretations offered for the several references to "officers" throughout the Constitution. See The Federalist Period at 139–44, 275–81; The

hostile amendments were rejected; the resolution as adopted called for the appointment of House and Senate committees "to wait on the President of the United States."[139]

By the time President Zachary Taylor died in 1850 the controversy was forgotten. Without a murmur of objection Millard Fillmore, who had been Vice-President, swore faithfully to "execute the office of President"; the Speaker, two Representatives, a Senate resolution, Fillmore's own messenger, and the Globe reporter all described him without cavil as "President of the United States."[140] Tyler's "shaky precedent," wrote Clinton Rossiter in 1960, "hardened into a rock against which no one has been disposed to butt his head from that day to this."[141]

A century and a quarter after Tyler's accession to the Presidency (or to its powers and duties) the twenty-fifth amendment finally solved the principal difficulty by separating the cases of death and of disability: If the President dies, resigns, or is removed "the Vice-President shall become President"; if he is disabled, the Vice-President ("as Acting President") shall assume his powers and duties so long as the disability continues.[142]

Aren't you glad? I am.

V. CASTING VOTES AND OTHER QUIDDITIES

The Vice-President, as I have remarked before, was and remains an anomalous officer with an executive title but without executive responsibility under the Constitution, whose macabre central assignment, as we have just seen, is to wait around in case something happens to the President.[143]

While he waits, as you know, the Vice-President is expected to perform the essentially ceremonial task of presiding over the Senate.[144] Even this modest attempt to prevent his becoming an actual vagrant (usually neglected in modern times though still honored during the years of which we speak) raised the hackles, as I have noted, of those who were especially sensitive to any hint of the commingling of executive and legislative authority.[145] As a result of such jealousies the Vice-President, at the time now under examination, found himself bereft by Senate action of some of the prerogatives commonly assigned to a presiding officer. These restrictions presented constitutional difficulties of their own, and I have alluded to them elsewhere.[146] One indubitable and impregnable power, however, remained in the Vice-President's hands, and it was the one that came closest to justifying the quaint institutional arrangements the Founders had devised. A rare issue of its interpretation arose during the period of this study.

Jeffersonians at 71–75, 82–86. In this case, however, such an approach might smack more of improving on than of explicating the Framers' designs.

[139]Cong Globe, 27th Cong, 1st Sess 4, 5.

[140]Cong Globe, 31st Cong, 1st Sess 1365–66.

[141]Rossiter, The American Presidency at 209 (cited in note 129).

[142]US Const, Amend 25, §§ 1, 3, 4.

[143]US Const, Art II, § 1 and Amend XII, XXV. On the tenacity of this peculiar institution see The Jeffersonians at 44–46.

[144]Id, Art I, § 3.

[145]See The Federalist Period at 11–12.

[146]See The Jeffersonians at 316.

There was a tie in the vote for Senate chaplain in 1850, and Vice-President Fillmore inquired whether he had the right to break it. The constitutional text suggests that he had:

> The Vice-President of the United States shall be President of the Senate, but shall have no vote, unless they be equally divided.[147]

Senator Calhoun reported that when he was Vice-President he had cast tiebreaking votes to defeat presidential nominations to office, including that of Martin Van Buren as Minister to Great Britain in 1832. John Berrien of Georgia said he saw no reason to limit the Vice-President's authority to cases of legislation. William King of Alabama said it had been so understood in the past but that he would acquiesce in a broader construction. Fillmore cast the decisive vote without objection.[148]

A different issue respecting vice-presidential powers arose in 1845 and again in 1847 when Vice-President George Dallas appointed a substitute to preside over the Senate while he was not there. The Constitution was clear, objected John Crittenden of Kentucky and George Badger of North Carolina; the Senate itself was to choose a President pro tempore "in the absence of the Vice-President."[149] Senate Rules did authorize either the Vice-President or the President pro tem to appoint a substitute, "but such substitution shall not extend beyond an adjournment."

That meant not beyond the end of the day, said Calhoun. Practice had settled that a single day did not amount to an "absence" within the meaning of the constitutional provision; the Vice-President was entitled to warm his feet. Crittenden thought the distinction geographical, not temporal: If the Vice-President was temporarily out of the chair, he was still viewed as presiding; if he was sick at home, he was absent. Samuel Southard, others pointed out, had appointed a substitute for an extended period when he was President pro tem and was taken ill. That was different, said Badger; Southard was a member of the Senate, not Vice-President. The rule, however, applied equally to both; and the spirit of the constitutional provision would suggest that if one President pro tem is absent the Senate should choose another.

In the course of this discussion Senator Webster called attention to yet another difficulty. Under the existing rule, he noted, the office of President pro tem terminated when the Vice-President returned to the Senate. This was unfortunate, he argued. There should always be a President pro tempore—not least in order to ensure an orderly succession to the Presidency.[150]

On Crittenden's motion David Atchison of Missouri was elected President pro tem, and the rules were referred to committee for possible revision or repeal.[151] It was 1890, however, before the rules were changed to provide for a permanent President pro tempore, Senator Turpie then arguing (over the objection of Senator George) that in directing the Senate to "choose a President pro tempore in the absence of the Vice-

[147]US Const, Art I, § 3.

[148]Cong Globe, 31st Cong, 1st Sess 128. For Calhoun's casting vote against Van Buren see Cong Deb, 22d Cong, 1st Sess 1324.

[149]US Const, Art I, § 3.

[150]For the origins of this practice see The Federalist Period at 11.

[151]See Cong Globe, 29th Cong, 1st Sess 95–96; Cong Globe, 29th Cong, 2d Sess 161–64.

President" Article I, § 3 specified his time of service, not of election.[152]

[152] 21 Cong Rec 2144–53.

7

All about Judges

We have spoken a lot about Congress, and a little about the President and his potential successor. It remains to say a few words about the third branch of the Federal Government.

The basic issues of federal judicial power were settled upon passage of the Judiciary Act in 1789.[1] After the great battle over judicial tenure in 1802,[2] Congress left the structure of the federal courts pretty well alone until long after the time of the present study. Occasional efforts to cripple the Supreme Court, as I have noted elsewhere, were beaten back without difficulty.[3] Thus as Jackson took office and as Buchanan left it the law governing the federal courts was very much as it had been in the days of President Washington.

Yet the courts did not escape controversy altogether between 1829 and 1861. Right off the bat we encounter the third impeachment of a federal judge in the nation's history—an event that raised knotty questions of freedom of expression and criminal procedure as well as the constitutional standard for conviction. The dogged but ultimately unsuccessful proceedings against yet another judge yielded additional insights into the meaning of the impeachment provisions, as did a handful of incidents involving the alleged misconduct of executive officials. The famous contretemps over the Wheeling Bridge engendered debate in Congress as well as the Court over legislative authority to set aside judicial decisions. Around mid-century, moreover, Congress began to grapple earnestly with the problem of devising adequate machinery for the resolution of claims against the United States, leaving us with a rich legacy of constitutional argument on the formidable issues that surrounded the creation of the original Court of Claims. Finally, the question of judicial independence raised its head yet again in the context of courts in the

[1] See The Federalist Period at 47–54.
[2] See The Jeffersonians at 11–22.
[3] See id at 329–32 and section III of chapter 4 of this volume.

territories, in the District of Columbia, and abroad. These various controversies form the subject of this chapter.

I. THE IMPEACHMENT OF JUDGE PECK

When Thomas Jefferson was President, the House impeached District Judge John Pickering and Supreme Court Justice Samuel Chase. Pickering was convicted, essentially of insanity and drink. Chase, accused of a spectrum of official misconduct, was saved by the requirement of a two-thirds vote for conviction. The case has stood ever since for the salutary principle that the Senate is not to remove a judge because it disagrees with his decisions.[4]

In April 1830, when Andrew Jackson was President, the House voted by the impressive margin of 123–49 to impeach James H. Peck, Judge of the federal District Court for the District of Missouri.[5] The charge, which James Buchanan of Pennsylvania presented to the Senate on behalf of the House managers ten days later, was that Judge Peck had summarily imprisoned and suspended an attorney named Luke Lawless for contempt of court for having published an article criticizing a decision the judge had rendered against his clients in a case involving a land claim.[6]

Little of the House debate on the motion to impeach was reported.[7] The attorney's criticism, Buchanan explained, had been "humble, tame, and submissive"; there was no basis to find it contempt. Ex parte contempt proceedings were dangerous, as they combined the functions of accuser and judge; Judge Peck's actions had offended the constitutional guarantees of press freedom and jury trial. A mere violation of law was not enough to support impeachment, Buchanan conceded, but Peck's actions had been "arbitrary and oppressive."[8]

Jabez Huntington of Connecticut, later to become judge of his state's highest court, gave a thoughtful speech against the motion to impeach. He agreed that the constitutional threshold of "high crimes and misdemeanors" did not require the commission of an indictable offense; "for if a judge should come on to the bench in a state of intoxication, or,

[4]See The Jeffersonians at 23–38.

[5]Cong Deb, 21st Cong, 1st Sess 818–19.

[6]Id at 411–13; HR Rep 385, 21st Cong, 1st Sess (1830). Judge Peck's opinion in the underlying land case is reprinted in HR Rep 325, 21st Cong, 1st Sess 5–23 (1830), Lawless's attack on it in id at 23–25, and the contempt citation in id at 27. Judge Peck's judgment in the land case was subsequently reversed, Soulard's Heirs v United States, 35 US 100 (1836). For the background and a summary of the impeachment proceedings by a commentator convinced that in most respects Peck acted correctly see Eleanore Bushnell, Crimes, Follies, and Misfortunes: The Federal Impeachment Trials 91–113 (Illinois, 1992).

[7]Much of the recorded discussion concerned Peck's request to produce witnesses and to present a written statement in his own defense, Cong Deb, 21st Cong, 1st Sess 736. The second request was granted, the first denied, several members insisting that the House was only to determine whether or not to file charges, not to conduct a trial. Id at 736–39, 746–53, 789. Peck's statement appears in HR Rep 359, 21st Cong, 1st Sess (1830), and in the full report of the proceedings (cited in note 11) at 11–45. For a transcript of the committee hearings that preceded the House debate see HR Rep 325, 21st Cong, 1st Sess (1830).

[8]Cong Deb App, 21st Cong, 1st Sess 1–5 (omitted speeches, following p 1148). See also Cong Deb, 21st Cong, 1st Sess 746–47 (Rep. Ellsworth). The impeachment article itself alleged that Peck had acted "with intention wrongfully and unjustly to oppress, imprison, and otherwise injure" Lawless, HR Rep 385, 21st Cong, 1st Sess 4; Peck insisted that if he had erred in imposing sanctions he had done so in good faith, HR Rep 359, 21st Cong, 1st Sess 41. The jury-trial argument would fail even today. Bloom v Illinois, 391 US 194 (1968).

while there, should employ himself, in playing games of chance, he ought . . . to be impeached." On the other hand, mere incompetence was not enough; "good behavior" was the absence of high crimes and misdemeanors for which an officer could be impeached. More specifically, an impeachable offense in the case of a judge was "an assumption of judicial power, exercised to the injury of an individual, and done *malo animo*." Thus

> [t]o sustain this resolution, the committee must be satisfied that Judge Peck had no power to imprison, and erase from the roll of attorneys the name of Mr. Lawless, for the causes that led him to do it; that the exercise of this power operated to the injury of Mr. Lawless; and that it was done with a corrupt motive.[9]

There was no doubt, Huntington continued, that Lawless had been injured by the sanctions Judge Peck had imposed, but there was no reason to think the judge had acted with an improper motive. Nor, in his view, had Peck acted illegally. It was the plain object of the offending article to influence related cases still pending before Judge Peck; and

> any publication, the object and design of which is to corrupt the fountains of justice, by its tendency improperly to affect the due administration of it in causes which are depending in the court of law or equity, is a contempt, authorizing a summary proceeding by process of attachment, punishable by fine and imprisonment, and, in the case of an attorney, by suspension from practice.[10]

The Senate heard testimony for nearly a month.[11] The House managers and lawyers for the respondent presented arguments at length. Members of the Senate maintained an inscrutable silence.[12] In the end they voted 22–21 against conviction.[13]

Though the testimony was prolix, there was no dispute over the facts. Nor was there much difference of opinion between the opposing advocates as to the definition of an impeachable offense. Former Attorney General William Wirt, arguing for Judge Peck, conceded that "a conscious usurpation of power for the guilty purpose of oppression" would suffice.[14] New York Representative Ambrose Spencer, for the prosecution, agreed

[9]Cong Deb, 21st Cong, 1st Sess 750.

[10]Id at 750–53.

[11]The testimony, along with arguments of the House managers and of Peck's lawyers not reported in the Register of Debates, was published separately in a volume of nearly 600 pages. Arthur J. Stansbury, Report of the Trial of James H. Peck (Da Capo, 1972) (first published in 1833).

[12]Senator Livingston moved at one point that Senators be permitted to assign reasons for their votes (Cong Deb, 21st Cong, 2d Sess 24), but the Debates do not reveal a vote on his motion.

[13]Id at 45. The vote was not exclusively on party lines. Jacksonians Forsyth and Hayne voted with opposition Senator Clayton to convict, Jacksonians Grundy and Tazewell with opposition Senator Webster to acquit. Id. For a further political breakdown of the vote see Bushnell, Crimes, Follies, and Misfortunes at 111–12 (cited in note 6).

[14]See Trial Report at 496 (cited in note 11), adding that the same was true of "an exercise of lawful power with excessive severity for the same guilty purpose." Cf the modern test for the liability of executive officers for damages arising from violations of the Constitution or statutes, which requires a violation of established law. Harlow v Fitzgerald, 457 US 800 (1982).

that mere error would not: "A judicial misdemeanor consists, in my opinion, in doing an illegal act *colori officii* with bad motives."[15] Buchanan said that either "[a] gross abuse of granted power" or "an usurpation of power not granted" would justify impeachment;[16] he thought criminal intention could be inferred from the act itself.[17] The real disagreement was over application of the common legal standard to the case, and that entailed arguments over two subsidiary constitutional issues: freedom of the press and summary punishment for contempt.

Every citizen, said South Carolina's George McDuffie for the House managers, had the right to criticize a judicial opinion; even the hated Sedition Act, which all agreed was unconstitutional, had made truth a defense and guaranteed trial by jury. The power to punish summarily, McDuffie added, was confined to the minimum necessary to prevent actual obstruction of court proceedings. "It must be a flagrant outrage in the face of the court," the reporter paraphrased him as saying, "to justify a summary punishment for contempt."[18]

No one denied the right to mere criticism, said Wirt for the defense—provided it was "decent," "temperate," and "fair."[19] But it did not follow, he insisted, that a judicial decision might be "vilely misrepresented . . . for the purpose of exposing both the opinion and the court to the contempt and ridicule of the world."[20] Wirt cited numerous English

[15]Trial Report at 290 (cited in note 11). Like Wirt, Spencer added that it was enough that the act in question, if improperly motivated, was "unwarranted in a particular case." Id.

[16]See id at 428–29. Compare Alexander Hamilton's definition of high crimes and misdemeanors as serious abuses of authority, The Federalist No 65. Charles Wickliffe of Kentucky, another manager for the prosecution, flirted at one point with the argument that no high crime or misdemeanor had to be shown. Wirt accused him of arguing that ignorance of the law was no excuse, but Wickliffe too echoed Buchanan's contention that "an evil and wicked intent" could be inferred from the facts of the case. Trial Report at 308–10, 320, 491–92 (cited in note 11). Wirt, for his part, acknowledged that "a judicial act may be so grossly and palpably illegal as to render it impossible to refer it to mistake." Id at 496.

[17]Id at 428. The difference between the two parties, wrote one later commentator, was that Peck's counsel insisted that a guilty intention had to be proved. DeAlva S. Alexander, History and Procedure of the House of Representatives 350 (Houghton, Mifflin, 1916).

[18]See Trial Report at 85–93 (cited in note 11). The quotation is taken from Cong Deb, 21st Cong, 2d Sess 10. Pollock mentions an early case in which a prisoner "ject un brickbat a le dit Justice, que narrowly mist." Frederick Pollock, First Book of Jurisprudence 302 (6th ed 1929), quoting a marginal note in James Dyer, Les reports des divers matters & resolutions . . . 188b (Rawlins et al, 1688). For the proposition that the power was *limited* to such cases, however, McDuffie cited no authority. As Buchanan pointed out (Trial Report at 432–33), the Pennsylvania legislature after a contrary judicial decision had forbidden summary proceedings for out-of-court publications concerning even pending cases (see 5 Pa Laws 55 (1812)), but there was as yet no comparable federal statute. The House of Representatives had asserted a broader authority to punish contempts against its own authority, but concern for legislative independence arguably provides a basis for distinction. See The Federalist Period at 232–38, discussing the case of Randall and Whitney.

[19]See Trial Report at 528–29 (cited in note 11), quoting from Francis Holt, The Law of Libel 170 (Stephen Gould, 1818).

[20]Trial Report at 529 (cited in note 11). Peck had put it more elegantly in his memorial to the House, id at 39: Liberty of the press did not include the right to vilify the courts, to misrepresent their opinions, or to bring them into disrepute. In the same document Peck painstakingly compared Lawless's paraphrases with the opinion itself in an effort to demonstrate that each of the attorney's eighteen points distorted what the opinion had said. Professor Bushnell singles out three of Lawless's assertions and concludes that Peck was right as to each of them. Peck had written, for example, that "the Lieutenant Governor of Upper Louisiana was not a sub-delegate" authorized to make land grants; Lawless alleged that Peck had said "a sub-delegate in Louisiana was not a sub-delegate" within the meaning of the relevant law. The consequence, as Peck put it, was to attribute an "absurdity" to the judge, or, as he said in connection with another of the alleged misrepresentations, to make

and American authorities to establish that it was contempt to speak or write "contemptuously of the court, or judges acting in their judicial capacity," that the offender could be tried summarily for out-of-court statements, and that it did not matter whether at the time of publication the case in question was still pending.[21]

If a federal judge had the gall to do now what Judge Peck did in 1826, there would indeed be a strong case for impeachment. The Supreme Court has made clear both that the first amendment affords great latitude even for what look like blatant attempts to influence the outcome of pending cases[22] and that, except in cases of contempt in the presence of the court, due process requires a full trial before a disinterested judge.[23] No judge could fairly plead ignorance of these precedents; Judge Peck's action would be a clear and deliberate abuse of authority today.

But the law was not so clear on either point in 1826, when Judge Peck cited Luke Lawless for contempt. As late as 1907, in *Patterson v Colorado,* Justice Holmes for seven members of the Supreme Court could flatly declare that "if a court regards . . . a publication concerning a matter of law pending before it, as tending toward . . . interference [with the administration of the law], it may punish it . . . ."[24] State reports throughout the nineteenth century contained decisions upholding summary contempt citations for extramural commentary on judicial actions,[25] occasionally saying that the same rule would apply even in cases that were truly finished, which the matter in Judge Peck's case was not.[26]

It is true that there were mitigating factors in Lawless's case not present in all of the precedents for summary contempt. Although the judgment was still on appeal and the same issues were pertinent to litigation instituted by other claimants, Judge Peck had al-

---

the reader think the judge was "either a dolt or a knave." See Peck's Memorial to the House, Trial Report at 23–25; Bushnell, Crimes, Follies, and Misfortunes at 94–95 (cited in note 6). For McDuffie's and Wickliffe's replies on the sub-delegate question see Trial Report at 95 and 318.

[21]See id at 513–22. The quotation is from 4 Blackstone at *285, in a chapter on summary punishments. The cited decision arguably most nearly in point is that of the Tennessee Supreme Court in the case of In re Darby, 3 Wheeler's Crim Cases 1 (1824), which involved suspension of an attorney for comments on a case that had been remanded to the court whose decision he attacked. The procedure followed in Lawless's case, which was essentially the issuance of an order to show cause, was that described by Blackstone (at *286–87) as applicable in such cases. See also Sir John C. Fox, The History of Contempt of Court: The Form of Trial and the Mode of Punishment (Oxford, 1927), discussing the origins of the then English practice of summary punishment for out-of-court contempt.

[22]Bridges v California, 314 US 252 (1941). Among the publications protected in *Bridges* was a statement by a powerful union leader in substance threatening a crippling dock strike in the event of an adverse decision. See also Craig v Harney, 331 US 367 (1947).

[23]In re Oliver, 333 US 257, 274–78 (1948).

[24]205 US 454, 462–63. Specifically singled out as punishable were "publications impugning their own reasoning or motives," which were involved in *Patterson,* as they allegedly were in the case of Judge Peck. Id. Of course, if freedom of the press protected only against previous restraints (as Blackstone had said and as Holmes strongly intimated in *Patterson*), there was no first-amendment violation in Judge Peck's case.

[25]E.g., In re Chadwick, 109 Mich 588, 67 NW 1071 (1896); Ex parte Barry, 25 P 256 (Cal 1890); State v Morrill, 16 Ark 384 (1855); People v Shuman, 64 Ill 195 (1872).

[26]In the *Chadwick* case, cited in the preceding note, the court rejected the contention that the case was no longer pending, noting that the decree had not yet been enrolled, that the court might grant a rehearing, and that the judgment might be appealed. 109 Mich at 602, 67 NW at 1076. The court went on to say, however, that whether the case was still pending was immaterial. See also Commonwealth v Dandridge, 4 Va 408 (1824), involving an insult delivered to a judge after the case in question was closed.

ready rendered his decision before Lawless published his article. Moreover, in contrast to publications overtly accusing judges of corrupt or mendacious actions or deliberate distortion of the law, all the article had expressly said was that Peck had made a number of errors in his ruling. It was a good thing that so many Senators were so concerned so early about freedom of the press and the right to fair trial.

Nevertheless it seems to me also a good thing that Peck was not convicted. As the thresholds for contempt by publication and for summary punishment should be high, so should the threshold for impeachment. We do not want to run the risk of compromising judicial independence by removing judges from office—or by making them fear removal—because the Senate disagrees with their decisions. Given the undeveloped state of the law at the time Judge Peck acted, I think it would be difficult to justify the conclusion that he acted in deliberate disregard of the Constitution; an impeachment proceeding is not an appropriate forum for law reform.

It was equally fitting that only a month after Judge Peck's acquittal, and in direct response to his case, Congress passed a statute declaring

> [t]hat the power of the several courts of the United States to issue attachments and inflict summary punishments for contempts of court, shall not be construed to extend to any cases except the misbehavior of any person or persons in the presence of the said courts, or so near thereto as to obstruct the administration of justice, the misbehavior of any of the officers of the said courts in their official transactions, and the disobedience or resistance . . . to any lawful writ, process, order, rule, decree, or command of the said courts.[27]

That took care of the procedural issue of summary contempt. Section 2 of the statute, which made it a federal crime to obstruct justice in ways not within this definition of the summary contempt power, dealt by unmistakable implication with the substantive question of free speech. For the new prohibition extended only to corruption and threats of force; it said nothing of mere publications.[28]

Judge Peck may not have broken the law when he punished Luke Lawless for criticizing his opinion, but Congress made clear he was not to do it again.

II. ANOTHER WHO GOT AWAY

In February 1857 the House Judiciary Committee recommended impeachment of a fourth judge, John C. Watrous of the District of Texas. The first charge was that in trying a particular case Watrous had been "oppressive and partial" and had "entirely disregarded the well-established rules of law and evidence." This looked like another appeal to Congress by a disappointed litigant, and it did not seem very promising. The second allegation appeared more serious: that Watrous had acquired an interest in property that was the subject of litigation in his own court.[29]

[27] 4 Stat 487–88, § 1 (Mar 2, 1831).

[28] Id at 488.

[29] HR Rep 175, 34th Cong, 3d Sess 1–5; Cong Globe, 34th Cong, 3d Sess 627–28. For the background of the controversy see Roger N. Conger, The Tomás de la Vega Eleven-League Grant on the Brazos, 61 SW Hist

The session was rapidly coming to a close, and the matter was postponed.[30] In the next Congress the committee was evenly divided,[31] and after several days of furious debate the House voted 113–86 that the evidence was insufficient to justify impeachment.[32] A third committee again urged impeachment in 1860,[33] but the matter was blessedly dropped after one Congressman said it was not worth the trouble to reopen a matter the House had already resolved.[34]

The dispute seemed to turn essentially on the facts. New Hampshire Representative Mason Tappan said that the first charge involved innocent errors at most and that there was no proof Watrous had ever meant to try his own cause.[35] Of greater interest for this study were the various suggestions that were made respecting the constitutional standard for impeachment.

In 1857, for example, New York Representative George Simmons asserted without contradiction that the committee had thought it sufficient that Watrous "has not fulfilled his duty as a judge in all respects, so as to entitle him to the confidence of the people."[36] Happily, the committee report itself enunciated no such flaccid and catholic criterion; it noncommittally accused Watrous, in the Constitution's own words, of "high crimes and misdemeanors."[37]

The 1860 report added a third charge against Judge Watrous involving alleged dealings in fraudulent land certificates, and in supporting this accusation the committee expanded upon its understanding of what constituted an impeachable offense. Although the acts alleged in the new charge were unconnected with Watrous's official duties, wrote Representative John H. Reynolds, they clearly constituted "misbehavior," and they demonstrated that he was unfit to be a judge: "It cannot be pretended that a person who deliberately sets about the violation of law for the purpose of gain, is fit to administer justice to others."[38]

The basic point was well taken; like extrajudicial treason, which is specifically mentioned in Article II, § 4, intentional participation in a fraudulent land scheme casts grave doubt upon a judge's ability to execute his duties with integrity.[39]

Q 371 (1958) (suggesting, id at 375, that the impeachment inquiry was instigated by disappointed squatters who had been evicted from the disputed land); Walace [sic] Hawkins, The Case of John C. Watrous (University Press in Dallas, 1950).

[30]Cong Globe, 34th Cong, 3d Sess 797–98.

[31]HR Rep 540, 35th Cong, 1st Sess 1 (1858).

[32]Cong Globe, 35th Cong, 1st Sess 2659; Cong Globe, 35th Cong, 2d Sess 102.

[33]HR Rep 2, 36th Cong, 2d Sess 2.

[34]Cong Globe, 36th Cong, 2d Sess 105 (Rep. Maynard).

[35]Cong Globe, 35th Cong, 2d Sess 17–22. Judge Watrous had in fact recused himself when the case came before him. See HR Rep 540, 35th Cong, 1st Sess 219. Texas Senator Sam Houston, after the 1858 House vote, flayed Watrous as part of a vast conspiracy, noted that the Texas legislature had condemned his actions, and offered a bill to abolish the District in which he sat, in order to get rid of him without traversing the hurdles of impeachment. Fortunately, however, the bill was never brought to a vote. Cong Globe, 35th Cong, 2d Sess 772–84.

[36]Cong Globe, 34th Cong, 3d Sess 628.

[37]Id at 627, 628.

[38]HR Rep 2, 36th Cong, 2d Sess 4.

[39]Cf the 1858 committee report, declaring it the House's duty to impeach a judge whenever, in the course of his official conduct, he was "guilty of actions which are inconsistent with an impartial discharge of the high duties entrusted to him." HR Rep 548, 35th Cong, 1st Sess 24.

The committee did not say, however, that this offense qualified as a "high crime or misdemeanor" within the meaning of Article II, § 4, as it might easily have done. Its reference to "misbehavior" suggests that it took as its lodestar not Article II but Article III's provision that judges should hold office "during good behavior," which as the 1858 committee had said was enforceable only through impeachment.[40] The implication seemed to be that it was easier to impeach judges than other "civil officers of the United States," though Article II seems to equate them.

One might say that was as it should be, since absent impeachment we may be stuck with the judges (unlike other officers) for the rest of their natural lives. Yet it is at least equally arguable that a more lenient standard for impeaching judges is precisely backward; the traditional explanation is that the good-behavior standard was intended to make it if anything *more* difficult to get rid of judges in light of the special urgency of their independence.[41] The current understanding is that "good behavior" is the absence of "high crimes and misdemeanors"; the two standards are one and the same.[42]

[40] Id. See US Const, Art III, § 1.

[41] See, e.g., The Federalist No 78 (Hamilton).

[42] See Raoul Berger, Impeachment 161–65 (Harvard, 1973) (criticizing this equation).

The possibility of impeaching an *executive* officer had arisen in 1832, when a customs collector in Wiscasset, Maine was accused of importuning an inspector to sign a false affidavit that he had received all fees that were owing to him for his services. Most of the Representatives who spoke said, or seemed to assume, that impeachment lay only for official misconduct or, as one put it, for crimes connected with the exercise of official duties; they differed as to whether the collector's conduct was private or public. See Cong Deb, 22d Cong, 1st Sess 2415–17 (Rep. Pearce); id at 2467–68 (Rep. Storrs) (both arguing that the allegations stated a case for impeachment); id at 2351 (Rep. Mitchell); id at 2483 (Rep. Kennon) (contra). Not every violation of law was cause for impeachment, Representative Slade added, but subornation of perjury was—and so were deliberate violations of official duty. Id at 2757–58. Speakers on both sides declared that the House had discretion whether to impeach if it found cause; as Representative Kennon said (id at 2482), the Constitution gave the House the power, not the duty, of impeachment. Accord id at 2759 (Rep. Slade). (That the power is prosecutorial seems to support this conclusion in light of long-standing tradition. But see Richard A. Posner, An Affair of State 189 (Harvard, 1999)). At its own request, the committee investigating the incident was discharged and the matter referred to the Treasury. Cong Deb, 22d Cong, 1st Sess 2251, 3103–4. Apparently nothing came of the investigation; the collector remained in office until 1836, when he was succeeded by another individual with the same surname. See Fannie S. Chase, Wiscasset in Pownalborough 122 (Wiscasset, 1941).

See also Representative John Bell's 1833 report, HR Rep 88, 22d Cong, 2d Sess 1, Cong Deb App, 22d Cong, 2d Sess 63, suggesting (contrary to prior assumptions, see The Jeffersonians at 113 n.192) that territorial judges were not "civil officers of the United States" subject to impeachment under Article II, § 4. Attorney General Felix Grundy confirmed this suggestion in 1839: "Territorial officers" were not "civil officers of the United States." 3 Op AG 409, 411. Grundy based his conclusion entirely on the less than overpowering ground that territorial judges had been held not to exercise "the judicial power of the United States" within the meaning of Article III. Id at 410. Did this decision mean there was *no way* to get rid of territorial judges before their terms expired? No, according to Attorney General John Crittenden in 1851, since the President was free to discharge them: Statutes prescribing four-year terms were meant only to ensure that judges serve *no longer* than four years, not (as one might have thought) to make them independent of the executive. 5 Op AG 288, 291. See also HR Rep 141, 32d Cong, 1st Sess (1852) (Rep. Lockhart), opposing a bill to provide for the election of territorial judges on the ground that they *were* "officers of the United States" and thus had to be appointed in accordance with Article II, § 2.

III. THE WHEELING BRIDGE

You know the story.[43] Virginia chartered a corporation to build a bridge across the Ohio River at Wheeling. A few of the tallest steamboats couldn't get under it during the highest floods,[44] and in 1852 the Supreme Court ordered it raised or razed in a suit brought by the state of Pennsylvania. For the bridge obstructed navigation, wrote Justice John McLean; it therefore offended both the compact between Virginia and Kentucky, which guaranteed free navigation of the Ohio, and the federal licenses of the steamboat owners, which conferred the right to negotiate navigable streams.[45] Chief Justice Taney seemed on strong ground in suggesting that the compact promised only equal access to out-of-staters and that the licenses did not require that particular streams be left navigable, but he was in the minority;[46] the statutory issues do not concern us here.[47]

The scene shifted to Congress, which the company had petitioned to legalize the bridge.[48] Congress obliged in the improbable context of a postal appropriation law:

> § 6. *And be it further enacted,* that the bridges across the Ohio River at Wheeling, in the State of Virginia, and at Bridgeport, in the State of Ohio, abutting on Zane's Island, in said river, are hereby declared to be lawful structures in their present position and elevation, and shall be so held and taken to be, any thing in any law or laws of the United States to the contrary notwithstanding.
>
> § 7. *And be it further enacted,* that the said bridges are declared to be and are established post-roads for the passage of the mails of the United States, and that the Wheeling and Belmont Bridge Company are authorized to have and maintain their said bridges at their present site and elevation; and the officers and crews of all vessels and boats navigating said river, are required to regulate the use of their vessels and boats, and of any pipes or chimneys belonging thereto, so as not to interfere with the elevation and construction of said bridges.[49]

[43]Would you like to know more? There is a whole book about it. Elizabeth Brand Monroe, The Wheeling Bridge Case (Northeastern, 1992).

[44]As its defenders emphasized, it was a full ninety feet above mean low water. Id at 44.

[45]Pennsylvania v Wheeling & Belmont Bridge Co., 54 US 518, 578 (1852). For the politics of this controversy see Harold M. Hyman & William M. Wiecek, Equal Justice Under Law 83 (Harper & Row, 1982):

> Western Pennsylvania economic interests [opposed the bridge], because the Cumberland Road would tie the commerce of the western states to an eastern depot at Baltimore. But if the road could remain effectively truncated by the river, . . . the lucrative western trade would be diverted northward to Pittsburgh and thence . . . to Harrisburg and Philadelphia.

[46]54 US at 583, 586, citing Willson v Black Bird Creek Marsh Co, 27 US 245 (1829).

[47]I have briefly addressed them in The First Hundred Years at 235 n.274.

[48]See Cong Globe, 32d Cong, 1st Sess 602 (Sen. Hunter).

[49]10 Stat 110, 112, §§ 6,7 (Aug 31, 1852). The two bridges were in series, over the east and west channels of the Ohio, separated by Zane's Island.

Pennsylvania went back to court, and the Justices upheld the statute 6–3.[50]

You know the arguments made by the majority and the dissent; let me tell you the arguments made in Congress during the debates on the bill. You will find them familiar; the Justices repeated them in their opinions. Once again congressional discussion anticipated the arguments of the Court.

There were three basic objections to the statute declaring the bridge lawful. Congress had no power to authorize internal improvements; by making navigation from Pittsburgh more costly than from Wheeling the law gave Virginia ports a forbidden preference over those of Pennsylvania;[51] Congress had usurped judicial power by attempting to set aside a decision of the Supreme Court.[52] Each of these objections was stated as a bare conclusion, and none of them holds water. Each was refuted in Congress and rejected by the Court.

To sustain legalization of the bridge it was not necessary for supporters of the bill to establish that Congress could promote land commerce by authorizing the construction of roads and bridges, although it had done so before.[53] The Supreme Court, said Maine Senator James Bradbury, had said the bridge was forbidden by federal statute; what Congress had enacted Congress could repeal.[54] Nor was there a forbidden port preference, added David Disney of Ohio in the House, unless every harbor improvement was invalid; the clause meant only "that in making your regulation for commerce you shall not make distinctions in favor of one port over another."[55] Finally, said North Carolina's estimable George Badger in the Senate, the bill did not say the Supreme Court was wrong; it merely altered the law for the future.[56]

[50]Pennsylvania v Wheeling & Belmont Bridge Co., 59 US 421 (1856). The dissenters were McLean, Grier, and Curtis. Justice Nelson wrote the majority opinion.

[51]See US Const, Art I, § 9.

[52]Cong Globe, 32d Cong, 1st Sess 2439 (Sen. Brodhead); id at 2441 (Sen. Chase); id at 2441–42 (Sen. Toucey); Cong Globe App, 32d Cong, 1st Sess 967 (Rep. Curtis); id at 1067–68 (Rep. Fowler). Cf Justice McLean's dissenting opinion, 59 US at 443–46.

[53]Most pertinently, Congress had not only authorized but constructed the Cumberland Road, which the Wheeling Bridge would carry across the Ohio. It would have been difficult for even so stingy an improver as Andrew Jackson to deny that such a bridge was of national rather than merely local importance. See The Jeffersonians at 114–22 and chapter 1 of this volume.

[54]Cong Globe, 32d Cong, 1st Sess 2439. Not every compact Congress had approved would be subject to supersession by federal statute, but this one was; for the subject of the modified provision was a regulation of commerce among the several states. Simple repeal would not suffice, however, to sustain the further provision of § 7 protecting the bridge affirmatively from damage from passing vessels. That looks suspiciously like the provisions to which President Monroe had unconvincingly objected in vetoing the Tollgate Bill in 1823. See The Jeffersonians at 278–81. For what it's worth, the modern Court would doubtless say it was also a regulation of vessels as instrumentalities of commerce. See United States v Lopez, 514 US 549, 558 (1995); cf Cong Globe, 32d Cong, 1st Sess 2439 (Sen. Bradbury) (arguing that Congress had "unquestioned power" to "regulat[e] the height of the chimneys of the boats navigating the river"). Even this argument would not sustain the additional provision ensuring the company the right to maintain the bridge, which as Senator Bradbury suggested (id at 2442) seemed to raise the general question of authority to promote internal improvements. Whether mere designation as a post road could give the requisite protection raised long-disputed questions respecting the limits of the postal power; having found the provision relevant to Pennsylvania's suit sustained by the commerce clause, the Supreme Court rightly refused to resolve them. 59 US at 431.

[55]"[T]hese unavoidable results which will flow from any action which may benefit one and injure the other," Disney added, "must take their natural course." Cong Globe App, 32d Cong, 1st Sess 1047.

[56]Cong Globe, 32d Cong, 1st Sess 2440. See also id at 2439 (Sen. Bradley); Cong Globe App, 32d Cong, 1st Sess 1044–45 (Rep. Disney). I said much the same thing in applauding the Supreme Court's later decision:

It would have been better if Congress had taken Senator Bradbury's advice to phrase the statute differently; to declare the bridge "lawful" after the Court had said it was not was to invite trouble.[57] Happily, the Court had the wit to see beyond the infelicitous choice of words and to uphold the law as an exercise of Congress's power to determine what was or was not an unreasonable obstruction of commerce by water. In so doing the Justices, as usual, added little to the arguments that had already been made in Congress.[58] The bottom line: It is for the courts to say whether a bridge violates existing law; it is for Congress to decide whether to allow it in the future.[59]

IV. THE COURT OF CLAIMS

The United States could not be sued without their consent. Chief Justice John Jay had hinted as much in *Chisholm v Georgia* in 1793 while inconsistently denying (until the country rose up in a body to correct him) that the same principle applied to individual states.[60] The consequence was that the only way Government creditors could get paid

---

"Congress's decision to authorize a bridge over the Ohio River did not contradict the Court's holding that earlier statutes had forbidden it." The First Hundred Years at 311 n.173. My praise here and elsewhere for the admirable Badger has nothing to do with the fact that I spent several happy formative years living in North Carolina. I quote the equally unbiased Thomas Wolfe, of Asheville:

> Old Catawba [North Carolina] is much better than South Carolina. . . . [I]n South Carolina . . . [t]hey do not have the mountain cool. They have dusty, sand-clay roads [and] great mournful cotton fields . . . . These people are really lost. . . .
>
> Old Catawba is just right. . . . They make all the mistakes that people can make. . . . They have Rotary Clubs and chain gangs and Babbitts and all the rest of it. But they are not bad. . . .

The Web and the Rock 13–15 (Harper, 1939). For another favorable assessment of Badger (noting that the Senate refused to confirm his nomination to the Supreme Court in 1853 because he believed Congress had power to ban slavery in the territories) see Alan Nevins, The Emergence of Lincoln: Douglas, Buchanan, and Party Chaos, 1857–1859 106 (Scribner's, 1950).

[57]Cong Globe, 32d Cong, 1st Sess 2439. See also Senator Toucey's complaint, id at 2441–42, that the bill would declare the bridge lawful without changing the law. Senator Brooke had not helped matters by trumpeting that he would "do everything I can, as a legislator, to nullify . . . the decision of the Supreme Court." Id at 2440.

[58]See 59 US at 431–35. One thing Justice Nelson did add was a refutation of Representative Fowler's argument (Cong Globe App, 32d Cong, 1st Sess 1067) that Congress had no power to alter an interstate compact it had earlier approved. If that was so, wrote Nelson, then with the consent of two states Congress could amend the Constitution by curtailing its own authority to regulate interstate commerce. 59 US at 433. The Court has long said that an Act of Congress supersedes a prior treaty (e.g., The Cherokee Tobacco, 78 US 616 (1871)); it would be strange if compacts enjoyed greater constitutional protection.

[59]As of 1992 the bridge survived and had been designated, appropriately, as a National Historic Landmark. Monroe, The Wheeling Bridge Case at 177 (cited in note 43).

[60]2 US 419, 478 (1793); see also id at 469 (Cushing, J). St. George Tucker disagreed with this suggestion: "The editor had supposed that that clause of the constitution, which declares that 'the judicial power shall extend to all cases, in law and equity, arising under the constitution,' &c. had prescribed a different rule of decision." 1 Tucker's Blackstone App at 363 n.†. Jay's dictum respecting the United States became holding in United States v McLemore, 45 US 286 (1846). See also 3 Story, § 1669. As the Court later recognized in the context of suits against states not precluded by the eleventh amendment, implicit immunity was supported both by tradition and by legislative history. Hans v Louisiana, 134 US 1 (1890); see The First Hundred Years at 14–20; The Second Century at 7–9. Cf the familiar implicit court-martial exception to the constitutional requirements of jury trial before a tenured judge. Dynes v Hoover, 61 US 65 (1857).

when the Administration rejected their claims was to press Congress to enact private bills. There was widespread agreement that this was a stupid way to pay the debts of the United States, and pressure mounted to do something about it. The upshot was the establishment of the first Court of Claims in 1855.[61]

Arguing in 1849 for a bill to establish a board of commissioners to advise Congress with respect to claims against the Government, Connecticut Representative John Rockwell sketched some of the deficiencies of the existing system. Claimants were given no hearing; many claims were never passed upon; a number of members invariably voted to reject claims. Fraudulent claims were difficult to detect, as the Government had no opportunity to contest them. Yet the House spent about one-third of its time in the consideration of private bills, in addition to the countless hours consumed in committee. No other "civilized country of the world" had "such an outrageous system"; ours was "about the worst that could be devised."[62]

Speaker after speaker agreed with this assessment, but there was no consensus as to the remedy;[63] the bill was defeated.[64] President Fillmore took up the cause in his first Annual Message in 1850:

> The difficulties and delays incident to the settlement of private claims by Congress amount in many cases to a denial of justice. There is reason to think that many unfortunate creditors of the Government have thereby been unavoidably ruined. Congress has so much business of a public character that it is impossible it should give much attention to mere private claims, and their accumulation is now so great that many claimants must despair of ever being able to obtain a hearing. It may well be doubted whether Congress, from the nature of its organization, is properly constituted to decide upon such claims. It is impossible that each member should examine the merits of every claim on which he is compelled to vote, and it is preposterous to ask a judge to decide a case which he has never heard. Such decisions may, and frequently must, do injustice either to the claimant or the Government, and I perceive no better remedy for this growing evil than the establishment of some tribunal to adjudicate upon such claims. I beg leave, therefore, most respectfully to recommend that provision be made by law for the appointment of a commission to settle all private claims against the United States; and as an *ex parte* hearing must in all contested cases be very unsatisfactory, I also recommend the appointment of a solicitor, whose duty it shall be to represent the Government before such commission and protect it against all illegal, fraudulent, or unjust claims which may be presented for their adjudication.[65]

[61]10 Stat 612 (Feb 24, 1855).

[62]Cong Globe, 30th Cong, 2d Sess 139–40. John Quincy Adams had said much the same thing to his diary in 1832. 8 JQA Memoirs at 480.

[63]See, e.g., Cong Globe, 30th Cong, 2d Sess 140 (Rep. Joseph R. Ingersoll); id at 163 (Rep. Strong); id at 166 (Rep. Meade); id at 170 (Rep. Schenck).

[64]Cong Globe, 30th Cong, 2d Sess 543. The vote was 85–98.

[65]5 Richardson at 77, 91–92 (Dec 2, 1850).

Congress did nothing. Fillmore repeated his request the following year, without success.[66]

By the time the Thirty-third Congress met for the second time in December 1854, the situation was getting desperate. The Senate, said Pennsylvania Senator Richard Brodhead, was now spending two full days a week on private bills, and doing it badly; barely half of all claims were ever acted upon.[67] As Chairman of the Claims Committee, Brodhead added, "I have not time to investigate the vast variety of cases which come before [it], and yet properly discharge my other duties . . . ."[68] This time Congress was prepared to remedy the situation; but how?

The bill Representative Rockwell was pushing in 1849 would have created a purely advisory commission to take evidence and then recommend adoption or rejection of private bills.[69] That would do no good, retorted Joseph Ingersoll of Pennsylvania; it would not expedite the resolution of claims to require creditors to surmount yet another hurdle before getting their money.[70] The real problem was that Congress was unsuited to the task of passing on individual claims, and it should be taken out of the process: Claims should be "submitt[ed] . . . to final determination before a proper board."[71] Virginia Representative Richard Meade would have gone a step further: On claims that would be justiciable between private parties the Circuit Courts too should be empowered to render final decisions against the Government.[72]

There was a flurry of objections. Neither a board nor a court, said Andrew Johnson of Tennessee, could be authorized to enter final judgments on claims against the United States. If the claimant prevailed, Congress would still have to decide whether to appropriate money to pay him; if he lost, he would still have the right to petition Congress for

[66]"Justice to individuals, as well as to the Government, imperatively demands that some more convenient and expeditious mode than an appeal to Congress should be adopted." Second Annual Message, 5 Richardson at 113, 137 (Dec 2, 1851).

[67]Cong Globe, 33d Cong, 2d Sess 70.

[68]Id at 107–8. For an excellent summary of the inadequacies of the private-bill process see William A. Richardson, History, Jurisdiction, and Practice of the Court of Claims of the United States, 7 So L Rev (NS) 782–83 (1882). The author was a judge of the Court of Claims. See also White, The Jacksonians at 158–59.

[69]For Rockwell's summary of the bill see Cong Globe, 30th Cong, 2d Sess 140.

[70]Id at 140. See also Cong Globe, 33d Cong, 1st Sess 74 (Tennessee Sen. James C. Jones); id at 107 (Mississippi Sen. Albert G. Brown). Virginia Senator Robert Hunter, who favored the establishment of a court with advisory authority, took issue with this assessment: The tribunal would facilitate Congress's task by laying out the evidence, and Congress would generally approve its decision. Cong Globe, 33d Cong, 2d Sess 109. A decision *against* the claimant, Georgia Representative Hiram Warner added in 1856, would provide a good ground for denial of a petition on the merits. Cong Globe, 34th Cong, 1st Sess 1245.

[71]Cong Globe, 30th Cong, 2d Sess 140. See also id at 171 (Ohio Rep. Robert Schenck); id at 379 (Kentucky Rep. Richard French) (limiting his proposal to claims not exceeding $5,000). President Fillmore, in the passage just quoted in the text, had appeared to endorse finality by urging the creation of a commission with authority to "settle" claims.

[72]Cong Globe, 30th Cong, 2d Sess 168. Like Representative French, Meade would have imposed a maximum jurisdictional amount of $5,000. See also id at 141 (New York Rep. Joseph Mullin), suggesting that ideally *state* courts should be given jurisdiction to render final judgments on claims against the Government. Senators John Pettit (Indiana) and Jones would echo Meade's suggestion (without either a jurisdictional amount or an alternate forum) in 1854. See Cong Globe, 33d Cong, 2d Sess 72, 74. Justice Story, in his treatise, similarly urged that ordinary courts be authorized to enter judgment on claims against the United States. 3 Story, §§ 1671–72.

relief.[73] Pennsylvania's William Strong (later to sit with distinction on the Supreme Court) denied that claims could be entrusted to the federal courts: They were suits neither in law nor in equity, and they did not arise under federal law.[74]

Why not? Some were based on statutes, or on the Constitution itself;[75] the modern Supreme Court would conclude that many claims by or against the Government were based on federal common law.[76] In the nineteenth century that seems not to have been so.[77] As Meade pointed out, however, Article III also extended the judicial power to controversies to which the United States were party—as they were in every suit to recover on a claim against the Government.[78]

In 1856, during a debate over what Congress should do with reports received from the new Court of Claims, Pennsylvania Representative David Ritchie argued that this provision included only proceedings in which the Government was *plaintiff*, suits against the United States did not fall within the judicial power.[79] His reason was sovereign immunity: Even *Chisholm v Georgia* had recognized that the United States could not be sued.[80] But no Justice in *Chisholm* or elsewhere had denied that Congress could waive this immunity. Senator Brodhead did question that conclusion in passing in 1854.[81] As James Bayard of Delaware would point out in 1860, however, the King of England had consented to suit since time immemorial.[82] Indeed the Supreme Court had already contradicted Ritchie's argument in the context of suits against states, although the

[73]Cong Globe, 30th Cong, 2d Sess 179. See US Const, Art I, § 9 and Amend 1. To make the decision final, added Senator Brodhead in 1854, would place the Treasury in the hands of the tribunal rather than of Congress. Cong Globe, 33d Cong, 2d Sess 70. Representative Bowlin agreed that the board's decision could not be made final, apparently because only Congress could appropriate funds; he had attacked even Rockwell's bill for an advisory board as "a base abandonment . . . of the treasury . . . to a few commissioners." Cong Globe, 30th Cong, 2d Sess 169, 168. See also id at 165 (Rep. Strong). Representative Meade conceded that the decision could not preclude petitions to Congress on rejected claims. Id at 167, 168. See also 1 Tucker's Blackstone App at 364, proposing to avoid the appropriation difficulty by amending the Constitution to permit payment from the Treasury on the basis of "a judicial sentence of a court of the United States" as well.

[74]Cong Globe, 30th Cong, 2d Sess 165.

[75]Strong himself declared that by refusing a remedy for the taking of property Congress denied an express constitutional right. Id at 163.

[76]See, e.g., Clearfield Trust Co v United States, 318 US 363 (1943); see Henry Friendly, In Praise of *Erie*—and of the New Federal Common Law, 39 NYU L Rev 383 (1964).

[77]See, e.g., Cotton v United States, 52 US 229, 231 (1850), declaring that the United States had "the same right to have [its property] protected by the local laws that other persons have"; Mason v United States, 260 US 545, 555 (1923), concluding that the measure of damages for the conversion of oil from federal land was a "local" matter governed by state law; Richard H. Fallon et al, Hart & Wechsler's The Federal Courts and the Federal System 698 (5th ed 2003), reminding us (by way of a quotation for the Government's brief in *Clearfield*) that in commercial cases in those days the federal courts applied the "general common law" under Swift v Tyson, 41 US 1 (1842).

[78]Cong Globe, 30th Cong, 2d Sess 168; see also id at 111 (Sen. Clayton).

[79]Cong Globe, 34th Cong, 1st Sess 1241.

[80]See note 60 and accompanying text.

[81]Cong Globe, 33d Cong, 2d Sess 70. In the next sentence Brodhead objected that many of the claims presented to Congress were "addressed to our discretion" and thus not of a judicial nature. If this observation was intended to explain why Congress could not consent to suit, it was inadequate; it did not apply to claims based upon contract, statute, or regulation.

[82]Cong Globe, 36th Cong, 1st Sess 983. See also *Chisholm*, 2 US at 460 (opinion of Wilson, J); Louis Jaffe, Judicial Control of Administrative Action 197 (Little, Brown, Student ed 1965); Cong Globe, 33d Cong, 2d Sess 73 (Sen. Pettit), adding that states too had been known to waive their immunity.

eleventh amendment—in contrast to Article III, which speaks without qualification of controversies to which the United States shall be "party"—declares flatly that suits by outsiders against states fall outside the judicial power.[83] As the Court would later explain, immunity (like limitations on personal jurisdiction or venue) is designed to protect the defendant; if the Government is willing to be sued, there is no reason to say nay.[84]

The Supreme Court, in 1933, would briefly embrace Ritchie's narrow interpretation of Article III, but for a different reason. It was conceded, Justice Sutherland would write, that Congress could entrust the resolution of claims against the Government to executive officers or reserve them for itself; they therefore could not be part of the judicial power.[85] But this reasoning was no better than Ritchie's, and it too was soon called into question.[86] The Court's own argument showed that there was an overlap between legislative and executive power; the very precedent on which the opinion relied had emphasized that Congress often had a choice between executive and judicial remedies.[87]

Until prodded by Congressman Meade, Representative Strong said nothing of the Article III clause respecting Government suits in 1849—all the more conspicuously in that he meticulously listed other clauses extending the judicial power to controversies defined by the character of the parties.[88] When pressed, he too explained that he believed that provision contemplated only suits in which the United States were plaintiff.[89] His reasoning, however, differed both from Ritchie's and from that of the Supreme Court. In denying that suits against the Government came within the judicial power at all or the federal-question clause in particular, Strong had earlier had this to say:

> What was a claim against the Government? How was it recovered? The party did not recover it by any compulsory process. It was not compulsory upon the Government; it was an appeal to the good faith of the Government, and, as a matter of course, could not be the subject of adjudication in a court of law. . . . [H]e regarded the Government as not responsible, under the principles of law and equity, in their constitutional signification, but as responsible under the faith which it owed to its citizens.[90]

Others had conceded that Congress should continue to pass upon claims founded on abstract "justice" as opposed to contract or law.[91] Strong was speaking of claims against the Government generally: *No* suit against the Government was a "case[] in law [or] equity."

[83]Bank of the United States v Planters' Bank, 22 US 904, 907–8 (1824) (alternative holding).

[84]Clark v Barnard, 108 US 436, 447 (1883).

[85]Williams v United States, 289 US 553, 580–81.

[86]See Glidden v Zdanok, 370 US 530, 531–32 (1962) (opinion of Harlan, J).

[87]Murray's Lessee v Hoboken Land & Improv Co, 59 US 272, 284 (1856).

[88]Cong Globe, 30th Cong, 2d Sess 165, mentioning among others the provisions respecting suits between states and between citizens of different states.

[89]Id at 168.

[90]Id at 165.

[91]See, e.g., id at 170–71 (Rep. Schenck); Cong Globe, 33d Cong, 2d Sess 73 (Sen. Pettit), distinguishing claims based upon mere "political right, such as meritorious services in such cases as those where you present medals and swords." As enacted the statute gave the Court of Claims jurisdiction over "claims founded upon any law of Congress, or upon any regulation of an executive department, or upon any contract, express or implied, with the government of the United States." 10 Stat 612, § 1 (Feb 24, 1855).

Why not? Because it was not a "case" at all. Why wasn't it? Because a judgment against the United States could not be enforced; collection depended on passage of an appropriation law, which Congress had no obligation to enact. That much had been settled by the debate on the Jay Treaty half a century before.[92] It followed that suits against the Government were not "controversies" to which the United States were party either, for they were not of a judicial nature. Any attempt to vest the determination of such claims in the courts would thus founder on the same reef that had wrecked Congress's plan for the adjudication of pension claims in *Hayburn's Case* in 1792:[93] The decisions of Article III courts could not be subjected to either executive or congressional review.[94] And thus advocates of judicial resolution of claims against the Government found themselves between a rock and a hard place. If the court's decisions were final, they would offend the appropriation clause of Article I, § 9; if they were not, they were dehors the judicial power.

Representative Meade thought the dilemma could be resolved by making appropriations in advance: "[T]he sums decreed to the claimants shall be paid out of any money in the treasury not otherwise appropriated."[95] Congress indeed had done precisely that with respect to the decisions of a commissioner on claims for property destroyed during the War of 1812.[96] As several speakers observed in 1849, President Madison had found the administration of this provision unsatisfactory and removed the commissioner, and the Act had been revised.[97] Mississippi Senator Albert Gallatin Brown (in 1854) seems to have been the first to argue that it was unconstitutional: "We are told, in the plain letter of the Constitution, that 'no money shall be drawn from the Treasury, but in consequence of appropriations made by law.'"[98]

Since both Meade's proposal and the 1816 law on which it was based *did* effectively provide for appropriations, further explanation was needed. Senators from opposite ends of the political spectrum attempted to provide it in 1860, in dissecting another proposal to

[92]See The Federalist Period at 211–17.

[93]2 US 409, 410–14 n.(a); see The First Hundred Years at 6–9.

[94]Chief Justice Taney would adopt this reasoning in a draft opinion prepared after Congress had provided for executive revision of Court of Claims judgments in 1863. See 12 Stat 765, 768, § 14:

> [N]o money shall be paid out of the treasury for any claim passed upon by the court of claims till after an appropriation therefor shall be estimated for by the Secretary of the Treasury.

The award of execution, Taney wrote, was an essential part of every judgment, and thus an Article III court could not review a judgment of the Court of Claims. 117 US 697, 702–3 (draft opinion in Gordon v United States). The Court's actual decision took a narrower ground. See note 103.

[95]Cong Globe, 30th Cong, 2d Sess 168.

[96]3 Stat 261, 263–64, §§ 10–11, 14 (Apr 9, 1816). See also Wilson Cowen et al, 2 The United States Court of Claims: A History 11 (US Judicial Conference, 1978), suggesting that a provision for payment out of a fixed sum specified in advance may have saved the constitutionality of a comparable scheme for the payment of claims arising out of the Mexican War, 9 Stat 393, 394, § 6 (Mar 3, 1849). That statute, however, did not require that prevailing claimants be paid out of the Treasury; it directed the Secretary to issue "certificates of stock" for the relevant amounts or to "pay the same in money, at the option of the United States."

[97]3 Stat 397 (Mar 3, 1817). See Cong Globe, 30th Cong, 2d Sess 165 (Rep. Strong); id at 305 (Rep. Rockwell). See also Cong Globe, 33d Cong, 2d Sess 106 (Sen. Cass).

[98]Id at 107.

strengthen the Court of Claims.[99] Brown himself offered a clarification of his earlier broadside: Congress could not appropriate a lump sum to pay unknown future claims.[100] The appropriation clause, added New Hampshire Republican John Hale from across the aisle, required Congress to vote separately on each claim.[101]

The problem, in other words, was one of the delegation of legislative power. The debate was not new; members of Congress had argued from the beginning over how specific appropriation laws were required to be.[102] Obviously Congress may not delegate the power to appropriate money either to the executive or to the courts; as Senator Brown insisted, Article I, § 9 requires that appropriations be made "by law." Yet the Government could hardly function if Congress could not appropriate money for specified purposes in advance, leaving it to executive officers or to the courts to determine precisely how to spend it; and that of course is what Congress has commonly done.

Meade's suggestion, in any event, would ultimately prevail. Subject to a provision for executive revision that the Supreme Court would say made the proceeding nonjudicial on grounds familiar from *Hayburn's Case,*[103] Congress in 1863 would make Court of Claims decisions "final" and authorize the Secretary of the Treasury to satisfy them "out of any general appropriation made by law for the payment and satisfaction of private claims."[104] The provision for executive approval was soon repealed,[105] and judgments of the modern Court of Federal Claims are paid from general appropriations today.[106] The Supreme Court has reviewed scores of money judgments against the Government without ever questioning the validity of lump-sum appropriations.

Meade proved to have the answer to the question of judicial authority as well. Once Congress began appropriating money in advance to pay Court of Claims judgments, the risk of legislative nullification was much attenuated,[107] and the Supreme Court had no difficulty in concluding that Article III judges could sit on the Court of Claims.[108]

[99]Throughout the debates on these technical questions, and especially (of all things) in 1860, neither political nor sectional divisions played a significant role in the discussion; the members seemed to be offering their honest opinions.

[100]Cong Globe, 36th Cong, 1st Sess 1123–24.

[101]Id at 985. The Senate passed the bill, with Meade's provision for advance appropriations in it, id at 1129; it died in the House.

[102]See The Federalist Period at 46, 68; The Jeffersonians at 4.

[103]Gordon v United States, 69 US 561 (1865). In announcing this decision, Chief Justice Chase was later reported to have said:

> We think that the authority given to the head of an Executive Department by necessary implication, in the 14th section of the amended Court of Claims Act, to revise all the decisions of that court requiring the payment of money, denies to it the judicial power, from the exercise of which alone appeals can be taken to this court.

United States v Jones, 119 US 477. 478 (1886). The offending provision is quoted in note 94.

[104]12 Stat 765, 766, § 7 (Mar 3, 1863).

[105]14 Stat 9 (Mar 17, 1866).

[106]31 USC § 1304 (2003).

[107]Congress might nevertheless repeal the appropriation law or forbid payment in a particular case. See Hart & Wechsler, The Federal Courts and the Federal System at 114 (cited in note 77).

[108]Glidden v Zdanok, 370 US 530 (1962). At the time of the *Glidden* decision judgments of the Court of Claims were final only as to claims not exceeding $100,000; Congress had reserved the right to decide after judgment whether larger claims ought to be paid. Relying on the infrequency with which Congress actually

When the proposal for a claims tribunal resurfaced in 1854, occasional Senators raised the opposite objection: *Only* an Article III court could resolve claims against the United States, for only judges enjoying the independence afforded by life tenure and irreducible salary could exercise the judicial power of the United States.[109] In general I have great sympathy for this type of argument.[110] The explicit purpose of the tenure and salary provisions was to ensure litigants an independent tribunal.[111] Indeed, as Virginia Senator Robert M.T. Hunter suggested in 1854, the need for independence from other branches of government is *greatest* when the United States are the other party, as they are when creditors sue the Government.[112]

This argument has force only if suits against the United States fall within Article III: The judicial power is exclusive only as to matters to which it extends. If Strong was correct that Congress's right to refuse appropriations meant that suits against the Government lay outside the judicial power, then clearly Article III did not forbid Congress to entrust their resolution to a less independent tribunal. The Supreme Court's later conclusion that suits on Government debts *did* fall within Article III revived the question, however, and the old-fashioned the-greater-includes-the-less argument that the opinions have employed to justify the resolution of such claims by Article I tribunals[113] has always struck me as fallacious. Yes, Congress may pay the debts itself by private bill; but Article III says in no uncertain terms that if Congress entrusts the decision to a court its judges must have tenure and an irreducible salary.

Congress avoided many of these constitutional conundrums when it established the Court of Claims in 1855.[114] For the statute took the cowardly way out, adopting in essence the modest reform that Representative Rockwell had urged in 1849. There were to be adversary proceedings before a tribunal with subpoena power;[115] testimony was to be taken, with an opportunity for cross-examination;[116] a solicitor was to be appointed to represent the United States.[117] But alas, this elaborate instrument of justice was to be set

---

refused appropriations in such cases, the Court held Article III judges could pass upon these claims too. See id at 570–71 (opinion of Harlan, J). See also United States v Jones, 119 US 477 (1886), upholding the Supreme Court's jurisdiction to review a Court of Claims judgment after the provision for executive review was repealed.

[109]Cong Globe, 33d Cong, 2d Sess 110 (Sen. Pratt); id at 111 (Sen. Clayton); id at 113 (Sen. Stuart); id at 114 (Sen. Douglas). Clayton carried this argument so far as to suggest that it was unconstitutional for Congress to pay Government debts by private bill, as it had done from the beginning. Id at 111. That strikes me as pushing a good argument too far. Congress has undisputed authority to pay the debts of the United States; Article I, § 8 expressly authorizes it to lay taxes for that purpose. Since the United States cannot be sued without consent, Congress need not vest authority in the courts. See Ex parte Bakelite Corp, 279 US 438, 451 (1929); Murray's Lessee v Hoboken Land & Improvement Corp, 59 US 272, 284 (1856) (concluding that Congress often had a choice between judicial and nonjudicial remedies).

[110]See David P. Currie, Bankruptcy Judges and the Independent Judiciary, 16 Creighton L Rev 441 (1983).

[111]See The Federalist No 78 (Hamilton).

[112]Cong Globe, 33d Cong, 2d Sess 109.

[113]See *Bakelite,* 279 US at 452–54.

[114]10 Stat 612 (Feb 24, 1855).

[115]Id at 613, § 3.

[116]Id, §§ 3, 5.

[117]Id at 612, § 2. There was no provision for jury trial; there is none in comparable proceedings today. The Supreme Court declared in 1880 that the seventh amendment did not require one, because suits against the Government were not "suits at common law" within the meaning of that provision: Since the United States

in motion only to produce a mouse: The court was to report its findings and conclusions to Congress, together with draft legislation in cases in which the court thought the plaintiff should prevail.[118] In short, the Court of Claims was merely to advise Congress whether or not it ought to satisfy a particular claim; the court had no power to resolve cases either for or against the Government.[119]

The only fly in this inconsequential ointment was that the new tribunal looked for all the world like an Article III court. Its judges were to be appointed by the President with Senate consent; they were to hold their offices during good behavior.[120] Whatever else *Hayburn's Case* may have meant for the resolution of claims against the United States, it certainly made clear that Article III courts could not give advice to other organs of Government.[121] Yet that is just what the Court of Claims was initially instructed to do. Thus unless the statutory assurance of tenure was dismissed as a mere repealable pledge[122]—and the debate strongly suggests it was not so intended[123]—the scheme was unconstitutional after all, for it gave nonjudicial functions to judges who could not exercise them.[124]

---

could not be sued without their consent, they could "prescribe the forms of pleading and the rules of practice to be observed in such suits" as a condition of filing them. McElrath v United States, 102 US 426, 440.

[118]10 Stat at 613, § 7.

[119]There was no doubt that Congress could set up an agency of some kind to advise it in the exercise of its legislative functions. In this case a statute so providing would be necessary and proper to the exercise of Congress's power to pay the debts. As an initial matter one might question Congress's decision (10 Stat at 612, § 1) to vest the appointment of these advisors in the President and the Senate, which is the constitutional default rule for "officers of the United States"; those who advise Congress arguably belong in the legislative department, and each House has authority to appoint its own officers. See US Const, Art I, §§ 2, 3; Art II, § 2; Buckley v Valeo, 424 US 1, 139 (1976), explaining that congressional officers are not "officers of the United States." Long practice, however, seems to have settled the constitutionality of this arrangement: Statutes had always required the Secretary of the Treasury to advise the House. See The Federalist Period at 42.

[120]10 Stat at 612, § 1. Their salary was not expressly made irreducible; if they were Article III judges, the Constitution did that for them. For Senator Hunter's fervent explication of the advantages of judicial tenure see Cong Globe, 33d Cong, 2d Sess 71.

[121]The Supreme Court had roundly reaffirmed *Hayburn's Case* in 1852. United States v Ferreira, 54 US 40. See also the famous Correspondence of the Justices, reprinted in Hart & Wechsler, The Federal Courts and the Federal System at 78–79 (cited in note 77). Alabama Representative Percy Walker turned this argument around in 1856: Congress was bound to accept the Court of Claims's decisions, since *Hayburn* had held no other body could review the decisions of an Article III court. Cong Globe, 34th Cong, 1st Sess 972. The difference between Walker's position and that suggested in the text is one of severability: In *Hayburn* it was the judges' authority that was struck down, not the revisory power.

[122]See Crenshaw v United States, 134 US 99 (1890), holding Congress free to repeal a statutory grant of tenure not guaranteed by Article III.

[123]In addition to the statements cited in note 109, see Senator Clayton's assurance (Cong Globe, 33d Cong, 2d Sess 111) that the committee reporting the bill had believed tenure was constitutionally required. See also Richardson, History of the Court of Claims at 783 (cited in note 68). Alabama Representative Percy Walker, during the 1856 debate, made clear he believed the Court of Claims was an Article III court. Cong Globe, 34th Cong, 1st Sess 971–72. Hunter's assurance that if the experiment did not work the judges could be abolished with their court does not detract from this conclusion; his apparent precedent was the controversial 1802 erasure of the new Circuit Courts (see The Jeffersonians at 11–22), which indisputably had been established under Article III. See Cong Globe, 33d Cong, 2d Sess 71, 114; see also id at 107 (Sen. Brodhead); id at 114 (Sen. Douglas).

[124]See Glidden v Zdanok, 370 US 530, 579 (1962) (opinion of Harlan, J) (discussing the congressional-reference jurisdiction of the Court of Claims). Senators Chase and Butler both argued that because the court's decisions were not to be final its functions would not be judicial (Cong Globe, 33d Cong, 2d Sess 112), but no

If that was true, it hardly mattered except to the judges, who would be left with nothing to do. For under the statute the decision whether to pay the claimant remained with Congress, and despite furious objections reports from the court were regularly referred to the Committee on Claims, with the understanding that Congress would not simply rubber-stamp the court's conclusions.[125] Faint heart, it is said, never won fair lady; nor did it relieve Congress in 1855 of the incongruous burden of private claims.[126]

V. GOOD BEHAVIOR

Not only in the controversy over the Court of Claims but also on more than one other occasion during the period in our sights Congress debated the question whether particular judges were required to have the independence guaranteed by Article III.

In 1836, for example, as the bill to establish the Wisconsin Territory was nearing enactment, Massachusetts Representative Caleb Cushing moved to amend it to provide that judges of the territorial courts would hold office for four years rather than during good behavior, as the committee had suggested. That would be unconstitutional, said Henry Wise of Virginia; the Constitution knew only tenure on good behavior. Not so, replied Ohio Representative Thomas Hamer; territorial judges had always been appointed for four-year terms. (This was not quite true; the first three territorial statutes had followed the pattern of the Northwest Ordinance and opted for good behavior.)

If that was the case, said Samuel Hoar of Massachusetts, it was the result of inadvertence: The Constitution was clear. Not so, Hamer responded: The tenure requirement applied only to courts of the United States, not to those of the territories. But territorial courts *were* courts of the United States, said James Pearce of Maryland, created and financed by the United States and exercising its judicial power. The committee that drafted the bill, Pearce added, had thought that precedents holding Article III protection inapplicable to territorial judges were wrong.

Isaac Toucey of Connecticut said the issue was not worth quarreling about since Wisconsin would soon become a state. Cushing thereupon withdrew his motion, and as

---

one is reported to have asserted clearly that for that reason the statute offended Article III. Senator Stuart contrived to contend that the constitutional requirement of an appropriation law meant that a tribunal could be judicial although its decisions were not final:

> [T]here is and can be no judicial tribunal which could issue an execution to satisfy a judgment out of the Treasury of the United States, so that test [of finality] in this instance must fail.

Id at 113. One would have thought, as Representative Strong had argued five years earlier, that the opposite conclusion followed from Stuart's premise: Since no judgment against the United States was final, no court could enter judgment against the United States.

[125]See, e.g., Cong Globe, 34th Cong, 1st Sess 1246 and the accompanying debate. See also White, The Jacksonians at 160–61: "Claimants were thus forced to try their cases twice . . . ."

[126]See the complaints registered in the House in 1856 and the Senate in 1860. E.g., Cong Globe, 34th Cong, 1st Sess 1247 (Rep. Havens); Cong Globe, 36th Cong, 1st Sess 987 (Sen. Fessenden); id at 1124 (Sen. Benjamin). Judge Richardson blamed the statutory requirement that all the evidence taken before the court be transmitted to Congress: With all the evidence before it, the committee felt called upon to read it; and thus (as Ingersoll had predicted) the reform was worse than useless, as claimants "were forced to try their cases twice." Richardson, History of the Court of Claims at 786–87 (cited in note 68).

enacted the statute provided for tenure during good behavior.[127] The experiment was not repeated during the period of this study, however; judges in territories created between 1836 and 1861 were given the conventional four-year terms.[128]

A second debate on the topic of judicial tenure took place in 1854, while Congress was wrestling with the same issue in the context of the Court of Claims, when the House Judiciary Committee reported a bill to codify the laws and reform the courts of the District of Columbia. Now that Alexandria had been restored to Virginia, explained Maryland Representative Henry May, there were more judges than necessary to handle the expected caseload; Chief Justice William Cranch, who had been there forever, was disabled; the court often divided 2–2 without possibility of appeal. The committee proposed to replace the existing courts and appoint new judges. A new court system always required new judges, May assured the House; you can't teach old judges new tricks.[129]

Opponents were horrified. District of Columbia judges, they protested, enjoyed tenure during good behavior under Article III; to turn them out of office struck at the heart of judicial independence.[130] In abolishing the Circuit Courts in 1802, May responded, Congress had settled that even a tenured judge held his office only while it existed. Moreover, he argued, courts of the District were indistinguishable from territorial courts, which the Supreme Court had held to be "mere legislative courts" not subject to Article III.[131] No respectable writer defended the 1802 precedent, retorted Thomas Eliot of Massachusetts, and as South Carolina Senator Andrew Butler had written in 1850 the territorial courts were different: The District of Columbia was not meant to be transitory.[132]

The House overrode these objections by a crushing vote of 113–35, but the Senate amended the bill so as to retain the incumbent judges. A conference committee proved unable to resolve the deadlock, and judicial reform was dropped from the bill entirely.[133] May's goal was finally accomplished in 1863, but the new judges were given tenure during good behavior.[134] The Supreme Court initially concluded that District of Columbia judges enjoyed tenure and irreducible salary and later reversed itself;[135] the reader will not be surprised to learn I think the Court was right the first time.

The question of nontenured judges ought also to have been debated in 1848, but it

[127]See Cong Deb, 24th Cong, 1st Sess 3222–24; The Jeffersonians at 113, discussing the early statutes; The First Hundred Years at 119–22, discussing American Ins Co v Canter, 26 US 511 (1828); 5 Stat 10, 13, § 9 (Apr 20, 1836). When Wisconsin became a state, one of its territorial judges was appointed to the new U.S. District Court there; the other two quietly left the Bench. See Alice E. Smith, 1 The History of Wisconsin 397–400 (State Hist Soc of Wis, 1973).

[128]9 Stat 323, 326, § 9 (Aug 14, 1848) (Oregon); 9 Stat 403, 406, § 9 (Mar 3, 1849) (Minnesota); 9 Stat 446, 449, § 10 (Sep 9, 1850) (New Mexico); 9 Stat 453, 455, § 8 (Sep 9, 1850) (Utah); 10 Stat 172, 175, § 9 (Mar 2, 1853) (Washington); 10 Stat 277, 280, § 9 (May 30, 1854) (Nebraska); id at 286, § 27 (Kansas); 12 Stat 209, 212, § 9 (Mar 2, 1861) (Nevada); 12 Stat 239, 241, § 9 (Mar 2, 1861) (Dakota).

[129]Cong Globe, 33d Cong, 2d Sess 116–20.

[130]Id at 120–23 (Rep. Eliot); id at 929 (Sens. Butler and Clayton).

[131]Id at 119. See *Canter,* 26 US at 546.

[132]Cong Globe, 33d Cong, 2d Sess 123, 121 (quoting S Rep 185, 31st Cong, 1st Sess 5–6 (1850)). See also Cong Globe, 33d Cong, 2d Sess 929 (Sen. Butler).

[133]Id at 128, 1086, 1146, 1184.

[134]12 Stat 762–64, §§ 1, 16 (Mar 3, 1863).

[135]See O'Donoghue v United States, 289 US 516 (1933) (holding the judges protected by Article III); Palmore v United States, 411 US 389 (1973) (overruling *O'Donoghue*).

was not. Four years earlier the United States had concluded a treaty with China whereby criminal and many civil matters involving American citizens in that country would be decided under U.S. law and by U.S. authorities—not, as the Supreme Court would later put it, by supposedly untrustworthy Chinese officials.[136] Congress implemented this treaty in 1848, investing the U.S. minister ("commissioner") and consuls with "judicial authority" to try Americans charged with criminal offenses in China and to resolve civil controversies between U.S. citizens there.[137]

The statute said nothing of indictment or jury trial, and of course the officers in question had neither tenure nor irreducible salary within the meaning of Article III. Alas, there was no discussion of these worrisome provisions; Congress was in a hurry to adopt them before the new commissioner left for China.[138] The Supreme Court, forty years afterward, would uphold a similar criminal provision against jury-trial objections on grounds of impracticability and the asserted inapplicability of the Constitution abroad—an argument that we have seen before[139] and that, as counsel for the defendant suggested, seemed to be "disproved by the existence and operation of the consular court itself." The Article III objection was not even raised.[140]

[136]8 Stat 592, 596–97, Arts XXI, XXV (Jul 3, 1844); see In re Ross, 140 US 453, 463–65 (1891).

[137]9 Stat 276, §§ 1–3 (Aug 11, 1848).

[138]Cong Globe, 30th Cong, 1st Sess 299, 633. Senator Davis of Massachusetts did say (id at 648) that the original bill raised ticklish questions that deserved further study, but his later amendment (which was adopted, id at 1008) did not eliminate those with which we are here concerned. The House had passed a similar bill the year before, also without debate. Cong Globe, 29th Cong, 2d Sess 535.

[139]See The Jeffersonians at 109–10.

[140]*Ross,* 140 US at 460, 464; see Louis Henkin, Foreign Affairs and the United States Constitution 305–7 (Oxford, 2d ed 1996). As the Court would say, apart from specific limitations on federal authority there was no constitutional difficulty with this scheme:

> The treaty-making power vested in our government extends to all proper subjects of negotiation with foreign governments. It can, equally with any of the former or present governments of Europe, make treaties providing for the exercise of judicial authority by its officers appointed to reside therein.

Id at 463.

8

More Miscreants

If people were angels, Madison said, there would be no need for government.[1] If federal officials were angels, there would be no need for impeachment procedures or for the disciplinary powers of the House and Senate over disorderly members. Alackaday, not all of them are angels, and these unpleasant procedures and powers have all too often been put to use—several times, as you have already seen, during the years from Jackson to Lincoln. Having already dealt with the panoply of actual and attempted impeachments of this period, we move on to a modest but colorful assortment of incidents involving demands for the punishment of members and others thought to have offended the privileges of one or the other House of Congress, concluding with a quick but illuminating debate on the intersection between congressional authority to obtain evidence in legislative investigations and the constitutional privilege against self-incrimination, hitherto conspicuously absent from these pages. One of the incidents in question is (I trust) still widely remembered. Yet not every reader, I suspect, is quite aware of just how much it has to teach us about the Constitution.

I. SAM HOUSTON

Samuel Houston, victor of the battle of San Jacinto in 1836, has come down to us as a hero of the Wild West. Having served two terms as a Tennessee Representative during the 1820's, he returned to Washington as a Texas Senator in 1846 and remained for thirteen years before becoming Governor of Texas—from which office he was deposed in 1861 for refusing to swear allegiance to the Confederate States of America.[2] Apart from his

[1]The Federalist No 51. For a recent dissenting view see Yves Simon, A General Theory of Authority (Notre Dame, 1980).

[2]For the story of Houston's valiant battle to keep Texas out of the Confederacy see Donald Braider, Solitary Star: A Biography of Sam Houston 303–11 (Putnam's, 1974).

military adventures, two things of note had happened to him between his two stints in the capital. He had twice been elected President of the Republic of Texas, and the House had cited him for contempt.

For there was a wild streak in the sometimes admirable Mr. Houston, as (if Hollywood is to be believed) was not uncommon in the days of the early West. In 1832 he had done something not unlike that which would more famously get South Carolina Representative Preston Brooks in Dutch a quarter of a century later.[3] He had lain in wait for a member of the House and beaten him with a stick for remarks made in the course of debate.[4]

Although the issue had initially been the subject of vigorous dispute, by 1832 there was little doubt as to the House's implicit authority to punish Mr. Houston. In the 1795 case of Randall and Whitney, after a full airing of the opposing arguments, the House had held a private citizen in contempt and imprisoned him for a week for trying to bribe several of its members.[5] Both the House and the Senate had exercised similar authority throughout the years.[6]

There was a great deal of debate over what to do about Houston. A month elapsed before the final vote was taken, and it was surprisingly close: 106–89.[7] His punishment was light. At the House's direction Speaker Andrew Stevenson publicly read him the following reprimand:

> Whatever has a tendency to impair the freedom of debate in this House . . . , or to detract from the independence of the representatives of the people . . . , must, in the same proportion, weaken and degrade not only the Legislature of the nation itself, but the character of our free institutions.[8]

Along the way the issues of authority debated in the case of Randall and Whitney were aired again without adding much to our understanding.[9] If bribery could be punished

[3]Brooks's notorious attack on Senator Sumner is considered in section III of this chapter.

[4]For the victim's complaint to the House see Cong Deb, 22d Cong, 1st Sess 2512 (Ohio Rep. William Stanbery). Houston basically admitted the facts, except that he asserted that the encounter was unplanned. Id at 2562, 2812. Houston thought Stanbery had accused him of fraud in connection with an Indian contract; Stanbery testified he had meant to impugn not Houston but Secretary of War John Eaton, though he did think Houston was in on the fraud. The testimony from the House investigation is excerpted in id at 2571 et seq and appears in full in the Journal. A House committee later exonerated both Houston and Eaton, over Stanbery's dissent. Id at 3854. For brief accounts of the entire incident see Clifford Hopewell, Sam Houston: Man of Destiny 124–31 (Eakin, 1987); Braider, Solitary Star at 110–14 (cited in note 2).

[5]See The Federalist Period at 232–38.

[6]For other early examples see id at 238 n.270 and 266–68; The Jeffersonians at 315 n.214.

[7]See Cong Deb, 22d Cong, 1st Sess 3015, 3017.

[8]Id at 3021 (May 14, 1832). Houston was also convicted and fined in court for assault, but President Jackson remitted the fine. Hopewell, Sam Houston at 131 (cited in note 4); Braider, Solitary Star at 114 (cited in note 2). See also Attorney General Benjamin Butler's opinion, 2 Op AG 655–56 (1834), concluding that the House's citation for contempt did not bar subsequent criminal punishment for the same act: The House was "protecting [itself] in the due exercise of [its] appropriate functions," not "vindicating the general law of the land," and thus Houston had not been twice placed in jeopardy "for the same offense" within the meaning of the fifth amendment.

[9]For the usual arguments in favor of the House's authority see, e.g., Cong Deb, 22d Cong, 1st Sess 2519–23 (Rep. Coulter); id at 2523 (Rep. Drayton); id at 2839–46 (Rep. Ellsworth); for the usual objections see, e.g., id at 2512–16 and 2822–35 (Rep. Polk); and especially id at 2597–2619 (Mr. Key, for the respondent).

summarily because it interfered with the House's exercise of its functions, so could an assault on a Congressman for what he had said on the floor.[10]

II. MISS OTIS REGRETS

Und wenn man immer in vornehmen Häusern gedient hat . . . , dann weiß man auch, was sich paßt und schickt und was Ehre ist, und weiß auch, daß, wenn so was vorkommt, dann geht es nicht anders, und dann kommt das, was man eine Forderung nennt, und dann wird einer totgeschossen.

THEODOR FONTANE, EFFI BRIEST[11]

When a member of Congress died, it was customary for the affected House to interrupt its proceedings in order to conduct a brief ceremony in remembrance of the departed colleague. The usual pieties were customarily lavished in advance. Senators and Representatives who had never opened their mouths were lauded as great statesmen; inveterate scoundrels were praised as major benefactors of mankind. The funeral itself was a simple and formal affair. The body would be brought in; the chaplain would offer an appropriate exegesis of the Scriptures; the company would then proceed to the Congressional Burying Ground, "where the remains of the deceased were deposited, with the usual solemnities, in the receiving vault."[12] Crape would be worn for a time, but by the next day the chamber would be back in business; life must after all go on.[13]

It was also customary to invite representatives of other branches of government, as well as the general public, to attend these solemn obsequies. When Senator John C. Calhoun died in 1850, for example,

> The galleries, and every avenue thereto, were crowded with spectators, and hundreds left the doors unable to gain admittance.
>
> At twelve o'clock, the House of Representatives, preceded by its officers, entered the Chamber, and took seats assigned them.
>
> Numerous officers of the army and navy, and many distinguished strangers, occupied the sofas in the lobbies.
>
> The Supreme Court of the United States entered the Chamber, and took seats at the left of the Vice President.

[10]See, e.g., id at 2512 (Rep. Vance); id at 2842 (Rep. Ellsworth). As I have said elsewhere, there was ample precedent for legislative punishment in such cases both in England and in the colonies. See The Federalist Period at 268 n.251.

[11]"And if you've always worked in high-class houses, then you also know what's right and proper and what honor is, and you also know that, if something like that happens, then there's no way around it, and then there comes what they call a challenge, and then somebody is shot dead."

[12]See Cong Globe, 31st Cong, 1st Sess 626 (Apr 2, 1850), describing the funeral of Senator Calhoun.

[13]See id at 624, 630.

> The President of the United States and the Cabinet soon followed; the President being conducted to a seat at the right of the Vice President.
>
> The diplomatic corps, which was very fully represented, occupied seats near the centre of the Chamber.[14]

This familiar protocol was followed in the main in February 1838, when Democratic Representative Jonathan Cilley of Maine died, "in the meridian of his life," at the age of thirty-five. The House and Senate adjourned after digesting brief encomiums and resolving to display the usual crape; the funeral service was performed by one gentleman of the cloth and the discourse preached by another; the funeral procession, which as usual included both Houses of Congress, the President and his Cabinet, foreign ministers, and members of the public, "moved from the Hall of the House of Representatives to the place of interment," where presumably the late Mr. Cilley was suitably inhumed.[15] There was just one departure from the traditional pattern. The Justices of the Supreme Court were officially not there.[16]

It was not as if they had not been invited. In formal resolutions adopted on the morning of the funeral they acknowledged the House's invitation and politely declined to attend. Was it because the press of judicial business precluded the Justices from leaving their chambers for the brief period of the ceremony? No. Was it because Mr. Cilley was no Calhoun but a mere unknown freshman beneath the notice of the august Court? No. It was because of what Cilley's colleague John Fairfield had delicately referred to as the "circumstances" of his death. For it was "well known," wrote the Justices in the terse preamble to their resolutions, that the unfortunate Mr. Cilley had been killed in a duel. Here is the text of the critical second resolution:

> Resolved, that with every desire to manifest their respect for the House of Representatives and the committee of the House by whom they have been invited and for the memory of the lamented deceased, the Justices of the Supreme Court, cannot consistently with the duties they owe to the public, attend in their official characters, the funeral of one who has fallen in a duel.[17]

The circumstances, it turns out, were even worse than the Court's order revealed. Representative Cilley had indeed been killed in a duel—and by one of his own colleagues in the House.

Born in New Hampshire in 1802, Jonathan Cilley was a graduate of Bowdoin Col-

[14]Id at 626.

[15]Cong Globe, 25th Cong, 2d Sess 199–200 (Feb 26–27, 1838).

[16]The reporter says they were in attendance, id at 200, possibly reprinting the prearranged program without counting heads. Read on!

[17]The Supreme Court's order, uncovered by one of the editors of the Green Bag 2d in the course of research on judicial oaths of office, can be found on microfilm in the National Archives under the title Minutes, Supreme Court U.S., vol H, p 3776. Perhaps the weasel word "official" serves to resolve the apparent discrepancy between what the Justices said they meant to do and what the Globe reported them as having done.

lege, a sometime newspaper editor, and a practicing attorney. Entering the Maine legislature in 1831, he served as Speaker of the state House of Representatives in 1835–36 and went to Congress in 1837—less than a year before his death.[18]

The remaining facts were brought out in the course of an investigation ordered by the House on the day following the funeral.[19] On February 12, 1838 Virginia Representative Henry Wise presented to the House an article from a New York newspaper charging another member of the House with corruption. The editor of the newspaper, Wise said, had vouched for the respectability of the anonymous source of this allegation, and the House ought to investigate the charge. Cilley opposed Wise's suggestion: If this was the same editor who had attacked the Bank of the United States until it loaned him a substantial amount of money and then become one of its staunchest supporters, "he did not think his charges were entitled to much credit in an American Congress."

The editor, J. Watson Webb, wrote a note to Cilley demanding an explanation and gave it to Kentucky Representative William Graves for delivery. Cilley declined to receive it, and Graves took umbrage at his refusal. Please to confirm, Graves wrote, that in declining to receive Webb's note you explained that you did so on the ground that "you could not consent to get yourself into personal difficulties with conductors of public journals, for what you might think proper to say in debate upon this floor," and that you intended neither disrespect to me nor "any personal objections to Mr. Webb as a gentleman." Cilley promptly replied that he had rejected Webb's note "because I chose to be drawn into no controversy with him," that he had "neither affirmed nor denied any thing in regard to [Webb's] character," and that he had intended no disrespect to Graves.

Graves contrived to find this response unsatisfactory: "[I]t does not *disclaim* any exception to [Webb] personally as a gentleman." Graves accordingly demanded to know "*whether you declined to receive his communication on the ground of any personal exception to him as a gentleman or a man of honor?* A categorical answer is expected." Cilley refused to answer the question: "I cannot admit the right on your part to propound the question to which you ask a categorical answer . . . ." Graves then issued the fateful challenge:

> As you have declined accepting a communication which I bore to you from Colonel Webb, and a by your note of yesterday you have refused to decline on grounds which would exonerate me from all responsibility growing out of the affair, I am left no other alternative but to ask that satisfaction which is recognised among gentlemen.

Cilley accepted the challenge: rifles at eighty yards.

With their seconds, friends, and surgeons, the parties met on February 24 "on the road to Marlborough, in Maryland." There they exchanged shots, which missed. Cilley's second inquired whether Graves was satisfied. Representative Wise, Graves's second, insisted that Cilley make a further disclaimer; Cilley refused. The parties fired a second time and missed again. Further negotiations failed to produce an agreement to terminate

[18]See Biographical Directory at 777.

[19]See Cong Globe, 25th Cong, 2d Sess 200–202 (Feb 28, 1838). The committee report, HR Rep 825, 25th Cong, 2d Sess (Apr 25, 1838), is also printed in the Globe for that session at 329–33.

the encounter. Wise then proposed, if both parties were still standing after the next shot, to shorten the distance between them. That proved unnecessary; on the third shot Cilley fell, "and in two or three minutes expired."[20]

The House committee, in a report presented by Isaac Toucey of Connecticut, recommended that Graves be expelled:

> It is a breach of the highest constitutional privileges of the House, and of the most sacred rights of the people in the person of their representative, to demand, in a hostile manner, an explanation of words spoken in debate; to be the bearer of such demand; to demand a reason for refusing to receive it, beyond the mere voluntary election of the member interrogated; or to demand, under any circumstances, any reason at all. . . . It is a still more aggravated breach of the privileges of the House, and of the rights of the people in the person of their representative, to challenge a member, and to slay him in combat, for refusing to comply with any such demand. It is the highest offence which can be committed against either House of Congress, against the freedom of speech and debate therein; against the spirit and the substance of that constitutional provision, that for any speech or debate in either House, the members shall not be questioned in any other place, and violates essentially the right of perfect immunity *elsewhere* for words spoken in debate *here,* which is essential to the independence of Congress, and to the exercise of constitutional liberty.

For their part in facilitating the duel the committee urged that the parties' seconds, both members of the House, be censured as well.[21]

As in the Houston affair, there appeared to be ample support for the House's authority—this time even without resort to the implicit powers exercised in the case of Randall and Whitney. For Article I, § 5 expressly empowered each Chamber of Congress to "punish its members for disorderly behavior" and, by a two-thirds vote, to "expel a member." Senator Blount had been unceremoniously expunged for extracurricular delinquency in 1798,[22] and the House itself had concluded in an earlier case that it was a breach of its privileges for one member to challenge another to a duel.[23] Adding that it was even worse actually to slay him, the committee in Graves's case adverted to no doubts about the House's prerogatives.

But Graves was not expelled, and neither Wise nor Cilley's second, Tennessee Representative George Washington Jones, was censured. The session ended without House

[20]HR Rep 25, 25th Cong, 2d Sess 2–10; Cong Globe, 25th Cong, 2d Sess 329–31.

[21]HR Rep 25, 25th Cong, 2d Sess 15–17; Cong Globe, 25th Cong, 2d Sess 332–33.

[22]See The Federalist Period at 275–76.

[23]See id at 238 n.270.

action or significant reported debate on the committee's proposal.[24]

It is an ill wind, however, that blows no good, and a little good may have come from Mr. Cilley's untimely death after all. In offering the initial resolution providing for an investigation Representative Fairfield had observed that, "aside from the peculiar circumstances of this case," the occasion presented

> an opportunity . . . for assailing the barbarous and inhuman practice of duelling—a practice which does violence to the laws of God, to the best feelings of our own nature, and to the dictates of reason—a practice which is entirely behind and unworthy of the age of civilization in which we live, and which should unite the earnest and faithful efforts of every friend to his species for its extermination.[25]

W. Cost Johnson of Maryland protested at once. If Fairfield was suggesting that Congress enact a law against dueling, "he would ask where, under the Constitution, you obtained the right to enact it." For dueling, he insisted, was "a matter which belonged to the States alone." New York Representative Amasa Parker corrected him: "Surely Congress has the power to act in reference to the District of Columbia."[26]

And so it came to pass. Within ten days after Cilley's death Vermont Senator Samuel Prentiss introduced a bill making it a crime to issue or deliver a challenge to a duel to any person in the District of Columbia, or for the latter to accept it;[27] in the following session a similar proposal became law.[28] One likes to think the Supreme Court's principled protest may have contributed, in some small way, to this small step forward in our halting campaign to civilize mankind.

III. THE CANING OF SENATOR SUMNER

In May 1856, in the course of an interminable and intemperate speech decrying what he termed "the Crime against Kansas," Massachusetts Senator Charles Sumner made disparaging remarks about his South Carolina colleague Andrew Butler:

> The Senator from South Carolina has read many books of chivalry, and

[24]The last relevant entry in the Globe was on July 4, when the subject was tabled. The House adjourned on July 9. Cong Globe, 25th Cong, 2d Sess 494, 505. The story is entertainingly told in Don Carlos Seitz, Famous American Duels, ch XIII (Crowell, 1929). See also Samuel Flagg Bemis, John Quincy Adams and the Union 377–79 (Knopf, 1956).

California Senator David Broderick was also killed in a duel (in 1859), but not in the capital and not by a member of Congress, although the free-soil position he had taken in Congress was said to have been the real cause of the encounter. The Senate took no action against Broderick's adversary, David S. Terry, who with poetic justice was himself killed some thirty years afterward by a bodyguard assigned to protect Supreme Court Justice Stephen Field. See Seitz, Famous American Duels, ch XVI (cited in this note); Cong Globe, 36th Cong, 1st Sess 748–49; In re Neagle, 135 US 1 (1890).

[25]Cong Globe, 25th Cong, 2d Sess 200.

[26]Id.

[27]Id at 206.

[28]5 Stat 318–19, § 2 (Feb 20, 1839).

> believes himself a chivalrous knight, with sentiments of honor and courage. Of course he has chosen a mistress to whom he has made his vows and who, though ugly to others, is always lovely to him; . . . I mean the harlot, Slavery.[29]

Consistent with his own conception of chivalry, South Carolina Representative Preston Brooks (a relative of Butler) accosted Sumner at his desk in the Senate chamber when that body was not in session and beat him within an inch of his life.[30]

Both the House and the Senate appointed committees to investigate the attack.[31] Both committees found that Brooks had offended the privileges of the Senate,[32] and both Houses agreed.[33] Yet Brooks escaped punishment by either Chamber. The Senate appears to have concluded that it had no jurisdiction to punish a member of the House of Representatives.[34] Though the House resoundingly defeated a resolution denying its authority to punish its members for offenses against the Senate, a motion to expel Brooks failed to attract the necessary two-thirds support.[35] Although the House later voted in a backhanded way that Brooks had offended both Houses and deserved to be punished,[36] no one moved to impose any further sanction.[37] Brooks resigned to protest the disrespect with which he had been treated, and his constituents promptly reelected him.[38]

[29]Cong Globe App, 34th Cong, 1st Sess 530. The "crime," as he depicted it, was the concerted effort of some Southerners and their supporters to win the territory for slavery by force and fraud. See Descent into the Maelstrom, ch 9.

[30]Henry Wilson, Sumner's Massachusetts colleague, reported the facts to the Senate the next day. Brooks never denied the assault; he was proud of it. House and Senate committees both found the facts to be substantially as Wilson had stated them. See Cong Globe, 34th Cong, 1st Sess 1279 (Sen. Wilson); id at 1317 (Senate Report); id at 1347 (letter of Rep. Brooks to the President of the Senate); id at 1348–49 (House Report) (containing the most detail); Cong Globe App, 34th Cong, 1st Sess 831 (Rep. Brooks). "Within an inch of his life" is my own phrase; the House committee said that Sumner, blinded, bleeding, and nearly unconscious, "remained for several days in a critical condition" from wounds that were "severe and calculated to endanger [his] life." Cong Globe, 34th Cong, 1st Sess 1348. Professor Donald, who has retold the whole tale, informs us "it was more than three years before he was able regularly to resume his Senate duties." David H. Donald, Charles Sumner and the Coming of the Civil War 312 (Chicago, 1960).

[31]See Cong Globe, 34th Cong, 1st Sess 1279 (Senate); id at 1292 (House).

[32]Id at 1317 (Senate), 1349 (House).

[33]The essence of the committees' findings was formally approved in each case. See id at 1317 (Senate); id at 1642–43 (House) (finding a breach of House privileges too).

[34]That was the explicit conclusion of the Senate committee, S Rep 191, 34th Cong, 1st Sess 3, and the Senate voted without further debate and without a division to accept the committee's report. Cong Globe, 34th Cong, 1st Sess 1317.

[35]The vote was 121–95. Cong Globe, 34th Cong, 1st Sess 1628.

[36]In the preamble to a resolution censuring another member, see note 38.

[37]Brooks was, however, fined $300 for the assault, apparently (for some odd reason) by a Baltimore court. See Donald, Sumner at 308 (cited in note 30).

[38]See Cong Globe App, 34th Cong, 1st Sess 831–33; Cong Globe, 34th Cong, 1st Sess 1863. At the same time the House did vote to censure Brooks's colleague Laurence Keitt, who with knowledge of Brooks's intentions had done nothing to prevent the attack (and whom the committee found to have prevented others from coming to Sumner's aid)—thus formally sanctioning the accessory but not the principal. Cong Globe, 34th Cong, 1st Sess 1641–43. Keitt too resigned and was immediately reelected, id at 1646, 1944. A second colleague also in the know but not in the Senate chamber at the time of the assault escaped the censure that the committee had recommended. See id at 1348–49, 1641. For a glimpse into the warped culture of Southern "honor" that nourished and applauded Brooks's act of savagery see Bertram Wyatt-Brown, Honor and Violence in the Old South (Oxford, 1986).

This remarkable dénouement seems to have been owing in no small part to the intense sectional hostility that pervaded Congress during the troubles in Kansas and on the eve of civil war.[39] Brooks's conduct had disgraced the House to which he belonged and grievously offended the other. The attack, the House committee concluded, was nothing less than "an aggravated assault upon the inestimable right of freedom of speech," asserting "for physical force a prerogative over governments, constitutions, and laws."[40] It deprived Massachusetts of the services of one of the Senators to whom the Constitution entitled it, said Joshua Giddings of Ohio in the House; it was an attack on the very principle of representative government.[41] It cried out, one might have thought, for punishment.

Numerous speakers argued, and the House committee agreed, that Brooks's attack was inconsistent with Article I, § 6 of the Constitution, which provides that for any "speech or debate in either House" no member shall be "questioned in any other place."[42] Brooks's defenders countered with some plausibility that the clause was meant to protect the legislature from other branches of government, not from individuals subject to ordinary criminal sanctions.[43] The general understanding that the clause was designed to ensure legislative independence and the fact that the Constitution ordinarily limits only official action lend credence to this position, and the English provision on which the clause was modeled was a response to encroachments by the Stuart Kings.[44]

[39]These troubles and that hostility will be pursued in due course in the ensuing volume. We cannot discuss everything at once.

[40]HR Rep 182, 34th Cong, 1st Sess 3; Cong Globe, 34th Cong, 1st Sess 1349.

[41]Cong Globe App, 34th Cong, 1st Sess 1117–21. See also id at 733 (Pennsylvania Rep. John Allison); Cong Globe, 34th Cong, 1st Sess 1577 (Ohio Rep. John Bingham). Representative Coke had put the matter pungently in Sam Houston's case in 1832: To permit a member to be beaten for his speech would "transfer . . . the power of legislation to the arena of ruffians or assassins." Cong Deb, 22d Cong, 1st Sess 2859.

[42]E.g., Cong Globe, 34th Cong, 1st Sess 1578 (Rep. Bingham); Cong Globe App, 34th Cong, 1st Sess 733 (Rep. Allison); id at 826 (Ohio Rep. Matthias Nichols); id at 890 (New Jersey Rep. Alexander Pennington); id at 945 (Maryland Rep. Henry Hoffman); HR Rep 182, 34th Cong, 1st Sess 4, Cong Globe, 34th Cong, 1st Sess 1349. This argument too had been made in the case of Sam Houston. E.g., Cong Deb, 22d Cong, 1st Sess 2517 (Rep. Jenifer); id at 2531 (Rep. Davis).

[43]E.g., HR Rep 182, 34th Cong, 1st Sess 16 (minority report), Cong Globe, 34th Cong, 1st Sess 1351 (Georgia Rep. Howell Cobb); Cong Globe App, 34th Cong, 1st Sess 735 (North Carolina Rep. Thomas Clingman); id at 809 (Rep. Cobb). Polk and Drayton had given the same response in Houston's case. Cong Deb, 22d Cong, 1st Sess 2823, 2848. Cobb's extravagant suggestion that to forbid private parties to "question" congressional speeches would preclude newspapers from commenting on them (Cong Globe App, 34th Cong, 1st Sess 809) not only reckoned without the later first amendment (which may have been declaratory on this point) but went beyond the purpose of the speech or debate clause; critical comment has less deterrent effect than physical assault and more redeeming social value to boot. Cobb's additional intimation that the clause protected only "proper and legitimate" speech (id at 1351) was frightening in the extreme: It would gut the provision by leaving it up to the courts to determine (as they would if there were no such provision) the propriety of congressional speech.

[44]1 Wm & Mary Sess 2, ch 2 (1689); see United States v Johnson, 383 US 169, 178, 181 (1966). Only the thirteenth amendment and the short-lived eighteenth plainly restrict private action. Blackstone had said generally that legislative privileges protected members of Parliament from "their fellow-subjects" as well as from the Crown (1 Commentaries at *164), but he was not speaking specifically of speech and debate. Early Massachusetts and Vermont provisions protected members only from "accusation or prosecution, action or complaint," but it is debatable which way that cuts. See Vt Const 1786, ch 1, art 16, Francis N. Thorpe, ed, 6 The Federal and State Constitutions, Colonial Charters, and Other Organic Laws of the States, Territories, and Colonies Now or Heretofore Forming the United States of America 3753 (Government Printing Office, 1909); Coffin v Coffin, 4 Mass 1 (1803) ; Mass Const 1780, pt 2, ch 1, § 3, Art 10, 2 Thorpe at 1899 (cited in this note).

Ohio Representative Matthias Nichols affected to think it absurd to argue that Brooks could beat Sumner on account of his speech but not sue him,[45] but he missed the point: In an action for defamation it is the court's judgment, not the plaintiff's institution of the action, that is the subject of complaint.[46] Better was the argument of New Jersey Representative Alexander Pennington that the purpose of the provision required that it be applied to private as well as public actions: A beating suppressed legislative debate as effectively as a lawsuit.[47] The response that the individual assailant could be prosecuted for assault was apt but not decisive, since as Pennington pointed out such an interpretation would arguably leave the legislature at the mercy of other branches.[48]

But the power of the House or Senate to punish Brooks did not appear to depend on the disputable question whether his action had offended the speech or debate clause.[49] For as we have seen the House had express authority under Article I, § 5 both to "punish its members for disorderly behavior" and to "expel a member," while both the House and the Senate had consistently asserted implicit power to punish those who endangered their authority by extracurricular efforts to corrupt or intimidate their members. Brooks's friends did not hesitate to renew all the old arguments against the existence of the latter authority,[50] and they were by no means frivolous; they were closely related to those made against summary proceedings for extramural contempt of court in the impeachment of

[45]Cong Globe App, 34th Cong, 1st Sess 826.

[46]Cf Shelley v Kraemer, 334 US 1, 18–20 (1948); New York Times v Sullivan, 376 US 254, 265 (1964).

[47]Cong Globe App, 34th Cong, 1st Sess 890. In 1826, when Henry Clay (then Secretary of State) challenged John Randolph to a duel for remarks made in a Senate speech, Clay's messenger acknowledged that "no one had the right to question him out of the Senate for any thing said in debate." Randolph agreed but replied that he would not "shield himself under such a subterfuge as the pleading of his privilege." His formal note accepting the challenge suggested a narrower ground for immunity:

> Mr. Randolph accepts the challenge of Mr. Clay. At the same time he protests against the *right* of any minister of the Executive Government of the United States to hold him responsible for words spoken in debate, as a senator from Virginia, in crimination of such minister, or the administration under which he shall have taken office.

The duel took place, and neither party was hurt; Randolph had made clear in advance his intention not to fire at his adversary. "It was as much as to say," wrote Thomas Hart Benton, "Mr. Clay may fire at me for what has offended him; I will not, by returning the fire, admit his right to do so." Benton, 1 Thirty Years' View at 70–77; see also Seitz, Famous American Duels, ch XII (cited in note 24).

[48]Cong Globe App, 34th Cong, 1st Sess 890. Defenders argued on the basis of British precedent that the immunity did not extend to private republication of congressional speeches. E.g., id at 735–36 (Rep. Clingman); id at 809–10 (Rep. Cobb) (citing 2 Story, § 863). Later Supreme Court authority supports them: Private publication, said a divided Court in 1972, was "in no way essential to the deliberations of the Senate." United States v Gravel, 408 US 606, 625 (1972). Pennington persuasively responded (as two of Brooks's confidants had testified) that the assault on Sumner was for the speech itself, not for its republication. Cong Globe App, 34th Cong, 1st Sess 891.

[49]Even if there had been a violation of that clause, as Representative Archer had argued in 1832, it did not necessarily follow that the House was the one to punish it; debate was important, but so was a fair trial. Cong Deb, 22d Cong, 1st Sess 2979.

[50]E.g., Cong Globe App, 34th Cong, 1st Sess 807 (Rep. Orr); Cong Globe, 34th Cong, 1st Sess 1350 (Reps. Cobb and Greenwood).

Judge Peck.[51]

From the Senate's point of view the only novelty in the Sumner affair was that the offender was a member of the other House. One might have thought that would make punishment easier, for as noted each House has explicit authority to punish or expel its members.[52] The Senate committee concluded, however, that the fact that the offender was a member of the House deprived the Senate of jurisdiction. British precedents were clear that the independence of each chamber precluded either from asserting any authority over members of the other; Vice-President Jefferson had stated the same rule in the Manual of Parliamentary Practice he had prepared for the Senate; and Article I, § 6 of the Constitution protected members of Congress from arrest while their Houses were in session, "in all cases except treason, felony, and breach of the peace." The Senate, the report continued, had no authority to punish "a breach of the peace, *as such.*"

> It cannot take any notice of the assault except as a breach of its privileges, and in this aspect it is not one of the cases in which the privilege from arrest is excepted.
>
> The Senate, therefore, for a breach of its privileges, cannot arrest a member of the House of Representatives, and, *a fortiori,* cannot try and punish him. That authority devolves solely upon the House of which he is a member.[53]

I must say every step in the argument from the constitutional immunity provision strikes me as fishy. Brooks *did* commit a breach of the peace, and it was for that act that the Senate was asked to punish him. If the public interest in criminal prosecution is great enough to justify encroaching on the operations of the House in such a case, so is the need to prevent disruption of the Senate. Moreover, the clause prohibits only arrest, not trial or punishment; it does not, for example, forbid civil actions for damages so long as the defendant is not prevented from attending Congress.[54] Finally, immunity from arrest is expressly limited to the time when the legislator is attending a session or traveling to or

[51]See section I of chapter 7. The most thought-provoking argument for Houston in 1832 had been his attorney's reminder that Congress had just passed a law restricting summary punishment for contempt of court and that the present case came within its spirit. Cong Deb, 22d Cong, 1st Sess 2607 (Mr. Key).

[52]US Const, Art I, § 5.

[53]S Rep 191, 34th Cong, 1st Sess 3, Cong Globe, 34th Cong, 1st Sess 1317, citing John Hatsell, 3 Precedents of Proceedings in the House of Commons 67, 71 (Payne, 1746); Thomas Jefferson, A Manual of Parliamentary Practice Composed Originally for the Use of the Senate of the United States 34 (Clark & Maynard, 1840): "Either House may request, but not command, the attendance of a member of the other." Representative Pennington, arguing that the House should take jurisdiction, added that Cushing's influential treatise had taken the same position. Cong Globe App, 34th Cong, 1st Sess 894, citing Luther S. Cushing, Elements of the Law and Practice of Legislative Assemblies in the United States of America §§ 732–33 (Little, Brown, 1856).

[54]Long v Ansell, 293 US 76, 83 (1934). The Articles of Confederation (Art 5) had protected members of Congress from "arrests and imprisonments" during sessions. See also 2 Story, § 857: "When a representative is withdrawn from his seat by a summons, the people, whom he represents, lose their voice in debate and vote . . . ." The distraction from duty incident to defending oneself in another forum might be thought counter to the purpose of the provision (cf Clinton v Jones, 520 US 681 (1997)), but it would be hard to call it an "arrest." On the question whether the penalties that could be imposed in congressional contempt proceedings included fines see 2 Story, § 846, and the English decisions there cited.

from it. Although one House is rather seldom in session without the other, the clause does not even forbid the Senate in all cases other than treason, felony, and breach of the peace to arrest a member of the House.

Be all that as it may, the precedent cited by the committee was pretty formidable, and no Senator appears to have contested the committee's conclusion that the Senate was without jurisdiction.[55] The Senate accordingly left the matter up to the other chamber,[56] where some Representatives argued that the House had no authority to punish Brooks either: It was not the House's responsibility to punish an offense against the Senate.

Once it was decided that Congress was not dependent on prosecutors and courts to protect its proceedings from obstruction, the conclusion that neither House had power to punish Brooks seems little short of absurd.[57] The House, as we know, rejected it, upholding its authority but imposing no formal sanction. Those who denied the House's authority tended also to deny the premise of legislative punishment for acts not committed in open session.[58] But they were asking those who disagreed with them on that long-settled issue either to reject the Senate's understanding of its own powers or to reach a conclusion they would regard as ridiculous, and that was a pretty tall order.

The words of the Constitution, in any event, appeared to support the House's authority: "Each House may determine the rules of its proceedings, punish its members for disorderly behavior, and, with the concurrence of two thirds, expel a member."[59] But this provision, said Brooks's defenders, should be read as a unified whole. It was all about orderly proceedings in the House and Senate; it did not authorize even expulsion, let alone other punishments, for whatever cause the members thought sufficient. "Disorderly behavior" meant violation of the rules the Chamber had adopted to govern its own proceedings; expulsion was the maximum penalty if the infraction was grave. As Albert Gallatin had argued in the case of Matthew Lyon in 1798, expulsion was a troubling remedy in a democracy, because it deprived the offender's constituents of their representation in Congress; the Framers should not be presumed to have empowered either House to apply it at will.[60]

This argument is not without plausibility. It is strongest in the case of punishments other than expulsion: "[D]isorderly behavior" does seem to suggest disruption of the House's own proceedings. As in the case of offenders who are not members of the avenging body, and as in the case of contempt of court, there is much to be said for leaving punishment to ordinary criminal proceedings when the government process is not actually impeded. As we have seen, however, there is also something to be said for allowing the

[55]Occasional Brooks partisans in the House did, in an effort to strengthen their conclusion that the House had no authority to act. See Cong Globe App, 34th Cong, 1st Sess 815 (Rep. Boyce).

[56]Cong Globe, 34th Cong, 1st Sess 1317.

[57]See, e.g., id at 1578 (Rep. Bingham); Cong Globe App, 34th Cong, 1st Sess 893 (Rep. Pennington), both arguing that the fact that the Senate could not punish Brooks made it imperative for the House to do so.

[58]E.g., Cong Globe App, 34th Cong, 1st Sess 814 (Rep. Boyce).

[59]US Const, Art I, § 5. There was no controversy over the meaning of the unspecific term "two thirds," since it made no difference to Brooks's fate; the vote to expel him fell short of two-thirds not only of the entire Senate but also of those voting on the motion. See the discussion of the same question in the context of constitutional amendments in The Jeffersonians at 58–64 and of the veto in section I of chapter 6.

[60]See, e.g., HR Rep 182, 34th Cong, 1st Sess 17–19 (minority report), Cong Globe, 34th Cong, 1st Sess 1352 (Reps. Cobb and Greenwood); Cong Globe App, 34th Cong, 1st Sess 813 (Rep. Boyce). For Gallatin's argument see The Federalist Period at 264.

legislature to protect itself against extracurricular obstructions. The argument for legislative authority had prevailed in the case of non-members; it is not obvious why the House should have less power to punish its own members than to punish outsiders for the same offense.

With respect to expulsion the text itself cuts against a restrictive interpretation, for in contrast to the authority to "punish" only for "disorderly behavior" the power to expel is expressly conditioned only on a two-thirds vote.[61] It is of course conceivable that expulsion was viewed only as the most severe "punish[ment]" for disorderly behavior, and it is hard to imagine why the House should be licensed to employ only the extreme sanction of expulsion, and not lesser penalties, in other cases. The opposite argument, however, is equally plausible: Since the power to expel is not so limited, there is no reason to think the Framers meant to limit lesser punishments to infractions of the procedural rules.

Precedent, moreover, was against Brooks, at least on the question of expulsion. Senator William Blount, as I have noted, had been expelled in 1797 for a plot to attack Spanish Florida.[62] Ohio Senator John Smith had escaped expulsion for complicity in the Burr conspiracy by a single vote not thought to reflect doubts as to the Senate's jurisdiction.[63] Matthew Lyon had avoided expulsion from the House for a conviction under the Sedition Act, and rightly so; but no one was said to have taken the position that he could be bounced only for "disorderly behavior." An earlier unsuccessful proceeding against Lyon for brawling had arisen while the House was in recess; his defenders conceded that a member could be expelled for conduct that did not disturb House proceedings directly if it rendered the offender "infamous."[64]

Advocates of expelling Representative Brooks cited these precedents,[65] and the House voted to sustain its jurisdiction.[66] Without conceding that the House may expel a member at will, I am inclined to think it was right. It is hard to believe the House would be without power to rid itself, for example, of a member who had committed treason. As

[61]See, e.g., Rawle at 46–48, concluding that Congressmen could be expelled but not otherwise punished for conduct outside of session. Similarly, Story linked the power to punish for disorderly behavior to the power to make rules, which would be "nugatory" without it, while asserting that a member could be expelled not only for "interrupt[ing] its deliberations by perpetual violence or clamour" but also for "disgrac[ing] the house by the grossness of his conduct." 2 Story, § 835. See also id, § 836:

> The power to expel a member is not in the British house of commons confined to offences committed by the party as a member, or during the session of parliament; but it extends to all cases, where the offence is such, as, in the judgment of the house, unfits him for parliamentary duties.

[62]See The Federalist Period at 275–76. Story cited Blount's case for the proposition that "expulsion may be for any misdemeanor, which, although not punishable by any statute, is inconsistent with the trust and duty of a Senator." 2 Story, § 836. See also In re Chapman, 166 US 661, 669–70 (1897).

[63]See The Jeffersonians at 142–43; 2 Story, § 836, opining that the arguments of Smith's counsel suggested the result was attributable to "some doubt as to the facts."

[64]See The Federalist Period at 263–66.

[65]See Cong Globe, 34th Cong, 1st Sess 1578–79 (Rep. Bingham); Cong Globe App, 34th Cong, 1st Sess 817 (Rep. Simmons); id at 824 (the remarkable Tennessee Rep. Emerson Etheridge), all arguing that the House could both punish and expel for whatever proved a member unfit. As Simmons noted, Cushing's treatise (cited in note 53) had said one House ought to punish a member who assaulted a member of the other.

[66]To be more precise, the House voted down a motion denying its jurisdiction. Cong Globe, 34th Cong, 1st Sess 1628. The vote was 145–66.

the first Representative James Bayard had said in the arguably analogous impeachment case against Senator Blount, a judge who shouldered a gun in an insurrection would be as unfit for the Bench as if he had abused the office itself.[67] It should not be an absolute bar to expulsion that the offense occurred outside the sessions of the aggrieved House.[68]

Yet the motion to expel failed; like Smith and Lyon, Brooks was saved by the salutary requirement of an extraordinary majority.[69] Are you sorry? I think I am. Gallatin was right that the power should be used sparingly. There might have been something unjust (though entirely congruous) in depriving South Carolinians of their spokesman in Congress because he had deprived Massachusetts citizens of theirs. The House was right not to expel Lyon for spitting at Representative Griswold, or either of them for continuing the fray. Even the assassination of Representative Cilley was the result of a fair contest, sanctified by long-standing if increasingly execrated custom, between consenting adults. Brooks's offense, I think, was far more heinous. Like Sam Houston, he assailed a defenseless man with a deadly weapon and with malice aforethought; and in each case the victim was a member of Congress.[70] I think both should have been punished, preferably by the offended Chamber, and by more than a slap on the wrist. Failing that, it seems to me on balance that Brooks ought to have been expelled from the House. But the question, I trust the reader will agree, turns out to be both intricate and perplexing; we do not get much guidance from the spare constitutional text.

IV. THE SINS OF ORSAMUS MATTESON

When New York Representative Orsamus Matteson was accused not long after the Sumner incident of encouraging attempts to bribe other members of the House, he resigned before expulsion proceedings could be completed, but the House censured him anyway—evidently concluding that its power to punish "disorderly behavior" was not limited to actual disruption of actual proceedings.[71] Reelected by his loyal constituents, Matteson was met in the next Congress by a second motion for expulsion. The House could expel a member for any reason it thought sufficient, supporters of the motion contended, or in-

[67]See The Federalist Period at 278. The case for expulsion is the stronger of the two, for the expulsion clause does not contain the limiting language "high crimes and misdemeanors," which is often equated with abuse of authority. The case Bayard imagined would actually be presented during the Civil War, though there were additional grounds for impeachment; but let us not get too far ahead of our story. See Eleanore Bushnell, Crimes, Follies, and Misfortunes: The Federal Impeachment Trials 115–24 (Illinois, 1992), discussing the case of Judge West H. Humphreys.

[68]The usual argument that legislative action is unnecessary because the courts are open is inoperative here; expulsion is not a remedy available in a judicial proceeding.

[69]Some doubtless agreed with Representative Clingman that Brooks's action was to be applauded. Cong Globe App, 34th Cong, 1st Sess 736, quoting Benjamin Franklin's unfortunate reference to the "liberty of the cudgel." See also, e.g., id at 805 (Rep. Orr). Representative Etheridge said he thought the heat of passion a mitigating circumstance (although three days had elapsed between Sumner's speech and the attack); if he had believed Brooks meant to kill Sumner, he would have voted for expulsion. Id at 825.

[70]The hypothetical case of cruelty to his slaves, raised by Brooks in his own defense (Cong Globe App, 34th Cong, 1st Sess 832), was for that reason a less compelling one for expulsion.

[71]Cong Globe, 34th Cong, 3d Sess 927–33 (Feb 25, 1857); HR Rep 179, 35th Cong, 1st Sess 3 (1858) (confirming that the clause in question had been the basis of the House's action).

deed for no reason at all.[72] Matteson's offense was serious, they said, and he had forfeited the respect of his colleagues; he was unworthy to associate with them; the House had a right to protect itself from contact with scoundrels.[73]

Matteson's defenders reiterated the argument (made in Sumner's case) that a member could be expelled only for disorderly conduct, which meant violation of House rules.[74] They added that he could not be punished twice for the same offense;[75] but, as Illinois Representative Thomas Harris said, expulsion was intended to purify the House, not to punish the offender.[76] Finally, they insisted, even an actual expulsion would not have disqualified Matteson from running for reelection; the people had a right to choose him again; to expel a member twice for the same conduct would deprive the voters of the right to choose their own Representative.[77]

A committee to which the matter was referred concluded that the power of each House to punish its members was not restricted to disruption of proceedings or breach of existing rules but extended to "any misconduct inconsistent with the character of a representative, while a member thereof"—that is, of the House that sought to inflict punishment.[78] The definition of wrongdoing in this standard was broad enough to include both Brooks's attack on Sumner and Matteson's alleged encouragement of bribery. In the committee's view, however, it was too late to expel Matteson, for he had committed no offense against the present House.[79]

The House tabled the whole subject after it was suggested that it was more important to discuss the bloody conflict then raging in Kansas,[80] and Matteson was never expelled. My own view is that the committee's criterion was too narrow: A member who undermines the legislative process by instigating bribes is no less indigestible in the next Congress than in the one he has already offended.

V. IMMUNITY

In 1795, as we know, in the case of Randall and Whitney, the House of Representatives had asserted implicit authority to protect the integrity of its proceedings by punishing attempts to bribe its members as contempt.[81] The Supreme Court confirmed the existence of this authority in *Anderson v Dunn* in 1821.[82] In 1853 Congress finally made it a crime to

[72]Cong Globe, 35th Cong, 1st Sess 311, 878 (Illinois Rep. Thomas L. Harris); id at 885 (Tennessee Rep. George W. Jones).

[73]Id at 882, 885, 1390 (Reps. Hughes, Curtis, and Craige).

[74]Id at 881–82 (Louisiana Rep. Miles Taylor, urging that the Rules be amended to forbid a repetition of Matteson's misdeeds).

[75]Id at 880, 884, 888 (Reps. Stanton, Nichols, and Ritchie).

[76]Id at 885. Less compelling was Hughes's argument that there was no double jeopardy because Matteson had resigned before the House could punish him, id at 882; for though he had not been expelled the first time, he had indeed been censured.

[77]Id at 879, 1390 (Georgia Rep. James Seward); id at 884 (Ohio Rep. Matthias Nichols). This argument would have been stronger, responded William Smith of Virginia, if Matteson had been reelected *after* the first disciplinary proceeding. Id at 883.

[78]HR Rep 179, 35th Cong, 1st Sess 3.

[79]Id at 4.

[80]Cong Globe, 35th Cong, 1st Sess 1392.

[81]See The Federalist Period at 232–38.

[82]19 US 204 (1821); see The First Hundred Years at 184–86.

offer a bribe to a member of Congress (or to any "officer of the United States"), or for the offeree to accept it.[83] That these prohibitions were necessary and proper to the operations of the Government appears not to have been called into question.

In January 1857, with this statute on the books, the *New York Times* published an editorial alleging corruption in the House of Representatives in connection with the disposition of Minnesota public lands.[84] Summoned by a select House investigating committee, J.W. Simonton, the Washington correspondent on whose report the editorial was based, refused to identify those members of Congress who, as he had asserted, had approached him in hopes of obtaining bribes.[85] He had promised not to reveal what they were about to tell him, Simonton explained, and he could not do so "without a dishonorable breach of confidence." The committee was not satisfied: It was "due to the dignity and reputation of the American Congress to purge itself" of members who had so "shamelessly prostituted their high and honored positions," and Simonton's testimony was essential to that end.[86] By a lopsided vote the House ordered him held in custody until the end of the session, unless he first purged himself of contempt.[87] All of this was standard; that Congress could imprison recalcitrant witnesses for contempt had been clear ever since *Anderson v Dunn.*[88]

At the same time, however, the committee proposed a new statute to improve the effectiveness of future investigations,[89] and Congress adopted it.[90] The first section made refusal to answer "any question pertinent to the matter of inquiry," or willful failure to produce subpoenaed papers, a crime punishable in federal court.[91] There was some sparring about the breadth of this provision, since it appeared to make no allowance for communications from attorney to client, husband to wife, or penitent to priest, or even for diplomatic secrets.[92] South Carolina Representative James Orr replied that parliamentary law recognized no attorney-client privilege and appeared to pooh-pooh the importance of confidentiality within the Executive Branch.[93]

The objection, I fear, could not so lightly be dismissed. Apart from impressive policy considerations, the modern mind will perceive arguable constitutional support for several of the suggested exemptions in the first and sixth amendments and the separation

[83]10 Stat 170, 171, § 6 (Feb 26, 1853). Earlier sections of the same law made it unlawful for federal officers to prosecute third-party claims against the United States, or for members of Congress to do so for pay. Id at 170, §§ 2, 3. (Section 8, id at 171, made these prohibitions inapplicable to "the prosecution or defence of any action or suit in any judicial court of the United States.") There was no reported discussion of the constitutionality of these provisions; to prevent conflicts of interest would appear to be necessary and proper to the functioning of all branches of the Government.

[84]The editorial is printed, with all its sleazy innuendoes, at Cong Globe, 34th Cong, 3d Sess 274.

[85]See id at 403.

[86]Id at 403–4.

[87]Id at 413.

[88]See id at 409 (Rep. Humphrey Marshall). Inevitably, a few speakers continued to deny the House's authority. See id at 404 (Reps. Walker and McMullin); id at 407–8 (Rep. Burnett, giving the usual reasons).

[89]See id at 404.

[90]11 Stat 155 (Jan 24, 1857).

[91]The newly prescribed penalties were expressly declared to be "in addition to the pains and penalties now existing," id, § 1; Congress did not attempt to divest either House of authority to impose its own sanctions.

[92]Cong Globe, 34th Cong, 3d Sess 431 (Rep. Dunn); id at 435 (Sen. Hale); id at 439 (Sen. Seward); id at 443 (Sen. Pugh).

[93]Id at 431.

of powers; long before 1857 a New York court had endorsed the first of these justifications, and more than one President had asserted the last.[94] More comforting, if true, was Georgia Senator Robert Toombs's assurance that the only privileges the proposal would disturb were those mentioned in the second section of the bill (of which more presently)—although there was nothing in the contempt provision itself to suggest that other privileges were meant to be preserved.[95]

Maine Representative Israel Washburn raised a related objection to the clause making it a crime to refuse to produce papers:

> I wish the Committee on the Judiciary to inquire whether this bill would be inconsistent with . . . the fourth article of the amendments, which provides that the right of the people to be secure in their person, houses, papers, and effects against unreasonable searches and seizures, shall not be violated . . .—whether, in fact, a more effective seizure of papers could be had in any way than under the form of this bill, by which parties may be compelled to produce and exhibit all their private papers under penalty of a year's imprisonment? . . .
>
> Unreasonable searches and seizures are not to be made, nor are any to be made without warrant upon probable cause, supported by oath or affirmation. Are you not by this bill dispensing with the conditions and requirements of the Constitution, and endeavoring to obtain the possession of private papers without warrant issued upon probable cause, and supported by oath or affirmation?[96]

Alack, in the haste to pass the bill and facilitate the pending investigation, no one condescended to answer Washburn's objection. It was by no means frivolous; Justice Joseph Bradley would echo it with eerie accuracy for a majority of the Supreme Court in *Boyd v United States* in 1886.[97] Concurring Justices would argue at that time that if such an order was a search and seizure it was not unreasonable; later decisions would conclude

[94]See, e.g., People v Phillips (NY Ct Gen Sess 1813), abstracted in 1 Western LJ 109, 112–13 (1843) (confession); Eric D. Green, Charles R. Nesson, & Peter L. Murray, Problems, Cases, and Materials on Evidence 619 (Aspen, 3d ed 2000) ("In the criminal context it may be asserted that the lawyer-client privilege is necessary to protect the accused's Fifth and Sixth Amendment rights to the effective assistance of counsel."); 3 Richardson at 36 (Dec 12, 1833) (President Jackson's assertion of executive privilege); United States v Nixon, 418 US 683, 703–7 (1974) (recognizing the constitutional basis of executive privilege).

[95]Cong Globe, 34th Cong, 3d Sess 440. Senator Seward had proposed an express provision to that effect, which Toombs branded as unnecessary. Id at 439–40. No one, however, suggested that the bill should permit a refusal to answer on the naked ground that the witness had promised to keep the requested information confidential, which the House had just decisively and persuasively rejected in Simonton's case. Nor would it be argued even today that a person in Simonton's position should be allowed to plead a journalist's privilege not to reveal his sources, for though he was a newspaperman by trade it was not in that capacity that he had received the information sought by the committee. By his own account he was approached as a potential intermediary in a criminal transaction, not a distributor of facts and opinions; there was no informant requiring anonymity to encourage divulgence. See the various opinions in Branzburg v Hayes, 408 US 665 (1972), discussing the basis of the asserted privilege, which the majority refused to recognize.

[96]Cong Globe, 34th Cong, 3d Sess 428.

[97]116 US 616.

that it was not a search or seizure at all.[98] The opportunity to contest a subpoena in court arguably justifies relaxing some at least of the requirements applicable to ex parte warrants;[99] the Court would uphold judicial subpoenas in 1906 because it would be "utterly impossible to carry on the administration of justice" without them.[100]

Apart from questions of privilege and seizure, there was widespread agreement that it was appropriate to make contempt of Congress a crime. Even those who doubted the House's own authority to punish contempt appeared to agree that a statute providing for prosecution before the courts would be necessary and proper to the exercise of congressional functions.[101] Indeed, as Maryland Representative Henry Winter Davis suggested, the bill seemed to remove the basis of their objections, as well as curing a number of other deficiencies in the existing law:

> The first section of the bill confers no summary power on any tribunal; it increases no power now existing in any committee, and confers no power to be exercised either by the committee or the House. It makes a mere substitution of a judicial proceeding for the ordinary proceeding by attachment by a parliamentary body. It substitutes a definite punishment for an indefinite punishment. . . . It substitutes the quiet formality of a judicial proceeding in lieu of the irregular proceedings which occurred in this House yesterday, in attempting to exercise such jurisdiction as is necessarily incident to any parliamentary investigation. It places in the court power to punish according to the gravity of the offense, and does not make it a question of time in relation to the beginning or the end of the session, whether the party shall be confined one day, one week, ten months, or two years, without any sort of reference to the merit or demerit of the party, and depending entirely on the accidental time of the duration of the Congress at which he may be called upon to testify.[102] . . . [It] makes the question a matter of calm judicial consideration and reflection, to be passed upon by a jury of his countrymen . . . .[103]

More controversial was the second section of the bill, which as enacted provided as follows:

> *And be it further enacted,* That no person examined and testifying before either House of Congress, or any committee of either House, shall be held to answer criminally in any court of justice, or subject to any penalty or

[98]See *Boyd,* 116 US at 641 (Miller, J, joined by Waite, CJ); United States v Dionisio, 410 US 1, 9 (1973): "It is clear that a subpoena to appear before a grand jury is not a 'seizure' in the Fourth Amendment sense . . . ."

[99]See Zurcher v Stanford Daily, 436 US 547, 570 (1978) (Stewart, J, dissenting).

[100]Hale v Henkel, 201 US 43, 73. I have discussed this question in somewhat more detail in connection with the *Boyd* decision; see The First Hundred Years at 444–46 and authorities cited.

[101]See Cong Globe, 34th Cong, 3d Sess 408 (Rep. Burnett); id at 436 (Sen. Toombs).

[102]It was generally conceded, as the Supreme Court had said in *Anderson,* 19 US at 231, that the House could not imprison a contemnor beyond the end of the session in which he was held in contempt. See Cong Globe, 34th Cong, 3d Sess 405–6 (Rep. Orr).

[103]Cong Globe, 34th Cong, 3d Sess 427. See also id at 437 (Sen. Trumbull).

> forfeiture for any fact or act touching which he shall be required to testify . . . , and that no statement made or paper produced by any witness . . . shall be competent testimony in any criminal proceeding against such witness in any court of justice; and no witness shall hereafter be allowed to refuse to testify to any fact or to produce any paper touching which he shall be examined by either House of Congress, or any committee of either House, for the reason that his testimony touching such fact or the production of such paper may tend to disgrace him or otherwise render him infamous . . . .[104]

In short, this was a typical immunity provision, requiring the witness to testify even with respect to matters tending "to disgrace him or otherwise render him infamous," in exchange for freedom from prosecution for what he revealed. In modern parlance it provided both transactional and use immunity: The informant could not be prosecuted for acts about which he testified, and the evidence he gave could not be used against him.

"How else," demanded Representative Orr in support of the proposed provision, "can you get the testimony" necessary to prove that a member of Congress, as alleged by Simonton, had solicited a bribe?

> Mr. Speaker, who makes these combinations? Are they made in market overt? Are they made in the presence of witnesses? Are they made in the open face of day? . . . Who knows of these bribes and rewards that may be tendered to members of Congress? The parties making them themselves. And how is the House and the country ever to put a stop to anything of the sort if a witness, when he is called by an investigating committee to testify his knowledge as to these facts, shall fold his arms and say, "I decline to answer that question, because it would criminate me?"

For bribery of a member of Congress, Orr reminded his colleagues, was now a federal crime.[105] The present investigation would come to nothing, Representative Davis added, "if witnesses are allowed to come before the committee and say that they have had arrangements with Congress, but they cannot reveal them without . . . subject[ing] themselves to punishment under the law of 1853."[106]

Nor, supporters argued, was there anything novel about the proposal. A number of states, said Senator Toombs, had adopted comparable provisions.[107] So, said Davis, had the British Parliament:

> On the one hand, the parliamentary law takes the party from under the protection of ordinary law, and compels him to disclose every fact whether it do or do not tend to show that he has been guilty of a crime; and on the other hand, it disables every party, and every instrument of ev-

[104]11 Stat at 156, § 2. A final proviso made clear that nothing in the statute exempted the witness from "prosecution and punishment for perjury committed . . . in testifying as aforesaid."

[105]Cong Globe, 34th Cong, 3d Sess 405.

[106]Id at 428. See also id at 437 (Sen. Toombs).

[107]Id at 436.

> idence, from going into the Court of King's Bench, and there testifying to a fact which the party may have himself confessed before a committee, or a House of Parliament. In that way it accomplishes the exact purpose of the ordinary administration of justice—throws a legal protection around a party against a legal prosecution, who, for great national and public purposes, is compelled to make a disclosure . . . .

Indeed, said Davis, there could hardly be any "reasonable objection" to such a procedure, "since it is an ordinary method used by the executive department of the Government in ordinary prosecutions, and the administration of criminal law":

> When an accomplice is placed upon the witness-stand, he is there so placed continually with the declaration of the executive Government beforehand, that if he shall fully and fairly disclose all the circumstances relative to the crime, he shall not be prosecuted for any fact that he may reveal himself to have been a participator in.

The immunity proposal, Davis concluded, amounted to "a parliamentary pardon" in advance.[108]

There were, however, objections; whether they were "reasonable" is another matter. Humphrey Marshall in the House and Lyman Trumbull in the Senate protested on the policy ground that the cost of the provision was excessive: It would make it too easy for offenders to escape justice.[109] Representative Orr saw it differently: "[I]t is more important that the House should purge itself than that an individual should be convicted before a criminal court."[110] Marshall argued that the provision would offend the constitutional ban on ex post facto laws by requiring a witness to divulge information previously received in confidence;[111] others rightly pointed out that it would punish only future refusals to testify.[112]

Other objections were more serious. What authority had Congress, Washburn inquired, to grant immunity from prosecution in state courts?[113] No one responded but Miles Taylor of Louisiana, who hazarded the conclusion that every state court would exclude coerced confessions; Washburn replied that "the bill implie[d] the reverse."[114] A better

[108]Id at 427–28, quoting Cushing, Legislative Assemblies, §§ 1001–2, 1005 (cited in note 53). Of the precedents invoked, that of state immunity laws was the most persuasive: Parliament was subject to no constitutional limitations, and bargains not to prosecute involved inducement to testify, not coercion. Senator Hale perceived the latter distinction, Cong Globe, 34th Cong, 3d Sess 436; as Toombs explained, it did not apply to the distinct precedent of state laws that required the witness to testify. Id at 436–37.

[109]Cong Globe, 34th Cong, 3d Sess 431 (Rep. Marshall); id at 437 (Sen. Trumbull). See also id at 442 (Sen. Pugh).

[110]Id at 432.

[111]Id at 430.

[112]See id at 430 (Rep. Taylor); id at 432 (Rep. Davis); id at 436 (Sen. Toombs). Senator Hale termed the provision retrospective in spirit if not in terms. Id at 435.

[113]Id at 428–29. See also id at 434–35 (Sen. Hale); id at 442 (Sen. Pugh).

[114]Id at 429. Nothing in the Constitution at the time, moreover, required them to do so. See Twining v New Jersey, 211 US 78, 113–14 (1908) (holding that not even the fourteenth amendment made the self-incrimination provision applicable to the states). The first case requiring a state court to exclude a confession coerced outside a legal proceeding (as a matter of due process) was Brown v Mississippi, 297 US 278, 285–86 (1936).

answer would have been that preempting state prosecutions, like preempting federal ones, was necessary and proper to ensuring the efficacy of congressional investigations.[115]

It was the unsavory John Quitman of Mississippi, a notorious freebooter himself, who first raised the most troublesome question: The fifth amendment declared that no person should be "compelled in any criminal case to be a witness against himself." By requiring a witness "to answer an inquiry which would throw infamy upon him," did not the bill offend this provision?[116] Senator John Hale of New Hampshire thought it did:

> [W]hen you undertake to pass this bill, you undertake to step over a barrier to which [the witness] has a right for his protection; you override his constitutional right, to require that he shall not be held to answer to any matter that may criminate himself.[117]

Once again it was Henry Winter Davis who attempted to justify the proposal. First, he argued, the constitutional ban on compulsory self-incrimination did not apply to legislative proceedings at all:

> The language there used is that no party in any criminal proceeding shall be compelled to give evidence against himself. It is plain, therefore, that that clause only applies to a case of a party indicted for crime—himself a defendant on the record, the party prosecuted—and in that proceeding he shall not be called upon or coerced to give testimony . . . which shall lead to a judgment against him.[118]

That seems wrong, as the Supreme Court would later hold, though no one said so at the time; to permit the Government to compel testimony in one proceeding and use it in another would deprive the constitutional provision of all force.[119] The text of the provision is no obstacle to giving it meaningful effect: If evidence a defendant is forced to provide elsewhere is used against him in court, he is "compelled . . . to be a witness against himself" in "a[] criminal case."[120]

Davis's second argument was better, and the Supreme Court would later adopt it. Even if the constitutional provision applied to compulsion exerted outside the criminal proceeding itself, he said, it would not be offended, for the purpose and effect of the bill were to protect the witness from criminal prosecution:

For the present law see Molloy v Hogan, 378 US 1 (1964) (overruling *Twining*); Murphy v Waterfront Comm, 378 US 52 (1964) (holding a federal court could not receive incriminating testimony compelled by a state and stating (id at 53 n.1) that the converse case would be decided the same way).

[115]The Supreme Court would accept this argument in Brown v Walker, 161 US 591, 606–8 (1896).

[116]Cong Globe, 34th Cong, 3d Sess 427.

[117]Id at 435.

[118]Id at 428.

[119]Counselman v Hitchcock, 142 US 547, 562–63 (1892).

[120]All right, I have reversed the order of the words, and the original language lends itself more easily to the conclusion that the compulsion itself must occur in the criminal proceeding: "[N]or shall any person . . . be compelled in any criminal case to be a witness against himself . . . ." Even in the original, however, it is not obvious what is modified by the adverbial clause "in any criminal case"; can it be illegitimate in such circumstances to paraphrase it so as to avoid an absurd result?

> He is, therefore, neither constrained here to give evidence against himself in a judicial proceeding in which he is defendant, nor to give evidence which may be used in any judicial proceeding which may hereafter be instituted. . . . I think, sir, we are free from constitutional objections.[121]

I think so too. As Davis suggested, the predicate for disagreeing with his first argument did not apply to his second: If evidence obtained elsewhere could not be used in a criminal proceeding, the defendant would not be compelled to be "a witness against himself" in "any criminal case." In the Senate, Hale protested that Davis's theory gave too little scope to the constitutional provision:

> It is not enough that you exclude [the witness] from matter that may subject him to criminal prosecution. . . . The protection of the law goes farther than that; and if it be not well settled, there is certainly very good authority for the position . . . that a man is not bound to answer to a matter that disgraces himself. Such, sir, is the authority of the best legal writers upon the law of evidence.[122]

Davis had anticipated this argument in the House. The alleged rule relieving a witness of providing evidence that might "tend to disgrace him or otherwise render him infamous," which the bill would expressly abrogate in congressional investigations, was not of constitutional dimension; it was "merely a rule of law adopted by the courts for the protection of a party, . . . subject at any moment to be modified by the courts according to their opinion, and by the statute law according to the opinion of the legislative body."[123] Senator Toombs agreed, and he argued that Hale's rule, if it was a rule, ought to be abandoned:

> Well, sir, shall society be defeated in punishing the crime that a man may cover his individual infamy? . . . I say if that was the common law, (which I deny, and the gentleman's own authority admits it to have been questionable,) it is competent for us and for the State to change the common law when it is requisite to do so . . . . If you believe protection for not making public the infamy of the infamous is a higher duty of the Legislature than bringing culprits to punishment, the reasoning of the Senator from New Hampshire is unanswerable . . . .[124]

The very existence of a separate rule, it might be added, reinforced the textual inference that the purpose of the constitutional provision was only to protect the witness from hav-

[121]Cong Globe, 34th Cong, 3d Sess 428. See Brown v Walker, 161 US 591 (1896), upholding a comparable immunity provision over four dissents.

[122]Cong Globe, 34th Cong, 3d Sess 435.

[123]Id at 428.

[124]Id at 437.

ing to help convict himself of crime.[125]

The House approved the bill 183–12, the Senate 46–3.[126] Posterity has ratified their interpretation of the relevant constitutional provisions.[127]

[125]Really? Is that consistent with what I have said about conflating the traditional categories of bankruptcy and insolvency laws, or of bills of pains and penalties and of attainder? See chapters 3 and 5.

[126]See Cong Globe, 34th Cong, 3d Sess 433, 445.

[127]Simonton himself, the cause of all the hullabaloo, was anticlimactically released from custody before the session ended, after making additional disclosures—whether in response to the new immunity provisions (which did not address his espoused ground for silence) the debates do not reveal. Id at 630.

9

Judging Congressional Elections

Article I, § 5 makes each House of Congress "judge of the elections, returns and qualifications of its own members." Other provisions give Congress additional powers relating to elections, and as we shall see in the next chapter they generated their share of controversy during the period here under scrutiny. One thing each House did as usual during this time, however, was to resolve an inordinate crop of disputes over particular elections, and with them I should like to begin.

Election contests may determine which party controls the House or Senate. They tend to be highly partisan and bloody. Sometimes they consume the better part (no, the greater part)[1] of a legislative session. Many such contests turn on questions of fact or of state law; they do not concern us here. Others raise challenging constitutional issues respecting eligibility, election procedure, and the like. We shall dig into them directly. Often, however, there are pesky threshold controversies with constitutional overtones as well; let me address them quickly ere we proceed.

I. THRESHOLD QUESTIONS

When the Twenty-third Congress first met in December 1833, each House was confronted with two claimants to a single seat. The initial question in each case was whether to seat one of them first and litigate later or to postpone seating until the controversy was resolved.

At first glance it may seem obvious that no one should be seated until it is decided who is entitled to sit. The House of Representatives took this position,[2] and William R.

[1]See Cong Globe, 36th Cong, 1st Sess 444 (Rep. Pennington): "I have been sitting here from five to six weeks, and a more wearisome or profitless time I never remember to have passed."

[2]Cong Deb, 23d Cong, 1st Sess 2160. The House dispute is reported under the name Letcher v Moore in M. St. Clair Clarke & David A. Hall, Cases of Contested Elections in Congress, 1789–1834 715–85 (Gales &

King of Alabama urged the Senate to do the same.[3] King supported his conclusion by pointing out that, if a member was provisionally given a seat ultimately found not to belong to him, an illegal vote might determine whether a bill passed or failed.[4] Ezekiel Chambers of Maryland replied that (under what we would call the de facto doctrine) an illegal vote would not invalidate the law.[5] But that was precisely the point; laws should not owe their enactment to those who have no right to vote.

Longtime House Speaker Henry Clay, now representing Kentucky in the Senate, offered the counterargument: To seat neither claimant until the dispute had finally been resolved would deprive a state in the meantime of one of its seats.[6] One of the Senate aspirants (Asher Robbins) had been seated in the preceding Congress; after what another Senator described as "a change in politics,"[7] the Rhode Island legislature had declared his reelection void.[8] Robbins thus had the prior claim, said one Anti-Jacksonian Senator after another; he should accordingly be seated until it was established that he had no right to sit.[9] North Carolina Democrat Willie Mangum turned the argument around: The Governor's certificate that Robbins's Democratic rival had won the seat should be accepted until disproved.[10] The Democrats, however, were in the minority. Robbins was seated pending a committee investigation,[11] which rejected the challenge to his election;[12] the Senate then voted (over Democratic objections) that he was entitled to his seat.[13]

In an 1849 dispute over the qualifications of James Shields as Senator from Illinois, where there was no pretender with a prior claim, the Senate accepted the state certificate of Shields's election pending resolution of the dispute.[14] In an 1840 House controversy over the New Jersey delegation John Quincy Adams had pointed out that this had been the English common-law rule,[15] and it seemed to make good sense. The House nevertheless adhered to its own precedent and refused to seat anyone until the dispute was decided.[16] The Senate continued to seat certified victors while challenges were pending

---

Seaton, 1834) [hereafter cited as Contested Elections, 1789–1834]. On the merits this dispute raised no constitutional question. It ended with a determination to seat neither contender, "it being impracticable for the House to determine with any certainty who is the rightful Representative." Id at 850; Cong Deb, 23d Cong, 1st Sess 4457.

[3]Id at 4. The Senate case is reported under the name Potter v Robbins in Contested Elections, 1789–1834 at 877–1009.

[4]Cong Deb, 23d Cong, 1st Sess 3.

[5]Id at 5.

[6]Id at 3.

[7]Id at 10 (Mississippi Sen. George Poindexter).

[8]See id at 1.

[9]Id at 2 (Sen. Poindexter); id at 3, 6–7 (Sen. Clay); id at 5 (Sen. Chambers); id at 7 (New Jersey Sen. Theodore Frelinghuysen).

[10]Id at 10.

[11]Id at 11, 19.

[12]Id at 804.

[13]Id at 1813. Everyone who addressed the question said the state legislature had no right to declare Robbins's election void, as it had attempted to do. Id at 6 (Sen. Clay); id at 7 (Sen. Frelinghuysen); id at 8 (Sen. Bibb); id at 9–10 (Sen. Mangum); id at 10 (Sen. Poindexter). The constitutional text proves at least that the legislature's decision was not conclusive: It is the Senate that is to judge the elections of its members.

[14]Cong Globe, 31st Cong, Special Senate Sess 329.

[15]Cong Globe App, 26th Cong, 1st Sess 152, citing 1 Blackstone at *180; see also Cong Globe, 26th Cong, 1st Sess 24–26 (Reps. Biddle and White).

[16]Id at 69.

throughout the period we are studying; on at least one occasion the House did so too.[17]

A further procedural complication had arisen during the 1833 House dispute. When Thomas Moore of Kentucky presented certificates attesting to his election, they were challenged as revealing both formal and material errors on their face.[18] Until the other members were sworn, Moore protested, the House did not exist; no one had the right to question his credentials.[19]

Finessed for the nonce when both contestants agreed to withdraw until the House could elect a Speaker,[20] this issue reemerged to generate a real Donnybrook when Democrats challenged the entire New Jersey House delegation in 1840. The Governor's certificate of election, protested Henry Wise of Virginia, entitled its bearers prima facie to their seats, and until the House was organized no one had a right to impugn them.[21] William Slade of Vermont took the argument a step further: Until a quorum had answered, no one could even decide whether to give the Governor's certificates prima facie effect.[22] The House clerk (himself a holdover from the preceding Congress presiding by parliamentary tradition until election of the Speaker)[23] chimed in to suggest it was not for him to usurp the House's function by deciding who was entitled to sit.[24] By not deciding whether to accept the certificate, Wise retorted, the clerk effectively decided not to seat the certified winners.[25] Not to seat them, added old John Pope of Kentucky, was to deprive New Jersey of its votes in the election for Speaker.[26]

Immobilized, the inchoate House in desperation placed former President John Quincy Adams in the chair so that it could decide whether to admit the certified claimants to their seats.[27] Adams then ruled that those with certificates could vote until the House decided otherwise.[28] Aaron Vanderpoel of New York objected that Adams had not been

[17]For Senate examples see Cong Globe, 32d Cong, 1st Sess 1–4 (Florida Sen. Stephen Mallory) and the instances from Illinois, Iowa, and Indiana noted in section III of this chapter. See also George H. Haynes, 1 The Senate of the United States: Its History and Practice 123 (Russell & Russell, 1960) (first published in 1938) [hereafter cited as Haynes], quoting a 1903 statement by Senator Hoar. In 1847, when the House received official notice that Archibald Yell of Arkansas had accepted an appointment as a volunteer colonel in the Mexican War, his successor was seated before the relevant committee reported that Yell had ceased to be a member. Cong Globe, 29th Cong, 2d Sess 341, 527. The merits of Yell's case are discussed in the text accompanying notes 142–49.

[18]See Cong Deb, 23d Cong, 1st Sess 2134–35, 2140 (Rep. Allan).

[19]Id at 2132.

[20]Id at 2135. Representative Allan objected that Kentucky was entitled to full representation for that important vote (id), but to no avail.

[21]Cong Globe, 26th Cong, 1st Sess 6–7. The New Jersey case is abstracted in D.W. Bartlett, ed, Cases of Contested Elections in Congress, 1835–1865 (HR Misc Doc 57, 38th Cong, 2d Sess) 19–33 (Government Printing Office, 1865) [hereafter cited as Contested Elections, 1835–1865].

[22]Id at 2–3.

[23]See id at 14 (Rep. Barnard).

[24]Id at 6.

[25]Id.

[26]Id at 9. All of the speakers quoted were Whigs. So were the contestants whom the Governor had certified as elected. New Jersey's votes were indeed significant, for the race for Speaker was a cliff-hanger; Robert M.T. Hunter, a states'-rights Whig from Virginia, was finally chosen on the eleventh ballot, New Jersey's competing delegations not voting. Id at 56. Pope had served in the Senate from 1807 to 1813; he had been in the House since 1837.

[27]Id at 18–20.

[28]Id at 20–21.

put in the chair to decide the question the House was debating,[29] and the House narrowly reversed his ruling—with both contested delegations participating in the vote.[30] There is more, but I shall spare you. Ultimately the House elected a Speaker (without the disputed New Jersey votes) and seated the Democratic challengers.[31]

One preliminary topic remains. In 1798 Congress had passed a statute regulating the taking of testimony in congressional election cases, but it had expired in 1804.[32] In 1842 Congress finally passed another.[33] President Tyler vetoed it, largely because it had been presented to him only forty-five minutes before Congress adjourned; he had had insufficient time, he said, to study its provisions.[34] Thus, Tyler added, he remained "uncommitted" as to similar measures that might be adopted in the future, "except so far as my opinion of the unqualified power of each House to decide for itself upon the elections, returns, and qualifications of its own members" had been expressed in his statement regarding the 1842 apportionment bill, which is discussed in the following chapter.[35] The curious who seek enlightenment in that earlier message will not find it; there Tyler merely paraphrased the constitutional provision.[36] Henry Wise of Virginia had made the same objection in more positive terms when the bill was before the House of Representatives: Each House being judge of its own elections, Congress had no right to interfere.[37] Implying that evidentiary rules were necessary and proper to the resolution of election disputes, John Campbell of South Carolina appropriately invoked the analogy of the federal courts: Congress does not usurp judicial power by prescribing rules of testimony for judicial proceedings.[38] It was a nice analogy, one might add—except that Article III contains no counterpart of the Article I, § 5 provision authorizing each House to "determine the rules of its own proceedings."[39]

[29]Id at 21.

[30]Id at 35.

[31]Id at 257. Why? Because, as the committee reported, they had received the greater number of lawful votes. Id at 241.

[32]1 Stat 537, 539, § 10 (Jan 23, 1798).

[33]See Cong Globe, 27th Cong, 2d Sess 969–70, 975.

[34]See 4 Richardson at 255, 256 (Dec 14, 1842).

[35]Id at 256.

[36]Id at 159, 160 (June 25, 1842).

[37]Cong Globe, 27th Cong, 2d Sess 968 (as paraphrased by Rep. Campbell).

[38]Id.

[39]President Fillmore, who did not share Tyler's reservations, later signed a bill providing that testimony relevant to election contests should be taken before a federal or state court and transmitted to the affected House (9 Stat 568 (Feb 19, 1851))—suggesting that Congress thought both that the House and Senate could be "judge" of their own elections without actually hearing the evidence (compare the question of the Senate's power to "try" impeachments, Nixon v United States, 506 US 224 (1993)) and that the recording of evidence for introduction in another forum was a task that could legitimately be entrusted to courts vested only with "judicial" power under Article III. The present statute, "patterned upon the Federal Rules of Civil Procedure," dates from 1969. 83 Stat 284 (Dec 5, 1869), 2 USC §§ 381 et seq (2003); see History of the United States House of Representatives, 1789–1994 36–37 (HR Doc 324, 103d Cong, 2d Sess) (1994); DeAlva S. Alexander, History and Procedure of the House of Representatives 321–22 (Houghton, Mifflin, 1916), reporting that the House often ignored the 1851 statute on the ground that, as Maine Representative Israel Washburn argued in 1858, the House as election judge was obliged to determine its own procedure (Cong Globe, 35th Cong, 1st Sess 734)—which was just what President Tyler had suggested back in 1842.

II. VACANCIES

A. Mississippi

The Twenty-fourth Congress expired March 4, 1837. Under Article I, § 4 the next Congress was to meet the first Monday in December, Congress not having specified a different day. To ensure that members of the new House would reflect the current preferences of the voters, Mississippi law postponed their election until November.[40] In early 1837, however, the economy went suddenly to pieces. To deal with the crisis President Van Buren called Congress into special session for September pursuant to Article II, § 3.[41]

To prevent Mississippi from being unrepresented at the special session, Governor Charles Lynch called a special election.[42] For Article I, § 2 authorized him to do so "[w]hen vacancies happen[ed]" in the representation of his state, and no one was qualified to represent Mississippi in the House. In accordance with his proclamation, Mississippi voters chose Congressmen to represent them during the special session. When they got to Washington, Virginia's veteran Representative Charles F. Mercer challenged their right to sit.[43]

Three arguments were made against seating the Mississippi claimants. The first was that only the legislature, not the Governor, could set the date of a special election.[44] As Hugh Legaré of South Carolina pointed out, the House had rejected this contention after full discussion in John Hoge's case over thirty years before.[45] The second argument, which was most pressed, was that no "vacanc[y]" had "happen[ed]" within the meaning of the special-election provision since no incumbent had resigned or died.[46] A similar argument had prevailed on occasion in the contexts of executive appointments and gubernatorial designation of Senators, in which the text more suggestively required that the vacancy "happen" while the legislature was not sitting.[47] As a Senate committee had said as recently as March 1837 in approving an earlier precedent that had refused to seat a Senator appointed for a special session,

> The principle asserted in that case is, that the Legislature of a State, by making elections themselves, shall provide for all vacancies which must

[40]The state statute is printed at Cong Deb, 25th Cong, 1st Sess 1062.

[41]3 Richardson at 321–22 (May 15, 1837).

[42]The Governor's proclamation appears at Cong Deb, 25th Cong, 1st Sess 1062–63.

[43]Cong Deb, 25th Cong, 1st Sess 559–60. Brief excerpts from the Mississippi proceedings can be found in Contested Elections, 1835–1865 at 9–16.

[44]Cong Deb, 25th Cong, 1st Sess 560.

[45]See id at 1187; The Jeffersonians at 75–77. Congress seems to have changed this rule in 1872, providing that elections to fill House vacancies should be held "at such time as is or may be provided by law for filling vacancies in the State . . . ." 17 Stat 28, 29, § 4 (Feb 2, 1872).

[46]Cong Deb, 25th Cong, 1st Sess 994 (Rep. Maury); id at 1112–13 (Rep. Towns). Special elections were for unexpected vacancies, said Maury; others could be dealt with by ordinary processes. Id at 1732. Special elections, added Kentucky Representative James Harlan, were for replacements, not for original members. Id at 1064. From the text one might have thought (as numerous speakers argued) that a vacancy occurred when the previous term expired. See, e.g., id at 1065 (Rep. Bronson); id at 1176 (Rep. Buchanan); id at 1200 (Rep. Howard).

[47]US Const, Art II, § 2; Art I, § 3. See The Federalist Period at 154 n.168; The Jeffersonians at 188, 316 n.214.

occur at stated or known periods; and that the expiration of a regular term of service is not such a contingency as is embraced in the second section [sic] of the first article of the constitution.[48]

In the case of presidential recess appointments, however, a succession of Attorneys General beginning with the legendary William Wirt rejected this argument on the ground, overpowering in the absence of such language or the anti-evasion policy that arguably inspired it, that the purpose of the provision was to ensure that offices were always filled.[49]

The third argument against the Mississippi delegation was the most bothersome, though for the moment it occupied little of the House's time. If there was a vacancy, argued Tennessee Representative Abram Maury, it was for the full two-year period specified in Article I, § 2; a state had no authority to elect a Representative for less than the constitutional term.[50] Thus the Governor had acted unconstitutionally in calling a special election for the special session alone, and thus the election was void; the Mississippi suitors had no right to their seats.

What a pity, if it was so. For the Governor's stratagem arguably made perfect sense. There would be no vacancy after the November elections. The only need was for someone to represent Mississippi during the special session. The Governor had no cause (and many argued no authority) to supersede the legislature's deliberate choice of a November contest for the regular term.[51] In the case of a *Senate* vacancy the constitutional text made clear that a Governor's "temporary appointment[]" was to last only until the legislature could choose a permanent replacement in the normal way.[52]

[48]Sen Journal, 24th Cong, 2d Sess 366–67, printing Senator Grundy's report in the case of Ambrose Sevier. The committee argued that Sevier's case was different in that at the time of his initial election the legislature could not have foreseen that his term would expire before its next meeting, since it had not yet been decided to which class of Senators he would belong. Apparently unpersuaded, the Senate tabled the motion to seat Sevier, and the session came to a close. Id. The earlier case involved Connecticut aspirant James Lanman in 1825 (Contested Elections, 1789–1834 at 871). Representative Pennybacker was right that Lanman's case was factually distinguishable (and so was Sevier's), since he had been appointed before the vacancy occurred. Cong Deb, 25th Cong, 1st Sess 998. The committee's reasoning, however, was broader. In a later debate North Carolina Senator George Badger questioned the reasoning of the *Lanman* decision: Given the purpose of the provision for recess appointments, the Governor should be able to appoint to a new term, because the end of the preceding term created a vacancy; Article I, § 3 provided that the seats of each class of initial Senators should be "vacated" at the end of the second, fourth, and sixth years. Cong Globe App, 30th Cong, 2d Sess 345.

[49]See 1 Op AG 631, 632–33 (Oct 22, 1823) (Attorney General Wirt); 2 Op AG 525, 526–28 (Jul 19, 1832) (Attorney General Roger Taney). See also 2 Farrand at 231 (Edmund Randolph), arguing that interim executive appointments were necessary "to prevent inconvenient chasms in the Senate." Successors of various political colorations tended to adhere to these opinions. See, e.g., the elaborate argument of Andrew Johnson's Attorney General Henry Stanbery, 12 Op AG 32, 34–38 (Aug 30, 1866). This argument was repeated, with corresponding citations, in the debate over the Mississippi election. Cong Deb, 25th Cong, 1st Sess 996 (Rep. Pennybacker); id at 1180–83 (South Carolina Rep. (and later U.S. Attorney General) Hugh Legaré); id at 1191–92 (Rep. Haynes); id at 1200–1201 (Maryland Rep. Benjamin Howard). See also HR Rep 2, 25th Cong, 1st Sess 3 (1837) (Rep. Buchanan, for the committee majority): "[A]ll the evils arising from vacancies by death or resignation would exist" if Mississippi's claimants were denied their seats.

[50]Cong Deb, 25th Cong, 1st Sess 1731. See also id at 1214 (Rep. John Quincy Adams).

[51]It was the legislature, after all, that was given explicit responsibility to prescribe "[t]he times, places and manner" of congressional elections. US Const, Art I, § 4. See Cong Deb, 25th Cong, 1st Sess 1064–65 (Rep. Harlan); id at 1108–10 (Rep. Towns); id at 1212–14 (Rep. J.Q. Adams); id at 1731 (Rep. Maury).

[52]US Const, Art I, § 3. Just how long such an appointment lasted in the absence of a legislative decision turned out to be a subject of heated debate. See section II C of this chapter.

Once the voters had chosen new Representatives in one election, however, it seemed wasteful and inefficient to hold another. In the case of the Senate a temporary appointment was necessary to ensure that the legislature, not the Governor, filled the position whenever it could. The House was different: Whether the election was special or general, it was the people who made the decision.[53]

The House voted 118–101 to seat the contested delegation; their election was not void.[54] One would like to think what was decisive was the purpose of the provision, or as Tennessee's Hopkins Turney said the gravity of denying the state its representation.[55] Would it be unduly cynical to suggest that the determinative factor may have been that the challenged suitors were Democrats, and that their party had a majority in the House?

But the shouting was not yet over. Having held a special election in July, Mississippi held its regular election in November. John Claiborne and Samuel Gholson, who had been seated for the special session, were defeated. Kentucky Representative John Pope moved to seat their victorious rivals, Seargent Prentiss and Thomas Word, who were Whigs.[56]

The Governor's proclamation, you recall, had invited the people to elect Representatives for the special session only; the most straightforward argument for not reseating the September Democrats was that their temporary mandates had expired. Vermont Whig William Slade, who unlike most of his party had argued that they should be seated for the special session, had made the argument then that would unseat them now: There was a vacancy only until the November election.[57]

Interestingly, only one advocate of seating the Whig claimants in the regular session repeated this argument.[58] One of Representative Maury's arguments against seating the Democrats in September had been that the Governor had acted illegally in attempting to shorten their term; consistency, if nothing else, made it difficult for the Whigs to repudiate his position. The Democrats, in turn, stood to gain by maintaining that their comrades had been elected for the full two years, as most of them had contended all along.[59] So there was a broad consensus when the regular session convened that Claiborne and Gholson had been chosen for the entire term; speakers on both sides declared their time of service could not constitutionally be limited.

This reluctance to argue that the Democrats' terms had expired placed the Whigs in an awkward position; they were forced to urge that the House rescind its earlier decision to seat their rivals, on the ground that the special election was void. Isaac Bronson, Democrat of New York, concisely defined the issue: Nearly everyone agreed the Governor could not limit the term of those chosen in special election to three months; the

[53]See Cong Deb, 25th Cong, 1st Sess 1106 (Rep. Turney).

[54]Id at 1216.

[55]Id at 1107–8.

[56]Cong Globe, 25th Cong, 2d Sess 56.

[57]Cong Deb, 25th Cong, 1st Sess 1738. See also id at 1194 (Rhode Island Rep. Joseph Tillinghast). Arkansas Representative Archibald Yell, who had won both special and general elections in 1837, was sworn in twice; he explained that he had been elected only for the special session the first time. Cong Globe, 25th Cong, 2d Sess 56.

[58]See id at 146 (Maryland Rep. Daniel Jenifer).

[59]See, e.g., Cong Globe App, 25th Cong, 2d Sess 68–69 (Georgia Rep. Charles Haynes); id at 125 (New York Rep. Isaac Bronson).

only question was whether in attempting to do so he had invalidated the election itself.[60] He had not, Bronson concluded; the attempted limitation was mere surplusage, as if the sheriff had inserted the wrong term in a newspaper notice announcing the election.[61] Besides, the House had already determined the matter by "solemn judicial decision"; though the parties might be different, the decision ought not to be reviewed.[62]

The House did rescind its prior determination, but it refused to seat the challengers.[63] Thinking they had been elected for two years, said Claiborne and Gholson, they had not campaigned for reelection; their supporters had boycotted the November contest.[64] Since that election therefore did not represent the views of the Mississippi people,[65] the House rejected the winners as well as the losers.[66] The state was without representation until May 1838, when Prentiss and Word triumphed in a third election and finally took their seats.[67]

It was all Mississippi's fault, said cantankerous old John Quincy Adams, if it ended up without voices in the House; the state should have chosen new Congressmen before their predecessors' terms had expired.[68] Indeed, James Buchanan implied, by postponing the regular election until November Mississippi had failed to live up to its constitutional duty: It was the state's obligation to see to it that its seats were always filled.[69]

[60]Id at 125.

[61]Id at 125–26. Buchanan's committee report had made this argument when Claiborne and Gholson had presented their credentials the first time, after agreeing that "[t]he gentlemen elected are members for the whole unexpired term of the twenty-fifth Congress, or they are not members at all." HR Rep 2, 25th Cong, 1st Sess 3 (1837). The conclusion that the Governor's innocent misrepresentation was immaterial seems questionable: The voters had thought they were choosing Representatives only for the special session.

[62]Cong Globe App, 25th Cong, 2d Sess 126. See also HR Rep 379, 25th Cong, 2d Sess 25–26, 29–30 (1838).

[63]Cong Globe, 25th Cong, 2d Sess 160. For the roll-call vote on the earlier motion to substitute rescission for a resolution rejecting the Whig pretenders see id at 150. The vote on that motion was 119–112.

[64]Id at 57 (Rep. Claiborne); id at 155 (Rep. Gholson); see also Cong Globe App, 25th Cong, 2d Sess 126–27 (Rep. Bronson).

[65]See id at 94 (South Carolina Rep. Robert Barnwell Rhett); id at 95 (Alabama Rep. Joshua Martin). Virginia Democrat James M. Mason, who like most Democrats had voted in September to seat Claiborne and Gholson, voted in January to rescind that decision: "[F]rom subsequent examination and reflection," he said, he "had come to the determination that the better plan would be to send both the delegations back to the people." Cong Globe, 25th Cong, 2d Sess 148, 150.

[66]By what authority? Rhett said it was the House's duty, "whenever it has reason to believe that an election has been unfair, and, therefore, might not be a correct expression of the popular will, to send it back to the people." Cong Globe App, 25th Cong, 2d Sess 94. But that had not been the general understanding; prior practice confirmed the inference from the state's responsibility to regulate the time, place, and manner of elections that in the absence of federal legislation the House in judging its members' elections was to look to state law. See The Federalist Period at 197 n.185. Rhett and Martin's alternative theory was arguably better: Though erroneous, the House's decision to seat Claiborne and Gholson was binding until rescinded; the November election was therefore void. Cong Globe App, 25th Cong, 2d Sess 93, 95. The weak point in this argument was that the earlier resolution had not made clear that Claiborne and Gholson had been seated for the whole term; it said only that as "duly elected members of the 25th Congress" they were "entitled to take their seats." Cong Deb, 25th Cong, 1st Sess 799, 1217.

[67]See Cong Globe, 25th Cong, 2d Sess 416.

[68]Cong Deb, 25th Cong, 1st Sess 1214–15.

[69]Id at 1176. Strangely, Mississippi did not act to prevent recurrence of this fiasco until 1856, when it provided by statute for a special election whenever Congress was called into special session after a term expired and before the next general election, "the persons so elected" to "serve for the entire term." Miss Laws 1856–57 (Adjourned Sess) 62, 72–73, Art 34 (Dec 16, 1856). This legislation removed two of the objections that had

What, then, did the House finally decide? That the resolution seating the Democrats was improper, and that neither they nor their adversaries were entitled to sit.[70] Why? There is no single answer. The resolutions were bare conclusions; members could have supported them for any of number of reasons. There appeared to be broad agreement, however, that special elections to fill House vacancies had to do so for the entire remainder of the unexpired term.

B. Kentucky

Fast-forward, if you please, to the Thirty-second Congress, in 1851. On December 17 of that year the great Henry Clay, three-time savior of the Union, announced his resignation, effective September 1, 1852. He had resigned from one or the other House before, but now he was old and ailing; this time it would be for keeps.

Pursuant to Article I, § 3 the Kentucky legislature elected a successor. Not a replacement; no one could replace Henry Clay. But Clay had had the foresight to give the legislature a grace period in which to make its own choice, in hopes of averting the second-best alternative of a temporary appointment by the Governor.

Clay had then had the bad taste to die on June 29, before his resignation became effective—and thus before the successor the legislature had named was supposed to take his place.[71] Seeing no alternative, the Governor made a temporary appointment—to last, as the Constitution seemed to provide, only until the legislature's choice could step in.[72] Here is the governing provision:

> [T]he Senate of the United States shall be composed of two Senators from each State, chosen by the legislature thereof for six years . . . , and if vacancies happen by resignation or otherwise during the recess of the legislature of any State, the executive thereof may make temporary appointments until the next meeting of the legislature, which shall then fill such

---

been raised in 1837 but not the third; it could still be argued that there was no "vacancy" to be filled within the meaning of Article I, § 2. In 1871 the Mississippi legislature finally put the matter to rest as far as that state was concerned by providing for congressional elections in November of each even-numbered year, five months before the outgoing Congress expired. Miss Rev Code 1871, § 360 (May 13, 1871). Congress took the matter into its own hands in 1872, pursuant to its Article I, § 4 authority to supersede state regulations respecting the time of elections. From 1876 on

> the Tuesday next after the first Monday in November, in every second year . . . , is hereby fixed and established as the day for the election, in each of [the] States and Territories, of Representatives and Delegates to the Congress commencing on the fourth day of March next thereafter.

17 Stat 28, § 3 (Feb 2, 1872). Congressional elections have been held on that Tuesday ever since. See 2 USC §§ 1, 7 (2003).

[70]Cong Globe, 25th Cong, 2d Sess 150, 160.

[71]See Cong Globe, 32d Cong, 1st Sess 1631. Clay was the last of the Great Triumvirate; Calhoun and Webster had gone not long before. See id at 1636 (Sen. Seward): "[T]he great lights of the Senate have set."

[72]See Senator Seward's concise statement of the foregoing facts, Cong Globe, 32d Cong, 2d Sess 93.

vacancies.[73]

Two principles emerge unmistakably from the constitutional language: A state should always have two Senators, and whenever practicable the legislature should choose them. James Jones, a self-educated farmer and Tennessee Whig, identified these twin purposes with singular clarity.[74] Thomas Jefferson Rusk, a freshman Democrat from Texas, echoed them concisely a few days later:

> Then in my opinion, we gather this—and it is a conviction from which I cannot escape—that it was the intention of the framers of the Constitution to vest primarily in the Legislatures of the States the power to choose the Senators . . . [and] to keep the Senate full . . . .

"I . . . cannot consent," said Rusk, "to give so technical a construction to the Constitution as to defeat the intention of its framers."[75] It will be well to keep this lodestar in view as we descend into the morass of technicalities that many of Mr. Rusk's fellow Democrats sowed in an effort to frustrate the purposes of the Constitution.

As both Jones and Rusk argued, Kentucky had done just what the Framers had envisioned. The legislature had filled the vacancy that would be created by Clay's resignation; the Governor had closed the earlier gap created by his unexpected death. David Meriwether, the Governor's interim appointee, should serve until September 1; Archibald Dixon, the legislature's choice, should replace him thereafter. Kentucky would always have two Senators, and the legislature would have chosen them whenever it could.[76]

That is what happened, and we can be glad of that. In the meantime, however, there was much thrashing and beating of wings. Neither Meriwether nor Dixon was permitted to serve without a struggle.[77]

No sooner was Meriwether installed in July 1852 than Senator Jesse Bright of Indiana (who like Meriwether was a Democrat) declared for future reference that he regarded the Governor's attempt to limit Meriwether's term as a nullity. The Constitution itself, said Bright, specified that an executive appointee was to serve until the legislature chose his successor; the Governor had no right to alter his constitutional term. Andrew Butler of South Carolina, another Democrat, agreed that the Governor had no authority to "limit the tenure of office under the Constitution of the United States." But, he said, the issue might never arise. It would be time enough to decide it if Mr. Dixon ever claimed the seat; there

[73]US Const, Art I, § 3. Since popular election of Senators was introduced in 1913, executive appointments (if authorized by state legislation) continue "until the people fill the vacancies as the legislature may direct." US Const, Amend 17.

[74]Cong Globe, 32d Cong, 2d Sess 14–15.

[75]Id at 93.

[76]One is tempted to suggest that the constitutional plan would be even better served if (as Seward mused at one point, id at 5) the legislature's choice were accelerated and its designee took office on Clay's death. The legislature had indicated who should be the next Senator, the argument would run, and it should make no difference when he stepped in. It is clear, however, that a Senator chosen for the Thirty-third Congress could not take over if his predecessor died while the Thirty-second was still in session; the period for which he was elected had not yet begun. Nor had that of Mr. Dixon begun when Clay died; he was chosen to take office on September 1, not whenever the seat became vacant.

[77]A highly truncated report of these proceedings is given in Contested Elections, 1835–1865 at 611–12.

was no need to reach out to resolve hypothetical questions.

Not so, said California Democrat William Gwin. "[I]f the Governor has put an improper limitation upon it," he said, "[i]t is no appointment at all," and Meriwether was not entitled to sit. Wrong, replied James Cooper, a Pennsylvania Whig. If the Governor's effort to limit Meriwether's term was improper, the limitation and not the appointment was void; it was "mere surplusage, which does not affect the Senator's right to the seat." Agreeing with Butler that the question of the validity of the limitation might never need to be decided, Cooper too urged that it "be passed over until the occasion presents itself"; and "[t]he conversation," the reporter tells us, "therefore dropped."[78]

The House, you remember, had grappled with a parallel question in considering the challenge to the Mississippi delegation in 1837. There too a Governor had attempted to limit the term of a member of Congress chosen by extraordinary process to the emergency that made it necessary. The predominant opinion in the House seemed to be that he had no power to do so; Article I, § 2 did not provide for temporary elections to the House.[79] Article I, § 3, in contrast, *did* provide for "temporary appointments" to the Senate. Moreover, the reason that section made emergency appointments temporary was that it was desirable that Senators be selected by the legislature, not the Governor. In naming Dixon to assume the position on Clay's retirement, the legislature had already picked his successor. The same consideration that had argued against limiting the Mississippi Representatives' terms argued in favor of limiting Mr. Meriwether's executive appointment: Just as it was pointless to require a second election after Mississippi voters had chosen new Representatives, it was pointless to require the Kentucky legislature to vote a second time after it had chosen a new Senator.

Having failed in his argument that the Governor's effort to limit Meriwether's term vitiated his appointment entirely, Gwin returned to the attack when Dixon presented his credentials from the state legislature for the following session in December 1852. As several speakers had suggested when Meriwether came to the Senate, the limitation itself (said Gwin) was void. Since the legislature had not subsequently met to choose his successor, he concluded, Meriwether was still in office; there was no vacancy for Dixon to fill.[80]

For reasons derived largely from the twin purposes of the constitutional provision, numerous Senators rejected Gwin's argument on the ground that the legislature had already chosen Dixon to sit from September 1; the vacancy the Governor was authorized to fill expired at that time.[81] Indeed a clear majority of Senators must have taken that position, for the Senate voted 27–16 to seat Dixon,[82] and no one repeated Gwin's earlier argument that Meriwether's appointment was void.

Ready to move on? No. For the alleged continuance of Meriwether's mandate was not the only asserted impediment to Dixon's pretension; Gwin and his fellow conspirators had another string to their bow. Dixon had no right to the seat, Gwin argued, because the

[78]Cong Globe, 32d Cong, 1st Sess 1783–84.

[79]See subpart A of this section.

[80]Cong Globe, 32d Cong, 2d Sess 1, 2. See also id at 62 (Connecticut Sen. Isaac Toucey); id at 91 (Illinois Sen. Stephen A. Douglas); id at 92 (Michigan Sen. Lewis Cass); id at 95 (Virginia Sen. James Mason).

[81]See, e.g., id at 4 (Ohio Sen. Salmon P. Chase); id at 14–15 (Sen. Jones); id at 47 (Kentucky Sen. Joseph Underwood); id at 72–73 (Mississippi Sen. Walter Brooke); id at 93 (Sen. Rusk).

[82]Id at 96.

legislature had had no authority to elect him. The term for which Clay had been elected had not expired when his successor was chosen, and he was still in the Senate; his resignation would not take effect until September. There was thus no vacancy to be filled; the legislature had no power to fill a vacancy that had not yet occurred.[83]

Absurd, cried Dixon's supporters, absurd. *Most* Senators, John Davis of Massachusetts reminded his colleagues, were chosen while their predecessors were still in office.[84] That was the only way, said Joseph Underwood of Kentucky, to be sure of avoiding the interregnum the Constitution was designed to prevent.[85] (It was the refusal of the Mississippi legislature to provide for electing Representatives in advance, you recollect, that had landed that state in the soup in 1837.) When the Governor of Arkansas had reappointed Ambrose Sevier while still a Senator to attend a special session after his term expired, Underwood added, the Senate had confirmed that a Governor had no power to make an initial appointment—but not because there was no vacancy until the earlier term was over. Rather the Senate, after a thoughtful committee report by Tennessee's respected Felix Grundy, had concluded that the legislature *ought* to have elected a successor in advance.[86]

Democratic foes of seating Dixon (for Dixon, as you may have gathered, was a Whig) were backed against the wall. Advance elections for *regular* Senate terms, argued Illinois's Stephen A. Douglas, were distinguishable, for they did not fill vacancies at all:

> Where a senatorial term has expired by its own limitations under the Constitution, and an absence of representation results from that cause, it is not a vacancy within the meaning of the Constitution.

In the absence of congressional action, Douglas concluded, a state might choose its regular Senators whenever it liked, for Article I, § 4 left it to the states to determine the time, place, and manner of their election. Dixon, however, had been selected to fill a purported vacancy created by Clay's future resignation; and at the time of his selection there was no vacancy to fill.[87]

One difficulty with this argument was precedent. As numerous speakers pointed out, it was common for members to resign in advance, as Clay did, and for the legislature to fill the resulting vacancies before they actually occurred.[88] When Clay himself had resigned once before (in 1842), observed North Carolina's Willie Mangum, the legislature had filled the prospective vacancy while he was still in office, and no one had complained.[89] Ah, said Douglas, but in those cases the vacancy previously announced had actually occurred.[90] Until the specified date arrived, added Isaac Toucey of Connecticut, Clay's resignation was necessarily conditional, and it was voided by Clay's death: No

[83]Id at 16. See also id at 17 (Sen. Bradbury); id at 62 (Sen. Toucey); id at 95 (Sen. Mason).

[84]Id at 75. See also id at 4 (Sen. Seward); id at 46, 59 (Sen. Underwood).

[85]Id at 46; see also id at 17–18 (Georgia Sen. William Dawson).

[86]Id 46–47; see note 48 and accompanying text.

[87]Cong Globe, 32d Cong, 2d Sess 90–91.

[88]See id at 4 (Sen. Brooke); id at 14 (Sen. Jones); id at 17–18 (Sen. Dawson); id at 75 (Sen. Davis); id at 93–94 (Sen. Seward).

[89]Id at 2. Originally elected to the Senate as a Jacksonian Democrat (see text accompanying note 10), Mangum had returned in 1840 as a Whig.

[90]Cong Globe, 32d Cong, 2d Sess 91.

Senator could resign his office after he died.[91]

The Senate had already concluded, in an 1815 contest, that a Senator could not revoke his resignation—at least not after the specified date had arrived.[92] But the more pertinent response to Douglas's distinction was that it made no sense in terms of the clear policies that underlay the vacancy provision. As Underwood and others argued, there was the same necessity for avoiding a gap in the state's representation when a Senator resigned as when his term expired and therefore the same justification for filling the seat before it was empty. Neither Douglas nor anyone else made the slightest effort to explain why the Framers would have wanted to create a system so inconsistent as the one he attributed to them.

Toucey did offer horror stories to show that filling offices after prospective resignations could not possibly have been the Framers' plan. What, he asked, if the entire Supreme Court were to resign effective several years in the future? To permit the incumbent President to fill their seats prospectively, Toucey suggested, would project his authority into the future at the expense of his successors; it would "install, with a degree of permanency unknown in any other department, the principles of the Administration about to go out by the verdict of popular opinion."[93]

The trouble with *this* argument was that it applied with even more force to anticipatory appointments for regular Senate terms.[94] Douglas conceded as much, and that seemed to put the last nail in his coffin. For the consensus that legislatures could elect Senators before their predecessors' terms had expired seemed to reflect (and I think correctly) the conviction that it was more central to the constitutional plan to avoid a gap in representation than to fret about hypothetical abuses of power—especially since, as Douglas acknowledged in the case of an expiring term, Congress could preclude abuses by regulating the time of election under Article I, § 4.[95]

As I have said, the Senate voted by a substantial margin to seat Dixon, despite the subtleties of Senator Douglas's partisan imagination. The breakdown was unusual for an election dispute and quite heartening. For several Democrats put party considerations to one side and joined Thomas Rusk in refusing "to give so technical a construction to the Constitution as to defeat the intention of its framers."

C. Vermont

Yet another question of the meaning of Article I, § 3's provision for filling Senate vacancies was presented shortly after the Thirty-third Congress met for its first regular session in December 1853. William Upham, whose term as Senator from Vermont was to expire in 1855, had died in January 1853, when the state legislature was not in session. The

[91]Id at 61.

[92]See Sen Journal, 13th Cong, 3d Sess 607–8 (Jan 20, 1815), Contested Elections, 1789–1834 at 869–70 (Case of Jesse Bledsoe). This precedent, much cited by Dixon's supporters, was distinguished by his detractors on the ground suggested in the text. E.g., Cong Globe, 32d Cong, 2d Sess 62 (Sen. Toucey).

[93]Id at 61.

[94]See id at 71 (Sen. Hale), noting the theoretical possibility (which he dismissed as so far-fetched as to be unworthy of consideration) that some overly ambitious legislature might attempt to appoint Senators for the next hundred years.

[95]Id at 90.

Governor had given Samuel Phelps a recess appointment, and Phelps had sat in the Senate until March, when a special session ended. Thereafter the Vermont legislature had held its annual session and adjourned without filling the vacancy. William H. Seward of New York, who like Phelps was a Whig, raised the question whether Phelps was still entitled to his seat,[96] and a lengthy debate ensued.[97]

Here again is the gist of the governing provision:

> [I]f vacancies happen [in the Senate] by resignation or otherwise during the recess of the legislature of any State, the executive thereof may make temporary appointments until the next meeting of the legislature, which shall then fill such vacancies.[98]

A vacancy had happened during the legislative recess, and the governor had made a temporary appointment. The question was when it expired.

Along the way to the Senate's decision to accept Archibald Dixon as Senator from Kentucky two Senators had opined that a gubernatorial appointment did not expire, as other speakers seemed to assume, the moment the legislature next convened. The phrase "until the next meeting of the legislature," they argued, limited only the period during which the Governor could make an appointment, not the length of his appointee's term. Precedent, they argued, supported this conclusion; both Robert Winthrop of Massachusetts (in 1851) and John McRae of Mississippi (in 1852) had been permitted to sit until their successors were actually chosen, although their state legislatures were already in session. In the case of *presidential* recess appointments, said New Hampshire's John Hale, Article II, § 2 specified that the commission itself expired at the end of the next legislative session. When the Framers intended to limit the duration of executive appointments, Phelps added in 1854, they said so.[99]

I must confess this interpretation had never occurred to me, but it seems correct; otherwise there would be yet another gap in representation whenever the state legislature convened while the Senate was in session, contrary to the purpose of the provision.[100]

The Judiciary Committee, to which the question of Phelps's status was referred, divided three to two.[101] Indiana Democrat John Pettit, for the majority, restated the reasons why Phelps was still a Senator. The limiting clause, he said, was ambiguous; it should be interpreted to accomplish its goal. "[T]he design of the framers," said Pettit, "was that

[96]Cong Globe, 33d Cong, 1st Sess 103.

[97]Phelps's case is briefly recounted in Contested Elections, 1835–1865 at 613–18.

[98]US Const, Art I, § 3.

[99]Cong Globe, 32d Cong, 2d Sess 4 (Sen. Brooke); id at 70–71 (Sen. Hale); Cong Globe App, 33d Cong, 1st Sess 357 (Sen. Phelps). Winthrop's case had been fervently debated after he presented his successor's credentials and withdrew, since some Senators were not convinced that the absent successor (Robert Rantoul) had accepted his election. The matter was finally tabled without a decision after Senator Hale pointed out that neither Winthrop nor Rantoul was claiming the seat. See Cong Globe, 31st Cong, 2d Sess 459–78 (1851). Two weeks later the nonchalant Rantoul appeared and was sworn in for the remaining ten days of the term, id at 660. He served as a Representative in the next Congress, until his death in August 1852.

[100]This argument, like others mentioned in this section, had also been made during the Winthrop controversy in 1851. See Cong Globe, 31st Cong, 2d Sess 462 (Sen. Hale); id at 462–63 (Sen. Walker); id at 463 (Sens. Rusk and Downs); id at 465 (Sen. Underwood); id at 466 (Sen. Bradbury); id at 477 (Sen. Mason); id at 478 (Sen. Baldwin).

[101]S Rep 34, 33d Cong, 1st Sess (1854), reprinted at Cong Globe, 33d Cong, 1st Sess 250.

there should be two Senators from each State in commission at all times ready for the exigencies of the public service." For the Framers had prescribed that each state was to have two Senators, and "in order to avoid anything like a hiatus, or vacancy" they had provided two distinct means of selecting them.

> When the Legislature is in session—is in a condition to act and to exercise the primary authority—it has power to do so; but, inasmuch as the Legislature is not always in that condition, and the State always has an executive, the Constitution has conferred upon the executive the right to make temporary appointments, so that the Senate can at all times be kept full . . . .

To hold that the Governor's appointee must "take his hat and walk out at the moment when the Legislature meets," Pettit concluded, would frustrate this purpose; for if he did the Senate would not be "composed of two Senators from each State, as the Constitution provides that it shall be." Thus until the legislature met the Governor could appoint temporary Senators, and they would remain in office until the legislature replaced them or their term expired.[102]

Mr. Pettit was an honest Democrat and a persuasive one.[103]

Phelps, who in accord with Senate practice had remained in his seat pending resolution of the controversy, ably repeated the relevant arguments,[104] and others supported him.[105] The whole idea of a temporary appointment, said Phelps's Vermont colleague Solomon Foot, was to keep the position occupied until it was permanently filled.[106]

Most Senators wouldn't buy it. "[U]ntil the next meeting of the Legislature," they argued, *did* limit the duration of a temporary appointment, not just the time during which the Governor could make it.[107] The precedents established only that the Governor's appointee could continue to sit while the legislature was in session. For the "meeting" of the legislature meant the entire session, not its commencement; the legislature could not be expected to fill the vacancy immediately.[108] The constitutional purpose was to ensure not that the seat always be filled (no provision could guarantee that), but rather that there always be someone with *authority* to fill it.[109] The dominant theme of the constitutional

[102]Id at 250–51, adding another precedent: In 1809 the Senate had formally resolved that Samuel Smith of Maryland, who had a temporary appointment, might continue to serve although the legislature had already convened. Sen Journal, 11th Cong, 1st Sess 381 (Jun 6, 1809).

[103]We have previously encountered him in opposition to the election of congressional chaplains, in chapter 5.

[104]Cong Globe App, 33d Cong, 1st Sess 356–69.

[105]Cong Globe, 33d Cong, 1st Sess 303–4 (Sen. Williams); id at 630–32 (Sen. Foot); id at 642 (Sen. Geyer); id at 644 (Sen. Walker); id at 645–46 (Sen. Clayton).

[106]Id at 632.

[107]Several Senators had argued in Winthrop's case that the Governor's appointment expired when the state legislature convened. Cong Globe, 31st Cong, 2d Sess 460 (Sen. Rhett); id at 463 (Sen. Borland); id at 464 (Sen. Berrien).

[108]For suggestions of this interpretation during the earlier Winthrop debate see id at 461 (Sens. Clay, Butler, and Davis)); id at 462 (Sen. Seward).

[109]Cong Globe, 33d Cong, 1st Sess 314–15 (Sen. Butler); id at 316–17 (Sen. Badger); id at 639–40 (Sen. Mason); id at 640–41 (Sen. Toucey); id at 643–44 (Sen. Stuart); Cong Globe App, 33d Cong, 1st Sess 120–26 (Sen. Bayard); id at 369–71 (Sen. Badger).

provision, said James Bayard of Delaware, was that the legislature should make the choice whenever it could; temporary appointments were meant for times when the legislature was unable to elect a Senator, not when it was unwilling to do so.[110]

It was not true, Bayard added, that the Governor could fill vacancies whenever necessary to avoid a gap in representation. The plain language of the provision showed that he could not do so if the seat became vacant while the legislature was in session. Moreover, it had long been established that, even if a vacancy arose while the legislature was in recess, the Governor could no longer fill it after the legislature had met and adjourned,[111] and that he could not make a temporary appointment at the beginning of a senatorial term.[112] If the legislature chose not to elect a Senator, said Mason and Toucey, the Governor had no business overruling its decision.[113]

That was a new one: The sovereign right of the state legislature to violate its constitutional duty.[114] In any case, said Foot, the fact that the Governor could not make a new appointment after the legislature met did not justify holding that the end of a legislative session terminated a valid appointment he had already made.[115] The fact that the constitutional text did not fully carry out the Framers' purpose, added Henry Geyer of Missouri, was no reason to construe doubtful provisions so as to exacerbate the problem.[116]

The Senate voted 26–12 that Phelps was no longer entitled to his seat.[117] Vermont had only one Senator between March 17 and October 13, 1854.[118]

III. THE THREE I'S

A. Illinois

In professional baseball, not so many years ago, there was a minor league known as the Three-I League—composed, as you would expect, of teams from the three adjoining states of Indiana, Illinois, and Iowa.[119] During the mid-1850's the same three states were

[110]Id at 121, 124.

[111]Of course not, rejoined Foot: He had authority to make appointments only "until the next meeting of the legislature." Cong Globe, 33d Cong, 1st Sess 631.

[112]Cong Globe App, 33d Cong, 1st Sess 121–22, 126 (Sen. Bayard). The relevant precedents are those of Kensey Johns and James Lanman, respectively. For Johns see 4 Annals at 77; The Federalist Period at 154 n.168; for Lanman see Contested Elections, 1789–1834 at 871. Others had questioned the *Lanman* decision on grounds similar to those advanced in favor of Senator Phelps. See the discussion of this issue in connection with the 1837 challenge to the Mississippi delegation, notes 46–48 and accompanying text.

[113]Cong Globe, 33d Cong, 1st Sess 640.

[114]See US Const, Art I, § 3: "The Senate . . . shall be composed of two Senators from each state, chosen by the legislature thereof . . . ."

[115]Cong Globe, 33d Cong, 1st Sess 631.

[116]Id at 642.

[117]Id at 646.

[118]See Biographical Directory at 158 nn.41–42.

[119]Its official name was the Illinois-Iowa-Indiana League, but the nickname was soon ubiquitous.

> Though it disbanded after the 1961 season, the Three-I League remains one of the most significant low minor league operations [Class B, in this case] in the history of the National Association of Professional Baseball Leagues.

linked together in quite another way, as all three faced challenges to the election of their spokesmen in the Senate.

Illinois was first at bat, when Lyman Trumbull presented his credentials in December 1855. Destined to become a Republican All-Star during the Civil War and Reconstruction, Trumbull at this time was a Democrat; but he was in the doghouse with a many of his teammates. Non-Democrats in the Illinois legislature had helped bring him to the plate, and influential Northwestern Democrats did their best to throw him out.[120]

It was Lewis Cass of Michigan, unsuccessful Democratic contender for the Presidency in 1848, who tossed Trumbull the first curve. As a Justice of the Illinois Supreme Court, said Cass, Trumbull was on the disabled list: Under the Illinois Constitution he was ineligible to the Senate.[121] No I wasn't, said Trumbull; I resigned from the court nearly two years before my election.[122] Yes you were, said the Governor of Illinois in a communication read to the Senate; judges were disqualified for a year after the term for which they were chosen expired, and you were sent to the Bench for nine years in 1852.[123]

John Crittenden, Kentucky Whig, argued that the ineligibility provision was inapplicable: Its purposes were to prevent judicial influence on the legislature's choice and legislative influence on the judges; neither was a concern in Trumbull's case, since he had been out of uniform for more than the prescribed year.[124] Henry Foote, Mississippi Democrat, agreed: The judicial term for which Trumbull had been elected was over, for he was no longer a judge.[125]

The state legislature, said Trumbull, found me eligible when it elected me to the Senate.[126] Who are we, asked Crittenden, to question the state's interpretation of its own constitution?[127] The legislature's interpretation was binding, added Mississippi's other Democratic Senator, Stephen Adams.[128] Sorry, Sir, but that ball was foul: The legislature's interpretation might be entitled to considerable respect, but the Senate was the umpire; the Constitution made each House judge of its members' qualifications.[129]

The meaning of the state constitution was not of much importance (except to the contending parties), but there was an alternative objection to Trumbull's disqualification that was. Article I, § 3 laid down the qualifications for Senators, and the list was exclu-

---

When times got tough, the league expanded into such exotic lands as Wisconsin, Nebraska, and Kansas, but to no avail; the loss of four "top" Iowa teams to a competing though inferior league "was a serious problem that could not be overcome." The information in this footnote was derived from the website of the Baseball Hall of Fame (http://www.baseballhalloffame.org) in August 2001.

[120]For an oversimplified and misleading account of Trumbull's case see Contested Elections, 1835–1865 at 618–21.

[121]Cong Globe, 34th Cong, 1st Sess 1. Following Senate precedent (see text accompanying notes 2–17), Trumbull was seated pending resolution of the challenge. Id at 1.

[122]Id at 58.

[123]Id at 343.

[124]Id at 548.

[125]Id at 581. The President's salary, Foote explained, could not constitutionally be reduced during his term; but that did not mean he could collect it after he resigned. Id at 582.

[126]Id at 467.

[127]Id at 548.

[128]Id at 582.

[129]US Const, Art I, § 5. Under this provision both the Senate and the House had consistently made independent determinations as to the construction of state laws. See note 66.

sive; the state had no power to make its judges ineligible to the Senate.[130]

Whigs like Seward and Crittenden made this argument; so did good Southern Democrats like Andrew Butler, James Mason, and Foote.[131] In William McCreery's case in 1807 a number of Representatives had drawn the same inference of exclusivity from the analogous provision of the preceding section governing eligibility to the House. Madison's insistence that the Convention had meant to afford the voters a broad range of choice had given McCreery the better of the argument then, and it gave Trumbull the better of it now.[132] George Pugh, an Ohio Democrat, argued that because Illinois could regulate the time, place, and manner of Senate elections it could instruct its legislature not to count votes for state judges,[133] but he was wrong; as we have seen, the Constitution made separate provision for the qualifications of the players.[134]

The House, said Butler, had decided in McCreery's case that the states could not add to the constitutional list of qualifications—age, citizenship, and residence.[135] No it hadn't, said Pugh,[136] and this time he was right.[137] Michigan Democrat Charles Stuart proposed that the Senate not decide it either but declare Trumbull elected because he was eligible as a matter of state law. At this suggestion, says the reporter, "expressions of dissent were heard all round the Chamber." Perceiving that the sense of the Senate was against him, Stuart did not press his suggestion.[138]

By the lopsided margin of 35–8 the Senate then decided that Trumbull was entitled to his seat.[139] No doubt some who voted to put him on base did so only on the basis of Stuart's state-law contention,[140] and it is impossible to say how many. From the reporter's observation and Stuart's reaction, however, that number cannot have been large. Add to this surmise the one-sided results of the poll, and one seems on far safer ground in

[130]The legislature could of course have refused to elect a judge, said Seward, but only by casting votes for someone else; neither statute nor state constitution could bind its hands in advance. Cong Globe, 34th Cong, 1st Sess 566–67.

[131]Id at 343 (Sen. Seward); id at 548–49 (Sen. Crittenden); id at 564–65 (Sen. Butler); id at 579 (Sen. Mason); id at 580–81 (Sen. Foote). See also id at 566 (Connecticut Sen. Isaac Toucey).

[132]See The Jeffersonians at 77–82; The Federalist Nos 52, 57. See also Cong Globe, 34th Cong, 1st Sess 549 (Sen. Crittenden); id at 566 (Sen. Toucey); Benton, 1 Thirty Years' View at 206–7, deploring the "misguided" practice of rotation in some states, "which brings in men unknown to the people, and turns them out as they begin to be useful":

> [E]very contrivance is vicious, and also inconsistent with the re-eligibility permitted by the constitution, which prevents the people from continuing a member as long as they deem him useful to them.

For the counterargument that the qualifications prescribed in Article I were mere minima designed to ensure a modicum of competence see Cong Globe, 34th Cong, 1st Sess 549–50 (Sen. Pugh) (adding that no fewer than sixteen states had established additional qualifications for Senators).

[133]Id at 550–51. Because Article II's provisions regarding the appointment of federal officers contained no similar provision, it proved little that, as Trumbull observed, states obviously could not prescribe qualifications for federal executives or judges. See id at 467 (Sen. Trumbull); id at 550 (Sen. Pugh's reply).

[134]See id at 581 (Sen. Foote).

[135]Id at 565.

[136]Id at 551–52.

[137]See The Jeffersonians at 81–82.

[138]Cong Globe, 34th Cong, 1st Sess 583–84.

[139]Id at 584.

[140]Stuart himself voted against seating Trumbull. Id.

Trumbull's case than in McCreery's in concluding that the incident stands for the proposition that a state cannot add to the qualifications laid down for members of Congress in Article I.[141]

B. Eligibility Encore

Whether the constitutional lists of qualifications for members of Congress were exclusive had also been in issue in 1844, when Tennessee Whig Spencer Jarnagin moved to refer to committee the question whether John Niles, Connecticut's new Democratic Senator, was out of his mind and thus incompetent to exercise his functions. John Fairfield of Maine questioned the Senate's authority to make such an investigation and added that in order to avoid setting what some would regard as a bad precedent Niles would waive any constitutional or legal objections to the inquiry. Senator Crittenden said the qualifications Article I, § 5 authorized the Senate to judge were those listed in § 3, namely age, citizenship, and residence, but he objected only to the form of the resolution, not to the Senate's authority. Ohio Democrat Benjamin Tappan made the argument we've been looking for: The Senate had no constitutional power to investigate the competency of its members. A bipartisan committee unanimously recommended that Niles be seated, and he was: Though suffering from both "mental and physical debility," the committee found, he was not of "unsound mind." As Senator Buchanan had predicted, this resolution enabled the committee to avoid deciding whether the Senate could exclude a member on grounds of insanity.[142]

Four other controversies during the period of this study raised additional questions respecting individual qualifications for members of Congress. The first two arose in early 1847, when two Representatives—Edward Baker of Illinois and Archibald Yell of Arkansas—were reported to have accepted appointments as volunteer officers to fight in the Mexican War. Ohio Representative Robert Schenck questioned Baker's right to keep his seat, since under Article I, § 6 "no person holding any office under the United States shall be a member of either House during his continuance in office."[143] The basic argument in Yell's case was the same: No one could continue to serve in Congress after accepting a military commission.[144]

As Representative Schenck pointed out in Yell's case, the House in 1803 had held John Van Ness disqualified because he was an officer in the militia. Officers of volunteer units—created by Act of Congress, "employed, provided, paid by the Federal Government" and placed by statute "on the same footing with similar corps of the United States

[141]Professor Haynes stated flatly that the Senate had so concluded. 1 Haynes at 174. See also Contested Elections, 1835–1865 at 618, 621. But see John C. Eastman, Open to Merit of Every Description? An Historical Assessment of the Constitution's Qualifications Clauses, 73 Denver UL Rev 89, 96 (1995), noting that five of the nine Senators who spoke in favor of seating Trumbull "found him eligible under the Illinois provision" and concluding that "[t]he grounds upon which Trumbull was seated . . . cannot be determined with any certainty." The Supreme Court would finally settle the question (against state authority) in U.S. Term Limits, Inc v Thornton, 514 US 779 (1995).

[142]See Cong Globe, 28th Cong, 1st Sess 564–65, 602.

[143]Cong Globe, 29th Cong, 2d Sess 115–16.

[144]Yell's appointment had come to the House's attention when a successor appeared to claim his position, and there was preliminary skirmishing over whether there had been a vacancy to fill before the House determined that Yell was no longer a member. Id at 339–41 (Reps. Rathbun, Cottrell, and Schenck).

army"—seemed to Schenck an a fortiori case.[145] Actually the case seems not so obvious to me, as § 5 of the statute provided that volunteer officers be "appointed in the manner prescribed by law in the several States and Territories," and under Article II, § 2 "officers of the United States" cannot be appointed by the states.[146] When official word of Yell's appointment was received, however, all opposition vanished, and his successor was sworn in.[147]

The elections committee subsequently reported that Baker's military commission had vacated his seat and that Yell's replacement, Thomas Newton, was entitled to his.[148] It was immaterial, the committee wrote, that Baker and Yell had been commissioned by the states; what mattered was that, having subsequently been mustered into federal service, they were paid by the United States and subject to presidential orders.

> The committee believe that to hold an office in the army of the United States is incompatible with the office of a member of Congress . . . . The constitution intended that the President should have no power to control the action of Congress in any respect . . . . To allow the two offices to be held by the same person would utterly destroy the independence of Congress . . . .[149]

The third controversy concerned Democrat James Shields, who had been a citizen of the United States for less than nine years when Illinois elected him to the Senate in January 1849 and on March 4 of that year, when the Senate met in special session. A select committee recommended that his election be declared void, Shields "not having been" a citizen for the time specified by Article I, § 3.[150]

Most Senators who spoke (regardless of party) said what mattered was Shields's status when his term (or his duties) began, not when he was elected. As Senator Stephen A. Douglas observed, the constitutional provision appeared to tie only residence, not age or citizenship, to the date of election; in accord with its apparent purpose, the clause said only that one should not "be a Senator" unless the additional qualifications were met.[151] Virginia Senator James Mason finally reported that the committee had found Shields ineligible because he *still* had not been nine years a citizen when he became Senator, and as amended to reflect this understanding the resolution was adopted.[152]

[145]Id at 340; see 9 Stat 9–10, §§ 1, 4 (May 13, 1846); The Jeffersonians at 71–75. For what it's worth, Van Ness had been an officer of the *District of Columbia* militia, though Schenck erroneously said otherwise. Id at 340.

[146]9 Stat at 10; see The Jeffersonians at 167.

[147]Cong Globe, 29th Cong, 2d Sess 341.

[148]Id at 527; HR Rep 86, 29th Cong, 2d Sess 3.

[149]Id at 1–3. No further action was taken; Newton was already in his seat, Yell had just been killed in action, and Baker had resigned. See Biographical Directory at 565, 2096; Cong Globe App, 30th Cong, 2d Sess 346 (Sen. Downs).

[150]Cong Globe App, 30th Cong, 2d Sess (Special Sen Sess of 31st Cong) 332–33.

[151]Id at 335. For the same conclusion see id at 333 (Sen. Turney); id at 335 (Sen. Butler); id at 336 (Sen. Webster); id at 337 (Sen. Seward); id at 338 (Sens. Webster and Calhoun); id at 340 (Sen. Berrien).

[152]Id at 346, 351. Note the remaining ambiguity: Calhoun, Berrien, and Mason said the critical date was when Shields's term began; Douglas said it was when he was sworn in. Cf earlier controversies over the relevant date under the similarly worded incompatibility clause of Article I, § 6, The Jeffersonians at 130 n.36, 315 n.214. See also The Annotated Constitution at 107 (citing S Rep 904, 74th Cong, 1st Sess (1935)): "While the

Finally, when Jefferson Davis was elected a Mississippi Senator for the second time in 1856, he was serving as Secretary of War. Apparently his eligibility had been called into question on the ground that, since he lived in Washington, he was no longer an "inhabitant" of Mississippi within the meaning of Article I, § 3, for he took the trouble to write a letter equating the constitutional term with domicile rather than residence. Felix Grundy of Tennessee, Davis acknowledged, had held himself ineligible under similar circumstances in 1839, but he was wrong: On James Madison's motion the Constitutional Convention had substituted "inhabitant" for "resident" in order not to exclude "persons absent occasionally for a considerable time on public or private business." Grundy had conceded that members of Congress and diplomats sent overseas remained "inhabitants" of their home state, Davis continued, and there was no basis for distinguishing Cabinet officers. The House had disqualified a government clerk stationed in Washington on the basis of Grundy's reasoning in 1824, but Davis's argument was the more persuasive, and he was seated without objection after his election.[153]

Other would-be Congressmen were challenged on the distinct ground that the geographical entity that had elected them had no right to representation. When William Gwin and John C. Frémont presented their credentials in September 1850, for example, several Senators objected on the ground that they had been elected before California was admitted to the Union. As Jefferson Davis put it, "The Constitution provides that Senators should be elected by the Legislature of a State, and if there was no State, there could be no Legislature of a State."[154]

As I have suggested elsewhere, the text of Article I, § 3 makes this argument look irrefutable.[155] As other Senators pointed out, however, it had been rejected before.[156] If the

language of the clause expressly makes residency in the State a condition at the time of election, it now appears established in congressional practice that the age and citizenship qualifications need only be met when the Member-elect is to be sworn."

Shields's case was complicated by the fact that, once it became clear he was not qualified, he had attempted to resign. Cong Globe App, 30th Cong, 2d Sess (Special Sen Sess of 31st Cong) 338, 342. You can't quit, said Webster and Butler (id at 340, 341); since your election was void ab initio, you had no office to resign. But he was sworn in, replied Douglas, and he voted; he was a Senator de facto and thus had the right to resign. Id at 343–44. See also id at 339 (Sen. Hale). This shadow-boxing was not so abstract as it appears; what lay behind it was the old argument (which most speakers on both sides seemed to accept) that there was no "vacancy" for the Governor to fill unless the seat had been occupied before. See id at 339–41 (Sens. Foote, Douglas, Berrien, and Butler). Contra, id at 344–45 (Sen. Badger); id at 347 (Sen. Mason); id at 351 (Sen. Dawson). Reelected by the legislature, Shields took his seat without objection on October 27, 1847, by which time he had been a citizen for more than nine years. See Johannsen, Douglas at 259–61; Douglas to Illinois Gov Augustus French, May 16, 1849, Robert W. Johannsen, ed, The Letters of Stephen A. Douglas 167–69 (Illinois, 1961); Biographical Directory at 1805. (Incidentally, who had the uncommon privilege of serving as U.S. Senator from three different states? The same James Shields, elected (for one term each) by Illinois, Minnesota, and Missouri. Id.)

[153]See Davis to John J. McRae, Feb 11, 1856, 6 Davis Papers at 8–11; 2 Farrand at 217–18, 239; The Jeffersonians at 316 n.214. See also James Buchanan's letter to Ellis Lewis, Jan 14, 1847, John Bassett Moore, ed, 7 The Works of James Buchanan 197 (Lippincott, 1909), concluding that his own sojourn in Washington as Secretary of State made him ineligible to continue as trustee of a Pennsylvania college under a similar provision: When the State Department clerk had been disqualified, "[t]he most distinguished lawyers of the House voted with the majority," and Buchanan thought they were right.

[154]Cong Globe, 31st Cong, 1st Sess 1792. See also id at 1791 (Sens. Turney and Mason).

[155]See The Jeffersonians at 226.

[156]Id at 226–27; see Cong Globe, 31st Cong, 1st Sess 1791–92 (Sens. Douglas and Foote).

words really compelled Davis's conclusion, it was too bad; the same policy that suggested the legislature could fill a vacancy before it happened suggested it could also elect Senators before it was the legislature of a state.[157] In any event, the Senate followed precedent; Gwin and Frémont were seated by a vote of 36–12.[158]

C. Indiana and Iowa

The Iowa and Indiana cases raised a wholly different question. Stripped of obfuscating details, the basic issue was the procedure by which Senators were to be chosen. The Constitution said that (except for certain recess appointments, which we have already considered) the state legislatures should elect Senators; it did not say how they were to do it.[159] Some states had required concurrent majorities in each House voting separately, as in the case of bills. Others, to minimize the risk of deadlock and consequent loss of representation, required a simple majority of all legislators, meeting in joint session.[160] It was generally agreed that the Governor had no part to play in the process; the Constitution required action by the legislature, not an act of legislation.[161]

Both Iowa and Indiana opted for joint sessions, which by 1857, when these controversies came to a head, was the almost universal practice; only Connecticut, it was said, still required separate approval by each chamber.[162] In each case, however, a majority of the state Senate had refused to participate in the joint session.[163] Two questions therefore were presented by both the Iowa and Indiana cases: Did the Constitution permit state legislatures to elect Senators by a simple majority of legislators in joint session? And if so, did the absence of a quorum of the state Senate preclude a valid election?[164]

[157]See text accompanying notes 83–95.

[158]Cong Globe, 31st Cong, 1st Sess 1792. There was a reprise of this controversy when Minnesota was admitted in 1858; the result was the same. See Cong Globe, 35th Cong, 1st Sess 2075–78 (Senate); id at 2310–15 (House). In contrast, when a "Delegate" from New Mexico presented himself in May 1850, a House committee said he ought not to be seated: Precedent recognized Delegates only from organized territories and on the basis of prior statutory authority. Cong Globe, 31st Cong, 1st Sess 1038–39.

[159]US Const, Art I, § 3.

[160]See Cong Globe, 34th Cong, 3d Sess 260 (Sen. Seward); id at 289 (Sen. Slidell). One day, said Senator Toombs, Congress would have to prescribe joint sessions in order to prevent a stalemate that could destroy the Senate. Id at 299. One day it did; see 14 Stat 243, § 1 (Jul 25, 1866) (requiring a joint session if a majority of each House failed to agree on a single candidate on the first vote).

[161]See Cong Globe, 34th Cong, 3d Sess 244 (Sen. Pugh, citing 2 Story, § 703); id at 245 (Sen. Geyer); id at 256 (Sen. Foster); Cong Globe, 35th Cong, 1st Sess 2924 (Sen. Pugh). Cf Herman V. Ames, The Proposed Amendments to the Constitution of the United States During the First Century of Its History, Am Hist Ass'n, 2 Ann Rep 1896 297–98 (reaching the same conclusion, despite conflicting practice, with respect to Article V's parallel provision for ratification of proposed constitutional amendments by state "legislatures"). In 1852 two Senators of different parties suggested that the question of the Governor's participation in Senatorial elections should be left to the states to resolve. Cong Globe App, 32d Cong, 1st Sess 1176 (Sens. Jefferson Davis and George Badger).

[162]See Cong Globe, 35th Cong, 1st Sess 2944–45 (Sen. Toombs).

[163]See Cong Globe, 34th Cong, 1st Sess 2 (Sen. Mason) (presenting a protest against seating Iowa Sen. James Harlan); Cong Globe App, 34th Cong, 3d Sess 193 (Sen. Trumbull) (presenting a protest against seating Indiana Sen. Graham Fitch); Cong Globe, 35th Cong, 1st Sess 2923 (Sen. Pugh) (explaining the Indiana situation).

[164]The Iowa case is excerpted in Contested Elections, 1835–1865 at 621–26, the Indiana case in id at 629–37.

A few Senators expressed the view that as an original matter the "legislature" should have been read to mean the two Houses acting independently[165]—by analogy to Article I, § 1, which defined Congress as consisting of "a Senate and House of Representatives." Nearly everyone agreed, however, that it was too late to go back to that interpretation; sixty years of practice had settled that Senators could be elected by joint ballot.[166] Just as convincing, in my judgment, was the recurring argument that whether to vote separately or together was a question not of who was to elect Senators[167] but of the manner of their election, which in the absence of congressional action the states were to regulate under Article I, § 4.[168]

The second objection to the Iowa and Indiana elections seems equally unpersuasive. There could be no action by the "legislature," it was argued, if one House was not there; for quite apart from the question how the legislature was to vote, the legislature (again like Congress) consisted of two Houses.[169] There was no doubt, however, that in each case a joint session had been announced and that the state Senate had had an opportunity to take part.[170] If applicable state rules required a quorum of each House in such cases, no doubt they should govern; for the state defined its own legislature as well as the manner of Senate elections.[171] No one pointed to any explicit requirement to that effect in either the Iowa or the Indiana case,[172] however, and the traditional concept of a quorum counsels

[165]See, e.g., Cong Globe, 34th Cong, 3d Sess 261 (Sen. Stuart). See also 1 Haynes at 81, suggesting that "the weight of constitutional authority" was that each House must vote separately, citing Kent and Story, who merely reported Kent's view without saying whether he shared it. See 1 Kent's Commentaries at 225–26; 2 Story, § 703. Andrew Johnson, of all people, had taken this position as a Tennessee Senator when the question arose in that state in 1841. The legislature, he argued, was "composed of two distinct bodies," intended to check one another; they could not do so if they sat together and the Senate was "dissipated in the more numerous body." See Leroy P. Graf et al, 1 The Papers of Andrew Johnson 58, 59 (Tennessee, 1967).

[166]See Cong Globe, 34th Cong, 3d Sess 243 (Sen. Toombs); id at 244 (Sen. Pugh, citing 1 Kent's Commentaries at 225–26; Cong Globe, 34th Cong, 3d Sess 254 (Sen. Foster); id at 261 (Sen. Stuart); id at 263 (Sen. Toucey); Cong Globe, 35th Cong, 1st Sess 2924–25 (Sen. Pugh). In March 1857 the Senate rejected a similar challenge to the election of Pennsylvania's Simon Cameron by joint ballot, on the basis of Judah Benjamin's committee report saying neither Pennsylvania law nor the "uniform practical construction" of the federal Constitution required a majority of each House. Cong Globe, 34th Cong, 3d Sess 387, 391.

[167]As suggested by Senator Bayard, Cong Globe, 34th Cong, 3d Sess 250.

[168]See id 243 (Sen. Toombs); id at 260 (Sen. Seward); id at 288 (Sen. Slidell). Cf the question whether the House could elect a Speaker by a simple plurality, text accompanying notes 133–42 of chapter 10. Missouri Senator Henry Geyer had a distinct and less satisfying theory: All constitutional references to legislatures required the concurrent action of both chambers, but a joint session was permissible because each House consented to its choice. Cong Globe, 34th Cong, 3d Sess 245–46. Accord id at 250–52 (Sen. Bayard); id at 292 (Sen. Benjamin); id at 293–94 (Sen. Fessenden).

[169]See id at 243 (Sens. Benjamin and Bigler); id at 250–52 (Sen. Bayard); id at 263 (Sen. Toucey); id at 292 (Sen. Benjamin).

[170]See id at 256 (Sen. Foster). In each case it was argued that the joint session had not been properly proclaimed or agreed upon (See S Rep 2, 35th Cong, Special Sess 2, 35 (in S Rep, 34th Cong, 3d Sess) (Indiana); S Rep 300, 34th Cong, 3d Sess 4–5 (Iowa)), but that raised a separate question; Foster was contending that the Senate could stymie a properly called session by staying away.

[171]See Cong Globe, 34th Cong, 3d Sess 290, 292 (Sen. Benjamin); id at 292 (Sen. Fessenden); id at 297 (Sen. Trumbull).

[172]The Indiana protest asserted the conclusion that a quorum of each House was necessary but did not substantiate it as a matter of state law. See Cong Globe App, 34th Cong, 3d Sess 193. See also Cong Globe, 34th Cong, 3d Sess 268 (Sen. Douglas); id at 290 (Sen. Benjamin, relying on the fact that the Iowa constitution repeated the federal requirement that the "legislature" elect Senators).

against the conclusion that a minority can frustrate the majority's will by refusing to attend.[173] Some objected that permitting the state House of Representatives to act when the Senate was missing enabled a single House to effect the election,[174] but that was inherent in joint balloting whenever one chamber was more numerous than the other.

Up to this point the Iowa and Indiana cases were virtually identical. There was one important difference between them, however. Unlike Iowa, Indiana at the time had no statute specifying that Senators be chosen by joint ballot; a provision to that effect had been repealed a few years before.[175] The most troubling argument against seating the Indiana Senators was therefore that Article I, § 4 required state legislatures (subject to congressional revision) to prescribe the manner of electing Senators by law; in the absence of such regulations there could be no lawful election.[176]

Supporters of the putative Indiana Senators pointed out that Ohio had never enacted a statute regulating Senatorial elections, and that Ohio's Senators had never been challenged on that ground.[177] That might have been only because nobody had thought of the problem, but there was House precedent in an arguably analogous case. In 1804, after extensive debate, the House had voted to seat John Hoge as Representative from Pennsylvania, despite strenuous arguments that the Governor could not call a special election until the legislature had prescribed the date on which it should be held.[178] If the obligation to call a special election implied authority to determine when to hold it (and, we may add, if the duty to elect a Speaker implied authority to decide how to do it),[179] then by the same reasoning the duty to elect Senators implied authority, in the absence of statute, to determine the manner of election.[180]

A counteranalogy surfaced nearly a century and a half after the Iowa and Indiana contests in the famous case of *Bush v Gore*.[181] Before that controversy was finally resolved, the U.S. Supreme Court had remanded one of the relevant cases to state court to explain whether in permitting the recount of certain votes given in the 2000 presidential election the court below had relied on state statutes or on the Florida constitution.[182] For Article II, § 1 provided—as Article I, § 4 did with respect to congressional elections—that presidential electors be chosen as the state "legislature" should direct. That provision, several Justices suggested during the nationally broadcast oral argument, meant just what

[173]See id at 263 (Sen. Brown) (asking rhetorically whether, if the U.S. Senate walked out of a joint session convened for counting electoral votes, the count would be void). More serious, if true, was Allan Nevins's assertion that no quorum of *either* House was in attendance at the contested elections. See Nevins, The Emergence of Lincoln: Douglas, Buchanan, and Party Chaos, 1857–1859 82 (Scribner's, 1950).

[174]See, e.g., Cong Globe, 35th Cong, 1st Sess 2943 (Sen. Wade).

[175]See id at 2924–25 (Sen. Pugh).

[176]See Cong Globe App, 34th Cong, 3d Sess 196 (Sen. Seward); Cong Globe, 35th Cong, 1st Sess 702 (Sen. Collamer). The same argument had been made and rejected when the House seated the first California Representatives in 1850. Cong Globe, 31st Cong, 1st Sess 1789 (Rep. Venable); id at 1791 (Rep. Toombs); id at 1795.

[177]Cong Globe, 35th Cong, 1st Sess 2924 (Sen. Pugh).

[178]Id at 2946 (Sen. Toombs); see The Jeffersonians at 75–77.

[179]See text accompanying notes 132–33 of chapter 10.

[180]See Cong Globe, 35th Cong, 1st Sess 2924 (Sen. Pugh, arguing that in the absence of statute the election was to be conducted however the members of the legislature might reasonably determine); id at 2945–46 (Sen. Toombs, arguing that the legislature did not have to prescribe time, place, and manner regulations in advance).

[181]531 US 98, 113 (2000).

[182]Bush v Palm Beach County Canvassing Board, 531 US 70, 78 (2000).

it said: Electors were to be chosen according to procedures prescribed by legislation, not by the state constitution or common law.[183]

Whether *Bush* was an appropriate case for invoking this argument may (almost) be put to one side.[184] But a more fundamental question can be raised about the remand in *Bush v Gore,* and it bears equally on the controversy over the Indiana election. For the constitutional provisions respecting the manner of presidential and congressional elections appear first and foremost to deal with a question of *federalism:* In each case it is the state, not the United States, that (at least in the first instance) is to determine how the choice shall be made. State legislatures seem to have been mentioned in order to highlight the contrast with Congress; I see no reason to think the Framers were concerned in either case with the separation of state powers.[185]

In any event, the Senate in 1857 clearly rejected the argument that state legislation was necessary to congressional elections, for it voted that the Indiana Senators were entitled to their seats.[186] It must follow, you say, that it seated the Iowa Senator as well. For Indiana presented the harder case; Iowa had the statutory regulation of election procedure that opponents of the Indiana claimants demanded.[187] Well, the Senate did seat him pending resolution of the dispute, as was its practice;[188] it unseated him thereafter following a committee investigation.[189] Why? By proceeding without the Senate, it was argued, Iowa had violated its own law requiring a joint session of both Houses;[190] Indiana had no such requirement.

Thus the Democratic majority in the Senate voted to reject Iowa's James Harlan and to seat Indiana's Graham Fitch and Jesse Bright. Would you care to guess to which party they belonged? Fitch and Bright were Democrats; Harlan was a Free Soiler. Election contests bring out marvelous arguments about the law, but it is not always the law that resolves them.[191]

[183]http:www.supremecourtus.gov/oral_arguments/argument_transcripts/00-836.pdf. See especially id at 31 (Rehnquist, CJ), 37–38 (Kennedy, J), 51–53 (Rehnquist, CJ and Kennedy, J), 58–59 (Scalia, J).

[184]I cannot resist observing that the Florida court's opinion seems to me a perfectly orthodox exercise in statutory construction. Palm Beach County Canvassing Board v Harris, 772 So 2d 1240 (2000).

[185]But the language of the provision, you ask? It *says* "legislature." Right. And the first amendment says "Congress" shall make no law impairing certain freedoms. Was the Supreme Court wrong to conclude that its purpose required that it be applied to judicial action as well? Bridges v California, 314 US 252 (1941); New York Times Co v United States, 403 US 713 (1971).

[186]Cong Globe, 35th Cong, 1st Sess 2981.

[187]See Cong Globe App, 34th Cong, 3d Sess 195 (Sen. Trumbull); id at 208 (Sen. Wilson); Cong Globe, 34th Cong, 3d Sess 244 (Sen. Pugh).

[188]Cong Globe, 34th Cong, 1st Sess 2. Fitch of Indiana was also was seated pending an investigation, which led to the conclusion that he was entitled to his seat. Cong Globe App, 34th Cong, 3d Sess 210, 215.

[189]The vote was 28–18. Cong Globe, 34th Cong, 3d Sess 299.

[190]Cong Globe, 35th Cong, 1st Sess 2935 (Sen. Sebastian).

[191]Reelected as a Republican to fill his own vacancy, Harlan would serve from 1857 to 1873, with two years off as President Johnson's Secretary of the Interior.

10

Other Election Issues

So much for individual contests over elections to the House and Senate. Three distinct issues relating to federal elections remain for consideration: Legislative *regulation* of congressional elections, selection of the Speaker of the House, and the counting of electoral votes for President and Vice-President.

I. DISTRICTS

As we know from regular encounters with the census taker, Article I, § 2 requires that an "actual enumeration" be made every ten years, to permit Representatives (and direct taxes) to be "apportioned among the several States . . . according to their respective numbers."[1] The decennial reapportionment process is not so mechanical as it looks, for whenever one essays to construct a microcosm on a scale of one to forty-odd thousand (as was the case in 1832) there will be fractions, and the number of seats is an integer.

Seats in the House of Representatives are power, and it is no wonder that interstate and partisan squabbles over their allotment are recurrent and intense. The first reappor-

[1]The usual issues of the legitimate scope of the census were raised during the period of this study, but the debates add little to our understanding. See, e.g., Cong Globe, 30th Cong, 2d Sess 627 (Sen. Westcott) (arguing that Congress's sole authority was to compile information relevant to the apportionment of Representatives and direct taxes); id (Sen. Underwood) (responding that other information might be necessary and proper to the consideration of possible legislation). See also Cong Globe, 31st Cong, 1st Sess 820 (Rep. Root); Cong Globe App, 31st Cong, 1st Sess 1244 (Rep. Stephens); The Annotated Constitution at 112. The 1830 statute modestly asked for the sexes and ages of the respondents and whether they were deaf, dumb, or blind; the 1839 law demanded "all such information in relation to mines, agriculture, commerce, manufactures, and schools, as will exhibit a full view of the pursuits, industry, education and resources of the country"; the 1850 version incorporated an intimidatingly exhaustive schedule of forms designed, as an earlier statute had prescribed, to achieve the same goal. 4 Stat 383–84, § 1 (Mar 23, 1830); 5 Stat 331, 336, § 13 (Mar 3, 1839); 9 Stat 402–3, § 1 (Mar 3, 1849); 9 Stat 428, 430, 433–36, § 10 and Schedules 1–6 (May 23, 1850). For earlier debates on this question see The Federalist Period at 19–20.

tionment, in 1792, had provoked both deep congressional division and a veto, from President Washington, on constitutional grounds.[2]

Issues that had been debated in 1792 were raised again when it came time to reapportion in 1832 and 1842. There were the usual questions of the ratio of Representatives to constituents, which determined among other things the number of seats to be apportioned.[3] Since the exponentially expanding population had eliminated any risk that the number of Representatives would exceed the constitutional ceiling of one to thirty thousand, this dispute was of constitutional significance only to the extent that some ratios produced greater deviations than others from the constitutional norm of an allocation proportional to population.[4]

Of more immediate constitutional import was the attempt to move closer to the constitutional goal by assigning an extra seat to each state whose excess population (after multiplying its adjusted population by the statutory ratio) was more than half the number required by the ratio itself.[5] Congress had adopted this system in 1792, but Washington had found it unconstitutional for reasons I have suggested were unconvincing.[6] Massachusetts Senator Daniel Webster made a determined effort to distinguish this precedent in 1832. Washington had complained that under the 1792 bill some states would receive more than one Representative for each thirty thousand inhabitants, and that was not the case under the 1832 proposal; Washington had complained that the 1792 apportionment could not be traced to a consistent standard, and Webster's proposal provided one.[7] A narrow majority of the Senate was persuaded, but the House was not; fractions were ignored again in the 1832 apportionment.[8] The same arguments were repeated in 1842,[9] and this time it was the House that yielded;[10] in a victory for the constitutional principle of equal apportionment, extra Representatives for states with surplus populations exceeding

[2]See id at 128–35.

[3]E.g., Cong Deb, 22d Cong, 1st Sess 1531, 1563–67, 1686, 1775, 1814, 1816.

[4]"Population" is an inexact term for the constitutional standard, since the well-known Convention compromise required inclusion of three-fifths of the slaves. US Const, Art I, § 2. There were occasional arguments that the Constitution required that the apportionment come as close as practicable to this standard. E.g., Cong Deb, 22d Cong, 1st Sess 523 (New Jersey Sen. Mahlon Dickerson); id at 857 (Sen. Clayton); id at 1766 (Rep. Adams); id at 3040–41 (Massachusetts Rep. Edward Everett); Cong Deb App, 22d Cong, 1st Sess 92–93 (Sen. Webster); HR Rep 463, 22d Cong, 1st Sess 49–51 (1832) (minority report of Reps. Everett and Vance) (drawing a persuasive analogy to the apportionment of direct taxes).

[5]In other words, fractions exceeding 50 percent of the ratio should be rounded up rather than down, as they had been before. See, e.g., Cong Deb, 22d Cong, 1st Sess 487–90 (Sen. Webster); Cong Deb App, 22d Cong, 1st Sess 92–98 (same).

[6]The Federalist Period at 133–35.

[7]Cong Deb, 22d Cong, 1st Sess 489–90; Cong Deb App, 22d Cong, 1st Sess 97–98. See also Webster's letter to Levi Lincoln, Feb 18, 1832, 3 Webster Correspondence at 152, 153: "I believe there is no Constitutional objection to this, & it is a near[er] approach to equality, I think, than can be attained in any other way"; James Kent to Webster, Apr 22, 1832, id at 168, noting that the New York legislature in 1791 had rounded off fractions to the nearest integer to maximize equality. For Senator Marcy's representative contrary argument see Cong Deb App, 22d Cong, 1st Sess 503–8; see also Representative Polk's adverse committee report, HR Rep 463, 22d Cong, 1st Sess 1 (1832).

[8]Cong Deb, 22d Cong, 1st Sess 866, 934, 936; see 4 Stat 516 (May 22, 1832).

[9]E.g., Cong Globe, 27th Cong, 2d Sess 526–27 (Sen. Walker); Cong Globe App, 27th Cong, 2d Sess 391 (Sen. Crittenden) (both supporting the constitutionality of awarding additional seats); id at 392 (Sen. Wright) (contra).

[10]See id at 649.

half the statutory ratio became the law of the land.[11]

A. Time, Place, and Manner

The big news of the 1842 apportionment law, however, was the inclusion of the following provision, which had not even been proposed in 1832:

> [I]n every case where a State is entitled to more than one Representative, the number to which each State shall be entitled under this apportionment shall be elected by districts composed of contiguous territory equal in number to the number of Representatives to which said State may be entitled, no one district electing more than one Representative.[12]

In plain English: Representatives must henceforth be elected from single-member districts, not by "general ticket" or, as we would be inclined to say, at large.[13]

Good, right? I have discussed the advantages of election by district (chiefly the enfranchisement of minorities and the protection of small states) in connection with repeated efforts to require that states be divided into districts for purposes of choosing the President, or his electors.[14] In that context the change could be effected only by constitu-

[11]5 Stat 491, § 1 (Jun 25, 1842):

> [F]rom and after the third day of March, one thousand eight hundred and forty-three, the House of Representatives shall be composed of members elected agreeably to a ratio of one Representative for every seventy thousand six hundred and eighty persons in each State, and of one additional representative for each State having a fraction greater than one moiety of the said ratio, computed according to the rule prescribed by the Constitution . . . .

The 1850 statute, which innovatively left it to the new Secretary of the Interior to apply the statutory formula to the findings of the coming census, preserved the principle of distributing seats to states with the largest fractions, though there were differences in detail. 9 Stat 428, 432–33, § 25 (May 23, 1850). The Interior Department had been created in 1849 to manage a variety of internal affairs (e.g., patents, public lands and buildings, Indian affairs, and the census) formerly entrusted to other agencies. 9 Stat 395 (Mar 3, 1849).

[12]5 Stat 491, § 2 (Jun 25, 1842). At one point, at Senator Benton's suggestion, the Senate voted (30–10!) without debate to require that districts be equal in population. Cong Globe, 27th Cong, 2d Sess 601. As Senator Walker said when the issue was reopened, the principle of equal representation was "so just and obvious, that no man could dispute the propriety of it"; the committee that had recommended it, he added, was unanimous. Id at 610. But the Whig majority regrouped (as Senator Buchanan tartly put it, id at 609, "King Caucus rules"), and the requirement of equal districts (which a horrified Tallmadge had said would require the division of counties, id at 609), was rejected after all. Id at 614. In 1872 Congress would require that districts "contain[] as nearly as practicable an equal number of inhabitants." 17 Stat 28, § 2 (Feb 2, 1872).

[13]Technically speaking, there is a difference. Although in both cases elections are held on a statewide (or citywide) basis, in the original general-ticket election all aspirants competed against each other in a single contest in which those at the top of the list were awarded seats; in the typical modern at-large election there are separate races for each individual post. See, e.g., 14 Pa Stat 271 (1792); City of Mobile v Bolden, 446 US 55, 59–60 (1980).

[14]See The Jeffersonians at 337–42. Representative Campbell restated these advantages in the debate over House districts in 1842. Cong Globe, 27th Cong, 2d Sess 445. See also id at 556 (Sen. Huntington) (stressing uniformity and the protection of minorities); HR Rep 909, 27th Cong, 2d Sess 8 (1842) (Rep. John Quincy Adams). Representative Atherton (Cong Globe App, 27th Cong, 2d Sess 399) protested that uniformity could hardly have been the Framers' goal, since they left the matter in the first instance to the states; but uniformity

tional amendment, since Article II, § 1 left the manner of choosing electors almost entirely to the states.[15] North Carolina Congressmen had begun by suggesting districting for House elections as well, but the quest for an amendment to this effect had been deflected by the argument that it was not needed: Congress could achieve its goal by simple legislation, since Article I, § 4 gave it full authority to "make or alter" regulations concerning "[t]he times, places, and manner of holding elections for Senators and Representatives."[16]

For surely, as most speakers agreed when the issue was debated in 1842, whether elections should be conducted by districts or by general ticket was a question of the "manner of holding elections"; it was the question of *how* the election should be held.[17] Imaginative members nevertheless managed to raise plausible if ultimately unpersuasive objections to this conclusion.

Several speakers contended that a congressional districting requirement would conflict with Article I, § 2's provision that Representatives be elected by "the people of the several states." The state was a unit for purposes of House elections, the argument ran; every voter had the right to participate in the choice of all of his state's Representatives.[18] On the merits, I think, there was little to recommend this argument. The reference to the "people" in Article I, § 2 was intended to contrast the state legislatures, which elected the Senate; there is no reason to believe it was meant to require statewide elections, which the

---

was expressly mentioned by Madison in the Virginia ratifying convention as one of the reasons for ultimate congressional authority. See 3 Elliot's Debates at 367 (cited by Rep. Summers, Cong Globe App, 27th Cong, 2d Sess 353).

[15]Proposals for constitutional amendments to require districting for presidential elections (as well as to require direct popular elections) continued to bud, and to wither, during the period of the present study. See, e.g., Cong Deb, 23d Cong, 2d Sess 216–17 (Sen. Benton); Cong Globe, 28th Cong, 1st Sess 686 (same). An offering by Andrew Johnson, in 1851, coupled popular election of the President with popular election of Senators and twelve-year terms for judges. Cong Globe, 31st Cong, 2d Sess 627.

[16]See The Jeffersonians at 337 n.132. The one exception (repealed when the seventeenth amendment provided for direct election in 1913) was "the places of choosing Senators." As Charles Cotesworth Pinckney told the South Carolina legislature in 1788, it would have been unseemly for Congress to tell state legislatures where to sit. 4 Elliot's Debates at 303.

[17]Apart from regulations of time and place, said Senator Tallmadge, "every thing else which is necessary to ascertain the will of the people in their choice of their Representatives is included in the term 'manner.'" Cong Globe App, 27th Cong, 2d Sess 512. See also, e.g., Cong Globe, 27th Cong, 2d Sess 445 (Rep. Halsted); id at 448 (Rep. Garrett Davis); id at id at 464 (Rep. Pendleton); id at 556 (Sen. Huntington); Cong Globe App, 27th Cong, 2d Sess 319 (Rep. Butler). As Representative Summers pointed out, Madison had cited districting as an example of a regulation of the manner of election in the Constitutional Convention. 2 Farrand at 240–41; see Cong Globe App, 27th Cong, 2d Sess 353. See also 1 Tucker's Blackstone App at 191. Representative Atherton, on the other hand, cited William R. Davie's remarks in the North Carolina convention to support his contention that the word "manner" had been understood to mean "either *viva voce* election, or election by ballot"—a most improbable conclusion, I should think, given the breadth of the language the Framers employed. In fact the implication that this was *all* that was included was Atherton's, not Davie's; the latter had said that the manner varied from state to state, as "[s]ome elect by ballot, and others *viva voce*," and that it would be "more convenient to have the manner uniform . . . ." 4 Elliot's Debates at 60–61; Cong Globe, 27th Cong, 2d Sess 470. See also id (Rep. Ferris) (making the obvious but seldom expressed point that no single Framer's understanding was determinative).

[18]Representative Payne put it succinctly: "If, then, the people of the several States were to elect them, what right had Congress to say that a district only should elect? for it could not be an election by a State, if a fraction only voted." Id at 453. See also id at 447 (Rep. Colquitt); Cong Globe App, 27th Cong, 2d Sess 583–84 (Sen. Bagby).

Framers never discussed.[19] Moreover, precedent afforded a crushing response to this suggestion, as numerous states had elected Representatives by district since 1788.[20]

Proponents of districting argued that precedent did more than simply refute the argument that each Representative must be chosen by the entire "people" of the state; it also established that districting fell within Congress's authority to regulate the "manner" of House elections. For the states derived their authority over the subject from the same clause; if the states could require district elections, Congress could too.[21]

Oh no, said Indiana Representative Andrew Kennedy. Article I was not the source of the states' authority to divide themselves into districts; the states had "inherent power" to regulate congressional elections.[22] Wrong, replied Daniel Barnard of New York and Nathanael Pendleton of Ohio: No government had inherent authority to regulate the operations of another.[23] New Hampshire Representative Charles G. Atherton tried another tack: State authority to require elections by district was implicit in the command of Arti-

[19]See id at 339 (Kentucky Rep. Garrett Davis):

> The object of this part of the clause is merely to designate the *body of the people* of the States, having certain qualifications, to be the electors of the *Representatives;* as the first clause of the third section declares that the *Senators* shall be chosen by the *Legislatures* of the States.

See also id at 352 (Rep. Summers); HR Rep 60, 28th Cong, 1st Sess (minority report) 3 (1844) (Rep. Davis), reiterating that the reference to the "people" was meant simply to provide for popular elections. The two provisions thus formed part of the great compromise between the large and small states at the Philadelphia Convention.

There was food for thought in Representative Colquitt's further suggestion that if Congress could require that Representatives be elected by districts it could do the same for Senators, as the Constitution gave it the same authority to regulate the "manner of holding elections" to both chambers. Cong Globe, 27th Cong, 2d Sess 447; see also id at 453 (Rep. Payne); Cong Globe App, 27th Cong, 2d Sess 583 (Sen. Bagby). "Many advocates" of the districting proposal, the reporter tells us, "cried out" that they claimed no such authority (Cong Globe, 27th Cong, 2d Sess 447). Garrett Davis later attempted to distinguish the two cases on the ground that Senators were to be selected by the "legislature" rather than the "legislators," and that the legislature was a collective body not subject to division. HR Rep 60, 28th Cong, 1st Sess 2–3 (1844) (minority report). Maybe the "advocates" were too quick to accept Colquitt's gambit: Maybe Congress could have required that Senators be chosen by districts as well.

[20]See, e.g. Cong Globe, 27th Cong, 2d Sess 448 (Rep. Garrett Davis); id at 453 (Rep. Barnard); id at 464 (Rep. Pendleton). See also 2 Elliot's Debates at 255 (Alexander Hamilton): "The natural and proper mode of holding elections will be, to divide the state into districts, in proportion to the number to be elected." The only attempt at a response was Representative Colquitt's suggestion that the "people" of the states waived their rights under Article I, § 2 when their authorized agents in the state legislature provided for election by districts. Cong Globe, 27th Cong, 2d Sess 447. Senator Bagby, in contrast, frankly contended that "the general-ticket system is the only constitutional mode of electing members of the House of Representatives." Cong Globe App, 27th Cong, 2d Sess 583.

[21]Cong Globe, 27th Cong, 2d Sess 448 (Rep. Davis); id at 453 (Rep. Barnard); id at 463 (Rep. W. Cost Johnson); id at 464 (Rep. Pendleton).

[22]Id at 449.

[23]Id at 453 (Rep. Barnard); id at 464 (Rep. Pendleton); see also Cong Globe App, 27th Cong, 2d Sess 352 (Rep. Summers). While by no means beyond dispute (whence, for example, did the states derive authority to elect delegates to the Continental Congress?), this argument seems to me more persuasive than the suggestion (made in the earlier controversy over the seating of Maryland Representative William McCreery) that the states could not prescribe additional qualifications for House members because the tenth amendment reserved only preexisting state authority. See The Jeffersonians at 78–79.

cle I, § 2 that Representatives be elected by the people of the several states.[24] Sure, if the Constitution had said nothing further on the subject; but that was equally true of other regulations of time, place, and manner that concededly fell within the parameters of Article I, § 4.

Thus there really seems no escape from the conclusion that to require elections by district was to regulate the manner of congressional elections—unless opponents of the districting proposal were right that to require district elections added to the qualifications of candidates or of voters, neither of which was within the competence of Congress.[25]

If a federal districting requirement did add qualifications, it was indeed unconstitutional. *Voter* qualifications were expressly committed to state law by Article I, § 2's provision that "the electors in each State shall have the qualifications requisite for electors of the most numerous branch of the state legislature";[26] and the better argument in McCreery's case in 1806 had been (as several Senators would repeat in Trumbull's case in 1855) that the catalog of *members'* qualifications in the same article (age, citizenship, and residence in the state) was exclusive.[27]

Georgia Representative Walter Colquitt stated categorically that the proposal before the House would require candidates to live in the districts they sought to represent,[28] but that was not true; as supporters of the proposal pointed out, it contained no such requirement.[29] More troubling was the argument that districting would add to the qualifications of voters by requiring *them* to live in a district in order to vote for its Representative. But it is not clear that this is what was meant by the Constitution's reference to the "qualifications" of the voters. All that provision need mean is that it is up to the states to determine who is entitled to participate in the process of congressional elections; for which Representatives the qualified voter is entitled to vote may perhaps be more properly viewed as a question of the manner of conducting elections.[30]

As a last desperate gambit occasional opponents of the districting requirement suggested that Congress had power to regulate the time, place, and manner of elections only if the states failed or refused to do so.[31] That is not what the Constitution says. Furthermore, as Kentucky Senator James Morehead pointed out, an amendment to that effect had

[24]Cong Globe, 27th Cong, 2d Sess 470.

[25]Id at 447 (Rep. Colquitt); id at 453 (Rep. Payne).

[26]See 4 Elliot's Debates at 61 (William R. Davie); id at 71 (John Steele).

[27]See The Jeffersonians at 79–82 and section III of chapter 9. Garrett Davis, who argued that the districting requirement was constitutional, conceded that Congress could not add qualifications for members. Cong Globe, 27th Cong, 2d Sess 448.

[28]Id at 447.

[29]Id at 453 (Rep. Barnard); Cong Globe App, 27th Cong, 2d Sess 319 (Rep. Butler). Representative Halsted's original proposal and a substitute offered by Representative Campbell (which was ultimately adopted) are printed in Cong Globe, 27th Cong, 2d Sess 446. Neither said anything about the residence of the members. Indeed, as Representative Butler noted, if districting itself added member qualifications to those listed in the Constitution, the laws of most states would be unconstitutional; for most states had chosen to elect Representatives by district, and the states had no more power than Congress to prescribe additional qualifications for members. Cong Globe App, 27th Cong, 2d Sess 319.

[30]This argument seems less attractive, however, in the context of residence requirements for the Representatives themselves, which were regarded in McCreery's case as qualifications; and this raises doubts as to the persuasiveness of the argument.

[31]E.g., Cong Globe, 27th Cong, 2d Sess 562 (Sen. Woodbury); Cong Globe App, 27th Cong, 2d Sess 341 (Rep. Goggin); id at 348 (Rep. Clifford); id at 584 (Sen. Bagby).

been proposed in 1789 and rejected by Congress—not because Article I already so provided but because it was a bad idea.[32]

B. Co-Opting the States

We come at last to the most prevalent, most important, and most plausible objection to the districting requirement. If districting was a question of the "manner" of holding elections, opponents argued, Congress was obliged to draw the districts itself; it could not order state legislatures to do so.[33] "The governing principle of the framers of the Constitution," said Pennsylvania Senator James Buchanan, "– the very key which unlocks its meaning—is, that the enumerated powers conferred upon Congress are to be executed by Federal, and not by State authority."[34]

Why? Buchanan did not elaborate. Rhode Island Representative Joseph Tillinghast offered a purely textual argument: Congress had the right to regulate elections, but not to require state regulation; the districting proposal "did not legislate, but called on the States to legislate, which was quite another thing."[35] New York Representative Charles Ferris thought the conclusion followed from the states' undisputed authority, confirmed by Article I, § 2, to regulate the manner of elections subject to congressional revision: "Power implied will;" the states must be free to make their own decisions.[36]

Behind these contentions lay a deeper concern for federalism and states' rights. If Congress insisted on ordering the states to carry out its policy, said New Hampshire Senator (and later Supreme Court Justice) Levi Woodbury, "the General Government is dependent on the States, as well as the latter being in other respects tributary to the General Government."[37] Indeed, added Mississippi Senator Robert Walker, the districting

[32]1 Annals of Congress at 797–802 (Aug 22, 1789). See also Cong Globe, 27th Cong, 2d Sess 577 (Sen. Morehead); Cong Globe App, 27th Cong, 2d Sess 408 (Rep. Pendleton); id at 457 (Sen. Crittenden); id at 749 (Sen. Graham). Cf McCulloch v Maryland, 17 US 316, 424 (1819), rejecting the argument that the National Bank could be "necessary and proper" to the execution of federal authority only if state banks were shown inadequate to the purpose. Maine Representative (and later U.S. Supreme Court Justice) Nathan Clifford tried to use the proposed amendment to show a contemporary understanding that the power was restricted to extreme cases, arguing that it might have been offered to remove doubts and rejected as unnecessary. Cong Globe App, 27th Cong, 2d Sess 349. Representative Barnard (id at 380) countered that in proposing an amendment New York had conceded but deprecated Congress's authority, and Clifford was unable to substantiate his exercise in wishful thinking.

[33]E.g., Cong Globe, 27th Cong, 2d Sess 446 (Reps. Tillinghast and Gamble); id at 448 (Rep. Houston); id at 452 (Reps. Kennedy and Payne); id at 464 (Rep. Pope); id at 470 (Rep. Ferris); id at 562 (Sens. Woodbury and McRoberts); id at 568 (Sen. Benton); id at 572 (Sen. Bagby); id at 577–78 (Sen. Buchanan); Cong Globe App, 27th Cong, 2d Sess 320 (Rep. Floyd); id at 347–48 (Rep. Clifford); id at 397 (Rep. Atherton); id at 467 (Sen. Wright).

[34]Cong Globe, 27th Cong, 2d Sess 577–78.

[35]Id at 446. See also id at 470 (Rep. Atherton); id at 452 (Rep. Kennedy): "Whatever power this Government exercises, it must exercise it itself; it cannot order the States to exercise it"; id at 568 (Sen. Benton): "[T]he import was clear that Congress was to act, not to command." But see id at 556 (Sen. Huntington): "Whatever Congress may do on the subject, is a regulation . . . ."

[36]Id at 470.

[37]Id at 562. What Woodbury had just said in a slightly different context seems equally applicable here and is reminiscent of much later Supreme Court arguments respecting co-optation of state officers: "He did not regard sovereign States as trained soldiers, to be dressed in a uniform livery as to every thing, and capable of being called up by Congress, as by an order of drill-sergeants, to review them and clip all their dress to our

proposal represented a return to the discredited principles of the Articles of Confederation; the Philadelphia Constitution had repudiated the authority of Congress to act directly on the states.[38]

These arguments must ring a bell for the twenty-first-century reader. Justice Sandra Day O'Connor stated the conclusion in *New York v United States* in 1992: "The Federal Government may not compel the States to enact or administer a federal regulatory program."[39] Justice Antonin Scalia gave the reason in *Printz v United States* five years later: Impressing state officers into service to enforce federal law was incompatible with "the independence and autonomy" of the states.[40]

Despite yowls of protest from dissenting Justices,[41] these were not the first occasions on which the Supreme Court had recognized the implicit immunity of state officers from federal co-optation. In 1861, in *Kentucky v Dennison,* the Court in an opinion by Chief Justice Roger Taney *unanimously* invalidated a 1793 statutory provision requiring "the executive authority" of each state to arrest and return fugitives from justice. Although Congress had implicit authority to implement the extradition clause of Article IV, Taney wrote,

> the Federal Government, under the Constitution, has no power to impose on a State officer, as such, any duty whatever, and compel him to perform it; for if it possessed this power, it might overload the officer with duties which would fill up all his time, and disable him from performing his obligations to the State.[42]

---

trim." Id. See also id at 567, where the same Senator Woodbury characterized the districting proposal as the latest in a "series of alarming encroachments by the General Government on the sacred rights of the States."

[38]Id at 573. See also id at 578 (Sen. Buchanan).

[39]505 US 144, 188.

[40]521 US 898, 928 (1997). Justice O'Connor picked up the Articles of Confederation argument in New York v United States, 505 US at 163–66, but I have never found it very convincing. The vice of the Articles was that Congress could not act against individuals, not that it could act against states.

[41]See, e.g., *Printz,* 521 US at 939 (Stevens, J, joined by Souter, Ginsburg, and Breyer, JJ, dissenting): "When Congress exercises the powers delegated to it by the Constitution, it may impose affirmative obligations on executive and judicial officers of state and local governments as well as ordinary citizens"; *New York,* 505 US at 211 (Stevens, J, dissenting): "[The] notion that Congress does not have the power to issue 'a simple command to state governments to implement legislation enacted by Congress' is incorrect and unsound."

[42]65 US 66, 107–8; see The First Hundred Years at 246–47. With obvious reference to the then recent decision in Prigg v Pennsylvania, 41 US 539 (1842), Illinois Senator Samuel McRoberts argued in the districting debate that the Court had already denied Congress's authority to conscript state officers to return fugitive slaves. Cong Globe, 27th Cong, 2d Sess 562. Since the question was not before the Court in *Prigg,* its observations cannot fairly be described as a holding. In the course of concluding that Congress had implicit authority to pass legislation implementing the fugitive-slave clause, however, Justice Story's opinion for the Court offered the following support to those opposing the districting provision:

> The clause is found in the national Constitution, and not in that of any state. It does not point out any state functionaries, or any state action, to carry its provisions into effect. The states cannot, therefore, be compelled to enforce them; and it might well be deemed an unconstitutional exercise of the power of interpretation, to insist, that the states are bound to provide means to carry into effect the duties of the national government, nowhere delegated or intrusted to them by the constitution.

As the last half of this quotation suggests, this immunity was an obvious corollary of the converse immunity recognized in *McCulloch v Maryland.*[43] For the Constitution recognizes the autonomy of the states as well as of the Federal Government; and the power to co-opt officers, no less than the tax power, is the power to destroy.[44]

South Carolina Representative Sampson Butler argued that the greater power of Congress to draw districts itself included the lesser power to require the states to draw them,[45] but we have wisely become leery of such arguments; the selective denial of Government benefits, for example, may do greater harm to individual rights than abolition of the entire program.[46] Kentucky Senator James T. Morehead supplied the requisite additional ingredient: It was *less* intrusive on state autonomy for Congress to require districting than to draw districts of its own.[47]

Maybe. For the state would then retain discretion as to how the districts should be defined; it would be precluded only from deciding whether there should be districts at all. This is the philosophy that underlies a number of modern federal programs, such as those for controlling air and water pollution, that enlist state cooperation in the implementation of federal policy.[48] The crucial element of these programs, however, is that they are *voluntary*. For a state may decide that the latitude to make substantive policy afforded by participation in federal enforcement is not worth the concomitant distortion of state priorities or diversion of state resources; I think the Supreme Court was right that state autonomy requires that states retain the option to decide whether their interests are best served by participation in the federal program.

Significantly, most defenders of the districting scheme shunned any direct challenge to the proposition that state officers were immune from co-optation by Congress; the basic

---

41 US at 615–16. The statutory provisions requiring state officers to return fugitives from justice or labor had been adopted without reported discussion, see The Federalist Period at 170–71, but constitutional objections had been raised in Congress on several occasions on which the conscription of state officials was proposed. See the Jeffersonians at 306 & n.147 and the other passages there cited.

[43]17 US 316 (1819).

[44]I have elsewhere argued that the case for immunity is *stronger* in the case of the states, which cannot protect themselves by legislation, as Congress can. See The First Hundred Years at 167. Similarly (even if the intrusion on state interests is no greater), modern case law is right to consider co-optation a more obvious breach of state autonomy than mere regulation of the state's own activities (compare *Printz* and *New York v United States* with Garcia v San Antonio Metropolitan Transit Authority, 469 US 528 (1985) (upholding application of the Fair Labor Standards Act to public workers)). A federal pollution control program could not achieve its goals if state-owned sources were immune from regulation; if Congress wants private sources to be controlled, it may regulate them itself. Silas Wright made the second half of this argument in 1842: Now that the United States could act directly on individuals, it had no need to co-opt the states. Cong Globe App, 27th Cong, 2d Sess 467.

[45]Id at 319.

[46]See, e.g., Speiser v Randall, 357 US 513 (1958). See also the discussion of limitations on political activities of federal officers and employees in chapter 5.

[47]Cong Globe, 27th Cong, 2d Sess 576–77.

[48]E.g., Clean Air Act, 42 USC §§ 7410 et seq (2000) (state plans to implement federal air-quality standards); Clean Water Act, 33 USC §§ 1251 et seq (2000) (state permit system to implement federal effluent standards).

defense was one of confession and avoidance.[49] In the first place, as many speakers emphasized, the statute as adopted did not (like the original bill) expressly require state legislatures to enact districting laws; it merely demanded that (in states entitled to more than one seat) Representatives "be elected by districts."[50] "Congress makes the principle," said Connecticut Senator Jabez Huntington, "and the Constitution makes it the duty of the States to conform to the principle. It is not Congress that exercises any control over the States; it is the Constitution."[51] "We exercise the constitutional power clearly given to us," added Senator John Crittenden of Kentucky, "leaving to the States the exercise of that power from which we have not excluded them by our action."[52]

For congressional elections were indeed a special case. Article I, § 4 did not simply empower Congress to regulate the time, place, and manner of House elections. It unmistakably *commanded* the states to legislate to the extent that Congress did not: "The times, places, and manner of holding elections for Senators and Representatives, shall be prescribed in each State by the legislature thereof . . . ."[53] Nor, proponents insisted, was the districting proposal unique in this regard. When Congress reapportioned congressional seats among the states, said Massachusetts Senator Isaac Bates, the states were obliged to adjust their laws accordingly;[54] if Congress set a uniform date for the election of Representatives, said New York Senator Nathaniel Tallmadge, state laws would have to be made to conform.[55]

The districting requirement, said Maine Senator George Evans, was analogous to the 1792 law setting a range of dates within which the states were to choose presidential

[49]Nathaniel Tallmadge of New York and Garrett Davis of Kentucky, both supporters of the districting proposal, expressly denied that Congress could order state legislatures to adopt election rules. Cong Globe App, 27th Cong, 2d Sess 339 (Rep. Davis); id at 512 (Sen. Tallmadge).

[50]5 Stat 491, § 1 (Jun 25, 1842); Cong Globe, 27th Cong, 2d Sess 446. Contrast Representative Halsted's original language: "[E]ach State shall be divided, by the Legislature thereof, into . . . districts . . . ." Id.

[51]Id at 556. See also id at 453 (Rep. Barnard); id at 464 (Rep. Pendleton); id at 577 (Sen. Morehead); id at 583–84 (Sen. Bates); id at 725 (Rep. Campbell); Cong Globe App, 27th Cong, 2d Sess 339 (Rep. Garrett Davis); id at 380 (Rep. Barnard); id at 408 (Rep. Pendleton).

[52]Id at 458. The districting provision was in uncanny conformity with the expectations of the Framers as stated by Madison in explaining the provision for congressional elections to the Virginia ratifying convention:

> [C]onsidering the State Governments and General Government as distinct bodies, acting in different and independent capacities for the people, it was thought that the particular regulations should be submitted to the former, and the general regulations to the latter.

3 Elliot's Debates at 367 (cited in Cong Globe App, 27th Cong, 2d Sess 341). Compare the institution of framework legislation ("Rahmengesetze") authorized by the German constitution (Art 75 GG), described in David P. Currie, The Constitution of the Federal Republic of Germany 50–52 (Chicago, 1994).

[53]See Cong Globe App, 27th Cong, 2d Sess 492 (Sen. Huntington); id at 512, 513 (Sen. Tallmadge); id at 750 (Sen. Graham); id at 793 (Sen. Bates); id at 560 (Rep. Campbell): "They are as much bound by that instrument to adopt the necessary measures to carry this law into effect, as they would be to regulate the elections in case such a law had not been passed."

[54]Id at 793; see also id at 788 (Sen. Miller); HR Rep 909, 27th Cong, 2d Sess 9 (1842) (Rep. Adams).

[55]Cong Globe App, 27th Cong, 2d Sess 513; see also id at 339 (Rep. Garrett Davis). If Congress prescribed that elections should be by ballot, Tallmadge continued, would it have to prescribe "the form of the ballot box, and how it shall be kept," and whether the ballot should be "written or printed"? Id at 513. If Congress drew the districts itself, added Representative Campbell in the same vein, opponents would complain that it had required the states "to appoint the managers of the elections, to provide the ballot-boxes, and to designate the precincts at which the elections shall be held." Id at 560.

electors; here too the statute narrowed the state's options in performing a constitutional duty.[56] It was also analogous, said Indiana Senator Albert White, to the 1792 militia law, which (pursuant to Congress's power "to provide for organizing, arming, and disciplining the militia") required the states to divide militiamen into divisions, brigades, and companies as their legislatures saw fit.[57]

Conspicuously missing from this list of analogies was the most salient of all, the 1793 statute expressly requiring the "executive authority" of the states to apprehend and deliver fugitives from justice or from slavery.[58] This was the statute the Supreme Court would soon strike down in *Dennison* as an invasion of state autonomy, and the Court had already questioned its constitutionality in *Prigg v Pennsylvania.*[59] As Justice Joseph Story wrote in *Prigg,* neither the fugitive-slave clause nor the extradition clause expressly imposed duties on state officers; both required that fugitives be "delivered up," but they did not say by whom.[60] Moreover, the fugitive statute, unlike the districting provision, explicitly imposed affirmative duties on state officers. It was thus the better part of valor not to stress the analogy between the two provisions, and it was generally ignored.

Later Supreme Court decisions, however, have vindicated the distinctions drawn by supporters of the districting proposal, and it seems clear it would be upheld today. In *Puerto Rico v Branstad,* in 1987, the Court unanimously overruled *Dennison* on grounds paralleling the arguments made in the 1842 districting debates.[61] Although the extradition clause speaks impersonally in the passive voice, the Court had no difficulty in concluding that it too imposed duties on state officers; for only the state, one might add, was in a position to ensure that the fugitive was "delivered up," as the clause required. Thus, as Justice Scalia wrote in reaffirming the general immunity of state officers from federal co-optation in *Printz,* the extradition clause was a special case: In ordering state officials to arrest and deliver fugitives Congress was merely implementing a duty the Constitution itself imposed.[62]

Thus I think Congress was within its rights in requiring in 1842 that members of the House be elected by districts. I also think the arguments made on both sides of the debate were remarkably refined and acute, as was so often the case during this period.

[56]Cong Globe, 27th Cong, 2d Sess 578; see also Cong Globe App, 27th Cong, 2d Sess 749–50 (Sen. Graham). See 1 Stat 239, § 1 (Mar 1, 1792); The Federalist Period at 136–37; US Const, Art II, § 1: "Each State shall appoint, in such manner as the Legislature thereof may direct, a number of electors . . . ; [t]he Congress may determine the time of choosing the electors, and the day on which they shall give their votes . . . ."

[57]Cong Globe, 27th Cong, 2d Sess 583; see also id at 573 (Sen. Bayard). See 1 Stat 271, 272–73, §§ 3–6, 10 (May 8, 1792); The Federalist Period at 157; US Const, Art I, § 8, cl 16. Cf the last clause of the provision just cited, expressly reserving to the states "the authority of training the militia according to the discipline prescribed by Congress." Smith of Connecticut argued that the militia was different because in its case the Constitution required both state and federal action (Cong Globe, 27th Cong, 2d Sess 584), but the essential provisions were the same: In each instance the Constitution gave Congress regulatory authority and imposed affirmative duties on the states.

[58]1 Stat 302 (Feb 12, 1793).

[59]See note 42 and accompanying text.

[60]US Const, Art IV, § 2; see the passage from *Prigg* quoted in note 42.

[61]483 US 219, 228.

[62]521 US at 909. The Seventh Circuit, in upholding the so-called Motor Voter law requiring states to register voters for congressional elections when they sought drivers' licenses, applied the same reasoning to the election provision of Article I, § 4. ACORN v Edgar, 56 F3d 791 (1995).

C. Undoing the Deed

Opponents of the districting requirement, however, did not take Congress's decision lying down. We will defy the law, they shouted; we will elect our Representatives by general ticket, and you will seat them.[63] This is rank nullification, supporters replied, and no more legitimate than South Carolina's defiance of the tariff in 1832: The states must obey federal law.[64] Not even the 1832 incident, said South Carolina's William C. Preston in the Senate, was precedent for nullification of the districting law; for unlike that measure the tariff his state had nullified was palpably and obviously unconstitutional.[65]

President Tyler signed the bill, but in so doing he gave aid and comfort to the enemies of the districting provision:

> When I was a member of either House of Congress I acted under the conviction that *to doubt* as to the constitutionality of a law was sufficient to induce me to give my vote against it; but I have not been able to bring myself to believe that a *doubtful opinion* of the Chief Magistrate ought to outweigh the solemnly pronounced opinion of the representatives of the people and of the States.
>
> One of the prominent features of the bill is that which purports to be mandatory on the States to form districts for the choice of Representatives to Congress in single districts. That Congress itself has power by law to alter State regulations respecting the manner of holding elections for Representatives is clear, but its power to command the States to make new regulations is the question upon which I have felt deep and strong doubts. I have yielded those doubts, however, to the opinion of the Legislature, giving effect to their enactment as far as depends on my approbation, and leaving questions which may arise hereafter, if unhappily such should arise, to be settled by full consideration of the several provisions of the Constitution and the laws and the authority of each House to judge of the

[63]Cong Globe, 27th Cong, 2d Sess 584 (Sen. Smith of Connecticut); id at 613 (Sen. Cuthbert). Disobedience, said Senator Buchanan, was the only way to test the constitutionality of the provision. Cong Globe App, 27th Cong, 2d Sess 450. See also Cong Globe, 27th Cong, 2d Sess 568 (Sen. Benton) (arguing that Missouri would have no time to draw districts prior to its August election, which was only two months away). Representatives Kennedy and Payne and Senator Bagby predicted that states would disobey the law; Senator Wright suggested that New York might; Senator Woodbury said the states would be justified in doing so. Cong Globe, 27th Cong, 2d Sess 452 (Rep. Kennedy) (reminding the House that Georgia had executed an Indian chief in defiance of a federal court); id at 453 (Rep. Payne); id at 563 (Sen. Wright); id at 567 (Sen. Woodbury); Cong Globe App, 27th Cong, 2d Sess 788 (Sen. Bagby). In any event, Benton added, if the districting proposal was adopted,

> it will soon die. The first day of the next Congress will see it die, in company with many others—such as the distribution law, the bankrupt law, and others. They will all be rubbed out together. [Expunged, said Mr. Woodbury.] Yes, sir, expunged! They will all go; all these acts of encroachment on the rights of the people and the States.

Cong Globe, 27th Cong, 2d Sess 568.

[64]Id at 584 (Sen. Kerr); Cong Globe App, 27th Cong, 2d Sess 459–60 (Sen. Crittenden); id at 513 (Sen. Tallmadge); id at 789–90 (Sen. Miller).

[65]Cong Globe, 27th Cong, 2d Sess 568.

elections, returns, and qualifications of its own members.[66]

Compulsory districting had been a party measure. Whigs favored it, Democrats opposed it, and the Whigs (for a change) controlled both Houses.[67] Normalcy was restored, however, when the Democrats recaptured the House in the 1842 elections, and (as Missouri Senator Thomas Hart Benton had predicted)[68] they lost no time in effectively nullifying their predecessors' decision.

Six states had elected Representatives by general ticket before the districting requirement was adopted.[69] Four of them—Georgia, Mississippi, Missouri, and New Hampshire—continued to do so in the 1842 election, after the requirement took effect.[70] When the Representatives from those states presented themselves at the commencement of the Twenty-eighth Congress, they were met with a protest signed by no fewer than fifty opposition members on the ground that they had not been elected in accordance with the governing law.[71]

The Committee on Elections, to which the question was referred,[72] concluded that the challenged members were entitled to their seats because the districting requirement

[66]4 Richardson at 159–60 (Jun 25, 1842). Tyler also expressed doubts as to the constitutionality of the provision giving states extra seats for fractions exceeding half the statutory ratio ("a question on which a diversity of opinion has existed from the foundation of the Government"), but he conceded that that provision "recommends itself from its nearer approximation to equality." Id at 160. The Whiglike deference to Congress displayed in this message was hardly characteristic of President Tyler, who typically wielded the veto with a ferocity previously associated only with Andrew Jackson. See the examples cited with respect to various aspects of the American System in chapters 1–4 and the discussion in section I of chapter 6. John Quincy Adams and South Carolina Representative John Campbell objected that the President had no right to explain his reasons for signing a bill (see HR Rep 909, 27th Cong, 2d Sess 1–2 (1842); Cong Globe App, 27th Cong, 2d Sess 558) but there was not much to that; the power to explain (as judges and members of Congress habitually do) seems implicit in the right to act. See id at 892 (Rep. Cushing); cf the discussion of President Jackson's protest against Senate censure in section II D of chapter 3.

[67]When the House voted on seating members elected in violation of the districting proviso, Representative Kennedy predicted two years later, "all the whig members would vote against the gentlemen who were elected under the general-ticket system, and all the democratic members would vote for them." Cong Globe, 28th Cong, 1st Sess 236. See also id at 254 (Rep. Brown of Virginia), declaring that all Democrats save Campbell of South Carolina—who "went over to the enemy" [!]—had voted against the districting requirement. I have made a half-hearted and fruitless effort to determine whether Democratic opposition was fueled by disparate election prospects as well as by principles of state rights; I leave this nonlegal inquiry to those who find pleasure in counting beans.

[68]See note 63.

[69]See Cong Globe App, 27th Cong, 2d Sess 319 (Rep. Butler).

[70]Georgia, however, had adopted districts for future elections. See Cong Globe App, 28th Cong, 1st Sess 197 (Rep. Stephens). Connecticut's legislature, meanwhile, in imitation of Virginia and Kentucky in 1798, had declared the districting provision unconstitutional. See Cong Globe, 28th Cong, 1st Sess 258 (Rep. Catlin). New Jersey and Rhode Island, which had formerly employed the general ticket, had changed their laws in response to Congress's direction.

[71]Cong Globe, 28th Cong, 1st Sess 10. There was much haggling over whether this protest belonged in the Journal, as Representative Barnard had not been allowed to present it. Ultimately the House voted to strike the statement from the Journal, id at 26; it remains, of course, in the Globe. Representative Newton objected that the Constitution required the House to keep a complete and accurate journal (id at 27); Representative Dromgoole distressingly replied that it was for the majority to determine what the Journal should contain. Id at 30. Compare the discussion of expunging the Senate's censure of President Jackson in section II E of chapter 3.

[72]Cong Globe, 28th Cong, 1st Sess 55.

was unconstitutional.[73] The accompanying report neatly summed up the arguments previously made to justify that conclusion;[74] the ensuing discussion went through the entire matter again without adding anything of significance on the merits.[75] The House then voted, essentially on party lines, to seat the contested members.[76] Virginia Representative George Dromgoole's motion that the House formally declare the general-ticket elections valid despite the statute was ruled out of order,[77] but it didn't matter; by holding that members chosen by general ticket had been properly elected, the House necessarily found the districting provision unconstitutional.

Had the House authority to nullify a statute passed by the whole Congress? Occasional Whig speakers said it had not.[78] But the House could not perform its duty of judging elections, majority spokesmen rejoined, without determining whether the election laws were valid.[79] This was one of the arguments Chief Justice Marshall had made to sustain judicial review;[80] it was what President Jackson had said to justify vetoing the extension of the Bank charter on constitutional grounds.[81] On this question I think the majority was right. The analogies are persuasive; the House had recognized from the beginning that it had the obligation, in passing on the elections of its members, to determine the validity of *state* election laws.[82] What South Carolina had done in 1832 was something else again: It had attempted to interfere with the enforcement of federal law against third parties.[83] As Stephen A. Douglas said, he "never supposed nullification to be the declaring a law void by a tribunal which was expressly empowered to declare it void."[84]

That was the end of the 1842 districting law, a worthy experiment that failed. It was never repealed, as the Whigs still had a majority (though a diminished one) in the Senate.[85] But three states went right on electing members by general ticket, and the law

[73]Id at 278.

[74]HR Rep 60, 28th Cong, 1st Sess (1844).

[75]See (if you insist) Cong Globe, 28th Cong, 1st Sess 236–79; Cong Globe App, 28th Cong, 1st Sess 115–307. While contributing nothing really novel, Alexander Stephens's fine speech (id at 196–201) may be the best single statement in defense of mandatory districting and will repay reading.

[76]Cong Globe, 28th Cong, 1st Sess 279–83.

[77]Id at 283.

[78]See Cong Globe App, 28th Cong, 1st Sess 254 (Rep. Summers); id at 312–13 (Rep. Vinton).

[79]See, e.g., id at 127 (Rep. Elmer); id at 191 (Rep. Jameson); id at 211 (Rep. Dromgoole); id at 267 (Rep. French).

[80]Marbury v Madison, 5 US 137, 177 (1803); see also The Federalist No 78 (Hamilton). Supporters of the House's authority repeatedly invoked the judicial analogy. E.g., Cong Globe, 28th Cong, 1st Sess 277 (Rep. Douglas): "Would gentlemen charge the Supreme Court with nullification, in case they decided that a law of Congress was invalid?" See also Cong Globe App, 28th Cong, 1st Sess 127 (Rep. Elmer); id at 191 (Rep. Jameson); id at 267 (Rep. French).

[81]See the discussion in section I of chapter 3. Representative Jameson also invoked this analogy. Cong Globe App, 28th Cong, 1st Sess 191.

[82]See id at 211 (Rep. Dromgoole); The Jeffersonians at 76–81. As Representative Douglas astutely observed, opponents of seating the contested members fully embraced this position, for they were forced to contend that the general-ticket laws were unconstitutional. Cong Globe, 28th Cong, 1st Sess 277.

[83]See the discussion in chapter 4.

[84]Cong Globe, 28th Cong, 1st Sess 277. Yes, this was indeed the Little Giant, then in his first term as a Democratic Representative from Illinois; the reporter spelled his name "Douglass," as the gentleman in question did until 1846. See Johannsen, Douglas at 876 n.7.

[85]See Cong Globe App, 28th Cong, 1st Sess 254 (Rep. Summers). A House bill to repeal the measure never got out of committee. See Cong Globe, 28th Cong, 1st Sess 283.

was never applied to deny any of them his seat. Since the requirement by its own terms applied only to elections held pursuant to the 1842 statute, it expired when the next apportionment was made ten years later, and the 1850 law omitted the districting provision.[86] It was reinstated in 1862, when the Republicans were in power.[87] In 1872 Congress finally appended the additional requirement that districts contain "as nearly as practicable an equal number of inhabitants,"[88] which again seems a perfectly legitimate and desirable regulation of the manner of conducting House elections under Article I, § 4—and which we have since been informed the Constitution requires.[89]

II. THE SPEAKER

The 1840 session, to which I adverted in the preceding chapter,[90] was not the only one of this period in which the House had difficulty in choosing its Speaker. In 1849, 1855, and 1859 the chamber was closely divided. Splinter parties and sectional animosities rendered consensus elusive. In each instance the process took from three to eight weeks and from 44 to 133 ballots.[91] During this time the House was at a standstill. As you would anticipate from the arguments that were made in the election contests earlier considered, several members insisted that the House could do nothing else until it elected a Speaker.[92]

What was the source of this peculiar abstemiousness? The Constitution required the House to "choose their Speaker and other officers,"[93] but it did not say it had to do so first.[94] There might be more important things to do than electing officers;[95] was the whole legislative machinery to be stalled because the House had yet to anoint its Clerk?[96] Louisiana Representative Miles Taylor protested at once that the House could do business

[86]9 Stat 428, 432–33, § 25 (May 23, 1850).

[87]12 Stat 572 (Jul 14, 1862).

[88]17 Stat 28, § 2 (Feb 2, 1872).

[89]Wesberry v Sanders, 376 US 1, 7–18 (1964), questionably relying on the requirement (US Const, Art I, § 2) that Representatives be elected by the "people" of the several states.

[90]See section I of chapter 9.

[91]See Cong Globe, 31st Cong, 1st Sess 66; 34th Cong, 1st Sess 337–42; 36th Cong, 1st Sess 650. The word "ballot" may give the wrong impression; each time the vote was viva voce. See Cong Globe, 31st Cong, 1st Sess 3; notes 111–12 and accompanying text. The happy winners, in chronological order, were Howell Cobb (D-Ga), Nathaniel Banks (W-Mass), and William Pennington (R-NJ). For a brief exposition of the background of the four great contests see M.P. Follett, The Speaker of the House of Representatives 51–63 (Longmans, Green, 1896).

[92]E.g., Cong Globe, 31st Cong, 1st Sess 62 (Georgia Rep. Robert Toombs); 36th Cong, 1st Sess 444 (Rep. Pennington). At one point the House went so far as to refuse to receive the President's Annual Message, though it later reversed itself. Cong Globe, 34th Cong, 1st Sess 123, 296. Indeed the Clerk initially ruled in 1849 that a motion to order the yeas and nays was out of order (Cong Globe, 31st Cong, 1st Sess 4), but that was fallacious; recording the votes was part of the process for choosing the Speaker, which all agreed the House had power to do. See also David Outlaw to Emily B. Outlaw, Dec 11, 1849, David Outlaw Papers, Southern History Collection, University of North Carolina at Chapel Hill, noting that members were not being paid, as no money could be drawn from the Treasury until the House was organized or at least had elected a Sergeant at Arms.

[93]US Const, Art I, § 2.

[94]The 1970 Illinois Constitution, in contrast, is explicit if Procrustean: When the House convenes, the Secretary of State shall preside for the [sole] purpose of electing a Speaker. Ill Const 1970, Art 4, § 6.

[95]See Cong Globe, 36th Cong, 1st Sess 521 (Massachusetts Sen. John Davis).

[96]See id at 497 (Sen. Crittenden).

without a Speaker,[97] as it indisputably did when that officer was elected but indisposed.

The short answer was statutory, as Pennsylvania Representative John Cadwalader revealed: The first statute Congress ever adopted required that the oath of office be administered to the Speaker, "and by him to all the members present, and to the clerk, previous to entering on any other business . . . ."[98] Standard doctrine, however, tells us that no legislative body can limit its own future authority;[99] if the Constitution allowed the House to do business before electing a Speaker, no statute would be likely to stand in its way.

Constitutional barriers were even asserted in early 1860 to the *Senate's* doing business before the House had a Speaker. Six weeks after Congress convened, with the House still in fetters, James Mason of Virginia objected to the Senate's voting on passage of a private bill. The legislative power, he argued, was vested in a Congress composed of two Houses.[100] The House of Representatives did not exist until it was organized, and thus there was no Congress either.[101] Mason took the inevitable next step a day later: So long as the House was in limbo, the Senate could not even initiate the legislative process by sending a bill to committee.[102]

It was scandalous enough for the House to twiddle its thumbs while the nation dissolved before its eyes; it was inexcusable for Mason to suggest that the Senate do nothing to hasten the adoption of legislation once the House was in a position to act.[103] No provision of the Constitution said that one House could not be in session when the other was not; Article I, § 5, which forbade one House to adjourn for more than three days without the other's consent, implied that it could. Indeed, Article II, § 3 expressly authorized the President to call one House into session without the other, and Presidents regu-

[97]Cong Globe, 34th Cong, 1st Sess 117.

[98]1 Stat 23, § 2 (Jun 1, 1789). Mere receipt of the President's message, Cadwalader argued, was not "business" within the meaning of this provision. Cong Globe, 34th Cong, 1st Sess 296.

[99]See Julian Eule, Temporal Limits on the Legislative Mandate: Entrenchment and Retroactivity, 1987 Am Bar Foundation Res J 379. Some later scholars have cast doubt on the existence of any such doctrine. E.g., Eric Posner & Adrian Vermeule, Legislative Entrenchment: A Reappraisal, 111 Yale LJ 1665 (2002).

[100]US Const, Art I, § 1.

[101]Cong Globe, 36th Cong, 1st Sess 494, 495. See also id at 519 (Florida Sen. Stephen Mallory). Representative Outlaw had privately taken the same position in 1949: Neither the House nor the Senate could act, and "so the wheels of Government so far as the Legislative branch is concerned are at a dead halt." David Outlaw to Emily B. Outlaw, Dec 5, 1849, in David Outlaw Papers (cited in note 92).

[102]Cong Globe, 36th Cong, 1st Sess 517. In support of this conclusion Mason and Mallory cited an earlier argument by Henry Clay that the Senate could take up *executive* (and by implication not legislative) business without the House, an 1855 Senate refusal to address legislative matters on grounds of practice (not constitutional compulsion), and Vice-President Fillmore's curt 1849 ruling that it was improper even to give notice of intent to introduce a bill until both Houses were organized. Id at 517, 519. (For Fillmore's ruling and the brief discussion that preceded it see Cong Globe, 31st Cong, 1st Sess 15; for Clay's argument and the Senate's corresponding resolution see id at 35–36.) When Mason repeated his objection, Crittenden protested that an issue of constitutional authority could not be made a point of order, and Vice-President Breckinridge submitted the question to the Senate. Cong Globe, 36th Cong, 1st Sess 522. Crittenden had made the same point earlier, id at 497. Crittenden seems right that questions of substantive power ought not to be raised by point of order, but Mason's objection went to the legislative process itself; I see no reason why constitutional questions of procedure should not be raised in this way.

[103]Senator Trumbull agreed the Senate could not proceed, but not because there was no Speaker; he thought Congress did not exist until the House notified the Senate that it was ready to conduct business. Id at 497.

larly did so at the beginning of their successors' terms.[104] Senators of all political stripes protested heartily against suspension of the Senate's functions. The President thought Congress was in session, said Maine Republican William Pitt Fessenden; he sent us his annual address.[105] The House must exist before it had a Speaker, added Judah Benjamin of Louisiana, since the Constitution authorized it to choose him.[106] Mason's objection was rejected by a resounding vote of 45–7, and the bill was sent to committee;[107] but the Senate passed no bills in the few days that remained before the House selected its Speaker.[108]

For in each of our three cases, mirabile dictu, the House managed to break the logjam and choose its presiding officer. Members tendered an imaginative assortment of expedients in efforts to do so. The Speaker should be chosen by lot.[109] (Laughed out of the chamber.)[110] He should be chosen by secret ballot.[111] (Disparaged as undermining party discipline, which was the point of the proposal.)[112] Three Speakers should be chosen, to preside on alternate days.[113] (Unconstitutional: Article I, § 2 for obvious reasons directs the House (in the singular) to "choose their Speaker.")[114] A temporary chairman should be selected (as in the 1840 contest over the New Jersey election) so that the House could proceed in an orderly way.[115] (Rejected after fears were expressed that the House might never be able to get rid of him.)[116] Until a Speaker was chosen, the House should not debate[117] or adjourn;[118] the doors should be locked;[119] members should not be fed[120] or even

[104]E.g., 5 Richardson at 426 (Feb 16, 1857) (President Pierce).

[105]Cong Globe, 36th Cong, 1st Sess 495. Are you saying, he asked Mason, that we cannot collect our per diem because the House is not ready to play? Id.

[106]Id at 495. Accord id at 497 (Sen. Crittenden). Other Senators speaking up for the Senate's authority included James Pearce (A-Md), id at 496; James Bayard (D-Del), id at 517; and Jacob Collamer (R-Vt), id at 521. Mason's colleague Robert M.T. Hunter (A-Va) thought the Senate had power to pass bills but advised against it by analogy to appropriations, which he said the Senate was competent to originate but which the House regularly refused to pass when it did. Id at 495.

[107]Id at 522.

[108]See Sen Journal, 36th Cong, 1st Sess 124 (Feb 6, 1860) (noting receipt of notice from the House that a Speaker had been elected); id at 130–31 (Feb 7, 1860), noting Senate passage of a joint resolution.

[109]Cong Globe, 31st Cong, 1st Sess 13 (Rep. Morse).

[110]Id (Rep. Root).

[111]Id at 6 (Rep. Ashmun); id at 14 (Rep. Schenck); Cong Globe, 34th Cong, 1st Sess 53 (Rep. Whitney).

[112]The euphemism of choice was deceiving one's constituents. See Cong Globe, 31st Cong, 1st Sess 14 (Rep. Venable); see his additional observations in id at 6. Secrecy, in any event, might well have been unattainable; under Article I, § 5 one fifth of the members could require that "the yeas and nays . . . be entered on the Journal."

[113]Cong Globe, 34th Cong, 1st Sess 85 (Rep. Colfax). Representative Evans had earlier suggested that two *temporary* chairmen should be appointed, likewise to preside on alternate days. Cong Globe, 31st Cong, 1st Sess 7.

[114]Cf US Const, Art II, § 1: "The executive power shall be vested in a President of the United States . . . ."

[115]Cong Globe, 31st Cong, 1st Sess 7 (Rep. McClernand); id at 32, 48 (Rep. Woodward).

[116]Id at 7 (Rep. Duer).

[117]Id at 34 (Rep. Dimmick). The House embraced this proposal "by an overwhelming 'aye'" (id) but continued to talk, not least about the proper interpretation of the rule. Toombs argued that debate could not constitutionally be forbidden and that until a Speaker was chosen the House could not adopt any rules. Id at 42, 61–63.

[118]E.g., id at 36 (Rep. Littlefield). The House so voted at one juncture but predictably relented. Cong Globe, 34th Cong, 1st Sess 83–84.

[119]Id at 139 (Rep. Mace).

[120]Id at 72 (Rep. English).

paid their salaries.[121] (Only the last of these suggestions was clearly inadmissible: Unless Mason was right that no House yet existed, Article I, § 6 required that members "receive a compensation for their services.") The House should vote by states, as it did when the electors were unable to choose a President.[122] (Fat chance: Recall the impossibility of persuading the large states to give up their *unfair* advantage in the choice of a President even when there was a quid for their quo.)[123] The Speaker should be chosen by committee,[124] or by the three candidates who had received the most votes.[125] (The House cannot delegate its authority to make decisions. Supreme Court decisions endorsing what the British call delegated legislation simply recognize that the power to execute laws necessarily implies interstitial policymaking.)[126] If all else failed, the entire House should resign so there could be new elections.[127] (Fat chance again, though parliaments in other countries can sometimes be dissolved if unable to agree on a government.)[128]

Two suggestions merited more attention, and one of them was twice adopted. The first was to strike the candidate with the fewest votes after each ballot so as ultimately to force a choice between two contenders.[129] That sounded promising. That is what is done in runoff elections for various offices across the country; it is what happens (and actually happened in 1837) under the twelfth amendment when the electors cannot agree on a Vice-President.[130] It works, however, only if voting is confined to the candidates who remain on the list, and it was suggested that the House could not prevent members from voting for whomever they pleased.[131]

This argument seems misguided. Even if the House was not yet a "House" empowered by Article I, § 5 to "determine the rules of its proceedings,"[132] it had express authority as we know to elect its Speaker; and it could not do so without determining the parameters of the election. Parliamentary rules habitually restrict the rights of members to vote or to speak; legislatures could get nothing done without them.[133]

[121]Cong Globe, 31st Cong, 1st Sess 35 (Kentucky Rep. John Mason).

[122]Cong Globe, 34th Cong, 1st Sess 317 (Rep. Crawford). See US Const, Art II, § 1 and Amend 12.

[123]See The Jeffersonians at 339–42.

[124]Cong Globe, 31st Cong, 1st Sess 47 (Rep. Butler); Cong Globe, 34th Cong, 1st Sess 328 (Rep. Steward).

[125]Id at 333 (Rep. Letcher).

[126]If you think otherwise, ask yourself whether you really believe Congress could authorize its committees to pass legislation. Preparatory labor is another matter; even the President may suggest legislation. Cf Nixon v United States, 506 US 224, 250–51 (1993) (White, J, concurring) (upholding the Senate's authority to take evidence by committee in impeachment trials).

[127]Cong Globe, 34th Cong, 1st Sess 27 (Rep. Letcher); id at 32 (Rep. McMullin) (urging that the House first vote appropriations).

[128]E.g., Basic Law for the Federal Republic of Germany, Art 63(4).

[129]For this and similar proposals see Cong Globe, 31st Cong, 1st Sess 32 (Rep. Williams); id at 44 (Rep. Savage); id at 63 (Rep. Meade); 34th Cong, 1st Sess 27 (Rep. Hickman); id at 69–70 (Rep. Stanton); Cong Globe, 36th Cong, 1st Sess 489 (Rep. Sickles).

[130]The Senate chose Richard M. Johnson of Kentucky. See Cong Globe, 24th Cong, 2d Sess 152, 166. The procedure for House selection of a President in like circumstances is a variant of this scheme. Representative Savage's resolution invoked these analogies, Cong Globe, 31st Cong, 1st Sess 44.

[131]Id at 32 (Rep. Root). This suggestion, Representative Outlaw wrote his wife, was "so manifestly unconstitutional, that it received no favour." David Outlaw to Emily B. Outlaw, Dec 5, 1849, in David Outlaw Papers (cited in note 92).

[132]Representative Toombs, for one, expressly denied that it was. Cong Globe, 31st Cong, 1st Sess 42, 61–63. For the contrary argument see Cong Deb, 34th Cong, 1st Sess 69–70 (Rep. Stanton).

[133]See The Federalist Period at 9–10; The Jeffersonians at 315 n.214.

The proposal for a runoff election was never adopted, but the alternate suggestion was: In 1849 and 1856 (for in the latter case the process erupted into the following year) the House determined by a simple plurality who was to be Speaker.[134] The objection that the House could no more delegate its authority to a plurality of members than to a committee[135] was off the mark. Whether a majority or a plurality sufficed, it was the House and not a group of its members that made the decision. The plurality rule specified not what body should choose the Speaker but how it should choose him, and as suggested in the preceding paragraph the House must have authority to determine the manner of electing its officers.[136]

House rules must of course be consistent with those laid down by the Constitution itself; the better objection was that the "House" authorized to choose a Speaker meant a majority of its members.[137] For traditionally legislative bodies acted by majority vote.[138] Surely, said South Carolina Representative William Porcher Miles when the plurality option was pushed again (without success) in 1860, the House could not agree to pass a bill without a majority.[139] That sounds right but not in point, for the choice whether or not to pass legislation is binary. For reasons made evident by the repeated struggles to choose a Speaker, the tradition of majority rule is not so firmly established when it comes to questions that may have more than two possible answers, such as elections. Since the

[134]See Cong Globe, 31st Cong, 1st Sess 63–66; Cong Globe, 34th Cong, 1st Sess 335–37.

[135]Cong Globe, 31st Cong, 1st Sess 43 (South Carolina Rep. Isaac Holmes); id at 63 (Rep. Toombs).

[136]See Cong Globe, 36th Cong, 1st Sess 444 (Rep. Pennington).

[137]See Cong Globe, 31st Cong, 1st Sess 42–43, 63 (Rep. Toombs); id at 43 (Rep. Holmes); 36th Cong, 1st Sess 447 (Rep. Miles). It took a quorum for the House to do almost anything, it was pointed out, and Article I, § 5 defined a quorum as a majority of all its members. Cf the argument respecting congressional regulation of the number of Supreme Court Justices needed to declare a statute unconstitutional, The Jeffersonians at 331.

[138]See Thomas Jefferson, A Manual of Parliamentary Practice composed originally for the use of the Senate of the United States 91 (Clark & Maynard, 1840), cited by Toombs at Cong Globe, 31st Cong, 1st Sess 63: "The voice of the majority decides; for the *lex majoris partis* is the law of all councils, elections, &c, where not otherwise expressly provided." See also David Outlaw to Emily B. Outlaw, Dec 22, 1849, in David Outlaw Papers (cited in note 92): "The Constitution declares the House shall elect a Speaker. Now what is the House. It is a majority of those who are present."

[139]Cong Globe, 36th Cong, 1st Sess 447. Resort to a plurality on that occasion was obviated when New York Representative George Briggs switched his support to the "Black Republican" Pennington on the forty-fourth ballot because Pennington was "not [John] Sherman" (the supposedly more radical Ohioan most Southern Whigs had sworn never to accept) and "we need a Speaker." Id at 654. Briggs's vote gave Pennington a majority of one, producing "a sensation in the Hall and galleries." Id at 650, 654.

At one point rabid Southerners had gone so far as to move to disqualify from the Speakership any member who "indorse[d] and recommend[ed]" an "insurrectionary" book entitled "The Impending Crisis of the South" by a North Carolinian named Hinton Helper. See Cong Globe, 36th Cong, 1st Sess 3 (Missouri Rep. John Clark). This motion was intended as a swipe at Sherman, who with a number of Republican colleagues had signed a letter speaking approvingly of the book, id at 16. Ohio Representative John Hutchins denied "the right of a minority or of a majority in this House to prescribe the rule by which my vote for Speaker shall be controlled or regulated." Id at 482. The Constitution itself prescribes no qualifications for Speaker, not even (unless it is implicit) membership in the House. See id at 483 (Rep. Washburn). Term limits for Representatives are distinguishable, since in the case of the Speaker the House is setting standards for itself; the question is whether it can bind itself in advance, as in the admission of states—or for that matter the plurality rule in selecting the Speaker. See The Federalist Period at 220–21 and note 142 of this chapter. For discussion of the freedom-of-expression debates engendered by Helper's book and Southern efforts to suppress it see Michael Kent Curtis, The Crisis Over *The Impending Crisis:* Free Speech, Slavery, and the Fourteenth Amendment, in Paul Finkelman, ed, Slavery and the Law 161 (Madison House, 1997).

Constitution was adopted, numerous members of Congress and presidential electors, to say nothing of state functionaries of one kind or another, have owed their offices to a mere plurality.[140]

Thus I think there would have been nothing wrong with the House's deciding to permit election of the Speaker by less than a majority of those voting even if it had left them the final decision. All reasonable objections were mooted, in any event, when the House overwhelmingly voted to confirm the plurality's choice.[141] Though a few uneducables still didn't get it, Speakers Howell Cobb and Nathaniel Banks were not really elected by mere pluralities after all. Even the bills Congress enacts, which are purely legislative, are commonly drafted by individual members or committees, or for that matter in the Executive Branch. A member may cast his vote for any reason he likes, including a prior commitment to honor the plurality's choice; nothing in the Constitution forbids either House of Congress to rubber-stamp someone else's decision.[142]

III. THE SNOWSTORM OF 1856

On December 3, 1856, it snowed in Wisconsin. There was nothing remarkable about that; it often snows in Wisconsin. But December 3 was the day on which, according to federal law, the electors were to meet in their respective states to choose a new President.[143] Because of the snow Wisconsin's electors were unable to reach the appointed place at the appointed time. A day later, on December 4, they doggedly arrived and cast their five votes for the Republican candidate, John C. Frémont. A certificate of these events was duly executed and shipped off to the President of the Senate, as the statute required.[144]

A few weeks later, as the Constitution provided, the members of the House and Senate sat together in the Capitol in Washington to proclaim the election of the President. For as it is written in the Scriptures:

[140]See Cong Globe, 34th Cong, 1st Sess 70 (Rep. Stanton). One thinks, to select an example at random, of the second President Bush's Supreme Court–assisted victory in Florida in 2000. See Bush v Gore, 531 US 98 (2000). (According to the website of the Florida Department of State, electors for George Bush received 2,912,790 votes, those for Al Gore 2,912,253, and those for Ralph Nader 97,488. http://enight.dos.state.fl.us/elections/resultsarchive/.) The postwar German constitution, to cite another instance, allows the President of the Federation to approve a parliamentary plurality's choice for prime minister. Basic Law for the Federal Republic of Germany, Art 63(4).

[141]Cong Globe, 31st Cong, 1st Sess 66; 34th Cong, 1st Sess 339–42.

[142]See Cong Globe, 34th Cong, 1st Sess 340 (Kentucky Rep. Humphrey Marshall); id at 341 (South Carolina Rep. William Boyce). Some argued no confirmation was necessary: Even if a majority had to approve the final decision, it had already done so by voting to abide by the plurality's future determination. Id at 340 (Reps. Clingman and Cobb); Cong Globe, 36th Cong, 1st Sess 446 (Maine Rep. Israel Washburn); id at 482 (Rep. Hutchins).

An unrelated question concerning the *rights* of the Speaker was also debated briefly during the Thirty-first Congress. Previous House rules had permitted him to vote only to make or break a tie, and members from both parties argued they were unconstitutional: The House had no authority to disfranchise either the Speaker or his constituents. Cong Globe, 31st Cong, 1st Sess 142–45 (Reps. Winthrop, McLane, McClernand, and Stanton). The rule was accordingly revised to say only that the Speaker was not *required* to vote except to make or break a tie, id at 145. See generally Follett, The Speaker of the House at 147–60 (cited in note 91), noting that several nineteenth-century Speakers insisted on occasion on their right to vote in other cases, and that no one ever objected.

[143]1 Stat 239, 240, § 2 (Mar 1, 1792).

[144]See Cong Globe, 34th Cong, 3d Sess 644; 1 Stat at 239–40, § 2.

> The President of the Senate shall, in the presence of the Senate and House of Representatives, open all the certificates, and the votes shall then be counted.[145]

The certificates were opened and read; the votes were counted by tellers appointed for the purpose.[146] Wisconsin, the members learned, had cast five votes for Frémont—on the wrong day. Wisconsin's votes are invalid, said numerous members; they may not be counted.[147] For the statute plainly required that the electors vote on December 3, not December 4; and the Constitution leaves no doubt that electors throughout the country must vote on the same day.[148]

A few members, to be sure, expressed doubts on the merits. *Force majeur,* they suggested, was always a sufficient justification for tardy compliance with legal duties.[149] Maybe so, although the constitutional requirement of uniformity looks pretty solid; the disfranchisement of a state is a serious matter.[150] But there was a threshold question that was much more interesting and important: Who should decide whether Wisconsin's votes should be counted?[151]

The President of the Senate, said Michigan Senator Charles Stuart, citing Chancellor Kent.[152] The Constitution, added John Thompson of Kentucky, directed that officer to

[145]US Const, Art II, § 1 and Amend 12.

[146]Cong Globe, 34th Cong, 3d Sess 644.

[147]Id at 646 (Sen. Douglas); id at 647 (Sen. Reid); id at 650 (Sens. Bell and Weller); id at 652 (Rep. Letcher); id at 653 (Sen. Butler); id at 653, 656, 672 (Rep. Orr); id at 659 (Rep. Bingham); id at 663 (Sen. Thompson); id at 665 (Sen. Crittenden) (noting that an individual voter would not be permitted to vote late if delayed by a storm); id at 666 (Sen Toucey).

[148]See US Const, Art II, § 1: "The Congress may determine the time of choosing the electors, and the day on which they shall give their votes; which day shall be the same throughout the United States." The uniformity requirement, you will observe, applies only to the "day" on which the electors vote, not to the "time" when they are chosen; Congress initially contented itself with requiring that they be designated within the thirty-four days preceding their meeting. 1 Stat 239, § 1 (Mar 1, 1792). The "time" of choosing electors, however, may be one day as well as thirty-four, and Congress made it so by statute in 1845: "[T]he electors of President and Vice-President shall be appointed in each State on the Tuesday next after the first Monday in the month of November . . . ." 5 Stat 721 (Jan 23, 1845); see 3 USC § 1 (2000). "The design of the [1845] law," explained Maine Representative Hannibal Hamlin, "was to prevent the interference of one State, or the citizens of one State, with the elections of another." Cong Globe App, 28th Cong, 1st Sess 434. See also 4 Elliot's Debates at 105 (James Iredell), supporting the constitutional provision in order to avoid "every danger of influence" or "combination." No one seems to have challenged the constitutionality of the statute; New Jersey Representative Lucius Elmer argued (erroneously) that it was constitutionally *required.* Cong Globe, 28th Cong, 2d Sess 15. Further provisions of the statute (5 Stat at 721) permitting states to fill vacancies when the electors met and to make a later selection if an election on the prescribed date failed to produce a choice needed no justification as necessary and proper to the election of a President (see The Federalist Period at 137, 289–90); they were mere exceptions to the general prescription that the "time" of selection was a single day.

[149]Cong Globe, 34th Cong, 3d Sess 647 (Sen. Seward); id at 648 (Sen. Hale); id at 653 (New York Rep. Solomon Haven); id at 657 (Wisconsin Rep. Elihu Washburn).

[150]Senator Stuart suggested that Congress settle the matter for the future by enacting a statute (necessary and proper to setting the date of election?) specifying "that electoral votes not cast on the day required by law shall not be counted." Id at 645. Neither House acted on his suggestion.

[151]See id at 644 (Sen. Nourse). Washburn of Maine urged that *this* question be resolved for the future by statute. Id at 657.

[152]Id at 664; see 1 Kent's Commentaries at 258–59:

open the certificates and count the votes.[153] Not so, others responded. The Constitution said only that the votes should be counted; it did not say by whom.[154] It should not be presumed that the Framers meant to empower any single individual to choose the President—least of all the President of the Senate, who in normal times was also Vice-President of the United States and often (you remember the 2000 election) a candidate for the Presidency himself.[155] For whoever decides which votes to count, it was argued, effectively selects the President.[156]

Thus, some contended, the members of the House and Senate should resolve disputes over the validity of electoral votes; for why else were they so solemnly required to assemble? And to whom could the Founders have safely entrusted this awesome responsibility, other than to the elected representatives of the states and the people?[157]

But each House must vote separately, some objected. Otherwise the House will outvote the Senate, since it has more members. By requiring both Houses to convene, the Framers must have intended them to have equal weight in making the decision.[158]

Wrong, said Maryland Representative Henry Winter Davis. The provision in question gave *no one* authority to decide which votes were valid. The task of the assembled Senators and Representatives was simply to report what votes had been cast. Whether those votes were lawful—and whether therefore a President had been elected—was for the House of Representatives alone to determine. For it was the House that the Constitution authorized to elect a President if the electors had not done so.[159]

Stop the train, said Jacob Collamer, Republican Senator from Vermont. We ought not to be discussing the validity of Wisconsin's votes at all:

> I presume, in the absence of all legislative provision on the subject, that the president of the senate counts the votes and determines the result, and that the two houses are present only as spectators, to witness the fairness and accuracy of the transaction, and to act only if no choice be made by the electors.

[153]Cong Globe, 34th Cong, 3d Sess 662–63. Representative Washburn offered a variant of this thesis that was no more appealing: Until Congress otherwise provided, the tellers should decide; for the statute said they were to count the votes, and neither House was authorized to interfere. Id at 657.

[154]Id at 652 (Rep. Humphrey Marshall); id at 664 (Sen. Hunter). Both Stuart and Kent acknowledged that the text did not answer the question. Id at 664.

[155]Id at 647 (Sen. Reid); id at 667 (Sen. Pugh). See also 1 Haynes at 242, rejecting the suggestion as absurd.

[156]See, e.g., Cong Globe, 34th Cong, 3d Sess 668 (Sen. Mallory). You remember the 2000 election. Bush v Gore, 531 US 98 (2000).

[157]Cong Globe, 34th Cong, 3d Sess 653, 672 (Rep. Orr); id at 655 (Rep. Marshall); id at 658 (Rep. Cobb); id at 659 (Rep. Bingham); id at 668 (Sen. Mallory).

[158]Id at 644 (Sen. Butler); id at 645 (Sen. Stuart); id at 645 (Sen. Toombs); id at 652 (Sen. Mason); id at 655 (Rep. Marshall). Senator Mason, the President pro tempore, specifically ruled that the joint session had no authority to determine the validity of votes, and that session ended without action on the question. Id at 653–54. To the ensuing question of what would happen if the two Houses disagreed, Representative Marshall had an answer: No vote should be counted unless both Houses agreed it was valid. Id at 655. Senator Thompson, who expressed his legal opinion with what he described as "great reluctance and diffidence," carried this reasoning to a point it could not reach: Because a per capita vote of all members would give the larger states overwhelming authority, the Senate alone must make the final decision. Id at 662–64. One might have wished for even more of that vaunted reluctance and diffidence from Senator Thompson.

[159]Id at 657–58. Senator Toucey made the same suggestion, adding that the Senate might also decide whether the President had been lawfully elected when it passed on his nominations for federal office. Id at 666.

> I very much doubt whether the framers of the Constitution ever intended to leave the subject of the presidential election to the House of Representatives, or the Senate, or either, or both of them. There was a great deal of debate in the convention that framed the Constitution as to the manner of choosing a President of the United States. . . . The Constitution vested in each House the power to decide upon the elections of its members; it provided carefully that it would not trust to the two Houses to elect a President.
>
> It seems to me that if we consult history at all, and consider the probability of things even as they fall within our own observation and experience, we shall find that there is very little practical difference between leaving the presidential election to Congress and leaving Congress to decide that election. . . . Disguise it as we may, . . . in deciding on the election of members of the two Houses of Congress, . . . the vote is a political one. . . .
>
> Under this view of the case it is, to say the least, exceedingly questionable whether, when the Constitution said, not that Congress should decide the election of the President, but that it should decide upon the elections of its own members, it at the same time meant to trust to these Houses, or either or both of them, the power of deciding the presidential election.[160]

Food for thought, yes? Prudently, Congress decided not to decide who should decide whether Wisconsin's votes were valid. For there was no need to decide. Whether Wisconsin was counted or not, the Democratic candidate (James Buchanan) had a clear majority of the electoral votes.[161] Each House voted simply to inform Mr. Buchanan and his running mate (John C. Breckinridge of Kentucky) that they had won the election.[162]

Thus, as in 1800, the great question was left unanswered. It would be resolved, insofar as a statute could resolve it, in 1887.[163] In the meantime Congress would grapple with the problem without statutory guidance during the 1877 crisis over the contest between Samuel Tilden and Rutherford B. Hayes, which Justice Joseph Bradley would ultimately resolve by adopting the essence of Senator Collamer's suggestion that it was not

[160]Id at 665. On the question of politics in election contests see DeAlva S. Alexander, History and Procedure of the House of Representatives 315, 324 (Houghton, Mifflin, 1916), noting the early onset of a tendency to consider election contests "entirely from a party standpoint" and adding that of the 382 cases decided through 1907 all but three were won by contestants from the dominant party.

[161]See Cong Globe, 34th Cong, 3d Sess 644, 646 (Sen. Hunter); id at 644, 645 (Sen. Mason); id at 647 (Sen. Seward). The same strategy had made it unnecessary to decide whether Missouri had become a state in time to cast votes in the presidential election of 1820. See The Jeffersonians at 247–48. It was employed again in the election of 1836, with respect to Michigan. See Cong Deb, 24th Cong, 2d Sess 698–701, 1582–85 (1837); HR Rep 191, 24th Cong, 2d Sess 2. The House report just cited also noted that several electors might have been federal officers at the time they were chosen and thus disqualified by Article II of the Constitution; finessing this difficulty in the usual manner, the committee added that it was unclear who was to decide whether to count the challenged votes and urged Congress to settle that question for the future. Id at 1–2.

[162]Cong Globe, 34th Cong, 3d Sess 668.

[163]24 Stat 373 (Feb 3, 1887); see 3 USC §§ 5, 15 (2000).

for Congress to determine the validity of electoral votes[164]—a position that had been well expressed in 1800 by that eminent South Carolinian who had been present at the creation, Senator Charles Pinckney.[165]

And thus the central message of the great snowstorm of 1856 was a reprise of that of the Great Committee debate fifty-six years before: Unless the electors are unable to make a choice, one ought to think at least twice before allowing Congress—or perhaps any other federal agency—to decide who is going to be President.[166]

[164]See Charles Fairman, Supplement to 7 History of the Supreme Court of the United States: Five Justices and the Electoral Commission of 1877 96–106 (Macmillan, 1988).

[165]See The Federalist Period at 288–91.

[166]No, the matter is not quite that simple. Representative Orr pointed out one obvious exception: What if a state certified more electoral votes than it was entitled to under Article II? Cong Globe, 34th Cong, 3d Sess 672. Ohio Representative John Bingham offered a dichotomy: Congress could determine whether the electors' votes were valid, but it could not go behind their election certificates to determine their qualifications. Id at 659.

Conclusion

We have reached the midpoint in our study of extrajudicial constitutional interpretation during the period from Jackson to Lincoln. Not, strictly speaking, the chronological midpoint, but one compounded of time and topic. Behind us are the great controversies of the first half of the period: those that led, as the title of Part I suggests, to the death of Henry Clay's ambitious American System, which had sought to harness the energies of the Federal Government to foster economic development. By 1845 that battle was essentially over. The Bank of the United States was gone, tariffs were about to be reduced again, federal aid for internal improvements had largely dried up, and distribution of land revenues had been suspended.[1]

It was the Democrats, led by their Southern wing, who killed the American System. Democrats controlled the Presidency during most of the period studied in this book, and for much of that time they controlled Congress as well. Southerners, in turn, controlled the Democratic Party. Democrats, especially Southern ones, tended to have a deathly fear of federal authority, and they construed it narrowly at every turn.

Sometimes, from the prevailing originalist perspective, they were right. The origins of the general-welfare and property clauses strongly suggest that tax revenues were to be spent only to carry out other enumerated powers, and that (apart from the specific constitutional policy of encouraging settlement) the public lands were viewed solely as an alternative to taxes.

On the tariff question the case for the Southern position was more shaky. That free trade generally enhances efficiency does not prove it constitutionally required; that pretextual taxes must be scrutinized lest they undermine limits on federal power does not disable Congress from achieving by customs duties what it could attain by direct regulation. The same is true of internal improvements. The mail cannot be delivered, nor

[1]In the case of railroads, improvements would enjoy a partial revival beginning in 1850, as explained in chapter 1.

troops moved from place to place, nor commerce conducted, without roads or canals. As Chief Justice Marshall had suggested in *McCulloch v Maryland,* one of the principal aims of the Constitution was to free Congress from dependency on the states to carry out its functions. Despite persistent efforts, the stubborn lighthouse precedent could not be explained away: Congress had recognized as early as 1790 that improved transportation facilities were essential to the promotion of trade.

Why did Southern Democrats of this period take such a grudging view of federal authority? In part, as Calhoun said, for purely economic reasons: The South, they thought, was being taxed to support other sections of the country. As I have noted elsewhere, however, opposition to aggressive measures such as those Senator Clay espoused also reflected Southern apprehensions of possible federal interference with slavery. John Randolph had said it hyperbolically back in the 1820's: The Government that can build roads can free the slaves.[2] Calhoun reaffirmed this concern during the tariff controversy in 1832: Even Nullification was really about slavery.

Although slavery thus forms the background of the issues of federal authority raised by the Jacksonian crusade against the American System, it seldom surfaced in the debates; the various components of the system were discussed largely in their own constitutional terms. As we shall see, however, slavery was an explicit subject of debate during the great controversy of the 1830's over the rights of petition and speech. Rather than pursue that controversy here, I have followed the economic struggles of the Jacksonian period down to the Civil War in the interest of tying up loose ends. I have dealt also with other run-of-the-mine issues respecting congressional and presidential authority, judicial and disciplinary proceedings, and federal elections in order to clear the decks for a more or less uninterrupted focus on the overriding and interrelated issues that dominated the second half of the period between Jackson and Lincoln: expansion, secession, and slavery.

Repetition is tedious, and we are only half through. What do we learn from the first half of our study? Many little things about particular disputes, and particular constitutional provisions, of which I shall not remind you. More generally, we confirm the lesson of earlier installments in this series that members of Congress, Presidents, and other executive officers have a good deal to tell us about the Constitution that we cannot afford to ignore.

Let us not tarry here. There is another story to be told, and I am eager to tell it. See you in volume four!

[2]41 Annals of Congress at 1308. For other early examples see The Jeffersonians at 347.

Appendix A

Dramatis Personae*

ADAMS, JOHN QUINCY, 1767–1848; Federalist, Republican, Whig
Minister to The Netherlands, Portugal, Prussia, 1794–1801
Senator from Massachusetts, 1803–8
Minister to Russia, 1809–14
Minister to England, 1815–17
Secretary of State, 1817–25
President, 1825–29
Representative from Massachusetts, 1831–48

ADAMS, STEPHEN, 1807–1857; Democrat
Representative from Mississippi, 1845–47
Senator from Mississippi, 1852–57

ALLEN, WILLIAM, 1803–1879; Jacksonian, Democrat
Representative from Ohio, 1833–35
Senator from Ohio, 1837–49
Governor of Ohio, 1874–76

ARCHER, WILLIAM S., 1789–1855; Republican, Whig
Representative from Virginia, 1820–35
Senator from Virginia, 1841–47

ATHERTON, CHARLES G., 1804–1853; Democrat
Representative from New Hampshire, 1837–43
Senator from New Hampshire, 1843–49, 1853

*Sources: Biographical Directory of the United States Congress 1774–1989 (Government Printing Office, bicentennial ed 1989); Biographical Directory of Federal Judges, 1789–2000 (Berman, 2001).

BADGER, GEORGE E., 1795–1866; Whig
Secretary of the Navy, 1841
Senator from North Carolina, 1846–55

BAGBY, ARTHUR, 1794–1858; Democrat
Governor of Alabama, 1837–41
Senator from Alabama, 1841–48
Minister to Russia, 1848–49

BAKER, EDWARD D., 1811–1861; Whig, Republican
Representative from Illinois, 1845–46, 1849–51
Senator from Oregon, 1860–61

BANKS, NATHANIEL P., 1816–1894; Democrat, American, Republican
Representative from Massachusetts, 1853–57, 1865–73, 1875–79, 1889–91
Speaker of the House, 1855–57
Governor of Massachusetts, 1858–61

BARNARD, DANIEL D., 1797–1861; Whig
Representative from New York, 1827–29, 1839–45
Minister to Prussia, 1850–53

BARRY, WILLIAM T., 1785–1835; Republican, Jacksonian
Representative from Kentucky, 1810–11
Senator from Kentucky, 1814–16
Postmaster General, 1829–35
Minister to Spain, 1835

BATES, ISAAC C., 1779–1845; Whig
Representative from Massachusetts, 1827–35
Senator from Massachusetts, 1841–45

BAYARD, JAMES A., JR., 1799–1880; Democrat
US District Attorney for Delaware, 1838–43
Senator from Delaware, 1851–64, 1867–69

BAYARD, RICHARD, 1796–1868; Whig
Senator from Delaware, 1836–39, 1841–45

BAYLY, THOMAS H., 1810–1856; Democrat
Representative from Virginia, 1844–56

BELL, JOHN, 1797–1869; Whig, American, Opposition
Representative from Tennessee, 1827–41
Speaker of the House, 1833–35

Secretary of War, 1841
Senator from Tennessee, 1847–59
Constitutional Union candidate for President, 1860

BENJAMIN, JUDAH P., 1811–1884; Whig, Democrat
Senator from Louisiana, 1853–61

BENTON, THOMAS HART, 1782–1858; Republican, Jacksonian, Democrat
Senator from Missouri, 1821–51
Representative from Missouri, 1853–55

BERRIEN, JOHN M., 1781–1856; Jacksonian, Whig
Senator from Georgia, 1825–29, 1841–52
Attorney General, 1829–31

BIBB, GEORGE, 1776–1859; Republican, Jacksonian
Senator from Kentucky, 1811–14, 1829–35
Secretary of the Treasury, 1844–45

BOTTS, JOHN M., 1802–1869; Whig
Representative from Virginia, 1839–43, 1847–49

BRADBURY, JAMES W., 1802–1901; Democrat
Senator from Maine, 1847–53

BRECKINRIDGE, JOHN C., 1821–1875; Democrat
Representative from Kentucky, 1851–55
Vice-President, 1857–61
Democratic candidate for President, 1860
Senator from Kentucky, 1861

BRIGHT, JESSE, 1812–1875; Democrat
Senator from Indiana, 1845–62

BRODERICK, DAVID, 1820–1859; Democrat
Senator from California, 1857–59

BRODHEAD, RICHARD, 1811–1863; Democrat
Representative from Pennsylvania, 1843–49
Senator from Pennsylvania, 1851–57

BRONSON, ISAAC H., 1802–1855; Democrat
Representative from New York, 1837–39
US District Judge for Florida and Northern Florida, 1846–55

BROOKS, PRESTON, 1819–1857; Democrat
Representative from South Carolina, 1853–57

BROWN, ALBERT G., 1813–1880; Democrat
Representative from Mississippi, 1839–41, 1847–53
Governor of Mississippi, 1844–48
Senator from Mississippi, 1854–61

BUCHANAN, JAMES, 1791–1868; Republican, Jacksonian, Democrat
Representative from Pennsylvania, 1821–31
Minister to Russia, 1832–34
Senator from Pennsylvania, 1834–45
Secretary of State, 1845–49
Minister to Great Britain, 1853–56
President, 1857–61

BURGES, TRISTAM, 1770–1853; Anti-Jacksonian
Representative from Rhode Island, 1825–35

BUTLER, ANDREW P., 1796–1857; Democrat
Senator from South Carolina, 1846–57

BUTLER, BENJAMIN F., 1795–1858; Jacksonian
Attorney General, 1833–38

BUTLER, SAMPSON H., 1803–1848; Democrat
Representative from South Carolina, 1839–42

CADWALADER, JOHN, 1805–1879; Democrat
Representative from Pennsylvania, 1855–57
US District Judge for Eastern Pennsylvania, 1858–79

CALHOUN, JOHN C., 1782–1850; Republican, Democrat
Representative from South Carolina, 1811–17
Secretary of War, 1817–25
Vice-President, 1825–32
Senator from South Carolina, 1832–43, 1845–50
Secretary of State, 1844–45

CAMPBELL, JOHN, ? –1845; Jacksonian, Nullifier, Democrat
Representative from South Carolina, 1829–31, 1837–45

CAMBRELENG, CHURCHILL C., 1786–1862; Jacksonian, Democrat
Representative from New York, 1821–39
Minister to Russia, 1840–41

CASS, LEWIS, 1782–1856; Democrat
Governor of Michigan Territory, 1813–1831
Secretary of War, 1831–36
Minister to France, 1836–42
Senator from Michigan, 1845–48, 1849–57
Democratic candidate for President, 1848
Secretary of State, 1857–60

CHAMBERS, EZEKIEL F., 1788–1867; Anti-Jacksonian
Senator from Maryland, 1826–34

CHASE, SALMON P., 1808–1873; Free-Soil, Democrat, Republican
Senator from Ohio, 1849–55, 1861
Governor of Ohio, 1855–60
Secretary of the Treasury, 1861–64
Chief Justice, 1864–73

CILLEY, JONATHAN, 1802–1838; Democrat
Representative from Maine, 1837–38

CLAIBORNE, JOHN F.H., 1809–1884; Jacksonian, Democrat
Representative from Mississippi, 1833–38

CLAY, CLEMENT C., 1789–1866; Democrat
Representative from Alabama, 1829–35
Governor of Alabama, 1836–37
Senator from Alabama, 1837–41

CLAY, HENRY, 1777–1852; Republican, National Republican, Whig
Senator from Kentucky, 1807–7, 1810–11
Representative from Kentucky, 1811–14, 1815–21, 1823–25
Speaker of the House, 1811–14, 1815–21, 1823–25
Secretary of State, 1825–29
Senator from Kentucky, 1831–42, 1849–52
Candidate for President, 1824, 1832, 1844

CLAYTON, JOHN M., 1796–1856; Anti-Jacksonian, Whig
Senator from Delaware, 1829–36, 1845–49, 1853–56
Secretary of State, 1849–50

COBB, HOWELL, 1815–1868; Democrat
Representative from Georgia, 1843–51, 1855–57
Speaker of the House, 1849–51
Governor of Georgia, 1851–53
Secretary of the Treasury, 1857–60

COLLAMER, JACOB, 1791–1865; Whig, Republican
Representative from Vermont, 1843–49
Postmaster General, 1849–50
Senator from Vermont, 1855–65

COLQUITT, WALTER T., 1799–1855; Whig, Democrat
Representative from Georgia, 1839–40, 1842–43
Senator from Georgia, 1843–48

COOPER, JAMES, 1810–1863; Whig
Representative from Pennsylvania, 1839–43
Senator from Pennsylvania, 1849–55

COOPER, MARK, 1800 –1885; Whig, Democrat
Representative from Georgia, 1839–41, 1842–43

CRAIG, ROBERT, 1792–1852; Jacksonian, Democrat
Representative from Virginia, 1829–33, 1835–41

CRITTENDEN, JOHN J., 1786–1863; Republican, Anti-Jacksonian, Whig, Unionist
Senator from Kentucky, 1817–19, 1835–41, 1842–48, 1855–61
US District Attorney for Kentucky, 1827–29
Attorney General, 1841–42
Governor of Kentucky, 1850–53
Representative from Kentucky, 1861–63

CUSHING, CALEB, 1800–1879; Whig, Democrat
Representative from Massachusetts, 1835–43
Minister to China, 1843–45
Attorney General, 1853–57
Minister to Spain, 1874–77

DALLAS, GEORGE M., 1792–1864; Jacksonian, Democrat
US District Attorney for Eastern Pennsylvania, 1829–31
Senator from Pennsylvania, 1831–33
Minister to Russia, 1837–39
Vice-President, 1845–49
Minister to Great Britain, 1856–61

DAVIS, GARRETT, 1801–1872; Whig, Unionist, Democrat
Representative from Kentucky, 1839–47
Senator from Kentucky, 1861–72

DAVIS, HENRY WINTER, 1817–1865; American, Unionist
Representative from Maryland, 1855–61, 1863–65

DAVIS, JEFFERSON, 1808–1889; Democrat
Representative from Mississippi, 1845–46
Senator from Mississippi, 1847–51, 1857–61
Secretary of War, 1853–57

DAVIS, JOHN, 1787–1854; Anti-Jacksonian, Whig
Representative from Massachusetts, 1825–34
Governor of Massachusetts, 1834–35, 1841–43
Senator from Massachusetts, 1835–41, 1845–53

DAWSON, WILLIAM C., 1898–1856; Whig
Representative from Georgia, 1836–41
Senator from Georgia, 1849–55

DISNEY, DAVID, 1803–1857; Democrat
Representative from Ohio, 1849–55

DIXON, ARCHIBALD, 1802–1876; Whig
Senator from Kentucky, 1852–55

DOUGLAS, STEPHEN A.,[1] 1813–1861; Democrat
Representative from Illinois, 1843–47
Senator from Illinois, 1847–61
Democratic candidate for President, 1860

DRAYTON, WILLIAM, 1776–1846; Jacksonian
Representative from South Carolina, 1825–33

DROMGOOLE, GEORGE C., 1797–1847; Jacksonian, Democrat
Representative from Virginia, 1835–41, 1843–47

DUANE, WILLIAM J., 1780–1865; Jacksonian
Secretary of the Treasury, 1833

ETHERIDGE, EMERSON, 1819–1902; Whig, American, Opposition
Representative from Tennessee, 1853–57, 1859–61

EVANS, GEORGE, 1797–1867; Whig
Representative from Maine, 1829–41
Senator from Maine, 1841–47

EWING, THOMAS, 1789–1871; Anti-Jacksonian, Whig
Senator from Ohio, 1831–37, 1850–51
Secretary of the Treasury, 1841

[1]Spelled "Douglass" until 1846.

Secretary of the Interior, 1849–50

FAIRFIELD, JOHN, 1797–1847; Democrat
Representative from Maine, 1835–38
Governor of Maine, 1839–43
Senator from Maine, 1843–47

FERRIS, CHARLES G., 1796(?)–1848; Jacksonian, Democrat
Representative from New York, 1834–35, 1841–43

FESSENDEN, WILLIAM P., 1806–1869; Whig, Republican
Representative from Maine, 1841–43
Senator from Maine, 1854–64, 1865–69
Secretary of the Treasury, 1864–65

FILLMORE, MILLARD P., 1800–1864; Anti-Mason, Whig, American
Representative from New York, 1833–35, 1837–43
Vice-President, 1849–50
President, 1850–53
American Party candidate for President, 1854

FITCH, GRAHAM N., 1809–1892; Democrat
Representative from Indiana, 1849–53
Senator from Indiana, 1857–61

FOOT, SAMUEL A., 1780–1846; Anti-Jacksonian
Representative from Connecticut, 1819–21, 1823–25, 1833–34
Senator from Connecticut, 1827–33
Governor of Connecticut, 1834–35

FOOT, SOLOMON, 1802–1866; Whig, Republican
Representative from Vermont, 1843–47
Senator from Vermont, 1851–66

FOOTE, HENRY S., 1804–1880; Democrat
Senator from Mississippi, 1847–52
Governor of Mississippi, 1852–54

FORSYTH, JOHN, 1780–1841; Republican, Jacksonian, Democrat
Representative from Georgia, 1813–18, 1823–27
Senator from Georgia, 1818–19, 1829–34
Minister to Spain, 1819–23
Governor of Georgia, 1827–29
Secretary of State, 1834–41

FREEMAN, JOHN D., 18??–1886; Unionist
Representative from Mississippi, 1851–53

FRELINGHUYSEN, THEODORE, 1787–1862; Anti-Jacksonian, Whig
Senator from New Jersey, 1829–35
Whig candidate for Vice-President, 1844

FRÉMONT, JOHN C., 1813–1890; Democrat
Senator from California, 1850–51
Republican candidate for President, 1856
Governor of Arizona Territory, 1878–81

GEYER, HENRY S., 1790–1859; Whig
Senator from Missouri, 1851–57

GHOLSON, SAMUEL J., 1808–1883; Jacksonian, Democrat
Representative from Mississippi, 1836–38
US District Judge for Mississippi, 1839–61

GIDDINGS, JOSHUA R, 1795–1864; Whig, Free-Soil, Republican
Representative from Ohio, 1838–59

GRAVES, WILLIAM J., 1805–1848; Whig
Representative from Kentucky, 1835–41

GRUNDY, FELIX, 1777–1840; Republican, Jacksonian, Democrat
Representative from Tennessee, 1811–14
Senator from Tennessee, 1829–38, 1839–40
Attorney General, 1838–39

GWIN, WILLIAM, 1805–1885; Democrat
Representative from Mississippi, 1841–43
Senator from California, 1850–55, 1857–61

HALE, JOHN P., 1806–1873; Democrat, Free-Soil, Republican
US District Attorney for New Hampshire, 1834–41
Representative from New Hampshire, 1843–45
Senator from New Hampshire, 1847–53, 1855–65
Minister to Spain, 1865–69

HALL, WILLARD P., 1820–1882; Democrat
Representative from Missouri, 1847–53
Governor of Missouri, 1864–65

HAMER, THOMAS L., 1800–1846; Jacksonian, Democrat
Representative from Ohio, 1833–39

HAMILTON, JAMES, JR., 1786–1857; Republican
Representative from South Carolina, 1822–29
Governor of South Carolina, 1830–32

HAMLIN, HANNIBAL, 1809–1891; Democrat, Republican
Representative from Maine, 1843–47
Senator from Maine, 1848–57, 1857–61, 1869–81
Governor of Maine, 1857
Vice-President, 1861–65
Minister to Spain, 1881–82

HARLAN, JAMES, 1820–1899; Free-Soil, Republican
Senator from Iowa, 1855–65, 1867–73
Secretary of the Interior, 1865–66

HARRIS, THOMAS L., 1816–1858; Democrat
Representative from Illinois, 1849–51, 1855–58

HARRISON, WILLIAM H., 1773–1841; Republican, Whig
Delegate from Northwest Territory, 1799–1800
Governor of Indiana Territory, 1801–13
Representative from Indiana, 1816–19
Senator from Indiana, 1825–28
Minister to Colombia, 1828–29
President, 1841

HAYNE, ROBERT Y., 1791–1839; Republican, Jacksonian
Senator from South Carolina, 1823–32
Governor of South Carolina, 1832–34

HOAR, SAMUEL, 1778–1856; Whig
Representative from Massachusetts, 1835–37

HOLMES, ISAAC, 1796–1867; Democrat
Representative from South Carolina, 1839–51

HOUSTON, SAMUEL, 1793–1863; Republican, Democrat, American
Representative from Tennessee, 1823–27
Governor of Tennessee, 1827–29
President of the Republic of Texas, 1836–38, 1841–44
Senator from Texas, 1846–59
Governor of Texas, 1859–61

HUNTER, ROBERT M.T., 1809–1887; Whig, Democrat
Representative from Virginia, 1837–43, 1845–47

Speaker of the House, 1839–41
Senator from Virginia, 1847–61

HUNTINGTON, JABEZ W., 1788–1847; Whig
Representative from Connecticut, 1829–34
Senator from Connecticut, 1840–47

INGERSOLL, JOSEPH R., 1786–1868; Whig
Representative from Pennsylvania, 1835–37, 1841–49
Minister to Great Britain, 1852–53

JACKSON, ANDREW, 1767–1845; Republican, Democrat
Representative from Tennessee, 1796–97
Senator from Tennessee, 1797–98, 1823–25
Governor of Florida Territory, 1821
Candidate for President, 1824
President, 1829–37

JARNAGIN, SPENCER, 1792–1853; Whig
Senator from Tennessee, 1843–47

JOHNSON, ANDREW, 1808–1875; Democrat
Representative from Tennessee, 1843–53
Governor of Tennessee, 1853–57
Senator from Tennessee, 1857–62, 1875
Military Governor of Tennessee, 1862–65
Vice-President, 1865
President, 1865–69

JOHNSON, CAVE, 1793–1866; Jacksonian, Democrat
Representative from Tennessee, 1829–37, 1839–45
Postmaster General, 1845–49

JOHNSON, RICHARD M., 1780–1850; Republican, Jacksonian, Democrat
Representative from Kentucky, 1807–19, 1829–37
Senator from Kentucky, 1819–29
Vice-President, 1837–41

JONES, JAMES C., 1809–1859; Whig
Governor of Tennessee, 1841–45
Senator from Tennessee, 1845–51

KANE, ELIAS K., 1794–1835; Jacksonian
Senator from Illinois, 1825–35

KEITT, LAURENCE M., 1824–1864; Democrat
Representative from South Carolina, 1853–60

KENNEDY, ANDREW, 1810–1847; Democrat
Representative from Indiana, 1841–47

KENNEDY, JOHN P., 1795–1870; Whig
Representative from Maryland, 1838–39, 1841–45
Secretary of the Navy, 1852–53

KENT, JOSEPH P., 1779–1837; Whig
Representative from Maryland, 1811–15, 1819–26
Governor of Maryland, 1826–29
Senator from Maryland, 1833–37

KING, WILLIAM R., 1786–1853; Republican, Jacksonian, Democrat
Representative from North Carolina, 1811–16
Senator from Alabama, 1819–44, 1848–52
Minister to France, 1844–46
Vice-President, 1853

LEGARÉ, HUGH, 1797–1843; Democrat
Representative from South Carolina, 1837–39
Attorney General, 1841–43

LETCHER, ROBERT P., 1788–1861; Republican, Whig
Representative from Kentucky, 1823–35
Governor of Kentucky, 1840–44
Minister to Mexico, 1849–52

LINCOLN, ABRAHAM, 1809–1865; Whig, Republican
Representative from Illinois, 1847–49
President, 1861–65

MANGUM, WILLIE, 1792–1861; Jacksonian, Anti-Jacksonian, Whig
Representative from North Carolina, 1823–26
Senator from North Carolina, 1831–36, 1840–43

MARSHALL, HUMPHREY, 1812–1872; Whig, American
Representative from Kentucky, 1849–52, 1855–59
Minister to China, 1852–54

MASON, JAMES M. 1798–1871; Democrat
Representative from Virginia, 1837–39
Senator from Virginia, 1847–61

MASON, SAMSON, 1793–1869; Whig
Representative from Ohio, 1835–43
US District Attorney for Ohio, 1850–53

MATTESON, ORSAMUS, 1805–1889; Whig, Republican
Representative from New York, 1849–51, 1853–59

MAURY, ABRAM P., 1801–1848; Whig
Representative from Tennessee, 1836–39

MAY, HENRY, 1816–1866; Democrat, Unionist
Representative from Maryland, 1853–55, 1861–63

MCDUFFIE, GEORGE, 1790–1851; Republican, Democrat
Representative from South Carolina, 1821–34
Governor of South Carolina, 1834–36
Senator from South Carolina, 1842–46

MCKEON, JOHN, 1808–1883; Jacksonian, Democrat
Representative from New York, 1835–37, 1841–43
US District Attorney for Southern New York, 1854–58

MCLANE, LOUIS, 1786–1857; Republican, Jacksonian
Representative from Delaware, 1817–27
Senator from Delaware, 1827–29
Minister to Great Britain, 1829–31, 1845–46
Secretary of the Treasury, 1831–33
Secretary of State, 1833–34

MCRAE, JOHN J., 1815–1868; Democrat
Senator from Mississippi, 1850–52
Governor of Mississippi, 1854–58
Representative from Mississippi, 1858–61

MEADE, RICHARD K., 1803–1862; Democrat
Representative from Virginia, 1847–53
Minister to Brazil, 1853–61

MERCER, CHARLES F., 1778–1858; Federalist, Anti-Jacksonian, Whig
Representative from Virginia, 1817–39

MERIWETHER, DAVID, 1800–1893; Democrat
Senator from Kentucky, 1852
Governor of New Mexico Territory, 1853–55

MILES, WILLIAM P., 1822–1899; Democrat
Representative from South Carolina, 1857–60

MILLER, STEPHEN D., 1787–1838; Republican, Nullifier
Representative from South Carolina, 1817–19
Governor of South Carolina, 1828–30
Senator from South Carolina, 1831–33

MOORE, GABRIEL, 1785–1845; Jacksonian, Anti-Jacksonian
Representative from Alabama, 1821–29
Governor of Alabama, 1829–31
Senator from Alabama, 1831–37

MOORE, THOMAS P., 1797–1853
Representative from Kentucky, 1823–29
Minister to New Granada, 1829–33

MOREHEAD, JAMES T., 1797–1854; Whig
Governor of Kentucky, 1834–1836
Senator from Kentucky, 1847

MORRILL, JUSTIN S., 1810–1898; Whig, Republican
Representative from Vermont, 1855–67
Senator from Vermont, 1867–98

NEWTON, THOMAS W., 1804–1853; Whig
Representative from Arkansas, 1846–47

NICHOLS, MATTHIAS, 1824–1862; Democrat, Republican
Representative from Ohio, 1853–59

NILES, JOHN M., 1787–1856; Jacksonian, Democrat
Senator from Connecticut, 1835–39, 1843–49
Postmaster General, 1840–41

NISBET, EUGENIUS, 1803–1871; Whig
Representative from Georgia, 1839–41

ORR, JAMES, 1822–1873; Democrat, Republican
Representative from South Carolina, 1849–59
Speaker of the House, 1857–59
Governor of South Carolina, 1866
Minister to Russia, 1872–73

OUTLAW, DAVID, 1806–1868; Whig
Representative from North Carolina, 1847–53

PAYNE, WILLIAM W, 1807–1874; Democrat
Representative from Alabama, 1841–47

PEARCE, JAMES A., 1805–1862; Whig, Democrat
Representative from Maryland, 1835–39, 1841–43
Senator from Maryland, 1843–62

PECK, JAMES H., 1790–1836
US District Judge for Missouri, 1822–36

PENDLETON, NATHANAEL G., 1793–1861; Whig
Representative from Ohio, 1841–43

PENNINGTON, ALEXANDER C.M., 1810–1867; Whig
Representative from New Jersey, 1853–57

PENNINGTON, WILLIAM, 1796–1862; Republican
Governor of New Jersey, 1837–43
Representative from New Jersey, 1859–61
Speaker of the House, 1859–61

PETTIT, JOHN, 1807–1877; Democrat
US District Attorney for Indiana, 1839–43
Representative from Indiana, 1843–49
Senator from Indiana, 1853–55

PHELPS, SAMUEL S., 1793–1855; Whig
Senator from Vermont, 1839–51, 1853–54

PIERCE, FRANKLIN, 1804–1869; Democrat
Representative from New Hampshire, 1833–37
Senator from New Hampshire, 1837–42
President, 1853–57

PINCKNEY, HENRY L., 1794–1863; Nullifier
Representative from South Carolina, 1833–37

POINDEXTER, GEORGE, 1779–1853; Republican, Jacksonian
Delegate from Mississippi Territory, 1807–13
Representative from Mississippi, 1817–19
Governor of Mississippi, 1819–21
Senator from Mississippi, 1830–35

POINSETT, JOEL R., 1779–1851; Republican, Democrat
Representative from South Carolina, 1821–25

Minister to Mexico, 1825–29
Secretary of War, 1837–41

POLK, JAMES K., 1795–1849; Jacksonian, Democrat
Representative from Tennessee, 1825–39
Speaker of the House, 1835–39
Governor of Tennessee, 1839–41
President, 1845–49

POPE, JOHN, 1770–1845; Republican, Whig
Senator from Kentucky, 1807–13
Governor of Arkansas Territory, 1829–35
Representative from Kentucky, 1837–43

PORTER, AUGUSTUS S., 1798–1872; Whig
Senator from Michigan, 1840–45

PRATT, THOMAS G., 1804–1869; Whig
Governor of Maryland, 1845–48
Senator from Maryland, 1850–57

PRENTISS, SEARGENT S., 1808–50; Whig
Representative from Mississippi, 1838–39

PRESTON, WILLIAM C., 1794–1860; Nullifier
Senator from South Carolina, 1833–42

PUGH, GEORGE E., 1822–1876; Democrat
Senator from Ohio, 1855–61

QUITMAN, JOHN A., 1799–1858; Democrat
Governor of Mississippi, 1850–51
Representative from Mississippi, 1855–58

RANTOUL, ROBERT, JR., 1805–1852; Democrat
Senator from Massachusetts, 1851
Representative from Massachusetts, 1851–52

REYNOLDS, JOHN H., 1819–1875; Democrat
Representative from New York, 1859–61

RHETT, ROBERT BARNWELL,[2] 1800–1876; Democrat
Representative from South Carolina, 1837–49
Senator from South Carolina, 1850–52

[2]Known until 1838 as Robert Barnwell Smith.

RITCHIE, DAVID, 1812–1867; Whig, Republican
Representative from Pennsylvania, 1853–59

RIVES, WILLIAM C., 1793–1868; Republican, Jacksonian, Democrat, Whig
Representative from Virginia, 1823–29
Minister to France, 1829–32, 1849–53
Senator from Virginia, 1832–34, 1836–44

ROBBINS, ASHER, 1757–1845; Anti-Jacksonian, Whig
US District Attorney for Rhode Island, 1812–16
Senator from Rhode Island, 1825–39

ROCKWELL, JOHN A., 1803–1861; Whig
Representative from Connecticut, 1845–49

RUSK, THOMAS J., 1803–1857; Democrat
Senator from Texas, 1846–57

SAUNDERS, ROMULUS M., 1791–1867; Republican, Democrat
Representative from North Carolina, 1821–27, 1841–45
Minister to Spain, 1846–49

SCHENCK, ROBERT, 1809–1890; Whig, Republican
Representative from Ohio, 1843–51, 1863–71
Minister to Brazil, 1851–53
Minister to Great Britain, 1870–76

SEVIER, AMBROSE H., 1801–1848; Jacksonian, Democrat
Delegate from Arkansas Territory, 1828–36
Senator from Arkansas, 1836–48
Minister to Mexico, 1848

SEWARD, WILLIAM H., 1801–1872; Whig, Republican
Governor of New York, 1838–42
Senator from New York, 1849–61
Secretary of State, 1861–69

SHEPLEY, ETHER, 1789–1877; Jacksonian
US District Attorney for Maine, 1821–33
Senator from Maine, 1833–36

SHIELDS, JAMES, 1806(?)–1879; Democrat
Governor of Oregon Territory, 1848–49
Senator from Illinois, 1849–55
Senator from Minnesota, 1858–59

Senator from Missouri, 1879

SIMMONS, GEORGE A., 1791–1857; Whig
Representative from New York, 1853–57

SIMMONS, JAMES F., 1795–1864; Whig, Republican
Senator from Rhode Island, 1841–47, 1857–62

SIMS, ALEXANDER D., 1803–1848; Democrat
Representative from South Carolina, 1845–48

SLADE, WILLIAM, 1786–1859; Anti-Mason, Whig
Representative from Vermont, 1831–43
Governor of Vermont, 1844–46

SMITH, WILLIAM, 1797–1887; Democrat
Representative from Virginia, 1841–43, 1853–61
Governor of Virginia, 1846–49, 1864

SOUTHARD, SAMUEL, 1787–1842; Republican, Anti-Jacksonian, Whig
Senator from New Jersey, 1821–23, 1833–42
Secretary of the Navy, 1823–29
Governor of New Jersey, 1832–33

SPENCER, AMBROSE, 1765–1848
Representative from New York, 1829–31

SPRAGUE, PELEG, 1793–1880; Anti-Jacksonian
Representative from Maine, 1825–29
Senator from Maine, 1829–35
US District Judge for Massachusetts, 1841–65

STANBERY, WILLIAM, 1788–1873; Jacksonian, Anti-Jacksonian
Representative from Ohio, 1827–33

STANTON, FREDERICK P., 1814–1894; Democrat
Representative from Tennessee, 1845–55
Governor of Kansas Territory, 1855–58

STEPHENS, ALEXANDER H., 1812–1883; Whig, Unionist, Democrat
Representative from Georgia, 1843–59, 1873–82
Governor of Georgia, 1882–83

STRONG, WILLIAM, 1808–1895; Democrat
Representative from Pennsylvania, 1847–51
Supreme Court Justice, 1870–80

STUART, ALEXANDER H.H., 1807–1891; Whig
Representative from Virginia, 1841–43
Secretary of the Interior, 1850–53

STUART, CHARLES E., 1810–1887; Democrat
Representative from Michigan, 1847–49, 1851–53
Senator from Michigan, 1853–59

SUMNER, CHARLES, 1811–1874; Free-Soil, Republican
Senator from Massachusetts, 1851–74

TALLMADGE, NATHANIEL P., 1795–1864; Jacksonian, Democrat, Whig
Senator from New York, 1833–44
Governor of Wisconsin Territory, 1844–45

TANEY, ROGER B., 1777–1864
Attorney General, 1831–33
Secretary of the Treasury, 1833–34
Chief Justice, 1836–64

TAPPAN, BENJAMIN, 1773–1857; Democrat
US District Judge for Ohio, 1833
Senator from Ohio, 1839–45

TAPPAN, MASON W., 1817–86; American, Republican
Representative from New Hampshire, 1855–61

TAYLOR, MILES, 1805–1873; Democrat
Representative from Louisiana, 1855–61

TAYLOR, ZACHARY, 1784–1850; Whig
President, 1849–50

TAZEWELL, LITTLETON, 1774–1860; Republican, Jacksonian
Representative from Virginia, 1800–1801
Senator from Virginia, 1824–32
Governor of Virginia, 1834–36

TEST, JOHN, 1771–1849
Representative from Indiana, 1823–27, 1829–31

THOMPSON, JOHN B., 1810–1874; Whig, American
Representative from Kentucky, 1840–43, 1847–51
Senator from Kentucky, 1853–59

TILLINGHAST, JOSEPH L., 1791–1844; Whig
Representative from Rhode Island, 1837–43

TOOMBS, ROBERT, 1810–1885; Whig, Democrat
Representative from Georgia, 1845–53
Senator from Georgia, 1853–61

TOUCEY, ISAAC, 1792–1869; Democrat
Representative from Connecticut, 1835–39
Governor of Connecticut, 1846–47
Attorney General, 1848–49
Senator from Connecticut, 1852–57
Secretary of the Navy, 1857–61

TRUMBULL, LYMAN, 1813–1896; Democrat, Republican
Senator from Illinois, 1855–73

TURNEY, HOPKINS L., 1797–1857; Democrat
Representative from Tennessee, 1837–43
Senator from Tennessee, 1845–51

TYLER, JOHN, 1790–1862; Republican, Jacksonian, Whig
Representative from Virginia, 1817–21
Governor of Virginia, 1825–27
Senator from Virginia, 1827–36
Vice-President, 1841
President, 1841

UNDERWOOD, JOSEPH R., 1791–1876; Whig
Representative from Kentucky, 1835–43
Senator from Kentucky, 1847–53

UPHAM, WILLIAM, 1792–1853; Whig
Senator from Vermont, 1843–53

VAN BUREN, MARTIN, 1782–1862; Republican, Jacksonian, Democrat
Senator from New York, 1821–28
Governor of New York, 1829
Secretary of State, 1829–31
Minister to Great Britain, 1831–32
Vice-President, 1833–37
President, 1837–41
Democratic candidate for President, 1840
Free-Soil candidate for President, 1848

VANDERPOEL, AARON, 1799–1870; Jacksonian, Democrat
Representative from New York, 1833–37, 1839–41

VENABLE, ABRAHAM, 1799–1876; Democrat
Representative from North Carolina, 1847–53

VERPLANCK, GULIAN C., 1786–1870; Jacksonian
Representative from New York, 1825–33

WALKER, ISAAC P., 1815–1872; Democrat
Senator from Wisconsin, 1848–55

WALKER, ROBERT J., 1801–1869; Democrat
Senator from Mississippi, 1835–45
Secretary of the Treasury, 1845–49
Governor of Kansas Territory, 1857

WASHBURN, ISRAEL, JR., 1813–1883; Whig, Republican
Representative from Maine, 1851–61
Governor of Maine, 1861–62

WATROUS, JOHN C., 1801–1874
US District Judge for Texas, 1846–57
US District Judge for East Texas, 1857–70

WEBSTER, DANIEL, 1782–1852; Federalist, Anti–Jacksonian, Whig
Representative from New Hampshire, 1813–17
Representative from Massachusetts, 1823–27
Senator from Massachusetts, 1827–41, 1845–50
Secretary of State, 1841–43, 1850–52

WHITE, ALBERT S., 1803–1864; Whig, Republican
Representative from Indiana, 1837–39, 1861–63
Senator from Indiana, 1839–45
US District Judge for Indiana, 1864

WHITE, HUGH L., 1773–1840; Jacksonian, Anti-Jacksonian, Whig
US District Attorney for Tennessee, 1808–9
Senator from Tennessee, 1825–40
Whig candidate for President, 1836

WICKLIFFE, CHARLES A. 1788–1869; Jacksonian, Democrat, Unionist
Representative from Kentucky, 1823–33, 1861–63
Governor of Kentucky, 1839–40
Postmaster General, 1841–45

WILKINS, WILLIAM, 1779–1865; Jacksonian, Democrat
US District Judge for Western Pennsylvania, 1824–31
Senator from Pennsylvania, 1831–34
Minister to Russia, 1834–35
Representative from Pennsylvania, 1843–44
Secretary of War, 1844–45

WINTHROP, ROBERT C., 1809–1894; Whig
Representative from Massachusetts, 1840–50
Speaker of the House, 1847–49
Senator from Massachusetts, 1850–51

WISE, HENRY A., 1806–1876; Jacksonian, Whig, Democrat
Representative from Virginia, 1833–44
Minister to Brazil, 1844–47
Governor of Virginia, 1856–60

WOODBURY, LEVI, 1789–1851; Jacksonian, Democrat
Governor of New Hampshire, 1823–24
Senator from New Hampshire, 1825–31, 1841–45
Secretary of the Navy, 1831–34
Secretary of the Treasury, 1834–41
Supreme Court Justice, 1845–51

WORD, THOMAS J., ?–?; Whig
Representative from Mississippi, 1837–38

WRIGHT, SILAS, 1795–1847; Jacksonian, Democrat
Representative from New York, 1827–29
Senator from New York, 1833–44
Governor of New York, 1844–46

YELL, ARCHIBALD, 1797–1847; Jacksonian, Democrat
Representative from Arkansas, 1836–39, 1845–46
Governor of Arkansas, 1840–44

Appendix B

Principal Officers, 1829–1861

VII. ANDREW JACKSON, MAR 4, 1829–MAR 3, 1837

Vice-President:
- John C. Calhoun
- Martin Van Buren, Mar 4, 1833

Speaker of the House:
- Andrew Stevenson, Dec 3, 1827–Jun 2, 1834
- John Bell, Jun 2, 1834–Mar 3, 1835
- James K. Polk, Dec 7, 1835

Secretary of State:
- James A. Hamilton, ad interim, Mar 4, 1829
- Martin Van Buren, Mar 28, 1829
- Edward Livingston, May 24, 1831
- Louis McLane, May 29, 1833
- John Forsyth, Jul 1, 1834

Secretary of the Treasury:
- Samuel D. Ingham, Mar 6, 1829
- Asbury Dickins (chief clerk), ad interim, Jun 21, 1831
- Louis McLane, Aug 8, 1831
- William J. Duane, May 29, 1833
- Roger B. Taney, Sep 23, 1833
- McClintlock Young (chief clerk), ad interim, Jun 25, 1834
- Levi Woodbury, Jul 1, 1834

Secretary of War:
- John H. Eaton, Mar 9, 1829
- Philip G. Randolph (chief clerk), ad interim, Jun 20, 1831
- Roger B. Taney, ad interim, Jul 21, 1831

Lewis Cass, Aug 8, 1831
Casey A. Harris, ad interim, Oct 5, 1836
Benjamin F. Butler, ad interim, Oct 26, 1836

Attorney General:
John M. Berrien, Mar 9, 1829
Roger B. Taney, Jul 20, 1831
Benjamin F. Butler, Nov 18, 1833

Postmaster General:
John McLean (continued)
William T. Barry, Apr 6, 1829
Amos Kendall, May 1, 1835

Secretary of the Navy:
Charles Hay (chief clerk), ad interim, Mar 4, 1829
John Branch, Mar 9, 1829
John Boyle (chief clerk), ad interim, May 12, 1831
Levi Woodbury, May 23, 1831
Mahlon Dickerson, Jun 30, 1834

VIII. MARTIN VAN BUREN, MAR 4, 1837–MAR 3, 1841

Vice-President:
Richard M. Johnson

Speaker of the House:
James K. Polk
Robert M.T. Hunter, Dec 16, 1839–Mar 3, 1841

Secretary of State:
John Forsyth (continued)

Secretary of the Treasury:
Levi Woodbury (continued)

Secretary of War:
Benjamin F. Butler, ad interim (continued)
Joel R. Poinsett, Mar 14, 1837

Attorney General:
Benjamin F. Butler (continued)
Felix Grundy, Sep 1, 1838
Henry D. Gilpin, Jan 11, 1840

Postmaster General:
Amos Kendall (continued)
John M. Niles, May 26, 1840

Secretary of the Navy :
Mahlon Dickerson (continued)
James K. Paulding, Jul 1, 1838

IX. WILLIAM HENRY HARRISON, MAR 4, 1841–APR 4, 1841

Vice-President:

John Tyler
Speaker of the House :
None
Secretary of State:
J.L. Martin (chief clerk), ad interim, Mar 4, 1841
Daniel Webster, Mar 5, 1841
Secretary of the Treasury:
McClintlock Young (chief clerk), ad interim, Mar 4, 1841
Thomas Ewing, Mar 5, 1841
Secretary of War:
John Bell, Mar 5, 1841
Attorney General:
John J. Crittenden, Mar 5, 1841
Postmaster General:
Selah R. Hobbie, ad interim, Mar 4, 1841
Francis Granger, Mar 8, 1841
Secretary of the Navy:
John D. Simms (chief clerk), ad interim, Mar 4, 1841
George E. Badger, Mar 5, 1841

X. JOHN TYLER, APR 4, 1841–MAR 3, 1845

Vice-President :
None
Speaker of the House:
John White, May 31, 1841–Mar 3, 1843
John W. Jones, Dec 4, 1843–Mar 3, 1845
Secretary of State:
Daniel Webster (continued)
Hugh S. Legaré, ad interim, May 9, 1843
William S. Derrick (chief clerk), ad interim, Jun 21, 1843
Abel P. Upshur, ad interim, Jun 24, 1843
John Nelson, ad interim, Feb 29, 1844
John C. Calhoun, Apr 1, 1844
Secretary of the Treasury:
Thomas Ewing (continued)
McClintlock Young (chief clerk), ad interim, Sep 13, 1841
Walter Forward, Sep 13, 1841
McClintlock Young (chief clerk), ad interim, Mar 1, 1843
John C. Spencer, Mar 8, 1843
McClintlock Young (chief clerk), ad interim, May 2, 1844
George M. Bibb, Jul 4, 1844
Secretary of War:
John Bell (continued)
Albert M. Lea (chief clerk), ad interim, Sept 12, 1841
John C. Spencer, Oct 12, 1841

James M. Porter, Mar 8, 1843
William Wilkins, Feb 30, 1844

Attorney General:
John J. Crittenden (continued)
Hugh S. Legaré, Sep 20, 1841, d. Jun 20, 1843
John Nelson, Jul 1, 1843

Postmaster General:
Francis Granger (continued)
Selah R. Hobbie, ad interim, Sep 14, 1841
Charles A. Wickliffe, Oct 13, 1841

Secretary of the Navy:
George E. Badger (continued)
John D. Simms (chief clerk), ad interim, Sep 11, 1841
Abel P. Upshur, Oct 11, 1841
David Henshaw, Jul 24, 1843
Thomas W. Gilmer, Feb 19, 1844, d. Feb 28, 1844
Lewis Warrington, ad interim, Feb 29, 1844
John Y. Mason, Mar 26, 1844

XI. JAMES K. POLK, MAR 4, 1845–MAR 3, 1849

Vice-President:
George M. Dallas

Speaker of the House:
John W. Davis, Dec 1, 1845–Mar 3, 1847
Robert C. Winthrop, Dec 6, 1847–Mar 3, 1849

Secretary of State:
John C. Calhoun (continued)
James Buchanan, Mar 8, 1845

Secretary of the Treasury:
George M. Bibb (continued)
Robert J. Walker, Mar 8, 1845

Secretary of War:
William Wilkins (continued)
William L. Marcy, Mar 8, 1845

Attorney General:
John Nelson (continued)
John Y. Mason, Mar 11, 1845
Nathan Clifford, Oct 17, 1846, resigned Mar 18, 1848
Isaac Toucey, Jun 29, 1848

Postmaster General:
Charles A. Wickliffe (continued)
Cave Johnson, Mar 6, 1845

Secretary of the Navy:
John Y. Mason (continued)
George Bancroft, Mar 10, 1845

John Y. Mason, Sep 9, 1846

XII. ZACHARY TAYLOR, MAR 4, 1849–JUL 9, 1850

Vice-President :
Millard Fillmore
Speaker of the House:
Howell Cobb, Dec 22, 1849–Mar 3, 1851
Secretary of State:
James Buchanan (continued)
John M. Clayton, Mar 7, 1849
Secretary of the Treasury:
Robert J. Walker (continued)
McClintlock Young (chief clerk), ad interim, Mar 6, 1849
William M. Meredith, Mar 8, 1849
Secretary of War:
William L. Marcy (continued)
Reverdy Johnson, ad interim, Mar 8, 1849
George W. Crawford, Mar 14, 1849
Attorney General:
Isaac Toucey (continued)
Reverdy Johnson, Mar 8, 1849
Postmaster General
Cave Johnson (continued)
Selah R. Hobbie, ad interim, Mar 6, 1849
Jacob Collamer, Mar 8, 1849
Secretary of the Navy:
John Y. Mason (continued)
William B. Preston, Mar 8, 1849
Secretary of the Interior
Thomas Ewing, Mar 8, 1849

XIII. MILLARD FILLMORE, JUL 10, 1850–MAR 3, 1853

Vice-President:
None
Speaker of the House:
Howell Cobb, Dec 22, 1849–Mar 3, 1851
Linn Boyd, Dec 1, 1851–Mar 3, 1855
Secretary of State:
John M. Clayton (continued)
Daniel Webster, Jul 22, 1850, d. Oct 24, 1852
Charles M. Conrad, ad interim, Oct 25, 1852
Edward Everett, Nov 6, 1852
Secretary of the Treasury:
William M. Meredith (continued)

Thomas Corwin, Jul 23, 1850
Secretary of War:
George W. Crawford (continued)
Samuel J. Anderson (chief clerk), ad interim, Jul 23, 1850
Winfield Scott, ad interim, Jul 24, 1850
Charles M. Conrad, Aug 15, 1850
Attorney General:
Reverdy Johnson (continued)
John J. Crittenden, Aug 14, 1850
Postmaster General:
Jacob Collamer (continued)
Nathan K. Hall, Jul 23, 1850
Samuel D. Hubbard, Sep 14, 1852
Secretary of the Navy:
William B. Preston (continued)
Lewis Warrington, ad interim, Jul 23, 1850
William A. Graham, Aug 2, 1850
John P. Kennedy, Jul 26, 1852
Secretary of the Interior:
Thomas Ewing (continued)
Daniel C. Goddard (chief clerk), ad interim, Jul 23, 1850
Thomas M.T. McKennan, Aug 15, 1850
Daniel C. Goddard (chief clerk), ad interim, Aug 27, 1850
Alexander H.H. Stuart, Sep 16, 1850

XIV. FRANKLIN PIERCE, MAR 4, 1853–MAR 3, 1857

Vice-President :
William R. King, d. Apr 18, 1853
Speaker of the House:
Linn Boyd, Dec 1, 1851–Mar 3, 1855
Nathaniel P. Banks, Feb 2, 1856–Mar 3, 1857
Secretary of State:
William Hunter (chief clerk), ad interim, Mar 4, 1853
William L. Marcy, Mar 7, 1853
Secretary of the Treasury:
Thomas Corwin (continued)
James Guthrie, Mar 7, 1853
Secretary of War:
Charles M. Conrad (continued)
Jefferson Davis, Mar 7, 1853
Samuel Cooper, ad interim, Mar 3, 1857
Attorney General:
John J. Crittenden (continued)
Caleb Cushing, Mar 7, 1853
Postmaster General:

Samuel D. Hubbard (continued)
James Campbell, Mar 7, 1853
Secretary of the Navy:
John P. Kennedy (continued)
James C. Dobbin, Mar 7, 1853
Secretary of the Interior:
Alexander H.H. Stuart (continued)
Robert McClelland, Mar 7, 1853

XV. JAMES BUCHANAN, MAR 4, 1857–MAR 3, 1861

Vice-President:
John C. Breckinridge
Speaker of the House:
James L. Orr, Dec 7, 1857–Mar 3, 1859
William Pennington, Feb 1, 1860–Mar 3, 1861
Secretary of State:
William L. Marcy (continued)
Lewis Cass, Mar 6, 1857
William Hunter (chief clerk), ad interim, Dec 15, 1860
Jeremiah S. Black, Dec 17, 1860
Secretary of the Treasury:
James Guthrie (continued)
Howell Cobb, Mar 6, 1857
Isaac Toucey, ad interim, Dec 10, 1860
Philip F. Thomas, Dec 12, 1860
John A. Dix, Jan 15, 1861
Secretary of War:
Samuel Cooper, ad interim, Mar 4, 1857
John B. Floyd, Mar 6, 1857
Joseph Holt, ad interim, Jan 1, 1861
Attorney General:
Caleb Cushing (continued)
Jeremiah S. Black, Mar 11, 1857
Edwin M. Stanton, Dec 22, 1860
Postmaster General:
James Campbell (continued)
Aaron V. Brown, Mar 6, 1857, d. Mar 8, 1859
Horatio King, ad interim, Mar 9, 1859
Joseph Holt, Mar 14, 1859
Horatio King, ad interim, Jan 1, 1861
Secretary of the Navy:
James C. Dobbin (continued)
Isaac Toucey, Mar 6, 1857
Secretary of the Interior:
Robert McClelland (continued)

Jacob Thompson, Mar 10, 1857
Moses Kelly (chief clerk), ad interim, Jan 10, 1861

Appendix C

The Constitution of the United States

We the people of the United States, in order to form a more perfect union, establish justice, insure domestic tranquility, provide for the common defense, promote the general welfare, and secure the blessings of liberty to ourselves and our posterity, do ordain and establish this Constitution for the United States of America.

ARTICLE I

Section 1. All legislative powers herein granted shall be vested in a Congress of the United States, which shall consist of a Senate and House of Representatives.

Section 2. The House of Representatives shall be composed of members chosen every second year by the people of the several States, and the electors in each State shall have the qualifications requisite for electors of the most numerous branch of the State legislature.

No person shall be a representative who shall not have attained to the age of twenty-five years, and been seven years a citizen of the United States, and who shall not, when elected, be an inhabitant of that State in which he shall be chosen.

Representatives and direct taxes shall be apportioned among the several States which may be included within this Union, according to their respective numbers, which shall be determined by adding to the whole number of free persons, including those bound to service for a term of years, and excluding Indians not taxed, three fifths of all other persons. The actual enumeration shall be made within three years after the first meeting of the Congress of the United States, and within every subsequent term of ten years, in such manner as they shall by law direct. The number of Representatives shall not exceed one for every thirty thousand, but each State shall have at least one Representative; and until such enumeration shall be made, the State of New Hampshire shall be entitled to choose three, Massachusetts eight, Rhode Island and Providence Plantations one, Connecticut five, New York six, New Jersey four, Pennsylvania eight, Delaware one, Maryland six, Virginia ten, North Carolina five, South Carolina five, and Georgia three.

When vacancies happen in the representation from any State, the executive authority thereof shall issue writs of election to full such vacancies.

The House of Representatives shall choose their Speaker and other officers; and shall have the sole power of impeachment.

Section 3. The Senate of the United States shall be composed of two Senators from each State, chosen by the legislature thereof, for six years; and each Senator shall have one vote.

Immediately after they shall be assembled in consequence of the first election, they shall be divided as equally as may be into three classes. The seats of the Senators of the first class shall be vacated at the expiration of the second year, of the second class at the expiration of the fourth year, and of the third class at the expiration of the sixth year, so that one third may be chosen every second year; and if vacancies happen by resignation, or otherwise, during the recess of the legislature of any State, the executive thereof may make temporary appointments until the next meeting of the legislature, which shall then fill such vacancies.

No person shall be a Senator who shall not have attained to the age of thirty years, and been nine years a citizen of the United States, and who shall not, when elected, be an inhabitant of that State for which he shall be chosen.

The Vice-President of the United States shall be President of the Senate, but shall have no vote, unless they be equally divided.

The Senate shall choose their other officers, and also a President pro tempore, in the absence of the Vice-President, or when he shall exercise the office of President of the United States.

The Senate shall have the sole power to try all impeachments. When sitting for that purpose, they shall be on oath or affirmation. When the President of the United States is tried, the Chief Justice shall preside: And no person shall be convicted without the concurrence of two thirds of the Members present.

Judgment in cases of impeachment shall not extend further than to removal from office, and disqualification to hold and enjoy any office of honor, trust or profit under the United States: but the party convicted shall nevertheless be liable and subject to indictment, trial, judgment and punishment, according to law.

Section 4. The times, places and manner of holding elections for Senators and Representatives shall be prescribed in each State by the legislature thereof; but the Congress may at any time by law make or alter such regulations, except as to the place of choosing Senators.

The Congress shall assemble at least once in every year, and such meeting shall be on the first Monday in December, unless they shall by law appoint a different day.

Section 5. Each House shall be the judge of the elections, returns and qualifications of its own Members, and a majority of each shall constitute a quorum to do business; but a smaller number may adjourn from day to day, and may be authorized to compel the attendance of absent Members, in such manner, and under such penalties as each House may provide.

Each House may determine the rules of its proceedings, punish its Members for disorderly behavior, and, with the concurrence of two thirds, expel a Member.

Each House shall keep a journal of its proceedings, and from time to time publish the same, excepting such parts as may in their judgment require secrecy; and the yeas and nays of the Members of either House on any question shall, at the desire of one fifth of those present, be entered on the journal.

Neither House, during the session of Congress, shall, without the consent of the other, adjourn for more than three days, nor to any other place than that in which the two Houses shall be sitting.

Section 6. The Senators and Representatives shall receive a compensation for their services, to be ascertained by law, and paid out of the Treasury of the United States. They shall in all cases, except treason, felony and breach of the peace, be privileged from arrest during their attendance at the session of their respective Houses, and in going to and returning from the same; and for any speech or debate in either House, they shall not be questioned in any other place.

No Senator or Representative shall, during the time for which he was elected, be appointed to any civil office under the authority of the United States, which shall have been created, or the emoluments whereof shall have been increased during such time; and no person holding any office under the United States, shall be a Member of either House during his continuance in office.

Section 7. All bills for raising revenue shall originate in the House of Representatives; but the Senate may propose or concur with amendments as on other bills.

Every bill which shall have passed the House of Representatives and the Senate, shall, before it become a law, be presented to the President of the United States. If he approve he shall sign it, but if not he shall return it, with his objections, to that House in which it shall have originated, who shall enter the objections at large on their journal, and proceed to reconsider it. If after such reconsideration two thirds of that House shall agree to pass the bill, it shall be sent, together with the objections, to the other House, by which it shall likewise be reconsidered, and if approved by two thirds of that House, it shall become a law. But in all such cases the votes of both Houses shall be determined by yeas and nays, and the names of the persons voting for and against the bill shall be entered on the journal of each House respectively. If any bill shall not be returned by the President within ten days (Sundays excepted) after it shall have been presented to him, the same shall be a law, in like manner as if he had signed it, unless the Congress by their adjournment prevent its return, in which case it shall not be a law.

Every order, resolution, or vote to which the concurrence of the Senate and House of Representatives may be necessary (except on a question of adjournment) shall be presented to the President of the United States; and before the same shall take effect, shall be approved by him, or being disapproved by him, shall be repassed by two thirds of the Senate and House of Representatives, according to the rules and limitations prescribed in the case of a bill.

Section 8. The Congress shall have power to lay and collect taxes, duties, imposts and excises, to pay the debts and provide for the common defense and general welfare of the United States; but all duties, imposts and excises shall be uniform throughout the United States;

To borrow money on the credit of the United States;

To regulate commerce with foreign nations, and among the several States, with the Indian tribes;

To establish a uniform rule of naturalization, and uniform laws on the subject of bankruptcies throughout the United States;

To coin money, regulate the value thereof, and of foreign coin, and fix the standard of weights and measures;

To provide for the punishment of counterfeiting the securities and current coin of the United States;

To establish post offices and post roads;

To promote the progress of science and useful arts, by securing for limited times to authors and inventors the exclusive right to their respective writings and discoveries;

To constitute tribunals inferior to the Supreme Court;

To define and punish piracies and felonies committed on the high seas, and offenses against the law of nations;

To declare war, grant letters of marque and reprisal, and make rules concerning captures on land and water;

To raise and support armies, but no appropriation of money to that use shall be for a longer term than two years;

To provide and maintain a navy;

To make rules for the government and regulation of the land and naval forces;

To provide for calling forth the militia to execute the laws of the Union, suppress insurrections and repel invasions;

To provide for organizing, arming, and disciplining the militia, and for governing such part of them as may be employed in the service of the United States, reserving to the States respectively, the appointment of the officers, and the authority of training the militia according to the discipline prescribed by Congress;

To exercise exclusive legislation in all cases whatsoever, over such District (not exceeding ten miles square) as may, by cession of particular States, and the acceptance of Congress, become the seat of the Government of the United States, and to exercise like authority over all places purchased by the consent of the legislature of the State in which the same shall be, for the erection of forts, magazines, arsenals, dockyards, and other needful buildings;—And

To make all laws which shall be necessary and proper for carrying into execution the foregoing powers, and all other powers vested by this Constitution in the Government of the United States, or in any department or officer thereof.

Section 9. The migration or importation of such persons as any of the States now existing shall think proper to admit, shall not be prohibited by the Congress prior to the year one thousand eight hundred and eight, but a tax or duty may be imposed on such importation, not exceeding ten dollars for each person.

The privilege of the writ of habeas corpus shall not be suspended, unless when in cases of rebellion or invasion the public safety may require it.

No bill of attainder or ex post facto law shall be passed.

No capitation, or other direct, tax shall be laid, unless in proportion to the census or enumeration herein before directed to be taken.

To tax or duty shall be laid on articles exported from any State.

No preference shall be given by any regulation of commerce or revenue to the ports of one state over those of another; nor shall vessels bound to, or from, one state, be obliged to enter, clear, or pay duties in another.

No money shall be drawn from the Treasury, but in consequence of appropriations made by law: and a regular statement and account of the receipts and expenditures of all public money shall be published from time to time.

No title of nobility shall be granted by the United States: And no person holding any office of profit or trust under them, shall, without the consent of the Congress, accept of any present, emolument, office, or title, of any kind whatever, from any king, prince, or foreign State.

Section 10. No State shall enter into any treaty, alliance, or confederation; grant letters of marque and reprisal; coin money; emit bills of credit; make any thing but gold and silver coin a tender in payment of debts; pass any bill of attainder, ex post facto law, or law impairing the obligation of contracts, or grant any title of nobility.

No State shall, without the consent of the Congress, lay any imposts or duties on imports or exports, except what may be absolutely necessary for executing its inspection laws: and the net produce of all duties and imposts, laid by any State on imports or exports, shall be for the use of the Treasury of the United States; and all such laws shall be subject to the revision and control of the Congress.

No State shall, without the consent of Congress, lay any duty of tonnage, keep troops, or ships of war in time of peace, enter into any agreement or compact with another State or with a foreign power, or engage in war, unless actually invaded, or in such imminent danger as will not admit of delay.

ARTICLE II

Section 1. The executive power shall be vested in a President of the United States of America. He shall hold his office during the term of four years, and, together with the Vice-President, chosen for the same term, be elected, as follows.

Each State shall appoint, in such manner as the legislature thereof may direct, a number of electors equal to the whole number of Senators and Representatives to which the State may be entitled in the Congress: but no Senator or Representative, or person holding an office of trust or profit under the United States, shall be appointed an elector.

The electors shall meet in their respective States, and vote by ballot for two persons, of whom one at least shall not be an inhabitant of the same State with themselves. And they shall make a list of all the persons voted for, and of the number of votes for each; which list they shall sign and certify, and transmit sealed to the seat of the Government of the United States, directed to the President of the Senate. The President of the Senate shall, in the presence of the Senate and House of Representatives, open all the certificates, and the votes shall then be counted. The person having the greatest number of votes shall be the President, if such number be a majority of the whole number of electors appointed; and if there be more than one who have such majority, and have an equal number of votes, then the House of Representatives shall immediately choose by ballot one of them for President; and if no person have a majority, then from the five highest on the list the said House shall in like manner choose the President. But in choosing the President, the votes shall be taken by States, the representation from each State having one vote; a quorum for this purpose shall consist of a Member or Members from two thirds of the States, and a majority of all the States shall be necessary to a choice. In every case, after the choice of the President, the person having the greatest number of votes of the electors shall be the Vice-President. But if there should remain two or more who have equal votes, the Senate shall choose from them by ballot the Vice-President.

The Congress may determine the time of choosing the electors, and the day on which they shall give their votes; which day shall be the same throughout the United States.

No person except a natural born citizen, or a citizen of the United States, at the time of the adoption of this Constitution, shall be eligible to the office of President; neither shall any person be eligible to that office who shall not have attained to the age of thirty-five years, and been fourteen years a resident within the United States.

In case of the removal of the President from office, or of his death, resignation, or inability to discharge the powers and duties of the said office, the same shall devolve on the Vice-President, and the Congress may by law provide for the case of removal, death, resignation or inability, both of the President and Vice President, declaring what officer shall then act as President, and such officer shall act accordingly, until the disability be removed, or a President shall be elected.

The President shall, at stated times, receive for his services, a compensation, which shall neither be increased nor diminished during the period for which he shall have been elected, and he shall not receive within that period any other emolument from the United States, or any of them.

Before he enter on the execution of his office, he shall take the following oath or affirmation:—"I do solemnly swear (or affirm) that I will faithfully execute the office of President of the United States, and will to the best of my ability preserve, protect and defend the Constitution of the United States."

Section 2. The President shall be Commander in Chief of the Army and Navy of the United States, and of the militia of the several States, when called into the actual service of the United States; he may require the opinion in writing, of the principal officer in each of the executive departments, upon any subject relating to the duties of their respective offices, and he shall have power to grant reprieves and pardons for offenses against the United States, except in cases of impeachment.

He shall have power, by and with the advice and consent of the Senate, to make treaties, provided two thirds of the Senators present concur; and he shall nominate, and by and with the advice and consent of the Senate, shall appoint ambassadors, other public ministers and consuls, judges of the Supreme Court, and all other officers of the United States, whose appointments are not herein otherwise provided for, and which shall be established by law: but the Congress may by law vest the appointment of such inferior officers, as they think proper, in the President alone, in the courts of law, or in the heads of departments.

The President shall have power to fill up all vacancies that may happen during the recess of the Senate, by granting commissions which shall expire at the end of their next session.

Section 3. He shall from time to time give to the Congress information of the state of the Union, and recommend to their consideration such measures as he shall judge necessary and expedient; he may, on extraordinary occasions, convene both Houses, or either of them, and in case of disagreement between them, with respect to the time of adjournment, he may adjourn them to such time as he shall think proper; he shall receive ambassadors and other public ministers; he shall take care that the laws be faithfully executed, and shall commission all the officers of the United States.

Section 4. The President, Vice President and all civil officers of the United States shall be removed from office on impeachment for, and conviction of, treason, bribery, or other high crimes and misdemeanors.

ARTICLE III

Section 1. The judicial power of the United States shall be vested in one Supreme Court, and in such inferior courts as the Congress may from time to time ordain and establish. The judges, both of the supreme and inferior courts, shall hold their offices during good behavior, and shall, at stated times, receive for their services, a compensation, which shall not be diminished during their continuance in office.

Section 2. The judicial power shall extend to all cases, in law and equity, arising under this Constitution, the laws of the United States, and treaties made, or which shall be made, under their authority;—to all cases affecting ambassadors, other public ministers, and consuls;—to all cases of admiralty and maritime jurisdiction;—to controversies to which the United States shall be a party;—to controversies between two or more States;—between a State and citizens of another State;—between citizens of different States;—between citizens of the same State claiming lands under grants of different States, and between a State, or the citizens thereof, and foreign states, citizens or subjects.

In all cases affecting ambassadors, other public ministers, and consuls, and those in which a State shall be party, the Supreme Court shall have original jurisdiction. In all the other cases before mentioned, the Supreme Court shall have appellate jurisdiction, both as to law and fact, with such exceptions, and under such regulations, as the Congress shall make.

The trial of all crimes, except in cases of impeachment, shall be by jury; and such trial shall be held in the State where the said crimes shall have been committed; but when no committed within any State, the trial shall be at such place or places as the Congress may by law have directed.

Section 3. Treason against the United States, shall consist only in levying war against them, or in adhering to their enemies, giving them aid and comfort. No person shall be convicted of treason unless on the testimony of two witnesses to the same overt act, or on confession in open court.

The Congress shall have power to declare the punishment of treason, but no attainder of treason shall work corruption of blood, or forfeiture except during the life of the person attainted.

ARTICLE IV

Section 1. Full faith and credit shall be given in each State to the public acts, records, and judicial proceedings of every other State. And the Congress may by general laws prescribe the manner in which such acts, records and proceedings shall be proved, and the effect thereof.

Section 2. The citizens of each State shall be entitled to all privileges and immunities of citizens in the several States.

A person charged in any State with treason, felony, or other crime, who shall flee from justice, and be found in another State, shall on demand of the executive authority of the State from which he fled, be delivered up to be removed to the State having jurisdiction of the crime.

No person held to service or labor in one State, under the laws thereof, escaping into another, shall, in consequence of any law or regulation therein, be discharged from such service or labor, but shall be delivered up on claim of the party to whom such service or labor may be due.

Section 3. New States may be admitted by the Congress into this Union; but no new State shall be formed or erected within the jurisdiction of any other State; nor any State be formed by the junction of two or more States, or parts of States, without the consent of the legislatures of the States concerned as well as of the Congress.

The Congress shall have power to dispose of and make all needful rules and regulations respecting the territory or other property belonging to the United States; and nothing in this Constitution shall be so construed as to prejudice any claims of the United States, or of any particular State.

Section 4. The United States shall guarantee to every State in this Union a republican form of government, and shall protect each of them against invasion; and on application of the legislature, or of the executive (when the legislature cannot be convened) against domestic violence.

ARTICLE V

The Congress, whenever two thirds of both Houses shall deem it necessary, shall propose amendments to this Constitution, or, on the application of the legislatures of two thirds of the several States, shall call a convention for proposing amendments, which, in either case, shall be valid to all intents and purposes, as part of this Constitution, when ratified by the legislatures of three fourths of the several States, or by conventions in three fourths thereof, as the one or the other mode of ratification may be proposed by the Congress: Provided that no amendment which may be made prior to the year one thousand eight hundred and eight shall in any manner affect the first and fourth clauses in the ninth section of the first Article; and that no State, without its consent, shall be deprived of its equal suffrage in the Senate.

ARTICLE VI

All debts contracted and engagements entered into, before the adoption of this Constitution, shall be as valid against the United States under this Constitution, as under the Confederation.

This Constitution, and the laws of the United States which shall be made in pursuance thereof; and all treaties made, or which shall be made, under the authority of the United States, shall be the supreme law of the land, and the judges in every State shall be bound thereby, any thing in the Constitution or laws of any State to the contrary notwithstanding.

The Senators and Representatives before mentioned, and the members of the several state legislatures, and all executive and judicial officers, both of the United States and of the several States, shall be bound by oath or affirmation, to support this Constitution: but no religious test shall ever be required as a qualification to any office or public trust under the United States.

ARTICLE VII

The ratification of the conventions of nine States shall be sufficient for the establishment of this Constitution between the States so ratifying the same.

AMENDMENT I (1791)

Congress shall make no law respecting an establishment of religion, or prohibiting the free exercise thereof; or abridging the freedom of speech, or of the press; or the right of the people peaceably to assemble, and to petition the Government for a redress of grievances.

AMENDMENT II (1791)

A well regulated militia being necessary to the security of a free State, the right of the people to keep and bear arms shall not be infringed.

AMENDMENT III (1791)

No soldier shall, in time of peace, be quartered in any house, without the consent of the owner, nor in time of war, but in a manner to be prescribed by law.

AMENDMENT IV (1791)

The right of the people to be secure in their persons, houses, papers, and effects, against unreasonable searches and seizures, shall not be violated, and no warrants shall issue, but upon probable cause, supported by oath or affirmation, and particularly describing the place to be searched, and the persons or things to be seized.

AMENDMENT V (1791)

No person shall be held to answer for a capital, or otherwise infamous crime, unless on a presentment or indictment of a grand jury, except in cases arising in the land or naval forces, or in the militia, when in actual service in time of war or public danger; nor shall any person be subject for the same offense to be twice put in jeopardy of life or limb; nor shall be compelled in any criminal case to be a witness against himself, nor be deprived of life, liberty, or property, without due process of law; nor shall private property be taken for public use, without just compensation.

AMENDMENT VI (1791)

In all criminal prosecutions, the accused shall enjoy the right to a speedy and public trial, by an impartial jury of the State and district wherein the crime shall have been committed, which district shall have been previously ascertained by law, and to be informed of the nature and cause of the accusation; to be confronted with the witnesses against him; to have compulsory process for obtaining witnesses in his favor, and to have the assistance of counsel for his defense.

AMENDMENT VII (1791)

In suits at common law, where the value in controversy shall exceed twenty dollars, the right of trial by jury shall be preserved, and no fact tried by a jury shall be otherwise re-examined in any court of the United States, than according to the rules of the common law.

AMENDMENT VIII (1791)

Excessive bail shall not be required, nor excessive fines imposed, nor cruel and unusual punishments inflicted.

AMENDMENT IX (1791)

The enumeration in the Constitution, of certain rights, shall not be construed to deny or disparage others retained by the people.

AMENDMENT X (1791)

The powers not delegated to the United States by the Constitution, nor prohibited by it to the States, are reserved to the States respectively, or to the people.

AMENDMENT XI (1798)

The judicial power of the United States shall not be construed to extend to any suit in law or equity, commenced or prosecuted against one of the United States by citizens of another State, or by citizens or subjects of any foreign state.

AMENDMENT XII (1804)

The electors shall meet in their respective States and vote by ballot for President and Vice President, one of whom, at least, shall not be an inhabitant of the same State with themselves: they shall name in their ballots the person voted for as President, and in distinct ballots the person voted for as Vice-President, and they shall make distinct lists of all persons voted for as President, and of all persons voted for as Vice-President, and of the number of votes for each, which lists they shall sign and certify, and transmit sealed to the seat of the Government of the United States, directed to the President of the Senate;—The President of the Senate shall, in presence of the Senate and House of Representatives, open all the certificates and the votes shall then be counted.—The person having the greatest number of votes for President, shall be the President, if such number be a majority of the whole number of electors appointed; and if no person have such majority, then from the persons having the highest numbers not exceeding three on the list of those voted for as President, the House of Representatives shall choose immediately, by ballot, the President. But choosing the President, the votes shall be taken by States, the representation from each State having one vote; a quorum for this purpose shall consist of a member or members from two thirds of the States, and a majority of all the States shall be necessary to a choice. And if the House of Representatives shall not choose a President whenever the right of choice shall devolve upon them, before the fourth day of March next following, then the Vice-President shall act as President, as in the case of the death or other constitutional disability of the President.

The person having the greatest number of votes as Vice-President shall be the Vice-President, if such number be a majority of the whole number of electors appointed; and if no person have a majority, then from the two highest numbers on the list the Senate shall choose the Vice-President; a quorum for the purpose shall consist of two thirds of the whole number of Senators, and a majority of the whole number shall be necessary to a choice. But no person constitutionally ineligible to the office of President shall be eligible to that of Vice-President of the United States.

AMENDMENT XIII (1865)

Section 1. Neither slavery nor involuntary servitude, except as a punishment for crime whereof the party shall have been duly convicted, shall exist within the United States, or any place subject to their jurisdiction.

Section 2. Congress shall have power to enforce this article by appropriate legislation.

AMENDMENT XIV (1868)

Section 1. All persons born or naturalized in the United States, and subject to the jurisdiction thereof, are citizens of the United States and of the State wherein they reside. No State shall make or enforce any law which shall abridge the privileges or immunities of citizens of the United States; nor shall any State deprive any person of life, liberty, or property, without due process of law; nor deny to any person within its jurisdiction the equal protection of the laws.

Section 2. Representatives shall be apportioned among the several States according to their respective numbers, counting the whole number of persons in each State, excluding Indians not taxed. But when the right to vote at any election for the choice of electors for President and Vice-President of the United States, Representatives in Congress, the executive and judicial officers of a State, or the members of the legislature thereof, is denied to any of the male inhabitants of such State, being twenty-one years of age, and citizens of the United States, or in any way abridged, except for participation in rebellion, or other crime, the basis of representation therein shall be reduced in the proportion which the number of such male citizens shall bear to the whole number of male citizens twenty-one years of age in such State.

Section 3. No person shall be a Senator or Representative in Congress, or elector of President and Vice-President, or hold any office, civil or military, under the United States, or under any State, who, having previously taken an oath, as a member of Congress, or as an officer of the United States, or as a member of any state legislature, or as an executive or judicial officer of any State to support the Constitution of the United States, shall have engaged in insurrection or rebellion against the same, or given aid or comfort to the enemies thereof. But Congress may, by a vote of two thirds of each House, remove such disability.

Section 4. The validity of the public debt of the United States, authorized by law, including debts incurred for payment of pensions and bounties for services in suppressing insurrection or rebellion, shall not be questioned. But neither the United States nor any State shall assume or pay any debt or obligation incurred in aid of insurrection or rebellion against the United States, or any claim for the loss or emancipation of any slave; but all such debts, obligations and claims shall be held illegal and void.

Section 5. The Congress shall have power to enforce, by appropriate legislation, the provisions of this article.

AMENDMENT XV (1870)

Section 1. The right of citizens of the United States to vote shall not be denied or abridged by the United States or by any State on account of race, color, or previous condition of servitude.

Section 2. The Congress shall have power to enforce this article by appropriate legislation.

AMENDMENT XVI (1913)

The Congress shall have power to lay and collect taxes on incomes, from whatever source derived, without apportionment among the several States, and without regard to any census or enumeration.

AMENDMENT XVII (1913)

The Senate of the United States shall be composed of two Senators from each State, elected by the people thereof, for six years; and each Senator shall have one vote. The electors in each State shall have the qualifications requisite for electors of the most numerous branch of the state legislatures.

When vacancies happen in the representation of any State in the Senate, the executive authority of such State shall issue writs of election to fill such vacancies: Provided, that the legislature of any State may empower the executive thereof to make temporary appointments until the people fill the vacancies by election as the legislature may direct.

This amendment shall not be so construed as to affect the election or term of any Senator chosen before it becomes valid as part of the Constitution.

AMENDMENT XVIII (1919)

Section 1. After one year from the ratification of this article the manufacture, sale, or transportation of intoxicating liquors within, the importation thereof into, or the exportation thereof from the United States and all territory subject to the jurisdiction thereof for beverage purposes is hereby prohibited.

Section 2. The Congress and the several States shall have concurrent power to enforce this article by appropriate legislation.

Section 3. This article shall be inoperative unless it shall have been ratified as an amendment to the Constitution by the legislatures of the several States as provided in the Constitution, within seven years from the date of the submission hereof to the States by the Congress.

AMENDMENT XIX (1920)

Section 1. The right of citizens of the United States to vote shall not be denied or abridged by the United States or by any State on account of sex.

Section 2. Congress shall have power to enforce this article by appropriate legislation.

AMENDMENT XX (1933)

Section 1. The terms of the President and Vice-President shall end at noon on the 20th day of January, and the terms of Senators and Representatives at noon on the 3d day of January, of the years in which such terms would have ended if this article had not been ratified; and the terms of their successors shall then begin.

Section 2. The Congress shall assemble at least once in every year, and such meeting shall begin at noon on the 3d day of January, unless they shall by law appoint a different day.

Section 3. If, at the time fixed for the beginning of the term of the President, the President elect shall have died, the Vice-President shall become President. If a President shall not have been chosen before the time fixed for the beginning of his term, or if the President elect shall have failed to qualify, then the Vice-President elect shall act as President until a President shall have qualified; and the Congress may by law provide for the case wherein neither a President elect nor a Vice-President elect shall have qualified, declaring who shall then act as President, or the manner in which one who is to act shall be selected, and such person shall act accordingly until a President or Vice-President shall have qualified.

Section 4. The Congress may by law provide for the case of the death of any of the persons from whom the House of Representatives may choose a President whenever the right of choice shall have devolved upon them, and for the case of the death of any of the persons from whom the Senate may choose a Vice-President whenever the right of choice shall have devolved upon them.

Section 5. Sections 1 and 2 shall take effect on the 15th day of October following the ratification of this article.

Section 6. This article shall be inoperative unless it shall have been ratified as an amendment to the Constitution by the legislatures of three fourths of the several States within seven years from the date of its submission.

AMENDMENT XXI (1933)

Section 1. The eighteenth article of amendment to the Constitution of the United States is hereby repealed.

Section 2. The transportation or importation into any State, Territory, or possession of the United States for delivery or use therein of intoxicating liquors, in violation of the laws thereof, is hereby prohibited.

Section 3. This article shall be inoperative unless it shall have been ratified as an amendment to the Constitution by conventions in the several States, as provided in the Constitution, within seven years from the date of the submission hereof to the States by the Congress.

AMENDMENT XXII (1951)

Section 1. No person shall be elected to the office of the President more than twice, and no person who has held the office of President, or acted as President, for more than two years of a term to which some other person was elected President shall be elected to the office of the President more than once. But this Article shall not apply to any person holding the office of President when this Article was proposed by the Congress, and shall not prevent any person who may be holding the office of President, or acting as President, during the term within which this Article becomes operative from holding the office of President or acting as President during the remainder of such term.

Section 2. This article shall be inoperative unless it shall have been ratified as an amendment to the Constitution by the legislatures of three fourths of the several States within seven years from the date of its submission to the States by the Congress.

AMENDMENT XXIII (1961)

Section 1. The District constituting the seat of Government of the United States shall appoint in such manner as the Congress may direct:

A number of electors of President and Vice-President equal to the whole number of Senators and Representatives in Congress to which the District would be entitled if it were a State, but in no event more than the least populous State; they shall be in addition to those appointed by the States, but they shall be considered, for the purposes of the election of President and Vice-President, to be electors appointed by a State: and they shall meet in the District and perform such duties as provided by the twelfth article of amendment.

Section 2. The Congress shall have power to enforce this article by appropriate legislation.

AMENDMENT XXIV (1964)

Section 1. The right of citizens of the United States to vote in any primary or other election for President or Vice-President, for electors for President or Vice-President, or for Senator or Representative in Congress, shall not be denied or abridged by the United States or any State by reason of failure to pay any poll tax or other tax.

Section 2. The Congress shall have power to enforce this article by appropriate legislation.

AMENDMENT XXV (1967)

Section 1. In case of the removal of the President from office or of his death or resignation, the Vice-President shall become President.

Section 2. Whenever there is a vacancy in the office of the Vice-President, the President shall nominate a Vice-President who shall take office upon confirmation by a majority vote of both Houses of Congress.

Section 3. Whenever the President transmits to the President pro tempore of the Senate and the Speaker of the House of Representatives his written declaration that he is unable to discharge the powers and duties of his office, and until he transmits to them a written declaration to the contrary, such powers and duties shall be discharged by the Vice-President as Acting President.

Section 4. Whenever the Vice-President and a majority of either the principal officers of the executive departments or of such other body as Congress may be law provide, transmit to the President pro tempore of the Senate and the Speaker of the House of Representatives their written declaration that the President is unable to discharge the powers and duties of his office, the Vice-President shall immediately assume the powers and duties of the office as Acting President.

Thereafter, when the President transmits to the President pro tempore of the Senate and the Speaker of the House of Representatives his written declaration that no inability exists, he shall resume the powers and duties of his office unless the Vice-President and a majority of either the principal officers of the executive department or of such other body as Congress may by law provide, transmit within four days to the President pro tempore of the Senate and the Speaker of the House of Representatives their written declaration that the President is unable to discharge the powers and duties of his office. Thereupon Congress shall decide the issue, assembling within forty-eight hours for that purpose if not in session. If the Congress, within twenty-one days after receipt of the latter written declaration, or, if Congress is not in session, within twenty-one days after Congress is required to assemble, determines by two-thirds vote of both Houses that the President is unable to discharge the powers and duties of his office, the Vice-President shall continue to discharge the same as Acting President; otherwise, the President shall resume the powers and duties of his office.

AMENDMENT XXVI (1971)

Section 1. The right of citizens of the United States, who are eighteen years of age or older, to vote shall not be denied or abridged by the United States or by any State on account of age.

Section 2. The Congress shall have power to enforce this article by appropriate legislation.

AMENDMENT XXVII (1992)[1]

No law varying the compensation for the services of the Senators and Representatives shall take effect until an election of Representatives has intervened.

[1]Proposed in 1789, this amendment was not ratified by three-fourths of the states until 1992. Although both Congress and the executive proclaimed that the amendment had been adopted, doubts as to its validity persist because of the long delay between proposal and ultimate ratification.

Index